PSYCHOANALYSIS
AND
CONTEMPORARY SCIENCE

PSYCHOANALYSIS
and
CONTEMPORARY SCIENCE
An Annual of Integrative
and Interdisciplinary Studies

VOLUME V, 1976

Volume editor
THEODORE SHAPIRO

INTERNATIONAL UNIVERSITIES PRESS, INC.
New York

Published by International Universities Press, Inc.
Copyright © 1977, Psychoanalysis and Contemporary Science, Inc.
Library of Congress Catalog Card Number: 72-84721
ISBN 0-8236-5145-2
Manufactured in the United States of America

CONTENTS

3 MEANING AND INTERPRETATION

4 THERAPEUTIC PROCESS AND OUTCOME

5 ADAPTATION AND STRESS

LIST OF CONTRIBUTORS

Barnaby B. Barratt, Ph.D., Society of Fellows, University of Michigan, Ann Arbor, Mich.

Ellen L. Gay, M.A., Clinical Psychologist, Delaware Guidance Services for Children and Youth, Wilmington; Doctoral Candidate in Education and Child Development, Bryn Mawr College, Bryn Mawr, Pa.

Leo Goldberger, Ph.D., Professor of Psychology; Director, Research Center for Mental Health, New York University, New York, N. Y.

Robert R. Holt, Ph.D., Professor of Psychology, New York University, New York, N. Y.

Marion C. Hyson, M.A., Doctoral Candidate in Education and Child Development, Bryn Mawr College, Bryn Mawr, Pa.

I. Charles Kaufman, M.D., Professor of Psychiatry, University of Colorado Medical Center, Denver, Col.

Steven Marcus, Ph.D., George Delacorte Professor in the Humanities, Columbia University, New York, N. Y.

Bruce F. McKeown, M.A., Doctoral Candidate in Political Science, Kent State University, Kent, Ohio.

Fred Pine, Ph.D., Professor, Department of Psychiatry (Psychology), Albert Einstein College of Medicine, Bronx, N. Y.

Judith Godwin Rabkin, Ph.D., Research Scientist, Epidemiology of Mental Disorders Research Unit, Psychiatric Institute, New York, N. Y.

Ruth C. Resch, Ph.D., Clinical Assistant Professor; Director, Infant-Toddler Observation Nursery, Downstate Medical Center, Brooklyn, N. Y.

Roger Reuben, M.A., Doctoral Candidate in Psychology, New York University, New York, N.Y.

Benjamin B. Rubinstein, M.D., Psychoanalyst, New York, N. Y.

George Silberschatz, M.A., Doctoral Candidate in Psychology, New York University, New York, N. Y.

Donald P. Spence, Ph.D., Professor of Psychology, Department of Psychiatry, Rutgers Medical School, Piscataway, N. J.

Elmer L. Struening, Ph.D., Director of Research, Epidemiology of Mental Disorders Research Unit, Psychiatric Institute and Columbia University, New York, N. Y.

Don R. Swanson, Ph.D., Professor, Graduate Library School, University of Chicago, Chicago, Ill.

Paul L. Wachtel, Ph.D., Associate Professor of Psychology, City College of the City University of New York, N. Y.

Preface

The Editors of *Psychoanalysis and Contemporary Science* have sought to provide a medium for the publication of integrative studies that bring psychoanalysis into closer contact with natural and social sciences as well as humanistic studies. In short, the editorial aim is to present our audience with the best in contemporary thought that utilizes, draws on, or expands psychoanalytic theory. Clinical and experimental studies and applied psychoanalytic presentations have been equally welcome and pursued.

Volume 5 brings together a group of papers gleaned from a year of concentrated editorial review. We believe they are all of high quality. They also represent a wide authorship by investigators and theoreticians, some of whom are familiar to our readers and others who are new to this area. The range of topics reflects some current trends in contemporary thought where psychoanalytic ideas and models are a potent and productive force. The application of psychoanalytic theory by each author represents a unique rethinking of some central analytic proposition, or its operationalization into a new method or experimental procedure. Others have reworked available data from many sources into syntheses that provide new insights.

While the scope of our editorial aim is large enough to encompass all areas of contemporary thought that overlap with psychoanalysis, each volume presents a narrower range of topics. We can compare Volume 5 to former volumes to witness the changing trends and concerns within our discipline. In addition to the familiar rewriting of theory in accord with other models, this volume shows a heavy emphasis on developmental studies using naturalistic and seminaturalistic observations. These encompass both humans and primates as subjects. A new interest in meaning is also evident in one author's reconsiderations of one of Freud's early case studies. The nature of evidence in psychoanalysis is explored in another contribution, as well as a systematic treatment of religious belief using a psychoanalytically derived strategy as its investigative hypothesis. A new interpretation of treatment results arises when available data from analytic studies are combined and compared to symptom-removal therapies, and the role of social change and stress in emotional illness has been integrated with psychoanalytic contributions in a new synthesis. This volume includes only one clinical contribution, and one experimental study.

We judge from the papers sent to us that there continues to be a significant intellectual movement devoted to psychoanalytic integration with other methods. However, the activities of psychoanalytically interested investigators are not likely to be static. Each volume will perforce reflect the dynamic and changing forces and climate of our science in relation to other intellectual and investigative movements.

We wish to remain an open vehicle for specialized knowledge while presenting material that is generally comprehensible. If some presentations prod the intellect and prove to be mind-stretching, it will provide what we consider to be a healthy antidote to the stale reworking of old ideas heaped on unexamined half-truths, and will permit the furtherance of a vital science of psychoanalysis. Moreover, if other presentations permit us to smile at our own extravagances, we might be pleased to have sufficient distance from our work to avoid stuffiness.

We continue to welcome innovation in ideas and methods so long as they fall within the confines of good scholarship, appropriate consideration of our audience, and reflect originality of thought.

THEODORE SHAPIRO, M.D.

1 Theoretical Studies

Benjamin B. Rubinstein, M.D.

Hope, Fear, Wish, Expectation, and Fantasy: A Semantic-Phenomenological and Extraclinical Theoretical Study

No one would deny, I presume, that the words "hope," "fear," "wish," "expectation," and "fantasy" play a significant role in psychological, including psychoanalytic, discourse. It therefore does not seem to be an idle pursuit to try to define them (and thus the activities they stand for) as precisely as one can. Precise definitions do not, as Freud (1915a, p. 117) apparently believed, lead to petrified concepts, but to greater clarity of thought than is otherwise attainable.

It is important to note that, again contrary to what Freud (1915a) seems to have believed, precision and tentativeness are not mutually exclusive. In fact, it adds to its precision if one can state clearly the respects in which a definition is to be regarded as tentative, and even if one can state merely that a clear definition is not possible for the time being. In certain analytic circles the temptation seems to be great to denigrate a quest for precision by equating it with compulsiveness. Even though an element of compulsiveness may well be involved, to any one who does not still cling to an outmoded "nothing-but" school of thought it does not detract from the importance of the quest.

I will briefly indicate the main features of the method I have chosen to employ and what I hope to achieve by employing it. For

3

one thing, I will not, in the manner of lexicographers, try to define *directly* the meanings of the words "hope," "fear," and "expectation." What I will attempt is a semantic analysis by which the meanings of these words will emerge from a juxtaposition of sentences in which they do and sentences in which they do not occur, the two sets of sentences being logically related to one another in a particular way. Hope and fear sentences will thus partly be juxtaposed with wish sentences, and expectation sentences partly with hope and fear sentences. For the most part it will not be necessary to spell out further the meanings that emerge; nor will it be necessary to examine specifically the meaning of the word "wish." The meaning of "fantasy" I will try to identify in a different way. We should note that the expressions "He wishes" and "He wants" will be treated as essentially synonymous, and likewise the expressions "He fears" and "He is afraid (of)," the expressions "He will not" and "He won't," and other similar pairs of expressions.[1]

I have spoken about semantic analysis. In fact, however, the analysis I will attempt has phenomenological as well as semantic aspects.[2] Although these aspects usually can be kept clearly separate from one another, for the sake of convenience I will speak about the analysis as semantic-phenomenological. This analysis is not an end in itself. One of my basic assumptions is that the semantic-phenomenological analysis involved in identifying the meanings of words like "hope" and "fear" will give a clue to the nature of the corresponding neural processes. This is by no means an obvious assumption. It seems to me, however, to be of enough interest for us to want to see where it leads. At this point let me say only that of course we cannot get at the neural processes themselves. What we can do is to use more or less crude, unavoidably tentative, models of such processes. For this purpose I will refer to a model I proposed a few years ago (Rubinstein, 1974). As I have

---

[1] In many instances the synonymity is not complete. The expressions "He wishes" and "He wants," for example, are not always interchangeable. We can say "He wishes you a happy birthday" but not "He wants you a happy birthday." Conversely, we can say "He wants the blue book over there" but not (at least not in contemporary English) "He wishes the blue book over there."

[2] Phenomenological analysis is primarily analysis of my own experience and, reasoning by analogy, my ascription of similar experience to other people when sufficiently similar conditions prevail.

done in previous publications (1965, 1967), we may refer to models of this sort as *protoneurophysiological*. To indicate their logical place in psychoanalytic theory we may also label them *extraclinical theoretical*.

Since it is customary in psychoanalysis to speak about unconscious wishes, the analyses about to be presented will naturally lead to the question whether it makes sense to speak also about unconscious hopes, fears, expectations, and fantasies. Here the phenomenological aspect of the semantic-phenomenological analysis will obviously not be of help. It is not unreasonable, however, to expect the semantic aspect of this analysis, together with the extraclinical theoretical analysis, to contribute at least to a tentative solution of this problem. Without at this point going into any detail I will merely indicate that the view of unconscious fears and fantasies these analyses lead to differs in some important ways from the view commonly held by analysts. I will also, in the end, sketch a theory of consciousness based on premises that have been indicated earlier in the paper.

For the most part I will present the semantic-phenomenological as well as the extraclinical theoretical analyses straight, without many explicit reservations. It is clear, however, that the method the indicated analyses add up to is fraught with uncertainties. These will become plain as we go along. It is possible that because of them I will be led astray on at least some points. This is a risk worth taking. In science nothing could be more deadly than not to move out of fear of making mistakes. Mistakes can always be corrected, even serious ones. And the commonsense adage that we learn from our mistakes still holds.

For the semantic-phenomenological analysis I will mostly use examples that are either schematic or quite trivial. This is in order not to deflect attention from my main concern, the meanings in particular contexts of the words "hope," "fear," "expectation," and "fantasy," to the content of the sentences in which they are embedded.

In these introductory remarks I have employed quotation marks when referring to particular words *as such*. This is commonly done to set off the words from (1) the corresponding concepts, and (2) these words when *actually used* to refer to the events they normally are used to refer to.

AN EXAMINATION OF THE CONSCIOUS ACTIVITIES REFERRED TO AS HOPE, FEAR, EXPECTATION, AND FANTASY

HOPE

A. A Semantic-Phenomenological Analysis of Hope

Let me begin with a word about hope and wish. Whereas we can wish without hoping, we canot hope without wishing. This is clearly brought out if we consider the following sentences. The sentence,

>   1. A wishes that P will recover, but he has no hope that P will in fact,

is perfectly acceptable, whereas the sentence,

>   2. A hopes that P will recover, but he has no wish for P to do so,

is self-contradictory.

The following sentence pair illustrates another difference between wishing and hoping. While the sentence,

>   3. A wishes to go to India, but he knows it is impossible,

is perfectly acceptable, the sentence,

>   4. A hopes to go to India, but he knows it is impossible,

is, like the previous hope sentence, self-contradictory.

The reason why the second hope sentence, sentence 4, is self-contradictory is that it is apparently part of the essence of hope that, if a person hopes for something, he must believe it is at least possible that what he hopes for will materialize. And this belief is ruled out by the second clause, the but clause, of the sentence in question. That hope indeed carries this implication is strongly suggested by the fact that we immediately—albeit reluctantly at times—give up hoping when we learn that what we hope for definitely cannot come true. Hope, in other words, involves as an essential component a prediction, a subjective assurance that the probability is greater than zero that what we hope for will come about. Wish, on the other hand, carries no such implication. We can wish regardless of whether or not we think that what we wish will ever occur.

It appears that, according to this analysis, the sentence,

>   5. A thinks there is hope that X will happen,

can be true only if the sentence,

>   6. A wants X to happen and he believes the probability is greater than zero that it will,

is also true. This is evident if we consider that, in the same way as in sentences 2 and 4, it is self-contradictory to assert sentence 5 and simultaneously negate either or both of the two clauses the conjunction of which forms sentence 6. Thus the following sentence,

>   7. A thinks there is hope that X will happen, but he does not want it to,

is self-contradictory, and so is the sentence,

>   8. A thinks there is hope that X will happen, but he believes the probability is zero that it will.

I will take a few concrete examples that fit this schema. If we consider the points just made, it becomes obvious that the sentence,

>   9. A thinks there is hope that it will rain tomorrow,

cannot be true unless the sentence,

>   10. A wants (would like) it to rain tomorrow and he believes the probability is greater than zero that it will,

is also true; and, similarly, if we claim that the sentence,

>   11. A thinks there is hope that P will recover,

is true, we implicitly affirm the sentence,

> 12. A wants P to recover and he believes the probability is greater than zero that P will.

Since the same relationship obtains between sentences 11 and 12 as between sentences 5 and 6 and between sentences 9 and 10, it is sufficient to characterize this relationship in reference only to sentences 11 and 12. I have already indicated that sentence 11 implies sentence 12. The implication is clearly contingent on the meaning of the word "hope" as it is used in sentence 11. We can, however, also describe the relationship between sentences 11 and 12 by saying that sentence 12 expresses *necessary conditions* for sentence 11 to be true. Thus, (a) *A's wanting P to recover* and (b) *his believing the probability to be greater than zero that P will in fact* both represent necessary conditions for us to claim truthfully that *A thinks there is hope that P will recover*. We should note, however, that on occasion the relationship between sentences 11 and 12 may be essentially linguistic. A can very well want P to recover and, without actually *experiencing* hope, determine that it is at least possible (i.e., that the probability is greater than zero) that P will in fact. It would seem that, when this is the case, sentence 12 spells out the conditions (or rules) governing the use of the expression ". . . there is hope that . . ." rather than the conditions under which hope is experienced. The same considerations clearly apply to the relationship between sentences 5 and 6 and between sentences 9 and 10.

A sentence beginning with "A hopes that . . ." seems to express hope more directly than a sentence beginning with "A thinks there is hope that . . ." I indicated that sentences of the latter type often do not express an *experience* of hope. It is, on the other hand, fairly clear that a sentence beginning with "A hopes that . . ." in most instances *does* refer to an actual hope experience. Thus, for example, as it seems to be most commonly used, in the case of the sentence,

> 13. A hopes that P will recover,

sentence 12 above spells out not only the conditions under which it is proper to use the expression "A hopes that . . ." but also the conditions under which hope is in fact experienced by A.

To say that the probability of an event is greater than zero obviously does not say anything about how much greater it is. In cases where the word "hope" is used without necessarily referring to experienced hope, the degree of probability is often expressed by phrases such as "A thinks there is some hope that ..." and "A thinks there is great hope that ..." But even if the degree of probability is not explicitly expressed, any sentence of the type "A thinks there is hope that ..." involves an implicit reference to some degree of probability, however vaguely defined. Accordingly, as revealed by phenomenological analysis, the most prominent aspect of the *experience* expressed in this type of sentence is a more or less clear awareness of at least roughly having assessed the probability of the hoped-for event. It is this awareness (which ordinarily is spoken about without the use of words like "probability") that in sentences 6, 10, and 12 the phrase "A believes" is meant to refer to when these sentences are taken *exclusively* as embodiments of the rules governing the use of the word "hope" in sentences 5, 9, and 11.

By contrast, in cases where hope is actually experienced, the probability assessment, although in some way experienced at first, together with the corresponding wish experience, soon fades as the experience of hope emerges. The latter may be more or less intense. It is worth noting that often there is an inverse relationship between the intensity of this experience and the firmness of the belief by the person in question in the hoped-for outcome. Take the sentence,

> 14. Although the outcome is still in doubt, A very much hopes that P will recover.

It appears that this sentence can be true (in the sense of referring to an actual experience) only if the sentence,

> 15. A wants P to recover and, although he knows that so far no definite opinion is warranted, he *wants* to believe that the probability is greater than zero that P will in fact recover,

is true also.

We can view the expression "to want to believe" in two (by no means mutually exclusive) ways. On the one hand, *wanting to believe* bespeaks a more intense (or turbulent) emotional state than simply *believing*. On the other hand, however, the phrase "A wants to believe" implies that A does not believe (or at least not very firmly), that he does not have—or, as far as one can tell, does not think he has—as good reasons for believing as when, in speaking about him, we use the phrase "A believes." We should note that the wish to believe is not a wish to believe in miracles—nor necessarily a denial of a fear that P may not recover—but rather a wish that closer examination (including watching the development of P's condition) will reveal reasons for believing that the probability is in fact greater than zero that P will recover.

Thus interpreted, the thought expressed in sentence 14, taken together with its explication in sentence 15, is perfectly rational. Consider, on the other hand, the following sentence:

16. A hopes against hope that X will happen.

As far as I can see, the necessary conditions for the use of this sentence are expressed in the sentence,

17. A wants X to happen and he wants to believe that the chances for it to happen are greater than he has reason to think they are.

The hope in this case is obviously *irrational*.

It follows from the above consideration that, whether hope is experienced or not, the corresponding wish and probability assessment are identified through semantic, not phenomenological, analysis. The distinction between experienced hope and the use of this word in the absence of the corresponding experience can, on the other hand, be made only through phenomenological analysis. Obviously this is also true of the more or less clear awareness of probability assessments and the absence of such awareness.

It is important to note that when, for all practical purposes, it is a foregone conclusion that something we want to happen will indeed happen, we generally do not speak about hope. We do not hope that X will happen when we have little or no doubt that it will. Thus for us to speak about hope, a wished-for outcome must be neither impossible nor a virtual certainty.[3]

The opposite of hope is hopelessness. I mentioned irrational hope. Obviously we can also, as in depression, speak about *irrational hopelessness*. This may conceivably be attributed to what we may think of as a paralysis of wishing or to an irrationally low assessment of the probability for fulfillment of any actually present wish. Exclamations like "What is the use!" clearly point to the second of these possibilities.

In the (hypothetical) case of paralysis of wishing we speak about hopelessness in a quite different sense of the word: if wishing does not occur, then obviously there is no possibility for hope to develop. This may happen in deep depression characterized by psychomotor retardation.

B. Hope: Outline of an Extraclinical Theoretical Model

Can we describe hope in terms of the extraclinical theoretical model referred to above? Here I must make a distinction that I have emphasized before (Rubinstein, 1974, pp. 101, 104, 106f.; 1976), namely, the distinction between a person and the organism this person is also, apart from being a person. In the above semantic-phenomenological analysis of hope, I regarded hope, when experienced as such, as an experience ascribable to a person. In the language of an extraclinical theoretical model, on the other hand, experienced hope is understood to be the experiential aspect of certain processes within the organism as which the person appears when looked at from the viewpoint of natural science. The same, obviously, is also true when the focal point of the experience is not hope but a more or less clear awareness of at least roughly having assessed the probability of the hoped-for event.[4]

---

[3] In the dictionaries I have consulted, hope is defined in roughly the way I have done here, but with less precision and without explicit reference to the probabilistic nature of the concept.

[4] In referring to the experiential *aspect* of certain processes I stand firmly on the ground of the identity theory of the mind-brain relationship. A person who does not want to commit himself to this theory may speak instead of the experiential *correlate* of the processes in question. For the problem with which we are right now concerned it does not seem to make much difference which of these views we adopt.

It is not that in these cases we have two parallel sets of events; rather, we have two alternative ways of looking at the experiences of human beings. These ways are mutually exclusive. When we ascribe, for example, hope to a person we think of it straight, as an experience of a particular kind, not as the experiential aspect of certain processes. Similarly, when we think about the experiential aspect of these processes we do not think about the experience we ascribe to the person. We may colloquially refer to a person's brain; but we do not seriously speak about particular processes in his brain. As soon as our attention moves in that direction we no longer think of the person but of the organism this person is also.

Metaphysically, an experience and the corresponding experiential aspect of certain processes represent one and the same event. But in the two cases it forms part of different *cognitive settings* or *frameworks,* each of which is defined by different sets of relationships.

This, no doubt, is a dualistic way of looking at things. As I just indicated, however, the dualism is merely descriptive, not metaphysical. A person is not an experiential entity apart from the existential entity we call an organism. And neither are experiences existential entities apart from the experiential aspects of certain processes.

But let me turn to our specific problem. I indicated above that the two clauses of sentence 12 ("A *wants* P to recover" and "A *believes the probability* to be greater than zero that P will in fact") spell out the necessary conditions for sentence 13 ("A *hopes* that P will recover") to be true. If we consider the points just made we can derive from these sentences the extraclinical theoretical hypothesis that *experienced hope* is the *experiential aspect of the integration in some manner* of

      (a) the initial wish process,

      (b) the more or less fully accomplished classification of any observation that can be so classified as evidence in favor of the hypothesis that the wish will be fulfilled at a later, more or less definitely specified time, and

      (c) the more or less fully accomplished classification of the total available evidence as indicating slight, moderate, or high probability of the actual occurrence of the wish fulfillment at the specified time.

An obvious analogy is a statement to the effect that the presence of hydrogen and the presence of oxygen are necessary conditions for the formation of water, hydrogen and oxygen being the elements from which it is formed. The analogy, of course, is only suggestive. Accordingly, it is not surprising that the hypothesis just stated, being based on an analogy of this sort, may seem somewhat arbitrary. On the other hand, I cannot think of an alternative that would be less arbitrary and will therefore, at least tentatively, accept the hypothesis as a part of the extraclinical theoretical model. I will briefly return to this question. At this point let me add that I use the phrase "integration in some manner" in a wide (and vague) enough sense to apply to any combination of two or more processes to form a process of greater complexity. For the sake of greater simplicity, in the following I will generally speak not about "integration in some manner" but merely about integration.

In the model the *wish to believe* referred to in sentence 15 can be accounted for without positing an actual second wish. What we have to posit, it seems, is the integration somehow of the following processes:

(a_1) the initial wish process,

(b_1) a readiness to classify, and an ongoing classification of, any observation that can be so classified as evidence in favor of the hypothesis that the wish will be fulfilled at a later, more or less definitely specified time,

(c_1) the establishment more or less as a fact of the hypothesis that the total evidence is not yet available, and

(d_1) the classification of the "anticipated" total evidence as indicating slight, moderate, or high probability of the actual occurrence of the wish fulfillment at the specified time.

It seems plausible that, when a person uses the word "hope" *without* actually experiencing hope (as often in sentences like sentences 5, 9, and 11), no integration occurs. In accordance with what I said above, the experience here is likely to be the experiential aspect of (some of) the processes involved in the probability assessment, i.e., the processes just indicated in points (b) and (c) [or points (b_1), (c_1), and (d_1), as the case may be]. In summary, we can thus say that, whenever the two clauses of sentences 6, 10, and 12 spell out the necessary conditions for the experience of hope, the corresponding processes are integrated (thus giving rise to this

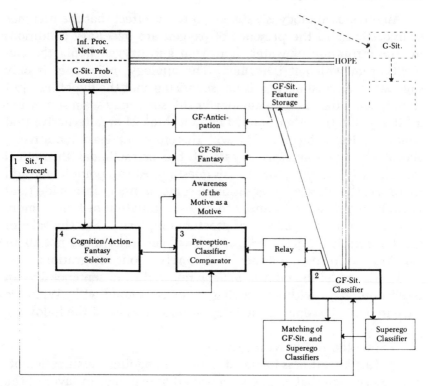

experience), whereas they are not when the clauses merely spell out the conditions for the proper use of the word "hope."

Figure 1 is a simplified and slightly modified version of Figure 5 in the paper in which I first presented some of the main features of the extraclinical theoretical model I indicated I would refer to here (Rubinstein, 1974, p. 132). A full explanation of the figure will be found in that paper. The main points in the present connection are (1) that a wish process involving conscious wishing is regarded as the experiential aspect of a *mismatch* between ongoing perceptual processes and what I have referred to as a *goal-situation classifier* (see Rubinstein, 1974, pp. 135, 136), and (2) that the various classifications and other processes referred to above [in points (b) and (c); and (b₁), etc.] are presumed to occur within a specific *information-processing network* (1974, pp. 139, 140). These classifications and other processes are thought to be set off and sustained by the wish process, but obviously are also dependent on the structure and functions of the network. In Figure 1 we find a box (box 2) representing the goal-situation classifier in the lower right quadrant of the figure, and a box (box 5) representing the information-processing network in its upper left quadrant. The first of these boxes is labeled "GF-Sit. Classifier" and the second "Inf. Proc. Network." The label "GF-Sit. Classifier" refers to the fact that in the model the goal-situation classifier is regarded as actually being a goal- and/or fulfillment-situation classifier. It is in this sense that, in the following, I will speak about goal-situation classifiers. The processes constituting the goal-situation classifier represent the *unconscious wish*. As I just indicated, according to the model the corresponding *conscious wish* is the experiential aspect of a mismatch between classifier and perception. The mismatch is presumed to take place in what I have referred to as a *perception-classifier comparator*, represented by a box (box 3) roughly in the middle of the figure. The perception, obviously, is of the prevailing situation at the moment the unrepressed goal-situation classifier is activated. In Figure 1 I refer to this situation as *situation T*. The perception of situation T is represented by a box (box 1) labeled "Sit. T. Percept." It is situated to the left and above the box representing the perception-classifier comparator. I have not here considered the fact, discussed in my 1974 paper, that perception is the outcome of a complex series of analytic, classificatory, and other processes.

Apart from having the function just mentioned, as the arrows originating in box 1 indicate, the situation T percept also serves to activate the goal-situation classifier. As depicted in Figure 1, situation T is supposed to be the prevailing situation not only when the wish becomes conscious but also at the time it occurs to A to speak about hope. In regard to its second function, situation T clearly is a situation, say, in the case of P, in which P's condition is recognized to be such that it makes sense to hope for his recovery. The label "Sit. T Percept" thus does not refer just to a simple percept but, in the example, also to the indicated recognition of P's condition. (The label "percept," therefore, is not quite accurate. I use it merely in conformity with Rubinstein, 1974, Figure 5, p. 132.)

In the previous communication I considered mainly wishes the fulfillment of which depends on instrumental action engaged in by the wishing person. In the cases we are now considering, the wish for rain and the wish for P to recover, the fulfillment of the wish depends on factors over which the individual has no control. The processes eventuating in the assessment of the probability that the wish will be fulfilled in these cases are, however, sufficiently similar to the processes eventuating in the assessment of the probability that some particular set of instrumental actions will succeed to permit us to "locate" both sets of processes in the same network. In accordance with the different type of wish considered here, I have, in box 4 of Figure 1, changed the label "Action-Fantasy Selector" (in Rubinstein, 1974, Figure 5, p. 132) to "Cognition/Action-Fantasy Selector."[5]

We can now move from the above transposition, in a *general* way, of the semantic-phenomenological analysis into the terms of an extraclinical theoretical model to a transposition of this analysis into the terms of the *particular* extraclinical theoretical model just outlined. I will consider only the relationship between sentences 12 and 13. It follows from the discussion of points (a), (b), and (c) above that in the model the processes represented by the goal-situation classifier, i.e., the process (or processes) referred to as (a), and those occurring in the information-processing network, i.e., the processes referred to as (b) and (c), are somehow integrated so as to form the processes the experiential aspect of which is hope. I will refer to the latter as *h-processes*. As we have seen, sentence 12 spells out the necessary conditions for the occurrence of the experience of hope, referred to in sentence 13. In the model, on the other hand, the processes represented by the goal-situation classifier and those occurring in the information-processing network represent not only the necessary conditions for the occurrence of the h-processes but also the elements the integration of which yields these very processes. This is not as odd as it may seem at first. Any part process, obviously, can be described as a necessary condition for

---

[5] Obviously, expressions like "classification," "evidence," "anticipation of total evidence," and "probability assessment" are metaphorical in the sense of being pointers to sets of unknown processes that presumably have some features in common with what these expressions stand for in ordinary parlance. It is in this sense that I will make use of these expressions later.

the occurrence of the larger, more complex process of which it is a part. Above I used the analogous relationship between hydrogen and oxygen, on the one hand, and water, on the other, to illustrate this point.

It is much simpler to view the h-processes this way than to posit a set of processes that are completely separate from the processes I have regarded as constituting the necessary conditions for their occurrence. The implication of the alternative just mentioned is that the processes represented by the goal-situation classifier and those occurring in the information-processing network would in some way *cause* the h-processes to occur, in which case they, at any rate, could not be said to be *logically* necessary conditions for the occurrence of these processes. Although more conventional, the hypothesis of a causal relationship cannot, on the basis of the available evidence, be judged to be more plausible than the hypothesis I have outlined above. I will therefore stick to the latter hypothesis which, as indicated, is that the h-processes represent the integration of the other two sets of processes mentioned. In its support we might invoke the commonly held doctrine of the ubiquitousness in the nervous system of integrative processes. But that, of course, is again only an analogy and as such no more than suggestive.

It is impossible for the present to speculate about how the integration may be accomplished. I can make only two points. According to our hypothesis, it is the *process of integration* and the *at least partly unknown factors responsible for its occurrence,* not the integrated processes, that are *causally* related to the h-processes. Among the factors determining whether the integration will occur, i.e., whether hope will actually be experienced, say, when A is about to speak about hoping that P will recover, are A's relationship to and feelings about P generally and his momentary mood and preoccupations. Thus P's doctor is much less likely to experience hope when he uses this word in reference to P's recovery than is a close friend or relative of P's.

The second point is that, when hope is experienced, the corresponding wish no longer is experienced as such. Accordingly, as I indicated above, only the active goal-situation classifier, not the mismatch between it and ongoing perceptual processes, is likely to be involved in the integrative process. In Figure 1 I have indicated the latter process by three parallel lines joining the word "HOPE" to the goal-situation classifier, on the one hand, and the information-processing network, on the other.

There is still another point to be considered. When we ascribe the experience of hoping to a person, we ascribe to him not merely this experience as such but the more complex experience that, in accordance with a view I have outlined elsewhere (Rubinstein, 1976, pp. 242, 243), we may refer to as a sense-of-being-a-person-hoping. The processes of which this sense is assumed to be the experiential aspect result from degrees of integration higher than those involved in the formation of the h-processes. At the present stage of knowledge, most constituents of these processes, as well as their mode of integration, we cannot fathom.

A word of explanation may be called for. The sense-of-being-a-person-hoping is immediately given, not the outcome of self-reflection. One cannot experience hope without in some way ascribing this experience to oneself. Hope does not exist out there somewhere, nor do we ascribe the hope we experience to somebody else. And the most immediate, totally unreflective experience of oneself is that of being a person, not just of existing in this form, a frozen generality, but of being a person doing and/or experiencing something.

I will not touch on this question further except to remark that when we ascribe fear, an expectation, or a fantasy to a person, in effect we ascribe to him a sense-of-being-a-person-fearing, a sense-of-being-a-person-expecting-(something), or a sense-of-being-a-person-fantasying.

Fear

A. A Semantic-Phenomenological Analysis of Fear

We will turn now to fear. It is instructive to contrast it with hope. Like hope, it has reference to future events. It is also related to wishing, but in a different way than is hope. Thus, the sentence,

18. A fears that Y will happen and he wishes it will,

is self-contradictory. To be afraid that Y will happen clearly involves a wish that it will *not*.[6]

In a way analogous to the case of hope, a person cannot fear
that something will happen unless he believes that the probability
is greater than zero that it will in fact. Thus, the sentence,

> 19. A fears that Y will happen,

implies the sentence,

> 20. A wishes that Y will not happen, but he believes the
>   probability is greater than zero that it will,

which means that sentence 19 can be true only if sentence 20 is also
true.

This is evident if we consider that it is self-contradictory simultaneously to assert sentence 19 and negate either or both of the two
clauses the conjunction of which forms sentence 20. Sentence 18
which, as we have just seen, is self-contradictory, represents the
simultaneous assertion of sentence 19 and the negation of the first
clause of sentence 20. The following sentence represents the simultaneous assertion of sentence 19 and the negation of the second
clause of sentence 20:

> 21. A fears that Y will happen, but he believes the proba-
>   bility is zero that it will.

This sentence obviously is self-contradictory.

On the other hand, in contrast to the corresponding situation in

---

[6] To account for certain ambivalences we must distinguish between (a) wishing for Y to happen, (b) not wishing for Y to happen, and (c) wishing for Y not to
happen. While (b) contradicts (a) in the sense that both expressions cannot be
true, i.e., in that (a) asserts the presence of a wish the presence of which is denied
by (b), the expressions (a) and (c) refer to different wishes which, although
contrary, can, because they are different wishes, coexist. It follows that A may
fear that Y will happen, thus wishing that it will not, and at the same time harbor
a wish for Y to happen. To be properly self-contradictory sentence 18 should be
formulated as follows: "A fears that Y will happen and he does not have a wish
for it not to happen." The formulation in the text is oversimplified.

the case of hope, virtual certainty that something we do not want to happen will happen does not preclude fear.

The following sentence represents a simple expression of *irrational fear*:

> 22. A fears that Y will happen, but he can present no acceptable reason for believing that the probability is greater than zero that it will.

In the case of fear there is no construction that would be analogous to the expression "A thinks there is hope that ..." The expression "A fears that ..." (or "A fears ..."), on the other hand, is used in three meanings, one of which roughly parallels the meaning of "hope" in "A thinks there is hope that ...," while the other two, although qualitatively different, parallel the meaning of "hope" in "A hopes that ..." Take (a) the sentences,

> 23. A fears it will rain tomorrow,

and,

> 24. A wishes it will not rain tomorrow, but he believes the probability is greater than zero that it will;

(b) the sentences,

> 25. A fears the lion will attack him,

and,

> 26. A wishes the lion will not attack him, but he believes the probability is greater than zero that it will;

and (c) the sentences,

> 27. A fears that P will not recover,

and,

> 28. A wants P to recover, but he believes the probability is greater than zero that P will not.

It is clear that sentence 23 implies sentence 24 in exactly the same manner as sentence 25 implies sentence 26 and sentence 27 sentence 28. Let us first consider sentences 23, 24, 25, and 26. Whereas sentence 25 refers to fear that is actually experienced, the word "fear" as used in sentence 23 does not ordinarily refer to actually experienced fear.[7] Accordingly, in most instances sentence 24 merely spells out the conditions in the given context for the proper use of the word "fear," while sentence 26 spells out not only these conditions but also the conditions (or rather, as we will see later, some of the conditions) under which in this case fear is actually experienced.

Let us turn now to sentence 27. The word "fear" may here be used in roughly the meaning it has in sentence 23, i.e., without referring to actually experienced fear (in the same manner as the word "hope" is commonly used in sentences such as 5, 9, and 11). Sentence 27 may, however, also be used in a sense in which the word "fear" *does* refer to actually experienced fear, although the fear in this case may differ in quality from the fear expressed in sentence 25.[8]

The important question is how to specify the conditions under which the word "fear" is used to refer to actually experienced fear. I will begin by considering only sentence 23, in which the word "fear" (in the meaning it most often has in this sentence) does not refer to actually experienced fear, and sentence 25, in which it does. A comparison of these sentences reveals that in the two cases the sentence structure is the same and so are the necessary conditions, as spelled out in sentences 24 and 26 respectively, for the use of the word. What distinguishes sentence 23 from sentence 25 is the *nature of the object or situation* that is said to be feared. It is obvious that, whereas in sentence 25 A is said to fear what we commonly refer to as a situation of *danger* (namely, being attacked by a lion), according to sentence 23 what he fears (namely, that it

[7] It may, however, if, as Dr. R. R. Holt (personal communication) has pointed out, A is a farmer who believes that it will rain the following day and that the rain will ruin his crop.

[8] Sentences 23, 25, and 27 do not present all possible uses of the word "fear." For example, the sentence "I fear (I am afraid) he came too late" does not necessarily imply that I wish he had not come too late and, since the word "fear" is used to make a particular kind of statement about a *known* past event, the sentence cannot imply a probability assessment.

will rain tomorrow) normally has no relation to what we ordinarily mean by "danger." It follows that, at any rate, in the cases we are considering, the actual experience of fear is somehow related to the recognition, or classification, of a perceived situation as a danger situation.

Considering the problem we will face when we move on to examine sentence 27, it is important to be more specific at this point. The danger sentence 25 refers to is clearly *physical*, i.e., the danger is one of physical hurt or mutilation, or perhaps of loss of life. In reference to sentences of the same type as sentence 25 I will say in a general way that the fear is directly related to the *probability of physical trauma*. If the probability is high enough, a situation of this kind normally elicits an *impulse to flight*. Thus fear and flight impulse are here intimately related to one another.

We are now ready to consider sentence 27. When the fear referred to in a sentence of this type is actually experienced fear, it is also related to danger, but to danger of a different kind than the danger described in sentence 25. According to sentence 27, A fears that P will not recover, which implies that he may die (or become an invalid). In a way that is analogous to the similar situation in the case of hope, A, obviously, is more likely to fear this possibility in a literal sense the closer he is to P, the more P means to him. Under these conditions P's death (if that indeed is the outcome) would be a personal loss to A. From A's point of view, as I just indicated, we can in this case too speak about danger; not, however, about physical but about *psychological danger*. Dangers of this kind include the threatened loss of position, of one's security, of self-esteem, of the respect or love of certain people, of a beloved person (such as P, as referred to in sentence 27). We can say that in these cases the fear is related to the *probability of psychological trauma*.

Here the most outstanding feature of the fear is that *normally* it does not elicit a flight impulse. We do not feel inclined to flee, say, when we learn that a person we love may be fatally ill.[9] Similarly,

---

[9] It is possible that in some cases there is an initial impulse to flee. But ordinarily it is soon squelched and can therefore for all practical purposes be disregarded.

if somebody is afraid of losing the love of a particular person, his impulse is not to run away. His first impulse in most cases is to try, in some manner, to forestall the threatened loss of love. He may, however, feel like running away when he realizes that he has actually lost, or has probably lost, the love of the person in question. But then he is not fleeing, or at any rate not in the sense of trying to avoid the trauma. His "running away" is rather a particular kind of reaction to its having occurred.

The fear related to the probability of psychological trauma is, as I have indicated, usually of a different quality from the fear related to a trauma that is strictly physical. We mostly refer to fear of this kind as *anxiety* or *apprehension*. I will speak about *normal anxiety*. The different quality most likely is related to the fact that, whereas fear in the face of physical danger somehow involves a flight impulse, normal anxiety does not.

It is noteworthy that the experience of normal anxiety (and sometimes of fear of physical trauma) may occur simultaneously (or in some kind of alternation) with the experience of hope. To state, in accordance with sentence 28, that the probability that P will not recover is greater than zero does not imply that the probability is zero that he will. The necessary conditions for hope, as spelled out in sentence 12, are thus present. It is only when the probability that P will not recover tends to approximate certainty that A's hope for P's recovery either vanishes or becomes irrational.

Apart from the two types of actually experienced fear I have discussed, there is a type of experienced fear the conditions for which are unknown—at least to the person experiencing the fear. It is also commonly referred to as anxiety. In contrast to the normal anxiety discussed above, it is always pathological. To distinguish it from normal anxiety I will refer to it as *clinically relevant anxiety*. Both normal and clinically relevant anxiety are of course varieties of fear. In contrast to the use of the word "fear," the expressions "normal anxiety" and "clinically relevant anxiety" are always used to refer to actual experiences.[10]

---

[10] In ordinary usage the distinctions between fear, normal anxiety, and clinically relevant anxiety are not as clear-cut as I have made them seem. For the sake of simplicity I will, however, stick to these distinctions. If the reader remembers how I use the words, he is unlikely to get confused.

B. Fear: Outline of an Extraclinical Theoretical Model

To begin with I will focus on normal anxiety, i.e., fear in the face of psychological trauma. Sentences 27 and 28 will again serve as examples. The assumption is that, exactly as in the case of hope, *normal anxiety* is the *experiential aspect of the integration in some manner* of the processes—the wish process and the processes involved in the probability assessment—corresponding to the psychological events the two clauses of sentence 28 have reference to. Normal anxiety is most likely to be experienced when an observation is made that lends itself to be, and accordingly is, classified as evidence against P's recovery. Some people, however, seem to have a greater readiness to make observations that can be classified as evidence against than observations that can be classified as evidence in favor of P's recovery (or of some similar event), while in others the opposite is the case.

Again, essentially as in the case of hope, when fear, i.e., normal anxiety, is not experienced the two clauses of sentence 28, although implied by sentence 27, obviously cannot be interpreted as representing necessary conditions for the experience of fear (i.e., normal anxiety) but merely for the proper use of the latter sentence (including the proper use of the word "fear" in it). Accordingly, the processes corresponding to the two clauses of sentence 28 are not integrated with one another.

Figure 2 is a greatly simplified version of Figure 1, representing the essential processes directly or indirectly involving the experience of both hope and normal anxiety as expressed in sentences 13 and 27 respectively. In the diagram, to be able to account for both experiences (which, as indicated above, may occur simultaneously or in alternation) I have divided the box representing the information-processing network into two parts. As in Figure 1, the three parallel lines converging, respectively, on the terms "HOPE" and "NORMAL ANXIETY" are meant to represent the integration of the processes represented by the boxes (or part boxes) from which these lines originate. The angular, partly dotted arrow in the left part of the figure represents in summary form the complex connection between the goal-situation classifier and the information-processing network diagrammed in Figure 1. In accordance with the point I made in my explanation of Figure 1 about the meaning

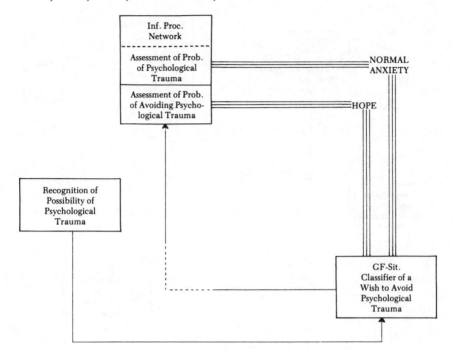

FIGURE 2

of the word "percept," I have labeled the percept box in Figure 2 "Recognition of the Possibility of Psychological Trauma."

It is important to note, as specified in Figure 2, that the same goal-situation classifier may be involved in both hope and normal anxiety. In the case I have considered I have labeled the classifier "Goal-Situation Classifier of a Wish to Avoid Psychological Trauma." The difference between hope and normal anxiety, according to the model, hinges on whether, as in hope, the probability of avoiding the psychological trauma is assessed or, as in normal anxiety, the probability of its occurrence is assessed. This difference between hope and normal anxiety in the extraclinical theoretical model is a reflection of the difference between sentences 12 and 28.[11]

---

[11] It may be of interest to note that the wish to avoid psychological trauma is derived from the first clause of sentences 12 and 28 by the following substitutions and generalizations:

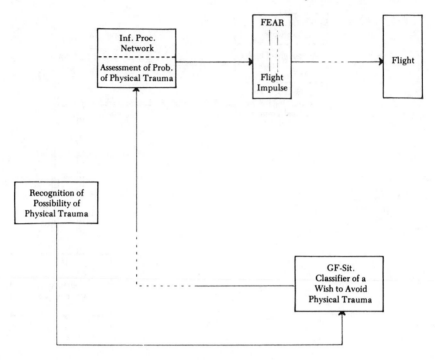

FIGURE 3

We will now move on to Figure 3. Except for the fact that they concern physical, not psychological, trauma, three of the boxes in this figure and the arrows connecting them correspond closely to the similarly placed boxes and arrows in Figure 2. Because in Figure 3 the possible occurrence of hope is not considered, there is no need, as in Figure 2, to divide the box representing the information-processing network into two parts.

    (a) A wants P to recover.
    (b) A wishes that P will recover.
    (c) A wishes that P will not *not recover*.
    (d) There is a wish that P will not *not recover*.
    (e) There is a wish for the nonoccurrence of P's nonrecovery.
      (e-1) A wish for the nonoccurrence of P's nonrecovery = a wish to avoid the occurrence of P's nonrecovery.
      (e-2) The occurrence of P's nonrecovery = the occurrence of a psychological trauma.
    (f) There is a wish to avoid psychological trauma.

As I have indicated, recognition of the probability of physical trauma—e.g., as spelled out in sentence 26 (the sentence about A's belief that the lion may attack him)—if this probability is high enough, instantaneously elicits a flight impulse which, provided the conditions permit it, leads to an appropriate form of flight. The two boxes in Figure 3 to the right of the box representing the information-processing network, together with the connecting arrows, depict this sequence. The dotted part of the arrow from the flight-impulse box to the flight box indicates that, between flight impulse and flight, information relevant to the possibility, and, if possible, the mode and direction of the flight, becomes an important determining factor.[12]

I am making two assumptions. One is that the experienced fear is the experiential aspect of the aroused flight impulse, the second that the instantaneous arousal of this impulse prevents the integration of the goal-situation classifier and the processes involved in the probability assessment. I will consider the second assumption first. It follows from this assumption that the implication, for example, of sentence 26 by sentence 25 must be interpreted as meaning that sentence 26 expresses the necessary conditions *exclusively* for the linguistically proper use of sentence 25 (including the proper use of the word "fear" in it). The situation, in other words, is exactly the same as when the word "fear" is used in the absence of any experience of fear or normal anxiety (as in sentence 23 and sometimes in sentences like sentence 27).

Let me turn now to the first of the two assumptions, the assumption that in the case of physical danger the experienced fear is the experiential aspect of the aroused flight impulse. If we disregard his instinct theory, this view is related to that of McDougall (1921, pp. 51, 52; 1928, p. 203), who regarded fear as an indicator of the aroused impulse to flee. It is also related to Köhler's view (1947, p. 105), according to which in a danger situation fear

---

[12] Since I am here concerned only with fear I have not considered cases where the probability of physical trauma can be reduced by means other than flight. In some of these cases fight may be an alternative to flight. In the case I am considering, namely, expecting to be attacked by a lion, fight, obviously, is ruled out as a possibility. That is, the probability of physical trauma is overwhelmingly great and, accordingly, the flight impulse is instantaneously elicited. The choice between fight and flight I regard as part of the function of the information-processing network.

and flight impulse arise simultaneously. It further has essential features in common with views about affects generally expressed by Austin (1946, pp. 108f.) and Hampshire (1971, pp. 143, 144). On the other hand, it differs from Freud's conception (e.g., 1926, p. 92) of fear as a signal of danger the function of which is to trigger flight. By not distinguishing between an impulse to flight and actual flight (or attempts at flight), Freud closed himself off from considering the possibilities that the "signal" (1) may not be a signal in any ordinary sense of this word, and (2), as I suggested above, may have dimensions beyond the purely experiential affective.

In his early theory of what I refer to as clinically relevant anxiety, Freud posited a direct transformation of libido into anxiety (1895, pp. 107ff.; 1915b, p. 155). Later, taking fear of physical trauma as his model, by his own admission (1926, p. 140) he became less concerned with the mode of production and the nature of the process of fear, including clinically relevant anxiety, than with the *purpose* of its production. Thus, according to Freud, fear is to flight as clinically relevant anxiety is to repression. And he carried the analogy far enough to posit in the latter case what, in the model I have proposed, is most readily thought of in terms of an unconscious assessment of the probability of physical trauma—primarily castration—as causally related to the anxiety. The unconscious threat of castration, he thought, emanated from the superego.

I will try to show later that it is not very meaningful to speak about an unconscious assessment of the probability of anything. At this point I will focus on another question. Even if we assume that the process of clinically relevant anxiety is identical with the process of fear, the above inference from the causation of fear to the causation of anxiety is by no means logically necessary. From the fact that A always leads to B, it does not follow that whenever B occurs A must also have occurred. Accordingly, it does not follow that, if in the indicated circumstances A is not consciously present, it must be present unconsciously. And, indeed, Freud himself allowed for the possibility of another explanation in certain instances. Recalling the old hypothesis referred to above, he thus stated that (clinically relevant) anxiety on occasion may arise directly from unutilized libidinal energy (1926, p. 141). The fact that in a later work (1933, p. 94) he again retracted this statement is irrelevant in the present connection.

This is not the place for a full-scale examination of Freud's theory of anxiety and repression. I must, however, at least indicate how, within the framework of the general model I am working with, this question can be handled. Freud used as his principal examples the well-known phobias of Little Hans and the Wolf Man. I will try to outline the main features of another phobia, namely, stage fright. The clinical data on which my construction is based are commonplace. I will assume that the clinical inferences that are involved have been reasonably well confirmed. I cannot be too emphatic in warning the reader that the following construction is highly tentative.

Stage fright is commonly regarded as related to an unconscious wish to exhibit oneself. That the wish is unconscious means that the corresponding goal-situation classifier—which in this case I will refer to as a *self-exhibition classifier*—is repressed and that as a consequence the conscious wish cannot emerge. The boxes and the connecting arrows in the lower right quadrant of Figure 1 illustrate the process of repression. Its main feature is that, as soon as the self-exhibition classifier is aroused, it is brought to interact with a classifier I have referred to as a *superego classifier*. In the case under consideration the two classifiers match, which means that the goal-situation the self-exhibition classifier is specifically tuned into belongs to a *class of prohibited situations*. According to the model, the match of the classifiers leads to *inhibition of the relay* situated in Figure 1 between the self-exhibition classifier box and the box representing the perception-classifier comparator. It is the inhibition of the relay that prevents the self-exhibition classifier from becoming conscious as a wish and thus constitutes the essential process of repression (see Rubinstein, 1974, pp. 136, 171, 172). We should note that anxiety is not involved in this process.[13]

[13] This clearly is contrary to Freud's view according to which, as I have indicated, it is anxiety that triggers repression. Some form of anxiety or fear may, however, have been involved in the *formation* of the superego classifier. Giving Freud's theory of superego functioning (as expounded in 1926) a *strictly histori-cal*, i.e., genetic, interpretation, we arrive at the view that, essentially through a specific learning process, the classifier has gradually developed in situations involving fear of psychological as well as physical trauma, namely, loss of love and corporeal punishment (castration?). The learning, according to this view,

I will posit next that, because acting (on a stage) provides an opportunity to exhibit oneself in a particular way, the repressed self-exhibition classifier in the presence of a wish to act is in some way integrated with the goal-situation classifier corresponding to this wish, thus becoming what I have referred to as a subclassifier of the latter classifier (Rubinstein, 1974, p. 114). I will refer to the goal-situation classifier of the wish to act as an *acting classifier*. This classifier, including its self-exhibition subclassifier, is not repressed. We must assume that the superego classifier is not discriminating enough to single out a matching subclassifier from a goal-situation classifier that *as such* it does not match and hence leaves unrepressed.

To account for the fact that anxiety is after all one of the distinguishing marks of a phobia, we must assume that the self-exhibition subclassifier of the acting classifier is at some point (unconsciously) recognized as such. I will posit—perhaps somewhat arbitrarily—that this happens at the stage of goal anticipation. The recognition that a self-exhibition classifier is a subclassifier of the acting classifier leads to the classification of the anticipated acting situation as a prohibited situation. According to the model, this classification activates the *flight impulse* and hence *fear*.

Figure 4, which is an elaboration of Figure 1 with all inessentials eliminated, illustrates the whole process. It should be read starting with the boxes representing the two classifiers in the lower right quadrant of the figure and following the mostly solid arrows leading to the relay, the perception-classifier comparator, etc., right to the box in the upper right quadrant labeled "Flight Impulse Activator." The label "GF_1-Sit. Classifier" stands for the self-exhibition classifier and the label "GF_2-Sit. Classifier" for the acting classifier. The integration of the two classifiers I have indicated merely by dotting the adjacent boundaries of the corresponding boxes and by the two-legged arrow representing the propagation of

consists mainly in the establishment of part classifiers by which recognition is achieved, first of prohibited situations (i.e., situations leading to trauma of one or both of the indicated kinds) and eventually of the principal features of the corresponding activated goal-situation classifiers. (It is not necessary in the present connection to discuss Freud's own theory of superego development, as set forth mainly in 1923.)

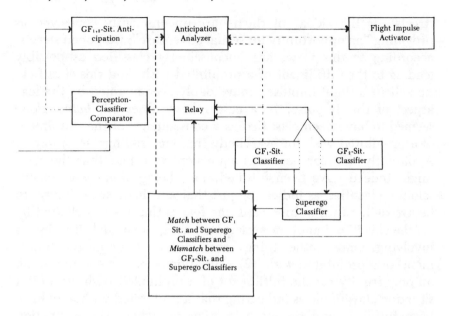

FIGURE 4

the integrated classifier process to the relay. The integration is also indicated by labeling the anticipation box "$Gf_{1,2}$-Sit. Anticipation." The broken arrows converging on the box labeled "Anticipation Analyzer" indicate some of the factors influencing the analysis and consequent classifications of the goal anticipation.

I will not dwell further on this phobia except to stress again that here the anxiety does not trigger repression. What it does accomplish is the avoidance of a goal-situation that, although acceptable in itself, is "contaminated" with features of a prohibited goal-situation. We can say clinically, i.e., in ordinary language, that unconsciously the acceptable situation has acquired the *meaning* of the prohibited situation. This locution, however, does not enhance our understanding of what is happening.

Not all phobias are alike. Let me take agoraphobia and fear of being alone as examples of phobias of somewhat different types. It will be simpler here to speak about the fulfillment of prohibited wishes instead of about prohibited goal-situations. I will be brief. As described by Fenichel (1945, p. 196), in *agoraphobia* open streets—or the "idea" of them—are unconsciously conceived as providing "an opportunity for sexual adventure"; i.e., open streets, according to this view, are unconsciously classified as possibly leading to the fulfillment of a prohibited wish, and this classification elicits a flight impulse, unavoidably accompanied by the fear aspect of this impulse. In a case I have observed, *being alone* seemed to have been classified as a consequence of the fulfillment of a prohibited wish for everybody (parents, siblings, etc.) to die. Apparently the fear here was equivalent to a fear that the wish might indeed have been fulfilled, i.e., being alone was unconsciously classified as indicating just that and had, accordingly, to be avoided.[14] In the three cases the fear is thus seen as elicited by (1) the classification of an anticipated acceptable goal-situation as involving, among other things, the fulfillment (or partial fulfillment) of a prohibited wish, (2) a situation classifiable as providing an opportunity for the fulfillment of a prohibited wish, and (3) a situation classifiable as indicating that a prohibited wish may have been fulfilled, and therefore in a world where the distinction between "may be" and "is" is obliterated, has been fulfilled. The classification in all cases is presumed to be unconscious. The third case is somewhat reminiscent of a distinction I have made between actual and metaphoric reality (Rubinstein, 1972, e.g., pp. 101f.).

One of the differences between the proposed schema and Freud's concerns the nature and functioning of the "superego." I have regarded the superego as a classifier of a particular kind. It is a salient feature of the proposed model that the assumed mode of functioning of this classifier removes the need to posit an anxiety

---

[14] The logic represented by this classification is somewhat peculiar. It follows the schema:

    (a) I want them to die.
    (b) If indeed they die, I will be alone.
    (c) I am alone.

Therefore:

    (d) They *may* have died.

Therefore:

    (e) They have "in fact" died.

signal to trigger repression. Freud clearly did not distinguish between a possible genetic and a permanent functional relationship. As soon as we make this distinction, we realize that there also is no need to posit unconscious assessment of the probability of "physical" trauma which, as I indicated and will elaborate on later, is a questionable concept. It is of interest to note that the clinical interpretations derivable from the two schemata need not appreciably differ from one another.

Another point is that the clinically relevant anxiety that in stage fright occurs as part of the essential symptom complex is not triggered in the same way as fear in the face of physical trauma. The process, however, is assumed to be the same, i.e., according to the model, the phobic anxiety is the experiential aspect of an aroused flight impulse.[15] The presumption that the causative factor is different in the two cases, the assessment of the probability of physical trauma in the one and a classification of an anticipated acceptable goal-situation as involving the fulfillment (or the partial fulfillment) of a prohibited wish in the other, is fully consistent with the simple logical point I made above to the effect that in different contexts the same event may be causally related to different factors. Obviously this consideration also applies to the other phobias mentioned.

We may note that in certain cases the relationship just indicated is reversed, i.e., the same causative factor may have different effects. Examples are examinations and job interviews which in some instances may give rise to normal anxiety (or apprehension) and in others to what we commonly refer to as *panic*. While the latter seems to involve a flight impulse, the former, in accordance with what ordinarily happens in the case of psychological trauma, does not. Panic in the indicated circumstances qualifies as clinically relevant anxiety. In some persons it apparently does, while in others it does not, result from an abnormal classification of the examination or interview situation, as the case may be. The extraclinical theoretical relationship, in situations like these, between normal

---

[15] There may be other forms of clinically relevant anxiety involving processes of different types. In a general way sentence 22 expresses a different form of clinically relevant anxiety than the form just considered. In the present connection, however, I will not pursue this question further.

anxiety and panic brings to mind a point Kubie made years ago (1947) that differences judged to be quantitative may really be qualitative. This, of course, is not always the case. As Koffka observed (1936, p. 404), fear is generally the more intense the less the possibility of flight. Koffka speaks about fear in cases of physical danger, but his point may apply as well, for example, to pre-examination panic in cases where the person very badly wants to flee but flight, i.e., his not appearing for the examination, is excluded.

I have distinguished between fear of physical trauma, normal anxiety, which is fear of psychological trauma, and clinically relevant anxiety. I have proposed that normal anxiety involves processes of a different kind than fear of physical trauma, and that fear of physical trauma and at least some forms of clinically relevant anxiety are experiential aspects of the same kind of process.

A brief summary of the most salient—and perhaps most questionable—extraclinical theoretical features of the three varieties of fear may be helpful. The above extraclinical theoretical description of normal anxiety is based on an interpretation in process terms of a particular type of logical relationship between two sentences, the one, sentence 27, referring to fear of psychological trauma and the other, sentence 28, to the logically necessary conditions for sentence 27 to be true. The extraclinical theoretical description of fear of physical trauma, on the other hand, is based on an interpretation of exactly the same logical relationship between two sentences, namely, sentences 25 and 26, but in process terms of an entirely different kind. The justification for the different interpretations in process terms of *logically* identical relationships derives from the fact that, whereas fear of physical trauma is *empirically* closely related to flight, fear of psychological trauma is not. The forms of clinically relevant anxiety I have considered resemble fear of physical trauma in that they are in the same way related to flight, but they differ from it in regard to at least the nature of their immediate causation.

Things may not be as comparatively clear-cut as I have made them seem. In a personal communication Joseph H. de Rivera has called my attention to the fact that in the case of some affects, contrary to what one might expect, the experienced affect may occur without an experience of the corresponding impulse. Thus, he claims, one can experience anger without experiencing even the shadow of an impulse to hit (or some equivalent angry act).

Since we are concerned with fear, I will discuss de Rivera's point in reference to this affect. Consider the statement, "The more frightened I am of Q the less I feel like running away from him." To the extent that this statement is felt to be self-contradictory it corroborates the hypothesis that the experience of being afraid does indeed involve an experience of wanting to flee in some sense of this word. A person who, on the other hand, claims to see nothing contradictory in this statement may back up his contention by adding either something like "... because I do not want to give in to my fear," or something like "... because the more frightened I am the more do I literally feel paralyzed." In other words, the person in question *explains away* the contradiction, i.e., *why*, contrary to what one would expect, he may not feel like running away, thus indirectly affirming that primarily the impulse is presumably present.

EXPECTATION

A. *A Semantic-Phenomenological Analysis of Expectation*

We will now consider the concept of expectation. As the word "expect" is commonly used, the sentence,

29. A expects Z to happen,

implies the sentence,

30. A believes the chances are considerably better than 50:50 that Z will happen.[16]

Accordingly, the sentence,

31. A expects Z to happen and he believes the chances are considerably less than 50:50, perhaps not much greater than zero, that it will,

[16] To say that the chances are better than 50:50 is equivalent to saying that the probability is higher than 0.5. The former expression, however, is closer to everyday speech and therefore preferable in the present connection.

is incoherent if not outright self-contradictory. This means that we cannot truthfully say that we expect something to happen unless we believe that the probability of its happening is quite high.

On the other hand, in contrast to hope and fear, expectation is independent of wishing. Thus, the sentence,

> 32. A expects it to rain tomorrow,

is as fully compatible with the sentence,

> 33. A wants it to rain tomorrow,

as with the sentence,

> 34. A does not want it to rain tomorrow.

Because it is compatible with both positive and negative wishing, expectation is compatible with hope as well as with fear. Thus, sentence 32, "A expects it to rain tomorrow," is as fully compatible with the sentence,

> 35. A hopes it will rain tomorrow,

as with the sentence,

> 36. A fears it will rain tomorrow.

The following sentences represent a special application of these relationships. Thus we can say,

> 37. A expects the good guys to win,

implying,

> 38. A hopes the good guys will win.

And we can also say,

> 39. A expects the bad guys to win,

implying,

40. A fears that the bad guys will win.

These implications clearly do not derive from the meaning of the word "expect" but from generalizations about what we think ought to and ought not to, and we hence want and want not to, happen. As I have indicated (Rubinstein, 1974, pp. 152f.), it appears that the dynamic effect on us—the suspense and the urge to know the outcome—of situations like those referred to in sentences 37-40 is due in part to the expectations as such, but in part also to the wishes, the hopes, and the fears that are involved in most cases. But not in all, as we will see presently.

Expectations of the kind we are considering generally remain active either until they have been matched by subsequent events or until it has been definitely shown that no events are likely to occur that will match them. Robbe-Grillet's short stories in *Snapshots* (1962) depend for their effect exclusively on aroused (essentially wish-, hope-, and fear-free) expectations that, when the story ends, have not been matched by the subsequent events and that remain for a while in an active state, because this is not what we expect of a short story. Thus we have here two sets of unmatched expectations, namely, expectations aroused by the content of the story and expectations aroused by the fact that what we are considering is a short story.

It may be of interest to pursue the relationship between hope and expectation a little further. Consider the sentence,

41. A hopes the good guys will win, but he believes the chances are considerably less than 50:50 that they will.

The hope expressed in this sentence may be irrational. But it is perfectly legitimate under the indicated conditions to speak about hope. Sentence 31, however, indicates that in this case it would be contrary to the meaning of the word "expect" to say that A expects the good guys to win. On the other hand, as I have mentioned, if it is virtually certain that something will happen, we cannot say that we hope it will happen. But we can still speak about expecting it to happen. When I peel an orange in order to eat it, I do *expect* it to taste like an orange; but, unless I suspect foul play, it would be inappropriate for me to say that I *hope* it will taste like an orange.[17]

I have indicated that, unlike hope and fear, expectation does not involve wishing and that, like hope and fear, it does involve an assessment of the probability of something's happening. The range of probabilities that allows us to speak about expectations, however, is narrower than the ranges of probabilities that allows us to speak about hopes and fears. If the probability of something's happening is minimal it may be irrational to speak about hope or fear, as the case may be, that this something will happen, but it would not be incorrect use of these words. In the case of expectation, on the other hand, if the chances of something's happening are assessed to be considerably less than 50:50, it would not be irrational, but simply incorrect use of the word "expect," to claim that we expect this something to happen. That is not to say, of course, that there are no irrational expectations. If a person A says he expects Z to happen, he implies that in his estimation the chances are better than 50:50 that Z will in fact happen. But if most competent people regarded the chances of Z's happening as at best minimal, then we would say that A's expectation was irrational.

Expectations (or perhaps some associated wishes) often involve (1) a more or less pronounced *disposition* to perceive and/or interpret any event that *can* be perceived and/or interpreted that way in accordance somehow with the related expectation, and (2) a *disposition*, or *set of dispositions*, to act accordingly. If the disposition first mentioned is very pronounced it may lead to irrational interpretations or even distorted perceptions. Thus the expectation expressed in the sentence,

42. M expects to be promoted,

involves a disposition on the part of M to interpret, for example, a friendly gesture by a superior at his job as a sign that he will indeed be promoted and, possibly, a disposition to act with greater assur-

---

[17] The expectation in a case like this corresponds to what I have, in a different connection (Rubinstein, 1974, p. 117), referred to as a predictive classification.

ance than before. M's interpretation may of course be mistaken. But it would not be irrational unless it were *merely subjective*, i.e., if no disinterested observer would agree with M about its validity (see Rubinstein, 1975, p. 21).

The expectation expressed in the sentence,

43. N expects to be rejected by any intelligent and attractive woman,

involves dispositions to perceive, interpret, and act of the same type as those involved in the expectation expressed in sentence 42. These dispositions easily make the expectation self-fulfilling. Expecting to be rejected by a particular intelligent and attractive woman, N may incorrectly see her behavior as rejecting and, acting accordingly, actually make her turn away from him. If he is sufficiently unaware of his own behavior, N would then see the woman's behavior as confirmation of his expectation.

The expectations considered so far may be referred to as *event-outcome expectations*. We can also recognize what may be called *expectations of probable continuation*. These are for the most part "silent." For example, without really being aware of it I expect the house next door to be in its usual place when I go out in the morning. And I expect, say, a conversation between nonpsychotic people to be reasonably coherent, i.e., I expect it to adhere to logical and syntactic rules, not continually to go off on tangents, to consist of statements by the people involved that in some way tie in with one another. It seems that my *orientation* in the world, the physical as well as the emotional place of everything in it, is defined largely by silent expectations of various sorts, including expectations of the types just indicated. These expectations, without which our world would seem quite chaotic, we generally become aware of only if something happens with which they are clearly mismatched. The absurdity of a play like Ionesco's *The Bald Soprano* (1950) derives from a relentless mismatch by subsequent events of nearly every expectation of probable continuation the play arouses.

Of the two sets of unmatched expectations in Robbe-Grillet's short stories referred to above, one set clearly comprises event-outcome expectations, while the other, mainly the expectation derived from the fact that we are concerned with a short story, is best classified as an expectation of probable continuation.

B. Expectation: Outline of an Extraclinical Theoretical Model

Since event-outcome expectation, as we have seen, involves probability assessment but not wishing, it would seem that in an extraclinical theoretical model it may be described as the experiential aspect of the processes occurring in the information-processing network, as depicted in Figure 1, by which the probability of occurrence of the event in question is assessed to be quite high (i.e., considerably higher than 0.5).

It appears, however, that one can experience the assessment of the probability as high without therefore experiencing the corresponding expectation. In discussing goal anticipation, I assumed that our perceptual space has "a temporal dimension, at some *after-now* point of which *not-now* events ... may be 'glimpsed,' more or less intangibly" (Rubinstein, 1974, p. 139). It is likely that to account fully for the experience of event-outcome expectations generally we will have to have recourse to a construction of this type.

The silent expectations of probable continuation are perhaps best described as organizations of object classifiers, situation classifiers, and related classifiers.[18] When they are aroused, the specific quality of their experiential aspects depends in part on the context in which they are aroused. When aroused in one context the *experiential aspect* of such an organization may be a *particular expectation*, when aroused in another a *sense of recognition and familiarity*, and when aroused in a third *bafflement* and perhaps *curiosity*. It is not difficult to envision the essential nature of the three contexts. To save space, I will leave that to the reader.

FANTASY

A. A Semantic-Phenomenological Analysis of Fantasy

I will say only a few words about fantasy. Whereas hope and fear are related to both wishing and probability assessment, and

---

[18] See Rubinstein (1974) for explanations of these terms.

expectation to probability assessment but not to wishing, fantasy, as the word is ordinarily used, is related to wishing but not to probability assessment. Fantasy often occurs if something one wants to happen does not, and also when there is little or no hope that whatever one wants will materialize. Fantasy typically does, but may not, involve imagery. In either event—as may be gathered from the foregoing remarks—it usually is closely related to the fulfillment of a wish. For the occurrence of fantasy it makes no difference whether a fantasied event is probable or highly improbable.

It is of interest that a fantasy, whether or not it involves imagery, may be more clearly articulated than the corresponding wish itself. For example, a young woman who was only dimly aware of *wanting* to have a penis nevertheless often *fantasied*, particularly when walking on crowded streets, that she did actually have one. In this case the fantasy, although clearly articulated as such, did not seem to involve unequivocally identifiable imagery. It was rather a *sense*, which the patient was unable to describe further, that she did have a penis. Some fantasies appear to be symbolically transformed wish fulfillments. A male patient who was filled with hostility toward both parents and to a lesser degree toward his siblings recalled that when he was around fourteen he used to fantasy that he was a submarine sailing into a harbor where he blew up every single ship. We may note in this connection that "harbor" and "home" are often linked metaphorically.[19]

Fantasies may be quite complex. For example, a patient once said that on her way to her analytic session she had a "quick fantasy" that if she were to stop talking about her feelings the analyst would rebuke her. This "fantasy" differs in two ways from the fantasies just considered. First, it has the quality of neither the imagistic nor the virtually imageless fantasies cited above. And indeed, on questioning, the patient said that really it was just a *thought* she had had about what the analyst would do. Second, it does not seem to be *directly* related to a wish fulfillment. I will return to this question in discussing unconscious fantasy.

---

[19] Although this fantasy is also quite suggestive of sexual symbolism, no data qualifying as evidence for a hypothesis to that effect could be identified in the material provided by the patient.

The following sentences illustrate the fact that in their occurrence fantasy, wish, and hope depend on different conditions. The sentence,

> 44. A *fantasies* about going to India because he knows he can't go,

is more likely to be true than the sentence,

> 45. A *wants* to go to India because he knows he can't go,

whereas the sentence,

> 46. A *hopes* to go to India because he knows he can't go,

being self-contradictory, obviously cannot be true.

B. Fantasy: Outline of an Extraclinical Theoretical Model

In the paper I have repeatedly referred to (Rubinstein, 1974) I discussed fantasy only as imagery (pp. 137-139). I will not repeat that discussion here except to indicate that if this form of fantasy is a goal-situation fantasy, as is usually the case, it arises through interaction of processes representing the corresponding goal-situation classifier with processes corresponding to activated elements of memories of previous goal situations. In Figure 1 the interaction is represented by arrows connecting, on the one hand, the goal-situation classifier (GF-Sit. Classifier) box with the box right above it labeled "GF-Sit. Feature Storage" and, on the other, these two boxes with the box roughly in the middle of the figure labeled "GF-Sit. Fantasy." In the previous paper I tried to justify the theory underlying this arrangement.

A simple way to account for imageless fantasy is to regard such a fantasy as the experiential aspect of a classification, say, of an A as being a B, the classification being inconsistent with what the individual in question knows to be the case, i.e., in essence with certain other, in some way related, fully accepted classifications. The experiential aspect of the classification is most simply described as a *sense*, known *not* to correspond to any reality, of A's being a B. The criterial attribute for being a B may be having a k (e.g., a penis), or receiving an *m* (e.g., a promotion), or doing *n* (e.g., solving a difficult problem). In these cases *A* is the fantasying person himself and the classification is thus a self-classification. It is clear from the cited examples that in most cases a goal-situation classifier is involved. It is not possible at this point to be more specific about the nature of the relevant processes.

The processes in the case of the patient who thought she would be rebuked by the analyst if she did not talk about her feelings include the classification of the two events as standing in a particular sequential relationship to one another. As I mentioned, I will consider this case more fully in discussing unconscious fantasy.

ON THE POSSIBILITY OF UNCONSCIOUS HOPES, FEARS, EXPECTATIONS, AND FANTASIES

According to Freud, the most characteristic unconscious activity is that of wishing. As he once put it: "The nucleus of the *Ucs.* consists of . . . wishful impulses" (1915c, p. 186). This statement obviously does not preclude the possibility of unconscious activities other than wishing. We may therefore ask if it is possible to hope, fear, expect, and fantasy unconsciously. It seems that we can attach the qualifier "unconscious" (or "unconsciously") to the verbal sign for any mental activity. *Grammatically* it makes as much—or, if you wish, as little—sense to speak, say about unconscious convictions and unconscious hopes as about unconscious wishes. The question, however, is not one of grammar but of the *nature* of the processes in question and/or of their component processes. In the following I will not consider the possibility of unconscious convictions or of any other unconscious mental activities the conscious counterparts of which I have not discussed above.

Among the characteristics Freud ascribed to unconscious mental activities, the most important in the present connection are that they proceed without consideration of degrees of certainty, of time relationships, and of reality (1915c, pp. 186, 187). Thus on the face of it the possibility of unconscious hopes, fears, and expectations seems pretty much to be excluded. The conscious activities of all three, as we have seen, involve probability assessments, i.e., as Freud put it, the assessment of *degrees of certainty.* The assessments are of the probability that certain things will *really* happen at *some point in the future*, which obviously means that they involve considerations of both reality and temporal relationships.

I will take one step beyond Freud and apply his characterization not just, as he did himself, to what he thought of as strictly unconscious, but also to what he thought of as preconscious (i.e., merely "qualitatively" unconscious) mental activity. At this point I can justify this step only by referring to the fact that intuitively it makes sense, at least to me. If, on the basis of mind-brain identity theory, we had to identify processes that could not be the processes they in fact are without having an experiential aspect, we would, I think, among others choose at least some of the processes involved in the assessment of probabilities and in the determination of temporal relationships and of what we call reality. With Freud (1915c, pp. 177-179) I would add feeling to this list, and, further, a number of other processes including the end point of the process of perception, certain phases of thinking, and choice.[20]

I will later, in a general way, touch on this question again. First, however, I will try to examine how the view just indicated fits the extraclinical theoretical model I am developing. Throughout this discussion I will not distinguish between unconscious and preconscious activities but will refer to both as unconscious. It will be clear from the context when I use the term "unconscious" in reference to repressed activities. As indicated in the above discussion of clinically relevant anxiety, I am not denying that the latter may function in ways that are specific to them only. Right now, however, I am not concerned with this question.

Although it should be clear from what I have said already, before proceeding it may not be redundant to point out explicitly that I have used Freud's view of the characteristics of unconscious mental activities not as he meant it to be used, but merely as a springboard to a view that, notwithstanding a certain superficial resemblance, in many ways differs from his. Once we realize that, we will be able to avoid a number of possible misunderstandings.

It may also not be redundant to point out that, as far as I can see, the difference between Freud's view and the one I have

---

[20] The determination of what we call reality obviously involves perceptions, probability assessments, etc. I mention it separately because it is often referred to separately in psychoanalytic theorizing.

adopted to a significant degree derives from the fact that I ascribe a greater functional importance to certain conscious phenomena than Freud did. This point has been at least implicit in much of what I have said above. It will become abundantly clear as we go along.

THE QUESTION OF UNCONSCIOUS HOPE

Let us start with *hope*. To the best of my knowledge psychoanalysts seldom, if ever, speak about *unconscious hopes*. And indeed, if we eliminate, in accordance with the above conception, the probability assessments that, as posited in the model, are involved in hoping, what we are left with is a wish—or rather, the goal-situation classifier corresponding to the wish. It thus follows from our premises that hope as such cannot occur unconsciously, only the goal-situation classifier of the wish involved in conscious hope. This, as I just indicated, is in full agreement with customary psychoanalytic usage of the word "hope."

THE QUESTION OF UNCONSCIOUS FEAR

In the case of *fear* the situation is different. Whereas Freud (1915c, pp. 177f.) strongly argued against the possibility of unconscious affects, Pulver (1971, 1974) and Brenner (1974, p. 551), among others, have adopted the opposite view. Neither of the latter two authors, however, has presented convincing arguments in favor of the view he advocates. Pulver's claim that *"unconscious affects* exist ... outside awareness" (1974, p. 78; emphasis in original) does not prevent him from also claiming that these unconscious affects "exist experientially." We can perhaps understand Pulver's indifference to this contradiction if we consider that in his rejection of Freud's commonsense view of the necessarily conscious nature of affects he insists that he does not want to be influenced by semantics (1971, p. 350). And it seems that indeed he is not. As we will see shortly, however, something may be said in favor of Pulver's general concept—but not as he phrases it.

Brenner, on the other hand, regards affects, including fear and anxiety, as "complex mental phenomena which include (a) sensations of pleasure, unpleasure, or a mixture of the two, and (b) thoughts, memories, wishes, fears—in a word ideas" (1974,

p. 535). He believes that both of these components of affect can be repressed and thus rendered unconscious (p. 552). It is difficult to see what might possibly be meant by *unconscious sensations* of pleasure or unpleasure. Does Brenner imply, as Pulver apparently does, that a mental event can exist *experientially* in an unconscious state?

If we consider the theory of repression outlined above, a glance at Figures 2 and 3 will convince us that, as in the case of hope, according to the model I have presented, unconscious fear, whether of psychological or of physical trauma, is constituted exclusively of the goal-situation classifier of a wish to avoid the trauma. If this is correct, we have no way of distinguishing, in cases like those illustrated by the figures just mentioned, between unconscious hope and unconscious fear. Thus the statement that unconsciously he is *afraid of* such and such and the statement that unconsciously he *hopes to avoid* such and such are both, in the language of the model, rendered by saying that unconsciously he *wants to avoid* such and such. The two conditions may, however, be associated with dispositions for the person in question to attend selectively to events classifiable as hopeful in the one case and to events classifiable as in some sense ominous in the other. We must not, on the other hand, lose sight of the possibility that, while fear may well be repressed and hence unconscious, hope is at least somewhat likely not to be.

In a previous discussion of hate I indicated that, while in some sense conscious, the hate may not be classified as such and hence may remain unrecognized by the person harboring it (Rubinstein, 1974, pp. 176, 177). It is at any rate plausible that fear may in a like manner not be classified as such and thus may be in this sense unconscious.[21] It seems that in discussing his findings, Pulver (1971, p. 353) has a similar idea in mind when he refers to "splitting of the ego" as a possible explanation. Although he rejects this and similar explanations, it may well be that what he calls unconscious affects are in fact affects that have not been classified as such by the persons entertaining them.

---

[21] It would be more correct to say, as in effect I did in the previous paper, that the fear is neither conscious nor unconscious. In the present connection, however, a less accurate wording will do.

The above considerations apply to what I have called normal anxiety and to fear of physical trauma. Ordinarily, clinically relevant anxiety, as I have defined the concept above, is not assumed to be unconscious. A phobia without the experience of anxiety is not a phobia but an avoidance reaction of a different type.

The following point is of interest. It is fairly common in psychoanalytic practice to speak about a patient as unconsciously being afraid of his own anger. This expression may be used in a number of meanings. For example, to say that a person is unconsciously afraid of something may mean that his fear is unconscious, in which case we can render, in terms of the model, what the speaker has in mind by saying that the person in question has an unconscious wish to avoid being angry or to avoid showing that he is angry. More interesting, however, is when we speak about a patient's unconscious fear meaning that, while his anger is unconscious, his fear is not. In this case, obviously, the anger is inferred and so is the connection between it and the actually experienced fear.

I will assume that these are reasonable inferences. I will assume further that anger is part of the experiential aspect of an activated impulse to hit (or otherwise harm) an adversary in combination with a goal-situation classifier of hitting (or otherwise harming) this person and presumably some constraining factors. We can then, in extraclinical theoretical terms, tentatively posit that, when a person experiences fear and the fear seems to be of his unconscious anger, the flight impulse is somehow, directly or indirectly, activated by the repressed active goal-situation classifier of hitting (or otherwise harming) an adversary or a person who unconsciously is a stand-in for an adversary.

THE QUESTION OF UNCONSCIOUS EXPECTATIONS

Expectations such as those expressed in sentences 37 and 39, namely, "A expects the good guys to win" and "A expects the bad guys to win," whether explicable in terms of hope (sentence 37), or fear (sentence 39), or neither (e.g., the sentence "I expect John and Mary, neither of whom I know well at all, to get married soon"), involve specific probability assessments and thus cannot, according to our premises, occur unconsciously. This is consonant with ordinary usage. Either a person watching a show *consciously* expects, say, the bad guys to win, or he just does not expect them to win.

The same consideration applies to the expectation of being promoted expressed in sentence 42. In this case, however, as in the case of any expectation involving specific perception and/or interpretation and/or action dispositions, we can *speak* about an *unconscious expectation* if we observe events qualifying as manifestations of the dispositions in question. When taken to be unconscious, the expectation expressed in sentence 43 is expressed in the following sentence:

> 47. Unconsciously N expects to be rejected by any intelligent and attractive woman.

According to our premises, this sentence does not imply that unconsciously N assesses the chances to be better than 50:50 of his being rejected by any intelligent and attractive woman he happens to meet. The only meaning—and most certainly the only testable meaning—of the sentence is expressed in sentence 48:

> 48. If N meets an intelligent and attractive woman he will perceive and/or interpret her behavior as rejecting of him and will act accordingly, i.e., he will withdraw, or behave awkwardly in some manner, etc.

The more fully (and, within certain limits, the more often) the prediction expressed in sentence 48 is confirmed by observation, the greater, by and large, the probability we as observers attach to the statement sentence 47 expresses.

As indicated, however, this does not mean that the occurrence of a process in every way like a conscious expectation, except that is is unconscious, is assigned a corresponding probability. What it does mean is simply that the greater the degree of confirmation of the prediction expressed in sentence 48 the more does it make sense *linguistically*, although not necessarily *factually*, to speak about an unconscious expectation. The reason for this usage seems to derive from a tacit convention according to which, whenever the dispositions involved in the corresponding conscious expectation are manifested in a sufficient degree (and their presence thus confirmed), we can speak *as if* the expectation itself were also present, even though in fact it may not be—and in the case of an "unconscious expectation" is not.

We may note that, making the same observations as an outside observer and following the same linguistic convention, when the prediction expressed in sentence 48 is reasonably well confirmed, N may ascribe to himself the "unconscious expectation" referred to in sentence 47. From an observer's point of view this is obviously not additional confirmation but merely a sign of agreement between observer and observed person on the validity of the inference involved and shared linguistic usage.

The following sentence is of some interest:

49. K expects always to be a loser.

On the face of it the sentence expresses a conscious expectation. However, if we were to ask K, "Do you expect always to be a loser?" he might be at a loss as to how to answer this question. If so, we might conclude that K's expectation is "unconscious," i.e., that the meaning of sentence 49 is to be explicated essentially in terms of dispositions such as those expressed in the following sentences:

50. K usually does not seem particularly surprised when he loses,

and

51. K apparently fails to take advantage even of seemingly very promising opportunities.

We should not, however, lose sight of the possibility that, while K is unable to answer the question, "Do you expect always to be a loser?," he might well, on particular occasions where it is possible for him either to win or lose, say that he really does not expect to win. In other words, before concluding in a case like K's that an expectation we believe to be present is likely to be "unconscious," we must be reasonably certain that we have not formulated our questions in so general a way as to make them difficult, if not impossible, to answer properly.

It is, however, also possible that K, without actually *classifying* his experience as one of expecting to lose in most situations in which he stands to lose something, does have an experience he might classify that way but, failing to do so, is only vaguely (and not more than preverbally) aware of this expectation and therefore is at a loss as to how to answer the question just cited. This consideration may very well also apply to other "unconscious" expectations.

It follows from the above considerations that, according to our premises, whereas neither unconscious hope nor unconscious fear can exist but only the corresponding wishes—or rather the isolated goal-situation classifier involved in the wishes—the term "unconscious expectation" can be used in reference to certain dispositions, namely, the same as those we have in mind when we speak about the corresponding conscious expectations, *and nothing else.* In comparison with the corresponding conscious activities, what is lacking in the types of unconscious mental activity we have considered is mainly the assessment of the probability of certain future events. In the case of at least these types of unconscious mental activity, thus, the corresponding conscious activities are not simply unconscious activities that have acquired the "quality" of being conscious, e.g., in the way Kris (1932-1952, pp. 305, 313) posited for unconscious (or preconscious) activities generally, namely, by some particular form of (energic) hypercathexis (see also Freud, e.g., 1915c, pp. 168, 194, 201f.).

The Question of Unconscious Fantasy

Freud did speak fairly often about *unconscious fantasies* (see, e.g., 1915c, p. 191). Obviously the expression cannot refer to unconscious imagery or to an unconscious "sense" of having something one wants corresponding to the conscious sense I referred to in discussing conscious fantasy. If the "unconscious fantasy" is supposed to be simply a "fantasy" of the fulfillment of a wish, then it seems to be impossible, from the point of view of possible processes, to distinguish it from an unconscious wish. In both cases what we have is merely the activity of an isolated (repressed) goal-situation classifier. Since such a classifier is a preliminary stage in the formation of both a conscious wish and a conscious fantasy, it is essentially a matter of stylistic preference if we want to speak about an unconscious wish or an unconscious fantasy. Indeed, it follows from the above discussion of these hypothetical activities that unconscious hopes and fears, if they may be said to occur, are likewise hardly distinguishable from unconscious fantasies.[22]

We may note that Freud also posited unconscious mental activities that, although functionally unconscious, have the characteristics of preconscious, and thus—according to his presuppositions—also of conscious, activities (1915c, pp. 190f.). Fantasies are often said to be unconscious in this sense. An example is the "fantasy" expressed in the following sentence:

> 52. Q has the unconscious fantasy that, if he does what R wants him to do, R will give him what he, Q, wants.

This sentence includes a reference to both a logical operation, namely, the formulation of an if-then relationship, and a probability assessment. If we assume that in general logical operations of the indicated type are as unlikely to occur unconsciously (in the descriptive sense of the term) as are probability assessments,[23] we must rule that either "unconscious fantasies" of the type expressed in sentence 52 do not exist or the corresponding concept can be broken down into terms that do not violate our presuppositions. It is not impossible to opt for the second of these possibilities. We will only have to be quite clear about the kinds of observed behavioral events (in the widest possible sense of the word "behavioral") on the basis of which an "unconscious fantasy" of the type we are considering is inferred and confirmed clinically. An examination of

---

[22] To distinguish between an unconscious wish, an unconscious hope, and an unconscious fear on the one hand, and an unconscious fantasy on the other, we might posit that in the case of the last-mentioned activity, and only in that case, appropriate elements in the goal-situation feature storage are alerted. This supposition, however, does not seem particularly credible. It cannot be confirmed clinically, nor does it explain anything that is not explained by regarding unconscious wishes and fantasies of the type we are considering as indistinguishable from one another.

[23] In the last section of the paper I will consider an important qualification of this statement to the effect that, whereas the process of assessment proceeds unconsciously, the initiation of the process and its end product are both conscious, at least in part.

this question must be left for another occasion. In the present connection I can only state flatly that, without appreciable loss of *verifiable meaning*, sentence 52 can be replaced by the following sentence:

> 53. Q has an unconscious wish for R to give him what he wants and a disposition, arousable by the wish, within certain limits to do what R wants him to do.

In this sentence, as we can see, there is no reference to an unconscious fantasy. What we have is an unconscious wish and a disposition causally related to the wish. This relationship presumably is not created *de novo* but is more likely a blind replay of a connection that in its general features has been established by experiences of the kind that may be expressed in some such sentence as "When I give him what he wants he is more likely to give me what I want than when I don't give him what he wants." We may call the configuration of unconscious wish, disposition, and the connection between them an unconscious fantasy. That, as far as I can see, is unobjectionable as long as we do not take this expression to mean that there are fantasies in every way like conscious fantasies except that they are not conscious.[24]

Arlow has claimed that "No sharp line of distinction can be made between conscious and unconscious fantasies" (1969, p. 25). This claim, however, is not based on an explicit theory of the processes that may be involved. According to the model I am presenting, the processes involved, even though they may have elements in common, are quite different. The concept of unconscious fantasy, of course, is more vivid than what I am substituting for it. But that does not mean that, taken literally, it is more accurate or has greater explanatory power.

It is obviously important to distinguish between an unconscious fantasy and unconscious determiners of a conscious fantasy. Take the patient referred to above, in the discussion of conscious fantasy, who had the "quick fantasy" that the analyst would rebuke her if

---

[24] It is an open question to what extent the hypothesis expressed in sentence 53, of the arousability of the disposition by the unconscious wish, is clinically verifiable. In the present connection I will leave this question open.

she did not talk about her feelings. I said that this "fantasy" does not seem to be *directly* related to a wish fulfillment. It may, however, be *indirectly* related to such fulfillment. There are at least two possibilities. The patient may have either (a) an *unconscious* wish not to talk about her feelings and a *conscious* anticipation of what would happen if indeed she did not, i.e., if she, unbeknownst to herself, were to act according to her unconscious wish, or (b) an *unconscious* masochistic wish to be rebuked by the analyst, to the fulfillment of which not talking about her feelings would then, again unbeknownst to herself, be the means. In either event the "fantasy" obviously is not unconscious, but the wish is, and in the second case the process by which a means-end relationship is utilized that presumably is pre-established, at least in its general features. Arlow (1969) has not analyzed his illustrative material in sufficient detail to allow us to determine whether or not some of the "unconscious fantasies" he lists may in fact be conscious fantasies with unconscious determiners.

If this analysis is correct, do we have to abandon the commonly held notion of the creative powers of "the unconscious"? In the next, and last, section I will consider this question, among others.

A NOTE ON CONSCIOUSNESS

In the preceding discussion I have repeatedly contrasted conscious with unconscious mental activities and have specified some of the ways in which they differ from one another. To round out the extraclinical theoretical model, which in part is founded on this contrast, a more general discussion of consciousness and some of the problems it presents is called for.

Elsewhere (Rubinstein, 1976) I have referred to psychologically relevant neural processes as M-processes and distinguished between ME- and MI-processes, i.e., processes that do and processes that do not have an experiential aspect. As indicated above (fn. 4), my reasoning in this paper is ultimately based on the identity theory of the mind-brain relationship. While on the basis of this theory, in conjunction with the fact that we do have experiences, we simply posit the existence of ME-processes, the mental activities constituting the MI-processes are themselves inferred. The *class* of ME-processes comprises what in a general way we refer to as consciousness.[25] The MI-processes, on the other hand, are what Freud referred to as descriptively or qualitatively unconscious. They include both repressed and not repressed M-processes and also M-processes involved in the activity of repression (and other activities geared toward the resolution of inner conflict).

I have assumed that the ME-processes differ from the MI-processes, not only from a psychological but from a physiological point of view as well, in the sense that in *principle* it should be possible to tell from a physiological examination alone which processes—or organizations of processes—do and which do not have an experiential aspect.

Another assumption I am making is that both ME- and MI-processes are essential to mental functioning. The question that interests us in the present connection is which way the ME-processes enter into the over-all mental activity. Quite generally I think one can say that in most sequences of M-processes, i.e., M-processes constituting particular mental activities, ME-processes are positioned at certain crucial points. We know next to nothing about these things. We can, however, make a few guesses. I will be brief.

Let me begin with a commonplace observation. We are generally aware of "formulating" what we want, what we want to say, what we want to do, the problems we want to solve, etc. The "formulation" is not necessarily a formulation in words, and in some cases it could not be. Before speaking, for example, we only have a *sense* of what we want to say. And we have a similar sense in regard to the other activities mentioned. But we have such a sense not only before the inception of a particular activity. Thus, in the case of speaking, when we say what we sensed we wanted to say we also

---

[25] We should not forget that, although often used as a spatial term, what the word "consciousness" stands for is an abstraction. The following example indicates that the corresponding concept can readily be interpreted as a class concept. The ordinary-language statement that a previously unconscious "idea" V entered consciousness at time t_1 can thus be rendered by saying that V, having prior to t_1 been a member of the class of MI-processes, at t_1 (through some transformation process) acquired characteristics that made it classifiable as a member of the class of ME-processes.

sense whether or not it came out right, whether or not we actually said what we had in mind to say. As I will try to show presently, the probability assessments that are involved, for example, in hope and fear are sensed in a similar fashion, either throughout the experience or, if they are integrated to form it, prior to their integration.

The variety of thinking we refer to as problem solving illustrates very well some of the points I have tried to make. As I have indicated elsewhere (Rubinstein, 1976, p. 241), it is a fairly commonly held view that the actual thought process proceeds without awareness. The problem, however, must be formulated consciously before the relevant MI-processes can begin to unfold. Stories abound about how the solution to a problem appeared in a dream or emerged clearly on awakening in the morning after fruitless attempts to find it the night before. It seems, however, that the solution could not have appeared unless the problem first had been formulated consciously. And I mean this in the nontrivial sense that, as far as one can tell, it is not possible for problems to be formulated unconsciously.

As just indicated, solutions seem to emerge directly from unconscious processing. It is striking, however, that we often know immediately whether they are right or wrong, i.e., if they actually are the sought-after solutions. That is, the checking is at least partly conscious. It is somewhat like not being able to think of a name. Various names, more or less resembling the name we are trying to remember, come to mind, but we *know* they are not right; and when the right name appears we *know* it is the right name. Clearly we are here faced with a matching process where both mismatch and match involve ME-processes. The phenomenon is not, as Freud (e.g., 1915c, p. 171) surmised, explainable by saying that consciousness functions like an organ of perception. This view implies that the mismatch and the match could have occurred without being perceived, i.e., without the involvement of ME-processes. My point is that, in a case like the one we are considering, they could not. Since ME-processes are involved, they must have a function in the over-all process. Freud's view is closely related to the epiphenomenalistic doctrine of the mind-brain relationship. My point, on the other hand, cannot be rigorously proven. But it seems to me more plausible than any alternative I know of.

The case of problem solving differs in some of its features from that of probability assessment in hope, fear, and expectation. While problems are discrete events and depend for their solution on as precise a formulation as possible, in hope, fear, and expectation the process of probability assessment is not preceded by a precisely formulated problem. In these cases we ordinarily do not explicitly ask questions like "What is the probability that such and such?" Take P to whom I have repeatedly referred to above. When A learns that P is seriously ill he asks a few questions about his condition, etc., and in this way gets the necessary data on the basis of which he can think (and perhaps say) that he *expects* P to recover, or *hopes* that he will, or *fears* that he may not, as the case may be. Without being itself conscious in its entire course, the assessment of a particular outcome probability—presumably through a process of matching—determines which of these thoughts (and statements) is most adequate. The matching process involves either a sense of rightness or of uncertainty, which means that it is at least in part an ME-process. It obviously corresponds to finding a solution in problem solving.

Let us take a closer look at the beginning of this sequence. It is not a very hazardous surmise that, like the "solution," the process that sets the sequence going is an ME-process of a particular kind. When he learns that P is ill, A, without necessarily putting his wish into words, wants to know the chances of P's recovery. This wish to know, whether articulated as such or merely sensed, together with the questions we have assumed he asked, corresponds to the formulation of the problem in problem solving. If this view is correct, A's wish to know, etc., can reasonably be identified as the ME-process that triggers the sequence of MI-processes which constitute the technical part, so to speak, of the probability assessment. I have taken it that the wish to know (which, incidentally, may not be a wish in the ordinary sense of the word) sets the stage for the probability assessment and that without this wish the latter could not occur. The reasoning here is exactly the same as in the case of problem solving. An obvious analogy is that in order to function computers need to be fed a program. They generate solutions, not the problems requiring these solutions.

Let us assume that by and large these considerations are sound. It then follows that, since they involve probability assessments, hope, fear, and expectation, as I have indicated, cannot occur unconsciously, i.e., without a particular kind of conscious involvement.[26]

In the discussion of unconscious fantasy I was led to ask whether creative powers can be ascribed to "the unconscious," as is commonly done. It seems fairly clear that so-called creative ideas, whether in the sciences, philosophy, or the arts, do not emerge in a void. A chance observation, such as Newton's proverbial falling apple, may give rise to a creative idea, but only if the person making the observation *recognizes* it as, in an unexpected manner, fitting into a particular framework, or as resolving a previously seemingly intractable contradiction, or as requiring a radical change of an existing framework and maybe its abandonment. It seems that the processes here are in large measure ME-processes involving matching and the resolution of mismatch. The analogy with problem solving is obvious. The starting point may not be an observation, however, but a more or less inchoate thought or image that, emerging from a series of what we may refer to as MI "primary-process" classifications, becomes a creative idea in the same manner as the type of chance observation just mentioned. I should add that the observation or the emerging idea may, as it were, simply bypass any existing framework and become the prime instigator of the creation of an entirely new framework into which it fits.

I mentioned MI "primary-process" classifications. I use this expression in reference to certain hypothetical processes related to those presumably involved in dream symbol formation and similar events (see Rubinstein, 1974, pp. 161-171). It is conceivable that they may result from what I have elsewhere figuratively referred to as a high degree of flexibility of class boundaries (Rubinstein, 1972, p. 104).

This is all quite obscure, and to speak with Kris (1932-1952) about regression in the service of the ego is not very illuminating. One thing is clear: both conscious and unconscious processes of various sorts participate in the formation of creative ideas, although not always in the same proportion. It also appears that in

---

[26] I must call attention to a certain ambiguity in the way I have used the term "probability assessment," namely, both in reference to a process and to the result of this process. If we pay attention to the contexts in which the term occurs, it will not be difficult to keep these meanings separate.

every case the over-all process involves some of the highest functions of which the human mind is capable.

We have seen—or surmised—that some mental activities apparently have to be conscious, at least in part, while others can only proceed unconsciously. In neither case is it a question of logical necessity. That is, however, the way things seem to be as revealed to introspection, i.e., on phenomenological analysis. The method, of course, is highly imperfect. But for now, at least, we have no other. And through it we can reasonably expect to arrive at some approximation of what may actually be the case.

The view that certain mental activities must be conscious (albeit not by logical necessity) seems foreign to psychoanalytic thinking. Even though Freud referred to consciousness as "a fact without parallel, which defies all explanation or description" (1940, p. 157), the main function he ascribed to it, apart from its being analogous to a sense organ, appears to be what he called a finely discriminating regulation of the displacement and discharge of cathexes (1900, p. 616). It is not easy to see what *specific* regulation this expression may refer to. Besides, being a class concept, "consciousness" obviously does not regulate anything. The fact that in Freud's view unconscious mental activities proceed without consideration of degrees of certainty, of time relationships, and of reality does not, as I have indicated, imply that activities characterized by these considerations are conscious, even in part. According to Freud, they need not be. He regarded them as normally preconscious, i.e., "qualitatively" unconscious (1915c, p. 188). He held the same view of thinking (1900, p. 617; 1915c, p. 202; 1940, p. 160). Indeed, he claimed—with somewhat greater circumspection than he ordinarily exhibited in these matters—that "Experience has taught us that there is hardly a psychical process, however complicated it may be, which cannot on occasion remain preconscious" (1940, p. 160). As I have tried to show, if we accept the model I have presented or some similar model, that cannot be the case.

CONCLUDING REMARK

Out of the multiplicity of semantic-phenomenological analyses and extraclinical theoretical speculations on the preceding pages some common psychoanalytic statements have emerged in a more specific and concrete form than the form in which they are usually presented. By making them emerge this way I hoped to be able to subject them to more rigorous testing than is otherwise possible. However, as I said in the beginning of this paper, the method I have employed is fraught with uncertainties. Accordingly, I may not have achieved my aim. But, if that is the case, I hope at least to have shown that there are weak links in our habitual ways of thinking. And if psychoanalysis is ever to become a science we cannot simply cover them over and go on as before.

REFERENCES

Arlow, J. A. (1969), Unconscious Fantasy and Disturbances of Conscious Experience. *Psychoanal. Quart.*, 38:1-27.

Austin, J. L. (1946), Other Minds. In: *J. L. Austin, Philosophical Papers*, 2nd ed., ed. J. O. Urmson & G. J. Warnock. Oxford: Oxford University Press, pp. 76-116, 1970.

Brenner, C. (1974), On the Nature and Development of Affects: A Unified Theory. *Psychoanal. Quart.*, 43:532-556.

Fenichel, O. (1945), *The Psychoanalytic Theory of Neurosis*. New York: Norton.

Freud, S. (1895), On the Grounds for Detaching a Syndrome from Neurasthenia under the Description of 'Anxiety Neurosis.' *Standard Edition*, 3:90-115. London: Hogarth Press, 1962.

——— (1900), The Interpretation of Dreams. *Standard Edition*, 4 & 5. London: Hogarth Press, 1953.

——— (1915a), Instincts and Their Vicissitudes. *Standard Edition*, 14:117-140. London: Hogarth Press, 1957.

——— (1915b), Repression. *Standard Edition*, 14:146-158. London: Hogarth Press, 1957.

——— (1915c), The Unconscious. *Standard Edition*, 14:166-215. London: Hogarth Press, 1957.

——— (1923), The Ego and the Id. *Standard Edition*, 19:12-66. London: Hogarth Press, 1961.

——— (1926), Inhibitions, Symptoms and Anxiety. *Standard Edition*, 20:87-174. London: Hogarth Press, 1959.

——— (1933), New Introductory Lectures on Psycho-Analysis. *Standard Edition*, 22:7-182. London: Hogarth Press, 1964.

——— (1940), An Outline of Psycho-Analysis. *Standard Edition*, 23:144-207. London: Hogarth Press, 1964.

Hampshire, S. (1971), *Freedom of Mind and Other Essays*. Princeton: Princeton University Press.

Ionesco, E. (1950), *The Bald Soprano*, trans. D. M. Allen. New York: Grove Press, 1958.

Koffka, K. (1936), *Principles of Gestalt Psychology*. New York: Harcourt, Brace.

Köhler, W. (1947), *Gestalt Psychology*. New York: Mentor Books, 1974.

Kris, E. (1932-1952), *Psychoanalytic Explorations in Art.* New York: International Universities Press, 1952.

Kubie, L. S. (1947), The Fallacious Use of Quantitative Concepts in Dynamic Psychology. *Psychoanal. Quart.*, 16:507-518.

McDougall, W. (1921), *An Introduction to Social Psychology,* 14th ed. Boston: Luce.

—— (1928), Emotion and Feeling Distinguished. In: *Feelings and Emotions,* ed. M. L. Reymert. Worcester, Mass.: Clark University Press, pp. 200-205.

Pulver, S. E. (1971), Can Affects Be Unconscious? *Internat. J. Psycho-Anal.*, 52:347-354.

—— (1974), Unconscious versus Potential Affects. *Psychoanal. Quart.*, 43: 77-84.

Robbe-Grillet, A. (1962), *Snapshots,* trans. B. Morrissette. New York: Grove Press, 1968.

Rubinstein, B. B. (1965), Psychoanalytic Theory and the Mind-Body Problem. In: *Psychoanalysis and Current Biological Thought,* ed. N. S. Greenfeld & W. C. Lewis. Madison: University of Wisconsin Press, pp. 35-56.

—— (1967), Explanation and Mere Description: A Metascientific Examination of Certain Aspects of the Psychoanalytic Theory of Motivation. In: Motives and Thought: Psychoanalytic Essays in Honor of David Rapaport. ed. R. R. Holt. *Psychol. Issues,* Monogr. No. 18/19:22-77. New York: International Universities Press.

—— (1972), On Metaphor and Related Phenomena. *Psychoanalysis and Contemporary Science,* 1:70-108. New York: Macmillan.

—— (1974), On the Role of Classificatory Processes in Mental Functioning: Aspects of a Psychoanalytic Theoretical Model. *Psychoanalysis and Contemporary Science,* 3:101-185. New York: International Universities Press.

—— (1975), On the Clinical Psychoanalytic Theory and Its Role in the Inference and Confirmation of Particular Clinical Hypotheses. *Psychoanalysis and Contemporary Science,* 4:3-58. New York: International Universities Press.

—— (1976), On the Possibility of a Strictly Clinical Psychoanalytic Theory: An Essay in the Philosophy of Psychoanalysis. In: Psychology versus Metapsychology: Psychoanalytic Essays in Memory of George S. Klein, ed. M. M. Gill & P. H. Holzman. *Psychol. Issues,* Monogr. No. 36:229-264. New York: International Universities Press.

Robert R. Holt, Ph.D.

Freud's Theory of the Primary Process— Present Status

During the past 25 years, I have devoted a good deal of my professional life to an attempt to understand and work with Freud's concepts of the primary and secondary process. The original mission of the Research Center for Mental Health, when George Klein and I founded it in 1953, was to investigate the psychoanalytic theory of thinking, and for a long time most of the empirical and theoretical research carried out under its auspices was more or less directly focused on that task. One reason we chose such a focus was that I had found it possible to operationalize the concept of the primary process in a way of scoring responses to Rorschach's ink-blots. Over the succeeding years, I have worked by fits and starts on the elaboration and application of the scoring manual that embodies an operational definition of the primary process (and of the closely related construct, adaptive versus maladaptive regression); after 10 informally duplicated revisions, it is about ready for formal publication, supported by a considerable body of research attesting to its empirical usefulness.

Near the end of the first decade of work, I found myself growing more and more frustrated in my efforts to understand the metapsychological underpinnings of Freud's theory of thinking, so I devoted increasing efforts to clarifying them for myself. The upshot was a series of papers in which I have tried to explore

Preparation of this paper was supported by a United States Public Health Service Research Career Award, Grant No. 5-KO6-MH-12455, from the National Institute of Mental Health.

Freud's thinking and writing, in part stylistically (Holt, 1974) and historically (e.g., Holt, 1967a), in part by an effort to sort through Freud's writings on a topic and search out a core of meaning (e.g., Holt, 1962), and in part by exploring philosophical issues implicit in the problems of metapsychology (e.g., Holt, 1965).

THE TWILIGHT OF METAPSYCHOLOGY

The obvious place to start this long critical task was the concept of psychic energy, for it was plain enough that throughout the years when he wrote about the theory of thinking, Freud laid major stress on propositions about the hypothetical energies of thought. In the terminology of his metapsychology, that was a treatment from the economic point of view; it consisted almost entirely in the assertion that the energies of the primary process were *freely mobile,* those of the secondary process *bound.* The meaning of these terms is hardly self-evident, and I found that the only way I could discover what Freud intended by them was to collect and study all the passages in which they occurred, looking for their systemic meaning in the contexts and ways in which these terms were used. Because I had not yet discerned some important components of Freud's cognitive style, I was dismayed to find him inconsistent, shifting his meaning from time to time with the needs of the moment and never taking stock or attempting to be system-atically inductive. Nevertheless, it became apparent that there was a core meaning in terms of his general model of the psychic apparatus and its functioning: ideas, images, and other "presenta-tions" were pushed through the model's network of pathways by energic quanta or charges called cathexes, and binding described a hypothetical closeness or stability of the relation between cathexis and presentation. When the two were easily separated, the energy was called free; when the cathexis clung fast, it was called bound. Free energy thus could easily be displaced—transferred from one idea to another—or condensed, a special case of displacement re-ferring to the transfer of more than one cathexis to a single idea.

Clear enough, except that Freud was vague and noncommittal about the nature of psychic (cathectic) energy, and I could not find a satisfactory treatment of that issue in the psychoanalytic liter-ature either. So I undertook its study, in the perspective of the history of the energy concept, and finally came to several unhappy conclusions (Holt, 1967a). Psychic energy shows a strong family resemblance to the vital force or entelechy of the vitalists, and is by its nature unmeasurable, enjoying a purely hypothetical existence in a separate metaphysical realm, safe from mortal observation, whether direct or indirect. Moreover, it shares some of these properties with the other central concepts of metapsychology, psychic force and psychic structure.

Again and again, I have had the experience of getting excited about a new topic, what strikes me as an original thought, or a way of looking at things more fruitfully, that subjectively seems to have derived primarily from my private inner experience. After a while, I look around me and discover that I am part of a social movement! Surely it was that way this time. Plenty of other people, many of them acting independently of one another, were beginning at about the same time to question basic assumptions of metapsychology and were subjecting it to a sometimes sympathetic but mercilessly analytical scrutiny.

And what was the result? To put it bluntly, this most general theoretical model of psychoanalysis has withered under the sharp light of methodological analysis. I do not see how it can recover from the blows it has been dealt. Interestingly enough, for fans of Kuhn (1970) who might like to look on this demise as a paradigm shift in psychoanalysis, the old theory's collapse cannot be attributed to embarrassment by data incompatible with it, which I believe is the usual case. One might almost say the reverse: metapsychology is going down at least in part because *no* data have ever been incompatible with it. It is untestable, formulated in terms of inscrutable forces, structures, and energies which cannot be measured *in principle*, not just because of the primitive state of our instrumentation. Unhappily, it is also internally inconsistent, vague or silent on critical issues, and hamstrung by such fallacies as anthropomorphism (Grossman and Simon, 1969) and reductionism (Yankelovich and Barrett, 1970). Worst of all, metapsychology turns out never to have been a satisfactory theoretical undergirding for clinical psychoanalysis. The latter deals with a world of meanings—the wishes, fears, dreams, and fantasies, the defensive strategies and adaptive efforts of people—not with the pseudophysicalistic world of energies and structures (Klein, 1975).

PHYSICALISM VERSUS MEANING

If any part of clinical psychoanalysis needs a theory designed in terms of meanings, it is the transformations of the dream work and the distorting operations of defenses that convert wishes and fears into symptoms and delusions. Indeed, Freud's central contribution in this realm of disordered thought lies precisely in his discovery of the *meaning* in what had seemed meaningless cognitive products. His masterwork is significantly entitled *The Interpretation of Dreams*, not "The Causes of Dreaming" nor even "A Dynamic and Topographic Explanation of the Dream." He taught us ways to find out what dreams mean, and the core of the secret is in those transformations of meaning he called the mechanisms of the primary process, first introduced as the devices of the dream work: condensation, displacement, and concrete visual representation of the abstract. Interpretation is the central operation of hermeneutics, a discipline of which psychologists rarely hear. Nevertheless, it had considerable currency in the intellectual world of the late nineteenth century, particularly in the work of Schleiermacher and his biographer, Dilthey (Hodges, 1968).

Hermeneutics was an attempt to create a rigorous philosophical discipline to guide the interpretation of written texts. It began with scriptural exegesis, from the Talmud to modern Biblical criticism, but was systematized and generalized by Friedrich Schleiermacher. So far as we know, however, Freud was uninfluenced by it; he was not even the kind of Jewish scholar (as Rapaport was, for example) who had studied the Talmud and who made frequent references to it.[1] Indeed, his whole manner of thinking and working was entirely different from the traditional exegetic model (Holt, 1974).

In any event, it is doubtful that Freud would have drawn much nourishment from hermeneutics even if he had studied it. His own intuitive understanding (*Verstehen*) seems to have been responsible for his ability to decode the transformation of meaning in dreams

---

[1] The indexes of the *Standard Edition* and of the Fliess letters (Freud, 1887-1902) contain no references to the Talmud, nor to hermeneutics or Dilthey. In his joke book, Freud (1905) quotes some jokes by one *E.* Schleiermacher, evidently not the same person; and the sole reference Freud made to the works of F. Schleiermacher (in his review of the prepsychoanalytic literature on dreams [Freud, 1900, pp. 49, 71, 102]) was to a passage from the latter's *Psychologie* on involuntary imagery, which has nothing to do with hermeneutics.

and other human products, and hermeneutics would not have offered him the theoretical resources to systematize and order his clinical discoveries. Indeed, its adepts never succeeded in making hermeneutics into the kind of discipline that would have offered a workable alternative to the physicalistic theories to which Freud was drawn. Despite their reductionism, they at least provided a model of the human being in a way that no hermeneutic theory did (see Barratt, 1976).

In a way, one might describe the famous Chapter Seven of *The Interpretation of Dreams* (1900), Freud's psychology of the dream process, as a triumph of mystification. It is at once a profound and insightful work, and a labyrinth of undefined terms, false empirical assumptions, and unclear assertions, wrapped in a beguiling package of masterly prose. The nature of the theoretical model never becomes fully intelligible, partly because at times Freud was engaged in a private debate with a missing antagonist who was unknown for over half a century—his unpublished earlier attempt at a model of the mind, the so-called "Project" (1895) written only for the eyes of Fliess—and partly because Freud was groping his way along in unrecognized metaphysical waters, forced by his unfamiliarity to invent the ground on which to find his theoretical footing. The amazing thing is not that he failed, but that he so nearly succeeded, and that he managed so skillfully to conceal the nature of what he was doing. For example, even though he was trying to conceptualize how mental phenomena arise in the brain, he took no consistent stand on the mind-body problem, though you would never know that from reading Jones (1953). The worshipful biographer attributes to Freud a consistent psychophysical parallelism of the sensible kind he had enunciated in his little monograph *On Aphasia* (Freud, 1891), but had abandoned by 1900. When you read works like *The Interpretation of Dreams* closely, looking for pronouncements on issues like the mind-body problem, you cannot fail to be struck by the way Freud managed to avoid committing himself without ever sounding evasive. Often he does it by his masterly use of figures of speech. The distinction between model and metaphor is not completely clear (Black, 1962), but in Freud's usage it is often apparent that he fell back on metaphor as a literary device where a scientific model-building attempt was called for.

By such means, Freud hid from himself as well as from others the fact that the fundamental terms of metapsychology made no place for meanings, constantly interpreting them *as if* they were hermeneutic rather than physicalistic. He was surely not unusual in this respect, for all of psychology was caught in a bind by the prevailing conception of the nature of science, which was narrowly reductionistic.[2] It has been well summarized by Whitehead (1925) as

> ... the fixed scientific cosmology which presupposes the ultimate fact of an irreducible brute matter, or material, spread throughout space in a flux of configurations. In itself such a material is senseless, valueless, purposeless. It just does what it does do, following a fixed routine imposed by external relations which do not spring from the nature of its being. It is this assumption that I call "scientific materialism" [p. 18].

As Yankelovich and Barrett (1970) put it, the effect was to induce scientists to believe that only matter and energy, which had the property of simple location in space and time, were "really real." Ideas and feelings, as such, could have only an epiphenomenal status—but interpreted as structures of energic cathexes, they seemed to be readmissible to the world of the real and thus of interest to serious scientists.

Much that is otherwise baffling in Freud's work becomes intelligible on the hypothesis that he was caught in this conflict: On the one hand, he had to maintain his loyalty to such spokesmen of reductionistic science as his own great teacher, Brücke, and to hew to an implicitly materialistic line in his metaphysical assumptions which made no place for the very kind of data he needed to work with. On the other hand, if he had squarely faced the fact that he was working with meanings, the only available methodological resources would have defined psychoanalysis right out of the realm of natural science, in which he had been trained and to which he felt a strong fealty, and into that of literature, philosophy, and other such "soft" intellectual pursuits which he enjoyed and felt a

---

[2] I remember being baffled, as a graduate student, by Boring's telling us how consistently his mentor and Freud's contemporary, Titchener, held to the position that meanings had no place in psychology—it was "the stimulus error" for a person to think, for example, that he perceived an object rather than a pattern of blues, grays, colds, and hards.

pull toward, but did not respect as approaches to truth. It may be that much of creativity can be seen as an attempt to reconcile contradictions (Rothenberg, 1971); be that as it may, Freud's metapsychology was a remarkable creative achievement, and I have come to realize that its properties that once struck me as so inexplicably confusing, inconsistent, and uncharacteristically devious were his unconsciously adopted means of achieving an only apparent resolution of a methodological dilemma. A true, transcendent synthesis is the only way to cope with such a contradiction as Freud's dual commitment, to scientific method—with what seemed an iron necessity for physicalistic reductionism—and to the meaningful universe of discourse in which his therapy and research into human lives were conducted. I mean transcendent not in any mystical sense, only in the sense that adopting a larger frame of reference makes it possible to see that what seems an inescapable logical contradiction can evaporate when one stops making certain implicit assumptions. Here the assumptions were philosophical, and the contradiction could not be escaped without explicitly facing and working through philosophical issues for which Freud had no stomach.

THE OBSERVATIONAL BASE OF THE CONCEPT OF THE PRIMARY PROCESS

Whatever the gaps in his philosophical training, Freud saw certain issues in the philosophy of science with extraordinary clearness. In his paper "On Narcissism," speaking of basic concepts such as instinct and libido, he wrote: "... these ideas are not the foundation of science, upon which everything rests: that foundation is observation alone. They are not the bottom but the top of the whole structure, and they can be replaced and discarded without damaging it" (1914, p. 77). The situation in which we find ourselves today is worse than these sensible words imply, however: not only do we lack a satisfactory high-level theory, we cannot even be sure of what our facts are. A fact is not merely an observation; it is an observation reported or recorded—that is, formulated—transferred from an experiential to a symbolized status, encoded into semantic symbols (words), presentational symbols (Susanne Langer's term for graphic or plastic representation), or purely conventional ones like those of mathematics. In psychology, we work almost entirely in the semantic realm, so we record most observations in words. But a word is a concept, and it therefore entails a theory, tacit or explicit.

Thus, I might claim that our task is to replace Freud's energic theory of the primary and secondary processes with a more defensible and satisfactory one; and indeed that is part of the task. But what *are* these processes that need an alternative explanation? Are they simple observables, like the rising of the sun or the running of the deer? As Freud used the terms most of the time,[3] the answer must be negative. They are remote from direct observation in two ways. First, they are inferred intervening variables that account for an observed output as the transform of assumed or inferred input, all of which entails a considerable theoretical model of cognitive functioning. Both the primary and secondary processes involve transformations of meaning, but in different ways: the secondary process is a type of information processing according to rules that are (at least to a first approximation) not difficult to specify; but the primary process covers a wider, more diffuse realm—impulse, affect, and behavior as well as thought—and operates by less easily specifiable rules. Second, in the way their boundaries are set much more is implicitly assumed, which needs to be explicated.

SOME ORIGINS OF FREUD'S CONCEPT[4]

Let us look at the latter issue first. It is not an easy point to make clear. If we tried to put ourselves in the position of a naïve observer who had never heard of Freud's ideas, and if we were exposed to the phenomena in which he discovered some unity, would we come up with the same groupings? Freud did not approach experience with any fewer preconceptions than anyone else. Language, commonsense psychology, and the formulations of psychologists and philosophers to whom he was exposed all tended

---

[3] As I shall demonstrate below (pp. 85ff.), some of the time he did treat them as observables.

[4] I do not try here to approach the question of origins in the manner of a historian of science, who would undoubtedly have begun by discussing Meynert's strikingly similar concept of a primary and a secondary ego, as well as other historical antecedents.

to encourage him to assume that thinking as we usually encounter it is a more or less unitary process: orderly, logical, realistic, proceeding in coherent ways from clear, definitive percepts and sharply formed concepts to specific conclusions or decisions. To be sure, the more you consider such thinking and attempt to describe precisely what you mean by it, the more complex it becomes and the more idealized; it begins to resemble less and less the actual cognitive processes of people like you and me in most of our everyday waking lives. Nevertheless, it was easy for Freud to believe that the learned professors who wrote the books on thought —men like Herbart, Brentano, Mill, and Lipps—knew what they were talking about so confidently and authoritatively, and so he could take it as established that this secondary process, as he called it, was a unitary system of thought so well known that he had little more to do than to allude to it. Before we turn our attention to the neglected night side of human cognition, on which Freud so quickly focused, let us take notice of his silent assumptions that conscious, waking, intelligible cognition forms a single system, and that everyday fallible deviations from the ideal type of scientific thinking are only quantitatively, not qualitatively, different from it.

Freud's letters to his fiancée show that in his late twenties he was already interested in dreams, before he had any exposure to psychiatric or even neurological patients. From adolescence he had been an avid reader of poetry and imaginative literature, and a devotee of the visual arts whose taste was not satisfied by the common man's demand for a good likeness. Dreams, poetry, non-photographic art—these human productions have in common a rich strangeness: all allude to the forms and contents of realistic experience without simply reproducing them. They are *strange* in that they are not faithful copies of what the assumed secondary process would yield, but still bear a resemblance to the latter, and *rich* in that so often they are elaborated, with as much added as has been taken away, and in that they have a mysterious[5] power to evoke emotional responses. It was a short step to the assumption that an allusive cousin of a prosaic waking cognitive product must

---

[5] I mean "mysterious" here only in the sense that the ways in which emotions are evoked are concealed, not obvious.

be a transform of it, hence the result of some *process of trans-formation*, which Freud came to call the primary process.

We know also that Freud had an excellent sense of humor, enjoying and collecting jokes and witty sayings long before he thought of writing a book about them. As he so aptly demonstrated, much verbal humor depends for its effect on allusion; hence it is not difficult to assimilate it to the same hypothesis that a distorting process has transformed an originally sober, straightforward thought.

At this point, I want to emphasize particularly the naïve *realism* that Freud implicitly assumed in his concept of the primary process. Paradoxically, it implied a realistic, straightforward, veridical cognition prior to the primary process. If the primary process distorts reality or logic, its theory requires the pre-existence of something veridical to be transformed. Is this odd implication merely the result of logic chopping, or is there any basis in the Freudian canon for it? Consider the following:

> ... we are driven to conclude that two fundamentally different kinds of psychical processes are concerned in the formation of dreams. One of these produces perfectly rational dream-thoughts, of no less validity than normal thinking; while the other treats these thoughts in a manner which is in the highest degree bewildering and irrational.... this second psychical process ... [is] the dream-work proper.... We have found from [the study of hysteria] that the same irrational psychical processes, and others that we have not specified, dominate the production of hysterical symptoms. In hysteria, too, we come across a series of perfectly rational thoughts, equal in validity to our conscious thoughts; but to begin with we know nothing of their existence in this form and we can only reconstruct them subsequently.... we discover by analyzing the symptom which has been produced that these normal thoughts have been submitted to abnormal treatment: *they have been transformed into the symptom by means of condensation and the formation of compromises, by way of superficial associations and in disregard of contradictions, and also, it may be, along the path of regression* [Freud, 1900, p. 597; his emphasis].

The "perfectly rational" and valid dream thoughts are the text that is reconstructed after the interpretation, which runs the distorting primary process backwards, as it were. It is quite evident in this remarkable passage that Freud conceived of the results of his therapeutic reconstructions of both dreams and neurotic symptoms as actually having existed unconsciously before the disguising work of the primary process came to bear on them.[6]

Elsewhere, he makes it clear that whenever a dream contains something that seems to be "a product of some ... higher intellectual function,"

> ... *these intellectual operations have already been performed in the dream-thoughts and have only been* TAKEN OVER *by the dream content.* A conclusion drawn in a dream is nothing other than the repetition of a conclusion in the dream-thoughts; if the conclusion is taken over into the dream unmodified, it will appear impeccable.... a calculation in the dream-thoughts ... is always rational.... [When] speeches made, heard, or read [are] revived in the dream-thoughts ... [their] wording is exactly reproduced [1901, pp. 667-668; Freud's emphasis].

At first, when I noticed these passages, I thought that Freud was only trying to contrast the obscurity of the dream with the intelligibility of its latent meaning; and no doubt that was part of what he was saying. Yet he does consistently speak as if the dream thoughts contain the most primitive wishes and are the products of unconscious mental functioning, which nevertheless is veridical, rational, and "impeccable."

Very well, you may say, it was not so bizarre of Freud to assume that a grown person might have a thought that was clearly and logically formulated but so abhorrent in its wishful content that he would have to disguise and transform it to make it consciously tolerable. But then why did Freud call "this second psychical process" the primary process? Doesn't the term contain a genetic hypothesis? Indeed it does. By the choice of this name, Freud tells us he meant to imply

> ... not merely considerations of relative importance and efficiency [efficacy?]. I intended also to choose a name which would give an indication of its chronological priority. It is true that, so far as we know, no psychical apparatus exists which

[6] He says so rather explicitly earlier in the same work: "It must be allowed that the great bulk of the thoughts which are revealed in analysis were already active during the process of forming the dream ... " (Freud, 1900, p. 280).

possesses a primary process only and that such an apparatus is to that extent a theoretical fiction. But this much is a fact: the primary processes are present in the mental apparatus from the first, while it is only in the course of life that the secondary processes unfold, and come to inhibit and overlay the primary ones; it may even be that their complete domination is not attained until the prime of life [1900, p. 603].

This is one of the key passages establishing the fact that Freud conceived of the primary process not only as a process of defense by means of cognitive distortion, but as a primitive mode by which the immature psychic apparatus functions. Another is the following conclusion to an extended and explicit discussion of this issue (about which Jones and Silberer had a controversy) in his book on jokes: "If we did not already know it from research into the psychology of the neuroses, we should be led by jokes to a suspicion that the strange unconscious revision [i.e., primary-process trans-formation] is nothing else than the infantile type of thought-activity" (1905, p. 170). As Gill comments, ". . . in this explanation he appears to equate infantile and even early childhood mental activity with primary-process functioning. . ." (1967, p. 285). What remains unclear is whether this developmental interpretation implies one or the other of the following two explanations for the fact that, in the beginning, children's thought has "archaic" char-acteristics: (a) in its crudest developmental forms, the psychic apparatus subjects veridical perceptions and correct logical thoughts to distorting transformations and does so naturally, some-times in pursuit of pleasure, but without being defensively moti-vated to do so; or (b) the earliest versions of the structures that underlie cognitive-affective functioning are crude and function crudely. At times, Freud does sound as if he might have had something like the latter formulation in mind, but he never made it explicit and probably never confronted the issues in just these terms.[7]

[7] In this connection, see Schimek's (1975, pp. 177-178) thoughtful discussion of these issues, in which he points out a fact I overlooked when I was writing my scoring manual, to be discussed below:"Symbolism, although now often listed as one of the characteristics of primary process ideation, is not on a par with the concept of displacement and condensation (it was never included in the theoreti-cal formulations of the seventh chapter of 'The Interpretation of Dreams')."

Recall, also, that Freud began theorizing about thinking in the attempt to understand the dreams and the neurotic symptoms of adults (notably himself), not as a part of a program of research on infants and young children. Indeed, he never mounted any such program, not even on his own children; he wrote to Fliess (on Feb. 2, 1897): "Why do I not go to the nursery and—experiment [on the question of whether there is a period in infancy when disgust is absent]? Because with twelve-and-a-half hours' work I have no time, and because the womenfolk do not back me in my investigations" (1887-1902, p. 192). His observations on his children's cognitive processes were quite incidental and unsystematic, therefore, and there is no record of his ever studying any others; he never analyzed a young child himself. His contributions to our understanding of childhood must seem all the more remarkable for having been the result mainly of retrospective reconstructions based on memories and fantasies supplied by adult patients.

One of the limitations of such a method, however, is an inescapably adultomorphic cast to the conception of the primary process. As I have argued elsewhere (Holt, 1967b), there are many reasons for supposing that primary-process thinking itself undergoes considerable developmental change, though Freud's cognitive developmental theory is well summarized in the last-quoted passage: the (presumably unchanging) primary process is gradually replaced, in conscious thought, by the secondary process (also conceived as essentially unchanging).

One piece of internal evidence that, even when he conceived of the primary process as the primitive mode of psychic functioning, Freud modeled it on adult dream work is the fact that he does not mention diffuseness, vagueness, or fluidity among its defining properties. Most students of children's thinking are impressed by these qualities, and by the slippery flightiness that makes it so difficult to approach the young child by methods that are designed for work with adults—including the Rorschach test. Freud was of course quite familiar with these elusive structural properties in dreams, even though his own, as reported in *The Interpretation of Dreams*, rarely have much vagueness or fluid unspecifiability. Where he does discuss such properties, he says that they are a means of conveying a content—e.g., that it is *unclear* who is the father of a baby (pp. 329-333)—or that they indicate a failure in the synthetic function of secondary revision, which he usually interprets as being motivated by resistance and defense.

> ... *there is an intimate and regular relation between the unintelligible and confused nature of dreams and the difficulty of reporting the thoughts behind them* [1901, p. 643; Freud's emphasis].

> The more obscure and confused a dream appears to be, the greater the share in its construction which may be attributed to the factor of displacement [p. 655].

> ... in the case of obscure and confused dreams ... The wish ... is either itself a repressed one and alien to consciousness, or it is intimately connected with repressed thoughts and is based upon them [p. 674].

To the best of my knowledge, nowhere does he say that vagueness or confusion are simply properties of primitive thought or of the primary process itself.

A DIGRESSION ON PERCEPTION AND COGNITION

It is important at this point for us to focus on a difference between Freud's and contemporary usage and theory. When Freud spoke about thinking or thought processes, he did not include perception, whereas we are likely to use the more general term, cognition, which often is construed to include perceptual processes, since in practice they can hardly be distinguished from thinking. Like his contemporaries in psychology and psychiatry alike, Freud assumed as a matter of course that perception is a simple matter of coming into contact with reality. We owe to Piaget (e.g., 1937) the phrase "the *construction* of reality," and so successful was the "New Look" movement in cognitive psychology during the years following World War II that psychologists now take it for granted that perceiving is an active process in which a person's motivational and structural properties play an intrinsic part. Ironically, the earliest and most extreme version of the New Look "viewed perception as expressing solely wish or need fulfillment.... This guideline was based on a vulgarized version of Freud's message..." (Klein, 1970, p. 7). The enthusiasts for a dynamic theory of perception did not notice that Freud made the prevailing assumption of "immaculate perception," that distortions are introduced subsequent to a veridical input of sensory images.[8] Those who tried to make experimental demonstrations of "perceptual defense" rarely quoted Freud directly even though he had described denial (or disavowal, as it is translated in the *Standard Edition*) in ways that made it sound like a perceptual process. No one seemed to notice that when he discussed "disavowal of reality," he usually made it not a part of seeing but subsequent to it. For example, "when a little boy first catches sight of a girl's genital region ... he sees nothing or disavows what he *has seen*" (1925, p. 252; emphasis added); and "They disavow the fact and believe that they *do* see a penis, all the same" (1923, pp. 143-144).

This position was quite consistent with the one he had earlier adopted toward the perceptual disturbances of hysterics, which were among the most prominent symptoms of that condition in the earliest years of Freud's practice: "... hysterically blind people are only blind as far as consciousness is concerned; in their unconscious they see" (1910, p. 212). That is, there is no disturbance in their basic processes of contacting reality, only in their becoming conscious of the input.

Even when he discussed the disavowal of reality by psychotics, Freud did not consider the possibility that the perceptual process itself was distorted. He began his paper on "The Loss of Reality in Neurosis and Psychosis" (Freud, 1924b) by noting that in psychosis the ego "withdraws from a piece of reality," a metaphorical statement that leaves the nature of the process as unclear as it had been in his earlier paper on the same topic (Freud, 1924a). He ended that brief note by asking what was the "mechanism, analogous to repression ... by which the ego detaches itself from the external world. . . . such a mechanism, it would seem, must, like repression, comprise a withdrawal of the cathexis sent out by the ego" (p. 153). That was equivalent to saying that the psychotic loses interest in, not perceptual contact with, external reality; in the later paper he added: ". . . neurosis does not disavow the reality, it only ignores it; psychosis disavows it and tries to replace it" (1924b, p. 185). The

---

[8] See, however, Schimek (1975), who independently comes to the same conclusion about Freud's theory of perception.

replacement takes place "by the creation of a new reality which no longer raises the same objections as the old one..." (p. 185). It becomes clear that this "new reality" is not perceptual but a delusional construction when he says: "Thus the psychosis is also faced with the task of procuring for itself perceptions of a kind which shall correspond to the new reality..." (p. 186), adding the probability that "in a psychosis the rejected piece of reality constantly forces itself upon the mind...." Thus, in the one context where he talks about the "creation" of a reality, it is clearly a "new, imaginary external world" (1924b, p. 187) defensively put in the place of the real world, which nevertheless continues to intrude via the (presumably still functioning) perceptual apparatus.

In his paper on "Fetishism," Freud (1927) makes it crystal clear that disavowal is not a perceptual process. He considers the situation in which "the boy refused to take cognizance of his having perceived that a woman does not possess a penis" (p. 153). First, he distinguishes *Verleugnung* (disavowal) from *Verdrängung* (repression) by limiting the latter to affect and applying the former to "the vicissitude of the idea." He goes on to criticize Laforgue's (1926) term "scotomization" as "particularly unsuitable, for it suggests that the perception is entirely wiped out, so that the result is the same as when a visual impression falls on the blind spot in the retina. In the situation we are considering, on the contrary, we see that the perception has persisted, and that a very energetic action has been undertaken to maintain the disavowal" (pp. 153-154). (Again, in the *Outline*, Freud spoke of the *"disavowal* of the perceptions..." [1940a, p. 204].) He even postulated a splitting of the ego in cases of extensive disavowal, such that one part maintains the original perception and related ideas while the other maintains a contrary belief system (1940b).

Let me summarize the conception of perceiving that is implicit in Freud's various incidental remarks, after noting that only in the unpublished "Project for a Scientific Psychology" (1895) did he undertake any substantial theorizing about this topic. A fundamental consideration, which Freud returned to many times, was his conviction (following Breuer, in his theoretical chapter in their joint book [Breuer and Freud, 1893-1895], and the generally received scientific opinion of the day) that consciousness and memory must be attributed to separate parts of the brain, since if neurons retained permanent records of their patterns of excitation (necessary for memory) they could not subserve the observable openness of perceptual consciousness to constant change. Indeed, this physiological-anatomical argument may have been responsible for Freud's persisting assumption that perception is a complete process antecedent to the involvement of memory, motivation, or other influences.

Anyhow, here is his notion of how perceiving takes place: an external stimulus in the form of physical energy impinges on a sensory surface, which reduces it in quantity but transmits its other properties (of which Freud spoke mostly about its *period* or vibratory frequency, but which presumably included its patterning or information content in other respects also) to the nervous system. After 1900, he tended to replace references to nerves and neurons by the term "system *Pcpt.*," partly because of the tangle he got into in 1895 and the following year or two in attempting to specify a neurological model of perception and of consciousness. Some of the time, he postulated separate systems for the latter two functions; for example:

> Excitatory material flows in to the *Cs.* sense-organ from two directions: from the *Pcpt.* system, whose excitation, determined by qualities, is probably submitted to a fresh revision before it becomes a conscious sensation, and from the interior of the apparatus itself [systems *Ucs.* and *Pcs.*], whose quantitative processes are felt qualitatively in the pleasure-unpleasure series ... [1900, p. 616].

At other times, he identified them (e.g., in the footnote to p. 541, added in 1919: "*Pcpt.* = *Cs.*"; "... the system *Pcpt.-Cs....* is turned towards the external world, it is the medium for the perceptions arising thence, and during its functioning the phenomenon of consciousness arises in it" [1933, p. 75]). The inconsistency (or complementarity; Edelheit, 1975) was characteristic, as was Freud's tendency to speak at times as if perceptions arise in the sense organs themselves. The separation is implied in his conception that perceptions could exist in a veridical but nonconscious form, as in hysterical anesthesia.

In one of Freud's earliest unpublished discussions of these matters (the letter to Fliess of Dec. 6, 1896), he takes from the beginning a developmental standpoint:

> ... I am working on the assumption that our psychical mechanism has come into being by a process of stratification: the material present in the form of memory-traces being subjected from time to time to a *re-arrangement* in accordance with fresh circumstances—to a *re-transcription*....
>
> I should like to emphasize the fact that the successive registrations represent the psychical achievement of successive epochs of life [pp. 233, 235].

Then he sets up the precursor of the picket-fence model of Chapter Seven, a linear diagram proceeding from *W* ("neurones in which perceptions originate, to which consciousness attaches"), through *Wz* ("the first registration of the perceptions; it is quite incapable of consciousness, and arranged according to associations by simultaneity"), *Ub* ("the second registration" arranged perhaps according to causal relations, perhaps corresponding to "conceptual memories"), *Vb* ("the third transcription, attached to word-presentations and corresponding to our official ego"; unlike the preceding, these can attain a "secondary *thought-consciousness* ... probably linked to the hallucinatory activation of word-presentations") and finally to *Bews* (evidently *Bewusstsein*, consciousness, though he does not say so).[9]

Perception is too evanescent to give us an integrated picture of reality; that must be attained through an organization of memory

---

[9] How strikingly similar is the following paragraph from Freud's last work, the *Outline:* "Conscious processes on the periphery of the ego and everything else in the ego unconscious—such would be the simplest state of affairs that we might picture. And such may in fact be the state that prevails in animals. But in men there is an added complication through which internal processes in the ego may also acquire the quality of consciousness. This is the work of the function of speech, which brings material in the ego into a firm connection with mnemic residues of visual, but more particularly of auditory, perceptions. Thenceforward the perceptual periphery of the cortical layer can be excited to a much greater extent from inside as well, internal events such as passages of ideas and thought-processes can become conscious, and a special device is called for in order to distinguish between the two possibilities—a device known as *reality-testing*. The equation "perception = reality (external world)" no longer holds. Errors, which can now easily arise and do so regularly in dreams, are called *hallucinations*" (1940a, p. 162; Freud's emphasis).

traces. It is easy for us to overlook this fact about Freud's thinking when he speaks about the "loss of reality" in neurosis and psychosis, for example; the reality that is disavowed is this internal construct within the realm of verbal memory, not reality as directly perceived. As Schimek (1975) points out, here is where Freud located the distorting effects of drives, not in perception. It is important to grasp this distinction between a veridical or autonomous perceptual process and a vulnerable process of forming an inner world (Hartmann, 1939) or vision of reality (Schafer, 1970). If Freud was a child of his time in retaining the "conflict-free" notion of perception, he led the way to our greatly broadened and deepened contemporary view of cognition in recognizing the distorting effects of wishes and defenses on this second stage of constructing an enduring picture of reality. And notice that Freud assumed some such construction of a reality in memory early in (preverbal) development, though he implied more than he ever explicated about the changing nature of the world of the child corresponding to the several systems of registrations ("at least three, probably more" [1896, p. 234]). Here is a basis in Freud's words for a Piagetian conception of successive stages in the child's construction of reality. But Freud, unlike Piaget, treated perception as invariant, undergoing no such successive developmental changes as memory.

It should not surprise us, therefore, to find Freud attributing clear, differentiated, veridical, adult perception to the infant, which could supply him with the grist for his distorting primary processing in the *Mnem.* systems, the *Ucs.*, or the id. And indeed he did very plainly assume precisely that, for example in the "Project" when he was discussing wishful memory in the nursing infant:

Let us suppose . . . that the mnemic image wished for . . . is the image of the mother's breast and a front view of its nipple, and that the first perception is a side view of the same object, without the nipple. In the child's memory there is an experience, made by chance in the course of sucking, that with a particular head-movement the front image turns into the side image. The side image which is now seen leads to the [image of the] head-movement; an experiment shows that its counterpart must be carried out, and the perception of the front view is achieved [1895, pp. 328-329].

Not only did Freud think of the infant as capable of highly differentiated and realistic perception, but he attributed to the nursling
a reversibility of thought processes that Piaget, by actual observations, found only in children several years older. But then, Freud
was willing to attribute adultomorphic secondary-process thinking
even to a simple, primitive organism:

> Let us imagine ourselves in the situation of an almost en-
> tirely helpless living organism, as yet unoriented in the world,
> which is receiving stimuli in its nervous substance. This or-
> ganism will very soon be in a position to make a first distinction
> and a first orientation. On the one hand, it will be aware of
> stimuli which can be avoided by muscular action (flight); these
> it ascribes to an external world. On the other hand, it will also
> be aware of stimuli against which such action is of no avail and
> whose character of constant pressure persists in spite of it; these
> stimuli are the signs of an internal world, the evidence of
> instinctual needs. The perceptual substance of the living organ-
> ism will thus have found in the efficacy of its muscular activity
> a basis for distinguishing between an 'outside' and an 'inside'
> [1915, p. 119].

I want to underline the fact that, in thinking of perception as a
straightforward, almost mechanical process by which any percipient organism comes into contact with the objective structure of
reality, Freud agreed with the prevailing psychological outlook of
his time.[10] Before approximately the last 50 years, psychologists
were remarkably uninterested in perception and slow to go beyond
the astonishingly varied discoveries of Helmholtz. As to child psychology, as recently as 30 years ago an authoritative manual (Carmichael, 1946) not only contained no chapter on perceptual development but had only a couple of index references to any aspect of
perception. One of these is to the hypothesis that childish mispro-
nunciations of words are attributable to "crude perception," not
further specified (p. 493); the other is to a section on perceptual

---

[10] Romanes, whose "book on animal intelligence [1882] is the first comparative psychology that was ever written" (Boring, 1950, p. 473), concluded in his
third and final book, published in 1888, "that 'simple ideas,' like sensory impressions, perceptions and the memories of perceptions, are common to all animals
and man" (p. 474).

learning which turns out to be a summary of experiments on problem solving, some of which required perceptual reorganization. None of the research cited antedates Köhler's (1917) celebrated demonstration of insightful learning in apes, which seems to have been its principal stimulus, and the major focus of all this subsequent research seems to have been on learning, not perception. Surely during Freud's scientifically formative years, the last quarter of the nineteenth century, developmental psychology paid no attention to the seemingly inaccessible perceptual words of children. And that was the era of anthropomorphic comparative psychology, in which it was a prevalent assumption that other animals perceived the world essentially as we do (Boring, 1950, pp. 472-476).

To go back a moment: When I began this bit of hypothetical reconstruction of how Freud may have arrived at the concept of the primary process, the point was to demonstrate that some preconceptions guided Freud in his choice of its limiting and defining properties. So far we have seen the following implicit assumptions: (1) The assumption of naïve realism—that all percipient organisms naturally and easily form phenomenal copies of external reality merely by being exposed to it, though young human beings, at least, also tend to distort the veridical input, for reasons yet to be discussed; (2) the assumption of a single kind of reality, namely the kind Freud himself and his mentors reported—a notably Euclidian, Apollonian world of pellucid air, clean sunlight, and crisply articulated, differentiated forms moving against stable backgrounds (in which the real always had the property of simple location, and object constancy was complete and reliable); (3) the assumption that young children, psychotics, and all of us in the course of constructing dreams, subject these veridical inputs to distortions in processing them internally, through operations Freud denoted as primary process.[11] Finally, I am suggesting also the

[11] In a personal communication, Merton Gill points out the fact that Pötzl's (1917) well-known experiment, to which Freud alluded approvingly (1900, pp. 181-182, in a footnote added in 1919), and others that have been stimulated by it (summarized by Fisher, 1960), "seem to represent the demonstration of a veridical input changed by primary processes." Some of these experiments do strongly suggest that there is a virtually photographic registration of pictures too

possibility that a kind of latent esthetic criterion may have directed Freud's attention differentially to attractively interesting transforms (or what appear to be transforms) of adult percepts, concepts, and trains of thought.

THE PHENOMENAL REFERENTS OF THE TERM PRIMARY PROCESS

Part of what I hope to have shown is that the factual basis for the concept of the primary process was quite diffuse, being *any cognitive or perceptual product that seemed for whatever reason to be the result of a distorting transformation.* That is, wherever the inferred cognitive processing fell short of the secondary-process ideal *and* any of the output seemed to violate reasonable expectations by appearing in some way unrealistic, quantitatively and—especially—qualitatively changed, Freud's first insight was to notice a similarity with other such products and to group them together. The collection became highly diverse, to say the least—dreams, delusions, and hallucinations, the peculiar or even bizarrely incomprehensible speech and drawings of insane persons and those suffering from deliria due to fever or drugs, the unrealistic myths and folk tales of "primitive" peoples, the play and imaginative chatter of children, works by the creators of all types of plastic and literary art, all sorts of neurotic symptoms—alloplastic as well as autoplastic—jokes and witticisms, slips of tongue and a whole range of other parapraxes or errors, and almost any manifestation of psychological defenses.

---

briefly exposed for the observer to become conscious of more than small fragments of them, while his subsequent dreams and mental images contain what look like derivatives of the unreported registrations modified by condensation and displacement. Yet the data do not coerce this interpretation; like most experimental findings, they are disconcertingly amenable to other interpretations, which do not assume separate processes of accurate registration and distorting transformation. We are up against the indeterminacy inherent in the fact that we have no way of learning about any perception other than our own except through verbal, graphic, or other responses by the perceiver, all of which require post-perceptual processing. I want also to note that Schimek (1975) has come to the same conception of the primary process as that which distorts an originally correct or veridical thought or percept.

Moreover, as time went on, Freud included even more in his concept. A thought product might appear quite ordinary, logical, and realistic; but if its producer were submitted to psychoanalysis and furnished the analyst with "associations" (further thoughts or other products stimulated by elements of the material under scrutiny), Freud could often find exactly the kinds of linkages he had originally traced in analyzing dreams as the defensive distortion of wishful fantasies, fears, or longings. Just as the work of secondary revision (the only secondary-process part of the dream work) at times smoothed out every telltale indicator of condensation and displacement in the manifest dream, so in the silent, subsurface phase of its generation a thought might have undergone primary condensations and displacements and still end up as unimpressively ordinary and reasonable. Freud and other analysts (notably Kubie, 1954) came at last to believe that there is an incessant stream of unconscious ideation, often accompanying conscious secondary-process thought and lending it color, idiosyncrasy, and emphasis even though it might not transgress the socially defined bounds of rationality and realism. Such a conception, attractive though it may be in its bold sweep and its capacity to explain many observations, cannot be given satisfactory empirical test. It can neither be proved nor disproved, which state of affairs relegates it to the status of a scientific curiosity or even that of a wholly negligible triviality.

Where, then, are we left in our search for the *facts* about the primary process? If it is entirely inferred, susceptible only of being constructed to fill a felt gap in a scientific model of a person's thinking, then we seem to be in hard straits. For the sad fact is that we never know and never *can* know all the inputs to this hypothetical process. We must construct most of them, as well as the nature of the transformations they have assumedly undergone, from meagre and in many ways suspect data: usually a cognitive product such as a dream text or the recountal of a pattern of acting out, plus whatever else the patient says in some conjunction with the critical material (e.g., occurring in the same analytic hour) or as a response to the request, "Tell me what you think of next." At times, but not often enough, the analyst has some independent corroboration of facts as alleged by the analysand, or may even offer his own hypotheses about presumably related or contributory

data when the patient is notably silent about facts known to both of
them. (For example, an analysand's dream may contain classic
birth symbols, while he fails to mention the analyst's obviously
perceptible pregnancy.) Even the Pötzl experiment or other experimental attempts to influence dream imagery by precisely known
presleep presentations fail to provide satisfactory information about
input (see Fisher, 1960). Fisher's papers (e.g., 1954, 1957) contain
many plausible and ingenious reconstructions of his subjects'
dreams, the day's residues for which included far more than the
briefly exposed slide (for example, things seen on the trip from the
ward to the experimental room), but also far less than the full
contents of the slide itself. Sometimes pictorial content expressly
chosen for its suitability to the safe indirect or allusive depiction of
the patient's known problems gave no sign of having ever been
admitted to preperceptual processing, much less used in constructing the dream's imagery. Clinical research would be much easier if
people only weren't so ornery!

I think it is safe to hazard that in the ordinary, reasonably
successful psychoanalysis, most dreams are analyzed either not at
all or in the most fragmentary way. If an analyst can find a single
useful linkage or hypothetical connection between something in the
dream and anything in the rest of what the patient says, he is doing
well enough, and training analysts generally warn against zealous
attempts at complete analysis of any dream.

Let me press this point home quite sharply: if you cannot
independently establish what all the inputs and outputs of a hypothetical process are, you can have *no* certainty that any one model
of the intervening processes is superior to any of a great many
others. Formally, the situation is analogous to the attempt to solve
a set of simultaneous equations with too many unknowns. Or
consider the famous black box problem. You are given a black box
with some wires leading in and others leading out. You may not
open the box or do anything other than put signals in and measure
what comes out, but must determine how it is wired inside. A hard
enough task, but think how much more difficult if your data
consist of a large number of values, *some* of which probably are a
subset of the inputs, and you have to decide even that from a study
of the outputs! This is indeterminacy with a vengeance.

A SCHEME FOR SCORING PRIMARY-PROCESS MANIFESTATIONS

Fortunately, however, Freud did not restrict his usage of the term primary process to inferred transformations, but also used it to refer to certain kinds of thought products. As Gill put it:

> Consistent with his distrust of formal definitions, Freud was not concerned to provide even a complete theoretical or conceptual definition of primary process, much less an explicit operational definition. Yet in his writings about dream work, joke work, and symptom formation he was concrete enough to enable the clinician to know how to use the concept of primary process in regard to specific thought products [1967, p. 265].

As I noted earlier, I used these works in setting up rules for identifying specific kinds of thought products—Rorschach responses—that might be called manifestations of the primary process. Because I was working with ordinary Rorschach protocols, without the benefit of "associations" from which to attempt a reconstruction of the processes by which each came about, I excluded all categories that implied such highly judgmental inferences. Nevertheless, I was able to find 60 specific types of primary-process manifestations. One third of them define various types and levels of wishfulness, as I now call it, though my original intent was to write operational definitions of degrees of neutralization. That last term was Hartmann's generalization and extension of Freud's idea of sublimation of libido, as a qualitative change in the psychic energy generated by the sexual instinct. He also linked this economic concept to the secondary process, as did Rapaport (1951), making explicit what was implied but never baldly stated[12] by Freud, that marked wishfulness of thinking was a hallmark of the primary process. Freud came this close: "... *a normal train of*

[12] Never, that is, in any published work; but his very first mention of the concept of the primary process, in the unpublished "Project," occurred in a discussion of how the ego is endangered by cathecting the memory of the need-satisfying object or situation of gratification so intensely as to give rise to an "indication of reality" from the ω(perceptual) system. Thus, his first definition of the primary process is "Wishful cathexis to the point of hallucination..." (1895, pp. 325, 326).

thought is only submitted to abnormal psychical treatment [i.e.,
the primary process] ... *if any unconscious wish, derived from
infancy and in a state of repression, has been transferred on to it"*
(1900, p. 598; Freud's emphasis). Taking Freud quite seriously, I
have proceeded as if the presence of verbally expressed wishes of the
kind usually considered to be infantile or repressed is a criterion for
calling the thought product primary process in nature. I made the
simplifying assumption that the libidinal and aggressive wishes
Freud described in his writings on instinct theory were all I needed
to worry about. (It has recently occurred to me that the wishes to
be taken care of and to be a grownup without having to wait are
probably good candidates that were omitted; but no great harm
has been done by their omission because they are rarely perceptible
in Rorschach responses, except in overtly oral forms, which *are*
picked up.) Finally, it seemed evident that something more than a
dichotomy (infantile versus adult) was called for, particularly since
there were so many socially acceptable, relatively unthreatening
and therefore not repressed, manifestations of orality, anality,
voyeurism, sadism, and the rest of them. So I called the more
primitive, raw, and blatant forms of these wishes, which one
would ordinarily expect to be repressed, Level 1 primary process,
and the more socialized forms Level 2 primary process.

The other 40 categories are structural or formal manifestations
of the primary process: types of condensation, displacement, symbolization, contradiction, and other miscellaneous kinds of distortion of perception or verbalization. My scoring manual requires 37
pages to define and exemplify these formal indications that the
primary process has been at work; here I can hope to do no more
than suggest the organization of the manual and the nature of the
scoring by the following extract, which presents about half of the
material concerning one category, Composition. (Its scoring symbol is C-co 1: the first letter indicates that it is a form of Condensation, and the final digit classifies it as one of the more blatant,
unsocialized, or direct manifestations of the primary process, which
are called Level 1.)

> COMPOSITION: Freud (e.g., 1900, p. 320) used this term
> to refer to one result of condensation—an image that is a
> composite of parts that do not actually belong together in

nature. We distinguish two types, depending on whether there is some external social support or precedent for the resulting unrealistic image. Distinguish carefully from C-a-c 2, Arbitrary Combination: in both types of responses reality is violated in that they bring together what does not belong together in literal reality. The difference, however, is that when this combination results in something with an organic unity or an unbroken boundary, it is considered a Composition, and when the incongruous elements are merely brought into juxtaposition, it is an Arbitrary Combination. Theoretically, it requires more violation of the integrity or object constancy of an image to invade its natural boundaries with a foreign element that is grafted on than merely to bring them into an unusual or even bizarre arrangement, which still respects the identities of the separate images. . . .

a. *Impossible fusions* (often cross-species): parts from two or more percepts are combined to make a new, hybrid organism. Score *only when* the composite image does *not* have some existence in a common cultural reality (usually people with animal parts or vice versa).

"Witches—they seem to have tails for some reason"; "dogs—kind of antennae for a tail"; "lady with a paw"; "a rabbit with bat's wings". . . .

b. *Improbable* (though theoretically conceivable) *fusions:* persons or animals with more parts than necessary (e.g., "a two-headed lobster"; "animal skin, a head at each end"; "two-*bodied* caterpillar"). Also, deformities or freaks that can occur in nature, e.g., "female form with hands sticking out of shoulders"; "baby with a moustache"; "men with long, pointed heads". . . .

c. A percept of a face with *parts organized in an unrealistic way:* mouth going vertically, horns next to nostrils, etc.; "face—but the mouth is where the nose should be"; "a mask, with the eyes upside down" [Holt, 1969].

I have introduced this much about my scoring scheme to make the following points: (a) It is possible to derive an extensive operational definition of the primary process from Freud's writings, thus to delimit a realm of empirical observations. (b) Since this operational definition is highly differentiated, not global, it is possible to ask how much empirical unity there is in this realm. Otherwise put, do the various specific varieties of the primary process form anything like an internally coherent system of thought?

In search of an answer to that question, let us consider the empirical relationship of the wishful to the structural indications of the primary process in Rorschach responses. If we add together all of a person's scores on the 20 types of wishful content, and all of his scores on the 40 types of structural or formal signs of the primary process, using a miscellaneous assortment of subjects, we can correlate the two arrays of scores. In a group of 305 Rorschachs, from 121 college students and other normals, 81 schizophrenics, and 103 neurotic and organically ill persons, the correlation between these two sums was .71. That is suspiciously high; but even when the inflating influence of the number of Rorschach responses is held constant, the partial correlation is still .50—not only highly significant, but large enough to indicate that it makes sense to consider wishfulness and such structural characteristics as condensation and displacement all part of one concept, the primary process.

Two factor analyses (summarized in Holt, 1966) have been done on some of my principal Rorschach scores, with remarkably congruent results. Heath (1965) analyzed data from a sample of 24 students at Haverford College; Kahn (1965) obtained his data from 43 convicted murderers. Both samples would ordinarily be considered too small to give replicable results, and despite differences in the kinds of other tests besides the Rorschach, in statistical method, and in subjects, the first two factors in each analysis are nevertheless recognizably the same. The first principal factor each time is most highly loaded with percentage of Rorschach responses containing Formal indications of the primary process, and with measures of the amount of the more extreme (Level 1) Content indications (wishfulness). The second factor is mainly defined by measures of intelligence but also includes percentage of the more socialized (Level 2) indications, mostly of wishfulness. The implication, I believe, is that Level 1 scores more defensibly indicate the primary process, while I may have encroached on the realm of the secondary process in my definitions of Level 2 scores, particularly those of Content indications. Otherwise, however, the statistical explorations of the various categories and scores derived from them support the proposition that Freud's descriptions of the empirical varieties of primary-process products (as applied to Rorschach responses) describe something unitary. His intuition seemingly enabled him to discern in his extremely variegated observations a single conceptual entity, which we might as well continue to call the primary process.

Thanks to the efforts of many of my students and colleagues, there now exists a considerable body of research using my scoring manual as a way of measuring primary-process thought and relating it to an impressive range of other variables. For example, in 10 independent studies (most of which are summarized in Holt, 1970) as many different experimenters have used my scoring system and the measures it yields of capacity for regression in the service of the ego to test Kris's hypothesis that that capacity is a necessary condition for artistic creativity. In a variety of different samples, using several criteria of creativeness, male subjects have yielded fairly consistently positive results, though female subjects have not.

I am glad to be able to say that there has been some theoretical yield, too, from about a quarter of a century of part-time empirical work on the problem of measuring the primary process, though it is of a rather negative kind. I am not speaking now about metapsychology, but about what might be called the clinical theory of thinking, lower-level statements about the primary process and related matters. Time and again, I sought in vain for theoretical guidance about decisions that had to be made: What kinds of wishes should be included in the content measure of what I originally called drive-dominated thought? As long as I didn't question the dual instinct theory, it seemed easy enough: anything sexual or libidinal in terms of the classical stages of psychosexual development, plus anything aggressive. Now that I have taken a hard look at the motivational theory of psychoanalysis and have found it wanting (Holt, 1975), I do not believe that it can any longer be considered a reliable guide.

The two degrees or levels of primary-process scores, alluded to above, embody a distinction that has proved useful, though it is quite without theoretical backup of more than the most general kind. These two levels dichotomize a continuum of control or socialization, concepts about which psychoanalytic theorists have written, though seldom relating them to the primary process. Indeed, the whole issue of the relation between the primary process and controls and defenses leaves a great deal to be desired in terms of clarity and specificity in the ways it has been discussed, except for a few books and papers like Schafer's (1954, 1958). This issue is important both practically and theoretically, for it is at the heart of the major distinction between adaptive and maladaptive regression: primary-process thinking used "in the service of the ego"—creatively, humorously, playfully, etc.—and the primary process as an indicant of pathological thought disorder.

The lack of specificity in the theory plagued me at every step of manual-construction, for writing scoring rules means setting boundaries in a world of continuous gradation, and only rarely have I been able to appeal to any criterion other than my own largely intuitive judgment about where to draw lines of definition that say, for example, when an image indicates a homosexual wish. "Two men dancing" is scored as an indication of the primary process if it is social or ballroom dancing, but not if the dance is part of a cultural ritual. If that decision appears arbitrary to you, let me confess that, though I can defend it, it feels all too arbitrary to me also.

When Joan Havel and I were first setting up the categories of formal manifestations of the primary process, we drew heavily on Rapaport's "pathological verbalization" scores from his chapter on the Rorschach (Rapaport, Gill, and Schafer, 1945-1946), on the grounds that schizophrenic pathology of thought was to be understood as a breakthrough of the primary process into consciousness. Many of his scores correspond nicely with the phenomenological varieties Freud described in his discussion of the dream work and joke work; thus contaminations and fabulized combinations were pretty clearly aspects of condensation, and clang associations were displacements. But what about peculiar, queer, and incoherent verbalizations? These specifically linguistic categories were among the best indicators of schizophrenic thought disorder, yet Freud said nothing about them. They are well correlated with other formal variables, even in samples that exclude schizophrenics, so I have continued to include them, although without theoretical backup.

The relation between the primary process and defenses is a ticklish and difficult one to handle. Gill (1963) showed that some defenses themselves functioned according to principles of the primary process (e.g., displacement in projection) but that they form a hierarchy corresponding to the continuum from the primary to the secondary process. How, then, should we handle a Rorschach response like this one: "Why do you show me these disgusting sexy pictures?" I think that most analysts would entertain the hypothesis that the subject is projecting his sexual wishes onto the blots or the examiner while strongly disclaiming them. I have followed the practice of scoring the remark as an indicator of the primary process because of the sexual wish (scored L 1 S), treating the rest of it as indicating a pathological attempt at control of that wish (Prj −) and letting the implicit displacement go unscored. Again, I can defend the decision, but wish that theory provided clearer guidelines.

Despite its premier status in defining the primary process, not all displacement should be scored because of the fact, so well developed by Gill (1967), that there are manifestations of displacement and condensation all along the continuum from the primary to the secondary process. This theoretical development was, initially, a shock to me, though I quickly recognized in it my familiar problem of distinguishing different levels of condensations and displacements, and of setting limits. It also reminded me that for a long time the only signs of displacement I could find in Rorschach responses were the Control categories of Remoteness, several ways in which a person can make wishful content less close to home (e.g., distant in time, space, level of reality). Such an operation seemed to be the replacement of a crude and direct wishful content by a more socially acceptable, safely controlled one—clearly an instance of secondary-process displacement. But if Freud's own fundamental definition of the primary process were thus to be overturned, what guidance was available?

In the foregoing I have tried to demonstrate that the term "primary process" has two somewhat different meanings. As an explanatory concept, it employs the apparatus of Freud's metapsychological model of psychic structures, forces, and energies, and

with the collapse of that model the corresponding meaning of the
primary process has lost its utility. As a descriptive concept, it
retains promise and usefulness, even though its empirical referents
are in some ways accidental, being based on Freud's personal
predilections and on traditions of intellectual culture. Empirical
demonstrations (just cited) of a moderate level of interrelationship
among its identifiable subparts suggest both that there is something
like the separate system of prelogical and wishful thought Freud
described, and that more than one such system may exist.

Freud intended his conceptualization of thinking to be mainly a
developmental one, but he did not follow through and elaborate it
by systematic observations of children at various developmental
levels. Overvaluing the economic or energic point of view as he
did, he tended to minimize the conception of various developmental stages or systems of thought without entirely abandoning it,
and simultaneously put forward the incompatible conceptualization of a continuum of thought from an ideal type of the primary
process to an opposite, secondary-process pole. In doing so, he was
wavering between two very general developmental models: the
phasic (the conception that growth takes place mainly through a
succession of internally integrated stages) and the *linear* (the conception that growth is mainly a matter of steady, small incre-
ments).

I believe that internal requirements of psychoanalytic theory
make the following definition—which entails the linear model—
the most satisfactory, and it is the one on which my scoring system
for the Rorschach is based. It starts from the position that the
primary process must be defined in terms of Freud's (1911) two
principles of mental functioning.

> Thus, the more thought (and also affect and behavior) can be
> characterized as an unrealistic seeking for immediate gratifica-
> tion, the more it is to be considered primary process ... And
> the more thought or behavior is organized by adaptive con-
> siderations of efficiency in the search for *realistic* gratification,
> the more it approximates the ideal of secondary process...
> [Holt, 1967c, p. 294 fn.].

The logic of the system seemed to leave this as the most consistent
definition, but it does raise difficult questions. Does the reality

principle actually imply clear logical structure as well as respect for the consensually established structure of reality? If the primary process is a joint function of wishfulness and unrealism, what do you do with discrepant cases—thought products that contain manifestly wish-related content but that are neither illogical nor inconsistent with reality? What about the reverse case, when a thought product shows no sign of wishful content but does fall short of secondary-process standards of logic and realism? In general, I have treated either criterion as sufficient, but once again drawing boundaries has been problematic.

In particular, several difficult issues are raised by the lack of clear theoretical guidelines for the classification of thought products as primary process on the basis of their formal properties, though they boil down to one question: Just because a form of thought is *not* unimpeachably secondary process in nature, is it necessarily primary process? Gill (1967) put it in the form of the question: Are there other mechanisms of the primary process besides condensation and displacement? He was able, to his own satisfaction, to reduce to condensation or displacement all other possibilities that had been suggested, including plastic representation, concretization, contradiction, symbolization, autistic logic, fragmentation, and timelessness. More precisely, he said: "If condensation and displacement as Freud described them in the dream work are seen as the characterization of id functioning from the economic point of view, the 'other' characteristics of id functioning are the result of looking at such functions from the several other metapsychological points of view" (1967, p. 294).

At the time, that seemed to me a good resolution. Since then, however, I have realized that it leaves us with only two distasteful alternatives in defining the limits of what is to be considered primary process: we can stick to the argument by authority, accepting everything that Freud said in describing unconscious and id functioning and nothing but what he said, or we can open the floodgates to all possible deviations from perfection. Partly, the hidden villain in the piece is the innocent-appearing proposition that the primary process and the secondary process are not really systems of thought, but hypothetical end points of a continuum. The trouble with that comes when you start describing real thought products and try to locate them with any degree of precision on the

continuum. There turn out to be at least two continua to begin
with, one of wishfulness and one of efficiency or realism; and the
attempt to formulate the latter suggests that it be divided into at
least two more continua, consistency with reality (as consensually
defined) and logical clarity.

Just as soon as you go from the theoretical level to the practical
one of classifying actual thought products, you find that even three
continua are not enough. For example, I have felt the need for four
rated continua: Defense Demand (related to the degree of wishfulness), Defense Effectiveness, Form Level, and Creativity of
Response. And none of the last three correspond directly to realism
or clarity of logical structure! Further, consider Defense Demand:
Is it tenable to take the position, as I have in my scoring manual,
that a response should be considered a primary-process manifestation merely because it contains evidence of wishfulness that is so
socialized and attenuated as not to raise an eyebrow at a polite tea
party? "Please may I have a cup of tea?" is surely such a remark,
yet it obviously meets the scoring criteria for the expression of an
oral wish, for rather immediate gratification.

You may counter that the problem here is that I am not taking
the continuum idea seriously enough, but insisting on applying an
outmoded dichotomy. Is it really outmoded? Do we not constantly
see clinical and research evidence that there is something like a
special system of thought that operates in dreams, symptoms, and
disordered thinking generally? I believe that we do, and that the
situation is exactly analogous to the paradox or antithesis between
typology and dimensional scaling in the field of personality assessment. Consider Loevinger's (1966) developmental types for a moment: they consist of configurations of traits, many of which have
been traditionally measured as separate continua, and which can
continue to be so treated despite the evidence that they are empirically clustered in a theoretically intelligible fashion. The appearance of meaningful and factually based developmental types
or clusters introduces a welcome order into the bewildering diversity of personality description, with its hundreds of continuously
varying, arbitrarily bounded traits. Is not something of the same
sort possible in the realm of thought?

Surely there is a great need for a typology comprising *several*
systems or forms of thought in addition to the primary and secon-

dary processes. The concept of the primary process was eagerly seized by psychopathologists, since it seemed to formulate so well the thought disorder of schizophrenia. Yet, as Rapaport, Gill, and Schafer (1945-1946) showed empirically, Freud's concept did not provide any help in clarifying theoretically the differences among various kinds of thought disorders in mania, in depression, and in schizophrenia, or even in distinguishing psychosis from neurosis: all are "breakthroughs" of the primary process. Similarly, it is all very well to say that "the child" thinks with the primary process, "the adult" with the secondary; but does that mean that only quantitative differences may be found in thinking at different developmental levels? Psychoanalytic theory provides for nothing more.

In the first attempt to apply my scoring scheme to thought products other than Rorschach responses, Goldberger (1961; see also Goldberger and Holt, 1958) found it possible to use the manual's criteria of the primary process in rating the free verbal productions of subjects kept in perceptual isolation (sensory deprivation) for eight hours. His ratings and mine attained a satisfactory degree of interjudge reliability, however, only after we made a further distinction. We were troubled by the fact that much of what his subjects said was vague, or concrete, or substandard in terms of grammar or rhetoric, or incomplete, or otherwise intellectually *déclassé*, without meeting any standard criteria of the primary process. We decided, therefore, to classify and scale these as forms of *regressed secondary process*, which we were able to distinguish from both well-controlled and poorly controlled primary process, and then to rate all three with reliabilities of about .9.

Once I had admitted the idea that there was regression from the secondary process not to the primary process but to developmentally earlier forms of everyday thinking, I began to have doubts about some of my "miscellaneous" formal signs of the primary process, like physiognomic responsiveness or the intrusion of irrelevancies—were they primary process or regressed forms of the secondary process? Psychoanalytic theory again gave no guidance, and the question remains unanswered.

From what I have presented so far, I hope to have made it clear that, in its present state, the theory of the primary process is in sad disarray. Its empirical referents are only generally specified, too imprecisely to give firm guidance to concrete attempts at measurement. Taken either as a low-level clinical theory or in its higher-level metapsychological guise, it is fundamentally lacking. As usual, Freud's clinical intuition had a good deal of validity, and his ideas about thinking have had both clinical and research utility, but they badly need reformulation.

In the present, already long communication, I cannot discuss in any detail an alternative conceptualization. Elsewhere I hope to present some specific proposals for a phasic developmental theory of cognition, which will be another in the lengthening list of attempts to unify the contributions to this topic of two towering figures, Freud and Piaget.

REFERENCES

Barratt, B. B. (1976), Freud's Psychology as Interpretation. *Psychoanalysis and Contemporary Science*, 5:443-478. New York: International Universities Press.

Black, M. (1962), *Models and Metaphors*. Ithaca, N.Y.: Cornell University Press.

Boring, E. G. (1950), *A History of Experimental Psychology*, 2nd ed. New York: Appleton-Century-Crofts, 1957.

Breuer, J., & Freud, S. (1893-1895), Studies on Hysteria. *Standard Edition*, 2. London: Hogarth Press, 1955.

Carmichael, L., ed. (1946), *Manual of Child Psychology*. New York: Wiley.

Edelheit, H. (1975), Complementarity as a Rule in Psychological Research. Paper presented at the Rapaport-Klein Study Group Meetings, June.

Fisher, C. (1954), Dreams and Perception. *J. Amer. Psychoanal. Assn.*, 2:389-445.

——— (1957), A Study of the Preliminary Stages of the Construction of Dreams and Images. *J. Amer. Psychoanal. Assn.*, 5:5-60.

——— (1960), Introduction to: Preconscious Stimulation in Dreams, Associations, and Images. *Psychol. Issues*, Monogr. No. 7:1-40. New York: International Universities Press.

Freud, S. (1887-1902), *The Origins of Psychoanalysis: Letters to Wilhelm Fliess, Drafts and Notes, 1887-1902*. New York: Basic Books, 1954.

——— (1891), *On Aphasia*. New York: International Universities Press, 1953.

——— (1895), Project for a Scientific Psychology. *Standard Edition*, 1:295-391. London: Hogarth Press, 1966.

——— (1896), Letter 52 to Wilhelm Fliess (December 6). *Standard Edition*, 1:233-239. London: Hogarth Press, 1966.

——— (1900), The Interpretation of Dreams. *Standard Edition*, 4 & 5. London: Hogarth Press, 1953.

——— (1901), On Dreams. *Standard Edition*, 5:633-686. London: Hogarth Press, 1953.

——— (1905), Jokes and Their Relation to the Unconscious. *Standard Edition*, 8. London: Hogarth Press, 1960.

———— (1910), The Psycho-Analytic View of Psychogenic Disturbance of Vision. *Standard Edition*, 11:211-218. London: Hogarth Press, 1957.

———— (1911), Formulations on the Two Principles of Mental Functioning. *Standard Edition*, 12:218-226. London: Hogarth Press, 1958.

———— (1914), On Narcissism: An Introduction. *Standard Edition*, 14:73-102. London: Hogarth Press, 1957.

———— (1915), Instincts and Their Vicissitudes. *Standard Edition*, 14:117-140. London: Hogarth Press, 1957.

———— (1923), The Infantile Genital Organization: An Interpolation into the Theory of Sexuality. *Standard Edition*, 19:141-145. London: Hogarth Press, 1961.

———— (1924a), Neurosis and Psychosis. *Standard Edition*, 19:149-153. London: Hogarth Press, 1961.

———— (1924b), The Loss of Reality in Neurosis and Psychosis. *Standard Edition*, 19:183-187. London: Hogarth Press, 1961.

———— (1925), Some Psychical Consequences of the Anatomical Distinction between the Sexes. *Standard Edition*, 19:248-258. London: Hogarth Press, 1961.

———— (1927), Fetishism. *Standard Edition*, 21:152-157. London: Hogarth Press, 1961.

———— (1933), New Introductory Lectures on Psycho-Analysis. *Standard Edition*, 22:5-182. London: Hogarth Press, 1964.

———— (1940a), An Outline of Psycho-Analysis. *Standard Edition*, 23:144-207. London: Hogarth Press, 1964.

———— (1940b), Splitting of the Ego in the Process of Defence. *Standard Edition*, 23:275-278. London: Hogarth Press, 1964.

Gill, M. M. (1963), Topography and Systems in Psychoanalytic Theory. *Psychol. Issues*, Monogr. No. 10. New York: International Universities Press.

———— (1967), The Primary Process. In: Motives and Thought: Psychoanalytic Essays in Honor of David Rapaport, ed. R. R. Holt. *Psychol. Issues*, Monogr. No. 18/19:260-298. New York: International Universities Press.

Goldberger, L. (1961), Reactions to Perceptual Isolation and Rorschach Manifestations of the Primary Process. *J. Project. Tech.*, 25:287-302.

———— & Holt, R. R. (1958), Experimental Interference with Reality Contact (Perceptual Isolation): I. Method and Group Results. *J. Nerv. Ment. Dis.*, 127:99-112.

Grossman, W. I., & Simon, B. (1969), Anthropomorphism: Motive, Meaning, and Causality in Psychoanalytic Theory. *The Psychoanalytic Study of the Child*, 24:78-111. New York: International Universities Press.

Hartmann, H. (1939), *Ego Psychology and the Problem of Adaptation*. New York: International Universities Press, 1958.

Heath, D. H. (1965), *Explorations of Maturity*. New York: Appleton-Century-Crofts.

Hodges, H. A. (1968), Wilhelm Dilthey. *International Encyclopedia of the Social Sciences*, 4:185-187. New York: Macmillan.

Holt, R. R. (1962), A Critical Examination of Freud's Concept of Bound vs. Free Cathexis. *J. Amer. Psychoanal. Assn.*, 10:475-525.

———— (1965), A Review of Some of Freud's Biological Assumptions and Their Influence on His Theory. In: *Psychoanalysis and Current Biological Thought*, ed. N. S. Greenfield & W. C. Lewis. Madison: University of Wisconsin Press, pp. 93-124.

——— (1966), Measuring Libidinal and Aggressive Motives and Their Controls by Means of the Rorschach Test. In: *Nebraska Symposium on Motivation, 1966*, ed. D. Levine. Lincoln: University of Nebraska Press, pp. 1-47.

——— (1967a), Beyond Vitalism and Mechanism: Freud's Concept of Psychic Energy. In: *Science and Psychoanalysis*, 11:1-41. New York: Grune & Stratton.

——— (1967b), The Development of the Primary Process: A Structural View. In: Motives and Thought: Psychoanalytic Essays in Honor of David Rapaport, ed. R. R. Holt. *Psychol. Issues*, Monogr. No. 18/19:345-383. New York: International Universities Press.

———, ed. (1967c), Motives and Thought: Psychoanalytic Essays in Honor of David Rapaport. *Psychol. Issues*, Monogr. No. 18/19. New York: International Universities Press.

———, ed. (1968), Foreword to *Diagnostic Psychological Testing*, rev. ed., by D. Rapaport, M. M. Gill, & R. Schafer. New York: International Universities Press, pp. 1-44.

——— (with the collaboration and assistance of J. Havel, L. Goldberger, A. Philip, & R. Safrin) (1969), Manual for the Scoring of Primary-Process Manifestations in Rorschach Responses, 10th ed. New York: Research Center for Mental Health, New York University. (Mimeographed.)

——— (1970), Artistic Creativity and Rorschach Measures of Adaptive Regression. In: *Developments in the Rorschach Technique*, Vol. 3, ed. B. Klopfer, M. M. Meyer, & F. B. Brawer. New York: Harcourt Brace Jovanovich, pp. 263-320.

——— (1974), On Reading Freud. Introduction to *Abstracts of the Standard Edition of Freud*. New York: Jason Aronson, pp. 1-79.

——— (1975), Drive or Wish? A Reconsideration of the Psychoanalytic Theory of Motivation. In: Psychology versus Metapsychology: Psychoanalytic Essays in Memory of George S. Klein, ed. M. M. Gill & P. S. Holzman. *Psychol. Issues*, Monogr. No. 36:158-197. New York: International Universities Press.

Jones, E. (1953), *The Life and Work of Sigmund Freud*, Vol. 1. New York: Basic Books.

Kahn, M. W. (1965), A Factor-Analytic Study of Personality, Intelligence, and History Characteristics of Murderers. In: *Proceedings of the 73rd Annual Convention of the American Psychological Association, 1965*. Washington, D.C.: American Psychological Association, pp. 227-228.

Klein, G. S. (1970), *Perception, Motives, and Personality*. New York: Knopf.

——— (1975), *Psychoanalytic Theory: An Exploration of Essentials*. New York: International Universities Press.

Köhler, W. (1917), *The Mentality of Apes*. New York: Harcourt Brace, 1924.

Kubie, L. S. (1954), The Fundamental Nature of the Distinction between Normality and Neurosis. *Psychoanal. Quart.*, 23:167-204.

Kuhn, T. S. (1970), *The Structure of Scientific Revolutions*, rev. ed. Chicago: University of Chicago Press.

Laforgue, R. (1926), Verdrängung und Skotomisation. *Internat. Z. Psychoanal.*, 12:54-65.

Loevinger, J. (1966), The Meaning and Measurement of Ego Development. *Amer. Psychol.*, 21:195-206.

Piaget, J. (1937), *The Construction of Reality in the Child*. New York: Basic Books, 1954.

Pötzl, O. (1917), The Relationship between Experimentally Induced Dream Images and Indirect Vision. *Psychol. Issues*, Monogr. No. 7:41-120. New York: International Universities Press, 1960.

Rapaport, D., ed. (1951), *Organization and Pathology of Thought.* New York: Columbia University Press.

——, Gill, M. M., & Schafer, R. (1945-1946), *Diagnostic Psychological Testing,* 2 vols. Chicago: Year Book Publishers.

Romanes, G. J. (1882), *Animal Intelligence.* London: Kegan Paul, Trench.

—— (1888), *Mental Evolution in Man.* London: Kegan Paul, Trench.

Rothenberg, A. (1971), The Process of Janusian Thinking in Creativity. *Arch. Gen. Psychiat.*, 24:195-205.

Schafer, R. (1954), *Psychoanalytic Interpretation in Rorschach Testing.* New York: Grune & Stratton.

—— (1958), Regression in the Service of the Ego: The Relevance of a Psychoanalytic Concept for Personality Assessment. In: *Assessment of Human Motives*, ed. G. L. Lindzey. New York: Rinehart, pp. 119-148.

—— (1970), The Psychoanalytic Vision of Reality. *Internat. J. Psycho-Anal.*, 51:279-297.

Schimek, J. G. (1975), A Critical Reexamination of Freud's Concept of Unconscious Mental Representation. *Internat. Rev. Psycho-Anal.*, 2:171-187.

Whitehead, A. N. (1925), *Science and the Modern World.* New York: Mentor, 1952.

Yankelovich, D., & Barrett, W. (1970), *Ego and Instinct.* New York: Random House.

Paul L. Wachtel, Ph.D.

Structure or Transaction?
A Critique of the Historical and Intrapsychic Emphasis in Psychoanalytic Thought

Psychoanalysis is not unique in its emphasis on the importance of childhood and its effort to understand a person's feelings and behavior in terms of his life history. A wide range of psychological theories suggest that early experiences are likely to establish lifelong patterns unless certain unusual subsequent events occur.

The precise way in which psychoanalysis treats the historical perspective in psychological inquiry is, however, distinctive—and controversial as well, especially in its explanation of the uniquely powerful influence of childhood experiences. There are many ways of understanding the continuities between early behaviors and experiences and those of later life, and many ways of conceiving of the seeming inappropriateness to current realities of much of day-to-day adult behavior. What is particularly characteristic of the psychoanalytic approach to these problems is its postulation of the persisting influence of certain childhood wishes and fears *despite later experiences which might be expected to alter them*. Repression, in the psychoanalytic view, does not merely prevent the person from being aware of what is being repressed; it also prevents the repressed desire or fantasy from "growing up," from changing in the course of development as do unrepressed desires or fantasies.

The analyst readily acknowledges that the child's conscious,

Portions of this paper appear in a different form in *Psychoanalysis and Behavior Therapy: Toward an Integration* (Wachtel, 1977).

unrepressed strivings may be altered or redirected as his values change and his conception of morality matures. New information and the dictates of logic often lead us to alter conscious choices and to give up efforts to achieve goals once highly prized. Those motives, however, which do not appear to be represented in consciousness seem far less responsive to the modifying influences of rational thought and contradictory information. The fantasies about and yearnings for the mother which often become apparent in the course of the psychoanalytic treatment of adult males seem appropriate for a naïve four-year-old, whose most important gratifications primarily depend on her, who has little experience with other women which would temper his queenly image of her, and who has hardly begun to develop the adult's complex view of people as having mixed strengths and weaknesses, beauties and warts. Though he consciously knows that she is now a middle-aged woman who is probably far less attractive than most women he meets, though he can readily report that she is often a tiresome nag and that he doubts she has given his father a good time in bed, though he knows that many others could gratify him far more than she could, he shows unacknowledged signs of longing for her with the same fervor he had when she was all the world to him, the holy center of his child's universe. His desire seems unmodified by his conscious perception and understanding of the realities of his life and the limited possibilities for gratification with his mother.

THE NOTION OF DISSOCIATED SYSTEMS

Freud's attempt to account for the persistence of such seemingly anomalous desires relied heavily on a conception of dissociation or disruption of integration in psychological functioning. The apparent immodifiability of certain aspects of our psychological life, in particular those aspects which were unconscious, in contrast with the responsiveness of much of our psychological functioning to changing circumstances, prompted Freud to build his model of mental functioning around an image of separate psychological systems, often influencing our experience and behavior in conflicting ways and thereby introducing disharmony into our efforts to find gratification and safety in the world.

In his earliest writings, when he was still concerned primarily with unconscious memories rather than wishes or fantasies, Freud (along with Breuer) indicated that repressing the memory of a traumatic event not only kept it out of awareness, but also prevented its interaction with the person's other ideas and memories. By remaining encapsulated and unintegrated with the rest of the person's mental functioning, it did not participate in the processes whereby memories of emotionally arousing events typically lost their original affective intensity (Breuer and Freud, 1893-1895).

Unrepressed memories underwent a wearing away of the associated affect through such "discharge" paths as crying, laughing, moving about, and taking action, as well as via thinking things through, which served to discharge both by relieving the push to think about them and by modifying their implications through comparison, putting things into perspective, etc. Repressed memories, on the other hand, by not undergoing such processes remained fresh, retaining in an unmodified way their original significance and intensity. The unconscious memories were viewed as "timeless," in contrast to unrepressed memories of events, which gradually lost their preoccupying significance as new events took center stage in the person's continuing life history.

Freud's description of the persisting influence of the past is reminiscent of the tales of woolly mammoths found frozen in the arctic ice, so perfectly preserved after thousands of years that their meat could be eaten by anyone with a taste for such regressive fare. Freud was extremely impressed with the "freshness" and vividness of the memories revealed after digging through layers of resistance. Their lack of access to usual associative pathways was seen as preserving them.

Some observations from other quarters tend to support the view that memories *can* somehow be stored in such a way as to lie dormant for years and then be extraordinarily powerful and vivid when they see the light of day. Penfield, for example, has reported that patients sometimes describe memories of almost hallucinatory vividness when certain regions of the brain are stimulated during surgery (e.g., Penfield and Roberts, 1959). Although his emphasis on localization of function has been questioned, and though many modern accounts of memory stress reconstruction rather than storage of exact copies of past experiences, observations of this sort do seem convergent with the kind of observation that so impressed Freud.

In a somewhat different vein, a friend and colleague of mine scared the wits out of her husband and several nurses when, on recovering from anaesthesia following the delivery of her child, she began to speak in gibberish while appearing to believe she was communicating. Fortunately there happened to be around a Hungarian-speaking resident, who readily identified the sounds she was making as decent, if somewhat simple, Hungarian sentences. She had been born in Hungary and spoke Hungarian for the first few years of her life, but came very early to the United States and as an adult spoke unaccented English and knew no Hungarian. Upon fully recovering from the anaesthesia she again communicated in excellent English, and to this day remains, in everyday life, blissfully ignorant of how one would ask the time of day in Budapest.

Such examples suggest that, whatever the exact means of storage, and apart from the question of whether what is recalled is the result of the activation of a replicative trace or the product of current active reconstructive processes, some record of past experiences can be stored for long periods without being subject to the kinds of wearing away or fusing of memory traces that so distress students at exam time and intrigue experimental investigators of memory.

The bearing of such observations upon the Freudian view of the timeless unconscious, however, is far from clear. Even at this early point in Freud's theorizing, when he thought his patients suffered from memories of actual events, the memories he was referring to were far from dormant. To push the previous metaphor a bit further, the woolly mammoths Freud saw frozen in the paleolithic layers of the psyche were trumpeting loudly enough to wake the dead, and certainly disturbed the sleep of the living. In Freud's view, the memories were not accessible to consciousness, but they were very active indeed. A continuous effort was thought to be needed to keep them from becoming conscious.

REPRESSION AND UNINTEGRATED SEXUAL DEVELOPMENT

When Freud's theoretical emphasis shifted from concern with

repressed memories of real events to repressed fantasies associated with unacceptable wishes and urges, the theoretical account of how the unconscious remained "timeless" was changed and elaborated, but the emphasis on repression as preventing integration as well as consciousness remained. In *Three Essays on the Theory of Sexuality*, Freud (1905) suggested that the sexual drive originally develops as a number of separate longings and urges which, in ideal circumstances, are integrated into a unitary genital urge at puberty. Thus Freud saw the complex nature of adult sexuality (in which full sexual activity and pleasure included oral and anal aspects as well as the involvement of the genitals, and in which sadistic, masochistic, exhibitionistic, and voyeuristic activities and pleasures are obvious) as the result of an integration of various urges which are apparent in the child as relatively separate motivational tendencies.

The successful integration of these "component instincts" was seen by Freud as interfered with by repression. When a component drive was repressed it was separated from the rest of development, persisting unconsciously in isolation while the other aspects of the instinctual life continued to be gradually shaped and molded by processes of development and the increasing influence of reality experiences upon the nature of our desires and the people, times, and places toward which they were directed. Thus, as Freud saw it, while most of our desires were "growing up," those which were repressed, and prevented from being integrated with the rest of the personality, remained active in their original primitive form.

DISSOCIATED SYSTEMS AND EGO PSYCHOLOGY

The close relation in Freud's thought between repression, the persistence of past psychological tendencies in unmodified form, and the conception of separate psychological systems is particularly evident after *The Ego and the Id* (Freud, 1923), in which he distinguished between "the coherent ego and the repressed which is split off from it" (p. 17). The split-off portion of our psychological functioning Freud of course designated as the id.

Freud clearly did not intend his conceptualization of these separate systems or structures as a formal theory. In the preface to *The Ego and the Id* he stated that the synthesis he was presenting there did "not go beyond the roughest outline" (p. 12). It is important to recognize this because current references to the "ego" in psychoanalytic works often treat the term not as an initial conceptual groping toward understanding of the organization and structure of psychological processes but rather as an entity given by nature. Questions are directed toward what the "ego" is like rather than toward whether it is a useful conception.

Such tendencies in psychoanalytic writing obscure the issues Freud was attempting to grapple with. The "ego" for Freud, when he was at his clearest and most consistent, was not an entity whose properties were to be studied. It was a tentative conceptual effort to bring together several theoretical issues which Freud sensed might be related. Implicit in Freud's writings are several definitions of the ego rather than one. These were not conflicting or incompatible definitions but rather foci or nuclei, vantage points from which the organization of psychological processes could be glimpsed. We must briefly examine these differing approaches to the ego concept in order to see clearly in what way Freud's use of it is relevant to our understanding of the psychoanalytic approach to the past and what alternative approaches are available to us.

ASPECTS OF THE EGO CONCEPT

Freud designated the ego as that part of the mind which is coherent and organized: ". . . the ego is an organization and the id is not" (Freud, 1926, p. 97). In referring to an organization, Freud was trying to come to terms with the fact that successful adaptation requires a coordinated effort in which various psychological processes must function together, as a unified system (much as synthesis and organization are characteristic of, and in some sense even define, life processes in general).

Though we may, for purposes of study and discussion, separately conceptualize such processes as motivation, perception, memory, etc., our survival depends upon these various aspects of our adaptational activity functioning *together*, as a system. When we are hungry, we must remember where to look for food, we must see the food in front of us, we must bring the food to our mouths, etc. If processes of motivation, perception, and motor

learning were not coordinated this could not happen. We would
be no more likely to search for food when our bellies were empty
than when they were full. We would be no more likely to initiate
movements toward the food we see than toward any other object
in our visual field. We would, in short, simply not function in a
way that would enable us to survive.

The property of organization or coordination in psychological
functioning, then, was represented in Freud's theorizing by the
conception of an organized *system*, the ego. From this perspective,
the id is defined by its separateness from this organization.
Psychological processes conceived of as part of the id are not
coordinated with the adaptational activities of the ego system.
Fuller elaboration of what this means requires us to consider a
second focus of Freud's conceptualization of the ego.

Freud described the ego as that mental system which starts out
from perception, or as he put it at another point, "that part of the
id which has been modified by the direct influence of the external
world."[1] He added that "For the ego, perception plays the part
which in the id falls to instinct" (1923, p. 25).

From this perspective, the ego is conceived as a system of
psychological processes whose functioning is in response to
environmental events. That is, what happens "out there," at least
as it is represented by our perceptual activity, has a considerable
influence[2] on just what thoughts are thought, what desires are
aroused, what desires are acted upon, etc., *if those thoughts,
desires, or other psychological processes or events are part of the
ego system.* Fantasies or wishes which are part of the id, however,
and therefore by definition not participating in the coordination
and organization of the ego system, are *not* conceived as
influenced by what we perceive of real external events. In other
words, they are not subject to reality testing. As conceived by

---

[1] This way of putting it implies that initially there is just id, that is, that all of
the psychological processes which constitute the ego are modifications of original
primitive instincts. Increased recognition of the problems such a formulation
gives rise to led Hartmann, Kris, and Loewenstein (1946) to postulate an original
undifferentiated ego-id.

[2] The ego is, of course, in the psychoanalytic view, also responsive to
influences other than environmental events, such as the arousal of id desires and
prohibitions of the superego.

Freud, these wishes and fantasies persist (unconsciously) despite being grossly unrealistic.[3]

They also are conceived as persisting despite being quite at odds with other important goals or ideas of the person. To put it somewhat facetiously, cognitive dissonance theory holds only in the ego. The ego, as an organized psychological system, is subject to the constraints of logic. Holding inconsistent ideas, or wanting incompatible things, creates a strain, and leads to alterations of one or another part of the system. But as Freud conceived things, id wishes or fantasies are not similarly organized. Wishes and ideas considerably at odds with other things we know persist without modification if they are not part of the ego system.

Still another perspective on what Freud was getting at in his conception of the ego as a system and the id as separate from it is provided by attending to the names Freud gave to these constructs. The Latinate terms "ego" and "id" obscure the phenomenological implications of the original names, *Das Ich* (the "I") and *Das Es* (the "it"). Thinking of *Das Ich* as the "I" instead of the "ego" highlights the view of the ego as an organization of psychological processes including, and strongly infused with, the feeling of self.

This is not to say that all psychological processes conceived as part of the ego system are experienced as part of the self, or acknowledged as what *I* am doing. On the contrary, the very observations which were most prominent in Freud's decision to recast his theory in terms of ego, id, and superego involve "ego processes" *not* experienced as self. The activities referred to by psychoanalysts as defense mechanisms are conceived of as part of the ego system, yet are often not acknowledged by the person as something he is doing. A tendency to try very hard to be nice when unacceptable hostile urges are stirred, or to become preoccupied with an irrelevant intellectual issue when a strange and disturbing feeling is aroused, is not likely to be part of the self-image of the person who exhibits it.

[3] More modern accounts of the id (e.g., Gill, 1963) do not present such a sharp dichotomy, developing instead Freud's implicit conception of a hier-archical layering of the personality and a gradual differentiation of more realistic and more primitive aspects of functioning. The conceptual issue central to this paper, however, is relevant to the latter model as well. See also fn. 4.

Yet the intimate conceptual link between the ego system and the experience of self is readily apparent in Freud's writings in more ways than just his choice of the name *Das Ich*. Freud, for example, stated that the ego is "first and foremost a body-ego" (1923, p. 27), pointing to the infant's explorations of his own body as the beginning sense of self that is very much at the core of the developing organization of the ego.

Additionally, the notion of the ego as the system from which the defenses emanate points to the ego as a system closely linked to self-feeling. From the earliest period of psychoanalysis, Freud was attuned to people's efforts to cast out of their experience what does not fit with their sense of who they are or want to be. The ego system is by no means synonymous with the sense of self, which is but one aspect or portion of the ego construct, but the sense of self is nonetheless a crucial feature distinguishing the ego as a system from the id which is excluded from it.

FURTHER IMPLICATIONS OF THE STRUCTURAL MODEL

In Freud's later formulations, then, those tendencies which are defended against are not merely kept unconscious; they are also dissociated from the coordinated system of processes that maintain the person's adaptation. Thus they are rendered relatively[4] unresponsive to new environmental input and cannot be experienced with a quality of self-feeling. In fact, from the perspective of the structural theory, it became increasingly apparent that certain ideas and strivings which were at least somewhat in awareness might still be best conceptualized as belonging to the id, and as having problematic consequences quite comparable to those of some more fully unconscious strivings. Repression— exclusion from awareness—was seen more clearly as but one kind

---

[4] It is necessary to recognize that Freud did not postulate *absolute* separation between the systems. He noted, in commenting on a figure he devised to represent this theoretical model, that "The ego is not sharply separated from the id; its lower portion merges into it" (1923, p. 24). Without *some* communication between systems one would have no way of accounting for the ability of repressed drives to influence behavior and create disturbance.

of defensive activity directed toward threatening ideas and inclinations.

People who rely on isolation and intellectualization as defenses, for example, are often able to report verbally desires or fantasies which other people cannot verbalize at all. These verbal reports, however, tend to be affectless and not to be integrated with other mental processes in the same way as tendencies not defended against. The intellectualizing person may tell us, for example, that he knows that a particular wish or fantasy he is reporting is illogical or at odds with what he knows is in his best interests. Yet it is clear that knowing it is illogical in no way changes his ideas. Logic as a modifying or regulating influence that coordinates most of his ideas seems to bounce off this particular one, as if it were not part of the regulated system of thought.

Further, while the idea defended against by isolation or intellectualization can sometimes be in awareness, it is nonetheless not experienced with a sense of its being part of the self. It is often experienced as a kind of inference, as something observed from outside rather than felt from within. ("It looks like I must be wanting..."; "I guess that means I'm trying to..."; "I seem to be feeling..." rather than "I want..." or "I feel..."). Thus it remains "it" (*Es*) rather than "I" (*Ich*).

It is just such observations which led Freud to change his description of the aim of the psychoanalytic process from "making the unconscious conscious" to "Where id was, there ego shall be." It is not enough that an idea be conscious. As we saw above, an idea can be conscious, at least to some extent,[5] and still be, functionally, part of the id. That is, it can still be excluded from the modifying influences that regulate those processes which are part of the organized adaptational system Freud called the ego. Such apparently conscious, yet defended-against, ideas play a similar role in psychological adaptation to that played by those ideas which in Freud's older theory were part of "the uncon-

---

[5] The question of what is "conscious" is not a simple one. Horney (1939), for example, talks of unconscious tendencies when a person is aware of some trend in his behavior but not of its pervasiveness or full implications for his functioning. Moreover, the distinction between "intellectual" and "emotional" awareness is not a very clear one, although common in the psychoanalytic literature.

scious." They are peremptory and unrealistic because they do not change over time in response to new environmental input, and are not modified by being put into perspective in the way ideas more familiar to us in our day-to-day living frequently are. Whether they become conscious is thus less important than whether they become part of the ego—that is, whether they are tamed by being integrated into a coordinated adaptational effort.

IMPLICATIONS FOR THERAPEUTIC EFFORTS

This ego-psychological model is certainly far more sophisticated than the model of dissociated memories in Freud's earliest psychoanalytic writings. It opened psychoanalytic concern to an enormously widened range of phenomena. But in many respects it remains merely a more sophisticated version of the "woolly mammoth" model.

This is particularly the case in the therapeutic technique of psychoanalysis, for much research on perception, cognitive styles, and adaptational strategies, undertaken in the name of psychoanalytic ego psychology, has had little impact on the theory of neurosis and even less on psychoanalytic technique. Analysts do pay far more attention now to the details of how the patient keeps some of his inclinations dissociated (that is, to the actual processes and activities of defense), and they are concerned with assessing how the patient's problems are exacerbated by defects in ego functioning, that is, by faulty thinking, reality testing, impulse control, etc. But the crux of the patient's problems is still thought to be in the split in the psychological functioning caused by his defending against childhood inclinations (and therefore in the persistence of unintegrated remnants of childhood which are impervious to the effect of new life experiences).

The continuity between modern formulations and the original view of the preservation of memories is especially clear in a passage from Stone (1961), which is particularly significant because Stone's volume represents one of the major attempts within the classical psychoanalytic tradition to modernize the role of the therapist. Stone writes that "true transference . . . retains unmistakably its infantile character. However much the given early relationship may have contributed to the genuinely adult pattern of relationships (via identification, limitation, acceptance of teaching, for example), its transference derivative differs from the latter, *approximately in the sense which Breuer and Freud ... assigned to the sequelae of the pathogenic traumatic experience, which was neither abreacted as such, nor associatively absorbed in the personality"* (p. 67; italics added). Thus Stone makes very clear that even modern conceptions of transference are directly related to the original "woolly mammoth" model—that of memories preserved in their original form by repression, and uninfluenced by later reality experiences or cognitive development.

The implications for therapy of this view of the intrapsychic preservation of the past are considerable. The patient's neurosis is seen as deriving most essentially from his continuing and unsuccessful efforts to deal with internalized residues of his past which, by virtue of being isolated from his adaptive and integrative ego, continue to make primitive demands wholly unresponsive to reality. It is therefore maintained by many analysts that a fully successful treatment must create conditions whereby these anachronistic inclinations can be experienced consciously and integrated into the ego so that they can be controlled and modified. The vehicle for such an effort is the transference neurosis, a shifting of the patient's neurotic preoccupations toward the person of the analyst. The transference neurosis, in its intensity and inappropriateness, reveals and highlights the infantile origins of the patient's concerns. Greenson (1967) states that the transference neurosis

> ... offers the patient the most important instrumentality for gaining access to the warded-off *past pathogenic experiences. The reliving of the repressed past* with the analyst and in the analytic situation is the most effective opportunity for overcoming the neurotic defenses and resistances. Thus, the psychoanalyst will take pains to safeguard the transference situation and prevent any contamination which might curtail its full flowering ... All intrusions of the analyst's personal characteristics and values will be recognized as factors which might limit the scope of the patient's transference neurosis. Interpretation is the only method of dealing with the trans-

ference that will permit it to run its entire course [pp. 189-190; italics added].

Greenson, like Stone, does indicate that the analyst need not, indeed should not, be cold, aloof, and utterly unresponsive. Stone recommends for the analyst a "physicianly commitment" to understanding and helping the patient, and Greenson devotes considerable space to describing how to facilitate a "working alliance" with the patient that enables the patient to cooperate in the difficult and frustrating task of being analyzed.

But for both Greenson and Stone these modifications of the harsher interpretations of Freud's recommendation that the analyst be a "mirror" or a "blank screen" are to be undertaken only to the minimum degree necessary to enlist the patient's cooperation. Both books are replete with warnings about the limitations in therapeutic change which accompany any therapist activity which might distort or restrict the transference neurosis. Greenson states, for example, that a "mode of behavior or attitude on the part of the analyst other than that of consistent, humane nonintrusiveness obscures and distorts the development and recognition of transference phenomena" (p. 272).

An analyst's decision to seek to evoke a transference neurosis, and to eschew the wide range of therapeutic interventions thought to limit the transference neurosis, means that the patient will experience a good deal of pain. For one thing, the transference neurosis itself is a painful thing. Violent emotions, of an intensity more characteristic of children than of adults, appear, often incomprehensibly.[6] Further, it is generally agreed that the transference neurosis cannot develop properly without a good deal of frustration (e.g., Menninger, 1958). An additional, related factor—the need for the analyst to remain as anonymous as possible in order to be able to demonstrate to the patient that his reactions to the analyst are displaced from the past—requires that

[6] The classical idea that the transference neurosis *replaces* the presenting neurotic problems suggests that the sum total of suffering might not increase. Greenson notes, however, that the patient's neurosis outside of the analytic situation often "merely pales and becomes relatively insignificant compared to the transference neurosis—*only to reappear* in the patient's outside life when another constellation dominates the transference picture" (p. 188; italics added).

the analyst intervene in the patient's life as little as possible except through interpretation. Thus many interventions which could bring immediate relief for particular current distresses are eschewed. Finally, adopting a strategy in which change is assumed to come about through the evocation and resolution of a transference neurosis includes the recognition that such a process requires years to be completed.

These privations are regarded as the course of choice, however, where the patient can stand them, because they are thought by analysts to lead to far more extensive and more lasting change than any other kind of treatment can achieve. Such an evaluation follows rather directly from the view that the effective cause of the patient's current neurosis is *tendencies within him which were locked in in the past and continue to exert a pressure unchanging in both quality and intensity and largely unresponsive to anything that happens in his current day-to-day living.*

If this view is correct, the most effective treatment would necessarily be one which makes possible the release of the locked-in tendencies so that they can be integrated with the rest of the personality and as subject to the limits of logic and reality as are our more mature inclinations. The classical psychoanalytic situation does seem to be the method par excellence for ultimately promoting in the patient the appearance of fantasies and strivings not directly expressible in any other way.

Within the classical framework, the only alternative to slowly and painfully uncovering the past within is to help the person to bury it more effectively and merely gain a respite from its disturbing pressures. Such a course of action may at times provide considerable relief to suffering people, and often in much less time and with far less suffering. In the view of most analysts, however, a substantial price is paid for this less demanding treatment. For one thing, by being helped to ward off the past better, rather than integrating it into his present personality, the patient continues to commit a substantial portion of his psychic resources to defensive activity—resources which in our complex era are sorely needed for the business of living. Attention paid to keeping oneself in check cannot be paid to other matters, and some limitation in the richness or effectiveness of the patient's living can be expected.

From another perspective, it is sometimes pointed out that the comfort achieved by such "supportive" measures is achieved by permanently cutting the patient off from sources of pleasure and creativity which are part of the human heritage. The infantile strivings are feared largely because they originally occurred at a time when the patient was both more dependent on powerful others and less able to control his impulses and discriminate appropriate from inappropriate opportunities. If accepted and integrated into the adult personality, these inclinations, instead of being a threat, could be modified and expressed in a more mature form, opening the way to greater creativity and richness in living rather than permanently barring such pleasures from the person's life.

Finally, therapeutic measures which do not uncover and resolve underlying conflicts are thought to produce changes of a precarious kind. If anything disturbs the still fragile equilibrium there is a potential for new disorders. Since his adaptive capacities are already strained by the unending necessity to devote part of his energies to defense, the patient treated nonanalytically is seen as especially vulnerable to the occurrence of illness, loss of his job, change in an important relationship, etc.

The reader is at this point likely to point out that there is a wide range of psychoanalytically inspired therapies between the poles of classical analysis and strictly supportive therapy. But from the classical framework these therapies appear to be best understood in terms of varying mixes of the two elements of uncovering and support (the latter including such means as suggestion, encouragement, strengthening defensive efforts, advice by the therapist, manipulation of environmental circumstances, etc.). If one examines, for example, the reactions of the psychoanalytic community to the efforts of Alexander and French (1946) to modify psychoanalytic technique, the most common criticism turns out to be that Alexander and French, although attempting an uncovering therapy, did not let the transference neurosis develop to the full extent. Modifications which, from the perspective to be discussed shortly, could be viewed as facilitating change and enhancing the effectiveness of psychoanalytically inspired efforts to bring about change, appear from the classical perspective to be compromises, useful with many patients but never capable of yielding as deep or extensive change as classical analysis if the patient is "analyzable" (see Bibring, 1954; Eissler, 1956, 1958; Gill, 1954; Greenacre, 1954; Rangell, 1954).

AN ALTERNATIVE ACCOUNT

If the argument thus far is correct, then the "woolly mammoth" model of intrapsychic preservation of the past is a key factor in the hesitancy of psychoanalysts to intervene in their patients' neurotic ways of living in any way other than by interpretation. It leads analysts to conclude that there is no fully satisfactory alternative to the lengthy, painful, and costly treatment method which has evolved from Freud's work. In its light, it appears perfectly obvious that there is an unbridgeable gap between psychoanalysis and such newer modes of active intervention as Gestalt therapy, the sex therapies, and various of the methods developed by behavior therapists; there would seem little basis for hope that any of these developments might enhance psychoanalytic theory or technique.

To be sure, if the observations which the psychoanalytic method has yielded require such a model to account for them, then these consequences must be accepted. One cannot reject the data simply because they lead to discouraging conclusions. The time seems ripe, however, to re-examine the question whether the observations made from behind the couch do in fact require such a model. I will argue that a workable alternative way of accounting for what has been observed does exist, and that its therapeutic implications are far more encouraging, and are deserving of trial and evaluation. Specifically, this alternative view suggests that rather than leading to superficiality, the integrating of active intervention techniques into psychoanalytic practice can enhance both the depth and the efficiency of the therapeutic process.

The analysis which follows owes much to Erikson, Alexander, Horney, and Sullivan, though its conclusions do not fully conform to the views of any of them individually. It starts with the question whether it is possible to account for the seemingly childlike quality of the fantasy life and secret strivings of neurotic patients without assuming that these are locked-in remnants of the past which can be changed only by gradually uncovering layer after layer of intrapsychic structure. Put another way, we may ask: Can the presence of these inclinations in the patient be accounted for by the way he is currently living his life, and might these manifestations change if his way of living changed?

WISHES AS INDEPENDENT AND DEPENDENT VARIABLES

From the traditional psychoanalytic focus an unconscious desire or fantasy is examined primarily as an independent variable, as something which, when present, has *effects* which are to be understood. But desires and fantasies can also be studied as dependent variables. One of the valuable contributions of the interpersonal approach to psychoanalysis, and of some existential writers as well, has been to emphasize that we always live *in situations*, that our perceptions, our feelings, and our behavior are in response *to* something. Rather than globally describing someone as an angry person, or as often struggling with hostile impulses, it is useful to ask *when* hostile impulses are aroused or *when* a conflict is evoked.

One does see a concern for the circumstances which evoke an impulse among Freudian writers as well, especially those with a more sophisticated knowledge of recent trends. Silverman (1972), for example, examines in fascinating detail the particular evoking conditions that arouse forbidden wishes. In one clinical example, he discusses a symptom in a childless and unmarried woman. She could readily identify the point of onset of the symptom: she had been reading an article when it began. But the content of the article seemed to bear no relationship at all to her conflicts or symptom. In the course of her analytic session, it occurred to her that the author of the article was named *Rothschild*, and that she had recently received a *birth announcement* from an old friend toward whom she had always felt considerable jealousy and rivalry. The friend's married name was Roth and it seemed to both patient and analyst that the author's name, *Rothschild*, had, without her awareness, stirred up her hostile and jealous thoughts about the new *child of Roth*. Interestingly, when she first received the birth announcement, and consciously felt jealous of her rival and a wish for her own child, no symptom occurred. Silverman suggests that the symptom was a consequence of such thoughts and feelings being aroused without her being aware of them.

Considerations of this sort by psychoanalysts reflect the growing concern in psychoanalytic ego psychology with the role of actual life events in influencing the clinical phenomena observed. But it is important to notice that, even in this very modern example, the role of environmental events is to evoke something lying in wait to be released. Although analysts may, in broad theoretical statements, acknowledge a wide range of ways in which the actual events in the patient's world are influential, in the concrete clinical examples in the literature one finds rather generally that when external reality is considered, it is primarily viewed as a source of triggers which can activate different parts of the already formed structure[7] that is the personality. One sees little emphasis on how that structure is perpetuated by the person's own actions and their consequences. The structure is, more or less, a given. The assumption that an understanding of the major features of the personality must be sought in childhood rather than in the person's current life situation seems to have inhibited inquiry into self-perpetuating processes which are a continuing part of the person's personality.

When we look closely at the situation which evokes a particularly troublesome impulse, we often discover that it is in large measure a self-created one. We discover that the desires which dominate our lives can be understood as *following from*, as well as causing, the way we live our lives. The patient whose excessive niceness and gentleness is seen as defending against extreme rage and vengeful desires can also be seen as feeling so angry and vengeful *because* he is so mild and unassertive. The frighteningly hostile fantasies and dreams which belie his meek exterior, and which lead him to strive ever more urgently to bolster that exterior, are ironically a *product* of the defense against them, for in tempting others to dominate and take advantage of him he feeds the conditions for further rage.

---

[7] Schafer (1972), in an important paper, has criticized the use by psychoanalysts of such terms as "internal" and "structure" as leading to reification and obscuring the *actions* that people take. I am in agreement with much that is presented in that paper. Since I am here trying to depict an established way of thinking, however, I shall use such terms, as they are the terms in which these ideas are cast and in which they are most readily recognizable. I do not view the use of such terms as desirable in efforts to formulate new theoretical positions.

Similarly, if a patient who seems compulsively to go out of his way to be active, independent, and responsible for others is found unconsciously to long for dependent gratification and to fear the extent of his passive yearnings, we need not assume that the conscious attitudes are simply a defense against desires from the past. We may valuably examine how this very pattern of compulsive activity and responsibility *creates* the so-called oral needs; by constantly taking on excessive burdens and simultaneously denying himself almost any opportunity to manifest normal dependence, he keeps himself continually yearning for dependence to an unusual degree (as he also continues to pursue this way of life largely because of the frightening strength of these continually created longings). By de-emphasizing the longing as a simple perpetuation of the past, we may see how it is brought about in the present, both by the patient's own behavior and by the behavior he evokes in others.

Let us look more closely at the details of how such patterns are perpetuated. Consider the first example cited, the person who is excessively meek and who also shows signs of intense disavowed rage. If, in the traditional fashion, we look back into his history, we may well seem to find there sufficient justification and understanding of his situation. We may uncover violent death wishes toward a parent, which he desperately attempted to cover up, and we may see a continuity in this pattern which seems to suggest that he is still defending against those same childhood wishes. We may even find images and events in his dreams which point to continuing violent urges toward the parent, and may discern many other indicators of warded-off rage toward that figure.

If we look in detail at his day-to-day interactions, however, we see a good deal more. We may find that his meekness has led him to occupy a job which is not commensurate with his real potentials and which he silently and resentfully endures. On the job and in his other social interactions as well, he is likely to be unable to ask for what is his due, and may even volunteer to do things which he really doesn't want to do. One can see this excessively unassertive and self-abnegating behavior as motivated by the need to cover up his strong aggressive urges, and that would be correct as far as it goes. But it is equally the case that such a life style *generates* rage. Disavowed anger may be a continuing feature of his life from childhood, but the angry thoughts which disturb his dreams tonight can be understood by what he let happen to him today.

Such a person is caught in a vicious circle. Having learned early to fear his anger, he has built up overt patterns of behavior designed to squelch and hide them. Even the smallest assertion seems dangerous because he senses[8] an enormous reservoir of violence behind it. Yet it is in just such excessive restriction upon his assertiveness that the conditions for further violent urges are created.

In one sense, he guards against his anger for good reason: as he is at any given moment, he *is* potentially explosive, he *is* resentful and full of hatred, he *would* be nasty and vindictive if he were not trying so hard to be otherwise. Ironically, if he were not so frequently bending over backward, if he could act with reasonable assertiveness and demand a fair return from others, he would discover that the underlying rage diminished. But because at any given moment real aggressive inclinations and fantasies have accrued from his way of living he is afraid to act assertively. So he once more squelches himself, thereby arousing the fierce resentment which will in turn motivate his further self-abnegation and lead once again to strong, if unacknowledged, resentment. In such fashion he perpetuates his personal myth that there resides within him an untouchable kernel of rage which is part of the essence of who he is. And in essence, this myth is often subscribed to by his analyst as well, in the analyst's notion that the anger is "in" the patient from the past, rather than a response to his present life circumstances.

A Comparison with the Classical Freudian View

These considerations are likely to seem familiar to the psychoanalytic reader. He has seen such links in his practice and has

---

[8] Here, as elsewhere in this discussion, the use of terms like sense, believe, fear, etc., does not necessarily imply a conscious experience. See Schafer's (1972) discussion of the false issue raised when such terms are taken to mean a concern only with what is conscious.

probably discussed them with his colleagues. Because they have such a familiar ring he may feel that such a point of view is well represented in the psychoanalytic literature, that it is part of what was added to psychoanalysis by the development of ego psychology, and that where psychoanalysis differs from other approaches is in integrating such a perspective into a broader and deeper framework rather than "reductionistically" emphasizing it to the exclusion of "hard-won" insights into the nature of primitive biological urges. I believe that the analyst who holds such a view will, if he re-examines the Freudian psychoanalytic literature with this focus, be surprised to discover just how rarely the perspective described in the past few pages is represented in either case reports or clinical descriptions. To put it plainly, such a point of view toward clinical data hardly ever appears in the orthodox psychoanalytic journals. While such a point of view is part of the commonsense understanding every analyst brings to bear on his work, it is not really well integrated into the *theory* which guides his work. This is especially true of the theory of therapeutic change, and it strongly influences the therapeutic options which seem "legitimate" to use.[9]

The absence of a genuinely interpersonal focus in psychoanalytic case reports follows a tradition begun by Freud. Fenichel (1940), in a review of Horney's *New Ways in Psychoanalysis*, claims that Freud's case studies are full of accounts of the vicious circles that Horney describes. I must confess that I have been unable to find very many such descriptions in my reading of Freud's case studies. Freud's genius lay in deciphering meanings, in discerning what is expressed by the patient's dreams, fantasies, associations, slips, and, to a somewhat lesser extent, acts.

Freud was not, however, a student of interaction sequences. When the patient's overt interpersonal behavior was the focus of his inquiry, Freud tended to find it of interest as a further vehicle

---

[9] Stone (1961, p. 18) points out that the analyst's theoretical conception of the analytic situation "has great influence and power, occasioning self-consciousness or even guilt, when its outlines are transgressed." Analysts of necessity will diverge from the pure classical model, but if varied interventions are viewed as deviations from an ideal, rather than being integrated into the theoretical model and modifying our view of what the ideal is, then our effectiveness in applying new insights is severely limited.

for expressing the patient's underlying dynamics. Rarely did he examine it for its *consequences*. Even in his strong focus on the transference, which would seem to imply great attention to the interpersonal, it is evident that Freud did not look very hard at interaction sequences nor consider how present behavior and its consequences perpetuate old patterns. The extreme degree of asymmetry in the analytic situation was designed to make it as clear as possible that the patient's behavior was *not* in response to anything that the analyst did, but stemmed instead from an almost inexorable assimilative process in the patient. The framework Freud provided did not emphasize examining how the patient's behavior was in response to the current behavior of others, and emphasized still less how the behavior of the other could itself be seen as a function of the patient's own acts.

Modern analysts do give some attention to these matters. The analyst's own emotional reaction to the patient, for example, is often used to provide a sense of how significant others in the patient's life are likely to feel in interacting with him. Even here, however, the analyst is more likely to use such insights to highlight what the patient is *up to* rather than what he provokes or confronts—"You'd like me to feel sorry for you" or "You're trying to get me to help you" rather than "You get people to feel sorry and help you out, and so you never get the chance to learn and try things out yourself."

Following through the latter way of understanding, the therapist might note that since the patient is deprived of chances to learn he is left with the feeling that *all he can do* is to get people to feel sorry for him and hope they will help him, and that this further perpetuates the circle. As long as he succeeds in eliciting help, he continues to *need* help. When the problem is viewed in this way, one is less likely to rely solely on interpretation. Helping the patient to undergo experiences which will break into the circle, perhaps via actively learning certain modes in a protected situation, begins to look like a useful course.

It may further be noted that even when the classical analyst does pay attention to interaction sequences in the fashion emphasized here, the very nature of the classical analytic situation guarantees that attention to such matters will be fleeting at best. In order to get a detailed picture of just what led to what in a particular sequence in the patient's life,[10] it is usually necessary to probe persistently, and to ask detailed questions of a sort not compatible with the emphasis on free association and nonintervention that one sees in even the most modern writings on psychoanalytic technique. Yet without a *great deal* of attention to present interpersonal processes, they are not likely to seem sufficient to account for the phenomena analysts observe. Only a detailed examination of the subtleties of interaction can provide a convincing alternative to the traditional psychoanalytic emphasis on the past. In the classical model inquiry is not aimed in that direction.

The perspective offered here does parallel in many respects the views of modern psychoanalytic ego psychologists. Rapaport (1958), for example, in his discussion of ego autonomy, stressed the concept of "stimulus nutriment." Pointing to such phenomena as the regressive alterations of functioning in stimulus-deprivation situations, and the modification of conscious superego functions in changed environments, Rapaport suggested that psychological structures often require environmental input to maintain themselves and that without such "nutriment" patterned psychological actions do not persist in their current form. Elsewhere (Rapaport, 1960) he even stated that "the vicious circle of neurosis crucially involves the fact that the patient persistently exposes himself to situations (stimulations) which tend to elicit his defensive behavior and to reinforce his defenses, and avoids other situations which would tend to elicit alternative behaviors and thus would facilitate giving up his defenses" (p. 892).

But while such discussions make clear that the view presented here is not alien to psychoanalytic thought, it is also necessary to recognize that Rapaport stops short of exploring the possibilities of the "stimulus nutriment" concept to the fullest. For Rapaport,

[10] The transference relationship in the classical analytic situation is no substitute for a detailed knowledge of the sequences in the patient's daily living. The ambiguous stance of the analyst, his efforts to minimize the kind of interaction with the patient that is characteristic of other kinds of relationships, make it extremely difficult to study via the medium of the transference relationship the patient's way of responding to and affecting the actual and manifest behavior of other people. The analyst, by interpreting and by remaining silent much of the time, truncates interaction sequences and produces instead expressive monologues.

while defenses and other ego structures are in part dependent upon environmental feedback, they are "maintained, *ultimately,* by *internal* (drive) stimulus-nutriment" (Rapaport, 1958, p. 737; italics added), and the question of *whether drives or motives themselves require stimulus nutriment* is never really seriously considered. In a sense, it is precisely this question that the alternative view presented here raises—what feedback is required for the patient to persist in (unconsciously) wishing for the same things he did as a child (i.e., what stimulus nutriment is required to maintain those structures[11] which psychoanalysis has designated as part of the id)? Persistent pursuit of this question has major implications not only for theory but also—and especially—for therapeutic intervention.

An Alternative Developmental Model

Viewpoints such as the one presented here are often criticized in the psychoanalytic literature for lacking a "genetic point of view," and hence as being incomplete or reductionistic. To be sure, the approach described here does place much less emphasis than does classical psychoanalysis on the need for the patient to understand his history in order to solve his neurotic dilemma. This approach is not, however, antidevelopmental. Whether detailed understanding of the history of a problem is necessary for *therapeutic* purposes is a question quite independent of whether *research and theory* should account for how such problems arise.

Preventing problems is ultimately far more humane and efficient than treating them after they have arisen, and for purposes of prevention, a knowledge of how problems develop, of the childhood roots and later transformations, is essential. More immediately, therapeutic work with children requires a sound knowledge of the modes of thought and action typical of various age groups, and of the concerns and dilemmas children of various ages are likely to confront. It is no comment on the need for a developmental point of view in psychological theory to consider

---

[11] Again, I do not here mean to endorse the term "structure" (see fn. 7), but rather to clarify the parallels and differences between Rapaport's view of how patterned psychological events are maintained and my own view.

whether therapeutic work with adults may be sidetracked by making that situation the arena for such research.[12]

A major focus on how the patient's current way of living perpetuates his problems does not imply that there is no continuity between present reactions and those of the past. The similarities are very clear. So too is the great importance of childhood in shaping the way of life that will be evident in the adult. Seeking correlations between childhood experiences and adult problems seems to me a valuable line of inquiry which can provide many useful leads.

But if connections or continuities are discovered, the question of *how these continuities are mediated* remains. In the more traditional developmental view in psychoanalysis, emphasis is placed on the layering of residues of past patterns in hierarchical fashion. The imagery is archeological. The focus is on the early structuring of the personality, and the personality patterns that have formed by the end of the Oedipal period are seen as set and relatively unresponsive to changing conditions.

The tendency for early patterns to be maintained can also be accounted for by a somewhat different view—one that also readily accommodates instances where change is rather striking (and more important, as discussed elsewhere [Wachtel, 1977], points to a wider range of ways in which change can be brought about). This view emphasizes that the kinds of experiences we have early in life, and our way of dealing with these experiences, strongly influences what further experiences we have, as well as how we perceive those experiences and how we deal with them.

The two-year-old who has developed an engaging and playful manner is far more likely to evoke friendly interest and attention from adults than is the child who is rather quiet and withdrawn. The latter will typically encounter a less rich interpersonal environment which in turn will decrease the likelihood that he will change. Similarly, the former is likely to learn continually that other people are fun and are eager to interact with him, and his pattern, too, is likely to become more firmly fixed as he grows. Further, not only will the two children tend to evoke different

[12] There is also, of course, the important question whether reconstructions from adult patients provide an *accurate* genetic picture. Even within psychoanalysis the most vital approach to studying developmental issues involves child observation and longitudinal studies rather than reconstruction.

behavior from others, they will also interpret differently the same reaction from another person. Thus the playful child may experience a silent or grumpy response from another as a kind of game and may continue to interact until perhaps he does elicit an appreciative response. The quieter child, not used to much interaction, will readily accept the initial response as a signal to back off.

If we look at the two children as adults, we may find the difference between them still evident, one outgoing, cheerful, and expecting the best of people, the other rather shy and unsure that anyone is interested. A childhood pattern has persisted into adulthood. Yet we really do not understand the developmental process unless we see how, successively, teachers, playmates, girl-friends or boy-friends, and colleagues have been drawn in as "accomplices" in maintaining the pattern.[13] And, I would suggest, we do not understand the possibilities for change unless we realize that even now there are such "accomplices" and that, if they stopped playing their role in the process, it would eventually alter.

We must also realize, of course, that it is not that easy to get the accomplices to change either. The signals we emit to other people constitute a powerful force field. The shy person does many sometimes almost invisible things to make it difficult for another person to stay open to him for very long. Even a well-intentioned person is, eventually, likely to help confirm the shy person's view that others are not really very interested.

Thus, from this perspective, the early pattern persists not in spite of changing conditions, but because the person's pattern of experiencing and interacting with others tends to recreate the old conditions again and again. In many cases the continuing process is subtle and not apparent without careful scrutiny. But on close inspection, each person may be seen to produce rather regularly a particular skewing of responses from others that defines his idiosyncratic interpersonal world. Even in seemingly similar situations we are each likely to encounter slightly different interpersonal cues so that the texture of one person's experience may be critically different from another's. We each then act (again) in a way that

---

[13] It should of course be understood that constitutional factors such as activity level may also play an important role.

seems appropriate to the particular state of affairs we have evoked, and we thereby create the conditions for others again to react to us in the same fashion and again set the stage for the pattern to be repeated. Rather than having been locked in in the past by an intrapsychic structuring, then, the pattern seems, from this perspective, to be continually being formed, but generally in a way that keeps it quite consistent through the years. It may appear inappropriate because it is not well correlated with the adult's "average expectable environment," but it is quite closely attuned to the person's idiosyncratically skewed version of that environment.

Emphasis on such a cyclical re-creation of interpersonal events, and on the real behavior of "accomplices" in perpetuating characterological patterns, does not imply that the person is perceiving every situation "objectively." Most clinicians have seen abundant examples of patients' distortions of what is going on, particularly in transference phenomena. Such aspects of psychological functioning must be included in any viable account of how neurotic patterns are perpetuated. But rather than relying on the metaphors which analysts have traditionally used in conceptualizing such phenomena, I prefer to think in terms of the Piagetian conception of schema; for such a conception implies that not only do we assimilate new experiences to older, more familiar ways of viewing things (as is implicit in the concept of transference), we also eventually accommodate to what is actually going on.

Thus, as in transference phenomena, new people and new relationships tend to be approached in terms of their similarity to earlier ones; and frequently, particularly in the special conditions of the psychoanalytic situation, one sees what appear to be quite arbitrary assumptions and perceptions. But in principle, I would suggest, accommodation is always proceeding apace and would, with nonreactive sources of stimulation, eventually lead to a fairly accurate picture of what one is encountering. The problem is that other people are *not* nonreactive. How they behave toward us is very much influenced by how we behave toward them, and hence by how we initially perceive them. Thus, our initial (in a sense distorted) picture of another person can end up being a fairly accurate *predictor* of how he will act toward us because, on the basis of our expectation that he will be hostile, or accepting, or sexual, we are likely to act in such a way as eventually to elicit such behavior from the person and thus have our (initially inaccurate) perception "confirmed." Our tendency to enter the next relationship with the same assumption and perceptual bias is then strengthened and the whole process is likely to be repeated.

Such a perspective enables us to understand both continuity and change in the same terms. In a large number of cases, this process of "distorted" perception, leading to a skewing of responses from others and hence to a "confirmation" of the problematic way of experiencing, continues for years and produces the phenomena so familiar to analytic observers. At times, however, a person appears who, by virtue of *his* interpersonal history and personal force field, intervenes (for good or ill) in the developmental process rather than simply confirming present directions.[14] The patient's behavior may make this process unlikely to persist, but if it does, it can be expected that he will eventually accommodate to this new input and show substantial change in an important aspect of his life. It is likely that many of the "spontaneous" cures which make the controls in psychotherapy research so tricky are the result of such accommodative processes.

By virtue of his training and his orientation to the patient's behavior, the therapist is frequently in a particularly good position to change rather than to confirm the patient's previous modes of experiencing others—though as Wolf (1966) argues, this may not happen nearly as frequently as we might hope. In particular, the psychoanalyst's less reactive stance (whatever its other limitations) does seem to reduce somewhat the likelihood of his acting in the same confirmatory ways as have previous accomplices in the patient's neurosis. The guarantee in this respect is far from ironclad, however. Frequently the seemingly bizarre and unrealistic reactions of the patient toward the analyst are understandable as symbolizations of what is actually, though covertly, going on between them. Even where this is not the case, the seemingly anachronistic reaction need not be viewed as the triggering of a tendency preserved in childhood from further possibilities of accommodating to new events; investigation from the point of

---

[14] Less dramatic instances of this sort, in which each person changes a bit, are common. Usually, however, the change is small, because each participant is free to leave rather than change. The more constrained to be together, the more each can alter the other.

view advocated here frequently reveals that *other* people throughout the person's life have participated in the kind of confirmatory
process I have described even if the analyst has not. Considerable
working through is then necessary because the disconfirming
experience with the analyst is at odds with a long series of
experiences which have produced expectations not readily
relinquished after just one or two disconfirmations. Assimilative
tendencies may be strong, even if not inexorable.

The earlier hypothetical example of the two-year-olds was
chosen to illustrate how striking continuities may be understood
according to a developmental model in which continuing
responsiveness to current happenings is stressed. In actuality, the
developmental course is likely to be more complicated and less
unidirectional than portrayed in the illustration. At least some
disconfirming events will probably occur, and the accommodation
which can then follow is likely to produce less monolithic
differences than depicted thus far. Complexity is introduced by our
ability to discriminate amongst the implications of different
situations, especially in view of the fact that not only may our overt
behavior differ from situation to situation but so may our fantasies,
wishes, and fears.[15] The presence of conflict and defense further
complicates the picture, introducing motivated misperceptions and
peremptory behaviors whose meaning is poorly understood or
misrepresented. As described above, patterns of conflict and
defense can also be viewed not just as the expression of an intrapsychic state of affairs but as part of a process in which feedback,
skewed by the very processes they maintain, plays a major role.
Thus, processes of defense and processes of adaptation interweave
complexly with the actual occurrences they produce or encounter.
Finally, it is important to understand the role of innate constitutional factors and of endogenously developing changes in shaping
the person's behavior and the world he encounters. The outgoing
two-year-old who is so charming may become just a pain in the

---

[15] It must also be recognized, however, that affect-laden interpersonal
situations are often exceedingly ambiguous and that our power to discriminate in
these situations is far less than in those where the cues are clearer. We must be
aware of broad consistencies deriving from how we construe subtle interpersonal
cues as well as the discriminations and situational differences in our reactions
which are also evident (see Mischel, 1973; Wachtel, 1973a, 1973b).

neck if at age four he exhibits an epigenetically programmed (Erikson, 1963) upsurge of intrusiveness beyond the ability of his parents and other important figures to tolerate. The course of his development could then alter considerably. Erikson in particular has illuminated how these various factors interact in the course of development.

Ties to "Early Objects"

In describing this view of development, there is one more issue it is important for us to consider at this point. Frequently, psycho-analytic exploration reveals that, often without awareness, the person remains tied in his fantasy life and in his secret strivings to figures from his early childhood. Typically, the discovery of such a tie is viewed as accounting for the inhibitions and symptoms of the adult. The pull of the past is regarded as the causal influence. We shall now consider an alternative way of understanding this common observation.

As an example, let us consider still another set of interlocking influences our two-year-old might encounter and then perpetuate. Suppose that he is not encouraged by his family to develop the skills which can help him gain greater independence from them. This need not take the form of outright prohibition or interference. Indeed, often the knot is tighter when not readily visible, as when an ambivalent parent gives explicit encouragement to the child's budding independence but in subtle ways undermines it. Perhaps the mother, without noticing it, is more frequently warm and attentive when the child sweetly says "I love you, Mommy" than when he shows her something he has put together; or cuddles him when he stands apart from the other children ("to make him feel better, so he won't be afraid to play") instead of helping him to initiate play or joining the group of children until her child is comfortable there. There are many ways in which, through ignorance or unacknowledged intent, a mother or father can bind and cripple a child while thinking he is encouraging independence.

When that is the case there is likely to be a point at which the child's fearful clinging is recognized as distinguishing him from his agemates, and not infrequently the parental reaction is likely to be a nagging, complaining, or insulting one, motivated by parental anxiety, embarrassment, guilt, or desperation. Even if the parent does not come out with "What's wrong with you? Why can't you be like the other kids?" or some similar assault, simply continuing to encourage him to participate in age-appropriate activities, when not accompanied by effective efforts to help him accomplish the transition, can be experienced as punishing and can cause the child considerable pain.

A child caught in such a developmental tangle is likely to remain more tied to his parents than most children his age. Having fewer alternative sources of gratification and security, he is likely to feel more than most the need to be Mommy's or Daddy's little boy. Not only is this likely to impede further the explorations and assertion needed to develop the skills which would get him out of this dilemma, it is also likely to make him afraid of expressing anger at or disagreement with his parents—and this in circumstances more likely than usual to arouse anger. So we can see an unhappy little child, afraid to venture forth, clinging to his mother in a way that angers her (even as it also may gratify), feeling frustrated and irritated, perhaps even—if it is the case—sensing the grasping intent in the mother's harmful cloistering, yet desperately trying to be a good boy so as at least to have *mother* securely, and therefore terrified of the anger that he is so frequently moved to express, as well as to hide, and which further confirms for him that he is no good.

If the dilemma confronting this child is in the "neurotic" range, then he will continue to grow despite all these inhibitions. There are enough countervailing forces in innate developmental processes, as well as in the expectations and reward structure of the larger social order, and even in other aspects of their own parents' behavior, for millions of children with such a history to grow up to become taxpayers, spouses, and parents and thus in a very general way functioning adults. It takes a rather extraordinary effort to inhibit cognitive and personality growth so completely that these rather minimal criteria of "normality" are not achieved.[16]

[16] These criteria are meant simply to point to the *kinds* of general achievements which tend to distinguish neurotic difficulties from more severe ones. It is in no sense meant to imply that people who do not marry, or do not have children, suffer from any personality disorder. My judgment would tend to be different, however, if the person were completely lacking in human relationships.

But the situation we have described takes its toll. The child does not "make it" without pain and struggle, and usually he does not make it without a price. In many respects he may advance along the way more slowly than his agemates, getting there eventually but always feeling a little bit behind or a little out of it, venturing less, mastering less, so again venturing less, etc.

One such person, whom I have discussed in more detail elsewhere (Wachtel, 1975), was at the time he began therapy a graduate student who had achieved fairly substantial academic success, but was almost completely unable to engage in even casual conversation with people at school without quite severe anxiety. His dreams and associations indicated rather strikingly the kind of intense ties to the mother which are often stressed and elaborated upon in the psychoanalytic literature, and which are often viewed as the primary cause of current life difficulties. I was struck, however, by the cumulative effects of a life history in which the experiences necessary to develop social skills and ease with people did not occur, and I suggested that even if his conflicted ties to his mother were historically earlier, and thus primary in that sense, the present causal nexus was far more complicated. Since his mother was at that time just about the only person he could be with without incapacitating anxiety, it made as much sense to think of his current preoccupation with her as a function of his dismal life situation as it did to consider the reverse, and more traditional, interpretation. A chain of events had occurred in his life which left him tied to his mother in many different aspects of his being, and this state of affairs seemed destined to continue so long as he did not have readily available alternatives. Such considerations led to the conclusion that direct efforts to train him in social skills and reduce his social anxiety might loosen the ties to his mother which seemed to "underlie" his anxiety.

Many cases in therapy are quite a bit more complex than the one discussed, but not necessarily different in principle. The patient discussed above was so seriously and obviously hampered in an important area of his life that his ties to his mother were manifest (though certainly not fully conscious in all their ramifications), and the way his current life contributed to these ties was fairly obvious if one is willing to adopt such a perspective. In many other patients, however, the tie may be wholly unconscious, evident only in dreams and in the pattern of associations. Further, such a patient may seem to be struggling with these strong, unconscious, regressive wishes and fantasies while his day-to-day functioning appears to be rather successful and independent.

Now, of course, if the patient were really living a completely free and successful life he would have no reason to be in therapy, and his therapist would have no reason to attribute any neurotogenic importance to any Oedipal wishes and fantasies he discerned in the patient's productions. Something must be wrong in the patient's life or such wishes and fantasies would be of no concern. In some instances, what at first is of concern is one or more isolated symptoms in an apparently otherwise psychologically healthy person, and it is these symptoms which the analyst sees as deriving from the patient's conflict over his continuing ties to people from the past. Such was the classic picture of neurosis. Freud originally analyzed symptoms, not character.

With the more careful scrutiny of the patient's way of life that has resulted from modern developments in theory, it has become increasingly more difficult to find instances of pure symptom neuroses with no characterological features. Indeed, one suspects that when such a state of affairs is evident, it is likely to be a case of the kind of simple conditioned reactions that were first put forth by behavior therapists as the model of all neuroses. But behavior therapists are increasingly recognizing that such simple neurotic responses are rarely as isolated from the patient's way of life as was first thought (e.g., Lazarus, 1968; Fodor, 1974), and certainly simple conditioned responses are not what analysts have in mind when they talk of neuroses.

In most instances, then, it is possible to find areas of inhibition, anxiety, or maladaptive behavior which are subtle equivalents of the more total and obvious life impairment evident in the patient discussed above. The patient may, for example, evidence reasonable social ease and competence in general, but be inhibited in making sexual advances. Or he may be able to initiate sexual activity quite easily, and "perform" adequately, but not experience complete sexual release and satisfaction. Or perhaps the sexual aspect of sexual relationships is fully satisfying but does not seem linked to an intimate sharing of personal feelings.

Any of these limitations in living could, if found to occur in conjunction with evidence of disavowed ties to parental figures, be attributed to the effects of those ties. That has traditionally been the analyst's understanding of such observations, and the inference drawn has been that one must work on untangling those ties in order to increase the patient's freedom in living. But again, it makes equal sense to consider, for example, how a longing for the ideal caretaker-beauty (mother) of childhood might be fostered by a current life style which excludes fully satisfying experiences of intimacy and sensual satisfaction.

The lure of the Oedipal imagery is strengthened each time the person has a frustrating or disappointing encounter. And in the course of growing up, many experiences accrue which keep this pattern going. Whatever role the vicissitudes of feeling for the mother may have played in starting the person on a life course which is in some important respects restricted, later interactions with other people tend to be significant in perpetuating it. If one is anxious or hesitant about sexuality or intimacy, one teaches one's partners to be similarly inclined. Satisfying sexuality and the experience of intimacy require mutual trust and understanding. If a person enters a new relationship in a hesitant way, the partner cannot long continue to be open with him, and he will find confirmed again and again throughout his life that his defensiveness in such situations is "justified," since he is inevitably disappointed and finds his partners tensing up or closing off in ways that hurt (and lead him to be hesitant again the next time and again evoke a complementary response from his partner).[17]

In this view, then, Oedipal longings, while "real," need not be the primary motor of the patient's current difficulties. One can acknowledge the evidence for their existence, and even intensity, without necessarily viewing them as the crucial center. Instead one sees the conflicts generated in the family leading to a continuing series of experiences which develop their own momentum and of which the Oedipal yearnings of the adult years are themselves a

---

[17] It should be clear that I am here describing something that does not necessarily go on consciously. Far from explicitly justifying a limited sex life on the basis of partners' responses, the person may well extol both his partners and his sex life for quite a while. Only careful scrutiny may reveal the particular dissatisfaction or lack of freedom in the person's life.

function. One would then expect that direct efforts to intervene in the events which perpetuate this vicious circle will, if successful, lead to a diminution of the hold that Oedipal yearnings and fantasies have on the person. Painstaking examination of the interpersonal signals given by the patient which disrupt intimacy would become at least as important as the painstaking analysis of regressive fantasies, and new methods to alter those signals and interactions, described elsewhere (Wachtel, 1977), would occupy a central position in efforts at change.

REFERENCES

Alexander, F., French, T., et al. (1946), *Psychoanalytic Therapy*. New York: Ronald Press.

Bibring, E. (1954), Psychoanalysis and the Dynamic Psychotherapies. *J. Amer. Psychoanal. Assn.*, 2:745-770.

Breuer, J., & Freud, S. (1893-1895), Studies on Hysteria. *Standard Edition*, 2. London: Hogarth Press, 1955.

Eissler, K. (1956), Some Comments on Psychoanalysis and Dynamic Psychiatry. *J. Amer. Psychoanal. Assn.*, 4:314-317.

——— (1958), Remarks on Some Variations in Psycho-Analytical Technique. *Internat. J. Psycho-Anal.*, 39:222-229.

Erikson, E. (1963), *Childhood and Society*, rev. ed. New York: Norton.

Fenichel, O. (1940), Review of K. Horney, *New Ways in Psychoanalysis*. *Psychoanal. Quart.*, 9:114-121.

Fodor, I. (1974), The Phobic Syndrome in Women: Implications for Treatment. In: *Women in Therapy: New Psychotherapies for a Changing Society*, ed. V. Franks & V. Burtle. New York: Brunner/Mazel, pp. 132-168.

Freud, S. (1905), Three Essays on the Theory of Sexuality. *Standard Edition*, 7:125-245. London: Hogarth Press, 1953.

——— (1923), The Ego and the Id. *Standard Edition*, 19:3-66. London: Hogarth Press, 1961.

——— (1926), Inhibitions, Symptoms and Anxiety. *Standard Edition*, 20:77-175. London: Hogarth Press, 1959.

Gill, M. (1954), Psychoanalysis and Exploratory Psychotherapy. *J. Amer. Psychoanal. Assn.*, 2:771-797.

——— (1963), Topography and Systems in Psychoanalytic Theory. *Psychol. Issues*, Monogr. No. 10. New York: International Universities Press.

Greenacre, P. (1954), The Role of Transference: Practical Considerations in Relation to Psychoanalytic Therapy. *J. Amer. Psychoanal. Assn.*, 2:671-684.

Greenson, R. (1967), *The Technique and Practice of Psychoanalysis*. New York: International Universities Press.

Hartmann, H., Kris, E., & Loewenstein, R. (1946), Comments on the Formation of Psychic Structure. *The Psychoanalytic Study of the Child*, 2:11-38. New York: International Universities Press.

Horney, K. (1939), *New Ways in Psychoanalysis*. New York: Norton.

Lazarus, A. (1968), General Discussion of Symposium. In: *The Role of Learning in Psychotherapy*, ed. R. Porter. London: Churchill, p. 245.

Menninger, K. A. (1958), *Theory of Psychoanalytic Technique*. New York: Basic Books.

Mischel, W. (1973), On the Empirical Dilemmas of Psychodynamic Approaches: Issues and Alternatives. *J. Abnorm. Psychol.*, 82:335-344.

Penfield, W., & Roberts, L. (1959), *Speech and Brain Mechanisms*. Princeton, N.J.: Princeton University Press.

Rangell, L. (1954), Similarities and Differences between Psychoanalysis and Dynamic Psychotherapy. *J. Amer. Psychoanal. Assn.*, 2:734-744.

Rapaport, D. (1958), The Theory of Ego Autonomy. *Collected Papers*. New York: Basic Books, 1967, pp. 722-744.

——— (1960), On the Psychoanalytic Theory of Motivation. *Collected Papers*. New York: Basic Books, 1967, pp. 853-915.

Schafer, R. (1972), Internalization: Process or Fantasy? *The Psychoanalytic Study of the Child*, 27:411-436. New York: Quadrangle.

Silverman, L. (1972), Drive Stimulation and Psychopathology. *Psychoanalysis and Contemporary Science*, 1:306-326. New York: Macmillan.

Stone, L. (1961), *The Psychoanalytic Situation*. New York: International Universities Press.

Wachtel, P. L. (1973a), Psychodynamics, Behavior Therapy, and the Implacable Experimenter: An Inquiry into the Consistency of Personality. *J. Abnorm. Psychol.*, 82:324-334.

——— (1973b), On Fact, Hunch, and Stereotype: A Reply to Mischel. *J. Abnorm. Psychol.*, 82:537-540.

——— (1975), Behavior Therapy and the Facilitation of Psychoanalytic Exploration. *Psychotherapy: Theory, Res., Pract.*, 12:68-72.

——— (1977), *Psychoanalysis and Behavior Therapy: Toward an Integration*. New York: Basic Books.

Wolf, E. (1966), Learning Theory and Psychoanalysis. *Brit. J. Med. Psychol.*, 39:1-10.

Don R. Swanson, Ph.D.

On Force, Energy, Entropy, and the Assumptions of Metapsychology

In a now classic and definitive paper, Rapaport and Gill (1959) set forth systematically the basic assumptions which underlie five metapsychological points of view. The authors did not of course attempt to explore many of the far-reaching consequences of this set of assumptions. It is my purpose here to show that a direct and elementary application of the principles they outlined for the dynamic and economic points of view illuminate a large number of additional metapsychological concepts and psychopathological phenomena.

The particular portions of the Rapaport and Gill work on which I shall focus are the following:

> Metapsychology proper thus consists of propositions stating the minimum (both necessary and sufficient) number of independent assumptions upon which the psycho-analytic theory rests. . . .

> The assumptions and their significance:

> *There are psychological forces.*

> This assumption underlies, for example, all the propositions concerning drives, ego interests, and conflicts. It is significant because it implies that we can study these forces by psychological methods of observation, without recourse to an organic substrate. . . .

Psychological forces are defined by their direction and magnitude.

This assumption underlies, for example, all the propositions concerning the strength of and the work performed by drives. It is significant because it postulates that in psycho-analysis, as in other sciences, all forces can and should be treated purely in terms of their magnitude and direction. . . .

The effect of simultaneously acting psychological forces may be the simple resultant of the work of each of these forces.

This assumption underlies, for example, the propositions concerning conflict, ambivalence, and the relationship of drives in the id. It is significant because it postulates that under certain conditions, certain simultaneously acting psychological forces follow the simple composition law of vectorial addition of forces. . . .

There are psychological energies.

This assumption underlies, for example, all propositions concerning the effects of drive forces, since—by universal definition—the work of a force always expends energy. . . .

Psychological energies follow a law of conservation. . . .

Psychological energies are subject to a law of entropy.

This assumption underlies, for example, all propositions concerning mobile cathexis and primary process: it is the statement of the pleasure principle in general terms. It is significant because it makes superfluous the postulation of a constancy 'principle' and a nirvana 'principle', since these 'principles' represent only the effects of the entropy (pleasure) principle operating under diverse structural conditions. . . .

Psychological energies are subject to transformations which increase or decrease their entropic tendency [pp. 155-157].

The concept of psychological force clearly plays a crucial role in metapsychological theory. What seems to be missing, however, is any cohesive discussion of what it is that psychological forces are assumed to act upon, and what the effect of such action might be. I shall suggest in this paper some possible formulations of these missing ideas.

We begin by noting that Rapaport and Gill used the language of physics (force, energy, entropy, work, vector) to clarify psychological concepts. It seems likely that they entertained at least the hope, if not the conviction, that the laws of physics could usefully be carried over in some way to psychological propositions. Let us pursue this line of reasoning.

Now it is not physics in general to which Rapaport and Gill made reference, but specifically the laws of classical mechanics, both statics (composition of forces by vector addition) and dynamics (conservation of energy as well as the relationship between energy change [work] and force). To invoke any aspect of classical mechanics implies an expectation that Newton's (1687) three laws of motion can somehow be brought to bear, for these laws are the foundation of classical mechanics. (They are incidentally summarized by Rosenblatt and Thickstun [1970, p. 266, fn. 1].) We shall be especially interested here in the second law, which can be expressed as the well-known equation:

$$\vec{F} = m \cdot \vec{a}$$

where $\vec{a}$ is the acceleration experienced by a body of mass m to which a force $\vec{F}$ is applied. (The arrows above $\vec{a}$ and $\vec{F}$ denote that they are vectors.) As noted earlier, all forces (even metaphorical ones) must be conceived in terms of something on which they act, and it would seem to have been an oversight of Rapaport and Gill not to mention what it is that psychological forces act upon. More plausibly, perhaps they considered the point too obvious to require explication. In any event, their intent must certainly have been that psychological forces act upon, or perhaps within, the psychic apparatus.

I must digress a moment to clarify the question of where the psychic apparatus is located. The evidence is persuasive that both Freud and Rapaport assumed that the patient's psychic apparatus was located somewhere inside the patient. Of course it is; the point would hardly be worth mentioning were there not some who think that the psychic apparatus is nothing more than an abstraction. How could an abstraction discharge psychic energy into the patient's soma, producing conversion symptoms, psychosomatic illness, or affects—all of which are directly measurable or experienceable? More cogently, if the psychic apparatus did *not* discharge psychic energy into the body organs, then the law of conservation of energy which Rapaport and Gill have postulated would be violated, for psychic energy is certainly discharged but according to their law it cannot simply vanish. Furthermore, the psychic apparatus is energized by libido, which originates in the soma. Freud put it unequivocally in his final, and in many respects clearest, definitive statement on psychoanalytic propositions—the *Outline of Psychoanalysis:* "There can be no question but that the libido has somatic sources, that it streams to the ego from various organs and parts of the body" (1940, p. 151). Where then could the ego be, if not in the patient's body? We can be less certain about exactly where in the body the ego and the rest of the psychic apparatus is located. Although the head would seem to be a plausible choice, we probably should not prejudge the issue. We might take note here of some remarks of psychotic patients which reveal unusual insight. A schizophrenic woman in treatment with a male therapist repeatedly expressed the wish to bite off his psychic apparatus. Unfortunately he was not able to ascertain the unconscious fantasy underlying this wish, and so we cannot draw any very specific inference about what location she had in mind, but the possibility that the psychic apparatus is bite-offable at least gives us food for thought. It is a not unreasonable conjecture that the Wolf Man may have believed that his psychic apparatus was located in his lower bowel; in this light his offer to defecate on Freud's head (Jones, 1955, p. 274), while indelicate to be sure, does have a certain logic. (This is not to say that such behavior should be encouraged.) In any event we should keep an open mind for now on the question of precisely where the psychic apparatus is located; conversely, we might also keep an open psychic apparatus on the question of where the mind is located.

Let us return now to Newton's second law, and consider what happens in the analytic setting. Drives are mobilized, and hence we have a psychological force, $\vec{F}$, applied to the psychic apparatus.

The latter must therefore accelerate. To understand in detail what happens, we need to know the mass of the psychic apparatus. The mass certainly cannot be zero for if it were the acceleration would be infinite—clearly absurd. Not only is the mass nonzero and finite, but I have actually made some measurements of it which I shall present shortly. We can proceed with confidence to explore the consequences of the second law of motion. The most immediate consequence is that the psychic apparatus must separate from the patient. For after all the patient is immobilized on the couch and the psychic apparatus is accelerating. Thus after the first few minutes of an analytic session, if all goes well we can assume that the patient's psychic apparatus is flying about the room somewhere. Incidentally, the recoil of the patient as the psychic apparatus is emitted is called by analysts a reaction formation; it is an expression of the third law of motion.[1]

The idea that the patient and his mental apparatus part company can be seen immediately to illuminate certain puzzling aspects of more familiar phenomena such as regression. The analytic setting facilitates regression, usually on the part of the patient. Regression may take the patient back to a point in time prior to the development of psychic structure. Such a regressed patient thus has no psychic apparatus. But then where did it go? It cannot just vanish, for we have already established that it has mass.[2] The preceding paragraph provides an answer to this question. Under the influence of psychological forces mobilized in the analysis, it has moved out of the patient but is still available to be analyzed.

How do we know that the psychic apparatus is actually present at the beginning of the analytic session? If it is detachable, it may have long since left. Unfortunately that does happen, but then

---

[1] "Lex. III. Actioni contrariam semper et equalem esse reactionem: sive corporum duorum actiones in se mutuo semper esse equales et in partes contrarias dirigi" (Newton, 1687, p. 13).

[2] Theoretically it might vanish. The possibility of completely converting the mass of the psychic apparatus into energy, as expressed by Einstein's equation $E = mc^2$, should not be lightly dismissed. In that case, however, not only will the psychic apparatus vanish, so will the patient, the analyst, and about 50 square miles of their surroundings, for such a conversion corresponds to the energy release of a fair-sized nuclear explosion. Should this actually be observed to occur, I would appreciate it being brought to my attention, for it would be a significant piece of data for metapsychological theory.

such patients are not analyzable and should be screened out in the diagnostic interview. What about the patient who has one but keeps leaving it at home? A possible remedy for such absent-mindedness is to tie the psychic apparatus with a string to some part of the body—a pierced earlobe, for example. Note, too, that a psychic apparatus tied with a string can be said to contain bound energy. Thus the patient is less likely to be overwhelmed with primary-process material, and so the analysis is facilitated. An additional advantage of such binding is that the patient can feel for the string to make sure that the apparatus is actually in place before having a session with the analyst.

I have oversimplified matters somewhat. The psychic apparatus is not completely free to dislodge itself (else many more would be lost than now seems to be the case). It is plausible to suppose, and Freud apparently thought along these lines, that the libido acts as sort of a glue to hold in the psychic apparatus. It is not difficult to imagine the consequence of excessively sticky libido. If sufficient psychical force is mobilized, and the psychic apparatus cannot move, it is conceivable that the entire patient will begin to accelerate. If this should be observed to happen during an analytic session, the prognosis is not good, and termination should be considered. Freud made precisely the same point: "We come across people, for instance, to whom we should be inclined to attribute a special 'adhesiveness of the libido'. The processes which the treatment sets in motion in them are so much slower than in other people because, apparently, they cannot make up their minds to detach" (1937, p. 241). (Freud obviously intended to say in the second sentence above, which may have been garbled in translation: "the treatment sets them in motion because they cannot make their minds detach.")

The above supposition about the entire patient accelerating is not implausible, as the following clinical anecdote indicates. An analyst, of the Kohuttite school, had in treatment a young man who persisted in believing that his feet did not quite touch the ground when he walked. The analyst in turn had persisted, quite mistakenly as it turned out, in attempting to understand and interpret the nature of this grandiose fantasy. It so happens that the patient is a friend of mine, and I can attest to the fact that indeed his feet do *not* touch the ground when he walks. (The analyst's failure to notice that the patient for many years actually floated into and out of the analytic sessions entitles us to suspect a counter-transference problem.) The correct diagnosis should be clear from the previous discussion. This patient is accelerating because of sticky libido. Now Freud (1917, pp. 348-349) connects "adhesiveness of the libido" with the sexual perversions. We see in the above case, of course, an intimate connection with Newton's second law of motion. But we should also recall that the second law explained regression. Thus we have now an independent proof, through physics, of the regressive nature of the perversions. The theory also points the way toward a cure—these people actually need to come unglued, and it is not unthinkable that soaking their heads may lead to significant therapeutic gain.

I shall now fulfill my promise to say more about measuring the mass of the psychic apparatus. We make use of a fundamental mathematical law called subtraction, overlooked for some reason by Rapaport and Gill. The sum of the masses of the patient and his psychic apparatus minus the mass of the patient alone equals the mass of the psychic apparatus. To make this perfectly clear, let B = mass of patient before detachment of the psychic apparatus, A = mass of patient after detachment of psychic apparatus, and m = mass of the psychic apparatus itself. We therefore deduce the very important equation:

$$m = B - A$$

The patient thus could be weighed at the beginning of a session and again after detachment of the psychic apparatus. This was done for a random sample of 50 patients drawn from a hat. (The sample was somewhat biased because about 30% of the patients we approached refused to get into the hat. The meaning of this refusal is still being analyzed.) We concluded that the weight of the average expectable psychic apparatus is 750 grams; the weights are abnormally distributed with a standard perversion of 300 grams. A project is underway to investigate possible correlations between the weight of the psychic apparatus and the nature of the patient's psychopathology. It would also be of interest to determine whether the weight of the psychic apparatus undergoes significant change during analysis. This study will be called a "project for a scientific psychology."

Notice that, knowing the mass of the psychic apparatus, we need only measure its acceleration during analytic sessions in order to deduce, from Newton's second law, the strength of the drives. This raises the question: Can the psychic apparatus be observed? The answer is "yes," but only by means of the analyst's own psychic apparatus; this is discussed in the literature in terms of introspection and empathy (see especially Kohut, 1959). (Empathy is often confused with entropy—actually the distinction is not important.)

We should reflect for a moment that the analyst's psychic apparatus is likely to be as detachable as the patient's. We picture it therefore as hovering about the room during an analytic session. This is undoubtedly what Freud meant in referring to "evenly suspended attention," (1912, p. 111) or what is also called "free-floating attention." He knew, of course, that attention couldn't float by itself; it had to be attached to a psychic apparatus. We may infer that the central idea expressed in this paper had been anticipated by Freud.

With this groundwork, we can now quickly illuminate a number of important additional metapsychological concepts, including transference, merger, object cathexis, fusion, internalization, introjection, incorporation, and narcissism.

During the session the patient's psychic apparatus may collide with that of the analyst. If the repression barrier is penetrated during the collision, transference results. If the two intertwine to the point of obscuring the boundaries, the outcome is called a merger. If the heat generated by the collision is sufficiently intense, fusion may occur. Occasionally the analyst's psychic apparatus will enter the body of the patient. If the patient swallows it, we have incorporation. Otherwise such entry is referred to either as introjection or internalization,[3] depending on the velocity of the impact. (High velocities prevent a transmuting internalization, so the apparatus remains as an introject.) Symmetrical things can, of course, happen to the analyst, and it is imperative to straighten out before the end of the session just who has which psychic apparatus.

Imagine that there is a vase on the analyst's desk. If it is struck by the patient's psychic apparatus, we say that the vase is ca-

---

[3] This clarification should be of assistance to Roy Schafer in the task of unwriting (1972) his book (1968).

thected. Object cathexis is defined as the amount of energy transferred to that object during a collision with the psychic apparatus. This quantity can be calculated directly, knowing the mass and velocity of the psychic apparatus, the mass and velocity of the object, and using the laws of conservation of energy and momentum.

Had Freud understood a bit more physics he probably would not have spent the decade from 1910 to 1920 confusing the ego with the self, and consequently muddling the theory of narcissism. The picture we now have occasions little excuse for such confusion. The ego, as part of the psychic apparatus, is flying around the analyst's office while the self is simply lying there on the couch. The psychic apparatus then occasionally strikes the patient, thus cathecting the self, according to our above definition. Kohut (1971) has written an important book expressing much the same idea.

In watching a psychic apparatus bounce around the room during an analytic session, one can hardly fail to get the impression that it is trying to escape. Of course it should be prevented from doing so if at all possible. Keeping the window closed is the most reasonable precaution one can take. This is what is meant by "optimal frustration" (Kohut, 1971, p. 50). Nonetheless, things aren't always optimal, and now and then a psychic apparatus does fly out. I shall attempt to make clear next the probable pathological sequelae. Many more careful observations will have to be made in order to understand precisely how the psychic force field surrounding the patient varies with distance, but it is plausible to suppose—and such measurements as are available do confirm—that the intensity of this force falls off with distance according to an inverse square law. In any event, once out the window a psychic apparatus apparently cannot be pulled back in by psychic force. It has mass, and so, under the influence of the earth's gravitational field, falls to the ground below. The most important variable, then, determining the outcome is the height of the analyst's office above street level. We denote this as h. The initial potential energy is mgh; this all becomes kinetic energy as the apparatus approaches the ground (g is the acceleration due to gravity). Equating $\frac{1}{2}mv^2$ with mgh, we can solve for the velocity of impact, v, which therefore is given by the square root of 2gh. For example, if the office window is 30 feet off the ground, the impact velocity is the square root of $2 \times 32 \times 30 = 1920$, or about 44 feet per second, which is 30 miles per hour. This calculation neglects air resistance, which is reasonable since we know the psychic apparatus to be egg-shaped (Freud, 1933, p. 78) and hence fairly streamlined.[4] (Thus there are exceptions to the usual rule of analyzing the resistance first; rules should not be applied blindly.) We assume next that the apparatus hits average expectable pavement (Hartmann, 1939, p. 35). The damage upon impact depends very much on whether it lands on its id, on its *Pcpt.-Cs.* system, or on its superego. The latter two possibilities are too dreadful to think about, so I have made calculations only for the first, the id. First- and second-floor offices are reasonably safe. Falls from the third and fourth floors are unlikely to be serious but may lead to a dented ego, minor character deformations, and occasionally a dislocated repression barrier. Traumatic neuroses are quite specific to falls from the fifth floor, while the sixth through eighth lead usually to vertical splits in the ego. (In referring to an ego split as vertical, the implicit assumption is made that the patient is horizontal—a point Kohut [1971, p. 176] fails to clarify.) From the ninth floor on up one must count on serious fragmentation. The least the analyst can do in this case is to go down with the patient and help him pick up the pieces. Some analysts consider this an undesirable parameter; it is no more than an act of humanity. Now if the psychic apparatus should strike a pedestrian instead of the pavement, the consequences tend to be less serious but nonetheless complicated. From the fifth floor or lower, there is no apparent damage, but the pedestrian does get cathected, and this interaction inevitably must be brought into the analysis. From the sixth floor and higher the result is a *folie à deux*.

Let us return now to our main point of departure, namely the specific assumption we make about what it is that psychical forces act upon. Certainly forces are of no use at all unless they act on something. This point was pivotal in the whole argument, and one

---

[4] We should not suppose that Freud's choice of an egg shape was accidental. In the same way that rough or irregularly shaped stones are worn smooth in a creek bed or in the ocean surf, the psychic apparatus must eventually become smooth and egg-shaped through the numerous collisions which it suffers in the normal vicissitudes of knocking about. That Freud was perceptive enough to give it this shape is additional persuasive evidence that his views remarkably anticipated those expressed in this paper.

for which Rapaport and Gill provide no guidance. Instead of applying force to the psychic apparatus as a whole, let us pursue the assumption that psychical forces act *within* the psychical apparatus, therefore upon only parts of the apparatus. Assuming the parts are connected,[5] this assumption would not make a great deal of difference to our argument since linear acceleration would still be imparted to the entire apparatus. However, if the psychic apparatus is fastened at some point, say with a thumbtack (technically this would be called a fixation), then it may not be able to detach itself from the patient. Instead, the moment of the psychic force about the point of fixation would impart angular momentum. That is, Newton's second law would take the form: torque equals moment of inertia times angular acceleration. Thus the psychic apparatus would be set spinning, a phenomenon much in accord with clinical experience. If we are dealing, then, with a spinning apparatus it is of course plausible to assume that the parts are discs, cylinders, wheels, and ellipsoids, with suitable linkages, and thumbtacks. I need go no further with this description, for I seem to have stumbled onto the kind of apparatus already thoroughly studied by Colby (1955). A detailed drawing of the apparatus appears as Figure 12 on p. 102 of his book. I could not improve on the imagery which his own description of it evokes:

> . . . —there are ten macro-systems, seven lying horizontally and three vertically. The vertical systems are three-dimensional cylinders while the horizontal systems are three-dimensional ellipsoids lying in a plane which cuts across the long axis of the cylinders. The model as a whole is a three-dimensional manifold. —Three-dimensional discoid cycle patterns are formed within and travel through the psychic apparatus, being carried by transport systems and being modified by storage systems [p. 85].

[5] The possibility that the parts are *not* connected may be of some general interest but is not highly germane to this paper, since a patient with such a psychic system would not be analyzable. We note, however, that if there are a lot of loose parts being accelerated by psychical forces and rattling around within the apparatus they should be detectable acoustically. One might well establish the exact location of the psychic apparatus with the aid of a stethoscope. See Reik (1948).

> While the sensor, receptor, proprial, environal, and emittor systems are three-dimensional ellipsoids and lie in a horizontal plane, the relinkor systems are similar to the transveyor system in that they are three-dimensional cylinders lying in a vertical plane [p. 100].

Colby does not make clear how the whole thing takes on an egg shape, but we can assume the point is relatively unimportant and simply a matter of good packaging and product design.

The hazard of analyzing patients with strong fixations is now apparent. If sufficient psychic torque around the fixation point is mobilized over a long enough period of time, the apparatus will spin so violently that it may begin to fly apart under the enormous centrifugal force that builds up. It is always best to loosen the fixations first, to permit the apparatus to detach itself from the patient and so reduce the risk of this kind of fragmentation. A clinical example will illustrate the unfortunate consequences of a series of technical errors on the part of the analyst. A female patient, aged 32, suffering from an extremely rigid pre-Oedipal fixation, began to emit high-velocity discs when she was 10 minutes into the sixtieth hour of her analysis. Clearly her relinkors were spinning wildly and throwing off percept segments (see Colby's Figure 12). The analyst should have immediately powered down the psychic forces, loosened the fixation, disconnected the transveyor, removed the psychic apparatus, and plunged it into an oil bath (which should always be kept handy for just this emergency) in order to damp out the spinning. Instead he lost his head and opened a window in order to let the discs out. We have been unable to get from him a coherent account of what happened next, and suspect he spent the rest of the session under his desk. The discs had been flying out no more than 20 minutes when an enterprising neighbor regrettably, but understandably, set up a skeet-shooting concession from a nearby window. This exacerbated an already deteriorating situation. The analysis had to be ended abruptly; both analyst and patient were hospitalized with double paranoia.

Colby's Figure 12, incidentally, is suggestive of the possibility that the psychic apparatus may be gyroscopically stabilized. In that event, a vertical split in the ego of a horizontal patient would remain vertical even when the patient stands up. More generally, any psychic split would remain invariant under rotations of the patient. Thus Kohut's afore-mentioned failure to clarify the orientation of the patient with respect to the verticality of an ego split may be inconsequential.

Finally I shall consider the Rapaport and Gill concept of entropy, as set forth in the last two italicized passages quoted earlier from their paper. The first of the two passages states that "psychological energies are subject to a law of entropy." One must assume they are referring to the second law of thermodynamics, stated as the principle that the entropy of a closed system cannot decrease—it must always increase or remain the same. But their statement is oddly worded and confounding, for one can hardly imagine how to apply this law to a system consisting of nothing but disembodied energies. Certainly we are far afield from physics at this point. Perhaps they mean only that energies are assumed to obey an entropylike law (let us reverse the direction of change, though, to make it more harmonious with a discharge principle). That is, in a closed system the amount of energy cannot increase—it must always decrease or remain the same. But if it decreases the assumed law of conservation of energy would be violated, and if we accept only the contingency that it cannot change we are simply restating the energy-conservation law.

Let me take a new tack now and attempt to discern the intuitive ingenuity behind their proposition rather than try to make sense out of it. Entropy can be interpreted as a measure of disorder, and the above-stated principle means that the disorder of a closed system must stay the same or else increase. Suppose we ask, does disorder increase during the analytic session? The answer is almost embarrassingly obvious. With a 750-gram psychic apparatus barging around the office at high speed, cathecting everything it touches, knocking over vases, and bumping into pictures, of *course* disorder increases. The law of entropy incidentally explains an additional fact—namely, why analytic sessions are best limited to less than an hour—in any longer period the office might well be reduced to a complete shambles.

We can see that the contributions made by Rapaport and Gill toward giving psychoanalysis a firm base in physics have led to many rewarding and unexpected theoretical insights. Surely this is only a beginning.

EPILOGUE—ON CONSERVATION, DISCHARGE, AND FIREWORKS

Once upon a time in the far north of Lapland a man named Joseph lived alone in a large secluded house. He was a frugal man. Electricity was expensive and the nights were long, so he was careful never to keep lights on in unoccupied rooms. When he moved from the kitchen to the living room he turned off the light in the kitchen and turned on the light in the living room. When he then went to the bedroom he turned off the light in the living room and turned on the light in the bedroom. Joseph was afraid of the dark, so never, never stayed in an unlighted room. The nearest neighbors were miles away, so when he wished to visit, or to go shopping in town, he would use his car. The car was small and economical, a two-door Soma. (The Soma is manufactured in Lapland and almost unknown elsewhere.) He kept it in a garage attached to one end of the house. He never went outdoors, except in the car, and he very seldom had visitors. When Joseph left the house in his car, he made sure that the garage light and all the house lights were off.

During the long Lapland night of the winter of 1923, a Martian scientist named Floyd was flying above the frozen countryside in his tripartite landing module when he was attracted by the lights in the house. He descended to a lonely mountain top nearby in order to observe the house more closely. He had no knowledge of electricity, nor of artificial illumination. His state of knowledge of the earth did not lead him to assume, or even suspect, that the house was occupied by a sentient being. His purpose was to observe carefully and to formulate a theory which would explain his observations. He saw only the house, the lighted windows, and the comings and goings of the car. He was a good observer, and a brilliant theoretician. Here is the essence of the theory which he developed, as set forth in a letter to his friend Felice.

The apparatus or organism which I have been observing is immobile except for a small object which can detach itself from one end and move great distances on the ground; each time it leaves it eventually returns and re-enters the apparatus. This object for lack of a better word I shall call the soma, and advance herewith a theory which, at least in part, accounts for its behavior.

The apparatus is divided into segments or rooms; each room can be in a state of excitation evidenced by a light visible from a window of that room. Each individual room spends most of its time in a state of quiescence. Since it seldom remains for longer than a few hours in a state of excitation, we can infer that there is a principle of discharge. Rooms tend to divest themselves of excitation. Within the apparatus as a whole we may say that there is some quantity of excitation in a state of flow; this quantity I shall call Q—it is a measure of the amount of light. The path of discharge can readily be followed by observing the succession of lighted windows as the quantity of excitation flows from room to room.

Most important, we can see also that there is a principle of conservation. If a room divests itself of its light, we may be certain that this same quantity of light appears elsewhere, and in fact almost invariably in an adjoining room. Whenever an impulse of light excitation has vanished from one room we are entitled and even obliged to search until we have accounted for it, for surely it will be found elsewhere. Just as the quantity Q cannot be destroyed, so also it cannot be created—for I have observed that never is there more than one lighted window at a time.

Only under one special circumstance is there no light at all visible, and that fact leads us to a most important discovery. Occasionally we can clearly follow the path of discharge from room to room until it reaches the end of the apparatus from which the soma can be emitted; if then the soma indeed is mobilized we find that the pulse of excitation has terminated. Clearly it has found expression in somatic discharge. Indeed we may plausibly say that that was its purpose from the outset. We can hardly avoid the impression that the entire flow of excitation culminating in the ejection of the soma has the quality of orgastic discharge, and so we may call our principle of discharge the pleasure principle. We may further state that the entire apparatus is energized by the soma, for it remains quiescent until the soma returns; upon re-entry, light energy in an amount Q streams from the soma into the apparatus, whereupon the state of tension, or unpleasure, is increased and the chain of excitations resumes its quest for a suitable path of discharge, and hence its pursuit of pleasure.

Many were the letters Floyd wrote to Felice. Many were the colleagues of Floyd who came to the mountain top to witness the things that Floyd had seen; and they saw too. They studied his theories and they were convinced. Upon this foundation greater and greater theories were built, and so many were the books they wrote that they filled the Martian libraries. They built new libraries; then they built libraries just to hold the indexes to the works of Floyd and his colleagues. And the indexes themselves needed indexes. And each winter night for years and years there were scientists on the mountain top carefully observing the house of Joseph and training other Martian scientists to see what they saw. They saw the light, they saw its path of discharge, and they saw the comings and goings of the two-door Soma.

Then one fine clear and crisp winter night Joseph, tiring of the loneliness of his life in that large secluded Lapland house, took a wife. There was a great celebration. Hundreds of friends came from afar and filled every room in his house. They danced in the street, and had a great feast outdoors, with 31 flavors of ice cream, and 31 colors of floodlights, and 10 pipers piping, and fireworks.......

REFERENCES

Colby, K. M. (1955), *Energy and Structure in Psychoanalysis.* New York: Ronald Press.

Freud, S. (1912), Recommendations to Physicians Practising Psycho-Analysis. *Standard Edition,* 12:111-120. London: Hogarth Press, 1958.

———— (1917), Introductory Lectures on Psycho-Analysis, Part III. *Standard Edition,* 16. London: Hogarth Press, 1963.

———— (1933), New Introductory Lectures on Psycho-Analysis. *Standard Edition,* 22:5-182. London: Hogarth Press, 1964.

———— (1937), Analysis Terminable and Interminable. *Standard Edition,* 23: 216-253. London: Hogarth Press, 1964.

———— (1940), An Outline of Psycho-Analysis. *Standard Edition,* 23:144-207. London: Hogarth Press, 1964.

Hartmann, H. (1939), *Ego Psychology and the Problem of Adaptation.* New York: International Universities Press, 1958.

Jones, E. (1955), *The Life and Work of Sigmund Freud,* Vol. 2. New York: Basic Books.

Kohut, H. (1959), Introspection and Empathy. *J. Amer. Psychoanal. Assn.*, 7:459-483.

———— (1971), *The Analysis of the Self.* New York: International Universities Press.

Newton, I. (1687), *Philosophiae Naturalis Principia Mathematica.* Imprimatur S. Pepys Reg. Soc. Praeses Julii 5, 1686. London.

Rapaport, D., & Gill, M. M. (1959), The Points of View and Assumptions of Metapsychology. *Internat. J. Psycho-Anal.*, 40:153-162.

Reik, T. (1948), *Listening with the Third Ear.* New York: Farrar, Straus.

Rosenblatt, A. D., & Thickstun, J. T. (1970), A Study of the Concept of Psychic Energy. *Internat. J. Psycho-Anal.*, 51:265-278.

Schafer, R. (1968), *Aspects of Internalization.* New York: International Universities Press.

———— (1972), Internalization: Process or Fantasy? *The Psychoanalytic Study of the Child*, 27:411-436. New York: Quadrangle.

Acknowledgment

I offer my sincere thanks to Professor Merton Gill, whose encouragement, even (or perhaps especially) when others flinched, remained steadfast. I am grateful also to Dr. George Klumpner for helpful suggestions. (He is not responsible, however, for my failure to act on several of his most urgent ones . . .)

This work was made possible by the refusal of the NSF, NIH, NIMH, NAS, YWCA, AMA, DOD, DIA, CIA, NSA, BSA, and the KGB to support any of the other projects which I had proposed.

2 Developmental Studies

Ruth C. Resch, Ph.D.

Natural Studies and Natural Observations: A Methodology

This paper had its genesis in a study of babies and toddlers who were separating daily from their mothers in the familiar setting of an infant day-care center. This setting provided a uniquely rich opportunity to study separation in very young babies as it occurred ordinarily in their lives. An equally compelling body of direct observational material was available: moment-by-moment behavior narratives sampled in a variety of situations. As a clinician devoted to the dynamics, nuances, and sequences in behavior, and as a researcher devoted to a clinical form of systematic study, I was pressed to try to solve some crucial methodological issues. This became a highly engaging and interesting problem in its own right: how to use observational material in a way that *optimizes* its richness and variety, and *incorporates* its limitations. This led to my developing a systematic research model fitted to studying the complexity that is contained in such observations.

The objectives of this paper are to underscore the importance of the *descriptive phase* and its necessary position within the whole scientific endeavor, and to demonstrate that the specific character of the setting, the phenomenon, and the data can determine new methodologies derived from biology. These will be more clinically useful for looking at natural data and natural data analysis. Methodology is a tool of research, and it is a highly maleable one.

My deep and affectionate thanks to Dr. Louise Kaplan, Fred Pine, Donald Spence, and Katharine Smith for their critical and thoughtful contributions to this work.

It can, and in fact must, be tailored to meet the particular character of the specific phenomenon, the nature of the questions that can be addressed to it, and the particular interests of the researcher.

The range of choice in methods for clinically sensitive study will be presented as quite broad. The more explicit ánd carefully analyzed these choices, the more thoroughly they are thought through, initially, in relation to one's particular purposes in study, the more productive the ensuing research. The point cannot be made too forcefully that methodology in human study can and must be molded to the phenomena of interest and not the other way around. It is my view that systematic methodology is often intrinsic to complex clinical phenomena and our interests in studying them. Consequently a sensitive analysis of the phenomena and the state of our understanding of it will illuminate *how* to study it.

In this paper I shall discuss the use and function of natural observational study as an integral—and for some issues, such as separation, an essential—part of the total scientific endeavor of understanding human behavior. The objectives of natural studies will be elaborated as different from *and* complementary to those of the traditional and major hypothesis-testing model.

Finally, I shall present a model for the use of natural observations and natural data analysis and illustrate it with aspects of a study of separation. Beyond the presentation of this model, however, I hope that the total discussion will be a stimulus to both clinicians and researchers to think in new ways—and perhaps with some pleasure in discovery—about methodology as intrinsic to the phenomena of interest to them.

PSYCHOLOGY AND METHODOLOGY: PHYSICAL-SCIENCE VERSUS ETHOLOGICAL-BIOLOGICAL MODELS

In its concern for scientific rigor as usually conceived, psychological, psychiatric, and developmental research has, for many decades, in large part left fallow the fundamentally important opportunities (and problems) of studying behavior in its natural everyday presentation. The high diversity, inconsistencies, multiple variables, and remarkable complexity of ongoing behavior have seldom been the very subjects of systematic study. When they are not partialed out, these confound traditional research methodologies, but taken together they are the everyday material of the clinician's work. This dichotomy presents major methodological problems for clinical research.

Two traditions in psychological study bear some examination for clinically minded researchers and for research-minded clinicians. One of these traditions is the dominance of the experimental model, with its implicit requirement for clear formulations that are often, functionally, beyond the current understanding of the phenomena we are interested in. The other is the physicalistic-mechanistic model that implies a particular philosophic view of the nature of the relationships among phenomena.

Research-minded clinicians, often certainly dissatisfied with experimentation as such, may also experience an incompletely understood malaise with the physical-science model.

Shakow (1959), speaking to clinicians, has placed both of these traditions in a historical context.

I have speculated about how much further advanced psychology as a science might now be if it had in the latter part of the last century permitted itself to be influenced primarily by the French hospital tradition of Charcot rather than by the physical-physiological laboratory tradition of Helmholtz. My thought was that because of the choice which academic psychology made in favor of the latter, the area of personality was passed over and the observational naturalistic stage of the development of science was skipped. This resulted in a predominant—and I think premature—emphasis on the experimental, the segmental, the rigorous and the molecular, with a parallel neglect of the molar and the less rigorously definable but more "meaningful" behavior ... I don't see how eventually we can be satisfied with less than full and accurate naturalistic accounts of the many classes of events surrounding the development of the infant and child—that is, reports on the phenomena without selection and without distortion. Such accounts call for actual presence at the events which are to be observed [pp. 47, 49].

These models were not merely adopted prematurely, they are also too limited for many kinds of problems and stages of work. Clinicians, because of their dominant interest in larger inferential patterns and meanings, frequently find these models not only narrow and limiting, but also lacking in synchrony with the scope of their interests.

It is not my intention here to present fully reasoned definitions or critiques of these traditions. Rather, it is to point out that they offer problems for many researchers. I would like to suggest that it is profitable to bear in mind that the experimental model, and the physicalistic-mechanistic world view associated with it, in fact represent *two different* issues. We may choose to separate them, and then to consider alternative models.

The research undertaking implies systematic ordering of data and standards of rigor for the testing of ideas. The usual experimental model offers a set of strategies and techniques for doing this, and it has the historic advantage of being clearly explicated and well defined. Thus it is a ready measure for assessing standards in research, something that is less true of other methodological models.

The physicalistic-mechanistic model, with respect to methodology, represents a particular view of the nature of relationships among phenomena. Many clinicians, interdisciplinary workers, and theoreticians may, in fact, not think in this way. Yet too often our research thinking automatically couples it with the experimental model. Yankelovich and Barrett (1970) and Chein (1972) have presented persuasive arguments on these issues.

Decades ago Klüver (1936) also, in effect, separated these two traditions. He retained the experimental tradition and suggested a "process" model, different from the physical-mechanistic model, to study certain relationships he observed in behavior.

In his relatively microscopic stimulus-response studies of monkeys with brain lesions, Klüver (1936) presented a closely reasoned argument for developing laboratory experimental methods that reflect the characteristics of particular relations between the organism and its environment. His experimental method of equivalent and nonequivalent stimuli is based on an observation that in many species "the *same* response may be elicited by widely different stimuli; the *same* stimulus may call forth widely different reactions . . . We are ultimately interested in functional equivalence, that is the factors bringing about or accounting for these forms of behavior" (p. 96). Klüver argued for applying such observations in a systematic way. In his view, it is not to prove the observation but rather to illuminate the *processes* that produce the differential phenomena.

From a quite different logic, Lewin (1936) argued for the scientific study of behavior in context. What I have called natural setting and natural phenomena, Lewin conceptualized together as "life space as a whole." A derivation of the totality of all possible events can proceed only from this. He argued for a shift of scientific psychology from objects and states to processes and changes of state. "The different kinds of behavior that occur in a certain situation are to be understood as belonging to a coherent system of 'possible' events that are in their totality an expression of the particular characteristics of this situation . . . the *derivation of the totality* of possible cases is valid not only for the behavior of the person within the situation but also for the possible changes of the person or of the situation itself" (p. 16; Lewin's italics).

Klüver and Lewin presented rather different working models, or views, of the relationships among phenomena; but both are process models.

I would argue strongly that the researcher must make explicit what his own view is of how phenomena go together. From this he can choose or create a model that will illuminate his data. The biological and ethological traditions offer process models that may be more compatible and fruitful ways for approaching and solving many clinical and developmental issues.

Once a model of the phenomena is chosen, then technique follows. Understanding one's implicit model of the nature of behavioral relationships is the first of a series of choices in realizing one's interests in doing research. Escalona (1968), for example, offers such a model for developmental research. It is applicable as well to conceptualizing many types of outcome or change problems.

Lewis and Lee-Painter (1974), Stern (1974), and Brazelton, Koslowski, and Main (1974), working in mother-infant interaction studies, offer highly interesting and diverse applications of process models. The implications for technical data-processing matters are quite different among these writers, and the ways in which they make use of experimental criteria synchronously with their own models are highly instructive.

Nikolaas Tinbergen, the "animal watcher," who has also studied childhood autism (E. A. Tinbergen and N. Tinbergen, 1972), has stressed (1973c) the importance for human study of the ethological method of direct observation of naturally occurring behavior. He emphasizes that there is little in the literature on human psychopathology and trauma that has a basis in comparative *normal* behavior. That is, in the hypothesis-testing model, the control is used as a *contrast* group—i.e., to establish that the observed pathology is in fact a deviation—and not for the purpose of discovering whether pathological patterns may have *characteristics in common* with normal adaptive sequences. The ethological methods of observing naturally occurring behavior, he asserts, make important contributions to this task. In his own studies of autism, for example, he observed that certain nonverbal behavior regularly seen in autistic children—avoiding of eye contact, spatial distancing, facial expressions, and gestures—are also seen transiently in normal children as parts of a fear response to the environment. His point is that observing patterns in naturally occurring behavior offers formal and functional explanatory possibilities not necessarily apparent either in current theory or in experimental methods.

Medawar, a biologist, agrees with Tinbergen, stating that "it is not informative to study variations of behavior unless we know beforehand the norms from which the variants depart." Pressing the point even further, he believes that experimental intervention of any sort produces "contrived behavior," which is itself a variant from the norm. "The [ethologists] studied natural behavior and were thus able for the first time to discern natural behavior structures or episodes ... Then, and only then, was it possible to start to obtain significant information from the study of contrived behavior—from the application or withholding of stimuli ..." (1967, p. 109).[1]

---

[1] Barker (1968) points to the same dichotomy in terms of "behavior units," which are "inherent segments in the stream of behavior," and "behavior tesserae," which are alien parts of the behavior stream formed by the intrusions of an investigator.

Purely observational methods, as Wright (1960) has pointed out, account for major discoveries of countless phenomena from "microorganisms to galaxies" in many areas of science. Yet, as Shakow also noted, psychology, in its pressure to be adequately scientific, has largely skipped the observational stage in its development. In a study analyzing the methods used in 1,409 child and adolescent studies published between 1890 and 1958, Wright (1960) found only 110 studies that had used "direct observations . . . of naturally occurring things and events." This is less than 8% of the total. Only a few of these studies dealt with the temporal, sequential, natural occurrence of behavior.

Observational studies have been carried out principally with children, and Hutt and Hutt (1970) suggest that this is a method of choice. Young children are among the groups of "uncooperative" subjects in terms of standard methods of testing, interviewing, and questionnaires, as well as for some types of experimentation. However, the most frequent use of direct natural observation in the published child literature was in the decades 1900-1909 and 1930-1939 (13% and 11% respectively) (Wright, 1960). It thus appears that the basic observational underpinning in developmental research—where it is so essential—has been surprisingly scant.

In the foreword to a two-volume collection of Tinbergen's papers, Medawar (1973) describes ethological methods thus far:

> The first stage in a behavioral analysis is, of course, to observe and record what is actually going on. This will involve intent and prolonged observation until what an untrained observer might dismiss as a sequence of unrelated behavioral performances is seen to fall into well-defined and functionally connected sequences or behavior structures. These behavior structures do not declare themselves in any obvious way. Their identification depends upon an imaginative conjecture on the part of the observer which further observation may or may not uphold [p. 9].

What Medawar is describing here, in ethological terms, are the observational, descriptive, and classificatory phases of a science. Fundamentally these phases have data-based hypothesis generation as their purpose.

The observational phase of a study establishes what there is to
explain in real life occurrences, and it generates new hypotheses
at a high rate as it goes along. The hypotheses that result are
also likely to be somewhere nearer the mark than hypotheses
that result from armchair speculation, textbook reading or
traditional theory ... An experiment merely chooses between
two hypotheses, it does not prove the correctness of either or
exclude many of the other possible hypotheses that it was not
specifically designed to test. Nor does an experiment determine
whether the tested effects play an important role in the occurrence of the phenomenon during real life [Blurton-Jones, 1972,
p. 11].

In Tinbergen's observations of autistic and normal children, he
demonstrates two aspects of ethological methodology that are of
special interest here: (1) analysis of natural observations into
behavior sequences and (2) natural experiments. He emphasizes a
reciprocal relationship between observation and experimentation,
"how fruitful the 'seesawing' can be" (1973c, p. 20). His collection
of studies on such diverse species as gulls, wasps, and butterflies
does indeed demonstrate the productiveness of an intimate working
back and forth among observations, natural and formal experiments (N. Tinbergen, 1972a, 1972b).

He makes careful observations—ethograms—of behavior in the
wild, and from them formulates descriptions of behavior patterns.
Taking those patterns as hypotheses, he then varies certain aspects
of the natural surround in order to determine the stability of the
pattern, its function, or the breadth of conditions in which it is
maintained. These he calls "natural experiments."

From these he may return to natural observation to check some
matters further, or he may proceed to more formal experiments of
a hypothesis-testing nature. The process becomes a branching one.
From the results of the formal experiments he may proceed to
further experiments, or return either to natural observations or
natural experiments as the unresolved questions dictate. In the
present context, an extremely important aspect of Tinbergen's
work is that there is a *continuum* of systematic study, from the
single clinical case study at one end to normative hypothesis-testing
work at the other. Figure 1 presents a conceptualization of such a
continuum.

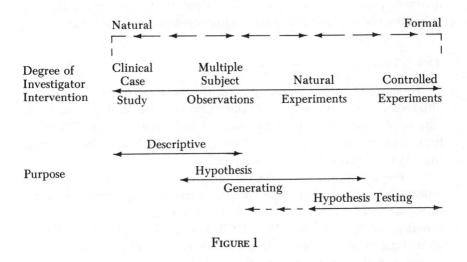

FIGURE 1

The basic tasks of the experimental method are to provide means for systematic ordering of data and rigorous testing of ideas. If we bear these tasks in mind as criteria for any methodology, this continuum should offer a more flexible set of possibilities for designing methodologies to suit the requirements of particular data, issues, and states of the art.

The model that will be presented in this paper occupies a position that cross-cuts the figure vertically through "multiple subject observations," "descriptive," and "hypothesis generating."

ELEMENTS OF NATURAL STUDY

Natural and observational studies can take a variety of forms and can be used for differing purposes. Specifying the great flexibility available for observational studies will serve as a basis for understanding how systematic method follows from careful analysis of and decisions about the form and purpose of one's study. Studies can be "natural" in four quite different ways: the *observational setting*, the *observed phenomena*, the *form of the data*, and the method of *analyzing the data*. These all represent choices available to the researcher. That is, any given study need not be natural in all of these ways. The important point is that the natural aspects of study can be used in a variety of ways tailored to different problems and phenomena. These will be discussed below, with illustrations from the separation and general literature.

THE SETTING

Researchers often choose not to use the controlled laboratory, and seek the real-life settings of the subjects to be studied. These are commonly used to eliminate some of the artificial conditions of laboratory experimentation that restrict the validity of findings and their generalizability to everyday behavior.

There are many examples of natural settings. With respect to separation, researchers have gone to nurseries, residential institutions, and private homes (see Spitz, 1945, 1946; Robertson and Bowlby, 1952; Heinicke, 1956, 1973; Shirley, 1942; Murphy, 1962). Clinicians study patients in hospital wards and in consultation rooms; social psychologists study the behavior of people in groups and street crowds. Ecological psychologists study children at home, at school, in camp (Simmons and Schoggen, 1972; Schoggen, 1972; Gump, Schoggen, and Redl, 1972). The British group of ethological psychologists study attachment behavior of babies with their mothers in parks (Anderson, 1972), play and social interaction in schools (Smith and Connolly, 1972; McGrew, 1972), separation from mothers in play groups (Blurton-Jones and Leach, 1972).

There are variations in the "naturalness" of the setting. For example, in a study of separation, Robertson and Robertson (1971) controlled some aspects of the setting by providing care for each subject in the Robertsons' home during a hospitalization of the mother. Thus they were able to combine more laboratorylike control conditions with a natural setting in which the separation was to occur. Research nurseries (e.g., Mahler's at the Masters Center, Galenson's at Albert Einstein Medical Center) are examples of an intermediate form between laboratory and completely natural settings. That is, they are specifically research settings, but designed to be *like* natural ones.

The naturalness of the setting can be quite independent of the rest of the method. That is, quite experimental studies can be carried out in such settings. For example, in an imaginatively designed study of the stare as a stimulus to flight, Elsworth,

Carlsmith, and Henson (1972) systematically varied certain conditions of the stare as random automobile drivers stopped for a red light at a metropolitan intersection, a natural setting. Their measure of flight—the phenomenon—used a natural condition: the time to drive to the far crosswalk line when the light turned green, comparing stare and no-stare conditions.

In the separation literature, Willis and Ricciuti (1974) carefully structured certain aspects of their babies' arrivals each morning in their day-care unit. The baby's outdoor clothing was removed at a dressing table in the hall. When ready, the parent knocked on the door, the familiar caretaker answered, and a "far greet" was observed and rated. After a few moments, the parent approached with the baby and a "near greet," during which the caretaker reached to take the baby, was observed and rated. In this study, while the setting was a natural, familiar one of daily care, the form of arrival—the phenomenon—was experimentally manipulated.

Similarly, Ricciuti and Poresky's (1973) study of attachment to the mother used the same familiar care setting, systematically varying approach and departure of familiar and relatively strange people.

THE PHENOMENA

The phenomenon of interest may also be observed as it occurs naturally in the life of the subject, rather than being produced by experimental intervention. In some of the separation studies referred to above, natural settings were combined with the natural occurrence of the phenomena, e.g., expected hospitalization of the mother, entrance into nursery school, the mother's departure in a playground. In sleep and dream studies, as another example, the phenomena being observed occur naturally while the setting is in the laboratory. In the Mahler research nursery there were both situationally induced separations and naturally occurring ones. Some were induced by calling the mothers out of the room for conferences, and others were naturally occurring when the babies crawled out into the hallway or when they were changed, at an appropriate age, to the toddler room where the mothers were not always present. Observation of the natural phenomenon may also be combined in many ways with other elements of the design.

Naturally occurring phenomena are also used to increase generalizability. That is, a restriction often affecting laboratory induction is whether the subject is experiencing and behaving as he ordinarily would, i.e., does the laboratory phenomenon observed have a direct relationship to real-life behavior? Often it does not.

The unnatural results of laboratory procedures, for example on separation phenomena, are highlighted by the experimental group at the University of Montreal. Shaffran (1974) reports a study in which she observed the natural approach of unselected strange adults to an infant. She found that the procedures commonly used in laboratory stranger studies coincided in *few* respects with the actual behavior of her strangers meeting an unknown infant. Infants, then, may never experience analogous conditions outside the laboratory.

The question must be asked, of course, to what life behavior are such studies generalizable? It is a critical question that can be applied to a great deal of laboratory study. Carrying the reasoning one step further beyond criticism: controlled hypothesis-testing procedures, if they are to produce generalizable results, must derive from and be synchronous with naturally occurring phenomena.

For example, Shaffran describes a number of different approach sequences by her strangers, some producing fear responses and some not. A repertoire of natural approach sequences (such as Tinbergen also describes) observed in natural conditions can lead to a series of controlled experiments. This mode of moving from the natural to the experimental is a scientific process which is the core of the model presented in this paper. The Shaffran study underscores the importance of the natural phenomena as a crucial informant of laboratory experimentation.

Not only experimentally induced phenomena but also experimental settings may produce "contrived" behavior in Medawar's sense. Especially in child studies, this may be a critical problem. Among many such studies, one by Dragsten and Lee (1973) illustrates this point. They compared social-contact behavior of 6- to 18-month-old babies in natural day-care settings with behavior under experimental conditions. They found that behavior differed markedly in the two conditions: In the experimental condition it was less diverse and more immature in form. For *some* developmental issues, and separation is among them, this distinction is crucial.

Babies, mothers, and alternate caregivers behave and respond to one another in a wide diversity of ways. Even with the same people, no two departures are quite the same. The setting itself— even the same physical one—varies considerably: what toys are out, which other people are there, what other activities are already going on. These conditions of variability in the behavior presentation of all the participants and in the setting are, in fact, *the standard* in which children at all ages, over time, experience separations from their mothers. Consequently contrived and delimited experimental studies will in themselves hardly tap the complexity of the experience, as separation is lived by children and their mothers.

THE FORM OF THE DATA

The naturalness of the *form* of the data is the extent to which it is unselected and uncategorized at the outset. Ordinarily, data to be recorded are preselected by some criteria and/or precategorized on some predetermined set of measures. For example, some separation studies select specifically the distress response, measuring in various ways the intensity, duration, and conditions of crying, clinging, and so on (see Ainsworth and Bell, 1970a, 1970b; Marvin, 1972; Lee et al., in preparation). Others, focusing on exploratory behavior, measure distances from the mother or strange examiner, and movement toward toys (see Ainsworth and Witting, 1969). More qualitative categories of behavior may be predetermined, and rated on the spot by trained observers (see Pine and Furer, 1963).

Wright (1960) describes six forms of natural data: (1) Diary description follows developmental phenomena longitudinally at more or less regular day-to-day intervals. A good example of this form is Piaget's (1936) observations of his own three children, from which he drew exquisite event samples (see below) for a number of his major studies. (2) Specimen description records of all behavior and the situation in continuous sequences. (3) Time sampling preselects behavior and situation variables and records (or counts) their occurrence in intermittent brief time units. (4) Event sampling records (or counts) given classes of behavior whenever they appear. (5) Trait sampling preselects dimensions of behavior and records in continuous sequences those dimensions whenever they appear. (6) Field-unit analysis selects variables of behavior or situation and records successive behavior units. These are quite different ways of tapping the naturally occurring "behavior stream." They are also choices of best fit, either in terms of the phenomenon or the goals of the study. Videotaping, audio-recording, and written narrative observations are means of obtaining natural data in any of these forms.

Generally, the more unselected, and in this sense natural, the form of the data, the more difficult and often unwieldy they are to evaluate and analyze. However, the advantage of natural obser-vation and data is precisely the minimum intrusion of selection at the outset. They can be relatively more invulnerable to measure-ment biases and errors due to preselection, thus achieving greater validity.

Shakow states the matter succinctly: "Since the data are naturalistic rather than experimental, they lend themselves to examination by hypothesis *after* collection. In fact they lend themselves to examination by a succession of hypotheses, since the data are not at all used up or modified by previous hypothesis-testing. This is perhaps the greatest advantage which nonobserver-distorted naturalistic data provide" (1959, p. 50).

The Data Analysis

Finally, and a central characteristic of the model to be pre-sented, a study may be natural in the method of analyzing the data and transforming them into conclusions. Exploratory studies, clini-cal case studies, and the use of clinical or observational vignettes are examples of a naturalistic use of data. These methods have in common a fundamental recognition that the state of the art in relating real-life behavior to theory in many areas of personality study is not advanced enough for meaningful reduction to numeri-cal analysis.

Ethologists, ecologists, and clinicians in initial phases of their work all use natural data-analysis methods in observing behavior and in hypothesizing structure, interrelationships, and classification. The level of data-relatedness versus abstraction from the data vary widely in these fields of study. In psychology, the observation of natural phenomena has been slighted in favor of achieving controls. In psychoanalysis, the problem of systematic analysis is analogously largely bypassed, left more loosely than necessary to single case studies and individual clinical acumen.

The intention in handling data naturalistically is to stay close to the intrinsic complexity of the data and to "allow them to speak for themselves," that is, to derive concepts *from* the data, in contrast to or preliminary to testing a concept by imposing it *upon* the data.

Starting from an educated naïveté, the data are used to *derive* salient variables and patterns that may then be fruitfully subjected to hypothesis testing and quantitative methods.

Ethological observers, such as Tinbergen and Lorenz, show in a vital way the fundamental merit of using extensive natural observations to discover natural patterns in behavior and natural sources of variation which can then be tested. They do not, however, detail the methodology specific to deriving such patterns from the behavior narrative (N. Tinbergen, 1963). The task of the model presented below is to formulate just such a systematic natural-data analysis.

Tinbergen's two small volumes of collected papers are, however, a superb case study in ethology of an important point I wish to make for psychological and developmental study. That is, natural observations can be analyzed in a systematic *hypothesis-generating* model that is not only instructive for hypothesis testing but can be crucial to the adequacy of formulation of the hypotheses themselves.

Anthony (1968) has presented several models for organizing natural observational data and drawing inferences from it. These models represent an effort to systematize clinical interpretation. They are focused on inferences regarding implicit dynamic or symbolic meanings in observational data.

In "Beyond the Pleasure Principle" (1920), Freud described several observations of an 18-month-old boy: first throwing his toys into a corner, then throwing a reel on the end of a string over the edge of his bed, and finally playing a peekaboo game with a mirror. These incidents were all accompanied by the verbalization "o-o-o-o" (*fort* in German = gone away).

Anthony schematized Freud's observations and method of interpretive inference. This schema is presented in Table 1.

In clinical practice we are now easily accustomed, in Freud's tradition, to this mode and degree of inference as a commonplace in formulating *diagnostic hypotheses*. However, as a conclusion about defensive structure in this boy, the reel observation is heavily interpreted. The main interpretations—the equivalence of the reel with the mother and the specific connection to separation from the mother—remain as hypotheses and are not confirmed as asserted by the data in Table 1. That is, the structured character of the behavior is an adaptation instituted in specific response to the absence of the mother is a *hypothesis* generated by the data. This observation is far too brief for adequate confirmation.

What *is* common to all three observations is the boy's preoccupation with the phenomenon of appearance and disappearance. He applies himself to this interesting problem very much in the manner of an experimenter, using different classes of objects—toys and his own body—under differing conditions. We are certainly observing a cognitive development occurring *in situ*, and research in object permanence and person permanence may help us infer that these observational bits at his age reflect his cognitive understanding of his mother's departure. In point of fact, however, the defensive relation of the behavior and its use in mastery of separation is not, as asserted, clearly indicated in these data.

Anthony, in his remarks about Freud's method, also makes this point:

> Many of his observations are ... masterpieces of a microtechnique ... He would start his observations with a meticulous and detailed description of an external event, build up evidence regarding its internal significance, construct tentative hypotheses and then look for external confirmation ... That it remains a four column analysis signifies that Freud showed not too much interest in the phenomenological sphere but tended to jump into the interpretive as soon as he was able to do so [1968, p. 106].

In his own model, Anthony divides the observation into large behavior-stream units, in the manner of Barker (1960). He then redescribes the observation in terms of organizing units, a process

TABLE 1

A FOUR-COLUMN ANALYSIS

Column 1	Column 2	Column 3	Column 4
Preobservational Data	The Behavioral Item	The Interpretation	The Confirmation
A "model" 18 month boy— well-behaved, obedient— close tie to mother—yet never cried when she left him. Threw his toys about emitting a gratified "O-O-OH!" (= gone away! according to mother)	Repeatedly threw wooden reel with string attached over side of cot. On its disappearance "O-O-OH!" On its reappearance, joyful "Da!" More pleasure with second part of game	Reel = mother. In place of her going and returning, child throws "her" away and brings "her" back (i) Mastery of separation (ii) Turning passive into active experience (iii) Revenge over being deserted	Interpretation confirmed by further observation in which child makes his mirror reflection disappear with the accompanying "Baby O-O-OH!" Speculation on the repetition compulsion

Reprinted by permission from Anthony (1968).

he terms "morphoanalysis." He describes effect, content, spatial relations, and expression.

A major limitation of the series of models that Anthony presents is that they are applicable only to individual cases and do not provide a schema for synthesizing multiple cases.

A HYPOTHESIS-GENERATING MODEL
FOR NATURAL DATA

This model is based upon the tradition of careful, detailed description of observed behavior that is exemplified by both the ethologists and Freud's now classic methods. It differs from the clinical Freudian in that symbolic dynamic interpretation is not its immediate goal. Its primary objective is the description of observed behavior and of the patterns that emerge in behavior sequences. When these are systematically organized, they serve as a basis for interpretation, hypothesis, and theory formulation.

An infant's use of symbol, metaphor, and defense is itself a developmental achievement in both cognition and organization of behavior. The description of the emergence of such patterning in behavior is itself the task of this model. When, for example, do such complex patterns emerge and under what conditions does the child come to use them, specifically in the situation of separation, with regard to the mother's departure?

This model is also analogous to Escalona's (1968) theoretical model for research design in developmental outcome studies. She proposes that the complex interaction of organismic variables and environmental variables produces "experience patterns." In her view, it is these patterns, "behavior-in-context," and not the individual organismic or environmental variables, that should show direct and consistent relationships with developmental outcome. Most child research, she points out, attempts to study the relationship of the *individual* variables to outcome, not that of the *patterns* to outcome.

Escalona's schematization of her model is shown in Figure 2.

The model proposed in this paper uses Escalona's concept of identifying behavior patterns and applies it to organismic variables in the study of a macroscopic process, here, changing behavior in the separation situation.

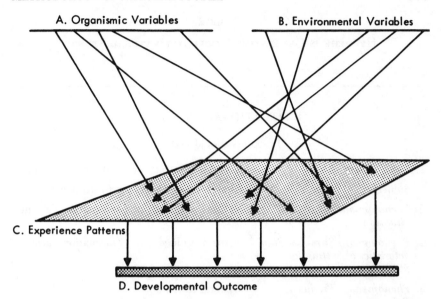

Reprinted by permission from Sibylle K. Escalona: THE ROOTS OF INDIVID-
UALITY (Chicago: Aldine Publishing Company); copyright © 1968 by Sibylle
K. Escalona.

FIGURE 2

Identifying salient developments in the data, i.e., the organismic variables that contribute to the behavior patterns—parallel
to Anthony's "morphoanalysis"—is a major descriptive task. What
developments appear in the total behavior stream of the separation
situation? What behavior comes to be used specifically, and in
what sequences, when the mother departs? Then, how do these
change over time? Finally, the model is designed for behavioral,
descriptive, natural analysis of *group* data, multiple observations.
Its goal is to identify the multiple contributing variables in the
phenomenon and to view them in their complex and changing
relationships across many observations, and, in this study, over
time. This model is presented in Table 2.

SITUATIONAL ANALYSIS

The situational analysis[2] is a schematic presentation of the

[2] The situational analysis is a further expansion of Anthony's adaptation from
Goodrich (1959).

TABLE 2

HYPOTHESIS-GENERATING MODEL FOR NATURAL STUDIES

I. SITUATIONAL ANALYSIS

Preobservational Data

1. *Type of Setting*	Natural, induced, or combination variant
2. *Subjects*	Characteristics germane to study issue
3. *Phenomenon: Behavioral Situation*	Natural, induced, or combination variant
4. *Phenomenon: Stimulus Characteristics of Setting for Study Issue*	Natural, induced, or combination variant
5. *Phenomenon: Predicted Behavior*	General statement
6. *Observer*	Method, conditions, and "set"

II. PROPAEDEUTIC ANALYSIS

A. Observational Process: Descriptive

7. *Type of Data*	Form: Written narrative, audio, video Type of record: Specimen, time, event, trait, field unit
8. *Morphoanalysis*	Identification of developmental elements in the stream of behavior which participate in the particular issue under study
9. *Identification of Patterns in Developmental Elements*	Coincident and successive behaviors within an observational segment

---

B. Informal Confirmation: Same Data

10. *Identification of Changes in Specific Presentation of Morphological Elements and Patterns over Time*	Application to successive observations

TABLE 2 *(Continued)*

11. *Preliminary Hypothesis Formulation*	Descriptive "fit" to data
	Reapplication of formulations in 8-10
	Substatistical criteria:
	  (a) Frequency
	  (b) Variability
	  (c) Validity
	  (d) Reliability (optional)
	  (e) Probability

12. *Reformulation*	Sharpening of descriptive results through successive reapplication and re-examination of the data Substatistical criteria (11)
13. *Firmly Data-Based Hypothesis Generation*	Final results of reformulation (12)

III. FORMAL SYSTEMATIC CONFIRMATION

New Data

14. *Formulation of Measures*	Using descriptive results from 8-10, apply to new data, e.g., constructing content of scales, categories
15. *Hypothesis Testing*	Hypotheses from 13 applied to new observational data Statistical criteria
16. *Experimental Methods*	Hypothesis testing: major and subquestions from 13 and 15 Statistical criteria

---

discussion of the types of natural study presented in the first part of this paper. The setting, the subjects, the phenomenon, and the method of observation should be viewed as independent aspects that can be varied in the degree of naturalness versus control. These decisions are choices of the investigator. Optimum use depends upon an astute and explicit analysis of the practicalities of what is available, the state of the art in the subject matter, and, finally, the purpose of interest to the researcher: hypothesis generation or testing.

PROPAEDEUTIC ANALYSIS

Data analysis with natural data can take many forms. Some developmental ethologists carefully record behavior in natural settings, and then analyze it in traditional statistical ways. Blurton-Jones and Leach (1972), observing mothers leaving their children in a play group, counted the frequency of certain types of behavior and compared criers and noncriers, across behavior modalities and behavior situations. Anderson (1972) carried out statistical analyses on time and distance parameters with various mother-child behaviors. He observed mothers and their babies playing in parks, natural miniseparations in the baby's movements to and away from the mother.

Quasi-experimental designs (Campbell and Stanley, 1966) may be used in conjunction with statistical counting methods. Wright (1960) outlines several major methods used in observational studies which range from simple to relatively complex and sophisticated: (a) ratings of behavior prevalence, which are summed across larger categories, (b) frequency counts, (c) duration scores, (d) frequency scores by time units, and (e) frequency of types within a behavior category. In these methods certain behaviors or behavior patterns are judged a priori as salient to the issues under study. The natural data are then scanned or divided into appropriate units.

An intermediate quantitative method that attempts to capture more qualitative features is the application of rating scales or clinical profile categories (see Heinicke et al., 1973; Pine and Furer, 1963) *to* the mass of the data.

Yet another method will now be proposed that occupies an intermediate position between strictly statistical applications and purely clinical methods. The propaedeutic[3] analysis of natural observations is the preliminary, careful, and systematic search in the natural phenomena for the variables relevant to the science. Both instruction and discipline should be emphasized as fundamental features of this method.

---

[3] "Propaedeutic: Pertaining to or of the nature of preliminary instruction: supplying the knowledge or discipline introductory or preliminary to some art or science: preliminarily educational." (*The Oxford English Dictionary*, Oxford University Press, 1971). (My thanks to Dr. Katharine Smith for bringing this descriptively pithy term to my attention.)

This portion of the model elaborates a process that is merely referred to by ethologists as "a behavior analysis." Although they name it, they do not present the method itself.

As Medawar has aptly stated (see above, p. 163), the initial process of pattern recognition cannot be easily illustrated, since it involves a series of "imaginative conjectures" by the researcher from the observations. There are many false starts that have to be discarded when further observations prove them to be unfounded. Others are poorly formulated and are successively reformulated from the data. So far the process is analogous to familiar, good clinical practice. The purpose of this analysis is systematically to press clinical synthesis from observational material several steps further.

Lewin's (1936) method of "gradual approximation" to define fundamental structures and processes is an applicable concept here. "The procedure . . . is to make the original structure more specific and differentiated . . . The representation in the first approximation will not be destroyed but only made more articulated by the second approximation since the whole situation is taken into account from the beginning" (p. 17).

The basic assumption of the propaedeutic analysis is that statistical principles may be applied substatistically in achieving successive approximations in identifying behavior patterns. It can be argued that this procedure is both defensible and essential when the purpose of analysis is data-based hypothesis generation, i.e., to retain the richness and complexity of the original natural observations while considerably increasing the rigor and systematic organization of the data.

The systematic research character of this analysis is delineated in the criteria for the formulation of descriptive hypotheses (see Table 3). These principles articulate a procedure by which to realize Medawar's "imaginative conjecture," used by the ethologists, or Lewin's "gradual approximations."

All of these principles (except multiple judges) were used in the separation study as criteria for evolving increasingly adequate hypothesis fit.

The efficacy of the initial formulations, as Medawar remarks, depends upon their appearance in further observations. As we know from clinical experience, a single observation can produce

TABLE 3

PROPAEDEUTIC ANALYSES:
SUBSTATISTICAL CRITERIA FOR HYPOTHESIS FORMULATION

Statistical Principle	Propaedeutic Analysis
Frequency	Appearance of the behavior or sequence in other observations
Variability	Accounting for negative instances of the behavior (a) Nonappearance (b) Different form or pattern (c) Changing context and associated variables
Validity	Quality of fit between repeated instances of observed behavior and the descriptive inference, hypothesis, or concept
Reliability	Multiple judges
Probability	Frequency of appearance relative to the sample size

inferences and hypotheses at many levels of abstraction. When other observations are searched, however, the same phenomena may or may not appear. Does a behavior sequence identified as important in one or several observations appear in others? When further observations are searched initially, the case is, more often, that the phenomena do not appear in quite the same form (low frequency, low validity). Through successive stages of examining and reworking the raw data, inferences and hypotheses regarding developmental patterns are discarded, reformulated, and sharpened (increasing frequency and validity).

In actual practice with natural observational data, and certainly with as broad a range of behavior as is seen in the separation situation, this process is repeated over and over to achieve the final hypotheses.

Negative instances further define the phenomenon. What are the conditions of the nonappearance of a behavior sequence when an initial formulation about it would suggest its appearance? The behavioral sequence may not appear in quite the same form, a kind of negative instance that requires reformulation of the initial statements. New forms of the phenomenon may be produced from changing context or changing associated developments, another type of negative data. A final form of negative data is behavior ordinarily observed under certain conditions (e.g., at certain ages) unexpectedly occurring in others. All of these forms of negative data must be searched and accounted for in the hypothesis development.

Interjudge reliability may also be used at this stage, but only as supporting the probability of hypothesis fit; it cannot be construed as proof. Applying rating scales or the like to the data from which they were drawn is not technically correct in hypothesis testing. However, multiple judges may be used as another guide to hypothesis fit (and in preparation of measures for use in later hypothesis testing).

Remaining very close to the behavioral data in successive reformulations of hypotheses is a form of internal verification—a measure of validity. A criterion used for this is the quality of illustration or "fit" to the inference. Do the numerous examples of behavior clearly make the same point, or, put another way, is the observed behavior accurately described by the inference being made?

When these criteria are applied, and the phenomena thus delineated appear with high frequency across the observations in the given sample, the probability of statistically significant findings is greatly increased.

These criteria are applied to the data in several steps:

1. The first formulations
2. Reapplication of the first formulations to the data
3. Reformulations as demanded by the re-examination of the data in (2)
4. Reapplication of the reformulations to the data
5. Successive and continued reapplications to the data followed by reformulations of hypotheses and concepts.

This analysis can be extremely sensitive clinically, but it differs from general clinical hypothesis generation in several ways. Detailed moment-by-moment behavior narratives (video or written) are the primary data across many observational periods. These narratives are reviewed repeatedly to correct and refine successive hypotheses regarding patterns, using substatistical concepts of frequency, variability, validity, probability (possibly reliability). Finally, this model is intended for descriptive behavioral hypothesis generation (primary behavior pattern recognition and structure), not for interpretive, dynamic hypothesis generation (clinical meaning).

The rigor of the propaedeutic analysis depends upon the total commitment of the researcher to the data: his willingness to immerse himself systematically in the behavioral narrative, and to stay with the behavior itself. It also depends upon the researcher's capacity to retain critical distance from his own processes of inference and hypothesis formation, a dogged willingness to review, to check and recheck his clinical hunches.

FORMAL SYSTEMATIC CONFIRMATION

With hypotheses, concepts, and questions now carefully formulated from the natural observations, high-probability hypothesis testing can be carried out. Hypothesis formulation in the propaedeutic analysis will yield descriptive results that will become the criteria or definitions for formal measures: for example, rating scales, categories of behavior, types of behavior sequences.

Some hypotheses will require new natural observational data. Other hypotheses will be already amenable to experimental methods, and such designs can at this stage be determined by knowledge of the necessary natural conditions.

Questions will also be raised—associated developments and the like—for which the original data may not be sufficient, and that require additional observational data, or a reimmersion in the original data from different points of view. Thus Tinbergen's (1973) "seesawing" becomes a highly productive way of working. Further propaedeutic natural studies may be done, natural experiments and formal experiments. The researcher may move among these methods with major questions and subquestions as the character of the formulations can now dictate.

Piaget's work on the development of thought in children is an example par excellence of the multiple use of the methodological continuum. In his use of what he terms the "clinical method" (1927) he retains a closeness to the natural flow of the child's thought by a highly judicious and sensitive use of direct observations, questioning, natural testing, and formal testing, pointing out the limits of validity in each of these steps. "The good experimenter must in fact unite two often incompatible qualities, he must know how to observe, that is to say let the child talk freely, without ever checking or side-tracking his utterance, and at the same time he must constantly be alert for something definitive, at every moment he must have some working hypothesis, some theory, true or false, which he is seeking to check . . . and the material it yields needs subjecting to the strictest criticism" (1927, p. 9).

From his highly detailed observations, coupled with tailored experiments, on his own three babies, to the interviews, discussions, and more formal experiments with older children in the later work, Piaget ranges among a wide variety of methods. They differ in their systematic character, and each is chosen to suit very particular goals and constraints. That is, he uses less formal methods for a purpose, retaining a closeness to the live phenomena even as he moves toward more formal hypothesis-testing methods.

The hypothesis-generating model is based on a conception of systematic scientific method as a continuum from natural to formal (see Figure 1 above). While the efforts of the observational researcher are intended to move increasingly to the formal, the continuum may be entered at any point. Which point depends upon choices that take into account (1) limitations of available data and setting, (2) intrinsic requirements of the phenomenon and subjects, as well as (3) the selected purposes of data analysis.

Once the continuum is entered, movement along it, as Tinbergen's metaphor suggests, may be—and perhaps in developmental research ought to be—multidirectional among a variety of methods, determined by the status of hypothesis formulation. The less formal methodologies should not be viewed as less scientific. When the systematic criteria are clearly defined and the differential purposes delimited, they in fact function as intrinsic and essential elements in the total scientific progression.

THE MODEL ILLUSTRATED: A SEPARATION STUDY

An application of the three parts of this model will be illustrated by the design considerations and outcome of a study of infants and toddlers who were separating daily from their mothers.

The growing literature on separation describes either the child's immediate distress in new and strange environments and unfamiliar laboratories (e.g., Shirley, 1942; Heathers, 1954; Ainsworth and Bell, 1970a, 1970b; Rheingold, 1969; Cox and Campbell, 1968; Maccoby and Feldman, 1972; Stayton and Ainsworth, 1973) or the longer-term and more traumatic distress seen in various kinds of institutionalization (e.g., Spitz, 1945, 1946; Schaffer, 1958; Robertson and Bowlby, 1952; Robertson, 1952, 1953; Bowlby, 1960, 1961, 1969, 1973; Heinicke and Westheimer, 1966).

The total sequence of the child's behavior attending the mother's brief departures in familiar settings has not been studied in the earliest years of life. The purpose of this study was to examine brief natural separations in order to illuminate the natural progression of separating as a developmental adaptive task.

I. THE SITUATIONAL ANALYSIS

Since it is through the mother's everyday comings and goings that the infant/toddler comes to separate temporally and spatially from her, homes are, of course, the ideal setting. For many practical reasons, studying the natural phenomenon at home presents major difficulties: getting cooperating families, making complex time arrangements to coincide with the mother's natural movements and departures, technical problems in observing unobtrusively, to name but a few.

The Setting

The Infant Day Care Unit[4] presented itself as a nearly ideal alternative for study. Its program was designed on a home model. Physically, it is made up of three small apartments and a pram room, furnished, except for the third-year rooms, like homes. Caregivers are selected for their maternal pleasure in caring for

[4] The Infant Care Unit of the Child Development Center of the Jewish Board of Guardians, New York City. My grateful thanks to Dr. Roy K. Lilleskov, Director, Ms. Thelma Mihalov, Administrative Director, and Dr. Helen M. Schur, for the wide variety of aid and thought they gave during the course of the separation study.

babies as well as for their attentiveness and sensitivity to individual needs. They become important attachment figures themselves. Close relationships with families are developed so that the nursery will be as much an extension of the child's own home as possible. In fact, the nursery is in the same building where most of the babies live. Finally, it has the advantage of having mothers' and caregivers' natural comings and goings on site. The practical coordination of being there to observe unobtrusively is thus enormously simplified.

In this setting more ordinary occurrences of separation into familiar and generally gratifying environments could be studied. The nursery context is one that specifically does not contain major disruptions in care, or stressors from stranger effects, but rather is one of continuity of both care and familiarity. It was precisely these homey qualities of the setting and the phenomena that drew my attention to studying the separations as developmental and adaptive processes rather than as disruptions.

The Phenomenon

From the point of view of the infant and toddler, the familiar day-care setting presents a rich array of emotionally important relationships and activities. The arrival situation, in its total sequence, is a very broad and complex behavioral context. A great deal of behavior can be observed that is clearly not distressed and that may or may not bear a relation to the departure of the mother. In the largest sense, the behavior seen reflects the baby's current developmental adaptations, that is, those that are externally provided by the environment and those that are generated by the infant himself.

What was studied as the emerging capacity to separate were those multiple developments that come to be used with increasing specificity, complexity, and structure by the baby in relation to the departure of the mother. The regular leaving of these infants in this nursery is regarded, *for these infants,* as a natural event in their lives. It parallels the periodic baby-sitting arrangements that children in this culture almost inevitably experience, often with some regularity. It is, in fact, via these sorts of separations that babies in general come, over time, to be able to part from their mothers.

The Observer

The arrival observations used in this study were written behavioral narratives, part of a series of observations collected in a framework of regular clinical developmental evaluation of each child and his progress in the nursery. Observations were also made regularly in play, feeding, and departure situations.

The observer set and training for all of the situations was behavioral and broadly developmental. That is, observers were trained to attend unselectively to the total presentation of behavior: motor behavior, motor coordination, vocalizations and verbalizations, emotions, interaction with caregivers and other children, sensory awareness and alertness, interactions with objects in manipulative, exploratory, and play behavior.

The observations were made without reference to particular developmental hypotheses and without respect to the particular content of the separation situation as a developmental phenomenon. In fact, systematic research issues were not being pursued during the period of these observations.

In addition to the author, the observers were a child psychoanalyst, the unit's administrating nurse, and several graduate students in developmental and school psychology.

In Table 4 the situational analysis for the separation study is summarized in terms of the model.

II. The Propaedeutic Analysis

To isolate separation behavior and study it alone, in its natural presentation, would have required predetermining and defining operationally beforehand what a separation "reaction" is, in the first three years of life, in order to distinguish it from the rest of the child's behavior. I chose to adopt a naïve and essentially atheoretical point of view in order to learn what the sequence of separation behavior is in its natural presentation and how it changes over time.

The Form of the Data

Studies that are natural in terms of the setting, the phenomena, *and* the form of the data permit any particular developmental issue

TABLE 4

SITUATIONAL ANALYSIS
SEPARATION STUDY

1. *Type of Setting*	Infant day-care program: daily, all-day, alternate care Familiar, regular part of the children's lives A natural behavioral setting
2. *Subjects*	Babies, ages 3 months to 3 years, regularly separating from their mothers each day Babies of "high-risk" families, but nursery developments within relatively normal ranges of health
3. *Phenomenon: Behavioral Situation*	Morning arrival: observation time 20-40 minutes Natural presentation
4. *Phenomenon: Stimulus Characteristics of Situation*	Arrival in the nursery Departure of the mother Both as they naturally occur, no experimental manipulation
5. *Phenomenon: Predicted Behavior*	Emergence of responses specific to mother's departure, increasing in complexity, leading developmentally to increasingly structured child-generated modes of adaptation
6. *Observer: Task and Set*	Trained observers, regular observations in a variety of situations, principally used for general developmental assessment, secondarily for research Observer attention unselectively to the total stream of behavior, to include generally relevant developmental behavior: motor, motor coordination, vocal, verbal, affect, sensory-perceptual, interpersonal activities, interaction with objects, play

to be viewed in its relation to the total behavioral context in which it occurs. The narrative observation used in this study is a natural "slice of life"; thus the behavior seen relates to a whole spectrum of developments, among them at times, separation.

The extensive behavioral description which is called an "ethogram" in ethology is termed a "specimen description" in psychology by Wright (first so named by Dresslar, 1901, quoted in Wright, 1960). "The observer is in no way deliberately selective. He is instead deliberately unselective in the sense that he aims to make a faithful record of 'everything' as it comes in the behavior and situation of the child" (p. 83).

The data for this study consisted of 20- to 40-minute written running specimen accounts of moment-to-moment behavior of each child, beginning with his appearance in the nursery and including details of interaction with children, adults, and objects in the environment. Behavior was recorded in detailed visual and auditory terms.

Interpretive description was elaborated by reference to observed behavior, or otherwise set apart in the narrative as observer impressions, "hunches," or questions. Hence the observer emphasis is on accuracy and specificity in recording the observed behavior of each child: what happened, when, where, with whom, or with what.

These observations were made by single observers only; the author's own observations were all completed before the data analysis was begun. Consequently, formal interobserver agreements were not systematically available. However, as Wright points out, "such records need as many reliability coefficients as they contain classes of statements about different facets of behavior and situations. Their reliabilities must differ from one to another of such categories" (p. 86). Observer reliability studies that have been carried out on natural observational records are of the specific categories of behavior under study and not of total records (see Jersild and Fite, 1939; Lafore, 1945; Tucker, 1940; Biber et al., 1942).

A total of 167 observations on 22 children ranging from 1½ to 40 months were recorded. From one to 20 observations were made on any one child.

This distribution has obvious limitations from the point of view of systematic hypothesis-testing research. I was prompted to develop a hypothesis-generating descriptive method precisely by this limitation in the data distribution, which prevented consideration of hypothesis testing. Years would be required to amass full longitudinal data, and yet many hours of richly detailed material were already available.

Many of the babies were observed repeatedly over time, but generally the data were used cross-sectionally. What behaviors appear at any given age level? Do they appear in the same form at other ages? In what ways do they change from one age to another? What new behaviors appear? The cross-sectional view of the data was extended across the age range under study; behaviors were compared and contrasted. Hence a developmental, process view of the behavior under study—i.e., longitudinal—was inferred. Normative use has been made of cross-sectional data, especially in time and event sampling studies (Wright, 1960).

Escalona et al. (1952), in their study of early personality development, used cross-sectional data in a similar way.

From the outset, we knew that if our cross-sectional data were to support our every hunch, if all the hypothesized relationships could be demonstrated to exist (for our sample), we would still have failed to "prove" anything. However, we would have accomplished some steps which may be essential preliminaries to the more rigorous study of developmental processes which will probably require longitudinal methods.

The dividing line between exploratory-descriptive research on the one hand, and validating research on the other, is not so sharp as our formulation may suggest. Absolute validation, which would imply among other things, completely accurate calculation of probable error and complete control of all relevant variables, is an illusion. The underlying imperfections of method, and of logic, are much the same for both types of research. Heuristically, the dichotomy has much to recommend it, especially as it helps to establish the inherent limitation of a research enterprise such as ours [p. 25].

Morphoanalysis

Using the propaedeutic analysis, particular developmental areas were identified from the observations as participating in distinct ways in the changing capacity to separate from the mother. These were briefly: (1) visual perception, (2) affects, especially distress, (3) motor and locomotor behavior, (4) play, (5) attachments (object relations), and (6) cognition: anticipation, conception of space and time, and symbolization. All of these were traced first as general developments and then as they came to be used specifically with respect to the mother's departure. The changing forms of distress behavior will be used to illustrate the model.

Patterns in Developmental Elements and Changes over Time

The appearance of distress changes in both form and frequency. The changing form was found to relate to achievements in the other areas identified above. Once distress begins to appear in these infants, it clearly does not appear all of the time. Other factors were found to supersede or modify the appearance of distress. These were the nursery setting itself, the multiple caregivers, changing relationships with them and with the other children, and emerging play interests. These came to have a strong drawing power, were gratifying to the toddlers, and at times were simply more interesting than the departure of the mother.

Periods of changing patterns were found in these children, and five successive stages were identified in the changing forms of distress. To illustrate and give a flavor of the transformation of the raw narrative data into these patterns, some observations and formulations from the second year of life will be presented below.

The observations are unedited continuous sequences taken from far longer narratives. The portion of the total protocol specifically relating to separation changed in duration from a few minutes in the first year to the major portion (or even more than a 40-minute narrative) in the third year.

In these children a gradual development was seen, from visual fixing and tracking accompanied by affective brightening and subduing, to brief focal distress at the departure of the mother, in the first year. Two separate forms of distress were seen in the second year: the brief, immediate distress continues to appear, and there also begins to appear a period of diffuse distress behavior extending well after the mother's departure.

While the immediate focal response to the mother's departure can be fairly intense, the period of diffuse distress following the mother's departure is generally not intense but is, rather, quite subdued. The babies may be somewhat more random in their play, less attentive to it. They may go from toy to toy, or from person to person, without connecting with anything especially pleasurable. They may have difficulty engaging with their surroundings, or they may encounter difficulties once they do so. There may be moments of rather immobile gazing about and seeming to turn inward. There may be somewhat more aggressive behavior, and nonspecific movements toward the door. There is frequently a generalized irritable dissatisfaction.

The combinations and sequences of these behaviors are quite varied. What is common to all of them is that ordinary modes of relating to the environment are disrupted for a time following the mother's departure. In these observations, this time period gradually lengthens over the course of the year. Focal and diffuse distress may or may not be seen together.

Obs. 60: Jim (12 months). Jim[5] continues to cry softly now and lies his head on J.'s bosom, resting there while still sobbing very softly. J. stands Jim on the sofa and he stops crying completely and he stares blankly out of the windows for a few seconds; his hands are touching a notebook, he tries to get it but cannot reach it. He finds the pair of pants his mother had left with J. before, takes them, looks at Obs. (who is sitting on the rocking chair next to the sofa) and shows them to Obs. *His face is still serious but does not show the tenseness it had before he started to cry.*[6] J. takes the notebook he was trying to read and he follows her attentively with his eyes. Jim *takes the pacifier* which is hanging from his neck, *puts it in his mouth,* sits down and *stares blankly at the empty room.* J. offers him her hand, he takes it but *without paying much attention to her; he sucks at the pacifier very hard while looking around.* J. puts the TV music box on the window sill. Jim stands up as soon as he sees it and starts manipulating the buttons. He looks at the different turning pictures *but his expression is still sober.* When the music stops he looks out the window. N. comes in, he turns his head and looks at the door. Cook approaches them and he looks at her with interest. J. and Cook start to talk out of the window to F. and Amy

Immediate focal distress

Diffuse distress

---

[5] Children are referred to by three-letter names, caregivers by initials, and mother as mother.

[6] Observations most salient to the point at issue are italicized.

who are playing in the park outside. Jim follows them
with great attention and leans out of the window to see
F. and Amy. J. turns around to Jim and hands him the
music box. Jim takes it and starts banging it against the
sofa. He stops for a second, *looks blankly out of the
window, and vocalizes very softly.* (Obs.: Bucatinsky)[7]

Approximately 7 minutes after his mother has left, Jim recovers
and begins to manipulate the music box with interest and concentration, swaying his body to the sound.

Jim is subdued in all aspects of his behavior. Motorically he is
relatively inactive, spending the whole of this 7-minute segment
sitting or standing on the couch. His attention alternates between
brief periods of interest in people and things and blank staring.
Along with these attentional shifts his affect is sober and muted. A
period of heightened distress is observed in his hard sucking on the
pacifier. In terms of object relations, he relates only briefly and
rather peripherally to the book, the observer, the caregiver, the
music box, other staff, and activities seen through the window.

In the following observation, immediate focal distress is not
observed. This child becomes very much occupied in watching
other toddlers' arrivals. Her emotions range from being rather
muted to open affective distress. While she attracts caregivers'
attention, and there are play sequences, she does not fully engage
herself with them; all are brief.

Obs. 75: Pat (15¾ months). Amy runs in ahead of her
mother and Pat *watches Amy's mother intently,* a toy
key bunch hanging from her mouth. Amy throws herself
on the floor crying bitterly and Pat watches her *and then
walks over to her. She looks puzzled* and chews on the
key. Somebody turns on the record player and S. starts
dancing with Amy and Pat. Amy's mother leaves and
Amy cries and fusses. *Pat looks at her with an astonished
and perplexed expression.* F. picks up Amy and Pat
follows them, her *expression changing from astonish-*

Diffuse
distress

---

[7] My special thanks to the observers at the Infant Care Unit: Thelma
Mihalov, R. N., Helen M. Schur, M.D., Blanca Masor, M.A., Miriam Bucan-
tinsky, M.A., and Inge King.

ment to sadness and almost crying. S. calls her and makes a few steps towards her but then *she looks* again *forlorn,* but then she apparently becomes aware of the music again or recalled the previous "dance," and she steps almost rhythmically alternatingly to the left and then to the right.

S. now takes her hand and *Pat looks at her sober-faced.* S. picks her up and lifts her on the couch and looks out of the window with her. Amy is right next to them, looking out too.

Max arrives and Amy calls him. Pat watches them with interest and then again moves with the music. She claps her hands when the music stops. Max now kisses his mother and *Pat watches them with a forlorn and then astonished expression.* J. comes in and Pat climbs off the couch slowly and carefully. She then makes a few dance steps, falls, gets up looking unperturbed, makes again a few dance steps and then watches J., who now plays with Amy on the floor. *She walks over to them very slowly.* J. smiles at her and Pat responds with a *long sober-faced gaze.* Amy points out something and Pat watches with her mouth open. F. walks out of the room and Pat makes dancing steps. Bet arrives and F. comes back and takes Bet and Pat to the Pram Room. J. is still sitting on the floor, talks to Pat, who has followed Bet and Max to the door. Max and Bet come back and Pat *watches them intently across the blocked entrance. She then plays with the doorknob.*

Amy fusses and Pat turns around and looks at her in consternation. She then lifts up her skirt, thus baring her chest. She looks intently at Amy who lifts her shirt in response. She then looks at J. N. passes by and Amy shouts. Pat turns around, looks at her and then at J., who is close by. The music plays again, S. claps her hands and Pat approaches Amy and dances a few steps with her. Still dancing, she looks around the room and then falls out of step. Amy stops dancing and walks away. *Pat watches her with a sad expression.* Amy shouts and N. enters the room and Pat follows. Amy

fusses as N. walks into the kitchen and blocks the
entrance. *Pat watches Amy with an astonished expression.* J. takes Amy on her lap and *Pat watches her,
looking sad.* J. stretches her arms out and pulls Pat
toward her. She embraces Pat and rocks with her and
Recovery   Amy. *Pat still looks sad,* but as Amy leaves Pat smiles
and *snuggles up to J.*   (Obs.: Schur)

Pat still looks sad as the observation ends after 12 minutes. She
smiles and snuggles as a caregiver takes her into her arms.

There are many observations during the second year when
there is little or no observable distress or disruption. The attachments, the sights, sounds, and activity potentials of the nursery
take the center of attention. Children move to other gratifications,
other interests, apart from the mother, her departure, and
separation from her. The care routines diminish considerably
during the arrival time at this stage; that is, feeding, diapering,
and putting to sleep. The caregivers now become, more and more,
play providers and, later, even more, play partners. Relationships
and activities with caregivers and other children become important
to the second-year toddlers.

Obs. 74: Kit (15½ months). Mother opens the door and
Kit looks at us with a broad smile on her face. She comes
in walking by herself, while her mother holds the door.
She smiles, stays in the middle of the room, looks at Obs.
and comes to Obs. with her arms extended and smiling.
Mother, who until now was staying at the door, walks to
the kitchen saying "Hello." Kit does not look at her; she
touches Obs.'s hand very quickly, smiles and *goes to
Sue, who is near the playpen. Sue reaches out for her,
and Kit puts her hand around Sue's neck; they stay like
that for a few seconds, looking at each other, Kit smiling
and Sue vocalizing.*   (Obs.: Mazor)

Obs. 108: Pat (20¾ months). Mother brings Pat, both
are smiling and laughing as they stop at the stoop and
mother takes Pat's jacket off. *At that moment, Amy
comes and both children greet each other joyfully.
There is a short interchange about their pacifiers and a*

doll. They both then run into the corridor, Pat's mother watches them smiling tenderly. Pat's mother then joins the girls announcing that she and Pat would put Pat's pacifier in her crib. They vanish into the bedroom while Amy re-enters the Red Room. Pat comes back with mother still holding the doll. Mother says, "Bye-bye, baby," smiling and lingering at the door. At that moment, J. comes and Pat jumps in excitement; she shouts and drops the doll. At that moment, mother leaves. One can hear her talk in the hallway. Pat shouts, "Bye-bye!" F. says, "Let me have the baby [doll], let me sew it and fix it," and she picks up the doll. Pat watches F. sewing, while Amy picks up the needles.

(Obs.: Schur)

Toward the end of the second year, the brief focal distress and the diffuse distress appear to consolidate into a few months of regular and prolonged focal distress. This happens despite the attentiveness of sensitive and experienced caregivers. After this stage, the children begin to develop complex social and symbolic methods for modulating feelings and behavior themselves in the separation situation.

The natural observations, together with the natural analysis, illuminated these developmentally changing forms of distress. These distress patterns would probably not have been recognized by the usual experimental or hypothesis-testing techniques, with a priori decisions about what constitutes distress behavior. The experimental literature of low-intensity nontraumatic separations does not deal with the total lengthy sequence of behavior after the mother's departure or with changes in these sequences over time. Negative instances—e.g., when babies do not show distress—which are a critical part of this model are not accounted for in the experimental literature, though the reported incidence is large.

The appearance of the brief focal distress of the late first year and the circumscribed period of prolonged focal distress of the late second year appear to belong in a developmental continuum of distress. When these forms of distress are viewed in their natural context, quite different associated developments suggest that they represent very different levels of coping in the separation situation.

Laboratory studies have concerned themselves with amount and specific types of distress (crying, searching, following) and with stranger and attachment effects, at different ages cross-sectionally. The laboratory assumption seems to be that distress is the same at all ages. Studying the natural daily separations of children and their mothers over long periods highlighted the importance of other developments as contributors to changes in the specific form of distress.

In addition, without the detailed moment-by-moment behavior narratives, the diffuse distress, for example, of the second year would not have been found. The experienced caregivers who were living these separations daily with these children did not connect this form of distress with the departure of the mother. The data suggest that this diffuse distress in the absence of the mother increases over the second year, eventually merging and consolidating with the emergence of prolonged focal distress at the end of the second year.

Nowhere does theory regarding separation suggest that there should be such a sequential change, and laboratory procedures would not have suggested these hypotheses.

The propaedeutic analysis for the separation study is summarized in terms of the model in Table 5. A fuller presentation of the separation study is made in the following paper.

III. The Formal Confirmation

It should be clear by this point that the propaedeutic, hypothesis-generating analysis is considered as a first major phase. What follows is a branching and increasingly systematic series of applications to observational and experimental data. It is important to reaffirm here Tinbergen's (1973) notion of "seesawing." The propaedeutic analysis not only leads in linear fashion to formal hypothesis testing and experimental methods, it also leads back into the observational data for further propaedeutic analyses. For example, the morphoanalysis in the separation study (see Table 5) defined many areas for detailed pursuit. The patterns and changes in patterns outlined there represent only some of the material that was and is yet to be delineated from the morphoanalysis of the data.

TABLE 5
PROPAEDEUTIC ANALYSIS
SEPARATION STUDY

A. Observational Process: Descriptive	
7. *Data*	Narrative report, detailed written Objective, descriptive, behavioral Specimen records
8. *Morphoanalysis*	Visual perception Affects: especially distress Motor and locomotor behavior Play Attachments Cognition: Anticipation 　　　　　Conception of space and time 　　　　　Symbolization
9. *Patterns in Developmental Elements*	Elements appear first as contextual general developments. Then stage-specific coordination of developments in each element appear with respect to the mother's departure.

B. Informal Confirmation	
10-13 *Data-Based Hypotheses*	Increasing complexity in patterns, as more of the elements become available for use and at higher levels in the separation situation Cognitive-perceptual-emotional focalization of the departure of the mother 　(a) Limited focalization—first year 　(b) Full focalization—second year Stages II and IV focalizations as necessary conditions for Stage V Stages in the development of distress behavior: 　(i) Early months 　(ii) Emergence of behavior focal to 　-　mother's departure: brief 　(iii) Emergence of variable distress behavior 　　　　Focal 　　　　Diffuse 　(iv) Emergence of prolonged focal distress behavior 　(v) Emergence of structured, child-generated modulations of separation behavior

The outgrowth of this portion of the separation study that is most clearly ready for the formal systematic confirmation stages of the model is outlined in Table 6.

DISCUSSION

A major point of this and the accompanying paper on the separation study is to stress the importance for both clinicians and researchers of immersion in natural observation—the scientific importance of a devotion to the details of ongoing behavior and behavior sequences in the real-life situation of uncontrolled variables. As a *clinical* approach, this view is basic to the psycho-

TABLE 6

FORMAL SYSTEMATIC CONFIRMATION: SEPARATION STUDY

Formulation of Measures	Scales of the several forms of distress
	Scales of changing associated play and attachments over the three years
Hypothesis Testing	Conditions of variability by stage
	Variability across stages
	Distress
	Play
	Attachments
	Focal distress and prolonged distress developmentally precede child-generated modes of adaptation.
Experimental Methods	(A) Object Permanence (persons), in immediate time and space by stage (age)
	(B) Object Permanence (persons), in remote time and space by stage (age)
	Object Permanence Type A developmentally precedes Type B.
	Autonomic nervous system studies of mother's movements toward and away from the baby in the early months of the first year of life

analytic tradition. What is being presented in these papers is a *systematic* approach to discerning the natural regularities that emerge across multiple natural observations, to evolve systematic descriptive formulations *from* the data that in turn lead sequentially to increasingly rigorous hypothesis testing.

The developmental sequences presented in these papers as beginning in the first year and reaching a degree of coordination in the late second year preparatory to more self-modulated behavior in the third year are not immediately suggested by theories of separation, cognitive development, affective development, or person or object permanence. In this study, visual perception, affects, motor behavior, play, attachment, and cognition (anticipation, conception of space and time, and symbolization) were identified in the observations as participating in important and changing ways in the development of the child's responses to separation. On the face of it, this is a fairly obvious list—once stated. Yet, via the natural study, they were seen in the separation situation first as general developments. Only later does each, and in its own time, come to be used specifically in connection with the mother's departure. Though each of these developments has its own course and line of emergence, they are used in the separation situation in changing ways, coordinating in different ways, at different levels of development (see Werner, 1948, 1957, and Pine, 1971).

While theory has not suggested the specific course of these developments, neither does experimental work necessarily give form to such behavior sequences. It deals only with already formulated hypotheses, and constructs designs to choose among them. Hypotheses are not generated by the experimental method except as byproducts, through theorizing about test failure or the implications of unexpected findings. It is unlikely that experiments would have led, except by chance, to the selection of those particular developments and the modes of coordination that were seen in the natural setting.

Much of baby behavior in general is highly situation-sensitive. This is certainly so of separating. Such behavior can be studied most effectively in its natural presentation in natural settings. And it is precisely these complex sequences and interactions that are of greatest interest to psychoanalytically oriented researchers and clinicians. A systematic hypothesis-generating model for natural studies enables the clinician to identify the important variables and study their changing patterning and coordination.

The research model that has been presented in this paper leads to recognizing the variate, sequential, coordinate, and hierarchical features in behavior patterns. The construction of hypotheses that can account for these features of behavior then follows. This model occupies an intermediate position on the continuum between systematic clinical thought and hypothesis-testing method. In effect, this model lies at a methodological interface between the traditional, careful, psychoanalytic clinical observation, developmental theory construction, and controlled validation.

It demands an adherence *to the data* in a continuous reformulation of hypotheses consistent with the data. To the extent that the researcher allows the data to speak for themselves and rigorously adheres to validation criteria within them, the method *may be* essentially atheoretical. An effortful intention to unbias oneself about the data can be a systematic analogue to free-floating attention. For the psychoanalytically oriented researcher, it is a method that can be extraordinarily fruitful in cross-fertilization between psychoanalysis and other behavioral and developmental sciences.

For example, in the separation study, the inference that a central relationship exists between person permanence and the immediate experience of separating evolved from the data. Piaget's cognitive theories were not a particular guide in my approach to these data, either in terms of play or of object permanence. And certainly the differentiation between the permanence of immediate persons and of remote persons arose from the data themselves, in the succession and duration of the different types of distress. The data themselves seemed to call for such constructs.

In fact, my initial interest was in how babies and toddlers deal with separation anxiety (coping, defense), i.e., anxiety at the mother's departure as a given. This construct has to be abandoned, since the babies and toddlers were clearly not always distressed. Nor could one necessarily posit from undistressed behavior that anxiety, formerly there, was being successfully and smoothly defended against or coped with. Thus I was compelled by the data to look at the development of distress itself, as a precursor, as it turned out, to the development of adaptive coping, or defenses, much, much later.

The heart of this methodology is the degree of critical doubt that the clinician or clinical researcher is willing to maintain, and the choice of appropriate tests to apply in seeking increasingly systematic validation of his ideas, from substatistical systematic internal testing to formal hypothesis testing. Doubt and the exercise of informed choice are crucial in this model.

The major point embodied in this paper and its companion piece is the importance for scientific study of lingering over the systematic propaedeutic phase—the rigorous utilization of the natural data themselves to provide a more powerful base for hypothesis generating and testing. The variety of methodologies that fall within this phase take their place on a continuum of purposes and rigor in a total conception of scientific method.

REFERENCES

Ainsworth, M. D. S., & Bell, S. M. (1970a), Attachment, Exploration, and Separation: Illustrated by the Behavior of One-Year-Olds in a Strange Situation. *Child Devel.*, 41:49-67.

——— ——— (1970b), Attachment and Exploratory Behavior of One-Year-Olds in a Strange Situaiton. In: *Determinants of Infant Behavior*, Vol. 4, ed. B. M. Foss. London: Methuen.

——— & Witting, B. A. (1969), Attachment and Exploratory Behavior of One-Year-Olds in a Strange Situation. In: *Determinants of Infant Behavior*, Vol. 4, ed. B. M. Foss. London: Methuen.

Anderson, J. (1972), Attachment Behavior Out of Doors. In: *Ethological Studies of Child Behaviour*, ed. N. G. Blurton-Jones. Cambridge: Cambridge University Press.

Anthony, E. J. (1968), On Observing Children. In: *Foundations of Child Psychiatry*, ed. E. Miller. Oxford & New York: Pergamon.

Barker, R. G., ed. (1960), *The Stream of Behavior*. New York: Appleton-Century-Crofts.

——— (1968), *Ecological Psychology*. Stanford, Cal.: Stanford University Press.

Biber, B., Murphy, L. B., Woodcock, L. D., & Black, I. S. (1942), *Child Life in School: A Study of a Seven-Year-Old Group*. New York: Dutton.

Blurton-Jones, N. G. (1972), Characteristics of Ethological Studies of Human Behaviour. In: *Ethological Studies of Child Behaviour*, ed. N. G. Blurton-Jones. Cambridge: Cambridge University Press.

——— & Leach, G. (1972), Behaviour of Children and Their Mothers at Separation and Greeting. In: *Ethological Studies of Child Behaviour*, ed. N. G. Blurton-Jones. Cambridge: Cambridge University Press.

Bowlby, J. (1960), Grief and Mourning in Early Infancy and Childhood. *The Psychoanalytic Study of the Child*, 15:9-52. New York: International Universities Press.
—— (1961), Processes of Mourning. *Internat. J. Psycho-Anal.*, 42:317-340.
—— (1969), *Attachment and Loss*, Vol. 1. *Attachment*. New York: Basic Books.
—— (1973), *Attachment and Loss*, Vol. 2. *Separation, Anxiety and Danger*. New York: Basic Books.
Brazelton, T. B., Koslowski, B., & Main, M. (1974), The Origins of Reciprocity: The Early Mother-Infant Interaction. In: *The Effect of the Infant on Its Caregiver*, ed. M. Lewis & L. Rosenblum. New York: Wiley, pp. 49-76.
Campbell, D. T., & Stanley, J. C. (1966), *Experimental and Quasi-Experimental Designs for Research*. Chicago: Rand McNally.
Chein, I. (1972), *The Science of Behavior and the Image of Man*. New York: Basic Books.
Cox, F. N., & Campbell, D. (1968), Young Children in a New Situation with and without Their Mothers. *Child Devel.*, 39:123-132.
Dragsten, S., & Lee, L. (1973), Infants' Social Behavior in Naturalistic vs. Experimental Setting. *Proc. 81st Ann. Convent. Amer. Psychol. Assn.*, 8:65-66.
Dresslar, F. B. (1901), A Morning's Observation of a Baby. *Pedag. Sem.*, 8:469-481.
Elsworth, P. C., Carlsmith, J., & Henson, A. (1972), The Stare as a Stimulus to Flight in Human Subjects: A Series of Field Experiments. *J. Pers. Soc. Psychol.*, 21:302-311.
Escalona, S. (1968), *The Roots of Individuality*. Chicago: Aldine.
—— et al. (1952), Early Phases of Personality Development: A Non-normative Study of Infant Behavior. *Monogr. Soc. Res. Child Devel.*, 17(1), No. 54.
Freud, S. (1920), Beyond the Pleasure Principle. *Standard Edition*, 18:7-64. London: Hogarth Press, 1958.
Goodrich, D. W. (1959), Observational Research with Emotionally Disturbed Children: Session I. *Amer. J. Orthopsychiat.*, 29:227-234.
Gump, S., Schoggen, P., & Redl, F. (1972), The Behavior of the Same Child in Different Milieus. In: *The Stream of Behavior*, ed. R. G. Barker. New York: Appleton-Century-Crofts.
Heathers, G. (1954), The Adjustment of Two-Year-Olds in a Novel Social Situation. *Child Devel.*, 25:147-158.
Heinicke, C. (1956), Some Effects of Separating Two-Year-Old Children from Their Parents: A Comparative Study. *Human Relat.*, 9:105-176.
—— Busch, F., Click, P., & Kramer, E. (1973), Parent-Child Relations; Adaptation to Nursery School and the Child's Task Orientation: A Contrast in the Development of Two Girls. In: *Individual Differences in Children*, ed. J. Westman. New York: Wiley.
—— & Westheimer, I. (1966), *Brief Separations*. New York: International Universities Press.
Hutt, S. J., & Hutt, C. (1970), *Direct Observation and Measurement of Behavior*. Springfield, Ill.: Charles C Thomas.
Jersild, A. T., & Fite, M. D. (1939), *The Influence of Nursery School Experience on Children's Social Adjustments*. New York: Columbia University Press.

Klüver, H. (1936), The Study of Personality and the Method of Equivalent and Non-equivalent Stimuli. *Character & Pers.*, 5:91-112.

Lafore, G. G. (1945), *Practices of Parents in Dealing with Preschool Children.* New York: Columbia University Press.

Lee, S. G. M., Wright, D. S., & Herbert, M. (in preparation), Aspects of the Development of Social Responsiveness in Young Children.

Lewin, K. (1936), *Principles of Topological Psychology.* New York: McGraw-Hill.

Lewis, M., & Lee-Painter, S. (1974), An Interactional Approach to the Mother-Infant Dyad. In: *The Effect of the Infant on Its Caregiver*, ed. M. Lewis & L. Rosenblum. New York: Wiley, pp. 21-47.

Maccoby, E. E., & Feldman, S. S. (1972), Mother-Attachment and Stranger-Reactions in the Third Year of Life. *Monog. Soc. Res. Child Devel.*, 37(1).

Marvin, R. S. (1972), Attachment and Communicative Behavior in Two-, Three-, and Four-Year-Old Children. Unpublished doctoral dissertation, University of Chicago.

McGrew, W. (1972), Aspects of Social Development in Nursery School Children. In: *Ethological Studies of Child Behavior*, ed. N. G. Blurton-Jones. Cambridge: Cambridge University Press.

Medawar, P. B. (1967), *The Art of the Soluble.* London: Methuen.

―――― (1973), Foreword. In: *The Animal in Its World: Explorations of an Ethologist*, N. Tinbergen. Cambridge, Mass.: Harvard University Press, pp. 9-12.

Murphy, L. B. (1962), *The Widening World of Childhood.* New York: Basic Books.

Piaget, J. (1927), *The Child's Conception of the World.* New York: Harcourt, Brace, 1929.

―――― (1936), *The Origins of Intelligence.* New York: International Universities Press, 1952.

Pine, F. (1971), On the Separation Process: Universal Trends and Individual Differences. In: *Separation-Individuation: Essays in Honor of Margaret S. Mahler*, ed. J. B. McDevitt & C. F. Settlage. New York: International Universities Press, pp. 113-130.

―――― & Furer, M. (1963), Studies of the Separation-Individuation Phases. A Methodological Overview. *The Psychoanalytic Study of the Child*, 19: 325-342. New York: International Universities Press.

Rheingold, H. L. (1969), The Effect of a Strange Environment on the Behavior of Infants. In: *Determinants of Infant Behavior*, Vol. 4, ed. B. M. Foss. London: Methuen.

Ricciuti, H. N., & Poresky, R. H. (1973), Development of Attachment to Caregivers in an Infant Nursery during the First Year of Life. Paper presented at the meeting of the Society for Research in Child Development, Philadelphia.

Robertson, J. (1952), Film: A Two-Year-Old Goes to the Hospital (16mm., 45 min.). London: Tavistock Child Development Research Unit. New York: New York University Film Library.

―――― (1953), Some Responses of Young Children to Loss of Maternal Care. *Nursing Times*, 49:382-386.

―――― & Bowlby, J. (1952), Responses of Young Children to Separation from Their Mothers. *Courr. Cent. Int. Enf.*, 2:131-142.

——— & Robertson, J. (1971), Young Children in Brief Separation: A Fresh Look. *The Psychoanalytic Study of the Child*, 26:264-315. New York: Quadrangle.

Schaffer, H. R. (1958), Objective Observations of Personality Development in Early Infancy. *Brit. J. Med. Psychol.*, 31:174-183.

Schoggen, P. (1972), Environmental Forces in the Everyday Lives of Children. In: *The Stream of Behavior*, ed. R. G. Barker. New York: Appleton-Century-Crofts.

Shaffran, R. (1974), Modes of Approach and the Infant's Reaction to the Stranger. In: *The Infant's Reaction to Strangers*, ed. T. G. Décarie. New York: International Universities Press, pp. 149-186.

Shakow, D. (1959), Research in Child Development: A Case Illustration of the Psychologist's Dilemma. *Amer. J. Orthopsychiat.*, 29:45-59.

Shirley, M. M. (1942), Children's Adjustments to a Strange Situation. *J. Abnorm. Soc. Psychol.*, 37:201-217.

Simmons, H., & Schoggen, P. (1972), Mothers and Fathers as Sources of Environmental Pressure on Children. In: *The Stream of Behavior*, ed. R. G. Barker. New York: Appleton-Century-Crofts.

Smith, P., & Connolly, K. (1972), Patterns of Play and Social Interaction in Pre-school Children. In: *Ethological Studies of Child Behaviour*, ed. N. G. Blurton-Jones. Cambridge: Cambridge University Press.

Spitz, R. A. (1945), Hospitalism. *The Psychoanalytic Study of the Child*, 1:53-74. New York: International Universities Press.

——— (1946), Hospitalism: A Follow-Up Report. *The Psychoanalytic Study of the Child*, 2:113-117. New York: International Universities Press.

Stayton, D., & Ainsworth, M. (1973), Individual Differences in Infant Responses to Brief Everyday Separations as Related to Other Infant and Maternal Behaviors. *Devel. Psychol.*, 9:226-235.

Stern, D. (1974), Mother and Infant at Play: The Dyadic Interaction Involving Facial, Vocal, and Gaze Behaviors. In: *The Effect of the Infant on Its Caregiver*, ed. M. Lewis & L. Rosenblum. New York: Wiley, pp. 187-213.

Tinbergen, E. A., & Tinbergen, N. (1972), Early Childhood Autism: An Ethological Approach. *Advances in Ethology*, 10:1-53.

Tinbergen, N. (1963), On the Aims and Methods of Ethology. *Z. Tierpsychol.*, 20:410-433.

——— (1972a), *The Animal in Its World: Explorations of an Ethologist*, Vol. 1. *Field Studies*. Cambridge, Mass.: Harvard University Press.

——— (1972b), *The Animal in Its World: Explorations of an Ethologist*, Vol. 2. *Laboratory Experiments and General Papers*. Cambridge, Mass.: Harvard University Press.

——— (1973), Ethology and Stress Diseases. *Science*, 185:20-26.

Tucker, C. (1940), *A Study of Mothers' Practices and Activities of the Children in a Cooperative Nursery School*. New York: Columbia University Press.

Werner, H. (1948), *Comparative Psychology of Mental Development*, rev. ed. New York: International Universities Press, 1957.

——— (1957), The Concept of Development from a Comparative and Organismic Point of View. In: *The Concept of Development: An Issue in the Study of Human Behavior*, ed. D. B. Harris. Minneapolis: University of Minnesota Press, pp. 125-148.

Willis, E. A., & Ricciuti, H. N. (1974), Longitudinal Observations of Infants' Daily Arrivals at a Day Care Center. A Technical Report from the Cornell Research Program in Early Development and Education. Unpublished.

Wright, H. F. (1960), Observational Child Study. In: *Handbook of Research Methods in Child Development*, ed. P. H. Mussen. New York: Wiley, pp. 71-139.

Yankelovich, D., & Barrett, W. (1970), *Ego and Instinct*. New York: Random House.

Ruth C. Resch, Ph.D.

On Separating as a Developmental Phenomenon: A Natural Study

Throughout life, separation appears as a succession of developmental tasks. From the infant's early emotional attachments to his family emanate those threads of development that eventuate in peer relationships. As early as the latency years, friendships, interests, and activities become increasingly separate from the family, less and less linked to it. In the school years teacher-student relationships support, distinct from the family, many aspects of autonomous ego development.

The major separation tasks of adolescence are widely recognized; those of adulthood, less so. The ending of formal education, the successive jobs, have different separation meanings and require different adjustments with each termination and new beginning. The recapitulation of the growth-separation process in sons and daughters resonates in the lives of parents. And, of course, in later life there are multiple variants of final separations and readjustments—the death of intimates, retirement, one's mode of approach to one's own death—as well as the more hidden separation tasks implicit in changing goals, hopes, and values over a person's life.

Thus the developmental task of moving to new phases of life and separating from old ones is repeated over and over in different forms. Differentiation of self from others and the capacity to part from the maternal figure are but the earliest forms. It is in both

My deep and affectionate thanks to Drs. Louise Kaplan, Fred Pine, Donald Spence, and Katharine Smith for their critical and thoughtful contributions to this work.

Mahler's stage-specific sense (Mahler, Pine, and Bergman, 1975) and in Erikson's life-cycle sense (1968) that the capacity to part from the mother is viewed as a developmental task—perhaps sometimes traumatic, but always and eventually a developmental necessity. The mastery of separation from the mother, then, is a centrally important beginning in a total life process.

With a few exceptions, theory regarding separation is generally derived from clinical findings, with adult and child patients, retrospective historical reports, experimental observations of children in strange environments, or direct observations of extremely high-stress, exceptional separation conditions. These data sources all emphasize the disruptive and pathogenic effects of traumatic separations, those that are beyond the child's synthetic capacities to cope. This study is concerned with the more ordinary separations that occur in familiar environments with familiar people, those separation experiences that contribute to constructive ego development and mastery.

The first significant discussion of early separation of the child from the mother, as an important developmental and psychological issue, was Freud's (1926), in "Inhibitions, Symptoms and Anxiety." From retrospective associations and memories of adult patients he inferred that early separations have an impact on later object relations. He conceptualized this effect chiefly as a *breach* in object relations. In that work he reformulated his concept of anxiety to include the anxiety that arises from loss of object and object love. He gave three examples: when a child is alone, or in the dark, or with unfamiliar people. The common condition in these instances is "missing someone who is loved and longed for" (p. 136). Anxiety, in his formulation, functions as a signal in these situations, as a safeguard against rising needs and their nonsatisfaction. Studies followed slowly upon this remarkable observation. The first ones were also retrospective (Levy, 1937; Bowlby, 1940, 1944; Bender and Yarnell, 1941; Fairbairn, 1941; Monroe, 1969).

It was not until World War II that direct observations were made of the experiences of children. A. Freud and Burlingham (1942, 1944), in their now classic studies, first drew attention to the difficulties toddlers and young children had in separating from their families in wartime London. Their observations were of the responses to a major break in family life, in conditions of crisis.

They wrote: ". . . it is not so much the fact of separation to which the child reacts abnormally as the form in which the separation has taken place" (1942, p. 208).

Spitz's reports, again based on natural observations, regarding institutionalized infants soon followed (1945, 1946). These had a profound effect on the handling of babies in residential institutions and hospitals. He brought forcefully to public attention the severe primary effects of maternal deprivation in early infancy (see also Goldfarb, 1943; Schaffer, 1958; Schaffer and Callender, 1959; Provence and Lipton, 1963).

The Tavistock series of studies extended these observations to brief but major separations in the lives of children aged 15 to 32 months who were hospitalized or placed in residential institutions during a hospitalization of the mother (Robertson, 1952, 1953; Robertson and Bowlby, 1952; Heinicke, 1956; Heinicke and Westheimer, 1966). In his major works, Bowlby (1969, 1973) reviews in great detail the literature on human and animal separation. In his own theorizing he discusses separation in terms of anxiety, loss, anger, and fear, chiefly in highly disruptive separations with multiple elements of the strange and unfamiliar. In his view, secure or anxious attachment is the only significant element modulating or heightening separation distress.

The experimental literature has chiefly dealt with separation in terms of strange environments (laboratories) and strange people (experimenters).

Mahler (1968, 1972; Mahler, Pine, and Bergman, 1975) was the first to undertake the work of synthesizing a concept of separation as itself a normal developmental phenomenon and in terms of a progressive unfolding over time. Beginning from observations of autistic childen who had never recognized the maternal relationship, Mahler began a new trend of work, viewing separation from a developmental standpoint. Her work has addressed the important issue of process, that is, direct observations of how a child normally differentiates himself from the mother and evolves into a relatively autonomous person, functioning separately both emotionally and physically. The "separation-individuation process" refers, in her work, to the child's growing awareness of himself as a separate person, that is, the *intrapsychic* differentiation of self from others—most centrally the mother.

Anna Freud (1965), in suggesting the concept of developmental lines, proposed several that are generally relevant to the issue of separation as a normal and necessary development: (1) from dependence to emotional self-reliance and adult object relationships; (2) from egocentricity to companionship; and (3) from the body to the toy and from play to work. Erikson's (1968) concept of life-cycle tasks enlarges the idea of developmental lines from childhood through phases of adult growth. He postulated stages of development throughout life, each of which poses and coordinates a fundamental life-cycle issue.

Following Mahler's work on the normal separation-individuation process, Pine (1971) has discussed the relationship of the temporal and spatial aspects of separating to the intrapsychic aspects. "Separation and being separate are, of course, related— physical separations being one of the stimuli to the child's dawning awareness of separate existence" (p. 113). From his studies of 4- and 8-year-olds, Pine has proposed a developmental line, on the model of A. Freud, specifically for separation: *"From (a) diffuse*

From (a) diffuse pleasure, distress, and delineation of body boundaries to (b) more differentiated gratification, anxiety, and object concept, and thence to (c) object relationship and structuralized defense and gratification [p. 116].

He further outlines a set of conditions for the achievement of a capacity to separate. "The main forces which have to be balanced are the child's anxiety about the mother's separations, his wishes for continued gratification and his knowledge of repeated (even if brief) separations" (p. 120). The solutions achieved in balancing these forces, Pine states, come to be used with regularity. Small amounts of anxiety are seen as necessary for progressive development.

Pine also views the dual developments of separation and stranger anxiety in their relation to the developing perception of separate others. "Stranger anxiety and separation anxiety at this period indicate that the child has developed some concept of a separate and differentiated self, mother, and 'other' " (p. 117). Pine further specifies the character of what has been achieved in the appearance of these two types of anxiety. The infant has become able to link a specific cognitive content with a specific affect. In terms of separation this is the connection of the absence of the mother with the feeling of, e.g., distress. Pine refers to this achievement as "focalization." In terms of Spitz's formulation of stranger anxiety (1965), the connection being made is between the perception that this is "not mother" and affective distress.

Pine defines a two-stage process with respect to separation. The first stage occurs in the first year and is the achievement of focal anxiety and focal pleasure in relation to the mother. The second, occurring at some time "later," is the achievement of regularized and repeated defense behavior.

The development from the focalization of the first year, however, to "later" organized defense or adaptive coping will be seen in this study as a long one. There are many intervening achievements, many resources that must emerge into general use, before such structured behavior becomes possible.

For Pine, Spitz, and Mahler, separation, psychic and spatial, is an achievement of the developing ego. It is a gradual emergence from the total biological and emotional dependence of earliest infancy to the autonomy and interdependence of adulthood.

In line with these writers, in the present study I view separating in a developmental context. That is, from small, daily-life separations in familiar settings with familiar people—at whatever age—grows the capacity to separate from the mother and to develop modes of coping, successfully or not so successfully, with the larger demands of major separations into unfamiliar settings with unfamiliar people.

Using a propaedeutic hypothesis-generating model, described in the preceding paper, natural observations were made of infants from 3 months to 3 years old who were being left daily by their mothers in an infant day-care program.[1] Detailed moment-by-moment observations were made of the 20-40 minutes following the arrival of the baby and the departure of the mother. In all, 167 separations were observed and studied across the age span of 3

[1] The Infant Care Unit of the Child Development Center of the Jewish Board of Guardians, New York City. My grateful thanks to Roy K. Lilleskov, M.D.; Helen M. Schur, M.D., and Thelma Mihalov, R.N., for their generous support in extending themselves, their ideas, and the resources of the ICU for this study.

months to 3 years. Regular observations were made in several kinds of situations, primarily for developmental evaluation of each child's status and progress in the program. A diversity of research was envisioned from the accumulation of such observations. The observations were made with no systematic hypotheses in mind regarding separation in particular. And they were made by a number of different trained observers over a number of years, thus in effect creating randomization of particular observer biases at particular times. In addition, observations were made in free-play, mealtime, and departure situations as well as in the arrival situation, so that the observers were attending to a wide variety of classes of behavior.

The kind of data analysis undertaken here was done after the observations were collected. The propaedeutic hypothesis-generating model is essentially a method of approaching "stream of behavior" data (Barker, 1960), deliberately eschewing a priori theory, searching the data for its internal patterns, and systematically checking and reformulating hypotheses within the data. While these data are not appropriate for statistical use (as described in the previous paper), substatistical criteria were used in systematically formulating hypotheses. Thus the various hypotheses generated and the illustrative observations presented below represent many observations, checked repeatedly against the total data base on principles of proportion, fit, and negation.

The developmental sequences and patterns are presented as rigorously generated, high-probability hypotheses from a very rich "stream of behavior" data base. Necessarily, hypothesis-testing with other data—either observational or experimental, as appropriate—must follow for formal validation.

From the observations particular developmental areas were identified as participating in the emerging capacity to separate from the mother. These are, briefly: (1) visual perception, (2) affects, especially distress, (3) motor and locomotor behavior, (4) play, (5) attachments (object relations), and (6) cognition: anticipation, symbolization, and conceptions of space and time.

In the observations these behaviors were found to make a *general* appearance in the arrival situation, first as developments nonspecific to the departure of the mother. Once each becomes centered upon the event of her departure, they then coordinate in changing ways over time, *specific* to her departure. The findings presented here are organized chiefly around distress behavior as it appears and changes in form and frequency during the first three years of life in these infants. Changes in the form of distress will be seen to relate to emerging achievements in the other areas. Once distress appears developmentally in these infants, it does not appear all of the time. Separating from the mother is seen in these observations, at times, as only *one among many* issues and interests for the baby and toddler. The nursery setting itself, the multiple caregivers, changing relationships with them and the other children, and emerging play interests—all of these come to be strongly attractive and gratifying to the toddlers. Any of them may supersede and modify distress. In many of the observations these other aspects simply seem to be more interesting than is the departure of the mother.

Different patterns of distress behavior were found at different ages in these children, and five successive stages in separation were identified:

I. Preconditions of separating
II. Emergence of behavior focused on mother's departure
III. Emergence of variable distress behavior
    A. Focal
    B. Diffuse
IV. Emergence of prolonged focal distress behavior
V. Emergence of structured, child-generated modulations of separation behavior

In this paper these five stages will be presented as a description of separating in a natural setting, a description of an evolving capacity that coordinates a number of achievements at changing levels of mastery. A selection of the narrative observations from which these hypotheses were developed will be presented to make the stages more vivid and to demonstrate the method of requiring the formulations to *follow from* what was seen in the observations. It should be borne in mind, however, that these formulations followed from multiple observations, not the single ones presented here. The illustrations below are sequential and unedited segments in themselves, but each is taken from far longer narratives.

STAGE I
PRECONDITIONS OF SEPARATING: ILLUSTRATIVE DATA

Obs. 14: Jon[2] (3½ months). Mother comes in, hands Jon to D. Mother complains about the morning. Jon gurgles as he is taken to the changing table. Once put down he quiets, watches Pat, who is wandering around. He has a pacifier in his mouth, makes some movements with arms and legs. He watches D. at the sink, eyes the observer standing at his head, smiles and gurgles in response to her smile.

D. takes off his sunsuit and Jon is placed to sitting for a moment and then laid down again. He begins crying and fussing a little. He is strapped in, joggled a little, but then is left on his own with his fussy crying while D. makes some preparations. He stops crying spontaneously, eyes observer briefly, watches D. come over to him. He gurgles as he is changed. He fingers his mouth and the pacifier in it. Then he lies almost motionless for a few moments, arms extended to the sides, watching observer watching him. S. comes into the room and he watches her, and then back to observer as S. disappears from his field of vision. There is increased noise at the sink and he looks there at D., then back at observer. He gurgles a little, contentedly, like little creaking sounds.

Jon is then picked up for feeding, lying in D.'s arms. He gurgles contentedly in anticipation. He tenses his whole body as he opens his mouth for the first bites of cereal.   (Obs.: Resch)

In this observation and others like it, the major point is that, in the earliest months of the first year, arrival is a casual matter for the baby. He is brought in, simply handed to the caregiver, and is at once immersed by her in the ordinary, expected, and taken-for-granted routines of care. This baby is taken to the changing table, clothes changed, and diapered, while at the same time the care-

---

[2] Children are referred to by three-letter names, caregivers by initials, and mothers as mother.

giver moves back and forth preparing his breakfast. Such routines are often carried out interchangeably by the mothers and the caregivers.

Here the mother leaves without notice and there is an absence of observed specificity of response in the infant to either mother or caregiver.

Incidental to these activities the baby sucks, mouths, and fingers his pacifier. He smiles, gurgles, fusses, and cries in response to immediate stimuli—the caregiver's smiling, being laid down, and being hungry. He is visually responsive to nearby sights and sounds.

VISUAL PERCEPTION: GAZE BEFORE THE MOTHER'S DEPARTURE

Infants begin to gaze at the mothers and caregivers as they move nearby, cooing and babbling in moments of content, vocalizing insistently in states of discomfort and apparent need arousal.

At first, pleasurable attention is centered on the mother's or caregiver's attentions to the infant just before the mother's departure. For example:

> Obs. 16: Tas (4½ months). D. admires her when Tas is brought in. *Tas turns toward D. and smiles broadly.*[3] There is a short conversation between D. and Tas's mother about Tas not yet having eaten this morning; then the mother leaves.   (Obs.: Resch)

> Obs. 18: Jim (4½ months). The mother has just taken his pants off and he looks at her intently and then moves his legs up, flexed at the hips and knees. He moves his arms quite vigorously, *looking intently at her.* She places the pacifier in his mouth and then she touches the musical mobile over his head as if she wants him to be aware of it. She looks sober-faced and *he looks at her.* Then she takes his shoes off and *he watches her intently,* then he gives J. a quick look. The mother pushes gently the socks up his legs, apparently to make them look tidy.

[3] Observations most salient to the point at issue are italicized.

He moves the legs up quite vigorously and he babbles shortly. She pats his legs, looking at him lovingly. He vocalizes again. She watches him and then says, "What?" in an uncertain intonation. She then pulls on the ring of the mobile which starts the music box.

The mother gives the impression as if she had a hard time to leave. She says "Okay," pinches his face, pats his chest, arms, and legs, then walks hesitantly to the door, looks at him. All the time *Jim has looked at her intently and sober-faced.*   (Obs.: Schur)[4]

Obs. 13: Jon (3½ months). Mother complains to D. that he won't eat for her and talks about feeding him juice. Jon begins fussing. Mother eventually comes over to the pen, stands watching him cry. D. says softly, "Mommy, don't let me cry." Mother then leans over and gives him his pacifier and stands talking to him about how she can't stay and has to go to work, but that she will come and talk to him and take him away somewhere, bye-bye! Her words are softly spoken and lulling. Jon is *quiet, watching her and listening.*   (Obs.: Resch)

Following the mother's departure, there is a sequence of play in which Jon pulls a mobile, watches it move, and then vigorously pulls it in different directions.

At times, small affective shifts can be seen together with the focal gaze, sobering, or alternate smiling and sobering, as the mother begins to move away.

VISUAL PERCEPTION: SHIFT IN GAZE AFTER THE MOTHER'S DEPARTURE

After the mother's departure the infant's gaze often shifts quickly to someone else in the room, usually the caregiver, sometimes others. This is frequently followed by visually refocusing or touching the caregiver. Combinations of these behaviors, accompanied by smiles, can be seen in the observations below.

   [4] My thanks to the observers over these years at the Infant Care Unit: Thelma Mihalov, R.N., Helen M. Schur, M.D., Blanca Masor, M.A., Miriam Bucatinsky, M.A., and Inge King.

> Obs. 13: Jon (3½ months). Jon is brought in by his sister. (She leaves.) D. takes him into her arms; *he turns toward her, smiles, handles her face.* D. kisses his fingers noisily. He *smiles,* turns and *gazes at F.* and Bet across the room. D. takes him over to see Bet, but he turns and *watches F.* He sits on D.'s lap on the couch, *looks with a serious expression at F.* as she talks to him. *Then he gazes at D.* She pinches his cheeks and *he smiles.*
>
> (Obs.: Resch)

In the above observation we see a succession of gaze shifts: first to the caregiver who receives him, then to another caregiver, and back again.

Following this sequence the caregiver leaves the room with the mother, and Jon is alone with the observer for a few moments.

> Obs. 13: Jon (3½ months). Obs. is sitting to his side, he turns and *watches* Obs., makes a *half-smile* when Obs. smiles. *He watches Obs. some moments,* looks around a little, still holding the soft lamb in the crook of his arm.
>
> (Obs.: Resch)

> Obs. 16: Tas (4½ months). *Tas looks at D.* and *looks at* Obs. (since Obs. is almost directly in front of her). She smiles when Obs. speaks to B., *but immediately looks back* at D. (Obs.: Resch)

The focal gaze before the mother's departure, and the shift in gaze after, appear in these infants before visual tracking of her departure.

The visual focusing seen in the three observations above is also accompanied by the positive smiling response in these infants. In these behavior sequences the affect is constantly positive, in contrast to the small variations in affect seen with the focal gaze before the mother's departure.

MOTOR KINESTHETIC BEHAVIOR

The visual perceptual focusing described above also appears to have some early counterparts in the bodily sensory sphere. Motor changes or disruptions in play or action sequences are sometimes observed at the moment of the mother's departure.

In these observations, the loss of pacifiers was frequent. This in itself is not a notable event. However, the high *proportion* of observations in which the pacifier fell out of the infant's mouth *just at that moment* was remarkable and thus highly suggestive.

> Obs. 18: Jim (4½ months). She says, "Okay," pinches his face, pats his chest, arms, and legs, then walks hesitantly to the door, looks at him. All the time, *Jim has looked at her intently* and sober-faced. *He now drops the pacifier.* (Obs.: Schur)

> Obs. 15: Tas (4½ months). Mother teases her with her pacifier, tickles her stomach. It is not altogether pleasurable, but not unpleasurable either to Tas. Mother says she will return on her break. *As mother leaves,* Tas is lying quietly gazing toward the window, has a pacifer in her mouth which she (Tas) takes out, sucking on the edge. *She loses the pacifier and begins to fuss, chews on her hand and then on her shirt. She is given her pacifier again and she quiets.* (Obs.: Resch)

It seems quite likely that on a more microscopic level there are many subtle shifts in body states and coordinations that participate in the centering of perceptual attention and then of emotion on the mother's departure. For mothers this stage of beginning differentiation is not entirely neutral either. Some mothers may linger a little longer on some days in a rather special moment. Some mothers softly babble explanations about leaving and coming back which clearly can have no verbal meaning for the baby at this stage. Yet these mothers may be responding to the shifts now beginning to take place in their babies.

STAGE I
DISCUSSION

In the earliest months of the first year the infant behavior seen in the arrival situation has very much the character of behavior seen at any other time of day. The caregiver's activities are chiefly centered on receiving the baby into the nursery—feeding, clothing, diapering, putting to sleep, according to need. The baby's response to these ministrations is not different from any other time—i.e., not specific to the arrival and separation aspects. In these observations separation at this stage is developmentally not at issue for these babies. It is not cognitively or emotionally registered or anticipated.

Care routines dominate the observations and also highlight the *functional* equivalence of the mother and the familiar alternate caregiver at this stage. In these earliest months the babies are not observed to distinguish between them. The babies are chiefly adapted *by* the environment to the departure of the mother via the effectiveness with which the caregiver assumes the mothering function.

The caregivers' fondling, handling, hugging and cooing, playing and talking, are major gratifications. Ordinarily part of a rich experience with a mother, they enhance continuity, a sense of well-being, in the change from the mother to the caregiver.

The body-oriented sensory play of the first months vividly illustrates the undifferentiated character of self and other. Clothing, straps, and body parts are sucked, mouthed, fingered, and felt interchangeably. The body is a source of play pleasure. It is moved, stretched, turned, wiggled; legs are kicked, lifted, touched, and gazed at; arms are waved, stretched; hands clasped and gazed at.

Structurally, play at this stage is a succession of very brief, fairly discrete, and rather simple sensorimotor activities. Toys are focused on, fall out of sight; people cross the child's vision, are focused on momentarily, and leave the room without being noticed. Body parts are moved, successively gazed at and observed. Objects and body parts are touched, felt, mouthed, and sucked. At this stage these activities seem to serve no other purpose than pleasure in visual, kinesthetic, and tactile sensation. In this sense we recognize them as "play."

Focusing of the gaze on the mother, together with small differential affective shifts just before her departure, serve, initially, to center attention on her particular movements to and away from the baby. In these observations these changes began to be seen around the fourth month.

At this early stage, the attachment to the mother is attended to, not the departure per se. The attachment to the caregiver as a maternal alternate is signaled as the infant's gaze and smile are directed toward her at arrival and she is visually sought after the mother's departure. Small disturbances in ongoing motor sequences are also seen after the mother's departure, e.g., losing balance, dropping pacifiers.

These phenomena all indicate a beginning centering of attention on an event which is *not yet* cognitively or emotionally significant.

Separating, in a familiar setting of continuity of maternal care, acquires a central meaning when the baby (1) has some perception of the mother as a separate person, (2) can distinguish her from other attachment figures, and (3) can further distinguish her movements, that she has moved away and left. The emergence of separating as a developmental issue is, then, dependent upon perceptual and cognitive as well as emotional developments. Feelings of distress may not be connected to the departure of the mother until these perceptual and cognitive capacities have become available to the infant.

STAGE II
EMERGENCE OF BEHAVIOR FOCUSED ON THE MOTHER'S DEPARTURE: ILLUSTRATIVE DATA

PERCEPTION: MOVEMENTS OF ATTACHMENT FIGURES

The first recognition of the mother's departure as an event appears to begin with an affective sensitization to the mother's and the caregiver's movements. This is seen, for example, in the following observation:

> Obs. 31: Pat (6 months). *The mother comes close again and talks to B. and Pat beams. B. moves away and Pat starts to cry,* but as *she comes back she starts babbling again.*
>
> D. now takes Pat out of the seat and removes the pants. Mother leaves and *brother comes close by again and says bye-bye. Pat squeals several times* and then he

makes brrr, brrr sounds, and she squeals again. B. now closes the straps again.

The mother comes back again—she had taken the wrong bag—and *Pat squeals and makes shouting noises. The mother leaves* immediately and *B. goes* to the back of the room, and *Pat watches the latter intently, half-smiling.*   (Obs.: Schur)

In this observation we see a succession of movements to and away from Pat. She now clearly takes notice of all these movements and responds directly to them. Her affective responses are differential, negative to those movements away from her and generally positive to those toward her. The quality of the affect at the second appearance of the mother is unclear in the observation. It could be positive, negative, or both. Its equivocal character still makes the same point—variety in Pat's response to movement around her.

Babies also notice the momentary departures of caregivers and respond to them. Similar, but rather milder, shifts of attention occur, for example as Tas shows when she is placed on the floor to play:

Obs. 46: Tas (9 months). The father brings Tas in and leaves immediately. She is placed on the floor next to a basket full of toys. She sits there, legs apart, sucking on a toy while D. plays with Jon and J. with Rob. She sucks and chews the toy. *She then watches J. and Rob intently as both leave the room. She is completely immobile. She then resumes the sucking* and chewing while watching D. and Jon.   (Obs.: Schur)

In these observations, crying and fussiness are not among the first types of distress to appear. The first indications are affective and motor shifts. These occur together with somewhat longer visual attention to the mother's whereabouts.

One type can be seen in Mar as a shift in aggressive balance in play:

Obs. 41: Mar (8¼ months). Kay extends her arm and touches Mar's dress; Mar does not react, she looks sober-faced. Mother watches them for a few seconds, then turns around and leaves. *Mar follows her with her eyes and looks after her, watching the door for a while.* F. comes up to her and gives her a rubber toy. Mar takes it in her hand *still looking very serious and starts banging it against the bars.*   (Obs.: Bucatinsky)

Some babies sadden and then brighten with alternating gratification. Some move to be physically closer to the mother.

Obs. 48: Pat (9½ months). *While mother walks with B. to the Blue Room, she [Pat] watches both sober-faced.* After a few seconds she sneezes and Obs. comments on it. Pat looks sober-faced alternatingly at brother, mother, and Obs. *The glance at mother is the longest; there is some* sadness to it. *The mother comes by* now, apparently in order to leave. *Brother hands Pat a rattle and she smiles* while shaking it. The mother now leaves, saying "Bye-bye." Pat looks at her for a second and then looks again at rattle. She shakes it and smiles, then touches the ball part of it lightly and then rubs it gently. She continues doing it while Obs. talks to her. *J. approaches* and Pat babbles and smiles joyfully.

(Obs.: Mihalov)

Obs. 38: Rob (8 months). Rob comes into the room in his mother's arm. They both stand at the entrance for a few minutes, mother is smiling, Rob's face is next to his mother and he is sucking his fingers. He looks into the room; *J. approaches them and talks to Rob, he smiles, J. wants to take him but Rob gets closer to his mother and his face frowns, he looks down.* Mother straightens him in her arm and Rob puts his fingers in his mouth, and *continues to look down and his fingers are in his mouth.* Mother sits down on a chair holding Rob on her lap. Rob *inspects the room with great attention* and looks at Obs. intently (Obs. is sitting next to them) for a few seconds. Jim approaches them, Rob looks at him seriously. Jim makes noises, Rob vocalizes slightly. Mother is holding Rob at a distance looking blankly into space. Rob starts moving his hands up; *he turns his head*

toward A. and Jim, who are talking very loudly, and
starts to scream.   (Obs.: Bucatinsky)

Distress in the form of crying appears late in the first year in these infants. It is relatively brief and, with the intervention of caregivers, does not extend beyond the first few minutes, as seen in Jon.

> Obs. 49: Jon (10 months). Jon's sister arrives with Jon in her arms, accompanied by two friends. *She starts to put Jon on the floor, but he begins to cry, and she picks him up again, making soothing, crooning sounds, kissing his palm. When he calms down,* she says, "You have to sit down with the other children; I have to go to school." One of her friends gives Jon a pacifier, saying: "Here's your bobo." Jon sucks on it moderately. His sister then hands him to J. and this time he does not cry. His sister says, "Bye-bye," and starts out the door, but comes back and lovingly kisses his cheek. *As she goes out the door, Jon begins to cry again.* His nose is running and J. says, "Let me get you a tissue." She opens a fresh box, and Jon reaches for the opening, as if to help her with it. As J. wipes his nose, he fusses again. He looks with interest at Tas, who is being given medicine. J. deposits Jon on the floor and *gives him a plastic pumpkin full of blocks. Although he takes it from her, he does not seem to be very interested in it. He shakes it a few times and then drops it.*
> *The pacifier falls from his mouth. He stands for a moment* and then sits on the floor. He seems *more content now, vocalizing cheerfully, "aah-eeieh," and clapping his hands.*   (Obs.: King)

The caregivers may, after the departure, spend special time with the babies in comforting, playing, feeding, and diapering. Life quickly resumes an "as usual" character after the brief distress at the mother's departure. The infants' behavior in subsequent activity does not appear to be different from their behavior in the same activities at other times.

MOTOR CHANGES: THE MOTHER'S DEPARTURE

As in Stage I, motor malcoordinations, or "play disruptions," also appear, but now at more complex levels. These may in turn lead to further distress.

Before the mother's departure Tas, early in this stage (7 months), is playing with a cradle gym with considerable interest and skilled coordination.

> Obs. 37: Tas (7 months). Tas gets the center ring into her mouth, gurgles, shakes the ring, drops it. She makes "ugh" sounds. She gets a wooden piece into her mouth with some difficulty; she has to coordinate maintaining her sitting balance while she leans rather far forward to get it to her mouth; quite deliberate.
>
> She turns away from the cradle gym, gets hold of a striped soft doll, pulls it to her, and begins chewing on the yarn hair. Her mother takes it away, saying she might choke, and gives her a terry-cloth doll.
>
> Tas gurgles happily, accepting the replacement; mother is pleased and talks to her a little as she continues handling and chewing on the doll. When Tas looks up at her mother with a big smile, mother says playfully, "Goodbye, yes, goodbye." Tas continues smiling, wrinkles her nose, shakes the doll exuberantly. Her mother continues with goodbye talk, reaches into the playpen, touches Tas on the face, and then goes out. Tas continues smiling, looks to the doll, shakes it, hugs it, and puts it again into her mouth....

However, just after the mother goes out a caregiver goes over to the pen and speaks to Tas. In looking up she does not maintain the coordination she had with the same action just a moment before. Compare also with the skill she showed in balance with the cradle gym previously.

> ... J. comes over to the pen, speaks to Tas. *In looking up at J., she loses her balance, falls over* backwards to a lying position, and begins fussing mildly. J. sits her up again and she continues fussing. J. rearranges the toys around her but she continues fussing. She stops when J.

picks her up and carries her momentarily, resuming when returned to the pen. J. tries to make her happy in the pen, making the hanging toy sound and offering her stuffed toys, talking, joggling various things to distract her. The fussing increases; she will have none of the distractions. J. picks her up again and she quiets immediately. She sits very quietly in J.'s arms as J. gets out cereal and makes it.   (Obs.: Resch)

The fussing is initially in response to falling over, and perhaps later a function of hunger, but not clearly to the departure of the mother. The loss of balance has certainly added to her general disequilibrium.

Disappearance as a Cognitive Development

Visual tracking evolves into locomotor tracking with the infant's increasing facility in crawling and then in walking. Rob demonstrates this development vividly with the departure of a caregiver shortly after his arrival:

Obs. 45: Rob (9 months). Caregiver walks momentarily out of the room, and *Rob crawls over to the chair she had been sitting in, looks at it, rocks it a little.* He crawls back to Tas's crib, pulls to standing, looks at her, then sits down with difficulty, then *crawls deliberately toward the door, intently looking towards the door.* He pulls up on the crib near the door and near Obs. *As the caregiver comes back into the room he sits, and crawls back into the room along after the caregiver.* He tries to pull up on her legs. He sits near the little sitting table for a few moments. He turns, looks at Obs. intently, then sits down in another direction, looks at another baby screeching in a crib, looks around at the caregiver, who brings a ring and block to him. He picks up the ring and fingers the block. He looks up at the caregiver intently, begins banging the ring against his foot and then the floor. *The caregiver leaves the room. Rob begins crawling purposefully around the room in an arc toward the door. He sees the caregiver and immediately sits back, moves back into the room,* pulls up on the sit-table. He bangs the ring on it and reaches toward the caregiver, fussing a little. She says, "Wait, Rob, wait," and he stops fussing. She tends the other baby and Rob sits, watching her go to the rocking chair. She says, "Come, Rob." He crawls toward her and she picks him up and wipes his nose. He fusses and shakes his head. He is put down and he fusses mildly as *he crawls after her* as she goes to Tas's crib. He pulls to standing, looks at Tas. Caregiver picks up Rob and sits with him in the rocking chair, *facing him away from her. He stretches his head and body all the way back so that he can see her face.* (Obs.: Resch)

His search for the disappearing caregiver also initially presents a cognitive problem, as he first looks for her in the rocking chair and then goes to the door by way of Tas's crib. This behavior shows an early stage in the development of object permanence, that is, a search for the object where it was last seen.

Particularly striking is Rob's persistence in locating the lost caregiver in space and vision.

STAGE II
DISCUSSION

During the latter half of the first year the focal gaze that was observed in Stage I before and after the mother's departure extends into visual tracking of the movements of people surrounding the baby. As these movements acquire increased meaning for the baby, differential affective responses emerge. The departure of the mother becomes a significant event, both cognitively and emotionally. As this double achievement occurs, the focal distress response appears in its first form.

In this stage mother and caregiver become clearly differentiated. In this infant care setting the experience has been that each baby selects a particular caregiver for special attachment. Much as Anna Freud recognized the need for special attachments in her older children by forming "family groups," this day-care program also altered its staffing structure to include special time between each baby and "his" caregiver.[5]

The departure of the mother is first visually, and later in this stage motorically, tracked as the child recognizes familiar movements leading to the departure. Her disappearance at the doorway becomes recognizable as a special class among her movements. Not until late in the first year does distress behavior begin to be seen in these infants; it is brief and not particularly intense. When the caregiver intervenes with body closeness and comforting, maternal care, or distraction with play, the distress quickly stops. This also highlights the still functional, but now differentiated, equivalence of mother and caregiver.

In terms of Pine's concept of focalization (1971) at this stage— the connection of a specific content with an affective state—these observations specify the behavioral details and the nature of that connection. What appears to be focalized is an *immediate* event, that is, the movement out of the door of now special attachment figures. A series of behaviors preceding this event now set it off as both perceptually and emotionally important. Only when the mother's going out of the door is no longer equivalent to her momentary disappearance to other parts of the room does distress behavior appear. The mother's movements come to be perceived as external to the baby, and not as solely determined by the infant's own actions. Temporally, her movement toward the door, even when the infant is in a relatively contented state of arousal, comes to mean something more than her disappearance into the kitchen or the bedroom. These developments, together with emerging differentiation in object relations, underlie the focal distress that develops during the second half of the first year.

These observations suggest that the focalization of the first year is limited by the cognitive meaning that the infant is capable of associating with the departure of the mother and the character of the distress. The specific cognitive content—the mother's departure —is of the nature of a dichotomy: here/not here. The focalization observed here may be of the mother's departure as a disappearance, experienced as immediate in both space and time. The

---

[5] Roy Lilleskov, M.D., and Thelma Mihalov, R.N., personal communication.

distress, also in response to an immediate event, is quite brief, and quickly alleviated by effective continuity of mothering care. The mother's departure is not yet cognitively organized by the infant as her leaving and being somewhere else that the baby can imagine. A full cognitive and affective focalization of her departure in this sense is not possible at this stage and will be hypothesized from these data as developing late in the second year.

A very imaginative experiment by Bell (1968) supports this interpretation. She hid mothers under successive sheets in the same manner that toys are hidden in object-permanence experiments. She showed that the 1-year-old infant is capable of object permanence with respect to persons. This is, however, only in an immediate sense with respect to time and space. That is, in the object-permanence experiment, the infant locates the mother who is hidden or disappears in *immediate space.* The progression of item presentation (in either person or inanimate object experiments) carefully and deliberately establishes the expectation in the infant that the mother is there to be found. What is being tested is the point at which, in a series of immediate disappearances, the baby loses this expectation.

In the separation situation the babies are observed to track the mothers and caregivers, visually and motorically, as they move about near the babies, from room to room, and the mother's morning departure. Bell's findings are consistent with a concept of limited focalization.

In the day-care situation of continuity of maternal care, the brevity of the distress and the ease of alleviating it suggest that these infants have little concept that the mother has left for a *length* of time and has gone somewhere else in space *not* accessible to them. That is, there is little concept of time and space beyond the immediate and directly experienced. In the more extended sense of space and time, object permanence with respect to persons (or object constancy) may be said to be incomplete.

There is additional support for this view of spatial-affective relationships at 1 year of age, in studies of infants' reactions to strangers (Goulet, 1974; Brossard, 1974). In these studies, infants in the late first year generally responded differentially to the approach movements of strangers—i.e., positively at a distance and intermediately or negatively closer by. Most of the infants who discriminated in this way had achieved both object permanence and causality with respect to persons. Goulet makes the point that the differential responses to autonomous movements of others are an advance in cognitive coordination and a step in objectivity beyond the egocentrism of earlier stages.

In the present observational data, distress behavior developed gradually over the second half of the first year, peaking in intensity at around 10 to 12 months. These findings are consistent with Benjamin's (1963) and Schaffer and Emerson's (1964) observations that separation distress appears later in the year than the 8-month stranger anxiety reported by Spitz (1950, 1965), and are consistent with experimental findings in the Cornell Infant Care program (Willis and Ricciuti, 1974).

Coordination between sensory modalities, such as between vision and prehension, or vision and sound, begins to be seen in the play amusements of the babies. The sensory, tactile, and body-oriented activities that dominate in Stage I are still frequently observed. New skills in sensory coordination and locomotion lead to greater variety and complexity in the structure of the play. The body sensory orientation now extends outward in space. Manipulation of and action upon objects become increasingly central pleasures.

Parallel to the increasing differentiation among people in the day-care setting, play objects become more clearly differentiated from the self. Toys are thrown about and retrieved; they are banged, rattled, and listened to; they are picked up, placed in containers, and noisily dumped out. Babies pull themselves up on doors, then open them and close them. The contents of cabinets are explored and emptied onto the floor. Games involving locomotion appear.

Increasing differentiation in play with toys in a sense coordinates with increasing differentiation among people. Play in *relation* to the caregiver is more frequently observed. Caregivers become part of the play, both as play objects themselves and as participants in play. They make simple demonstrations of toy properties or action possibilities; babies observe, and enjoy the sight of and relationship to the caregiver. The babies urge repetitions and sometimes try to copy.

Structurally, play is more complex and varied. Play activities are now less often relatively discrete actions as in Stage I. They are now often combined into brief, related sequences.

The stage of coordination in play appears to be parallel to the status of development in separating. Piaget (1936), in a discussion of intelligence, highlights in terms of early sensorimotor coordination, the emerging situation seen in separating: "When an object can be simultaneously grasped and sucked or grasped, looked at and sucked, it becomes externalized in relation to the subject quite differently than if it could only be grasped. . . . As soon as there is coordination, on the contrary, the object tends to be assimilated to several schemata simultaneously. It thus acquires an ensemble of meanings" (p. 121).

And so it is with the separating experience. The focalization described by Pine as a linking of cognitive content (departure) with an affective state (distress) can now be specified more microscopically from these data. When the mother can be discriminated from other attachment figures and can further be perceived in independent movement in space, the psychological-perceptual coordination is analogous to Piaget's coordination of sensory modalities. The mother's movements can then acquire differential meanings they did not have before. As seen in the Stage I observations, this simple level of discrimination is the prerequisite for the emergence of separating as a psychological issue. For the infant, this is the beginning of the separating progression.

In Stage II the baby extends differential perception of mother's and caregiver's movements to their disappearances. This is the cognitive side of the focalization achievement. On the affective side the familiar caregiver is clearly distinguished from the mother, though retaining considerable functional equivalence in caregiving. With this differentiation, the infant now connects a specific affect, distress, with the mother's disappearance.

STAGE III
EMERGENCE OF VARIABLE DISTRESS BEHAVIOR:
ILLUSTRATIVE DATA

Beginning in the early part of the second year, two separate forms of distress are observed: immediate distress at the mother's departure (as in Stage I), and diffuse distress that now extends after her departure.

While the immediate response to the mother's departure can be fairly intense (crying), the period of diffuse distress following her departure is generally not intense, but rather quite subdued. The babies may be somewhat more random in their play, less attentive to it. They may go from toy to toy, or from person to person, without connecting with anything especially pleasurably. They may have difficulty engaging with their surroundings, or they may encounter difficulties once they have done so. There may be moments of rather immobile gazing about and seeming to turn inward. There may be somewhat more aggressive behavior, and nonspecific movements toward the door. There is frequently a generalized irritable dissatisfaction after the mother's departure, of the kind seen in some of the Stage II observations above *preceding* her departure.

The combinations and sequences of these behaviors are quite varied. What is common to all of them is that ordinary modes of relating to the environment are disrupted for a time following the mother's departure.

Disruptions in Initially Engaging Relationships or Play

In Jim, immediate focal and diffuse distress behavior appear together, on this day.

Obs. 60: Jim (12 months). Jim continues to cry softly now and lies his head on J.'s bosom, resting there while still sobbing very softly. J. stands Jim on the sofa and he stops crying completely and he stares blankly out of the windows for a few seconds; his hands are touching a notebook, he tries to get it but cannot reach it. He finds the pair of pants his mother had left with J. before, takes them, looks at Obs. (who is sitting on the rocking chair next to the sofa) and shows them to Obs.; *his face is still serious but does not show the tenseness it had before he started to cry.* J. takes the notebook he was trying to read and he follows her attentively with his eyes. Jim *takes the pacifier* which is hanging from his neck, *puts*

Immediate focal distress [margin label]

Diffuse   *it in his mouth*, sits down, and *stares blankly at the*
distress   *empty room.* J. offers him her hand, he takes it but
              without paying much attention to her; he sucks at the
              pacifier very hard while looking around. J. puts the
              TV music box on the window sill. Jim stands up as soon
              as he sees it and starts manipulating the buttons. He
              looks at the different turning pictures *but his expression*
              is still sober; when the music stops he looks out of the
              window. N. comes in, he turns his head and looks at the
              door. Cook approaches them and she looks at her with
              interest. J. and Cook start to talk out of the window to
              F. and Amy, who are playing in the park outside. Jim
              follows them with great attention and leans out of the
              window to see F. and Amy. J. turns around to Jim and
              hands him the music box. Jim takes it and starts banging
              it against the sofa; he stops for a second, looks blankly
              out of the window, and vocalizes very softly.

                                                    (Obs.: Bucatinsky)

Approximately seven minutes after his mother has left, Jim,
recovering, begins to manipulate the music box with interest and
concentration, swaying his body to the sound.

   Jim is subdued in all aspects of his behavior. Motorically he is
relatively inactive, spending the whole of this 7-minute period
sitting or standing on the couch. His attention alternates between
brief periods of interest in people and things and blank staring.
Along with these attentional shifts his affect is sober and muted. A
period of heightened distress is observed in his hard sucking on the
pacifier. In terms of his relationships to people and things around
him, he relates only briefly and rather peripherally to the book, the
observer, the caregiver, the music box, other staff, and activities
seen through the window.
   In the following observation, immediate focal distress is not
observed. This child becomes very much occupied in watching
other toddlers' arrivals. Her emotions range from rather muted to
open affective distress. While she attracts caregivers' attention, and
there are play sequences, she does not fully engage herself with
them; all are brief. In this child, a little older, the diffuse distress
lasts longer.

Diffuse
distress

Obs. 75: Pat (15¾ months). Amy runs in ahead of her mother and Pat *watches Amy's mother intently,* a toy key bunch hanging from her mouth. Amy throws herself on the floor crying bitterly and Pat watches her *and then walks over to her. She looks puzzled* and chews on the key. Somebody turns on the record player and S. starts dancing with Amy and Pat. Amy's mother leaves and Amy cries and fusses. *Pat looks at her with an astonished and perplexed expression.* F. picks up Amy; and Pat follows them, her *expression changing from astonishment to sadness and almost crying.* S. calls her and she makes a few steps towards her but then *she looks* again *forlorn,* but then she apparently becomes aware of the music again or recalled the previous "dance," and she steps almost rhythmically alternatingly to the left and then to the right.

S. now takes her hand and *Pat looks at her soberfaced.* S. picks her up and lifts her on the couch and looks out of the window with her. Amy is right next to them, looking out too.

Max arrives and Amy calls him. Pat watches them with interest and then again moves with the music. She claps her hands when the music stops. Max now kisses his mother and *Pat watches them with a forlorn and then astonished expression.* J. comes in and Pat *climbs off the couch slowly and carefully.* She then makes a few dance steps, falls, gets up looking unperturbed, makes again a few dance steps, and then watches J., who now plays with Amy on the floor. *She walks over to them very slowly.* J. smiles at her and Pat responds with a *long, sober-faced gaze.* Amy points out something and *Pat watches with her mouth open.* F. walks out of the room and Pat makes dancing steps. Bet arrives and F. comes back and takes Bet and Max to the Pram Room. J. is still sitting on the floor, talks to Pat who has followed Bet and Max to the door. Max and Bet come back and Pat *watches them intently across the blocked entrance. She then plays with the doorknob.*

Amy fusses and Pat turns around and looks at her in consternation. She then lifts up her skirt, thus baring her chest. She looks intently at Amy, who lifts her shirt in response. She then looks at J. N. passes by and Amy shouts. Pat turns around, looks at her and then at J., who is close by. The music plays again, S. claps her hands, and Pat approaches Amy and dances a few steps with her. Still dancing, she looks around the room and then falls out of step. Amy stops dancing and walks away. *Pat watches her with a sad expression.* Amy shouts and N. enters the room and Pat follows. Amy fusses as N. walks into the kitchen and blocks the entrance. *Pat watches Amy with an astonished expression.* J. takes Amy on her lap and *Pat watches her, looking sad.* J. stretches her arms out and pulls Pat toward her. She embraces Pat and rocks with her and Amy. *Pat still looks sad,* but as Amy leaves Pat smiles and *snuggles up to J.*   (Obs.: Schur)

Beginning recovery (margin note)

Pat still looks sad as the observation ends after 12 minutes. She smiles and snuggles as a caregiver takes her into her arms.

PLAY DISRUPTION

Other children are initially more able to engage the environment but show disruption and irritability in these efforts. Other events that occur may add to the distress in various ways at this time.

Obs. 60: Rob (12¼ months). They proceed to accompany grandmother down the hall. They come back almost immediately, Rob now with his pacifier in his mouth. F. puts him down. S. calls him, dangling the keys. He disregards her. F. picks him up and sits down on a rocker with him on her lap. She gives him the clock. *He moves the clock back and forth and then drops it.* He tries to get off the chair and F. helps him. He tries to get on the little rocker, by stepping on the seat. *He is unsuccessful and gives it up almost immediately.* He then *watches, solemn-faced,* Amy, Pat, and Bet playing with the shape ball. He tries to get it. Pat pulls it away from him. He looks first amazed and then frightened,

Diffuse distress (margin note)

and walks away. *He cries and looks at F., who at that moment does not notice him. The moment she notices him he stops crying.* F. picks him up. *He looks solemnly* at Pat, who is lying on the floor, then looks around the room and then makes clucking sounds. D. comes by and he vocalizes, "Ada, ada," and *stretches his arms toward her.* She picks him up, and removes the pacifier. *He sucks his index finger.* She then tosses him up and he smiles. She then takes him on her lap and he vocalizes. She hugs him and then continues playing with him by pulling him alternately closer and pushing him slightly away. *He remains solemn.* He then watches the children playing on the floor for a moment. D. kisses him and *he cuddles up to her and smiles.*   (Obs.: Schur)

Rob finally begins playing with a toy 5 minutes after the mother's departure. The length of time is relatively brief, consistent with his just beginning the second year.

VARIABILITY IN APPEARANCE OF STRESS

There are frequent observations during the second year in which there is little or no observable distress or disruption. The attachments, the sights, sounds, and activity potentials of the nursery take the center of attention. Children move to other gratifications, other interests, apart from the mother, her departure, and separating from her.

Obs. 72: Rob (15 months). She hands him to J., saying, "Bye, Rob," and she goes.

Watches Kay start to play — Another caregiver takes Rob from J., asking him, "Hungry?" Rob directs his gaze at Kay, who is shaking a plastic block which rattles. Rob is wearing two shirts, and the caregiver takes off the outer one and puts him on the floor. Kay has abandoned the blocks, and Rob picks up the one she was playing with and also shakes it.

Hugs caregiver — The caregiver is sitting on the play steps; Rob goes to her and hugs her legs. She picks him up and holds him on

Sits on her lap — her lap. He looks sober-faced and sleepy. The caregiver gives him two wooden sticks she has been holding and he puts one into his mouth for a moment and then takes it out. The caregiver guides his hands and hits the sticks against each other. He now does the same independently. After a moment, he puts one back into his mouth. Then he drops one of the sticks. Kay picks it up and hands it back to him. Rob smiles faintly.

Imitation and play with sticks

He has gotten down from the caregiver's lap and is squatting on the floor, rolling a ball. He stands up, walks to a chair which is blocking the entrance to the kitchen. He pushes at the chair, and the caregiver says, "No, Rob," as she leaves the Red Room. Rob follows her to the door, but it closes before he reaches it. He wanders into the kitchen on the side which is not blocked, comes back out, goes to the door, reaches both hands up to the doorknob and tries to turn it. The caregiver returns and Rob, appearing content, says, "Dadadada," as he walks around. He again wanders into the kitchen, still saying, "Dadada." He tries to climb into the feeding chair. He is still carrying the sticks and occasionally hits them against each other.

Follows caregiver to door

Plays with sticks

(Obs.: Schur)

In this observation, Rob immediately gets interested in what another child is doing. Then he goes and hugs a caregiver and is taken onto her lap briefly. She gives him two sticks and shows him a simple game which he repeats during the rest of the sequence. The caregiver leaves, he follows, and appears to welcome her back without particular distress. There are many small gratifications for this child during this time.

In these infants and toddlers, who are growing up in like-age groups of children, other children clearly become early objects of attachment, i.e., friends. The engagement in these relationships is also of some importance in the arrival situation.

Obs. 74: Kit (15½ months). Mother opens the door and Kit looks at us with a broad smile on her face. She comes in walking by herself, while her mother holds the door. She smiles, stays in the middle of the room, looks at Obs., and comes to Obs. with her arms extended and smiling. Mother, who until now was staying at the door, walks to the kitchen saying, "Hello!" Kit does not look at her; she touches Obs.'s hand very quickly, smiles and *goes to Sue, who is near the playpen. Sue reaches out for her, and Kit puts her hand around Sue's neck; they stay like that for a few seconds, looking at each other, Kit smiling and Sue vocalizing.* (Obs.: Masor)

Obs. 108: Pat (20¾ months). Mother brings Pat, both are smiling and laughing as they stop at the stoop and mother takes Pat's jacket off. *At that moment, Amy comes and both children greet each other joyfully. There is a short interchange about their pacifiers and a doll.* They both then run into the corridor; Pat's mother watches them smiling tenderly. Pat's mother then joins the girls, announcing that she and Pat would put Pat's pacifier in her crib. They vanish into the bedroom while Amy re-enters the Red Room. Pat comes back with mother, still holding the doll. Mother says, "Bye-bye, baby," smiling and lingering at the door. *At that moment, J. comes and Pat jumps in excitement, she shouts, and drops the doll.* At that moment, mother leaves. One can hear her talk in the hallway. Pat shouts, "Bye-bye!" F. says, "Let me have the baby [doll], let me sew it and fix it," and she picks up the doll. Pat watches F. sewing, while Amy picks up the needles.

(Obs.: Schur)

STAGE III
DISCUSSION

Beginning about the second year and extending through most of it, the response to the separation from the mother begins to vary in both form and regularity. The babies are expanding their experience of the event. Separation behavior now lasts longer and is more clearly observable: behavior preceding the mother's departure and anticipating it, distress directed to her departure, and new forms of distress sometimes extending long after her departure. Separation behavior is more sharply viewable in terms of sequences: before, during, and after, a simple indicator of increasing complexity in structure.

The increasingly gratifying and differentiated attachments in the nursery to both caregivers and other children, as well as broadening interests in the play activities available, are major contributors to this variability in distress.

When distress does appear, two forms are observed: (1) immediate focal distress as seen in Stage II, and (2) diffuse nonfocal distress which gradually increases in duration in the course of the second year. Diffuse distress is seen in a variety of disruptions and disturbances of ordinary performance levels. Some babies have initial difficulty engaging the environment from the moment of entrance into the nursery, before and after the departure of the mother. Other babies are able to engage initially with people and play activities but are not able to sustain them at usual levels. Some of the behavioral indicators of diffuse distress—abstracted gaze, staring, lessened interest in people and play—are similar to those described by Mahler (1972) as "low-keyedness" in the absence of the mother during the practicing subphase of differentiation.

In Stage III the emergence of distress behavior following the mother's departure, which gradually *lengthens* over several months, may be an indicator of the status of development in both affective experience and in object permanence. The diffuseness of the distress suggests limits in the toddler's capacity to connect the now more extended feelings occurring later with the mother's departure or with her absence.

Waving to the mother and watching her departure now underscores the departure as more than casual. That is, the mother is not coming back shortly. These motor and visual tracking activities indicate the infant's expanding understanding of the mother's departure. In this stage a shift is taking place from a perception of her departure as an immediate event toward the understanding that she exists in other space (unseen and not in the toddler's here and now) and through time in her absence. That is, the toddler can now watch her go out the door and down the hall. A few moments later she can be seen and waved to from the window as she leaves the building. The few moments delay may indicate development in cognitive spatial mapping of the mother's movements. This may be a connecting link between object permanence of immediate persons and object permanence of remote persons.

At this stage the infant, in addition to showing focal distress at the mother's *departure*, now shows diffuse distress in her *absence*. In the course of the second year these toddlers experience diffuse distress over an increasing length of time after the mother's departure. The mother may be said to be missed or longed for in her absence. Two aspects of the separation experience have become differentiated: the mother's departure and her absence. The capacity to experience feelings over time in the absence of the mother is an emotional achievement of this stage. This is a partial achievement, since these feelings are as yet diffuse and unfocalized.

In Stage II the caregiver's intervention was immediately effective in ending focal distress at the mother's departure. In this stage the caregiver's intervention in diffuse distress does not have the same automatic effectiveness. During the period immediately following the mother's departure on these days, the caregiver for a time is not *as* satisfying a substitute as she is at other times: she is now less functionally equivalent to the mother. This is a clear indication of the increasing emotional differentiation of the two.

Some observations at this stage suggest that a hierarchy of attachments is emerging. Toddlers are seen to respond differentially to the departures of mothers and those of other caregivers, showing more or less distress depending on who is going.

When distress behavior does not appear, the recognition of the mother's departure or a sense of loss is superseded by the interests and pleasures of the nursery itself: great variety in play, more differentiated relationships to caregivers and to other children. In this stage caregivers become more clearly providers of play, beyond basic care. The absorption in the characteristics of play materials and the pleasure in exploratory action are very much like the "practicing subphase" described by Mahler. The world is the baby's "oyster." She observes her babies moving in independent and elated activity, yet still remaining well within the maternal orbit.

Many new gratifications and pleasures are available to the toddler, in relationships with caregivers, other toddlers, and play activities. On many days these simply supersede distress and missing the mother at her departure.

In the first part of the second year, play is still fragmentary: brief sequences of behavior are strung together. In this stage, a variety of locomotor, manual, sensory, and social explorations are going on simultaneously. The succession of sequences often seems determined by what happens to catch the infant's eye or ear; sometimes the sequences are related by continuities in sensory or motor schemata. The body as an instrument of action is of intense interest in this stage, in contrast to the earlier stages when play seems to be dominated by sensory experience of the body itself.

In the course of the second year, play sequences lengthen and begin to be organized increasingly by single preoccupations or "themes." The play often illustrates and certainly is often a medium for extending cognitive developments, via intense exploration, manipulation, and little experiments.

This lengthening in play sequence—that is, the capacity to string together multiple and coordinated sensorimotor elements into more sustained play—coincides with the lengthening in the distress response following the mother's departure. As play activities are more sustained in time, important feelings can also be experienced over more extended periods. These developments may underlie the fuller focalization of the mother's departure that occurs in the next stage.

STAGE IV
EMERGENCE OF PROLONGED FOCAL DISTRESS:
ILLUSTRATIVE DATA

Toward the end of the second year, toddlers rather suddenly begin to have difficulty, for a period of a few months, in initially engaging in play at all, or in engaging in gratifying relationships with other children and caregivers. Affective discharge is both much more intense and much more prolonged than before. Little sustained play is seen; what play there is tends to be disjointed and sporadic. Distress typical of this stage is seen in Amy.

> Obs. 113: Amy (21 months). *Amy is crying as she comes down the hall. The crying increases when she sees F.* They come in and mother goes with her to sit on the couch. Amy stands beside her mother on the couch, crying; then she puts her head over on her mother's shoulder and stops crying. *F. tickles Amy as she goes*

over behind mother to raise the window shade. Amy
starts crying again. She sits down beside her mother,
who has said very little during this time but now and
then gives Amy a little pat. *Amy throws her pacifier
forcefully onto the floor.* A record is put on. . . .

Various toys are now successively offered, and she loudly refuses. After some minutes, the caregiver hits on something that
begins to engage Amy's interest.

. . . F. lays out a blanket on the floor and puts a soft toy
in the middle of it and merely gestures to Amy that it is
for her. Amy points to it and leans forward, saying
". . . Down there." F. says, "Then go." Amy instead
leans onto her mother's lap, *a little fussy again.* Mother
jiggles her legs; Amy is pleased, a small smile on her face
as she stops fussing for some moments. She *resumes and
quiets again.* She is lying in her mother's lap part of the
time, looking in Obs.'s direction. Amy sits up looking at
F., *begins fussing again a little, gets up,* restless. . . .

After trying to get into her mother's pocketbook and being put
off, she goes away to the closet with a caregiver to get a pocketbook
of her own. Mother quietly but very obviously sneaks out.

. . . *Amy returns to the room, looks at the empty couch,
around the room to the door, then back at the couch and
then to the door again. She looks at F. and cries,
"Mommy!"* F. says, "She'll be back." *Amy continues
fussing a little. The door opens and C. comes in. Amy
looks at her and lets out a short cry.* It seemed quite clear
to the observer that when the door opened again Amy
had expected/wanted her mother to walk in and that
her cry was in disappointment. . . .

On discovering the mother's departure, Amy shows a natural
sequence in object permanence. She sees the empty couch, looks at
the door where she now knows her mother leaves, though she has
not seen her do so this time. She rechecks the couch and the door,
and then in her yell demonstrates her knowledge of what has
happened.

Her response to the entrance of another caregiver suggests that she understands that her mother is elsewhere and has thus achieved some capacity to anticipate her actual return. Another sequence of this sort occurs a little later in the same observation.

> ... Amy now has a ball, rolls it in the blanket on the floor, and then rolls herself into it, wrapping the blanket around herself and rolling around on the floor. The blanket comes off and F. puts it back on. Amy makes a little peekaboo game with the blanket with F., then sits up and says, "Peekaboo" and slowly pulls the blanket off her head. *She hears a noise in the hall, turns and smiles broadly, says sweetly, "Hi!" She runs to the door; Pat's brother comes in. She goes out into the hall and begins crying.* S. picks her up and brings her in her arms. Amy says, "Hike hike" to S., and S. does put on the record, keeping Amy in her arms and walking around the room in a semidance/march. *Amy holds on around S.'s neck, listening to the music, still not yet very happy.* (Obs.: Resch)

The familiar peekaboo game as a prototype of disappearing is also seen in this sequence.

This observation ends 25 minutes after Amy's arrival, and she is not yet at all happy. Some assuaging of her distress is seen, but means of finally ending it do not seem to appear by the end of this observation period. In this observation, the modulations are almost wholly externally provided—physical body closeness and offering of activity.

> Obs. 133: Tom (25½ months). His father was kneeling beside him trying to push him gently into the room while *Tom desperately tried to stay with his father. He wailed, struggled, whined, giving the picture of frantic despair.* His father talked with a soft voice to him and everybody in the room tried to coax Tom in, pointing out different toys. Somehow after about a minute or two the father left and M. picked up Tom, who *continued to cry bitterly*, desperately, *and tried to open the door.* She carried him to the window, saying something

to the effect that they could see papa from the window. All the time Tom had been *holding on tight to his training cup*. Then M. sat down with Tom on her lap; *he continued to cry* in a high-pitched, *medium loud tone; it sounded desperate and angry and whiny*. He tried to *struggle out of her arms, shaking his whole body and kicking, making motions to throw the cup*, which M. prevents. He then looks at Obs. and then around the room, then throws the cup and stops crying.

He runs toward the kitchen. Cook says a word and Tom *starts crying again, tries to open the door, kicking and stomping* and then back to the kitchen where he *kicks the refrigerator. His angry crying is now interrupted by coughing. . . .*

While continuing to sob, he looks at a book with the caregiver; 13 minutes after his arrival he finally allows the caregiver to remove his snowsuit. He piles dolls in the caregiver's lap over the next few minutes, then throws a toy "with force" into the crib.

. . . B.'s lap is by now quite loaded with toys and she suggests to put them on the couch next to her (she had been sitting on the rocking chair and Obs. on the couch).

Tom pats the couch slightly, saying "Aqui, aqui." He then puts the blocks into the ferris wheel and watches how their weight makes the wheel turn, and he looks at B. now smiling; after a while he turns the wheel with both hands, getting excited; he makes it go faster. "Eh, eh!" And he turns it more gently. All the time he accompanies his action now with chatter.

(Obs.: Schur)

At the end of the 20-minute observation, he is smiling for the first time with his engagement in making the ferris wheel turn. The indications of excitement may suggest that some distress still remains.

This observation and others later in the day show that he still responds to briefer departures of caregivers too with distress. But it is less intense and not as prolonged as with the father.

STAGE IV
DISCUSSION

Toward the end of the second year there occur a few months of frequent, intense, and prolonged distress. The diffuse distress of Stage III is observed to lengthen from a few minutes to 25-40 minutes. Rather suddenly, over a week or two, this shifts into intense focal distress at the mother's absence, lasting the same length of time and possibly longer. The 40-minute observation time was often not long enough to include the end of this distress.

At this time the caregivers offer themselves and activities in a close, intense, personal relationship. They concentrate on distractions in favorite play activities, which for some children are repeated over and over every morning. They frequently take the toddlers out—trips to the park or shopping. In the face of this intense distress they try all manner of methods to re-establish the important attachments, interests, and pleasures that these children have come to enjoy.

Despite the extra effort and concern of the caregivers, however, there seems to be a kind of inevitability to this heightened distress. While the caregivers' closeness appears to be important to the toddlers, their effectiveness as alternate gratifiers is strikingly low—for a time an often discouraging fact for the caregivers.

During this period the play, symbolic development, and language seen at other times of day are strikingly diminished in the separation situation.

This now longer and more intense distress in the mother's absence suggests a major change in the focalization of separation.

Complete focalization of separating from the mother is conceptualized from these observations as being completed only when the child reaches a stage when (1) "not here" has a meaning beyond immediate space and time, (2) the mother's disappearance is understood to extend in time and she is understood to exist elsewhere in space, and (3) feelings can be experienced focally through time. The developmental achievements of the first two years may be stated in terms of increasing organization in the focalization of the mother's departure.

The affect and the cognitive content both change in organization over the second year. The distress becomes (1) more intense,

(2) more differentiated (departure and absence; focal and diffuse), and (3) of longer duration. And (4) alternate familiar caregivers lose their gratifying caregiving equivalence to the mother as they become more differentiated in function. These affective changes integrate into a prolonged focal response at the end of the second year (20-25 months). The cognitive content, on the other hand, changes from a perception of the mother's immediate disappearance to an increasingly differentiated understanding of her movements in time and other space, inaccessible and unobservable.

These observations suggest that focalization as described by Pine (1971) is not limited to the first year, but has a developmental progression which extends over the first two years. This line may be described as follows: *From the association of distress with the mother's departure to the association of distress with her absence.*

Only when the perceptual and cognitive developments take place that permit an understanding of the movements of persons outside immediately observable space and time can the child be said to have a complete *intellectual* grasp of the meaning of separating from the mother. When these achievements are attained, the toddler can then fully experience in *affective* terms the spatial and temporal features of separating from the mother: her departure and her absence.

The intensity of Stage IV may be augmented as well by its following upon the greater differentiation and variety of attachments that the toddler is now capable of forming. As the toddler's autonomy increases in the "rapprochement" phase of differentiation, Mahler (1972) describes an accompanying need in the toddler for periodic return to the mother for "refueling" in her nursery setting, in which the mothers are present. The situation may be similar in the day-care separations. In the course of the second year these toddlers do gain major gratifications from their independent interests and relationships in the day-care setting. And for most of the second year, these can at times supersede concern with the mother's departure. Independence and autonomy of movement have a strong pull in the practicing subphase of psychological differentiation (Mahler, Pine, and Bergman, 1975). As the second, more extensive focalization of the mother's departure at the end of the second year takes place, the primary importance of the attachment to the mother is fully asserted and supersedes the attachments of the nursery.

McDevitt (in Mahler, Pine, and Bergman, 1975) has characterized the "rapprochement crisis." The toddler's increasing capacity for and appreciation of his own autonomous activity come into conflict with his lack of achieved emotional autonomy. Dramatic fights with the mother are described in the rapprochement subphase of differentiation.

In the separation situation in this study, the heightened need for refueling in the rapprochement crisis may be an additional emotional source of the toddler's sudden, intense, and inconsolable distress at the mother's departure and in her absence.

Some symbolic dramatic play is seen in the arrival observations at this time, but informal comparisons with observations later in the day suggest that it appears much less often in the separation situation. There appears to be differentially less use of emerging cognitive resources in the arrival situation as compared to more general play levels later in the day, e.g., amount and level of language use in play, reasoning in language use, problem solving in play, exploration of cause and effect relations, as well as symbolic and dramatic play.

However, some preliminary trends toward structured coping behavior may be seen, e.g., as imitative identifications.

In the arrival observations, however, these play sequences, when they do appear, are not used by the toddler in relation to the mother's departure. They have much more the character of general developments in symbolic play preliminary to the more active use of play in relation to separation that appears in the next stage.

The full focalization of the mother's departure that is seen in Stage IV, then, seems to be based upon and can only follow the achievement of object permanence of persons in nonimmediate space and time. This change in level of achievement in object permanence, from immediate time and space to remote time and space, can be seen as an example of Kaplan's (1972) application of Piaget's concept of "vertical décalage" to the development of object constancy. "Vertical décalage," she writes, "describes adaptations which repeat at later stages of development patterns analogous to those experienced at a preceding stage" (p. 324). "As the child's object relations increase in complexity and attain higher levels of organization there will be corresponding extensions in the nature of object constancy" (p. 333). These changes she extends through latency, adolescence, and into adulthood.

In these data the vertical décalage is represented in the two achievements in object permanence: permanence in immediate time and space, and then in remote time and space. Analogously, Pine's focalization of the first year is repeated again late in the second year as the connecting of new levels of cognitive content with new levels of affective differentiation. At this stage the intense focalization is seen as a culmination of the preceding stages and as an essential precursor of the developments in self-modulation that occur in the next stage.

STAGE V
EMERGENCE OF STRUCTURED CHILD-GENERATED MODULATIONS OF SEPARATION BEHAVIOR: ILLUSTRATIVE DATA

Verbal communication and dramatic play appear in the separation situation and are used to reinstitute gratifying relationships in the nursery, to share thoughts, feelings, and experiences. Communication, play, and highly differentiated relationships are now used by the children in a wide variety of ways to modulate behavior, their own and their mother's, in the separation situation.

Speech by now is generally mastered and becomes a rich form of communication. Topics of conversation are wide and varied. Talk often revolves around personal appearance, hairdos, clothing, events at home, and reminiscences both from home and previous experiences in the nursery.

> Obs. 141: Bet (29¼ months). Bet runs into the room; she has a slight frown on her face. Nep greets her, also F. and C. and Sam nearby. She watches without response as she is told that it is juice time. She does not go herself and is guided to the table. When she sits she becomes animated, jumps up and down, saying she wants a pink vitamin, and drinks her juice. She is attentive to everything, the activity and the talk around the table. She makes "Mmmm" sounds plus other vocalizations and

screeches. Her earrings are mentioned by C. and she immediately touches both ears, leans forward and says something. She leans back in her chair, puts her feet up, and asks for a cookie. She is told they can have cookies in the afternoon snack. Bet gets up and points at a painting of hers on the wall. C. names who did which paintings and Bet says she painted the green on the big one. They talk about how C. painted their feet so that they could make footprints. Bet exclaims, *"Me* painted feet." Bet gets off the chair and sits on the steps nearby. (Obs.: Resch)

Obs. 185: Pam (37½ months). Pam is left at the door. She runs in, smiles broadly, shows her sunglasses to C. and then to B., who takes her to the mirror to look at herself. He makes much of the sunglasses and there is a lot of laughing and pleasurable talk. Pam comes back across the room with the glasses on, gets up on the couch with C. Max hugs her from behind and Pam instantly bursts into tears. There is general talk about telling Max "No" when you don't like what he does. Pam stops crying and puts the glasses back on. B. talks to her about how he can see her eyes through the dark glasses. She watches him intently. She is sober-faced now. She is sitting on her knees, watching as B. puts his own glasses on Max, then Nep. C. asks Pam about how her sister Lor is. Pam corrects C. about the symptoms, "No, no, her foot hurts." She is very eager to talk about Lor and does so animatedly. Several times she repeats "And and and" in a stutter in the process of beginning a new thought. Then she takes the glasses off, still standing beside C., looks around the room. "Lor has a blue one," she says in a very loud voice. The glasses go off and on as she talks to Nep. She is very emphatic. C. offers juice, and Pam and others yell "Yes!"   (Obs.: Resch)

Play in the separation situation at this stage virtually blossoms in length and complexity. Sequences of actions are combined into long thematic units. Cognitive and motor skills are directly pursued and extended in these activities; multiple and highly differentiated social relationships are often incorporated; fantasy and symbolic functions are used in dramatic play.

The capacity to engage in fantasy play as make-believe at this stage implies developmental advances in both cognition (symbolization) and object relations. That is, enough stability is achieved in the differentiation between self and other, in both the cognitive-perceptual and emotional sense, to allow a further elaboration in assuming imagined roles deliberately. These roles may be very obvious and direct expressions of immediate primary needs, or they may be less direct and highly transformed games.

An explicit game that is close to the primary needs and gratifications of the moment is shown early in Nep's arrival.

> Obs. 165: Nep (33¼ months). Mother says, "I'm going to leave now." [After 7 minutes of staying close to mother] Nep says, "I want to play baby." Mother immediately responds, "Okay," sits down, and takes Nep onto her lap. Nep sticks her bottle into her mouth, leans back on her mother, drinking contentedly. Both sit quietly and contentedly, relaxed, watching Max and his mother across the room. When Nep has drunk most of the bottle and has taken it out of her mouth, mother starts to put her down, saying "Okay, so you've done your little baby for the day." She sets Nep on the floor, takes the bottle to the kitchen and then to the sink to rinse it out. Nep sits on the floor for a few moments vocalizing and fingering the little toys she has in her hands. Her mood is the dreaminess of a little baby who has just been fed. Suddenly she gets up and runs over to C. and says to her, "My mother will come later." C. says, "Yes, that's right," and they go into the kitchen together. (Obs.: Resch)

The announcement of a game allows both mother and child to return to an earlier mode of gratification, to reinstate a symbiosis-like union. This is followed by a dreamy state of satiation. The child then follows her mother's ending of the "little baby" game with an assertion of a more mature, age-appropriate understanding that mother will return later, and now institutes a connection with her teacher.

There have been many discussions before this particular morning of Nep's spending the day at school while her mother works. Here she uses this achievement to end the regression with the mother, to master this day's departure, and to institute her day's ties with the caregiver. The achievement here is a multiple one of understanding explanation and causal relationships based upon cognitive, language, and communication developments, as well as an emotional readiness (still in process for Nep) to assimilate such explanations.

In contrast to Nep's behavior, a child's immediate needs and conflicts regarding separation may be more transformed and embedded in the structure and theme of play.

Kit's entry into the nursery has involved a prolonged struggle with her mother over submitting, giving, and withholding. In the following observation Kit plays out this theme in her subsequent activity with Nep. Kit has fought taking off her coat, refused to join the reading of a story, refused to get off her mother's lap, refused to go with a caregiver for the morning's juice. At this point a more transformed sequence of play begins as Kit sits down by a box of discs.

> Obs. 137: Kit (27½ months). She sits down, looking suspiciously at Nep, who is standing next to her, smiling broadly. After a while, Kit smiles at her and both laugh loudly. Kit asks her, "Do you want some?" Nep nods her head yes; Kit smiles, opens the box and starts putting them back. Nep helps her, and both girls are smiling broadly. When they finish Kit asks, "Want more?," looking right at Nep's face with a serious expression. Nep says "Yes," and Kit again takes them out while Nep picks them up one at a time and shows them to the Obs. Then Kit says, "Put them all back," and Nep does it. Then she closes the box, saying, "No more," and for a few seconds stares at the picture on the box. Nep reaches out for the box and Kit screams "No!," and then asks very softly, "Want more?," while opening the box and taking three discs out, chattering all along. She takes one and looking smilingly at the Obs. says, "Cookie," and puts it close to her mouth. Obs. asks her if they taste

good and Kit laughs. She mouths the disc, still smiling, and then announces, "No more." She puts the discs back into the box, closes it, and puts it on her lap, holding it with both hands. She sits quietly for a moment, staring at a caregiver who is at the other table. Then she says, "I want my juice," in a firm tone of voice. . . .

The back and forth sequence of offering and limiting continues, and an eating play accompanies the "Want more?-No more."

. . . Kit picks up one disc and gets her index finger through the hole; then she does the same thing with the other hand. She moves her fingers up and down, smiling broadly and singing, "Mommy, Daddy." Suddenly she stops, frowns, and asks, "Where is Mommy?" C. explains that Mommy is working. Kit starts to whine. C. adds that she'll come to pick her up after her nap. Kit throws the discs and grabbing the box shakes it angrily. She takes the top off and puts it on her face.

(Obs.: Masor)

A peekaboo game follows. In this example the symbolic usages are minor in contrast to the real relationships with her mother being re-enacted in a game context. That is, Kit directly controls Nep's getting or not getting the discs rather than, for example, playing out a fantasy with a doll.

The discs here are not objects of focal exploratory manipulation, as in earlier stages. They become symbols, for a time, when they are cookies. But their dominant usage in this sequence is as a medium of exchange in a relationship: "No more-Want more?" In a dynamic sense Kit may be enacting her mother and Nep enacting Kit's role in relation to her mother. Aside from the discs being transformed into cookies, there is little imaginary quality of a made-up game or a fantasy. It is a direct playing out of giving and withholding, in a game context. She has enough emotional appreciation of the relationship with the mother (i.e., some degree of mental representation of it) to be able to enact it after the mother's departure. She is possibly working at mastery by shifting sides, enacting mother.

The developmental achievement beyond the preceding stage illustrated here is that memory and perception have coordinated to produce an internal representation sufficient (at the very least) to reproduce the relationship 10 minutes later. There also seems to be enough differentiation for Kit to be able to shift roles. She enacts the mother's dominant active role; she makes Nep submit.

Kit, via this play, arrives at accepting (more accurately, demanding) the juice she could not engage with earlier. The problem of the absent mother then emerges, and she asks for an explanation, connects her anger with the mother's departure, and finally plays out the issue of disappearance/reappearance in the familiar peekaboo game. She and Nep then go off happily, running and yelling, to climb the steps. (All this is accomplished in the 20 minutes following the mother's departure.)

Fantasy play emerges as a yet further symbolic transformation of primary needs and conflicts. These children are seen to engage in evolving such fantasies together. The spontaneous "staging" of these fantasies implies considerable social sensitivity and subtlety. In the following observation, Bet (27½ months) and Nep (33¼ months) were being observed during their arrivals. Max, whose slow development warranted his remaining in the nursery beyond the third year, is 46 months old at this observation.

> Obs. 136: Max comes along to Bet and Nep and makes a monster expression. Bet shrieks and then both Bet and Nep cry. Bet's cry turns into a laugh. Since Nep is still afraid of Max, C. suggests that Nep read with her and let them play monster. Bet says to Max, "Okay, I want to play," and they run off to the kitchen-office area, shrieking. Nep comes creeping after them in long, slow steps, crouched over and making small growling sounds. Then they all three come running out and around the room, shrieking. They stop in a little group facing one another, make little threatening sounds and gestures to one another which build louder and louder, then burst out into running and shrieking across the room again. They repeat this sequence several times. Bet hits her knee against something and Nep stops and examines it with the stethoscope hanging around her neck. They

return to the sequence of threatening sounds, leading to running and screaming, but Nep gets interested in asking about Bet's toenails. (Obs.: Resch)

All three children make themselves the monster and live out how it is to be both threatened and threatening. This living out is different for each child. Max has special difficulties in modulating expressions of anger and aggression, and is frequently frightening to the other children. Here, with the girls' cooperation, his aggression is for the moment quite socially acceptable. For Max, the game is one of playing at aggression without dire effects, a game of mastering its modulated expression.

The easy and fluid transition between preoccupations (needs and gratifications), reality and fantasy (make-believe), allows play now to be a resource for living out, learning, and mastering developmental tasks, among them, in this arrival situation, the relation to the mother and the mastery of separation. The monster play is an example of a fantasy transformation.

In the following example, play becomes a medium for a child to shift from a mode of passively experiencing separation to an active stance of self-assertion. Jos first entered the nursery during his third year and regularly comes into it tentatively, physically constricted, watchful, and easily disrupted in his pursuit of intended activities (Stage III behavior).

> Obs. 176: Jos (35¾ months). A caregiver and Lyn come in from the Red Room. Jos smiles. As Lyn comes over he stretches his arms out to the side as he did with another caregiver (a gesture seeming to imply, "Look what I did, and what next?"). He half smiles at her, a slightly impish expression on his face now. Lyn comes into the block corner and Jos breaks into a full smile. He approaches her, his lips slightly puckered, trying to get his face close to hers, as though he wants to kiss her. But she is moving on into the block corner. Lyn is smiling. Presently she gives the blocks Jos has laid out a hard kick, looking at him to see the effect. He laughs. A few moments of excited play follow in which Lyn breaks up the rows of blocks, Jos following, yelling with pleasure.

Lyn begins to hit Jos, a big smile on her face. Jos yells with pleasure; both run. Lyn comes back and hits him again. He yells; they run. He is physically much more active and assertive now. He strides after Lyn with a cardboard block in his hands, wide, big strides. He is holding the block up near his face, eyeing Lyn over it, making a playfully threatening roaring sound. This playful taunting back and forth continues some moments more; Jos delighted to stimulate its continuation. He looks at Lyn with a bright, impish expression, looking intently at her, waiting for her next move. He does not make moves or overtures to get Lyn to taunt him. He makes it clear to her that he is highly interested by his eager expression and an anticipatory tension in his stance. He has said nothing throughout the observation.

(Obs.: Resch)

Jos has been alone for 10 minutes with a caregiver and the observer; he is delighted at the arrival of a peer, a very competent little girl.

As in the monster example, there is a subtlety of social communication here. Jos seems to have issued a challenge which Lyn engages by aggressively kicking his blocks apart. The whole sequence is clearly a *game* of aggression. Jos moves dramatically from his passive behavior to a highly pleasurable stance of active aggressor. Neither child takes the aggression as a serious matter, that is, as a *drive reality*. Yet its transformation into a game allows it to have an *emotional reality* that is highly pleasurable for both, and allows Jos to loosen up considerably.

The developmental advance illustrated in these examples is that emotions and drives have become sufficiently objectified to be capable of transformation into imagined and playful games. They are manipulated and enlarged in dramatic and thematic fantasies. Nep *becomes* the baby; she and the others *become* the monster intentionally and deliberately. There seems to be little doubt about who they "really" are (i.e., the cognition of reality). The aspect of emotional differentiation of self and other, however, varies in the situations. Nep's "little baby" game allows her to recreate an early union with her mother that temporarily loses its game quality. In the monster game, the game reality is never lost once gained by all three.

Children at this stage can be seen to play at sadness, crying, being hurt, and so on. Dramatic play is used to play out a wide array of preoccupations in the separation situation and does not appear until the child can symbolize, i.e., until words, thoughts, actions, objects, or people become capable of standing for others.

All of these play sequences are characterized by fantasy, game, and pretense, but there are qualitative differences in the examples. That is, the monster, the "little baby," and the discs are all symbolic representations, but they are quite different in the extent to which they transform the child's preoccupations or remain quite close to the needs and gratifications of the moment. Important issues are being dealt with, but they differ in degree of transformation, closeness to the drives expressed, and the degree of fun and pleasure immediately experienced.

Many of the elements that have been discussed at this stage— increasing differentiation and variety in social relationships, an increasingly complex social awareness, and complexity in sustained fantasy play—come together in the following observation. Lyn is observed at the end of the third year, after she has left the nursery and is in the 3-year-old group in a city day center.

> Obs. 190: Lyn (37 months). Lyn comes into the room with her two brothers and another boy. She is holding the hand of the oldest one and walks with her head slightly down, smiling shyly. Looks up at Obs., still smiling in the same way when passing by, and moves her right hand, like saying "Hi!" Looks right in front of her, this time with a more open smile, and walks by herself to the teacher, who is at one of the tables with a child. Lyn gets close to her and reaching out first with her face, gives the teacher a short kiss. The teacher greets her warmly, hugs her, and suggests she take off her jacket and find something to do. Lyn nods her head, and smiles while looking at the materials on the table (puzzles). Turns around and stares at the different areas of the room with a brief smile on her face. Starts to walk

toward the door, both hands on the buttons of her jacket, a sober expression on her face. Her oldest brother says, "Come, I'll take off your jacket." She takes a few steps toward him, looking at Obs., with a broad smile while he takes her jacket off. Lyn is intently involved with her eyes in a group of three children who are playing in the block corner.

After a second or two, she takes her brother's hand and looking at him says, "Come here." They walk to the fish tank, which is on the other side of the room; Lyn is talking while pointing at the fish. Both are smiling. Lyn turns around and, half-jumping, half-walking, goes to the doll corner. Looks at the different toys there, then at Obs., smiles and waves her hand. Bends down in front of the toy cabinet and gets the toy bottle. The youngest brother walks to her and says, "A kiss." He gives her one and Lyn hugs him and stamps one on his eye. The boy laughs and Lyn, smiling broadly, gives him another kiss on his cheek. The other boy comes by and kisses her, but Lyn just looks at him and smiles. The three boys start to walk out and Lyn looks at them with a broad smile and waves goodbye to them. The oldest brother turns around and waves goodbye to her, and Lyn, still smiling, says "Bye!" She follows them with her eyes until they are out of sight, now frowning slightly with a thoughtful expression. Lyn stays in the same position for a few seconds, her mouth slightly opened and staring blankly.

Suddenly she turns around and picks up a doll. Puts the doll on her arm and looking at it with a smile walks around the doll corner. Sits down and holding the doll on her lap puts the bottle in the doll's mouth. She does it very gently, smiling briefly and looking at the doll. A boy comes by and there is a short verbal interchange between them. Lyn stands up, saying "I am the mommy," in what sounded like an explanation, then walks to the toy cabinet and gets a spoon. Sits down again and with the doll lying on her lap, she puts the spoon into the bottle, looks at the doll, then at the bottle, and back at the doll saying, "Don't cry, your food is ready." Starts to feed the doll with the spoon, very carefully, and places the spoon on the doll's mouth, smiling at it. Puts the spoon into the bottle and then takes it to the doll's mouth. This goes on for a while, Lyn seems totally involved in her activity, not looking even once at the boy who is standing beside her watching. She stands up, puts the doll on the chair and announces, "I have to change her diaper." Walks to the table, picks up a piece of cloth which is there, looks at it very seriously, opens it up and leaving it on the table, walks toward the doll, picks it up, smiling at her broadly and says to the boy, "I have a diaper." Both of them go now to the table and Lyn puts the doll down. Takes a tissue and wipes her legs, lifts the doll's skirt and with a big smile says, "She's clean." Gives the doll a kiss and leaving it on the table goes to the toy cabinet. Looks through the different things, and finally she picks up a dish and two cups and puts them on the table. The boy asks, "Is it for me?" Lyn says, "No, it is for the baby. Do you want one?" The boy shakes his head, no.

Lyn walks to the mirror, takes a chair and sits right in front of it. Looking at the mirror she sticks out her tongue slightly and smiles. Takes a brush and makes as if she is brushing her hair. She is looking at the mirror and smiling broadly. Takes a toy lipstick and puts it on her mouth. Looks more closely at the mirror, opens and closes her mouth, and finally breaks into a laugh. Stands up, picks up the doll, and says, "Now we'll go for a walk." Holding the doll in her arm she starts to walk through the room, staring at the group of children who are at a table in front of her. Jumps back to the doll corner, puts the doll in the carriage, and very softly she says, "Now you are going to sleep." Looks at the doll for a second, smiling briefly.

Then she turns back and runs to the table. She says something to the teacher. Lyn gets a chair and takes it to the table and sits down. She gets some dough and makes a ball. A girl beside her says something and both laugh. Lyn makes two holes with her fingers and shows it to the other girl. A conversation goes on between them while Lyn smashes the dough.   (Obs.: Masor)

Lyn moves remarkably smoothly from one activity sequence to another; each has its own organization and subtlety; and each is completed before the next is begun. In most of the children behavior in the arrival situation remains more fluid and open during the third year; for the most part they do not seem to achieve quite the high level of organization and stability that Lyn does.

STAGE V
DISCUSSION

After the few months of regular, prolonged, focal distress around the end of the second year, distress behavior again becomes highly variable in both form and frequency. When focal distress does appear in this stage, it is not often the intense discharge in crying seen in Stage IV; nor is the extended diffuse response of Stage III often seen in these observations.

In this stage cognitive, and social, achievements that were strikingly absent in the separation situation in Stage IV become richly available. Developments in language, thought, symbolic representation, and fantasy that are observable during other parts of the day much earlier become dramatically available in the separation situation around the beginning of the third year.

Play, social play, and social relationships become strikingly differentiated, complex, organized, and structured in the third-year observations. They come together in highly complex ways via the relationships and play opportunities that are also available to these children in a familiar nursery setting. The sequences of play become long and intricate in cognitive content. They progress beyond the sensorimotor explorations of the second year.

Play reproductions of events and relationships, symbolic and fantasy play in Piaget's (1945) terms, appear in the separation situation. These new cognitive functions become available and are used for modulating the expression of extended distress which begins the development of structured coping mechanisms. They incorporate and balance drive preoccupations and gratification in a variety of more and less transformed ways. Play now has considerable structure, which is seen in (1) organizations of now very lengthy sequences of (2) thematically integrated play, and (3) coordination with complex social relationships. Such play provides multiple gratifications and serves multiple adaptations, including the capacity to separate from the mother.

Play at this stage seems to incorporate the beginning of self-modulation and defense development with respect to separation.

Pine discusses the structured nature of defense development as

... indicated by its being repeated (predictable, regularized) and actively produced (intended) by the child. It is not random, and the child has sufficient stake in it to reproduce it in a variety of related circumstances.... psychic acts which come to have multiple functions ... for drive satisfaction, defense, and adaptation to external ... reality achieve considerable permanence ... such organizations of behavior reflect not simply mindless growth of complexity, but serve a dynamic function in reconciling diverse aims [1971, p. 119].

Behavior in the arrival situation is now more frequently modulated by efforts of the children themselves. These take the form of lengthy anticipations of the mother's departure, actively keeping her around longer, a variety of uses of the caregiver, and play after the mother's departure. Distress, when it appears, may be incorporated and embedded in these activities over a fairly long period.

With language development, there may now be direct discussions with the mothers and caregivers about the mother's departure. These can take many forms, from imploring her not to leave yet, to involving her in specific play until she leaves, to discussion with the caregivers during the day about where she is and when she will be back.

The immediate arrival period often includes some form of close personal relationship, generally with the caregiver. There is often personal talk, revolving around things that are brought from home, clothes, appearance, sometimes bruises and hurts, and events and personal possessions at home.

With the achievement of full focalization in Stage IV, the appearance of distress once more becomes highly variable, and child-generated modulations of behavior are observed. The successive stages of differentiation and focalization of distress precede, and may be necessary precursors to, the appearance of modulating strategies.

SUMMARY DISCUSSION

This study used natural direct observations of babies separating from their mothers daily in a familiar setting with familiar caregivers, to describe and elaborate the developmental sequences and achievements of normal separating. A propaedeutic hypothesis-generating methodology was developed as a means of discerning and systematizing naturally occurring patterns and regularities of behavior in narrative observational data (presented in the preceding paper).

Using this method, a developmental progression for separating was proposed from the data: from the limited and full focalizations of the first and second years as necessary precursors, to the development of adaptive coping behavior in the third year. Natural observations have been presented to illustrate major aspects of this progression and to amplify the use of the methodology.

This work forms an important descriptive link between the observational literature on traumatic separations of infant or toddler from the mother and the literature on the normal intrapsychic process of separation-individuation.

The stages that have been delineated in terms of the coordination of developments and their increasing complexity beautifully exemplify, in terms of separation behavior, Werner's (1957) theory of development as increasing in differentiation, articulation, and hierarchic integration. These data may also be described in terms of this theory as they enlarge and provide behavioral detailing for Pine's developmental progression for separation: *"From (a) diffuse pleasure, distress, and delineation of body boundaries to (b) more differentiated gratification, anxiety, and object concept, and thence to (c) object relationship and structuralized defense and gratification"* (1971, p. 116).

In terms of the distress component of this developmental line, these observations have provided a substantial and detailed behavioral description of how distress behavior emerges and changes over time in the daily-life experiences of a group of infants and toddlers. The changing patterns in distress behavior coordinate with cognitive and perceptual achievements, increasing differentiation and pleasure in relationships with others, and the changing uses of play. A series of stages describing the focalization of distress has been presented in detail.

The developmental line of gratification is "from (a) diffuse pleasure ... to (b) more differentiated gratification ... to (c) structuralized ... gratification." For most of the first year, in the homelike setting of the nursery and with its caregiver emphasis on alternate mothering, the dominant gratifications are those multiple ones which surround the basic care functions of feeding, diapering, putting to sleep, providing warmth and general protection. The fondling, handling, cooing, babbling, talking, and playing with the infants that accompany and surround these routines are major and rich sources of gratification. They are diffuse pleasures for the infant at the early stages (I and II) in the separation progression. They are intimately intertwined with the contextual, taken-for-granted routines of daily life. Gratifications are not specifically related to separation in this familiar consistent setting. They are maintained by the caregivers and are not disrupted by the departure of the mother.

Both the confident expectation, and the real experience, of a continuity of gratifying care probably differentiate the normal development of the capacity to separate from the mother from the experience of traumatic separation.

As play evolves out of the bodily sensory modalities dominant in the first year and into the sensorimotor explorations dominant in the second year, play in itself and play in relation to adults and other children become great pleasures in the separation situation. As the caregivers' specific caretaking functions wane in the morning arrivals, their provision of play opportunities, and participation in the toddlers' play, increase. The stimulus of the sights, sounds, and activities of the nursery and the multiple gratifications of play are significant contributors to the variability in the appearance of stress. Over the second year play increases in complexity, relationships with caregivers have more varied components, other children become friends (not, of course, without conflict), and other children's play becomes an interesting part of the child's own play. Thus overlaid on the basic, intimate, caregiving functions is a more differentiated and complex array of play, mastery, and social pleasures. The toddlers increasingly structure and determine these gratifications themselves, but not yet in specific relation to the departure of the mother at Stage III. The structuring with respect to separation is chiefly externally provided by the caregivers' making themselves and play opportunities available in the arrival situation.

At the beginning of the third year, language, symbolic representation, and fantasy increase almost geometrically the complexity of play and social gratifications. For the toddler, the caregiver, while still maintaining her intimate care functions, further differentiates into playmate, teacher, confidante. The child's social play with other children can often be seen to contain remarkably subtle communication. The gratifications available at Stage V are extremely wide, and are organized in complex ways by the children in the separation situation. At Stage V the children themselves select and organize gratifications specifically in relation to the departure of the mother.

The third element of Pine's progression is the self/object relationship: "From (a) diffuse ... delineation of body boundaries to (b) more differentiated ... object concept ... to (c) object relationship ..." In these observations, in the first months the caregiver is functionally equivalent to the mother and not significantly differentiated from her, given the familiar nursery context of complete assumption of mothering functions during the time the infant is there. The play of the first months highlights the undifferentiated body orientation of the baby. Following the perceptual discrimination of the caregiver from the mother, the infant begins to notice their comings and goings and then to take particular notice of the mother's departure. There are, in these data, a series of perceptual-kinesthetic phenomena that precede the appearance of distress.

As the infant selects a particular caregiver, distress appears at the mother's departure late in the first year. Through the second year, the caregiver's functions expand into play and amusement provision and to participation as a playmate. The infant has now achieved object permanence in nonimmediate space and time: the present caregiver and the absent mother are clearly differentiated. In the third year, the child's relationships with caregivers in the separation situation become genuinely socially interactive, with many nuances and variations. At this stage the child actively institutes these relationships and uses them in a variety of ways, specifically in relation to the mother's departure, in allaying distress, gaining substitute gratification, and pursuing autonomous interests in her absence.

The normal separating sequence begins in the infant's earliest perceptions and experiences of the mother's movements toward and away. It evolves through a series of stages coordinating and advancing developments in cognition (e.g., discrimination of persons, disappearance, object permanence, space and time perception) and affect (first the mother's disappearance, and then her absence, toward object constancy).

The emerging capacity of the infant and toddler to separate temporally and spatially from the mother is then understood as a developmental progression.

Elaborating Pine's formulation (1971) from the five stages described, a developmental line for focalization of distress behavior may be stated as follows:

From (a) a perceptual and kinesthetic recognition of mother's movements in nearby space to (b) affective and cognitive focalization of the mother's immediate departure to (c) diffuse distress in her absence to (d) affective and cognitive focalization of her absence to (e) the use of cognitive and symbolic resources to modulate and structure feelings and activities in the mother's absence.

In fact, these stages incorporate a series of progressions in sensorimotor, perceptual, affective, attachment, play, and cognitive functions. These coordinate in changing ways at each successive stage.

Other sublines, then, may be stated briefly as follows:

1. Visual perception: From focal gaze to visual tracking.
2. Auditory perception: From focal attention to language assimilation.
3. Motor: From kinesthetic-responsive to motor-active in locomotor tracking and gestures maintaining proximity and then to independent pursuits in action, learning, and mastery.

4. Affective: From nonfocal to focal to self-modulated.
5. Cognitive: From object permanence of persons in immediate space and time to object permanence of persons in remote space and time.
6. Differentiation: From self-object differentiation to increasing differentiation among people, events, and sequences of experience.
7. Play: From disturbance responsive to externally provided play to autonomous production to utilization as expressive, modulating, and organizing.

The baby successively coordinates achievements in these areas at different levels of mastery. In the separation situation they appear first as general developments, and then come to be used specifically in connection with the mother's departure and then with her absence. The general progress toward increasing complexity occurs over long periods of time. Similarly, the use of these achievements in connection with separating evolves over a long period.

Toward the third year, in these observations, the capacity to separate involves those modulating and structuring behaviors that developmentally follow focalization. Those behaviors instituted by the child as adaptations to separating serve to balance feelings, autonomy, gratifications, and attachment. The beginnings of the development of structuralized defense formation (Pine, 1971) with respect to separation are then seen.

The coordination of developments presented in the progression of stages elucidates developmental precursors and the behavioral applications of psychoanalytic theories of structure (see Nagera, 1967; Gill, 1963; Holt, 1967) as well as of ethological formulations of functional hierarchies of behavior (see Lorenz, 1973; Tinbergen, 1951). In Stage I the structural beginnings were in the coordination of sensory modalities with affect. The developments necessary to and underlying the two-stage focalization are understood in these data as complex and subtle differentiations and integrations of distress and its cognitive contents. In fact, this two-stage focalization may be thought of as separation organizers in Spitz's use of the term "organizer" (1959). When the separation event can be specified cognitively and emotionally by the infant in terms of disappearance and absence, then anticipatory, modulating behavior becomes fully possible to the toddler.

The integration and structuring of perceptual, cognitive, and affective processes culminates in Stage IV. The full focalization of distress (focal anxiety), together with emerging achievements in language communication, symbolic functioning, and differentiated social relationships, provide the basis for the emergence of child-generated modulations of separation behavior (defense). This organization, together with the new resources now available, make possible the development of individualized and situation-specific adaptations to the immediacy of the mother's departure and to the time-space aspects of her absence.

The achievement of relative stability and regular use of these structured organizations in Pine's terms of defense is probably a long-term, open-ended development. It is in a sense parallel to the open-endedness (Mahler, Pine, and Bergman, 1975) of the final phase of the separation-individuation process. These data are highly suggestive in terms of defense and structure developments. However, to make formulations that are fully data-based requires more propaedeutic observational study in the third and fourth years.

The infant's separation distress can then be viewed in terms of its natural emergence as part of a process of discrimination and the differentiation of people and of experience. Changes in distress behavior are indicators of stage achievement in progressive development in the child. Distress, in this view of stages, indicates in part what is right with the child and by no means altogether what is wrong in the environment—the mother's or the caregiver's handling—as producers of distress.

Persons permanence in immediate space and time, and then person permanence in remote space and time, are cognitive achievements. The capacities to feel and focalize feelings of loss at the departure and the absence of the mother, and then to be able to pursue autonomous pleasures and learning, are emotional achievements. The syntheses of these cognitive and emotional achievements are essential for the ensuing developments in modulating and structuring distress. The status and character of distress behavior is, in part, then, an indication of the status of these achievements—as adaptive signs.

These stages are presented as a succession of essential integrations for normal infant development. Because of the regular and daily nature of the separations, in these children the stages may be emerging very close to the earliest possible time. In this paper I have postulated a sequence of stages, not the ages at which they emerge. Children with different experiences of mother departing, in familiar and unfamiliar circumstances, will probably achieve these stages and make use of the coordinating developments at different rates.

For example, a few of the children we have observed entered the nursery during their third year. They seemed to respond successively at Stages III and IV before moving toward V, though they had available many of the complex coordinate developments of Stage V. Both the focal and diffuse distress were more intense in these children because the caregiver was clearly differentiated from the familiar family but as yet had no functional equivalence to the mother. For these children integration of strange people and a strange environment was clearly a more prolonged aspect of the Stage IV focalization.

At the beginning of this paper this work was conceived as a connecting link between the literature of intrapsychic separation-individuation and that of traumatic separation. The implication of the normal progression described here for traumatic separations (those that are prolonged and in strange settings) is that qualitatively different consequences are to be expected at the successive stages. That is, the resources an infant, toddler, or young child brings to and can use in response to the demands of major separations will depend first upon the achievements in the stages described here in separating in familiar environments with familiar people. The character of the distress and the nature of the adaptive failures and symptoms that ensue are likely to show considerable concordance with the characteristics of the stage achieved in the normal progression and the integration achieved in all of the sublines.

REFERENCES

Barker, R. G. (1960), *The Stream of Behavior*. New York: Appleton-Century-Crofts.

Bell, S. (1968), The Relationship of Infant-Mother Attachment to the Development of the Concept of Object Permanence. Unpublished doctoral dissertation, Johns Hopkins University.

Bender, L., & Yarnell, H. (1941), An Observational Nursery: A Study of 250 Children in the Psychiatric Division of Bellevue Hospital. *Amer. J. Psychiat.*, 97:1158-1174.

Benjamin, J. D. (1963), Further Comments on Some Developmental Aspects of Anxiety. In: *Counterpoint*, ed. H. S. Gaskill. New York: International Universities Press, pp. 121-153.

Bowlby, J. (1940), The Influence of Early Environment in the Development of Neurosis and Neurotic Character. *Internat. J. Psycho-Anal.*, 21:154-178.

――― (1944), Forty-Four Juvenile Thieves: Their Character and Home Life. *Internat. J. Psycho-Anal.*, 25:19-52, 107-127.

――― (1969), *Attachment and Loss*, Vol. 1. *Attachment*. New York: Basic Books.

――― (1973), *Attachment and Loss*, Vol. 2. *Separation, Anxiety and Danger*. New York: Basic Books.

Brossard, M. D. (1974), The Infant's Conception of Object Permanence and His Reactions to Strangers. In: *The Infant's Reaction to Strangers*, ed. T. G. Décarie. New York: International Universities Press, pp. 97-116.

Erikson, E. (1968), *Identity, Youth and Crisis*. New York: Norton.

Fairbairn, W. R. D. (1941), A Revised Psychopathology of the Psychoses and Psychoneuroses. In: *Object-Relations Theory of the Personality*. New York: Basic Books, 1954.

Freud, A. (1965), Normality and Pathology in Childhood: Assessments of Development. *The Writings of Anna Freud*, Vol. 6. New York: International Universities Press, 1965.

――― & Burlingham, D. (1942), Annual Report (January, 1942) [Young Children in Wartime]. *The Writings of Anna Freud*, Vol. 3. New York: International Universities Press, 1973, pp. 142-211.

――― ――― (1944), Infants without Families. *The Writings of Anna Freud*, Vol. 3. New York: International Universities Press, 1973, pp. 543-664.

Freud, S. (1926), Inhibitions, Symptoms and Anxiety. *Standard Edition*, 20: 87-172. London: Hogarth Press, 1959.

Gill, M. M. (1963), Topography and Systems in Psychoanalytic Theory. *Psychol. Issues*, Monogr. No. 10. New York: International Universities Press.

Goldfarb, W. (1943), Infant Rearing and Problem Behavior. *Amer. J. Orthopsychiat.*, 13:249-265.

Goulet, J. (1974), The Infant's Conception of Causality and His Reactions to Strangers. In: *The Infant's Reaction to Strangers*, ed. T. G. Décarie. New York: International Universities Press, pp. 59-96.

Heinicke, C. M. (1956), Some Effects of Separating Two-Year-Old Children from Their Parents: A Comparative Study. *Human Relat.*, 9:105-176.

――― & Westheimer, I. (1966), *Brief Separations*. New York: International Universities Press.

Holt, R. R. (1967), The Development of the Primary Process: A Structural View. *Psychol. Issues*, Monogr. No. 18/19:345-383. New York: International Universities Press.

Kaplan, L. J. (1972), Object Constancy in the Light of Piaget's Vertical Décalage. *Bull. Menninger Clin.*, 36:322-334.

Levy, D. (1937), Primary Affect Hunger. *Amer. J. Psychiat.*, 94:643-652.

Lorenz, K. (1973), Analogy as a Source of Knowledge. *Science*, 185:229-234.

Mahler, M. S. (1968), *On Human Symbiosis and the Vicissitudes of Individuation*, Vol. 1. *Infantile Psychosis*. New York: International Universities Press.

—— (1972), On the First Three Subphases of the Separation-Individuation Process. *Psychoanalysis and Contemporary Science*, 3:295-306. New York: International Universities Press, 1974.

—— Pine, F., & Bergman, A. (1975), *The Psychological Birth of the Human Infant*. New York: Basic Books.

Monroe, A. (1969), Parent-Child Separations. *Arch. Gen. Psychiat.*, 20:598-604.

Nagera, H. (1967), The Concepts of Structure and Structuralization. *The Psychoanalytic Study of the Child*, 22:77-102. New York: International Universities Press.

Piaget, J. (1936), *The Origins of Intelligence*. New York: International Universities Press, 1952.

—— (1945), *Play, Dreams and Imitation in Childhood*. New York: Norton, 1951.

Pine, F. (1971), On the Separation Process: Universal Trends and Individual Differences. In: *Separation-Individuation: Essays in Honor of Margaret S. Mahler*, ed. J. B. McDevitt & C. F. Settlage. New York: International Universities Press, pp. 113-130.

Provence, S., & Lipton, R. C. (1963), *Infants in Institutions*. New York: International Universities Press.

Robertson, J. (1952), Film: A Two-Year-Old Goes to the Hospital (16mm., 45 min). New York: New York University Film Library.

—— (1953), Some Responses of Young Children to Loss of Maternal Care. *Nurs. Times*, 49:382-386.

—— & Bowlby, J. (1952), Responses of Young Children to Separation from Their Mothers. *Courr. Cent. Int. Enf.*, 2:131-142.

Schaffer, H. R. (1958), Objective Observations of Personality Development in Early Infancy. *Brit. J. Med. Psychol.*, 31:174-183.

—— & Callender, W. M. (1959), Psychological Effects of Hospitalization in Infancy. *Pediatrics*, 24:528-539.

—— & Emerson, P. E. (1964), The Development of Social Attachments in Infancy. *Monogr. Soc. Res. Child Devel.*, 29, No. 3.

Spitz, R. A. (1945), Hospitalism. *The Psychoanalytic Study of the Child*, 1:53-74. New York: International Universities Press.

—— (1946), Hospitalism: A Follow-Up Report. *The Psychoanalytic Study of the Child*, 2:113-117. New York: International Universities Press.

—— (1950), Anxiety in Infancy: A Study of Its Manifestations in the First Year of Life. *Internat. J. Psycho-Anal.*, 31:138-143.

—— (1959), *A Genetic Field Theory of Ego Formation*. New York: International Universities Press.

—— (1965), *The First Year of Life*. New York: International Universities Press.

Tinbergen, N. (1951), *The Study of Instinct*. New York: Oxford University Press, 1969.

Werner, H. (1957), The Concept of Development from a Comparative and Organismic Point of View. In: *The Concept of Development: An Issue in the Study of Human Behavior*, ed. D. B. Harris. Minneapolis: University of Minnesota Press.

Willis, E. A., & Ricciuti, H. N. (1974), Longitudinal Observations of Infants' Daily Arrivals at a Day Care Center. A Technical Report from the Cornell Research Program in Early Development and Education. Unpublished.

Ellen L. Gay, M.A., and
Marion C. Hyson, M.A.

Blankets, Bears, and Bunnies: Studies of Children's Contacts with Treasured Objects

*I'd kill myself if anything
ever happened to that blanket.*
—A mother

The study described in this paper is an effort to apply a promising method to a little-researched and complex phenomenon in child development. Normal children under 4 often develop a tenacious attachment to a tattered blanket, a grimy piece of cloth, or a stuffed animal. Sometimes the child and his blanket[1] are literally inseparable; more often the child will go to it at intervals during the day, stroke or cuddle with it for a while, and then—seemingly refreshed—return to other activities.

Because children so frequently become devoted to these objects, and because the objects may play a role in the development of attachment, separation-individuation, and understanding of the world of things, we became interested in exploring this subject further in a controlled but naturalistic research study. For this purpose, we decided to adapt the "symptom-context" method

---

The authors, who took part equally in this paper, wish to thank Samuel Snyder, Ph.D., and Lester Luborsky, Ph.D., for the many suggestions and comments they contributed to the study.

[1] The term "blanket" will be used throughout this paper to represent all kinds of inanimate objects to which children may become attached—diapers, rags, pieces of fuzz or fur, stuffed animals, etc.

developed by Luborsky (1967; Luborsky and Auerbach, 1969) to analyze the elements preceding and following the appearance of a patient's symptom during a psychotherapy session. Our use of this method does not imply that a child's cuddle with her blanket is a pathological "symptom." We did, however, see some tantalizing similarities in the recurrent nature of the behavior and in the presence of characteristic patterns of situations and feelings surrounding the emergence of a symptom and a child's contact with her treasured object.

We hoped, then, that this preliminary study would accomplish two ends. First, we hoped that it would help us learn more about the ways in which young children use their treasured objects in coping with stress and in dealing with developmental issues in their lives. Second, we hoped to find out whether this particular method would be a useful way to analyze the context of this and many other recurring behaviors, both normal and disturbed.

THEORY AND RESEARCH

Our reading of the theoretical and research literature concerning the function of the treasured object in childhood revealed a number of widely varying opinions about this attachment but very little controlled, empirical research to back them up.

The theoretical explanations of children's treasured objects can be grouped into four general categories: the behaviorist view, the ethological position, the pathological view (regarding the object as a fetish), and the "presymbolic" view (a composite of a number of theorists' views of the object's role in relation to the child's developing mental structures).

The behaviorist view of the treasured object is the most parsimonious. Although behaviorists in general have not been concerned with the subject, Bijou and Baer (1965) describe the blanket as a "generalized reinforcer" which, through being paired with such things as warmth, sleep, and tactile stimulation, eventually becomes reinforcing in itself. Simple as it is, this explanation leaves unexplored a number of issues having to do with the very specific nature of the attachment, the calming effect of the blanket at times of stress, and the reason for the child's outgrowing the attachment.

The second perspective from which attachment to a treasured object can be examined is that of ethological theorists such as Bowlby (1969), who has closely examined the child's attachment to his mother as a primary survival mechanism. Bowlby briefly discusses clinging to a blanket as a substitute form of attachment behavior when the mother is unavailable; he doubts that the blanket has any broader significance. However, a look at the implications of his theory might suggest that, if indeed the blanket contributes to such characteristically human behavior as the manipulation of symbols and the freedom to explore, it could have a "survival value" beyond that of a mere mother substitute.

The mother's absence is regarded in a less literal and more sinister light by Sperling (1963), who asserts that a profound, qualitative disturbance in the mother-child relationship results in a child's becoming attached to a fetish—an inanimate object such as a "security blanket." Greenacre (1960, 1969) questions the generality of this explanation, and draws some useful distinctions between the normal treasured object of childhood and the pathological fetish. Perhaps, like most aspects of development, attachment to a treasured object can be either normal or pathological, depending on its over-all effect on the child.

The "presymbolic view" (Gay, 1976) does not represent one theorist or even one theory. Rather, it is an attempt to synthesize a number of ideas which are consistent with one another and which describe the treasured object in relation to the child's developing mental structures. Under this umbrella can be placed many psychoanalytic writers (e.g., Winnicott, 1958; A. Freud, 1936, 1965; Tolpin, 1971). Piaget's description of the stages in a young child's understanding of objects (see Flavell, 1963) is a complementary perspective from which to look at "blanket" attachment.

Of course, each contributor to this view of the treasured object has his or her own emphasis, but a reading of their work shows a number of points on which they might be in general agreement:

1. The child's attachment to the treasured object is positive and healthy. It enhances normal psychological development.

2. The uses and purposes of the treasured object change as the child develops; at any given time, the particular use the child makes of his blanket both reflects and contributes to the development of mental structures and object relationships. Even the

regressive, "babyish" behavior often seen in children's contacts with their blankets may actually serve an adaptive function.

3. The treasured object reflects and plays a part in separation-individuation (see Tolpin, 1971). It aids the child in the process by which he comes to see himself as distinct from other people. With the help of his "portable soother," he can tolerate separations from his mother while beginning to internalize some of her role as regulator of tension and allayer of fears.

4. The treasured object reflects and plays a part in the development of "object permanence," the process by which the child comes to know that people and objects other than himself are constant regardless of whether he can see or touch them. The very young child may become seriously distressed when his mother or blanket cannot be found; later he may tolerate separation from the mother if a "fuzzy reminder" is nearby; still later the blanket itself may be discarded without a qualm.

5. The treasured object reflects and plays a part in the child's growing ability to fantasize—to create and manipulate representatives or symbols of absent objects. On the same day, the blanket may be mother, a whip, a ball, a cape—and just a blanket.

6. The treasured object is uniformly soothing. The child always considers it as a comfort, a secure base, or a helper. These are the main reasons his blanket is so important to him.

In an earlier theoretical paper, one of us (Hyson, 1974), working within the presymbolic framework, began to explore the possible relationship between normal defensive processes and the child's use of a treasured object. Hyson speculated that the regulatory function of the blanket is analogous to the function of defenses in lessening anxiety and facilitating the child's eventual adaptation to reality, and that indeed a child's contacts with his blanket may sometimes be visible signs of defensive processes at work. Descriptions in the literature of the circumstances surrounding a child's contacts with his blanket—states of worry, conflict, exhaustion, etc.—sound very much like the kinds of inner and outer threats that give rise to defense mechanisms and coping behaviors both in children and in adults.

If this relationship in fact exists, Hyson reasoned that it should be possible to describe a child's various uses of his blanket as analogues of the various mechanisms of defense (as described, for instance, by A. Freud, 1936). One child may cover her head with her blanket when frightened—seemingly using the blanket to help her deny the existence of the feared object; another child may project his fears onto his teddy bear and assert that teddy is afraid robbers are coming in the window. Hyson speculated that children of different ages may use their treasured objects in characteristically different ways, reflecting different stages of growth in ego and cognitive processes as well as individual differences in over-all coping style and hierarchy of defenses.

Various criteria have been proposed for evaluating the normality of defenses in children; these, too, can be used in assessing the role of the beloved blanket in a child's development. Using these criteria (A. Freud, 1965; Lampl-de Groot, 1957), Hyson suggests that a child's contacts with his blanket can be considered normal if they ultimately help him adapt to or cope with reality (even if by a temporarily regressive or reality-distorting route) and if they do not hinder the over-all course of his development.

It is obvious, then, that the various theories about children's treasured objects raise a great many questions. Answers to some of these have been empirically sought.

Parental reports have been used by Stevenson (1954) and Busch (1974) to describe children's typical patterns of attachment. Some informal observations of children with their blankets have been made (Busch, 1974) and individual case studies have been reported (e.g., Roiphe and Galenson, 1975). While these data basically support the presymbolic view of the normal, adaptive function of the blanket, the accuracy of parental reports and the representativeness of the clinical cases can certainly be questioned.

Using a controlled experimental setting, Weisberg and Russell (1971), Passman (1974), and Passman and Weisberg (1975) have investigated the tendency of children to move to their special blanket in preference to other objects or the mother, as well as the effect of the presence of the blanket in facilitating exploratory behavior and discrimination learning. Again, their research suggests that the blanket can have an adaptive and positive role in development.

This survey of the existing theory and research on treasured objects influenced several decisions that we made in planning our study.

First, we were attracted by the presymbolists' emphasis on the role of the blanket in the child's efforts to deal with anxiety and other kinds of stress. We were particularly interested in testing Hyson's ideas about the relationship between normal defensive processes and the child's use of his blanket, and in extending this investigation beyond defense to include other forms of coping as well. To do these things we needed to look closely at patterns of stress, regression, and other variables *before*, *during*, and *after* the child's contact with the blanket.

Second, we wanted to pursue the notion, suggested by Hyson, that children of different ages might use their special objects in ways cognitively and emotionally appropriate to their stage of development (and to deal with issues specific to that stage of development). We therefore decided to study children of different ages—2½- to 3-year-olds and 4½- to 5-year-olds.

Third, we found in the literature a stress on pure theory, clinical observation, or—at the opposite extreme—rigorously controlled studies in a laboratory setting; we saw a need for a naturalistic but controlled study of real children in real homes with real blankets.

RESEARCH METHOD

It is no simple matter to find ways of checking what meanings a treasured object such as a "security blanket" has for its owner. Many researchers have complained about the difficulties of obtaining clear empirical evidence for intrapsychic causes of behavior. The multiple sources of many behaviors, the problems of observer bias in determining what intrapsychic meanings an observable behavior has, and the impossibility of isolating for study one behavior or affect from other connected ones are all well-documented research obstacles (Meehl, 1973; Waelder, 1964).

The method we adapted for our purposes—the "symptom-context" method—was one Luborsky (1967) devised to study the contexts in which patients' symptoms emerge during psychotherapy or psychoanalytic sessions. Luborsky has for some time been interested in testing the psychoanalytic hypothesis that frightening or unacceptable thoughts or feelings that enter consciousness may be followed by the emergence of a symptom, which both alleviates anxiety created by the thought and takes the thought's place. Luborsky has studied such symptoms as momentary forgetting and periodic stomach upset by examining the patients' verbalizations before and after the symptom emerges. These verbalizations are then compared with "control" verbalizations drawn from interview material far removed from the appearance of the symptom. Luborsky's research suggests that there are both general and individual patterns in symptom emergence. Some indicators, such as "helplessness," precede symptom emergence in nearly all cases (Luborsky and Mintz, 1974). Still, each patient is quite consistent in displaying his own specific worries before symptom emergence, and these fears or worries represent core issues for that patient.

The symptom-context method seemed a happy choice for studying possible stress-reducing effects of the child's treasured object. It is a method which allows one to keep track of the play of observable behavior and emotions before, while, and after the child is touching the blanket or teddy. Individual children can be studied in detail, so that a given child's particular pattern of blanket use can be charted. Furthermore, children can be compared, and common patterns can emerge. Since each child serves as his own control, periods of blanket use can be compared with periods of nonuse.

We thought also that our adaptation of Luborsky's method would test its potential for examining other recurrent child behaviors. A sturdy means of discriminating the stages of feelings and behavior surrounding particular events would offer almost unlimited possibilities for the study of, for example, tantrums and crying, expressions of affection, mastery play, messy play, fantasy play, repetitive withdrawal, compulsive behavior, periodic hyperactivity, and enuresis.

The major alteration of the symptom-context method for our study was that observation notes on children in their homes were used instead of transcripts from psychotherapy sessions. Luborsky rates the patient's verbalizations before and after the appearance of the symptom; we rated an observer's detailed sequential notes on the child's behavior, her apparent emotions, verbalizations, and interactions with others. Segments of observation notes on the child's behavior before she made contact with the blanket, while she was touching it, and after she had given it up, were compared with each other and with controls on a number of scales of stress and regression.

Luborsky has had to depend on getting appropriate tapes or transcripts of psychotherapy sessions in order to do his work. For this reason, he has generally studied one subject at a time. We decided to use four children in this preliminary study. The amount of time and work required for observing and rating discouraged us from using a larger sample; and we believed that four children, two in each of two age groups, were enough to allow us to test some hypotheses, and the utility of the method for our purposes.

PARENT INTERVIEWS

The theoretical literature on treasured objects and on coping and regressive behavior in children gave us some ideas about items we might include in our ratings of our observations. To ground these ratings more firmly in reality, we decided to interview 20 parents of children attached to blankets or other inanimate objects (and the variety was certainly astounding). At the same time we hoped to use the interviews to collect some general information about this subject and to find four children to observe at home. To avoid biasing our home observations, the parents of the four children chosen for observation were not interviewed in depth.

The parents were predominantly middle- to upper-middle-class mothers of nursery-school children, who had responded to a letter requesting their participation in our study. The ages of the children discussed ranged from 2 to 7, including some siblings. Our interview consisted of an open-ended, semistructured telephone conversation based on the questions listed in Appendix 1.

In general, the results of our interviews tended to corroborate other reports in the literature (Stevenson, 1954; Busch, 1974).

A look at the most relevant interview findings will provide an introduction to the ratings we derived from them. (The number of responses was 20 except when otherwise specified.)

1. Age of first attachment

	No. of responses
0-6 months	6
6 mo.-1 year	5
1-2 years	6
2-3 years	3
3-4 years	0
4-5 years	0

Children develop these attachments early; the distribution from birth to 2 years was fairly even, with no children reported as developing an attachment after age 3. Two mothers noted *very* early and specific attachment (within the first month); one baby chewed the corners of his crib blanket at 3-4 weeks; another refused to go to sleep in a strange place until the mother discovered that he was used to the cotton crib sheet she placed over him at home. Several mothers voluntarily mentioned special circumstances which accompanied the "real" beginning of attachment: weaning, a new sibling, hospitalization.

2. Physical appearance of object (5 parents reported more than one object)

	No. of responses
Blanket with silky binding	11
Other blanket	5
Diaper	1
Rag, cloth, or sheet	1
Stuffed animal	6
Other	1

The winner in popularity is certainly the blanket with a silky binding, the binding being the part to which the child is most attached. A number of children are reported to have more than one object; in four of five such cases, the second object is a stuffed animal. One mother believed that her child used his blanket for comfort and security and his bear for companionship, the bear being a more "socially acceptable alternative" at the grocery store and library. A number of children had multiple objects—several identical diapers, cloths, or blankets—often representing the mother's attempt to avoid a crisis if one should be lost.

3. Similarity of object to mother's clothing while nursing

	No. of responses
Yes	5
No	2
Not discussed in interview	13

This relationship has been suggested in the literature, but most mothers had not thought about the possibility; in some cases the subject did not come up in the interview. However, five mothers were quite convinced that the child became attached to a specific object because it resembled the clothing the mother wore while nursing him. One mother usually nursed the baby with her sweater pushed up and resting against the baby's nose; the child now sniffs her woolly blanket and rubs it against her nose (she did not begin doing this until she was weaned). Another mother remembers wearing silky robes while nursing her baby; the child now rubs the silky binding of her blanket and sometimes rhythmically strokes her mother's stockings or scarf if the blanket is not available.

4. Association of object with thumb, pacifier, bottle

	No. of responses
Always	3
Sometimes	9
Never	2
No response	6

It seems that, for many children, the blanket has oral associations. This finding, too, corroborates the theoretical literature (e.g., Winnicott, 1958). Only two children were reported as *never* sucking thumb, pacifier, or bottle while using the object, and of these, one sucks the blanket itself. Some mothers reported that thumb-sucking declined with increasing age, although the blanket attachment remained.

5. Physical manner in which object is used (6 parents reported more than one mode)

	No. of responses
Tactile—rubs, strokes	8
Oral—chews, sucks	3
Smells, sniffs	2
Holds or hugs	7
Covers body with it	5
No predominant mode	0
Other	1

Although a number of children use their object in more than one way, most of them seem to be attracted to the tactile aspects of the loved object; they stroke it, rub it, or hug it. Two children sniff their blankets—something that Busch (1974) did not see. One mother commented that her child, who strokes the binding of his blanket, seems to be basically a tactile, sensuous person—he loves to stroke his mother's fur hat, and his favorite stuffed animal has a particularly soft, fuzzy texture. It would be interesting to explore these preferences further; perhaps children who become attached to blankets have a greater need for sensory stimulation than those who do not.

6. Role of parents in attachment

	No. of responses
Definitely encouraged original attachment	6
No role in first attachment but feels it is a good thing	5
Ambivalent	7
Negative	0
Not discussed in interview	2

Considering that all the respondents were volunteers, it is understandable that none of them expressed clearly negative feelings about their children's treasured objects. What was interesting was the amount of ambivalence and the reasons for it, stated or implied. One mother, involved in a LaLeche nursing group, seemed to feel that intense attachment to an object was an effect of premature weaning, and that her child did not need his teddy bear as much as other children did because his needs were so fully satisfied. Several mothers expressed feelings of rejection when their child turned to a blanket for comfort rather than to them; others tolerated the attachment only within certain limits (e.g., at bedtime).

Generally there seemed to be a concern about the possibility of the child's developing a pathological dependence on the object, as well as some concern over what others might think of the child— and the parents. Conflicts within families over the blanket were also reported; for instance, an orderly father who teases his son about the "filthy" blanket, and visiting grandparents who try to discourage the child's attachment.

7. *Physical changes in object since original attachment*

	No. of responses
Original object—no change	7
Original object with modifications (e.g., new binding)	4
Substitute for original object but similar (e.g., new teddy)	6
Entirely different object	2
Not discussed in interview	1

As a group, the children seem remarkably consistent in their affections. Only two children have entirely different objects now; most of the changes reported were wrought out of necessity and such domestic tragedies as the trashman taking the blanket away, or the teddy bear being left in a gas station washroom. Particularly striking are the persistence and ingenuity of parents in devising substitutes and replacements, showing their sensitivity to the importance of the object to the child. One mother has knit numerous satin-edged blankets; another mother and father spent a year and a half looking for a perfect replacement for a disintegrating teddy.

8. *Reaction of a child to loss of object*

	No. of responses
Extreme anxiety, agitation	3
Moderate distress	9
Not much reaction	1
Not discussed in interview	7

Most parents reported moderate distress in the child when the blanket is missing. Some mothers mentioned that, with increasing age, the child is less upset by the blanket's disappearance; this observation has cognitive as well as emotional implications. Some children are ambivalent about their need for the object; one little girl is in the habit of throwing down her blanket and doll, saying, "I don't need them any more," but her mother noted that she always changes her mind at bedtime.

Many of the parents' answers to earlier questions suggest the lengths to which they have gone to insure that even moderate distress is avoided.

9. Child's personality (dimension of dependence/independence)

	No. of responses
Dependent, fearful, shy	6
Independent, outgoing	10
Not discussed in interview	4

This question was intended to explore the validity of the Linus stereotype—the neurotic, fearful child clinging to his security blanket for dear life. Judging by parents' responses to an open-ended question about their child's personality, this stereotype is far from accurate. Especially striking were the spontaneous comments by some parents expressing surprise that it was *this* child (the outgoing one) who had become so attached to a "security blanket" rather than a shy, reserved sibling. Certainly these parental reports need to be validated by other measures.

10. Times when child needs and uses object

Since many parents mentioned a great number of ways in which the child used his blanket or bear, these ways are listed below in descending order of frequency.

	No. of responses
Tired, sleepy	20
Separation	15
Fantasy play	14
TV watching	9
Injured or sick	7

Dominated or scolded	6
Interaction with others	4
Fearful, anxious	3
Cranky, upset	2
Angry, frustrated	2

The answers to this question were most useful in suggesting items for our rating scales and in corroborating theoretical discussions of the function of the treasured object. Generally the child's use of his blanket seemed varied and flexible (unlike descriptions of rigid, fetishistic attachments). Several parents offered descriptions of the child's use of his object which did not fit easily into any of the above categories. The issues of control and balance came up frequently. One child seems to see her blanket as a means of differentiating herself from a very capable older sister (who does not have a blanket). Another child uses his blanket as a way to control others, and as something over which he has exclusive control. "Bugsy never gives him any lip," said one mother, explaining the appeal of her son's toy rabbit. Two mothers mentioned that their children seem to use their objects as a means of controlling themselves when they become "wild" or "hyperactive." One 4-year-old boy has to have a 15-minute session alone with his blanket after nursery school; the mother of a 6-year-old feels that he needs his teddy bear for "quiet times to balance himself."

The child's fantasy play with his treasured object often shows a belief in its magical powers. "Superman" or "Batgirl" play is common, with the blanket used as a cape. Other children build protective structures such as tents and hideouts with their blankets. Several children insist on being totally covered with the blanket at bedtime as a protection against monsters, snakes, and other nighttime dangers. Children are sometimes willing to share the blanket's power, however. One child gives her blanket to friends to sniff (they are not always appreciative); another offered his blanket to his mother when he saw her crying.

RATING SCALES

These descriptions by parents of the circumstances surrounding their child's contacts with his blanket were helpful to us in devising items for scales to be used in rating our observations.

In creating these scales, we expected to find—and did find—that some items were far more useful than others in rating the observations. We also realized after the fact that we should have included items that we omitted. While the present study is thus less "tidy" than it might be, it may also be more useful as a basis for further research.

From the parent interviews, and from a theoretical base influenced by the presymbolic view, we devised three clusters of items (see Appendix 2 for a fuller description), 18 scales in all.

A. Individual scales (these rated the child—affects and behaviors)

Anxiety
Fearfulness
Tiredness, sleepiness
Physical and verbal passivity
Upset
Anger
Habits (thumb-sucking, rocking, etc.)
Frustration
Lability of affect
Aimless physical activity
Age-inappropriate use of language

B. Interactional or environmental scales (these rated the child in relation to the situation or interaction)

Separation (actual or discussed)
Interactional conflict
Control (child feels controlled by or fails to control others)
Unfulfilled need
Affront
Need for closeness

C. Miscellaneous scale

Regression/Progression—any situation (often fantasy play) in which child shows behavior which contrasts infantlike aspects with adultlike aspects (e.g., playing Superman with a blanket cape)

Early in our ratings of observation notes it became apparent that some children behaved in "babyish" or age-inappropriate ways (e.g., whining, crawling, "bathroom talk") which were not being tapped by scales such as Tiredness, Passivity, Age-Inappropriate Use of Language, etc. We therefore devised an additional, nineteenth scale, General Regression, to rate age-inappropriate behaviors that did not fit into the other categories.

In our analysis of the ratings, we combined the individual scales for "Upset" and "Angry" when it became apparent that they were measuring essentially the same affect.

Each of our observation-note segments was rated on all of these scales as follows:

     0 = absence of behavior, affect, or situation
     1 = some of behavior, affect, or situation
     2 = a large amount of behavior, affect, or situation

HYPOTHESES AND QUESTIONS

Although we considered this an exploratory study (because of the small number of children observed and the absence of similar research), our theoretical views and the reports of parents we interviewed led us to expect to find certain things when we applied our scales to the observation notes and analyzed the results.

1. We expected to find an increase in stressful behavior or situations immediately before the child seeks contact with his blanket. This finding would be consistent with Hyson's view of contact with the blanket as a way of coping with inner and outer stress.

2. We expected to find that contact with the blanket indeed makes the child "feel better"—and thus expected a lower number of stress indicators immediately following contact with the blanket. This finding would be consistent with the view of the blanket as a way of coping with stress.

3. We expected to find age differences in the kinds of factors that precipitate contact with the blanket, although we were not sure just what the pattern would be. These differences would be consistent with theories of cognitive and psychosexual development.

4. We also expected to find strong individual differences.

In addition to these expectations, we had a number of questions, the answers to which we could not predict with certainty:

1. Which of our scales would prove to be most (and least) helpful in discriminating control segments from "blanket" segments?

2. Would our home observations reveal factors that clearly were missed by our scales?

3. And, most generally, would the method prove workable, appropriate, and useful in understanding the dynamics of a child's day-to-day use of her treasured object?

PROCEDURE

After our initial brief interviews with the parents, we selected four children to observe by considering how likely it was that we would see a good amount of interaction with the treasured object during a morning or an afternoon observation. Our plan was to go to each child's home twice and observe and write notes about him or her for 2 hours each time. To get observational reliability, we (two observers) simultaneously wrote notes on a nursery-school child not in our study, stopping at 10-minute intervals to check how closely our observations were matching in global and molecular content, in balance between affect and content, and in reports of interactions with others. Though we have no quantitative measure of our reliability, we were satisfied that we were seeing and recording essentially the same things.

Following this practice session, two observers watched and wrote notes on four children for a total of 16 hours (two 2-hour observation periods for each child). MH observed two boys, aged 2½ to 3 years, and EG observed two girls, aged 4½ to 5 years. The sex difference was not planned, and it was not specifically examined, since none of the literature on treasured objects suggested sex differences in use of the blanket.

After the observation sessions, the observers marked off on their notes the periods of interaction with the treasured object. Then 100-word sections of notes were marked for the periods just *before* the child's moves to the object and *after* she had temporarily given the object up.[2]

---

[2] Some pre and post segments had to be less than 100 words each, because there were times when treasured-object contacts were so close together that fewer than 200 words intervened.

For each contact with the object, then, there were three observation-note segments: *pre, during,* and *post.* From the residual observational material, separated as much as possible from the object-contact segments, we randomly selected control segments corresponding to each object-contact segment.[3] The object-contact segments and the controls were matched in length. The six types of segments, then, were pre, during, post, pre control, during control, and post control.

The observation notes were typed, cut into segments, and pasted on sheets. Specific references to the child touching, picking up, or putting down his blanket were left out, so that the "during" segments and their controls could not be readily discriminated from each other by the rater. The number of segments ranged from 22 to 55 for a 2-hour observation period.

Interrater reliability between the two observer-raters was achieved by talking over the scales and trying them out, first on the observations of a child in nursery school, and then on extra observation notes on the four children. After the first few attempts, agreement was over 90%. Periodic rechecks of interrater reliability showed continuing agreement of 90% or better. For this reason, and because the rater who had observed a given child had more information about that child (i.e., she remembered material from actually having been there), each observer rated her own observations.

We made rating sheets so that each segment could be easily rated on the 19 indicators, and marked down 0, 1, or 2 in the appropriate boxes.

RESULTS

There are a number of ways to analyze our ratings. We will begin by discussing the most general effects and then look at the patterns of the individual children.

The most general kind of analysis we performed was averaging

---

[3] As it turned out, there was not enough observational material on two of the children, Ben and Sally, to select control segments for all of the experimental ones. The reason was that they contacted their treasured objects so frequently that an insufficient quantity of material was left in between. We handled this problem by assigning controls to the pre and post segments but not to the durings.

all the ratings before, during, and after contact with the blanket and comparing those averages with averages of ratings for the control segments. This analysis yielded a distinctive pattern common to all four children, showing a buildup of the content and affects measured by our scales *before* the children go to their objects. The conditions measured appear to reach a peak while the child is holding or using the object and then to decline after he leaves the object. This effect can be seen in Figure 1.

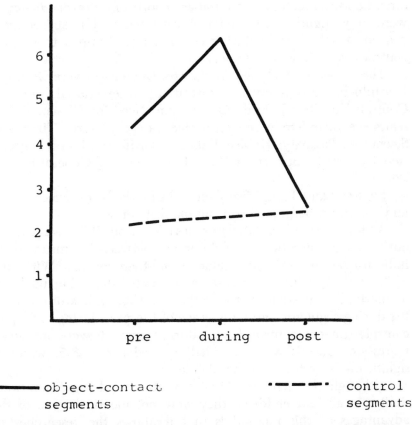

object-contact segments · control segments

FIGURE 1. Mean ratings of the four children on all scales. These ratings were calculated by adding all ratings for each category of segments (pre, post, etc.) and dividing by the total number of segments in each category. Because of insufficient observational material, controls for the during segments were not obtainable for two of the four children. For this reason, during controls are not included in this figure.

As we looked more closely at the individual scale ratings, however, it became clear that to average all scales is misleading. Some of the indicators were primarily responsible for the buildup *before* blanket contact, and others tended to account for the high averages *during* contact.

What emerged was that, for all subjects, indicators of *stress* were very prevalent before contact with the treasured object, declined somewhat while the children were with their objects, and then sank to control level after the blankets were given up. On the other hand, indicators of a number of sorts of *regressive behavior* were only slightly above control level before blanket contact, peaked at a high level during contact, and dropped to roughly control level following contact.

The scales we included in the *stress* category were: Anxiety; Fearfulness; Upset/Anger; Frustration; Interactional Conflict; Control; Unfulfilled Need; Affront; and Need for Closeness. The scales we included in the *regressive* category were: Tiredness/Sleepiness; Passivity; Habits; Lability of Affect; Aimless Physical Activity; Age-Inappropriate Use of Language; and General Regression.

Figures 2 and 3 graphically show the marked difference in stress and regression before and during blanket contact.

A *t* test for two correlated samples (Ferguson, 1971) was carried out to test the significance of difference between the mean stress-indicator ratings in the *pre* segments and their controls. With an *n* of 4, $t = 2.45$, which is significant at better than the .05 level. Similarly, the difference between the regression-indicator means in the during segments and an average of the pre, during, and post control segments (controls for the during segments were few, so all regression controls were included) yielded a *t* of 8.5, which is significant at better than the .005 level.

Although the general patterns of stress and regression were similar in all four children, they were not identical. One of the advantages of this method is that it allows the researcher or clinician to focus on individual differences as well as group effects. To describe these individual differences, we will now look at each of the four children in turn, basing our conclusions on three kinds of data. First, we can use the observation notes to provide a rich picture of the child's distinctive style of using his treasured object.

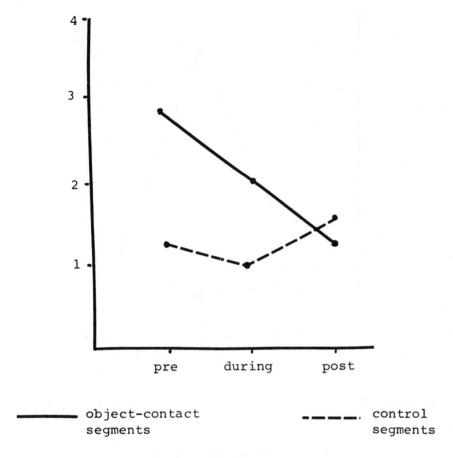

FIGURE 2. Mean stress ratings

Second, we will look at some differences in each child's graphs of stress and regression. Third, we will examine the particular scales that figured most prominently in each child's ratings.

Timmy. The observation notes show Timmy to be a sturdy, mischievous child of 2½ who spent a great deal of time darting about from playroom to kitchen to bedroom (with the observer scribbling frantically behind). His attention span is still very brief, and he was easily frustrated by the often difficult activities he chose. His investigations often led him into trouble; for instance, he broke the television set by fiddling with the dials, and he dropped some toys into his milk, spilling it in the process.

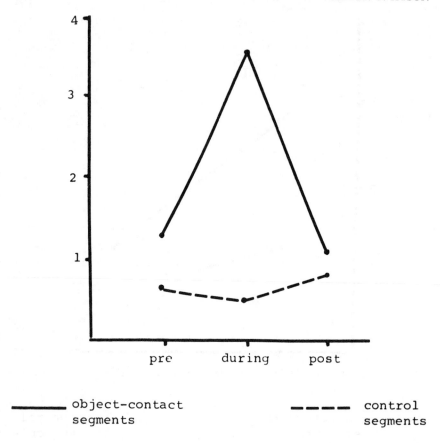

FIGURE 3. Mean regression ratings

Timmy's treasured objects are a well-worn, satin-bound blanket and, secondarily, a knit "puppy." The blanket figured prominently in television-watching episodes (where he seemed to use TV and blanket together as calming devices), in preparing to leave the house at the end of the morning, and as a comfort when he was scolded sharply by his mother. His behavior with the blanket was markedly regressive; he usually lay down with it, stroking or cuddling it in a "babyish" manner. He also used it for retaliation; at one point, perhaps feeling generally bossed around, he hit the observer with his blanket.

The observations showed that, like many 2-year-olds, Timmy vacillates between dependence and independence, between frustrated whining and peremptory commands. Balance is not his strong point; perhaps his blanket helps him come closer to it.

Figures 4 and 5 show Timmy's ratings on stress and regression.

These figures show the basic pattern that surrounds the use of the treasured object in all four children. However, it is worth noting that the decrease in stress in Timmy's post segments is less marked than it is for Ben and Sally. He is often still upset after a session with his blanket. This difference suggests that for Timmy the blanket is a less effective calming device than it is for some other children.

An even clearer picture of Timmy's use of his treasured object is shown in his ratings on individual scales (see Table 1, p. 296).

Table 1 shows which kinds of issues and feelings were most likely to precede, accompany, and follow Timmy's contacts with his blanket. In the pre segments, the scales measuring Upset/ Anger, Interactional Conflict, and Control were rated highest. Like many 2-year-olds, Timmy seems to be engaged in a series of skirmishes involving issues of conflict and control. His cuddles with the blanket, accompanied by the indicators of Tiredness, Passivity, Habits, Lability of Affect, and General Regression, appear to serve as a way of retreating from the difficulties of this struggle for autonomy. The presence of high ratings on Upset/Anger in the during segments reflects his occasional tendency (seen in the observations) to use the blanket as a weapon or a "safety valve."

Ben. Ben is slightly older but a good deal smaller and more frail-looking than Timmy. As an infant he was seriously ill with an intestinal blockage which required surgery at 7 weeks; his mother attributes his now devoted attachment to his pacifier and bunny to the unhappy feeding experiences he had in his first few months. He made a good recovery, however, and now is a pleasant, quiet little boy who still walks with a bit of a toddle.

Turning to the observation notes, the theme of submission seemed to run through both of Ben's observation sessions; during one he was bossed around by an older sister and her friend; during the other he played second fiddle to a more assertive friend of the same age (of whom he is very fond), and ended the morning with a tantrum over not being allowed to stay outdoors. In all of these situations his bunny (and a piece of fur from the bunny's disintegrated predecessor) seemed to provide an escape and release when

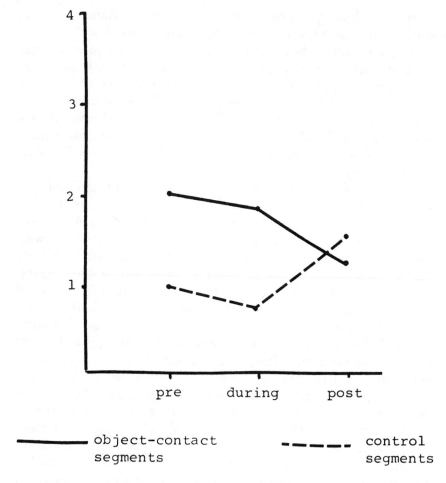

FIGURE 4. Stress ratings for Timmy

things got too difficult, and enabled him to express feelings that his verbal limitations and rather timid nature did not otherwise permit him.

Like Timmy, Ben sometimes lay down and cuddled with his bunny; in contrast to Timmy, however, he also used it in rich symbolic play or in friendly interactions with other people. Both active coping efforts and more reality-distorting defensive maneuvers could be seen in Ben's flexible and varied contacts with his treasured object.

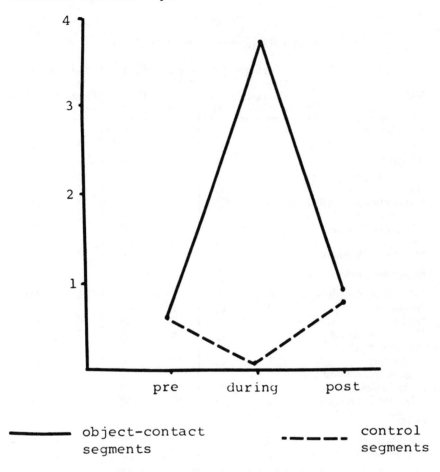

4

3

2

1

pre   during   post

——————— object-contact   ▬ ▬ ▬ ▬ control
          segments   segments

FIGURE 5. Regression ratings for Timmy

The curves of stress and regression for Ben (Figures 6 and 7) show a marked decline of all indicators in the post segments, confirming the impression from the observation notes of the effective way in which Ben uses his bunny to soothe himself and to cope with stress.

Ben's ratings on individual scales (see Table 2, p. 299) show a distinctive individual pattern. Like Timmy's, Ben's pre segments are rated high on Interactional Conflict and Control; in addition, Ben's ratings are very high on Upset/Anger and Separation. The observation notes show that Ben's family was packing for a trip

TABLE 1

TIMMY'S RATINGS ON INDIVIDUAL SCALES

Scale	Pre Segments Object-Contact Control $n=12$ $n=12$		During Segments Object-Contact Control $n=12$ $n=12$		Post Segments Object-Contact Control $n=12$ $n=12$	
Stress Scales						
Anxiety	1	(1)	1	(0)	0	(0)
Fearfulness	2	(1)	1	(0)	0	(0)
*Upset/Anger	4	(2)	7	(2)	1	(4)
Frustration	1	(4)	0	(1)	3	(4)
*Interactional Conflict	6	(2)	3	(0)	1	(2)
*Control	6	(0)	5	(3)	2	(4)
Unfulfilled Need	0	(1)	1	(2)	3	(2)
Affront	1	(1)	0	(0)	3	(0)
*Need for Closeness	2	(0)	3	(0)	0	(0)
Regression Scales						
*Tiredness, Sleepiness	0	(0)	7	(0)	0	(1)
*Passivity	0	(0)	7	(0)	1	(1)
*Habits	0	(1)	6	(0)	0	(0)
*Lability of Affect	3	(2)	8	(0)	3	(0)
Aimless Physical Activity	1	(2)	2	(0)	0	(0)
Age-Inappropriate Use of Language	1	(0)	2	(0)	0	(1)
*General Regression	2	(1)	10	(0)	2	(2)
Other						
Separation	0	(0)	3	(0)	1	(0)
Regression/Progression	2	(0)	0	(2)	1	(0)

Note. Numbers were arrived at by summing the ratings of all segments within each pre, during, post, and control category.

* These scales seem particularly important and discriminate especially well between object-contact and control segments.

during one session and much of his play with his bunny—putting him half in and half out of a suitcase, etc.—was an attempt to deal with this situation.

Again, our impression (from the observation notes and the graphs) of the effectiveness of Ben's use of the bunny to cope with stress is confirmed by this table. Not one of the stress indicators is rated higher in the post segments than in the pre segments, whereas for Timmy several were rated higher.

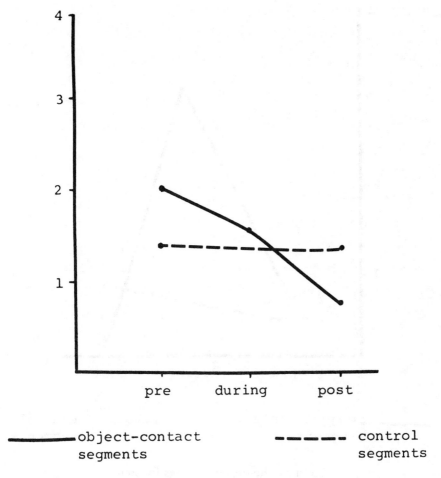

FIGURE 6. Stress ratings for Ben

Ann. Ann is an agile little girl who had a friend, Lena, over to play during all of the first observation session. The two girls danced, listened to records, and played "dirty" (lots of "BM") and sexy ("Let's take down our pants") games. Ann was acutely aware of the observer and seemed to be playing out a drama of control, approval, and rejection with her and Lena. For instance, she wanted always to be able to be Lena's boss, and when this sometimes didn't work, she acted as though she felt rejected and inadequate. By the same token, she seemed to interpret the observer's "just watching and working" as disapproval, and began

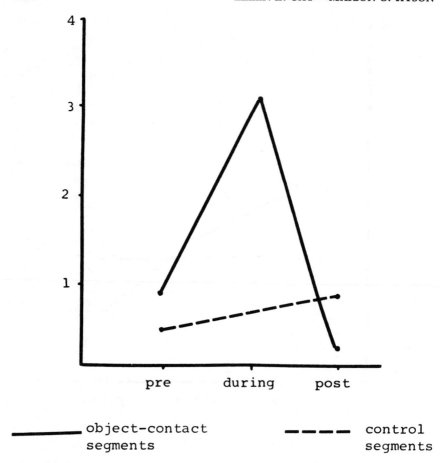

FIGURE 7. Regression ratings for Ben

to treat her as though she were a "mean mother." It was not always apparent to the observer what precipitated Ann's move to her blanket (a white, well-used item with very frayed edges) during the first observation. Twice she was frightened at the possibility of being hurt right before taking the blanket; once she took up her blanket when she moved to another room; and once she picked it up as she was about to turn on the TV. There were indications that she sometimes used the blanket in the context of changing to a new, more mature set or attitude. For example, after playing regressed bathroom games for a while, she picked up her blanket and

TABLE 2

BEN'S RATINGS ON INDIVIDUAL SCALES

Scale	Pre Segments		During Segments [a]	Post Segments	
	Object-Contact $n=16$	Control $n=16$	Object-Contact [b] $n=18$	Object-Contact $n=16$	Control $n=16$
Stress Scales					
*Anxiety	4	(0)	6	0	(0)
Fearfulness	0	(0)	1	0	(0)
*Upset/Anger	13	(7)	5	4	(10)
Frustration	2	(3)	3	1	(2)
*Interactional Conflict	3	(1)	0	1	(4)
*Control	9	(3)	6	5	(4)
Unfulfilled Need	1	(3)	3	0	(0)
Affront	1	(0)	0	0	(1)
*Need for Closeness	3	(4)	5	2	(0)
Regression Scales					
*Tiredness, Sleepiness	3	(2)	11	1	(1)
*Passivity	4	(1)	14	0	(4)
Habits	2	(0)	2	0	(1)
Lability of Affect	1	(1)	6	1	(2)
Aimless Physical Activity	1	(0)	1	0	(3)
Age-Inappropriate Use of Language	0	(0)	0	0	(0)
*General Regression	2	(1)	10	0	(0)
Other					
*Separation	8	(2)	7	2	(2)
Regression/Progression	0	(0)	1	0	(0)

[a] Because of the frequency of Ben's contacts with his bunny, there was not enough material to provide controls for the during segments.

[b] Since Ben was holding his object at the beginning and end of the observation periods, pre and post segments are lacking for those during segments.

* These scales seem particularly important and discriminate especially well between object-contact segments and control segments.

announced that she was now going to get dressed. She held the blanket for a while, and then, after putting it down, did stop the silly play and got dressed.

Ann was alone with the observer during nearly all of the second observation period. Though she again became involved with the observer, there was not as much provocativeness and not as much controlling behavior. For the most part Ann watched TV, played alone, and used the observer's presence, if not her active involvement, in her play. Ann talked, showed the observer her games and toys, dressed dolls to show the observer, etc. Moves to the blanket seemed twice to be touched off by an affront from Sacha the Afghan dog (easily three times Ann's size), once by a permanent move to a different room, and once (at least) by a sensed rejection by the observer. After this last move, Ann began throwing the blanket at the observer and stuffing it into her handbag. It was as though the blanket were endowed with special retaliative power that could do the job of revenge that Ann herself did not dare or felt unable to do. The stress and regression indicators for Ann are presented in Figures 8 and 9.

As with Timmy, Ann's stress indicators do not decline in the post segments as steeply as they do for Ben and Sally. Also, Ann's indicators of regression do not approach the control level in the post segments. Perhaps Ann's blanket is not as effective a stress reducer as are Ben's and Sally's. It may be, however, that the buildup and decline of Ann's stress and regression around her blanket take longer than the time periods studied. The use of 200-word pre and post segments might have given a better indication of this matter.

Ann's ratings on all the scales are presented in Table 3.

The scale which contributed most heavily to stress before Ann took up her blanket was Unfulfilled Need, which in her case meant that she appeared to feel rejected. Control was also prevalent but did not discriminate between object-contact and control segments as well as Unfulfilled Need. Among her important regression indicators were Lability of Affect, Passivity, Habits, and General Regression.

Sally. Sally can't really be described in a few sentences. She was extraordinarily taxing to observe, because she desperately wanted to play with the observer and tried every tactic she could think of to break down the "scientific detachment." Her ploys ranged from snuggling up close on the couch to calling the observer nasty names to asking a barrage of questions to pinching, licking, and kissing the observer's toes. All the while, Sally was utterly delightful.

Sally's "object" was a series of pieces of cloth about 15 inches

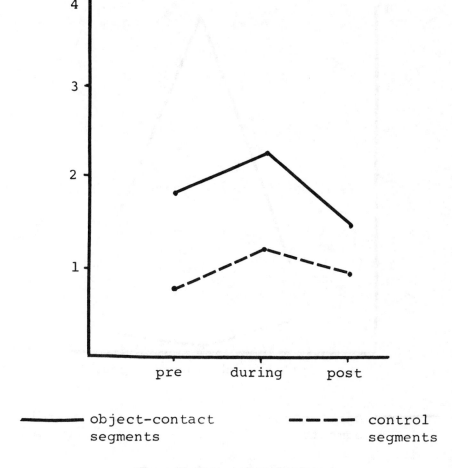

FIGURE 8. Stress ratings for Ann

square. These she deposited in various locations in the house. One was close at hand most of the time. While she held or touched one of them a number of times during the first observation period, she did so only once in the second period.

Sally also had a habit of pausing now and then and briefly sucking the thumb of one hand while twiddling her hair with her other hand. Since there was only one blanket episode in observation II, we examined the pre, during, and post segments of the "suck" episodes in this observation. Controls for the during

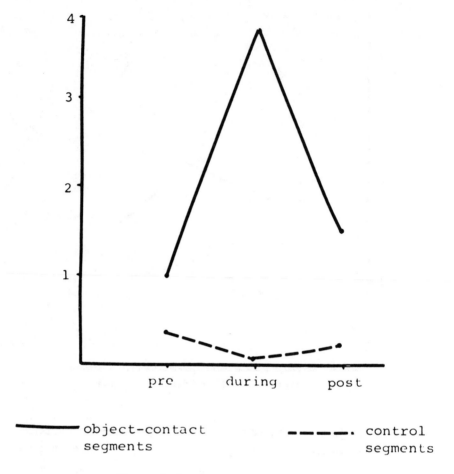

FIGURE 9. Regression ratings for Ann

segments were not chosen because there was not enough control material to match all object-contact segments. See Figures 10 and 11 for Sally's stress and regression indicators.

Ratings of both "suck" and "cloth" segments are higher than the control ratings. Total averages are somewhat lower for the "suck" than for the "cloth" contexts. See ratings on the individual scales in Table 4 (p. 306).

Some of the scales noticeably discriminated between object-contact/suck segments and control segments. Those that did so for the "cloth" segments were Anxiety, Upset/Anger, Lability of Affect

TABLE 3

ANN'S RATINGS ON INDIVIDUAL SCALES

Scale	Pre Segments		During Segments[a]		Post Segments	
	Object-Contact $n=12$	Control $n=12$	Object-Contact $n=4$	Control $n=4$	Object-Contact $n=12$	Control $n=12$
Stress Scales						
Anxiety	1	(1)	1	(0)	2	(1)
Fearfulness	3	(2)	0	(0)	1	(0)
*Upset/Anger	2	(0)	1	(0)	2	(0)
Frustration	2	(0)	1	(0)	1	(1)
Interactional Conflict	2	(1)	1	(0)	1	(1)
*Control	5	(4)	2	(0)	3	(2)
*Unfulfilled Need	5	(0)	1	(2)	2	(3)
*Affront	2	(0)	1	(2)	1	(1)
Need for Closeness	0	(0)	0	(0)	0	(0)
Regression Scales						
Tiredness, Sleepiness	0	(0)	1	(0)	0	(0)
*Passivity	2	(1)	3	(0)	3	(0)
*Habits	0	(0)	2	(0)	0	(0)
*Lability of Affect	4	(2)	2	(0)	6	(1)
Aimless Physical Activity	0	(0)	1	(0)	1	(0)
Age-Inappropriate Use of Language	0	(1)	0	(0)	1	(0)
*General Regression	6	(0)	4	(0)	5	(1)
Other						
Separation	0	(0)	0	(0)	0	(0)
Regression/Progression	0	(1)	2	(0)	1	(1)

[a] Eight of the 12 during segments were so short that they could not be rated.

* Scales that discriminate particularly well between object-contact and control segments.

(in the pre and during segments), and Unfulfilled Needs (in the pre segments). The picture for the "suck" contexts was unaccountably different. Here the Control and General Regression scales were the only ones that clearly discriminated the pre "suck" segments from controls. This difference in indicators for the "cloth" and "suck" segments certainly urges one to conclude that Sally uses her cloths to cope with certain kinds of stress and the thumb for others. This

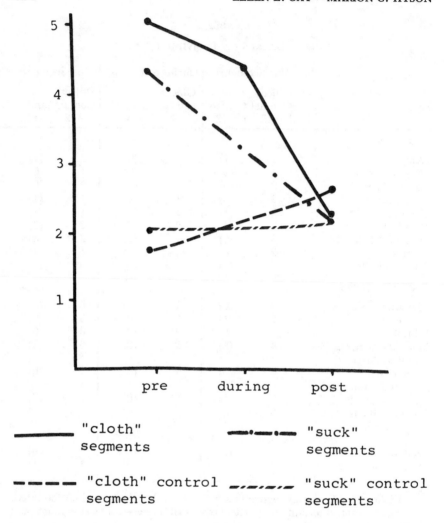

FIGURE 10. Stress ratings for Sally

may be so; however, most of the "cloth" episodes occurred on a
different day from the "suck" ones. It may just be that the pattern
of stress was different on the two days.

DISCUSSION

What do these findings tell us about the significance of
children's contacts with their blankets and bunnies? Although the

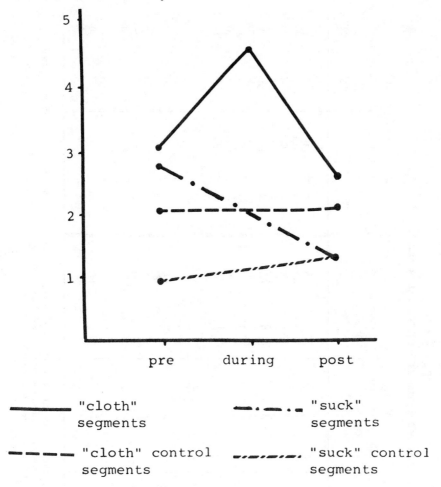

FIGURE 11. Regression ratings for Sally

number of subjects was small in this preliminary study, we were able to learn a good deal about treasured objects and about the value of this method for the study of recurrent behaviors.

Turning first to the over-all implications of our study, there are three findings to discuss.

First, the graphs and individual scales show a great deal of stress immediately *before* blanket contact. This finding tends to confirm both theoretical and parental reports of children's use of "security blankets" in response to tension, uncertainty, conflict,

TABLE 4
SALLY'S RATINGS ON INDIVIDUAL SCALES

| | "Cloth" Context [a] | | | | | "Suck" Context [a] | | | |
| | Pre Segments | | During Segments | Post Segments | | Pre Segments | | Post Segments | |
Scales	Object-Contact n=7	Control n=7	Object-Contact [b] n=4	Object-Contact n=7	Control n=7	Suck n=6	Control n=6	Suck n=6	Control n=6
Stress									
*Anx.	7	(4)	6	5	(4)	2	(3)	1	(3)
Fearf.	0	(0)	1	0	(0)	0	(0)	0	(0)
*Ups/Ang.	4	(1)	3	1	(3)	2	(0)	4	(3)
*Frust.	2	(0)	0	1	(1)	1	(2)	0	(1)
Int. Conf.	1	(0)	0	0	(1)	2	(1)	0	(0)
* **Control	7	(5)	3	6	(4)	14	(1)	6	(3)
*Unf. Need	9	(2)	2	4	(5)	5	(5)	4	(3)
*Affront	3	(0)	1	0	(1)	0	(0)	1	(0)
Need Cl.	2	(0)	1	1	(3)	0	(0)	2	(2)
Regression									
Tired. Sl.	0	(1)	0	0	(0)	0	(0)	0	(0)
Passiv.	0	(1)	1	2	(0)	0	(0)	0	(0)
*Habits	0	(0)	2	2	(0)	1	(0)	0	(0)
*Lability	9	(5)	5	4	(5)	5	(5)	3	(3)
Aiml. Act.	1	(0)	1	1	(2)	1	(1)	0	(0)
*Inapp. L.	3	(1)	3	2	(1)	2	(1)	0	(1)
* **Gen. Regr.	8	(6)	5	5	(6)	8	(4)	4	(3)
Other									
Separ.	1	(2)	1	0	(0)	1	(1)	0	(0)
R/P	0	(0)	0	0	(1)	1	(0)	0	(1)

[a] Three of the seven during segments for "cloth" contexts and all of the "suck" during segments were so short that they could not be rated.

[b] There are no controls for the during segments because of insufficient observational material.

* Scales that discriminated between "cloth" contexts and their controls.

** Scales that discriminated between "suck" contexts and their controls.

and other stressful states. This pattern is markedly similar to more general descriptions of coping processes as responses to stress, anxiety, or perceived threat.

Second, the ratings of the segments *during* which blanket contact occurred show a great increase in regressive behavior and a corresponding decline in stress. It seems that regression (accompanied by the blanket) is often the means the child chooses to cope with stress, although we will see that it is only one of several possible modes that children may employ. The use of the blanket, then, is often accompanied by behavior typical of an earlier stage of development. Frequently the child's behavior with his blanket reminds one of his earlier behavior when fed and cuddled by his mother. Again this is consistent with theories about the maternal associations of the blanket (Winnicott, 1958) and about the role of the blanket in the child's growing ability to soothe himself as the mother used to (Tolpin, 1971).

Third, our ratings show a marked decline in *both* stress and regression after the child puts the blanket down. Thus the blanket seems to be a successful means of coping with stress. The regressive behavior we saw during blanket contact is temporary and often restricted to the context of the child's usually brief snuggles with his blanket. Although the scales were not designed to measure "exploratory" or "mastery" behavior, a review of the observation notes shows evidence of occasional increases in this kind of behavior immediately after blanket contact (e.g., block building, getting something for one's self, a counting game).

Our analysis of the four children's ratings has shown many individual differences, but we have not yet commented on age or sex trends. We chose to study two 2-year-olds and two 4-year-olds and, although the numbers are too small to be conclusive, there were some differences.

Both the ratings on specific scales and (more sensitively) the observation notes suggest that different *kinds* of stress precede a move to the blanket in the younger and older children. For example, Interactional Conflict was prominent in the pre segments for Timmy and Ben, but not for Ann and Sally. On the other hand, several scales, such as Affront and Unfulfilled Need, were more prominent in the pre segments for Ann and Sally. In the same vein, the observation notes for the younger children show a good deal more overt conflict (often battles over autonomy or the mother's refusal to meet the child's demands), whereas the older children often turned to their blankets after a more subtle, sensed rejection or feeling of guilt. This difference is consistent with theories of psychosexual development as well as with cognitive theories of increasing internalization of impulses and feelings. During blanket contact, the ratings of the younger children showed more Tiredness, Passivity, and Need for Closeness than did those of the older children. Again, the observation notes describe the 2-year-olds as frequently lying down with their blankets and stroking them in a "babyish" manner. This behavior changes with increasing age.

The fact that our younger subjects were boys and our older ones girls raises the possibility that age difference and sex differences are confounded, of course. The girls did seem intensely aware of their "femaleness" with respect to the female observer, and both girls showed off their bodies, dressing and undressing. They seemed more concerned than the boys with involving the female observer in their play, turning to provocative and "naughty" tricks when a direct approach failed. These age and sex variables will be sorted out and further explored in another study (Gay, 1976).

We have seen that children turn to their treasured objects to cope with stress. We have seen that the ratings of segments during which children are holding these objects reveal a great deal of behavior that can be described as "regressive." But this generalization does not tell the whole story. Again, the observation notes are useful in preserving the richness and variety of ways that blankets help their owners, including but not limited to regression.

In fact, our observations of children and their treasured objects revealed three separate modes of coping with stress: a purely regressive use of the object, a use of the object as a magical weapon or protector, and a use of the object (often in fantasy play) as a means of working out inner conflicts and developmental concerns.

The first type—the regressive use—is reflected most prominently in the ratings of the "during" segments. The child's holding or fondling of the object often appears in a constellation of immature behaviors—lying down as if sleeping, passivity, thumbsucking—which contribute heavily to the high number of regression indicators in the "during" segments. Often such encounters are brief; having coped with the stress by a temporary retreat to babyhood, the child turns to more active pursuits.

The second type of use is somewhat more active and progressive than the first. In these instances, the child behaves as if he believed the object were endowed with magical possibilities either of protecting him or of holding power over others. Timmy reached for his blanket as if it were a talisman when dinosaurs or monsters were discussed. When Ben walked past the observer with his bunny's ears held over his eyes, it was almost as though he thought she would disappear if he could not see her. Similarly, using her blanket as a weapon to throw at the observer seemed to endow the lowly blanket, and Ann, its owner, with special powers.

The third kind of use is potentially the most progressive of all, with its emphasis on flexible and highly adaptive coping. In these cases, the child seems to be using his special object in fantasy play to work out questions or concerns appropriate to his stage of development. After listening to a discussion between his sister and a friend concerning birth and his own surgery, Ben told his mother that he wanted to "play kangaroo" and "have bunny be the baby"—while trying to stuff a rather large bunny into a very small pocket. The same child seemed to deal with his ambivalence about separation by trying to pack his bunny in a suitcase while assuring himself of its presence by leaving its ear sticking out.

It is possible that the sorts of indicators that are prevalent and their distributions may yield valuable information about how well a child uses the treasured object to cope with stress, and may therefore indicate something about the psychological health of the child.

While the four children we observed show similar patterns of distribution of indicators in the pre, during, and post object-contact segments, there were some individual differences in the relative amounts of indicators in the pre and post segments.

For two children, the ratings on regression indicators were considerably higher in the pre segments than in the posts. For the other two, the ratings on regression indicators were about the same for the pre and post segments. Differences like these are most likely indicative of varying patterns of intensity and duration of stress and the effectiveness of the blanket in alleviating it. If one reasons that a drop in indicators following use of an object means that a youngster has used the blanket or stuffed animal to regain equilibrium or to master a stressful situation, it would follow that a greater drop may mean a quicker or more complete return to equilibrium or better mastery.

Thinking about normality and pathology in connection with treasured objects raises another interesting issue. Some of the work Luborsky (1967; Luborsky and Mintz, 1974) has done rating the symptom contexts of psychologically disturbed adults shows a pattern of buildup and decline of indicators before and after a symptom emerges, which is similar to the pattern we found around blanket contacts. One wonders what, if any, relationship there is between symptoms and developmental patterns such as the use of treasured objects. Can the use of a "security blanket" be a symptom of disorder in some cases? How might one empirically investigate this question? Where does one draw the line between normal regression and disturbed regression? Possibly the analyses of the buildup and decline of relevant indicators around the use of objects and around other normal recurrent behaviors and symptoms will help give concrete answers to these questions. A start might be to look more closely at the sorts of behaviors that follow use of the treasured object in normal and disturbed children.

As expected, we confronted a number of methodological difficulties in carrying out this study. Some of them could be cleared up in further studies.

To begin with, the observation-note method used to gather information about our children's uses of the treasured object is one which has inherent limitations for assuring observer reliability. It is impossible to jot down everything a child does and says, let alone all other relevant factors such as affect and environmental circumstances. This means that an observer must pick and choose. While one can draw up observation rules specifying the sorts of material that should have priority, no two observers are likely to agree completely. An observer who knows shorthand would help. It might also be possible eventually to develop an observation instrument that observers could use to record behavior more concisely and objectively while they are watching the child.

We also found that the scales we had developed were not always sufficient to pick up important antecedents of contact with treasured objects. Our ratings did not always reflect our intuitive understanding of the reason for a child's need for his object. For example, one child at times seemed self-conscious before he picked up his object, and we had no scale that quite got at this construct. At other times, we felt that events leading to a need for the object built up for quite a while and could not be tapped by a look at the 50 or 100 words before contact. Some of these difficulties could be cleared up by refining our scales and changing the length of segments to be studied. Types of scales that seem to be needed are scales tapping self-consciousness, sensed rejection, and change to a more mature set, as well as scales that would tap such themes of behavior as sexual play and mastery play.

A technical problem we had in preparing our observation notes for rating was that observational material between object contacts was not always sufficient to provide 100-word pre and post segments. This was particularly so with the younger children, who went to their objects more often and stayed with them longer than the older children. Furthermore, the more often a child made contact with her object, the less observational material was available for control segments, and thus in some cases there were not enough control segments to match all the experimental ones. One additional difficulty in preparing segments for rating was that pre segments could not always be clearly separated from durings. A child might begin a search for the bunny, get distracted and do something else for a while, and then resume the search. In such a case, it was hard to decide whether the start of the search should be included in the pre or in the during segment. These are all problems that are inherent in the method we used. One can only hope to be able to find a way for each case, by shortening the length of segments, or by some other means, to solve the individual technical difficulties.

Despite the snags encountered in this pilot study, we were encouraged by the results. The method proved to be a good mix of qualitative and quantitative research approaches, combining rich naturalistic observations with more precise rating and comparison of clearly defined segments of behavior. The subject chosen for study, children's contacts with treasured objects, turned out to be a fascinating source of insights into the many resources that children employ to cope with stress. We were barely able to begin to examine the variety of differences in individual children, in children of different ages and sexes, in children with differing degrees of adjustment. Certainly both the method and the subject are worth exploring further.

APPENDIX 1: TELEPHONE QUESTIONNAIRE

In a rather unstructured manner, ask parents the following questions (these all can refer to more than one child in family):

1. Does your child have a particular toy, blanket, stuffed animal, etc., that he/she is very much attached to? Describe it.

2. In what ways does the child enjoy, play with, or use the object? Follow this up as necessary with:

a. Are there particular times (of day or types of incidents) when the child will go to the object? When sleepy? Upset? Afraid? As part of fantasy? When embarrassed or challenged? What follows? How long does he stay with the object, what does he do with it, and what does he do when finished with it?

b. Will he/she use object only on some days and not on others?

c. How does he/she use object when involved in separation from parents, e.g., when left with baby-sitter or taken to school?

d. Is object used in interaction with other people, e.g., a parent or other children? Does this use differ with different people?

e. How does the child use object—aggressively? as comfort? Apparent feelings of child toward object—do they change with time?

f. Does child ever go to object rather than parent when upset, afraid, etc.?

3. Discuss history, chronology of use or attachment to object— changes in object or use of object. How did attachment begin? What role, if any, did parent have in forming the attachment?

4. What is your feeling about child's attachment to object? Why do you think he/she needs it? How do you handle issues around it? Do you feel there will be a time when the child will be ready to give up object?

5. Did you yourself have an object as a child? Spouse? Other children in family?

6. Child's other habits (be sure not to make this sound negative)

—e.g., thumb-sucking, rocking, etc. Chronology? Any imaginary friends? Associated in any way with the object?

7. Child's reaction when object unavailable.

8. Describe child's personality—shy, clinging, aggressive, anxious, controlling, etc.

APPENDIX 2: RATING SCALES

Scales are rated 0 (absence of behavior or affect), 1 (some of the behavior or affect), or 2 (a large amount of the behavior or affect). An "S" in front of the scale indicates that it was later included in the *stress* category; an "R" means that the scale was later put into the *regression* category.

Individual Scales (rate just the child)

1. (S) *Anxiety*—apprehensiveness, fearfulness where there is no clear cause.
2. (S) *Fearfulness*—distinguish this from anxiety by evidence of presence of or talk about something feared by the child.
3. (R) *Tiredness, Sleepiness.*
4. (R) *Physical and Verbal Passivity.*
5. (S) *Upset*—unhappy, cranky, irritable, crying.
6. (S) *Anger.*
7. (R) *Habits*—sucking (fingers or something else), rocking (rhythmically, in habitual way), systematically stroking or rubbing something over a part of the body, repeatedly smelling, etc.
8. (S) *Frustration*—child seems to feel he cannot do something right, or he is trying to do something and cannot. Negative reaction to an obstacle (perceived or real) in the way of mastery or success.
9. (R) *Lability of Affect*—mood swings.
10. (R) *Aimless Physical Activity*—running around in driven but aimless manner; or abrupt, undirected movements.
11. (R) *Age-Inappropriate Use of Language*—baby talk, silly talk, or nonsense words, talking in a fake voice, loss of control of logical verbal processes. Regressive use of language (not baby talk as part of a fantasy role) is implied by this scale.

Interactional or Environmental Scales (rate child in relation to the situation or interaction)

1. *Separation*—separation about to occur, is occurring, or is being discussed. This may be separation from a place or a person. Rate 2 if there is either high frequency or high intensity on this scale.

2. (S) *Interactional Conflict*—argument, disagreement or conflict. Someone may be angry at the child or the child angry at someone else.

3. (S) *Control*—interaction involving the issue of control. E.g., mother or a friend tells the child to do something or the child tells another to do something. The implication is that the child appears to feel controlled by the other person or that he or she is unsuccessful at controlling the other person.

4. (S) *Unfulfilled Need*—child's need or desire is unfulfilled by other person. Indicates desire and is turned down or rejected. May rate strong affect even if need is finally filled. Scale rates need for goods or for nurturance. Example: child asks mother for a cookie and is turned down.

5. (S) *Affront*—child embarrassed or "put down" by another person. May imply a sudden embarrassment or somewhat alarming surprise. Example: another child says to the target child, "That's dumb," or "You don't do it that way, you dumb-dumb."

6. (S) *Need for Closeness*—desire for closeness, hugging, kissing, being held by or holding another, especially mother.

Miscellaneous Scale

Regression/Progression—any situation where the child shows a behavior which contrasts infantlike aspects with adultlike aspects. This may include imitation or fantasy about adult behavior in which mastery beyond the child's years is implied and in which there is characterization of both adult and infant roles.

Examples: (a) child plays "Superman" with his own blanket wrapped around himself as a cape (security versus he-man power);

(b) child covers dolls with her own baby blanket (nurturing versus being nurtured);
(c) child dresses, protects, or mothers a baby doll.

Additional Scale

(R) *General Regression*—behavior or affect which shows regression from the child's present age level or optimal developmental level.

REFERENCES

Bijou, S., & Baer, D. (1965), *Child Development*, Vol. 2. New York: Appleton-Century.

Bowlby, J. (1969), *Attachment and Loss*, Vol. 1. New York: Basic Books.

Busch, F. (1974), Dimensions of the First Transitional Object. *The Psychoanalytic Study of the Child*, 29:215-229. New Haven, Conn.: Yale University Press.

Erikson, E. (1963), *Childhood and Society*, rev. ed. New York: Norton.

Ferguson, G. (1971), *Statistical Analysis in Psychology and Education*. New York: McGraw-Hill.

Flavell, J. (1963), *The Developmental Psychology of Jean Piaget*. Princeton: Van Nostrand Reinhold.

Freud, A. (1936), *The Ego and the Mechanisms of Defense*, rev. ed. New York: International Universities Press, 1966.

——— (1965), *Normality and Pathology in Childhood: Assessments of Development*. New York: International Universities Press.

Gay, E. (1976), A Study of the Treasured Objects of Early Childhood and the Contexts in Which They Are Used. Dissertation proposal, Bryn Mawr College.

Greenacre, P. (1960), Further Notes on Fetishism. *The Psychoanalytic Study of the Child*, 15:191-207. New York: International Universities Press.

——— (1969), The Fetish and the Transitional Object. *The Psychoanalytic Study of the Child*, 24:144-164. New York: International Universities Press.

Hyson, M. (1974), The Child's Treasured Object: The Development of Defenses and Cognitions as Seen in Blankets and Bears. Unpublished paper, Bryn Mawr College.

Lampl-de Groot, J. (1957), On Defense and Development: Normal and Pathological. *The Psychoanalytic Study of the Child*, 12:114-126. New York: International Universities Press.

Luborsky, L. (1967), Momentary Forgetting during Psychotherapy and Psychoanalysis: A Theory and Research Method. In: Motives and Thought: Psychoanalytic Essays in Honor of David Rapaport, ed. R. R. Holt. *Psychol. Issues*, Monogr. No. 18/19:177-217. New York: International Universities Press.

——— & Auerbach, A. (1969), The Symptom-Context Method: Quantitative Studies of Symptom Formation in Psychotherapy. *J. Amer. Psychoanal. Assn.*, 17:68-99.

———— & Mintz, J. (1974), What Sets Off Momentary Forgetting during a Psychoanalysis? Investigations of Symptom Onset Conditions. *Psychoanalysis and Contemporary Science*, 3:233-268. New York: International Universities Press.

Meehl, P. (1973), Some Methodological Reflections on the Difficulties of Psychoanalytic Research. In: Psychoanalytic Research: Three Approaches to the Experimental Study of Subliminal Processes, ed. M. Mayman. *Psychol. Issues*, Monogr. No. 30:104-117. New York: International Universities Press.

Passman, R. (1974), The Effects of Mothers and "Security" Blankets upon Learning in Children (Should Linus Bring His Blanket to School?). Paper presented at meetings of the American Psychological Association, New Orleans.

———— & Weisberg, P. (1975), Mothers and Blankets as Agents for Promoting Play and Exploration by Young Children in a Novel Environment: The Effects of Social and Nonsocial Attachment Objects. *Develop. Psychol.*, 11:170-177.

Roiphe, H., & Galenson, E. (1975), Some Observations on Transitional Objects and Infantile Fetish. *Psychoanal. Quart.*, 44:206-231.

Sperling, M. (1963), Fetishism in Children. *Psychoanal. Quart.*, 32:374-392.

Stevenson, O. (1954), The First Treasured Possession. *The Psychoanalytic Study of the Child*, 9:199-217. New York: International Universities Press.

Tolpin, M. (1971), On the Beginning of the Cohesive Self: An Application of the Concept of Transmuting Internalization to the Study of the Transitional Object and Signal Anxiety. *The Psychoanalytic Study of the Child*, 26:316-352. New York: Quadrangle.

Waelder, R. (1964), *Basic Theory of Psychoanalysis*. New York: International Universities Press.

Weisberg, P., & Russell, J. (1971), Proximity and Interactional Behavior of Young Children to Their "Security" Blankets. *Child Devel.*, 42:1575-1579.

Winnicott, D. (1958), *Collected Papers*. New York: Basic Books.

I. Charles Kaufman, M.D.

Developmental Considerations of Anxiety and Depression: Psychobiological Studies in Monkeys

In this paper I describe some of my studies of monkeys in an effort to illuminate our understanding of anxiety and depression, with particular emphasis on two topics, the processes of adaptation and the functional transition from the biological to the psychological level of organization. From use of the experimental paradigm of mother loss, data are presented to document three main conclusions. First, the infant reacts to this stress adaptively, using both inborn and acquired coping mechanisms. Second, in the course of development the infant's reactions become psychobiological rather than purely biological as the inborn biological response systems of flight-fight and conservation-withdrawal are elaborated cognitively, motivationally, and affectively into the organismic states of anxiety and depression respectively. Third, depression is basically a state of helplessness.

PSYCHOANALYSIS AND PSYCHOBIOLOGY

Among the principal contributions of psychoanalysis to human understanding, in demonstrating that symptoms have meanings

The research reported here has been supported by U. S. Public Health Service Grants, MH 4670 and MH 18144; National Science Foundation Grant, BMS 75-01147; and grants from the Grant Foundation, all to the author.

For suggestions regarding the manuscript I wish to thank Drs. Janice Norton Kaufman, Robert N. Emde, and David R. Metcalf.

and arise from psychological forces, was the provision of a theoretical framework within which human development, normal and abnormal, could be viewed scientifically. For the most part, until recently, psychoanalysts have studied psychopathological phenomena in terms of the psychological forces that create them and their ultimate determination by life experiences, notably in childhood. This has been an extraordinarily fruitful and clinically rewarding approach. Central to this approach is the concept of ontogeny and its crucial role.

This is not to say that psychoanalysis has overlooked the role of hereditary influences—quite the contrary. Freud always assumed that the "instinctual drives," which provide the motivational basis of behavior in psychoanalytic theory, arise from genic influences. He also recognized that ego forces had genic determination, a viewpoint which Hartmann (1939) elegantly elaborated. As a result, for the past several decades there has been an increasing emphasis within psychoanalysis on those ego functions which are autonomous. This has meant more attention to processes, apparatuses, and mechanisms, such as in the extensive work being done in studying perception, cognition, sensorimotor integration, language, etc. It has meant also an increasing inquiry into very early life, such as studies of the physiological and behavioral patterns of the newborn and their changes during subsequent phases of development. There has been a search for species-typical patterns but also for the manifestations of individual differences— and in all cases an attempt to correlate these with later patterns of behavior, an effort which integrates concepts of maturation and development.

Meanwhile, recognition of the inadequacy of a dichotomous nature-nurture conceptualization has led to the appreciation of development as a continuing process in which genetic influences determine not so much the specificity as the range of potentialities. In this respect, awareness of the continuous interaction of the growing organism with many independent-variable influences, some internal such as hormones, other environmental, especially animate objects, has led to numerous studies of these influences on infant development, including of course the mother-child inter-action. Over-all, then, a major current of psychoanalytic research has been and is strongly biological in orientation. This in no way gainsays the peculiarly human significance of the psychological aspects of behavior. It simply reflects the belief that a more thorough understanding of psychological manifestations, forces, and structures can be gained from a more total biological knowledge of the human, a perspective we consider *psychobiological*.

Furthermore, having adopted a biological approach to an understanding of human behavior, it seems reasonable to expect that this would be furthered by understanding the biological bases of behavior in nonhuman species. This is so because, with all its apparent discontinuities, there is nevertheless an obvious continuity in evolutionary development. Knowledge of the principles, mechanisms, and apparatuses of nonhuman behavior is bound to allow certain valid extrapolations to the human. In this regard a major reward from comparative research is the light it sheds on the problem of adaptation.

ADAPTATION

The key to the meaning of behavior is to be found in the processes and mechanisms of adaptation. It should be noted that adaptation refers to both evolutionary and ontogenetic phenomena, and that the distinction is not always clearly apprehended. On the one hand, the behavioral patterns of the human may be seen as adaptive propensities which evolved phylogenetically through the pressure of natural selection. Studies of nonhuman species and of humans may help us to understand the adaptive role of behavioral *differences*. For example, the human infant has a smiling response, whereas the monkey infant does not. The smiling response of the human baby has obvious survival value through its influence on the mother, increasing her maternal behavior. This function we presume to have been favored by selection pressure. However, it poses a question. Is there some characteristic of the human mother (that is different from the monkey) that required the evolutionary development of the smiling response in the infant to ensure survival? In other words, what does this difference in infant behavior imply about the difference between the mothers, human and monkey? Does the human baby *have* to smile to survive? The question may not be so ominous as it sounds. The answer may, for example, be related to the human mother's loss of hair and clingability and the infant's lesser ability to cling, placing a greater burden on the mother to *behave* maternally, with the smile serving to motivate her.

Ontogenetic adaptation, on the other hand, is the story of individual development based on individual experience. From this perspective, human behaviors may be seen as adaptive (or maladaptive) responses to experience, of course within the genetically determined range. For example, the smile at first occurs automatically in response to a moving visual gestalt abstracted from two eyes and a nose. It then usually becomes selectively focused on one or a few specific human beings, notably the mother, and it takes on a strong emotional connotation as part of a dyadic interaction. Despite the universality of the smiling response, its role in further individual development depends on individual life experience with all its vicissitudes, and illustrates ontogenetic adaptation with all its implications for complexity of individual development. In growing up, each child adapts to its surround, which of course has many common elements in each family, culture, and society that, together with the shared genes in a population, help explain the commonalities of behavior.

*Mal*adaptive manifestations are also important. At the evolutionary level they usually lead to extinction. At the onto-genetic level they are of great consequence since they constitute behavioral pathology. The difference between an adaptive and a maladaptive response arising under similar conditions may be exemplified by the following. A canary in nest-building mood, deprived of a supply of feathers, the usual nest-building material, may build a nest with straw or other material. This behavior is not species-typical, but it is adaptive. It provides a nest for the eggs to come. Even the canary's plucking feathers from itself to build the nest may still be adaptive. If, however, on subsequent occasions, when other feathers are available, it continues to pluck its own feathers, this behavior is maladaptive and constitutes behavioral pathology. An example from human behavior involves a man with heart disease. To the extent that denial of his illness prevents him from experiencing anxiety, an acute attack of which, with its outpouring of adrenalin and other physiological changes, might kill him, the denial is adaptive. If, however, he attempts to run a mile as part of the denial, this behavior is maladaptive since the exertion will very likely kill him.

BACKGROUND TO THE STUDIES

In addition to the intrinsic value of comparative research there is a further reason to study nonhuman animals, namely, the opportunity to perform experiments which for ethical and other reasons cannot be carried out with humans.

In the light of the above considerations I determined to study animal behavior and decided to use nonhuman primates as experimental subjects, since phylogenetically they are our closest relatives. (The apes are least removed in evolutionary distance but were not available for experiments, so I chose macaques, monkeys who are reasonably close in phylogeny. See footnote 3 below for a comment on animal models.) As an experimental paradigm I chose the separation of an infant from its mother by removal of the mother. There were two reasons for this choice.

MOTHER LOSS AND ADAPTATION

First, loss of the mother is a crisis the study of which should illuminate the processes of adaptation. Let us remember that in the course of evolution a series of successful adaptations led to an improved system of reproduction and greater viability of offspring. The adaptations involved the change from external fertilization to internal fertilization by copulation, the development of the amniote egg, the development of the placenta and viviparity, and finally, the development of mammary glands and milk.

What also evolved, and this is very important, was *improved parental care*—a system of feeding and protection involving increased closeness and a shared experience, leading to a new kind of durable bond which makes more complex development possible (Kaufman, 1970). Generally, among higher primates multiple births are the exception, and the single offspring is likely to survive. There is also a long period of caretaking and growing up, so that the more complex central nervous system may mature and allow the development of the full variegated and plastic behavioral repertoire.

Making possible this long maturation and experiential development are: (1) the superior parental care, and (2) the immaturity of the neonate, who is thus not too fixed at birth. The immaturity means that the neonate is relatively helpless, so to speak. Note that this statement is not intended to imply a *feeling* of helplessness at this stage; it is simply a description of the functional status of the neonate.

This neonatal helplessness has two major consequences. One, the dependence upon the mother (and perhaps others) for support of the life systems guarantees that multiple interactions will occur, leading to the development of both significant relationships and strategies of relating; these in turn will determine the nature of the life experience for the individual, the structure of the group, and the rules of the social system. In other words, there is a feedback relationship between the social system and the individual, each making the other possible. Two, there is a danger. There is vulnerability to the loss of the mother's caretaking (from whatever reason). This loss poses a diverse set of dangers: (a) for the infant, the problem of survival; (b) for the mother, the loss of a major investment if the infant does not survive; (c) for other relatives, the loss of investment of, if nothing else, shared genes; and (d) for the group, the loss of integrity. The loss of the mother is thus a challenge to all and, therefore, a test of adaptability for all. Its usefulness in studying adaptation, then, was my first reason for choosing this experimental situation.

MOTHER LOSS AND DEPRESSION

There is one other major consideration for using this experimental paradigm or model, namely, the relationship that it has to the problem of depression in humans. First of all, we know that in humans the loss of a love object is reacted to with grief and then mourning. Furthermore, we know that phenomenologically and psychologically there is great similarity between such grief and mourning and depression. Third, we know that human beings often react to a loss with depression. The differences between such depression and grief and mourning are in either the extent and duration of the reaction or the nature of the loss. Depression may follow not only the loss of a love object but also the loss of status, or faith, or honor, etc. Finally, we know that in human infants and children there are dramatic reactions to the loss of the mother.

The first observer to compel attention to the deleterious effects of mother loss was Spitz, who described two syndromes in institutionalized infants. In one, which he called "anaclitic depression," the syndrome arose in the second half of the first year of life when mothers who had raised infants from birth were removed. After an initial period of apprehension and weepiness, such infants showed withdrawal, rejection of the environment, retardation of reaction to stimuli, slowness of movement, loss of appetite, increased finger sucking, insomnia, a reluctance to assume an erect posture or perform locomotion, and a "physiognomic expression ... difficult to describe ... [which] would, in an adult, be described as depression" (Spitz, 1946, p. 316). If the mothers were returned within three to five months there was an immediate and dramatic effect. "They suddenly were friendly, gay, approachable" (p. 330) and subsequently recovered fully. If the mothers did not return, the other, more malignant, syndrome developed. The latter, which he called "hospitalism," was first seen in infants who lost their mothers permanently and were cared for by very busy nursing personnel. It was characterized by massive failure of development, both mental and physical, frequent illness, marasmus, cachexia, and often early death (Spitz, 1945).

NORMATIVE STUDIES

There were, then, two important areas, adaptation and depression, that might be studied experimentally by separating monkey mothers from their infants. However, since my knowledge of monkeys, in 1961 when I started my first primate laboratory, was very limited, I decided that it was essential to learn more about normal monkey behavior and infant development before attempting any experimental manipulations. In setting up the laboratory I adopted two strategies which were quite uncommon in 1961. The first was to study animals living in social groups rather than individually or paired in cages, as was then the custom. Since monkeys in the field are very social animals it seemed that only in a social group would we be able to study the complexity and adaptiveness of their behavior. The other strategy adopted was that we would study two species of a single genus, in other words, two closely related species, since it seemed that this would provide a more adequate base for comparison, extrapolation, and generalization than would the study of only one monkey species. Accordingly, we set up the laboratory with social groups of two species of macaques, the pigtail (*M. nemestrina*) and the bonnet (*M. radiata*).

Initially each group consisted of wild-born animals—a breeding male and four or five breeding females—housed in a large pen with one-way glass windows for observation.[1] For the first five years we carried out normative studies of social behavior. As babies were born into the groups we were able to study maternal behavior, the mother-infant interaction, and infant development.

Since the two species belong to the same genus, we anticipated that they would show many common attributes, including structural aspects of the central nervous system and potentialities for learning and social development. We also expected that they would show some salient differences which would be markers of their separate evolutionary adaptational achievements.

We found that they do indeed share many behaviors and social characteristics. And we also found some striking differences. The first was immediately manifest in the different spatial configurations shown by social groups of the two species. Invariably, bonnet adults tend to remain physically close to each other, often in huddles (Figure 1), whereas pigtails, although they show the same ability to form a cohesive group, do not usually make physical contact with neighbors (Figure 2) except to engage in a dynamic social interaction such as mating, grooming, or fighting. At night pigtails often sleep lying down, whereas bonnets sleep sitting up, maintaining physical contact with each other. This difference in spacing has been shown by every group we have formed, using animals captured at different times and different places, and this

[1] The techniques of observation, data collection, data analysis, and a taxonomy of behavior for these two species are described in Kaufman and Rosenblum (1966, 1969a). In the studies to be cited I was aided by colleagues and research assistants. I especially want to thank Andrew J. Stynes, who has collaborated with me throughout, and Leonard A. Rosenblum, who worked with me from 1961 to 1968.

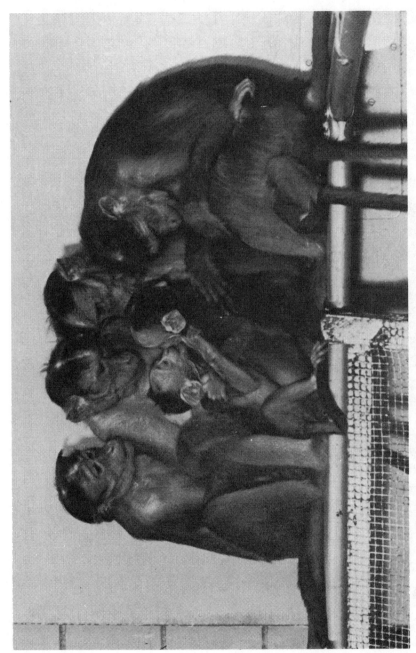

FIGURE 1. A typical huddle of bonnet macaques, including mothers and infants.

FIGURE 2. A group of pigtail macaques showing the typical spacing out and lack of physical contact except between mother and infant (from Kaufman, 1975).

difference has persisted despite a variety of manipulations, such as varying the ambient temperature over a wide range, and depriving the animals of food or water.

The tendency to propinquity among the bonnets is not affected by pregnancy or delivery. After a baby is born its mother returns to close contact with her neighbors, whereas pigtail females with infants tend to remain apart from other females. Both provide their infants with the intensive care characteristic of higher primates, but the bonnet does it in the company of her peers, whereas the pigtail mother does it in relative isolation (Kaufman and Rosenblum, 1969a). The bonnet mother permits considerable attention to her infant (Figure 3), whereas the pigtail mother jealously guards her infant from the attention of others (Figure 4). As a result, even in the first month of life bonnet infants have significantly more social interaction with animals other than their mothers than do pigtail infants.

Over the next few months, infants of both species begin to initiate departures from their mothers. Our data indicate clearly that most of the early breaks in contact are initiated by the infant (Kaufman and Rosenblum, 1969a). The initial breaks are brief and do not take the infant very far away from the mother, who watches closely the whole time. Gradually the infant spends more time away from the mother, but it tends to remain on the same level of the pen. Meanwhile, the mother rarely fails to watch her infant when it is away from her, and quickly retrieves it if she perceives any threat to it. Mothers of both species show other protective behaviors as well, such as restraining the infant from leaving and guarding it as it moves about. A comparison of the total amount of *protective* behavior by the mothers of the two species shows that the pigtails are far more protective (Figure 5).

Soon the infants leave their mothers behind by moving to other levels of the pen. The frequency and duration of these vertical departures increase dramatically after the first month and reach a high asymptotic level in the eighth month. As with the early breaks, it is the infants, not the mothers, who are responsible. When we compare both the frequency and total duration of these maximal distance departures in the two species, we find clear evidence of a distinction between pigtail and bonnet infants. From about the third month of life onward, bonnet infants consistently

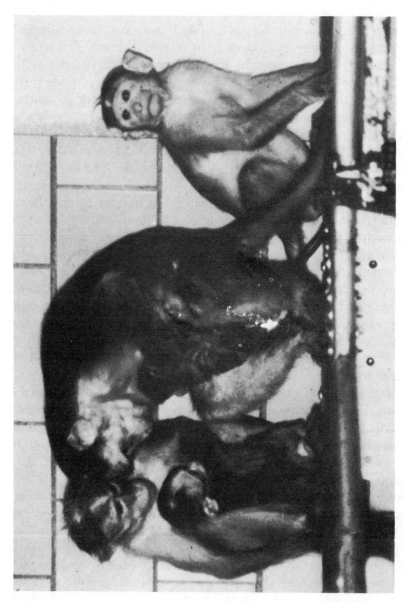

FIGURE 3. A bonnet mother cradling her newborn infant while approaching with interest another mother-infant pair (from Kaufman, 1975).

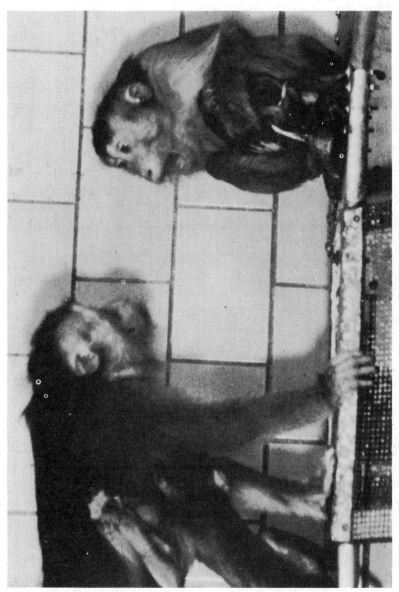

FIGURE 4. A pigtail mother cradling her newborn infant (with cord and placenta still attached) and giving an open-mouth threat to another mother who is approaching too close (from Kaufman, 1975).

PROTECTIVE BEHAVIORS

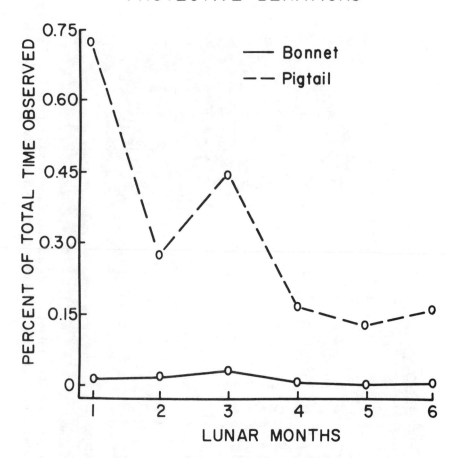

FIGURE 5. Mean duration in the two species of maternal protectiveness (*departure restraint, guard,* and *retrieval*) over the first six months of life.

spend more time than pigtails away from their mothers and at different levels of the pen. This behavior appears to signify a greater relative security of bonnet infants in their physical and social environment, and a real difference in the nature of their attachment to their mothers as they mature. Consistent with the increased security of the infants is the fact that retrieval, which reflects maternal apprehension about a separated infant, appears considerably less often, peaks earlier, and wanes more rapidly in bonnet than in pigtail mothers. We could say that bonnet mothers *let* their infants go and that bonnet infants *go*.

In both species, as the infants grow into the middle of the first year of life, maternal solicitude wanes. Mothers become less protective of their infants. They encourage them to depart and even deter them from returning. They deprive their infants of the nipple, and when an infant is too persistent the mother punishes it by gentle biting. A comparison of the total amount of these various maternal *abdyadic* behaviors shows a far greater amount by the pigtails (Figure 6).

To recapitulate, the bonnet mother retrieves and protects less, weans less, and punishes less. She appears to allow, but not necessarily to coerce, her offspring to develop increasing freedom and independence. The pigtail mother is at first more protective and later more punitive, a combination that fosters in her infant a closer attachment to or dependence upon her.

Concurrently, as the first year of life progresses, the infants of both species display a growing interest in the inanimate environment and in their peers, while physical capacities, dexterity, and coordination continuously improve. The initially tentative and hesitant movements away from the mother are soon transformed into repeated playful practice of its physical prowess, an activity which we term exercise play. These playful behaviors then become increasingly focused on peers, and thus toward the end of the first year of life social play is the most common infant behavior that does not involve the mother. Although the two species spend the same total amount of time in play, it should be noted that pigtail infants engage in more exercise play whereas bonnets engage in more social play.

From these data it is clear that a developmental difference between pigtail and bonnet dyads exists from birth. The preference for physical contact among bonnet adults is reflected in a relatively relaxed maternal disposition. While providing good care to their infants, bonnet mothers are less restrictive and more tolerant. They allow infants to go and to return. As a consequence, in the course of development bonnet infants have different experiences than do pigtails. Their social interactions begin earlier, and they are freer to approach other members of their group, whether peers or

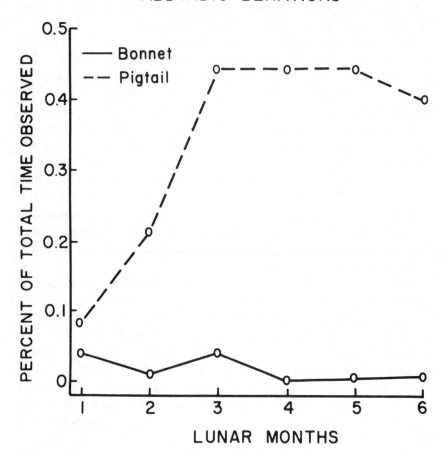

FIGURE 6. Mean duration in the two species of maternal abdyadic behaviors (*weaning, punitive deterrence, infant removal,* and *contact deterrence*) over the first six months of life.

adults. They are less dependent on their mothers in that they leave them more often and go further away. They engage in more social play, whereas the pigtails spend more time in solitary play.

I wish to suggest that it is the mother's behavior, within the context of the characteristic social structure, which provides the experience for the developing infant that perpetuates (through ontogenetic realization) the species-characteristic difference in spatial patterning and temperament. Since this pervasive difference between the two species appears to be as characteristic as the difference in the length of their tails, we must assume that it arose as an adaptation to selective pressure and has long since been genetically encoded. The hypothesis suggested, then, is that species-typical, genetically determined behavior, such as is manifested in this difference between the two species, develops in each generation as a consequence of species-typical life experience.

Another major difference between the species became obvious only as we followed several groups for over a decade, into the third and fourth generations. In a pigtail group, now containing 34 animals, all but two having been laboratory-born, we find that social behavior occurs primarily within a clan, that is to say, among a mother and all her descendants. This is not true in a comparable multigeneration bonnet group. Considering the usual kinds of positive social interactions, such as physical contact, proximity, grooming, and play, pigtails interact much more with clanmates than do bonnets. In fact, pigtails interact primarily with clanmates, whereas bonnets do not.

This difference between the species also appears to be explained as an effect of the characteristic maternal behavior on the development of the young, in line with the hypothesis previously offered. The protective, restrictive behavior of the pigtail mother, combined with her intermittent rejection, create in the infant an intense attachment to her and a strong tendency to remain close to her (Hinde, 1974; Kaufman, 1974a). The attachment is intensified when siblings are born (Kaufman and Rosenblum, 1969b) and then spreads to include the siblings, who are similarly closely attached to the mother. The same process applies to the next generation. The maternal clan is thus the primary social structure of the pigtails (Figure 7).

The social structure of the bonnets is different. The primary unit is not the maternal clan, but the larger group. Peer relations appear to be as important as clan relations. Conviviality with all the members of the group is an early enduring characteristic (except during dominance encounters). Special closeness to the mother does not appear to last long beyond infancy. Bonnets seem to form equivalent bonds with all *familiar* animals.

FIGURE 7. A pigtail maternal clan of three generations, mother on the right with her youngest infant, another offspring in the center, and the oldest offspring on the left, with her own infant.

SEPARATION STUDIES

A final major difference between the species became evident when we carried out our separation studies. In these experiments the mother was separated from the infant and removed to a cage in a distant location. The infant was left in its home pen with all the animals it had ever known. First, I will describe the reaction seen in the great majority of pigtail infants whose mothers were removed when they were between four and six months of age. The immediate reactions of both mother and infant to physical separation were loud screams and massive struggling to regain each other. When the infant was put back in the pen it was highly agitated (Figure 8).

Pacing, searching head movements, frequent trips to the front door and windows, sporadic and short-lived bursts of erratic play, and brief movements toward other members of the group seemed to be constant. No adult attempted to comfort the infant. Cooing, the rather plaintive distress call of the young macaque, and intermittent screeching, were frequent. This reaction persisted throughout the first day. All observers were struck by a sense of acute distress.

After 24-36 hours the pattern changed strikingly. The infant sat hunched over, almost rolled into a ball, with its head often down between its legs (Figure 9). When the face could be seen, it seemed that the facial muscles had sagged, which together with the configuration of forehead and mouth, created the same appearance of dejection and sadness that Darwin (1872, p. 182) described and believed "to be universally and instantly recognized as that of grief" (Figure 10). Movement virtually ceased except when the infant was actively displaced. The movement that did occur appeared to be in slow motion, except at feeding time or in withdrawal from aggressive behavior, when it could be quick. The infant appeared to be moping much of the time, rarely responded to social invitation, rarely made a social gesture, and play behavior virtually ceased. The infant seemed to be largely disengaged from the environment and to derive little comfort from the presence of others (Figure 11). Occasionally the infant would look up and plaintively "coo." A strong feeling of dejection, withdrawal, and social isolation was communicated to all observers.

FIGURE 8. An agitated pigtail infant, grimacing and screaming while fleeing from an abusive rebuff by an adult female he had approached (from Kaufman and Rosenblum, 1967b).

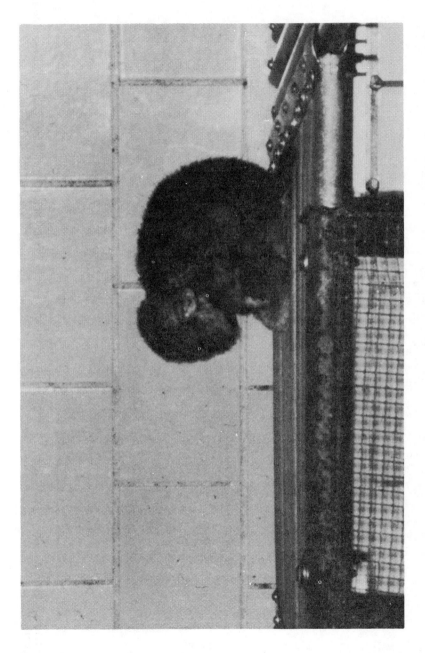

FIGURE 9. A pigtail infant showing the collapsed posture typical of the second stage of reaction to separation.

FIGURE 10. A pigtail infant showing the characteristic posture and dejected facies (from Kaufman and Rosenblum, 1967b).

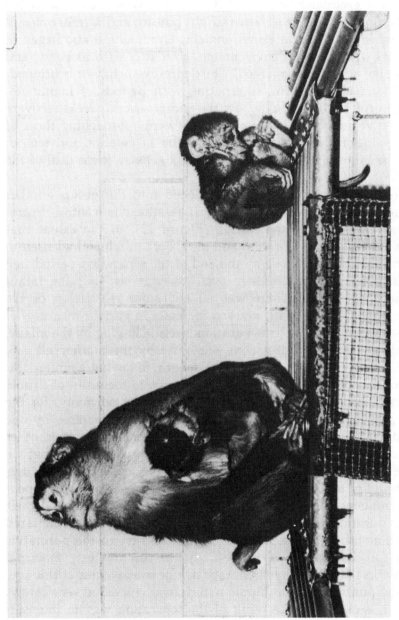

FIGURE 11. A pigtail infant with characteristic posture, completely disengaged from the mother-infant pair nearby (from Kaufman and Rosenblum, 1967b).

The state of dejected withdrawal persisted for five to six days, and then gradually began to lift. The recovery started with the infant's resumption of a more upright posture and a resurgence of interest in the inanimate environment. Gradually, it also began to interact with its social environment, primarily with its peers, and then play activity re-emerged. The depressive behavior continued, but in an abated form, alternating with periods of inanimate-object exploration and play. By the end of several weeks recovery seemed virtually complete; play levels were approaching those of preseparation, movement was increasing in amount and tempo, and the infant appeared to be alert and active a great deal of the time.

When the mother was reintroduced into the group another dramatic change occurred. Physical reunion via ventral-ventral contact was intense and lasting (Figure 12), to the extent that inanimate-object exploration and play, both of which had risen to near preseparation levels by the end of the separation period, fell during the reunion month to even lower levels, i.e., the infant became less active. There was an enormous reassertion of the dyadic relationship, with marked increases in various measures of closeness compared to preseparation levels. Clinging by the infant, nipple contact, and protective enclosure by the mother all rose significantly. Even in the second month following reunion this trend was still evident. This significant rise in measures of dyadic closeness is quite striking when we realize that normally, for the age periods involved, these particular behaviors *decrease* by one third to one half. The increased closeness was manifested in other ways as well. A measure of mother-infant spatial relations that we have found valuable in our normative studies concerns departures by infant or mother from the other to a different level of the pen. The frequency of such other-level departures fell 80%, and their mean duration fell 43% in the month following reunion compared to the month before separation, again contrary to the normative data for the ages involved. Finally, in this context, maternal behaviors that normally discourage dyadic cohesiveness at this age, such as punishment and nipple withdrawal, appeared very rarely. Thus it is clear that the result of the separation was an intensification of the mother-infant relationship, with each partner acting to maintain physical closeness.

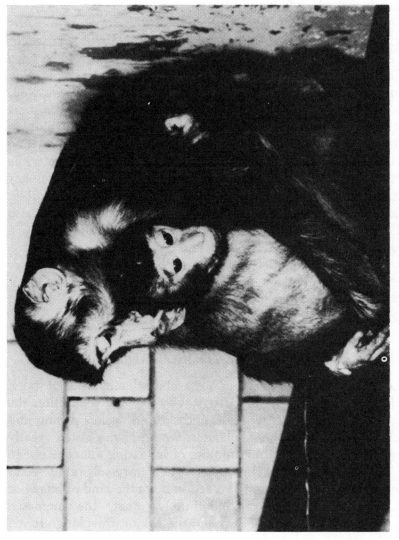

FIGURE 12. Reunited pigtail mother and infant in close ventral-ventral contact (from Kaufman and Rosenblum, 1969b).

HUMAN COMPARISONS

It seems clear that the pigtail monkey's reaction[2] to loss of the mother is strikingly similar to the anaclitic depression in human infants described by Spitz.

Human studies by others—for example, Robertson and Bowlby (1952), Schaffer and Callender (1959), Bowlby (1960b), Provence and Lipton (1962), Heinicke and Westheimer (1965)—have been confounded by age differences and by the fact that the separation was not only from the mother but from the usual homesite as well. Even so, it seems clear from all the studies that from about six months of age on, separation from the mother is disturbing to children, that the initial response is agitation, and that if there is no alleviation as by substitute mothering, this gives way after a while to depressive behavior. The reactions of human and monkey infants to separation, then, are phenomenologically comparable. The similarity is found not only in the form of the behavior but also in the succession of stages—an initial agitation followed by a depressive withdrawal. Heinecke and Westheimer (1965), in a study of older children, delineated five stages of reaction, which we have not seen in monkeys, but their conceptualization is very apt and fitting. They called the stages "successive efforts at adaptation."

REACTION TO SEPARATION AS ADAPTATION

Let us now consider the reaction to separation in terms of stages of adaptive response. In the first stage following separation the infant gave frequent distress calls and showed restless pacing and searching. In the wild these behaviors would have assisted greatly in reuniting the infant with its mother or in getting someone else to take over the mothering functions. Their survival value seems evident. However, this agitated reaction is not the kind of behavior that can profitably go on indefinitely. First, the increased movement and vocalization augment the risk of provoking attack,

[2] It should be noted that other observers, at the University of Wisconsin (Seay, Hansen, and Harlow, 1962; Seay and Harlow, 1965) and at Cambridge University (Hinde, Spencer-Booth, and Bruce, 1966), have found roughly comparable reactions in another macaque, the rhesus.

either from conspecifics or from predators. Second, the markedly heightened activity is exhausting. Thus, after a relatively short period of time, the agitated reaction comes to an end, an adaptive change in organismic state.

The second stage also may be seen as having survival value. There is an obvious conservation of energy and resources. This is not depletion of energy or massive fatigue because in certain circumstances the infant moved rapidly and appropriately, e.g., when food was put into the pen or when an act of aggression was directed at it. Conservation is achieved through the marked inactivity, as well as by the posture (body rolled almost into a ball), which probably cuts down heat loss by reducing the exposed body surface. The posture, which reduces the infant's size, and the paucity and extreme slowness of movement, make him less of a visual stimulus to other animals and thus less likely to provoke attack. The posture also would reduce exposure to adverse elements such as wind and rain. Finally, the reduced body exposure and the hidden face markedly reduce sensory input to the infant.

Just as the agitation reaction has time-limited survival value, the energy-conserving withdrawal reaction, if it continued indefinitely, would have a host of deleterious effects. This state of minimal action and interaction sharply curtails experience of the outside world and would virtually bring further development to an end. An animal growing physically larger but otherwise not acquiring the personal and social skills of his species would not survive long, or would survive only as an outcast with little possibility of successful reproduction. The consequences of prolongation of this reaction were tragically evident in the babies with the hospitalism syndrome described by Spitz (1945). Not only did further development cease, but there was regression and ultimately no fitness for survival. This outcome illustrates the fact that, in the human, evolutionary adaptation has accentuated the role of the mothering figure to an exquisite degree. The human infant cannot survive without a mother. The monkey infant, on the other hand, from an early age *is* capable of surviving without a mother, and this capacity was shown by the third stage of reaction: the recovery from depressive withdrawal. The monkey infant is able to survive because of its considerable locomotor ability. This provides the means by which the monkey, on its own, is finally enabled to re-engage the environment so as to find new sources of comfort, with a reasonable likelihood of success not only in surviving but also in resuming development, acquiring new knowledge and new skills, and achieving social growth through interaction with peers and adults.

I suggest, then, that the reaction to separation consists of stages which are successive efforts at adaptation by changes in organismic state, and that the first two stages are similar in human and pigtail monkey infants. In so doing I am aware that in any attempt to explain both monkey and human behavior the complexity of the explanatory hypothesis necessary for the human case must be limited. I believe that explanation is possible in this instance because in the young of both species the mediating neural mechanisms are similar and relatively undifferentiated. In fact, there is evidence that these neural mechanisms may be common to most vertebrates (Riss and Scalia, 1967).[3]

BIOLOGY—"FLIGHT-FIGHT" AND "CONSERVATION-WITHDRAWAL" AS COPING MECHANISMS

In further consideration of the first two stages, from both the phenomenological and adaptive points of view, they appear to be explicable by a theoretical construction of George Engel's, the historical development of which is interesting. Engel and Reischman (1956), in their classic study of the child Monica, were struck by the fact that in the presence of a stranger Monica would abruptly turn away and even fall asleep, while showing profound reduction in the secretion of hydrochloric acid by the stomach. They saw this behavior as a manifestation of a primary regulatory process for organismic homeostasis, designed to conserve resources in the face of possible depletion. This biological response pattern was ultimately labeled "conservation-withdrawal." After finding a variety of other comparable manifestations and noting that they usually followed a response pattern of active engagement in

---

[3] This is not the place to explore in detail the use and relevance of animal models. However, the likelihood that an animal model of a behavioral disorder will allow extrapolation to man would seem to depend on the extent to which the phenomena in question share common biological and psychosocial structures and mechanisms. Behavioral similarity alone is not sufficient.

stressful situations, Engel (1962a) concluded that the central nervous system is organized from birth to mediate *two opposite patterns* of response to a mounting need. The first, or "flight-fight," pattern involves activity and environmental engagement to avoid danger or control sources of supply. The second, or "conservation-withdrawal," pattern is activated when the high energy expenditures of the "flight-fight" reaction threaten exhaustion; it is characterized by withdrawal from the environment and inactivity, thereby conserving energy. Engel found neurophysiological support for his theory in Hess's demonstration (1957) of separate *ergotropic* and *trophotropic* zones in the diencephalon and mesencephalon underlying the two patterns of response. Gellhorn (1967, 1970) independently provided evidence of reciprocal systems which activate and inactivate the organism in relation to both environmental and internal fluctuations.

The human and pigtail infants' initial reaction of agitation appears to be a manifestation of the "flight-fight" pattern. The subsequent stage of depressive behavior appears to be a manifestation of the "conservation-withdrawal" reaction.

PSYCHOBIOLOGY—DEVELOPMENTALLY ACQUIRED COPING MECHANISMS

To recapitulate, these two response systems for dealing with organismic stress, based on vertebrate neural systems of organization, are available from birth and may be called upon quite automatically when their thresholds are exceeded. These are *coping mechanisms* of an inborn nature, i.e., phylogenetic adaptations. They are called into play only as they are required. They may not be required if they are superseded by developmentally acquired coping mechanisms, i.e., ontogenetic adaptations. For example, we have seen that the infant's initial reaction to mother loss is agitated searching, calculated to regain the mother. If this fails, what happens *then* depends on the infant's ability to deal with the loss of the mother and/or to find a substitute mother. These two factors are related. Being able to turn to someone else is an aspect of coping, and being comforted by someone else may increase the capacity to cope. We assume that much coping is experientially determined. It is based on acquiring knowledge and skills, on overcoming obstacles and surmounting stresses. It is based on the successes of the individual past, made possible, of course, by genetically determined potentialities for learning that were selected in the course of evolution, i.e., successes of the species' past.

We may illustrate the development of coping by considering the response of bonnet infants to mother loss. Bonnet infants react initially the same way as pigtail infants, with agitation—pacing, searching, and vocalization. What happens then is on the whole strikingly different from pigtails. Bonnet adults provide comfort and security to the bereft bonnet infant. Figure 13 illustrates a female with an infant of her own who has literally adopted two separated infants, carrying them and nursing them along with her own. An adult bonnet *male* (in this case the father) may also carry, comfort, and sleep with a bereft bonnet infant (Figure 14). Even if outright adoption does not occur, there is nevertheless considerable physical contact, proximity, and even ventral-ventral contact between a separated bonnet infant and the remaining adults. With this degree of comfort and support bonnet infants, although their play behavior decreases, simply never display the massive postural collapse, the dejected appearance, and the total social withdrawal characteristic of pigtail infants.

Thus we have found that bonnet and pigtail infants four to six months of age differ in their coping ability, the most obvious manifestation being the difference in reaction to mother loss. The explanation of this difference too appears to lie principally in their different experiences during the first months of life. Bonnet infants from the beginning have much wider social encounters than pigtails. They literally know more animals better, including adults. They have been away from their mothers more than have pigtails and have had a head start in social play. They have a better knowledge of their surround and a greater repertoire of behavior. They are more secure in the environment, both inanimate and animate. Among pigtails we have found that the ones with the greatest coping ability tend to be the offspring of the dominant females. The explanation is similar to the explanation of the difference between the bonnets and pigtails: the offspring of dominant females are more privileged, have had more social encounters than other infants, and have had a wider experience of

FIGURE 13. A bonnet female with two separated infants she adopted and her own infant. She cared for and nursed all three, one of whom has nipple in its mouth.

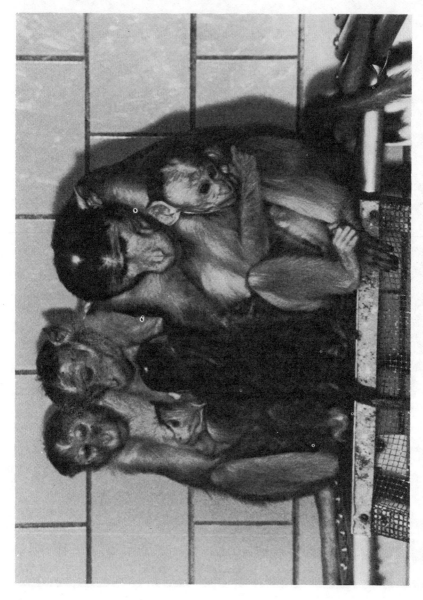

FIGURE 14. A bonnet male holding a motherless infant whom he protected and cared for.

the inanimate environment, i.e., they have had more opportunities to do things and acquire skills.

REACTION TO SEPARATION AND AFFECTS

Let us turn now to another important aspect of the separation reaction, the affective, since it has been suggested (e.g., Freud, 1926; Bowlby, 1960a, 1960b; Engel, 1962a, 1962b; Kaufman and Rosenblum, 1967a, 1967b) that both anxiety and depression are related to separation. The problem of affects is a difficult and complex one, being in the first place a biological problem that Darwin, Freud, and many others have attempted to clarify. To begin with, affects are biological organismic states. They come to serve as regulators of social living as well as of inner, ultimately psychic, life. The behavioral manifestations of affect serve to communicate to others the organism's needs and states. Affect states also include systems of internal regulation. These functions of outward communication and inner regulation, which we assume were selected for their survival value, are exercised automatically in response to the conditions for which they were evolved, without necessary psychic participation, at least initially.

Engel (1962a, 1962b) has suggested that the organismic reaction patterns of flight-fight and conservation-withdrawal are the precursors of affect states, specifically that they are the biological anlagen of anxiety and depression. Earlier I detailed the survival value of these organismic states as they were manifested in separated pigtail infants, in terms of their communicative and regulatory aspects. There is one other critical characteristic of affects, namely, the subjective or experiential aspect, the *felt* emotion, regarding which our data need to be examined in terms of the hypothesis that these reaction patterns are the biological substrate of the affects associated with anxiety and depression. Since subjective reports from monkeys are unavailable, as they are also from human infants, our interpretation of the data is limited to what we can see in the monkeys and what we can feel empathically in ourselves as we observe them.

In the first stage we see agitation, restless seeking, repeated crying, and an anguished face, while we sense a feeling of panic and distress. It is difficult not to associate this organismic state with anxiety.

In the next stage we observe withdrawal, rejection of the environment, retardation of reaction to stimuli, slow movement, a collapsed posture, minimal locomotion, and the face Darwin associated with grief, while we sense feelings of dejection and despair. It is difficult not to associate this organismic state with depression.

In the human we know that these powerful feeling states, when once discriminated by the developing ego, then function as signals, as indicators of the total psychic situation, as calls for appropriate regulation. Freud made it clear, for example, that the ego learns to recognize anxiety as a signal of danger and a call for regulation. He said, "Anxiety has an unmistakable relation to *expectation*" (Freud, 1926, pp. 164-165). He was thus describing an evaluating mechanism, based on experience, which activates regulating mechanisms to maintain homeostasis. In this, as in so many other instances, he was anticipating more recent theories of organismic function. Pribram (1967), for instance, has proposed a neuro-psychological theory of emotion according to which the organism's continuing stability depends on neural programs or plans (i.e., a set of genetic and experiential memory processes) which organize the perceptions and behavior of the organism. He describes two mechanisms, a "test" (or matching) mechanism to sense incon-gruities between plans and current input, and an "operate" mechanism to appraise changes effective in decreasing the incongruity. Input to the organism which is sufficiently incon-gruous can interrupt the ongoing plans, thereby producing "e-motion." Various regulatory mechanisms then act to reduce the incongruity; either old plans are used to restore the status quo ante and to "gate out" new input; or new plans are developed which incorporate the incongruity, what Piaget might call accommoda-tion, a form of ontogenetic adaptation. I find Pribram's theory useful in understanding our data.

A DEVELOPMENTAL PSYCHOBIOLOGICAL HYPOTHESIS—CONSERVATION-WITHDRAWAL, HELPLESSNESS, AND DEPRESSION

Development in the human or monkey infant proceeds through the progressive elaboration of new plans and repertoires of behavior. To begin with, the infant's plans are largely dependent on the constant interventions of the mothering figure, whose separate identity has not yet been established by the infant. As self-object differentiation occurs, and the mother becomes important for herself, we may speak of the mother-infant unit as having shared plans of action. The sudden disappearance of the mother interrupts the shared plan and for the infant creates perceptual incongruity, a situation of danger.

For the four- to six-month-old monkey infant, losing his mother is a problem of great magnitude for two reasons. First, it threatens his very capacity for survival, since at that age he is still very much dependent on her for protection, guidance, shelter, and, to some extent, food. Second, her loss is also a crisis because the monkey infant at that age has not only long since discriminated his mother as a separate object in his world, he has become very attached to her. A libidinal bond has been forged. In Schneirla's terminology, the bond is now of a "psychosocial" type in which the *meanings* rather than the immediate physiological effects of stimuli are functional (Tobach and Schneirla, 1969). In other words, the mother is important to the infant because of his feelings for her, for what she means to him, in addition to what she does for him. The infant's reaction to mother loss, as observed, may be understood from this perspective too.

When the infant is confronted by the loss of his mother, the situation is appraised as one of incongruity and *uncertainty*, accompanied by feelings of apprehension and anxiety. The flight-fight response system is activated, producing searching, calling, and a great effort to find the mother. If he finds her, or she him, the whole reaction ends. If he secures a substitute to comfort him, the uncertainty and apprehension are reduced. If somehow he has already developed the capacity to tend himself and to wait, this too will reduce the agitation, and he will experience less apprehension. If, however, he neither finds the mother nor secures a substitute, nor has the capacity to tend himself, the situation becomes one which to the infant now appears *unmanageable* (however that decision is arrived at, and whether or not it is the most accurate appraisal), rather than uncertain. In this situation the infant feels pessimistic, helpless, and depressed. Conservation-withdrawal occurs, with the collapsed posture, reduced activity, social withdrawal, etc.

The majority of pigtail infants we have studied failed to secure substitute mothering of a comforting type and apparently found the situation unmanageable; helpless, depressive affects and conservation-withdrawal resulted. Bonnet infants, with their greater ability to cope, including the ability to secure comforting from others, did not find the situation so unmanageable, did not feel so helpless, and showed far less conservation-withdrawal.

What has been described is the hypothesized relationship between the two biological response systems described by Engel and the two organismic states akin to anxiety and depression that were observed in four- to six-month-old monkey infants separated from their mothers. I suggest that in these infants we are seeing the emergence of psychological function from its biological base. It is not hypothesized that psychological aspects are present from the very beginning of life. We know, for example, that very young human infants respond to stressful situations with intense crying (i.e., flight-fight reaction); further, that if the stress is unrelieved the infant will ultimately stop crying, become quiet, and probably fall asleep (i.e., conservation-withdrawal). We do not attribute any particular psychological functions or experiences to this behavioral sequence, which we understand (with Engel) as the automatic successive evoking of the two available biological response systems. Comparable biobehavioral reactions occur in monkey neonates. Some months later, however, the situation has changed.

By four to six months of age, before any separation experience, the monkeys we studied showed considerable evidence of cognitive development, including clear discrimination of all the members of their social group. They knew how to delay gratification, e.g., in waiting their turn for water or solid food. They displayed a number of seemingly discriminable affective states—fear, anger, interest, and surprise. Finally—and of great importance—they showed a strong attachment to their mothers, what in the human child would probably be called object love.

In infants with this degree of psychological development, the reaction to mother loss is, then, not *simply* or *only* the activation of biological response systems. First, as we have seen, reactions vary, depending on the totality of available coping mechanisms. Second, even when the biological response systems are activated, the total organismic reaction differs from the neonatal b·cause the experiencing organism has changed. What was a purely biological reaction has become also a psychological reaction. That it may shortly become *essentially* a psychological reaction is demonstrated, I believe, by another experiment we carried out (Kaufman, 1973; see also Rosenblum, 1971).

Before describing this experiment, let us try to conceptualize the experience of the infant who becomes depressed during separation, and offer a suggestion about the further developmental role of this experience. If a four- to six-month-old has found loss of his mother unmanageable, so that the conservation-withdrawal reaction was the only possible adaptation, he has suffered a severe psychological trauma, specifically a situation with which he could not cope (except by the conservation-withdrawal reaction), and in which he experienced an overwhelming feeling of helplessness. From that time on, whenever faced with a situation which appears to be unmanageable (however that decision is arrived at, and whether or not that is the most accurate appraisal), the infant who has experienced helplessness before will probably experience it again, and elements of the conservation-withdrawal reaction will probably be re-evoked.

The Caged-Mother Return Study

Two pigtail mothers were simultaneously removed from a group. The infants of both showed initial agitation and then depression, but the depressive phase was mild in one infant and severe in the other. Each then recovered over the next several weeks until they appeared to be behaving normally, for example, playing a good deal of the time. Then the mothers were put back into the pen for 30 minutes, one at a time, but *inside a cage* so that reunion was impossible. Each infant ran immediately to the cage when it contained its own mother but not the other mother. Each vocalized and tried unsuccessfully to get to its mother inside the cage. Then, the infant who had been mildly depressed stopped trying and resumed playing, but the infant who had been severely depressed now again collapsed into a ball, showing the typical face of grief, and remained withdrawn and immobile until the cage with its mother was removed, whereupon within moments it got up and resumed playing. On many days during the next eight weeks the mothers, inside a cage, were each reintroduced into the pen for 30 minutes. Each time the first infant, after a cursory look, continued what it was doing, but each time the second infant, after looking at its caged mother, cooed, collapsed into a ball, usually closed its eyes, and remained withdrawn and immobile until its mother was removed, whereupon it quickly resumed playing. For 23½ hours of those days, it explored and played and ate and slept like the other infants, but during the half hour of its mother's caged presence it showed the depressive response.[4] An identical experiment was carried out with two bonnets. Upon separation both infants showed agitation, but then each was adopted, one to a greater extent than the other. Later, when their mothers were returned in a cage, each infant ran to its *adoptive* mother; one remained with her until the cage was removed, whereas the other soon resumed playing.

How shall we interpret these results? It seems clear that the return of the caged mother was a stressful stimulus to all infants, a reminder of the separation experience, creating again a situation of uncertainty and anxiety. In response the bonnets ran for security to their new "mothers." The first pigtail tried to return to its caged mother, but when it could not, it resumed playing. *These infants all responded to their anxiety by using the coping techniques they had learned and used before.* The second pigtail, who had originally shown a protracted conservation-withdrawal reaction to the loss of his mother, with severe depression, a very traumatic experience, had acquired no new coping mechanisms. It responded to the inaccessible mother with a recurrence of depressive withdrawal. Yet it seems unlikely that each time the mother was returned in a cage the conservation-withdrawal reaction in its biological entirety was automatically turned on and then off when

---

[4] The caged-mother return experiment may cast light on the relation among object love, object constancy, and memory. The fact that the depressive response reappears whenever the caged mother is visible, and disappears when she is not, suggests that the infant has excellent recognition memory but no or poorly sustained evocative memory. If object constancy depends upon evocative memory, then this experiment suggests that object love does not depend upon object constancy. Out of sight, out of mind, does not preclude a love-object relationship when in sight. In the human we know that this is not the final developmental stage of object relationship. In the monkey we need more data.

she was removed. It is far more likely that her every reappearance served to remind the infant of its helplessness, reproducing the depression with some behavioral aspects of the conservation-withdrawal response. This experiment suggests that it is the *state of helplessness* that is the critical mechanism underlying the depressive response, both in the original experience and in the repeated experiences. It suggests further that the response to mother loss changes developmentally from a biological reaction into a primarily psychological (i.e., psychobiological) reaction, both in terms of the intervening mechanisms and the felt experience. It changes, that is to say, from flight-fight and conservation-withdrawal to anxiety and depression.[5]

The problem of affects may be illuminated further by these separation studies, if we consider the behavior of infant and mother upon reunion, namely, the remarkable increase of closeness. We could call this a regression in the sense that the behavior is typical of a much younger infant and its mother, but this does not help us to understand it since it occurs not in the face of frustration but rather of gratification, and furthermore, we have no reason to suspect an earlier process of fixation. It appears to be regressive only because the behaviors shown are those usually shown by younger infant-mother pairs.

It is reasonable to assume that the initial reaction is motivated by the joy of reunion to be seen in any two individuals who have been apart, such as lovers or even friends. Physical closeness and

[5] Further experimentation is necessary to document the developmental changes. For example, it would be informative to separate much younger infants whose psychological development is minimal. The difficulty is that younger infants are dependent on mother's milk for nourishment and might not survive. A major reason for choosing to separate at four to six months was the fact that infants of that age are already eating solid food. Another approach is to study the biological reaction in terms of its physiological parameters. This we are already doing. My colleague, Martin Reite, has developed a surgically implantable telemetry system for monitoring seven channels of physiological data—heart rate, body temperature, three channels of EEG, eye movement, and muscle potential. We have already found (Reite et al., 1974) dramatic changes in heart rate, body temperature, and sleep patterns during separation. At present Reite is investigating to what extent the depression reproduced by the return of the caged mother is accompanied by the same physiological changes as the original depressive response. The similarities and differences, together with the temporal relationship between the behavioral and the physiological changes, should clarify the relationship between the psychological and biological aspects of the response.

hugging are typical. In these monkeys, however, the behavior continues for several months: they stay close to each other; they make frequent physical contact; the infant does not go as far away as infants of that age usually do, and he does not stay away as long; he does not explore or play as much as agemates, or even as much as he himself did in the last week of his separation when he appeared to have largely recovered from the devastating effects of the mother's absence; and the mother desists from weaning and punishing behaviors. The explanation I suggest is that the distressing experience of apprehension and anxiety upon separation leads to a new plan to avoid a massive repetition. The infant must constantly see, feel, smell, or otherwise sense the mother because every loss of the perception of her is an immediate reminder of the previous incongruity and uncertainty produced by her absence, a reminder which includes the subjective emotion. It seems reasonable to speculate that *signal* anxiety is now operating to keep them close and minimize the danger of another separation. This places signal anxiety in the broad context of adaptive behavior and not only in the narrower confines of neurotic behavior. As time goes on this extra closeness finally wanes. Presumably the specific anxiety that separation will occur again becomes attenuated in the continued proximity of the pair. However, another study suggests that some proneness to anxiety persists. Hinde (1972), who separated rhesus macaque infants from their mothers, has found that even after two years, previously separated animals, who in all other ways appear normal, show more evidence of anxiety than nonseparated controls when confronted by strange objects in a strange cage, although not in their home cage. Apparently they still have difficulty in the face of perceptual incongruity and uncertainty.

It remains to clarify the meanings of three terms that have been used and the relations among the referents of these terms: *conservation-withdrawal*, *helplessness*, and *depression*.

Conservation-withdrawal refers to a biological reaction pattern, including both the underlying bodily processes (physiological and biochemical) and their manifest appearance and behavior. The circumstances that evoke it may vary; it may be more or less successful as an adaptational effort; it may in the course of development be accompanied by awareness of associated feelings and achieve mental representation; but as a somatic response it must always be viewed within a biological frame of reference.

Helplessness is less easy to circumscribe. First, it refers generally to the functional status of a neonate (see p. 322); the organism is unable to maintain its life systems without the aid of a caretaker. No awareness of state is implied. In a related vein, it refers, in situations of acute stress, to the state of the young organism which is unable to cope or can attempt to cope only by resorting to automatic emergency measures, e.g., the conservation-withdrawal reaction (see p. 352). These states of helplessness have no psychological referents and no direct relationship with depression.

It is helplessness as a psychobiological state that is most relevant to the problem of depression (also a psychobiological state).[6]

Earlier I cited Freud's comment that anxiety is related to expectation (see p. 350). It should be noted (1) that expectation in this context is a cognitive representation of an egocentric contingent relationship between plans and outcome; and (2) that it is based on an appraisal. The appraisal involves an estimate of coping ability in the given circumstances, generally based on previous experience. If it leads to the expectation (cognitive representation) that course of action A will manage the situation, then appropriate action follows. If, however, the appraisal leads to a cognitive representation of an uncertain contingent relationship, this expectation that coping may or may not suffice identifies the situation as one of danger and produces a state of fear or anxiety. I believe that this is what Freud meant by relating anxiety to expectation. We can add that depression is also related to expectation. If the appraisal leads to the expectation that nothing the organism can do will affect the outcome, this cognitive representation of helplessness produces a state of depression.

Helplessness as a psychobiological state is more than a cognitive representation. At a conference in 1970 I stated that "helplessness has cognitive, affective, and motivational aspects. Helplessness is a perception, an awareness, an appraisal, a feeling state, and, at the same time, it is a tendency to behave in a given way. I view the

---

[6] In one frame of reference both these states are *psychological*. It is our view of them in relation to biological processes that changes the frame of reference to *psychobiological*.

state of helplessness as a kind of unified psychobiological structure [in which] . . . motivational, cognitive, and affective processes are interdependent parts" (Kaufman, 1974b, pp. 252-253). The early prepsychological functional state of helplessness achieves mental representation in the course of development as the expectation (described above) that nothing can be done to affect the outcome. This cognitive representation undermines the motivation to act because of the belief that action will not avail. This negative cognitive set is experienced affectively as pessimism, discouragement, despondency, and despair. The motivational, cognitive, and affective aspects all go together. By the same token, as suggested by Engel and Schmale (1972), the bodily changes in the biological reaction of conservation-withdrawal (which occurs universally in functional states of helplessness) achieve mental representation as feelings of fatigue, weakness, and lack of energy and interest in the outside world. *The psychobiological state of helplessness represents all these threads woven together developmentally*, including the somatic manifestations of conservation-withdrawal.

Helplessness, from this perspective, is the basis of depression. In its simplest, most uncomplicated form, *depression* is isomorphic with helplessness. As such, it is a universal reaction to a ubiquitous existential reality—the inevitable succession of frustrations and losses. In normal development, omnipotence fails, and a major adaptational achievement is the development of adequate reality testing, including assessment of the self. Goals and aspirations are shaped on the wheel of experience, with episodes of depression serving a major developmental function in setting limits. However, in seeming to extoll the developmental virtue of helplessness, we cannot overlook the fact that even "normal" depressions are painful—the mood dysphoric, the will ebbing, the outlook gloomy, and, not infrequently, some biological manifestations of conservation-withdrawal, such as disturbed sleep and appetite.

To comprehend depressive *illness* we need to add to the basic state of helplessness a set of biological and psychological complications. At the far end from simple depression is classic melancholia—severely depressed mood, psychomotor disturbance, anhedonia, anorexia, loss of energy, sleep disturbance, poor concentration and slowed-up thinking, loss of self-esteem, self-reproach, suicidal thoughts, and a variety of biochemical and neurophysiological disturbances demonstrable in the laboratory, as well as, in all probability, evidence of a family history of melancholia. Depending on both genetic and ontogenetic experiential factors, episodes of depressive illness may show differences in duration, frequency, relation to mania, etc., as well as greater or lesser evidence about the specificity or intensity of psychological conflict. However, as Bibring (1953) pointed out, we must "make a clearer distinction between: (1) the basic or essential mechanism ...; (2) conditions which predispose to and help to bring about depression; (3) the attempts at restitution ...; (4) conditions which complicate the basic type of depression such as aggression or orality; and (5) the secondary use which may be made ... of ... depression" (p. 40).

This presentation borrows heavily from Bibring and in turn offers confirmation of his ideas. He first formulated the thesis "that depression is an ego-psychological phenomenon, a 'state of the ego,' an affective state" (p. 21). He then defined depression "as the emotional expression (indication) of a state of helplessness and powerlessness of the ego" (p. 24). The basic mechanism is "the ego's shocking awareness of its helplessness" (p. 39). He contrasted depression with anxiety as "diametrically opposed basic ego responses" (p. 34). In response to danger the ego "mobilizes the signal of anxiety and prepares for fight or flight. In depression, the opposite takes place, the ego is paralyzed because it finds itself incapable to meet the 'danger' " (pp. 34-35). Dynamically, he did not view depression as resulting from a conflict between ego and id, or superego, or environment, but rather as stemming from a tension within the ego itself; there is a collapse of self-esteem as the ego feels helpless to live up to its narcissistic aspirations. He described basic depression as "a state of the ego whose main characteristics are a decrease of self-esteem, a more or less intense state of helplessness, a more or less intensive and extensive inhibition of functions, and a more or less intensely felt particular emotion" (p. 27).

Clearly, Bibring's conception, while cast in purely psychological terms, without any reference to biological systems, is consistent with the psychobiological formulations presented in this paper. He described a dynamic state, helplessness[7] of the ego, with

---

[7] Helplessness has been studied and stressed by several other investigators as well. Engel and Schmale in a series of papers (e.g., Engel and Schmale, 1972;

affective, cognitive, and motivational aspects, as the basis of depression. Of course, in monkeys we must be hesitant to speak of an ego. However, if we keep in mind (1) that the ego is a hypothetical construct defined by its functions, and (2) that these monkeys showed considerable psychological function, we might consider the monkeys to possess some coherent, if primitive, mental organization. Also, since we hesitate to attribute narcissistic aspirations to monkeys, it might be better to think of them as having personally organized plans for living. In that case, the perceived inability to carry out those plans would be comparable to feeling helpless to live up to narcissistic aspirations.

SUMMARY

Studies of monkeys are presented in an attempt to clarify (1) processes of adaptation, (2) the transition from the biological to the psychological level of organization, and (3) the problems of anxiety and especially depression.

Two closely related species of monkeys were found to show great behavioral similarity but also significant differences.

Schmale and Engel, 1975) have related the affects of helplessness and hopelessness to conservation-withdrawal and depression via the intervening psychological response of "giving up." They distinguish the depressive manifestations of giving up (the affects of helplessness and hopelessness) and of conservation-withdrawal (fatigue, weakness, and lack of energy) from the clinical syndromes of depression, which they view as psychologically more complex disorders of adaptation. Their formulations and those presented here obviously overlap but they also differ, most strikingly in their view that the monkey's reaction to separation is a model of conservation-withdrawal but not of depression. Seligman (1975) has proposed a theory of "learned helplessness" which is largely concordant with the views expressed in this paper. In his original research he administered to dogs random shocks that the dogs were unable to avoid by anything they did. His theory is that such dogs learn that trauma is uncontrollable. This cognitive representation then reduces the motivation to respond, interferes with learning successful responses, and increases emotionality, producing first fear, when the subject is unsure that the trauma is uncontrollable, and then depression, when the subject decides that the trauma is uncontrollable. His theory differs from mine in two principal ways. First, he does not see fit to include the biological reaction of conservation-withdrawal in his scheme. Second, in considering the reaction to mother loss, he attributes little significance to the libidinal tie (the object relation) to the mother. By viewing the mother solely in terms of her reinforcing properties, he is able to say that it is not reinforcement per se but control over reinforcement that is critical to the infant.

Although these differences are presumably genetically encoded, evidence is presented that these species-characteristic differences are ontogenetically realized through species-typical life experience, centering primarily on differences in maternal behavior.

The reaction of monkey infants to mother loss is similar to that of young human infants. It is explained as consisting of successive efforts at adaptation, using whatever coping mechanisms are available, including some which are inborn and some which are developmentally acquired. Inborn are two biological response systems mediated by central nervous system organizations. The first, flight-fight, is an ergotropic reaction calculated to find the mother or secure a substitute for her. The second, conservation-withdrawal, is a trophotropic reaction, calculated to save the organism for better times. Developmentally acquired coping mechanisms include turning for comfort to other adults and making do on their own. These latter coping mechanisms are seen primarily in only one of the two species; this difference between the species is one of those accounted for by differences in species-typical life experience.

From a developmental psychobiological perspective, it is hypothesized that the two inborn biological response systems are the precursors of anxiety and helplessness (depression), respectively, which are viewed as organismic states that arise through the interwoven cognitive, affective, and motivational elaboration of the biological systems. One value of such research, then, is the opportunity to study the emergence of psychological aspects from the biological.

Finally, evidence is presented to suggest that the psychobiological state of helplessness is the basis of depression. Depression in its simplest form is considered to be isomorphic with helplessness, but to comprehend depressive illness we need to add to the basic state of helplessness a set of biological and psychological complications.

REFERENCES

Bibring, E. (1953), The Mechanism of Depression: In: *Affective Disorders*, ed. P. Greenacre. New York: International Universities Press, pp. 13-48.

Bowlby, J. (1960a), Separation Anxiety. *Internat. J. Psycho-Anal.*, 41:89-113.

———— (1960b), Grief and Mourning in Infancy and Early Childhood. *The Psychoanalytic Study of the Child*, 15:9-52. New York: International Universities Press.

Darwin, C. (1872), *The Expression of the Emotions in Man and Animals*. New York: Philosophical Library, 1955.

Engel, G. L. (1962a), *Psychological Development in Health and Disease*. Philadelphia: Saunders.

———— (1962b), Anxiety and Depression-Withdrawal: The Primary Affects of Unpleasure. *Internat. J. Psycho-Anal.*, 43:89-97.

———— & Reischsman, F. (1956), Spontaneous and Experimentally Induced Depressions in an Infant with a Gastric Fistula. *J. Amer. Psychoanal. Assn.*, 4:428-452.

———— & Schmale, A. H. (1972), Conservation-Withdrawal. In: *Physiology, Emotions and Psychosomatic Illness*. Amsterdam: Elsevier, pp. 57-85.

Freud, S. (1926), Inhibition, Symptoms and Anxiety. *Standard Edition*, 20:87-156. London: Hogarth Press, 1959.

Gellhorn, E. (1967), *Principles of Autonomic-Somatic Integrations*. Minneapolis: University of Minnesota Press.

———— (1970), The Emotions and the Ergotropic and Trophotropic Systems. *Psychologische Forschung*, 34:48-94.

Hartmann, H. (1939), *Ego Psychology and the Problem of Adaptation*. New York: International Universities Press, 1958.

Heinicke, C. M., & Westheimer, I. J. (1965), *Brief Separations*. New York: International Universities Press.

Hess, W. R. (1957), *The Functional Organization of the Diencephalon*. New York: Grune & Stratton.

Hinde, R. A. (1972), *Social Behavior and Its Development in Subhuman Primates*. Condon Lectures. Eugene: Oregon System of Higher Education.

———— (1974), Mother/Infant Relations in Monkeys and Humans. In: *Ethology and Psychiatry*, ed. N. F. White. Toronto: University of Toronto Press, pp. 29-46.

———— Spencer-Booth, Y., & Bruce, M. (1966), Effects of 6-Day Maternal Deprivation on Rhesus Monkey Infants. *Nature*, 210:1021-1023.

Kaufman, I. C. (1970), Biological Considerations of Parenthood. In: *Parenthood*, ed. E. J. Anthony & T. Benedek. Boston: Little, Brown, pp. 3-55.

———— (1973), Mother-Infant Separation in Monkeys: An Experimental Model. In: *Separation and Depression*, ed. J. P. Scott & E. C. Senay. Washington, D.C.: American Association for the Advancement of Science, pp. 33-52.

———— (1974a), Mother/Infant Relations in Monkeys and Humans: A Reply to Professor Hinde. In: *Ethology and Psychiatry*, ed. N. F. White. Toronto: University of Toronto Press, pp. 47-68.

———— (1974b), Panel Discussion. In: *The Psychology of Depression*, ed. R. J. Friedman & N. M. Katz. Washington, D.C.: Winston, pp. 251-253.

———— (1975), Learning What Comes Naturally. *Ethos*, 3:129-142.

———— & Rosenblum, L. A. (1966), A Behavioral Taxonomy for *Macaca nemestrina* and *Macaca radiata:* Based on Longitudinal Observations of Family Groups in the Laboratory. *Primates*, 7:205-258.

———— ———— (1967a), Depression in Infant Monkeys Separated from Their Mothers. *Science*, 155:1030-1031.

———— ———— (1967b), The Reaction to Separation in Infant Monkeys: Anaclitic Depression and Conservation-Withdrawal. *Psychosomat. Med.*, 29:648-675.

———————— (1969a), The Waning of the Mother-Infant Bond in Two Species of Macaque. In: *Determinants of Infant Behaviour*, Vol. 4, ed. B. M. Foss. London: Methuen, pp. 41-59.

———————— (1969b), Effects of Separation from Mother on the Emotional Behavior of Infant Monkeys. *Ann. N. Y. Acad. Sci.*, 159:681-695.

Pribram, K. H. (1967), Emotion: Steps toward a Neuropsychological Theory. In: *Neurophysiology and Emotion*, ed. D. C. Glass. New York: Rockefeller University Press, pp. 3-40.

Provence, S., & Lipton, R. C. (1962), *Infants in Institutions*. New York: International Universities Press.

Reite, M. L., Kaufman, I. C., Pauley, J. D., & Stynes, A. J. (1974), Depression in Infant Monkeys: Physiological Correlates. *Psychosomat. Med.*, 36:363-367.

Riss, W., & Scalia, F. (1967), *Functional Pathways of the Central Nervous System*. Amsterdam: Elsevier.

Robertson, J., & Bowlby, J. (1952), Responses of Young Children to Separation from Their Mothers. *Courrier Centre Internationale de l'Enfance*, 2:131-142.

Rosenblum, L. A. (1971), Infant Attachment in Monkeys. In: *The Origins of Human Social Relations*, ed. H. R. Schaffer. London: Academic Press, pp. 86-113.

Schaffer, H. R., & Callender, W. M. (1959), Psychologic Effects of Hospitalization in Infancy. *Pediat.*, 24:528-539.

Schmale, A. H., & Engel, G. L. (1975), The Role of Conservation-Withdrawal in Depressive Reactions. In: *Depression and Human Existence*, ed. E. J. Anthony & T. Benedek. Boston: Little, Brown, pp. 183-198.

Seay, B., Hansen, E., & Harlow, H. F. (1962), Mother-Infant Separation in Monkeys. *J. Child Psychol. Psychiat.*, 3:123-132.

———————— & Harlow, H. F. (1965), Maternal Separation in the Rhesus Monkey. *J. Nerv. Ment. Dis.*, 140:434-441.

Seligman, M. E. P. (1975), *Helplessness*. San Francisco: Freeman.

Spitz, R. A. (1945), Hospitalism. *The Psychoanalytic Study of the Child*, 1:53-74. New York: International Universities Press.

———————— (1946), Anaclitic Depression. *The Psychoanalytic Study of the Child*, 2:313-342. New York: International Universities Press.

Tobach, E., & Schneirla, T. C. (1969), The Biopsychology of Social Behavior in Animals. In: *The Biologic Basis of Pediatric Practice*, ed. R. E. Cooke. New York: McGraw-Hill, pp. 68-82.

3 Meaning and Interpretation

Donald P. Spence, Ph.D.

Clinical Interpretation: Some Comments on the Nature of the Evidence

As we listen to the stream of associations from an analytic patient, we hear an almost continuous flow of linked ideas. They seem to resolve themselves into a number of strands—sometimes few, sometimes many. But ask a friendly critic to listen to the same material: he hears a mixture of unrelated words and has the impression that the patient simply skips from one topic to the next. Who is right?

To put the problem in these terms helps to show how quickly we lose sight of the fact that the links between ideas in clinical material may be imposed from outside and are not always inherent in its structure. Since we find it so easy to see connections between disparate ideas, we assume that the connections are contained in the structure, which is to say that other judges would hear the material in much the same way. But would they? Would 12 friendly critics independently arrive at the same underlying structure, or would each hear his own favorite melody?

A suspicion that the latter is often the case comes from a recent study by Hartvig Dahl (personal communication) on hypothesis formation. A group of analysts listened to the early hours of a case and interrupted the reading whenever any one of them decided that enough evidence had accumulated to support one among a set of possible hypotheses. Each of these interruptions was defined as a "call," and many single calls were heard—in fact, it was rare for the group to decide in unison that such and such a hypothesis could be supported at such and such a point. Dahl found that a judge's confidence was significantly higher on his own calls than on those of his colleagues. This finding suggests that, to a large degree, each man hears the material in his own way, and that we must be cautious about assuming that there is a pattern in the material, waiting to be discovered. That there is such a pattern is the assumption implied by Freud's archeological metaphor, and the major portion of this paper is addressed to an examination of its strengths and weaknesses.

I

To see a connection between two ideas can be abstractly formulated as a species of pattern matching. Pattern matching is one of our primary means of dealing with qualitative data. Rather than saying that x is equal to y (as with quantitative data), we say that x looks like y, x resembles y, x reminds us of y, etc. In almost no case is the match an exact one; nevertheless, we behave as if it were, as if the partners in a match share a common meaning.

Metaphor and simile are frequent examples of pattern matching. The sentence "Sam is a bear before breakfast" gains its power from the fact that we can readily match Sam's behavior with that of a bear, make allowances for the obvious differences, and (from what remains) learn something about Sam. The sentence "Sam is a swordfish before breakfast" fails because there is no obvious match between Sam and the swordfish, not even were Sam to have a long nose and somewhat scaly skin. Similes operate in the same way: The sentence "Sam is like a lion" is a plausible expression, for it is based on a possible match. The sentence "Sam is like a swordfish" implies an impossible match and is probably nonsense.

Pattern matching is particularly frequent in dream interpretation when we try to link associations to fragments of the dream. Once again, we must have an implicit match for the association to be understood—either manifest in the material, developed in further associations, or contained in our shared conventions. An association of "swordfish" to a dream of a potbellied stove is merely baffling (and presumed nonsense) until we learn that the dreamer is thinking of a restaurant with a stove in one corner and a swordfish hanging on the wall; then a match is possible and the association becomes intelligible. A dream about getting off a train and watching it disappear is understood to be about termination of treatment because of the agreed-upon convention that changes in time are frequently expressed by changes in space.

It begins to become clear that a large part of clinical activity consists of pattern matching, and pattern implies form. We are constantly looking at forms and transforms—monitoring matches made by the patient in his associations; making matches between the patient's material and our own associations; matches between a theme during the current hour and a previous event; between a dream and a day residue; and any number of other comparisons. The ability to make these matches is part of our clinical skill. The extent of the match determines our clinical satisfaction with the material; thus, we might challenge an unclear association on the one hand, and take pride in a persuasive match on the other. To a certain extent, the match must occur easily; if it has to be worried into position, so to speak, we suspect an element of word play and feel unhappy with the outcome.

Thus it would appear that the structure does indeed lie in the material and that all we are doing, when we make a match, is calling attention to what has been there all along. We are simply drawing attention to what is latent, and should not be accused of imposing external forms on the material. But consider the following example. A patient dreamed of a dog charging across the lawn and hurling himself at the screen door. Missing the door, he hit the side of the house and fell down, stunned. Later that day, the patient, while driving to work, narrowly avoided being hit by a car from the side. The analyst might argue that the dream was a clear anticipation of the narrow escape—an instance of precognition, if you will. The pattern of dog-hitting-house can be mapped onto the pattern of car-hitting-car. But can it? There is a certain formal similarity between the two events, but only because we have chosen to focus on those aspects which have to do with missing and hitting. We could just as easily select the dog and the car as the principal ingredients and say there was no correspondence. Because we have no systematic basis for comparison, we choose the most appealing points of correspondence. Because each specimen is rich in detail, we can usually find points of overlap. Thus we build into the comparison the results we are looking for.

Our problem, in general, stems from the fact that we are

always dealing with essentially ambiguous pieces of behavior, rich in meaning, the meanings often overlapping and not hierarchically arranged. By that I mean that no meaning is clearly foremost in importance—until indicated by us or by the patient. The hierarchy does not reside in the material. We approach these ambiguous specimens with our own framework of beliefs and ideas, in the context of our own immediate experience, and from our private perspective of recent and distant happenings. Just as the boy with a new hammer sees the world as a collection of nails, waiting to be pounded, so we cannot help being sensitized to the themes which resonate with our own concerns, and tend to resolve the ambiguity of the dream specimen in terms of our favorite set of categories.

Frequently this choice of categories is made silently, outside of awareness, and the certainty which follows on the resolution of ambiguity is projected onto the material. We are relieved because we have found a match; the strength of that relief, the feeling that we have found the right answer, is falsely attributed to the material and generates the idea that, like Michaelangelo's *David*, it was simply waiting all this time to be discovered. Simply chip away the excess marble and there it is! But clearly our feeling is often wrong: we often impose more structure on the material than we like to admit.

II

Problems of the kind I have been discussing have been faced by literary scholars for several centuries, and a tradition of explication has developed which I would like to summarize briefly. The explication of a literary text can be roughly divided into two stages: a phase of preunderstanding in which some hypotheses are formed about the general meanings of the text, and a phase of critical analysis in which these hypotheses are put to the test. I think there are some striking points of similarity between the way the scholar works in making a given explication and the way a clinician goes about analyzing a piece of clinical material.

The first phase is dominated by three impressions: a sense of excitement, a sense of clarity, and a sense of certainty. The investigator has made a discovery and his sense of conviction carries the day; there is no need to be concerned about the details.

We are all familiar with this excitement; it appears quite often in clinical settings. Ask why a particular interpretation is true, the discoverer will frequently reply, "Isn't it obvious?" This remark is related to Dahl's finding that the "caller" showed more confidence in his own discovery than did the rest of the group—the caller, in other words, found the hypothesis obviously supported while the rest of the group were more skeptical. The feelings of clarity and certainty are interdependent: the simpler the idea, the more certainty is attached to it.

In the second phase of explication, the reader begins a more systematic analysis. First, he will try to establish the form, period, and genre of the piece in question—which is to say, what type of composition was intended and when was it written? (I am borrowing heavily from a general discussion of the problems of interpretation by Hirsch [1967].) For example, a poem (one type of form) implies something different from a piece of prose, and it has been shown that rewriting a piece of prose in the form of verse can produce subtle and rather systematic changes in its connotations. As Hirsch makes clear, a poem is read more generally; it is therefore taken to be more abstract and sweeping than a piece of prose, even when the words are identical.

Going further, the reader might ask, if a poem, what period? Knowledge of period helps to delimit the meanings of certain expressions. If we know that we are working with an eighteenth-century poet, and we find the word "compact," we rule out the sense of small car (as in "He drives a green Ford compact").

Knowledge of period, form, and genre helps to make explicit our intuitive preunderstanding of the text. We may have some early sense of what is being said; asking about the period, form, and genre forces us to make this sense explicit and to relate it to known conventions. We place the text in both a historical framework and in a meaning framework; we say this poem is about a restaurant, or this poem was written by a blind man, and immediately certain details take on a sharper focus. Hirsch has described how he read one of Donne's poems to his class when they were convinced it was written by a dying man (an assumption which he believes was provably wrong) and shows how this belief colored, and was supported by, specific words in the poem. Given an overriding hypothesis, a particular interpretation stood out boldly, and was difficult to ignore. A similar error caused an anthropologist to make a public confession when he found that a faulty generic view of a poem had caused him to misconstrue it; rather than an old folksong, it turned out to be a nineteenth-century love poem (see Hirsch, 1967).

Once the genre has been established, Hirsch suggests four criteria for explication:

1. Legitimacy. "The reading must be permissible within the public norms of the *langue* in which the text was composed." In other words, it must be true to the larger conventions of that particular genre.

2. Correspondence. "The reading must account for *each* linguistic element in the text" (my italics).

3. Generic appropriateness. "If the text follows the conventions of a scientific essay, it is inappropriate to construe the kind of allusive meaning found in casual conversation." In other words, the different parts of the text must each belong to the same genre; one cannot invoke one genre to explain one part and a second to explain another.

4. Coherence. The explanation must hang together. (All taken from Hirsch, 1967, p. 236.)

Now let me turn to some examples of clinical interpretation and see whether these literary concepts make our task any easier. I will begin with a dream reported by Witkin (1969) in an experiment on the role of presleep stimuli on dreaming. It is a particularly useful example for our purpose because we are in the position of being able to compare the dream with a film which preceded it by several hours, and (presumably) influenced its form and content. The stimulus was the well-known subincision film by Róheim; it shows a tribal initiation of four young men, all naked. Each victim is placed on the backs of two other men who are positioned on all fours. The underside of the victim's penis is cut with a sharp stone. The film is in black and white. Here is the dream:

"I can tell you about the sense of it rather than anything particular concerning it. I think I was in a car and I was being, uh, quote, you know, 'taken for a ride'. And in the back seat of a large black car. I don't know what I had done to merit it, and, uh, I mean by 'taken for a ride' I was about to be exterminated. I, I, the sense of it was they were taking me away. I was being sent away

... I don't remember whether the car was moving, or where it was heading, or who was in it, uh, except I was not alone. I was in the back seat" (Witkin, 1969, p. 311).

Reading the dream in the context of the experiment, we notice in ourselves a certain excitement or elation of exactly the kind I have been describing as characteristic of the first phase of explication—the phase of preunderstanding. The idea of being taken for a ride, with all of its gangland implications, seems to fit exactly with the castrating theme of the film. Once this larger theme has been established—once we have, in effect, defined the dream as belonging to the genre of castration dreams—then the rather neutral details take on a new and sharper meaning. Let me quote from Witkin's subsequent comments on the spontaneous recall. The subject: "Everything was black." Witkin: "As was everyone in the film." Subject: "I know there were other people in the car, all males." Witkin: "Again, as in film." Subject: "Flanked by people ... there were two gentlemen, once on each side of me in the back." Witkin: "Corresponding to the two men holding the initiate in one of the scenes of the film" (p. 311).

In the inquiry following the sleep session, the subject, asked for associations to the word "exterminated," thought of the Jews during World War II. Somewhat later, asked about his memory of the subincision film, he said he thought it might be a circumcision, but remained undecided: "I knew they weren't Jewish [laugh] so I really don't know" (p. 312).

The links are suggestive but somewhat fragmentary, and raise the question of selection. In the inquiry, the experimenter queries the subject about circumcision, and it is this question which elicits the remark about the tribe members not being Jewish. Similarly, in the postsleep inquiry, the experimenter asks about the word "exterminated" and produces the material about the Jews in World War II. The link between film and dream, mediated by references to Jews in both cases, is somewhat suspect because of the possible effects of selective cueing. And the reliance on selective cues seems to violate the "correspondence" rule which states that *each* element in the dream must be accounted for by some element from the presleep stimulus. Once that rule is set aside, the way is open for selective interpretation with all of its pitfalls.

Now suppose, for purposes of argument, that we grant a better-than-chance degree of correspondence between the subject's dream and the presleep stimulus; how does it compare with some controls? The control dreams were picked at random from a recent book on psychoanalytic technique by Greenson (1967); I looked up the word "dream" in the index, picked the subhead with the largest number of choices ("transference"), and picked the first two dreams cited. I present them here because they should give us a further check on the good and bad points of our explication.

Control Dream I (Greenson, 1967, p. 231): "I am driving down a huge mountainside in a truck. I am sitting in the rear and the truck is being driven by a man who seems to be the leader of a caravan. We make a pause and as he helps me down he sticks his tongue in my ear."

Suppose we had heard this dream following the subincision film: Wouldn't we have been impressed by the apparent overlap? Parts of this dream are rather similar to parts of the film; once we defined it as belonging to a class of castration dreams, we could have further supported our hypothesis by pointing to the parallel between being a passive passenger and a passive victim, and by pointing to such suggestive equivalences as tongue and penis; the parallel between sitting *on* the rear (in the film) and sitting *in* the rear (in the dream); and the word caravan, which implies Arabs, and the black aborigines of the film. There are other links I have probably missed; what I want to show is how easily specific parts of one sequence can be matched to parts of another. Once again, without the safeguard of one-to-one correspondence, the way is open for adventitious matches. And if we had been able to query the dreamer about suggestive parts of the dream, we might well have produced additional links to the film.

Here is Control Dream II (Greenson, 1967, p. 250): "I come to my first analytic hour, but you seem different, you look like Dr. M. You lead me into a small room and ask me to undress. I am surprised and ask you whether you're supposed to do that as a classic Freudian. You assure me it is all right. I get undressed and you begin to kiss me all over. Then you finally went down on me. I was pleased but I kept wondering if it was all right."

The links between this dream and the film are so many that one might think that it too came from Witkin's experiment. It did not; but it points an obvious moral. If links between unrelated sequences of behavior—the subincision film and this patient's dream—are so relatively easy to find; if, in other words, the base rate is so high, how can we separate meaningful connections from mere noise?

What has happened? In the case of the experimental dream, our expectation that the film would have an effect has supplied us with a misleading classification. We assume that the dream of being taken for a ride belongs to the larger genre of castration dreams; this reading then gives a particular interpretation to the phrase "being taken for a ride" and to the other, more ambiguous details, and we feel that our case is made. Not until we look at the control dreams do we begin to have doubts about our initial assumption. If we assume, as seems more parsimonious, that all three dreams belong to a doctor-patient or experimenter-subject genre, then (a) we have accounted for such similarities among the three as the passivity of the dreamer; (b) we have reinterpreted the phrase "being taken for a ride" as a comment on the experimental situation and its ambiguous demands; and (c) we have brought into question the evidence for any effect of the presleep stimulus. And note the similarity to standard literary procedures. We have taken a critical specimen, compared it to two knowns, established the features in common, and arrived at an explanation which best fits all three cases.

III

Once you have been impressed by the power of preunderstanding in molding the elements of a dream or a text, you can never return to the decoding metaphor without a certain amount of skepticism. The code is broken only by smuggling in many hidden assumptions. No matter how clever the account, no matter how many pieces of evidence support it, we can never get away from the suspicion that the preunderstanding was generated in part by some of the dream elements, and therefore we are always faced by a kind of circularity that is very hard to ignore. And then we have a second problem: the base rate of correspondence between unrelated bits of behavior is so high that we are unable to separate the true links from those generated by chance.

How can we break out of this circularity—what has been called the hermeneutic circle (Hirsch, 1967, p. 76)? Let us go back to Freud's archeology metaphor. He meant it quite literally. We begin with a piece of behavior which existed at some time in the past. Erosion over time has caused gaps in the patient's recollections; distortions imposed by different defenses cause further gaps and perhaps introduce some transformations. Our job is to take the bits and pieces remaining in the present and reconstruct the original specimen. The metaphor implies reversibility. The original specimen was decomposed into small pieces; if we can find all the pieces, we can put it back together. If reversibility can be established, it may provide a way out of the hermeneutic circle.

Reversibility is a measure of what might be called the inevitability of a pattern match. The amount of reversibility in our interpretation tells us something about its truth value. I think we frequently behave as if our interpretations are highly reversible. Watching the material unfold, we have a sense of inevitability; as we watch the transformation of a dream into its network of associations, we are impressed by the lawfulness of the process. But in how many cases can we go from the associations back to the dream? Taking Freud's associations to one of his lesser-known dreams as our starting point, how many of us could reconstruct the dream to within 75% of its original form? We are apt to be much more impressed by cases in which the associations, given to a naïve judge, are reassembled into the original dream than by those cases where such a reconstruction fails, just as we are more impressed by the archeologist whose artifacts can be successfully reassembled.

But the fact is that we rarely check for reversibility directly. No need to, we say; the patient's later associations are confirmation enough. But if we bear in mind how easy it is to discover communalities in unrelated pieces of material, it is clear that this kind of confirmation is not sufficient.

It frequently happens that we think we are applying the reversibility rule when we are, in fact, doing something quite different. Suppose, in an analytic hour, we find a certain connection between a patient's dream and a preceding significant event—say, the analyst's being five minutes late on the preceding day. We check our interpretation by giving the dream and the event to a colleague and asking if he sees any connection. From what I have said about the molding effect of a preunderstanding, it is immediately obvious that we are stacking the deck. Given this pair of events, it would be impossible *not* to see a connection, and any confirmation of this sort is essentially worthless. We have, in effect, defined the dream as belonging to the genre of dreams-about-analyst-being-late; given this genre, our friendly judge sets about confirming it from individual details, and he is almost sure to succeed. (When, we might ask, has it been possible to say this dream and this event are *not* related? Or, to extend the point, to say that this dream could *not* have taken place before such an event? Just as possible pattern matches are embarrassingly easy to find, negative pattern matches are a near impossibility.)

Somewhat better but still not definitive is the application of another rule, which I will call repeatability. Consider the following situation. We hear a dream fragment at a case conference, and all participants are asked to arrive at an independent formulation. We go around the table and hear each formulation in turn. Suppose that the dream in question was the dream I quoted from Greenson in which the patient is led into a room and asked to undress. The first analyst says that the patient has an unconscious wish to be raped. The second analyst says that the patient has an unconscious fantasy that if she does what the analyst wants she will get a baby. The third analyst says that the patient has the unconscious fantasy that she is intellectually inferior to men. The fourth analyst says that the patient has the unconscious fantasy that she will become pregnant through her ear by listening to the analyst. And so on. Our friendly critic hears impressive agreement, tantamount to reversibility. And there is, to be sure, a certain kind of overlap among the different formulations, but it is misleading. The formulations are on such a general level that they could not really be contradictory; once we assume a general category, as given by the manifest dream, all interpretations can be found consistent with it. But consistency is not identity, and does not imply that we have reconstructed the latent dream thoughts.

A much stricter test would take the following form. Given one (or more) of the interpretations, can we reconstruct the original dream? If the dream is a translation of the latent thought into the manifest content, we should be able to translate back to the latent thought, imposing all the standards we would require of any other kind of translation. First and foremost, we require reversibility, or interchangeability. *"Defense de fumer"* means "no smoking," and vice versa. Reversibility underlies all good translation; where reversibility fails we have schoolboy trots and the kind of instructions which accompany Japanese abacus sets. I defy you to go from the English instructions back to the Japanese original.

Reversibility, it seems to me, is one way to break out of the hermeneutic circle because we are matching our explication against an external criterion—the assumed original. But it is putting the analytic situation to a very strict test. Are there any other alternatives?

IV

So far we have been talking about a certain type of hermeneutics, according to which our job, when faced with an unknown text, is to restore the original meaning which once (as in Freud's archeological metaphor) existed in fact, but which has become so disguised, distorted, and formally rearranged that it is no longer visible in its original form. The opposite position presents hermeneutics as a kind of demystification, a reduction of illusion, based on the assumption that things are seldom what they seem. In this mode, interpretation is asking the question, "What *could* it be?" as opposed to asking "What is it?" The first approach—the reconstructive mode—lends itself to a search for *the* primal scene at a specific point in time when the child was witness to an explicit event. (Paul Wachtel [this volume, p. 103] calls this version the "woolly mammouth" hypothesis, arguing that we pretend that the past has been buried in its original form, much as the woolly mammoth is preserved in the ice, and that analytic work will help us to find him again.) In the second approach the analyst adopts what Ricoeur (1970, p. 32) calls interpretation as an exercise of suspicion: he assumes an attitude of benevolent skepticism in an attempt to go beyond superficial appearances, but—and this is the important distinction—does not expect to find the original message.

These two points of view have a bearing on the general problem of pattern matching and on the specific issues of reversibility and repeatability. If we believe that we are engaged in the reconstruction of original meanings—in a search for the specific event which, for example, was the source of this symptom, for the specific day residue which has led to this dream—then we must apply the reversibility test because we are assuming a causal sequence. These shards, says the archeologist, can be rearranged to make this pot. The manifest remains, cleaned of cobwebs and isolated from pebbles and other pieces of foreign matter, can be put back together to form the original object—a clear case of reversibility. This model can be illustrated by the following experimental paradigm. Suppose we expose a subliminal stimulus and ask the subject to make a drawing. We are assuming a causal link between the stimulus and the drawing; we are also starting from the idea that the original event—the stimulus—actually existed in fact. If we then give the drawings, intermixed with a set of unrelated pictures, to a naïve judge to select the ones caused by the subliminal stimulus, we are posing a reversibility test because we must go from drawing back to stimulus.

If, on the other hand, we take the second position—that a manifest piece of behavior is multidetermined *and nothing more*—then the reversibility test seems inappropriate because we are not claiming a discrete and explicit source. Repeatability is encouraging but not essential; it may even be irrelevant because, if we take this position seriously, you can argue that your associations are just as good as mine, and that there are probably an almost infinite number of other constructions which could be placed on the material with just as much intrinsic plausibility. Just as Chomsky is fond of saying that the number of possible sentences is infinite, so we can assume that the number of possible (and plausible) explanations is infinite. In the light of this fact, we should understand that consensus is not a criterion of validity, and that a patient's agreement is more often a mark of passivity than a confirmation.

V

We are beginning to realize that all too frequently the "archeological object" does not exist in a confirmable form. Our reconstructions are usually poor approximations, what Freud called constructions or imaginative recreations of what might have been.

The suspected seduction, for example, turns out to be a fantasy, a creation of the patient at a younger age, an elaboration of an ambiguous situation. Even though the reversibility rule seems the best on logical grounds, it fails in many clinical instances because the unconscious source of the derivatives is usually unknowable. The archeology metaphor was a reasonable analogy so long as Freud believed that actual childhood events were causal factors in the development of the neurosis; once he adopted the view that a fantasy was the crucial stimulus, the archeology analogy lost much of its usefulness and even became misleading. In partial recognition of this change, Freud (1937) revised his metaphor and spoke of construction rather than reconstruction.

To put the problem in these terms is to see that the psychic past, unlike the geologic past, is essentially out of reach. The psychic past can be construed in a wide variety of ways, many of them equally plausible, but almost all impossible to check in any rigorous way. Glover's (1931) famous distinction between exact and inexact interpretations seems almost irrelevant when we are working in this domain, because exactness, by definition, must be ruled out, and the majority of our constructions are equally inexact. But none are clearly false. Just as it is almost impossible to generate a negative pattern match, so is it equally difficult to generate a clearly false interpretation.

Does this mean that all our formulations are equally true? Not at all. For the reasons set forth earlier, there are clear differences between formulations based on the analyst's superficial preunderstanding of the material and those based on a more systematic level of analysis. But these checks take place in the present, not in the past. And since the pattern we are trying to match no longer exists in reality, we have no way to test whether one formulation will prove to be better than another. We can only be on guard against pattern matches based solely on subjective feelings of conviction— indeed, the experience that such and such is an *obvious* reading of the material should be a warning that further explication is probably necessary.

One important safeguard comes from restricting our field of inquiry to the current analytic situation. Gray (1973) has discussed the crucial difference between the psychic event, as experienced by the patient during the hour, and its referent in the outside world—

the difference between the patient's associations as speech acts, to use the current linguistic label, and as carriers of information. We can focus on either or both aspects of his productions; Gray argues that our analytic work is carried further when we focus on the association as a psychic event and examine its relation to other events within the hour. I would add that such a focus also reduces the danger of misreading the material and drawing erroneous conclusions from it. Given the patient's distortions, some of which are, in fact, encouraged by the analytic method ("say whatever comes to mind"), the truth value of his reports on the "outside" is much less than perfect. By contrast, we have a much surer grasp of what happens "inside" the treatment situation, and interpretations based on this material are probably on much surer ground.

Gray gives as an example a patient, given to making impulsive decisions, who announced during an analytic session that she had just persuaded her boss to let her take a week-long business trip during the coming month. Gray lists three possible responses to this announcement.

(a) Point out to the patient that this would interrupt her analysis;

(b) Suggest that it would be important to analyze such an impulse before carrying it out, in order to know whether it is determined primarily by analytic reasons;

(c) Or, on the other hand, use could be made of what had just preceded these remarks—it was in this instance an expression of mild disappointment over the difficult location of the analyst's office. For instance, I could show the patient that her thoughts of being many miles away followed immediately the expressions of disappointment. This detail could then be analyzed. Thus, it might be revealed that she is indicating in this way that disappointment and criticism connected with the analyst are being experienced as unsafe; or some other equally important dynamic meaning of the *reference* to the trip could thus be demonstrated [Gray, 1973, p. 480].

The more we focus on *what* he is pointing at in contrast to *how* and *when* he is pointing, the smaller our chances of validating any interpretation or pattern match, and the greater our chances of imposing our own structure on the material without realizing what we are doing. Comparing material "outside" and "inside" the hour, Glover's distinction takes on much more significance. If we focus on the outside (*referent*), we run the danger of being misled by the patient's distortions; as a result we can misconstrue its meaning and make an inexact interpretation. If we focus on the inside (*reference*), we are making direct observations of sequence and context, our data are free of distortion, and we are in a much better position to assess their truth value. As a result, we can make an exact interpretation and, as a consequence, hasten the analytic work.

Consider a recent example from Ramzy (1974) in this connection. Some time before the hour in question, the analyst announced that he would be taking a two-week vacation. The week before the vacation was to begin, the patient began the hour as follows:

> Well, before I came up here I went back home since I forgot to leave a cheque with my cleaning lady. Well, she wasn't around and when I was driving up here I was kind of worried. She is sort of an old lady, maybe in her late 50s or early 60s. Maybe she's sick or some such. So I was telling myself while I was driving up here I better go and call some friend of mine and see what happened to her. And immediately it also struck me that: 'Well, what if she is really sick and can't work?' That would be kind of horrible. In Kansas a cleaning lady is not so easy to find, especially the one that you don't have to tell her what to do and she will just automatically do. Well, then I began to think, 'What did I do before I found her?' I remember before I found her there was another one I had, then she moved out to California. Well then, what happened before the one I had? Well, well, thinking of it, that was very funny because now I remember before I had all these cleaning ladies and when I first came to Kansas; every couple of months or so I would get really depressed because wherever I lived it is going to be so dirty and so messy and sometime I have to really get enough energy to really do a thorough cleaning for a whole week practically. So I haven't faced this for quite some years and I didn't remember how it used to be. It was pretty horrible.

In any event, I hope nothing happened or else it will be a big hunting job [Ramzy, 1974, p. 546].

After another 15 minutes in which the patient changed the subject to problems he had experienced with his students, their abilities, and related issues, the analyst made the following interpretation:

"Your earlier thoughts about the cleaning lady which occurred to you on the way here and your worry over losing her make me think that they may be connected with my upcoming absence for the next two weeks, starting next Monday" (p. 546).

Although the coming vacation is obviously important to Ramzy, its status in the analysis, as we will see, is quite another matter. Although Ramzy implies that his interpretation grew out of the patient's opening remarks (see p. 548), there is no clear correspondence between the two sets of patterns. It seems more likely that the interpretation, rather than growing out of the early remarks, was there all the time, waiting, so to speak, for some material to link up with. And as we have seen, links are always fairly easy to find.

Because the interpretation is not solidly based on material from inside the hour—because, for example, the analyst cannot point to a clearly contingent speech act within the session which might have contributed to the patient's concern about the cleaning lady—the interpretation is never accepted, as shown by the subsequent interchange. Despite the fact that Ramzy implies that his interpretation follows logically from the material (p. 548), there are many other explanations for the patient's concern, including (1) the discovery, just before the hour, that the cleaning lady had not arrived; and (2) previous experience with a cleaning lady's absence, which turned out to be a prelude to her moving away.

In more formal terms, Ramzy was making a pattern match between his upcoming vacation and the patient's concern about losing his cleaning lady. The vacation was a fairly explicit proposition inside the analyst's head; it was less clearly shared by analyst and patient and, because we do not have the previous material, we cannot decide how clearly or how frequently it was announced. Given its overriding importance to the analyst, it became a readily available preunderstanding which could be applied to whatever material came along, just as the theme of the subincision film was dominant in Witkin's experiment and was freely applied to the subsequent dream. Furthermore, we can say that Ramzy failed to stay inside the hour by using an event—his coming vacation—that was not clearly established as true in the current session and whose status, as a causal factor, was therefore ambiguous. He was also guilty of using his certainty as the criterion of a pattern match: because it seemed obvious to him ("it is probably too obvious that the analyst's inferences . . . were conclusions reached from the very material he heard" [p. 548]), he assumed that his pattern match was correct. I would suggest that his interpretation did not derive from the material in the hour but was established by his upcoming vacation and its importance to him, and that it was therefore brought in from outside.

As it turned out, the patient had misremembered the analyst's vacation plans, and assumed that he would be leaving a week later: not the next Monday but the Monday following. The misremembering is used by Ramzy (see p. 548) to validate his interpretation, but this conclusion is also open to question, and, when added to his general proposition, does not make it any more probable. Again, what seems to have happened is that the analyst formed an overriding formulation which he applied to a suggestive set of free associations. And when he states that "The validity of these inferences is, of course, further enhanced when partial information, such as that contained in this sample, is put within the proper sequence and the total context of the preceding stages of the analysis, the patient's past history and his current way of life" (p. 548), our confidence is not necessarily increased. If we enlarge our pool of data, we can always find additional matches, but their significance diminishes as the possibilities for random matches are increased. (And this danger points up the advantage of staying within the restricted bounds of the current analytic situation.)

VI

I have gone to some lengths to show how difficult it is to arrive at a truly reversible pattern match, and how easy it is to use subjective certainty as the criterion for deciding truth value. I have suggested that reconstruction is frequently an irrelevant metaphor because we rarely, if ever, make contact with the psychic past, and

I have supported Gray in suggesting that anything outside the analytic situation is open to many kinds of distortion and therefore difficult to assess.

Finally, I have pointed to a crucial asymmetry in pattern matching. While it is unbelievably simple to find matches (and therefore easy to overestimate their true occurrence), it is hard, if not impossible, to find nonmatches. Lack of fit is much harder to establish than partial fit, and therefore we are left with no true test of overlap. About the best we can do is to compare a possible match, as I have done several times in this paper, with control matches; if the latter are just as convincing as the former, we have reason to worry. (And such comparisons are, of course, almost never made in clinical practice.)

Where does all this leave us in dealing with patients? I would like to argue for constructions as against reconstructions; for the second hermeneutic position, in which we ask (of a dream or set of associations) what *can* it be? rather than what *is* it?[1] The therapeutic question changes, then, from the problem of discovering the hidden meaning to the problem of facilitating the analytic work. Under these conditions, timing may be more important than content; a range of options, presented to the patient in a rather tentative way, may achieve more, in terms of analytic work, than a specific interpretation, forcefully delivered and energetically defended.

One reason to de-emphasize content stems from the fact that any piece of material is amenable to a wide range of constructions. A second reason stems from the possibility that the truth value of an interpretation may make less difference than we are fond of assuming. Glover's (1931) well-known paper alarmed analysts about the dangers of being wrong (not completely wrong, of course, but only "inexact"); to be inexact, he said, would increase the strength of the resistance. But data on this point have never been systematically collected. We need to explore the conditions under which the truth value of an interpretation makes a clinical difference. These conditions may, in fact, represent a rather small

[1] Compare Harré's distinction between *modal* transforms, which are alternative ways of conceptualizing certain events, and *causal* transforms, which imply a provable connection between the event and the model (discussed in Cheshire, 1975, p. 110).

subset of all utterances. It seems quite possible that, in certain states of consciousness, the patient may not even register the exact wording of an interpretation and that tone, rhythm, and empathic involvement may play a more important role. Useful material may be produced by the patient, but in response more to form than to content. At other times, the content of an interpretation may even be false, yet therapeutically useful because it touches on some key issue that has never been raised; one can imagine, for example, how an interpretation which brings together two unrelated themes might arouse a number of possibly fruitful associations without being true in any specific sense. If we can isolate the conditions under which truth value is important, we can make our procedures even more sophisticated and spare the analyst the burden of searching for the precise word at all times.

I would like to make it very clear that I am not trying to caricature or belittle the process of interpretation. Inspired interpretation is a truly creative act, a unique event. But pedestrian interpretation is something quite different, and because our language is rich and highly interrelated, associations are always easy to find. What I wish to emphasize, above all, are the logical pitfalls in the process, and how easily we can be fooled into thinking that we have uncovered the single structure in a set of associations. Most of the time there are many such structures, all partially correct, and the therapeutic problem is, first, to be sensitive to alternatives, and second, to choose, on the basis of clinical issues, which one to present to the patient.

In an analysis of the process notes of a single case, Horowitz (1976) was able to isolate the gradual emergence, in the first 100 hours, of more and more explicit statements of criticism, blame, and opposition. They became more explicit in a lawful way; their frequency increased significantly over time. At the same time, they were applied to more and more significant people: relatives in the early hours of the therapy, and therapist, husband, and colleagues in the later hours. This structure was not, apparently, central to the therapist's view of the case; it was not the subject of the majority of his interpretations and appeared to change independently of them. It was even described, but one clinician familiar with the case, as an epiphenomenon. The therapist saw quite a different structure emerging and responded accordingly;

his description of the case did not focus on the change in the form or the object of the patient's statements of criticism, blame, and opposition.

Which is figure and which is ground? Which is the epiphenomenon? Suppose another therapist treated this patient—would still a third structure appear? If we extend the concept of multiple determination to include multiple structure, we have introduced a new difficulty. So long as we believe that only one structure lies hidden in the material, any clue, no matter how elusive or conjectural, is evidence that we are on the right track, and inspires the belief that a stronger clue lies right behind it. If only one pattern waits to be discovered, we have the right to exercise as much ingenuity as possible and take advantage of whatever associative combinations happen to come along.

But as soon as we concede that many patterns may coexist in the same structure, the picture changes. Something more than partial correspondence is needed, because we have no way of distinguishing the right pattern match from all the others. As soon as we concede that more than one pattern may exist, we must solve the further problem of which match is correct. And since there may be no satisfactory answer to this question, we need to be particularly cautious about our conclusions.

REFERENCES

Cheshire, N. (1975), *The Nature of Psychodynamic Interpretation.* London: Wiley.

Freud, S. (1937), Constructions in Analysis. *Standard Edition,* 23:255-269. London: Hogarth Press, 1964.

Glover, E. (1931), The Therapeutic Effect of Inexact Interpretation. *Internat. J. Psycho-Anal.,* 12:397-411.

Gray, P. (1973), Psychoanalytic Technique and the Ego's Capacity for Viewing Intrapsychic Activity. *J. Amer. Psychoanal. Assn.,* 21:474-494.

Greenson, R. R. (1967), *The Technique and Practice of Psychoanalysis.* New York: International Universities Press.

Hirsch, E. D., Jr. (1967), *Validity in Interpretation.* New Haven: Yale University Press.

Horowitz, L. (1976), Two Classes of Concomitant Change in a Psychotherapy. Presented at a conference on Communicative Structures and Psychic Structures, Downstate Medical Center, Brooklyn, January 15-17.

Ramzy, I. (1974), How the Mind of the Psychoanalyst Works: An Essay on Psychoanalytic Inference. *Internat. J. Psycho-Anal.,* 55:543-550.

Ricoeur, P. (1970), *Freud and Philosophy*. New Haven: Yale University Press.
Witkin, H. A. (1969), Influencing Dream Content. In: *Dream Psychology and the New Biology of Dreaming*, ed. M. Kramer. Springfield, Ill.: Charles C Thomas.

Steven Marcus, Ph.D.

Freud and Dora:
Story, History, Case History

I

It is generally agreed that Freud's case histories are unique. Today
more than half a century after they were written they are still
widely read. Even more, they are still widely used for instruction
and training in psychoanalytic institutes. One of the inferences that
such a vigorous condition of survival prompts is that these writings
have not yet been superseded. Like other masterpieces of literature
or the arts, these works seem to possess certain transhistorical
qualities—although it may by no means be easy to specify what
those qualities are. The implacable "march of science" has not—or
has not yet—consigned them to "mere" history. Their singular and
mysterious complexity, density, and richness have thus far
prevented such a transformation and demotion.

This state of affairs has received less attention than it merits.
Freud's case histories—and his works in general—are unique as
pieces or kinds of writing, and it may be useful to regard them from
the standpoint that this statement implies. I shall undertake, then,
to examine one of Freud's case histories from the point of view of
literary criticism, to analyze it as a piece of writing, and to determine whether this method of proceeding may yield results that
other means have not. The assumption with which I begin, as well

A shorter version of this essay appeared in *Partisan Review*, Winter, 1974;
and a different version appeared in *Representations*, New York, Random House,
1976.

as the end that I hope to demonstrate, is that Freud is a great writer
and that one of his major case histories is a great work of literature
—that is to say, it is both an outstanding creative and imaginative
performance and an intellectual and cognitive achievement of the
highest order. And yet, as we shall see, this triumphant greatness is
in part connected with the circumstance that it is about a kind of
failure, and that part of the failure remains in fact unacknowledged and unconscious.[1]

"Fragment of an Analysis of a Case of Hysteria" (1905a), better
known to future readers as the case of Dora, is Freud's first great
case history—oddly enough, he was to write only four others. It
may be helpful for the reader if at the outset I refresh his memory
by briefly reviewing some of the external facts of the case. In the
autumn of 1900 Dora, an eighteen-year-old young woman, began
treatment with Freud. She did so reluctantly and against her will,
and, Freud writes, "it was only her father's authority which
induced her to come to me at all" (p. 22).[2] Neither Dora nor her
father was a stranger to Freud. He had made separate acquaintance with both of them in the past, during certain episodes of
illness that characterized their lives if not the life of the family as a
whole. (Freud knew other members of the family as well.) Dora's
father was a man "of rather unusual activity and talents, a large
manufacturer in very comfortable circumstances" (p. 18). In 1888
he had fallen ill with tuberculosis, which had made it necessary for
the family to move to a small town with a good climate in some
southern part of Austria; for the next ten years or so that remained
their chief place of residence. In 1892 he suffered a detached retina
which led to a permanent impairment of his vision. Two years later
he fell gravely ill—it was "a confusional attack, followed by
symptoms of paralysis and slight mental disturbances" (p. 19). He
was persuaded by a friend to come to Vienna and consult with
Freud, who was then a rising young neurologist and psychiatrist.
Freud settled upon the diagnosis of "diffuse vascular affection," a
meningeal disturbance associated with the tertiary stage of syphilis;

---

[1] The empirical rule that literary criticism generally follows is to trust the tale
and not the teller; indeed, it was the empirical rule pursued by Freud himself.

[2] Page numbers refer to Freud (1905a). The Strachey translation has been
checked against the text in *Gesammelte Werke*, 5:163-286. In a few places the
translation has been corrected; such corrections are indicated by brackets.

and since the patient admitted to having had a "specific infection" of syphilis before he married, Freud prescribed "an energetic course of anti-luetic treatment, as a result of which all the remaining disturbances passed off" (p. 19). By 1899 his constitution had sufficiently recovered from the tuberculosis to justify the family's leaving the health resort and moving to the town in which his factory was situated; and in 1900 they moved again and settled permanently in Vienna.

Despite this long and protracted history of illness—he also at one time had apparently been infected with gonorrhea, which he may have passed on to his wife—Dora's father was clearly a dominating figure: vigorous, active, energetic, enterprising, and intelligent. Nothing of the sort could be said of Dora's mother, who from the accounts received of her by Freud appeared to his imagination as

> . . . an uncultivated woman and above all as a foolish one, who had concentrated all her interests upon domestic affairs, especially since her husband's illness and the estrangement to which it led. She presented the picture, in fact, of what might be called the 'housewife's psychosis'. She had no understanding of her children's more active interests, and was occupied all day long in cleaning the house with its furniture and utensils and in keeping them clean—to such an extent as to make it almost impossible to use or enjoy them [p. 20].

The immediate family circle was completed by a brother, a year and a half older than Dora, who hardly figures in the account rendered by Freud and who seems to have escaped from his childhood and family experiences without severe disablements. In adult life he became a leading figure in Socialist politics and apparently led an active, successful, and distinguished career up to his death many years later.

As for Dora herself, her afflictions, both mental and physical, had begun in early childhood and had persisted and flourished with variations and fluctuating intensities until she was pre-presented to Freud for therapy. Among the symptoms from which she suffered were to be found dyspnea, migraine, and periodic attacks of nervous coughing often accompanied by complete loss of voice during part of the episode. Dora had in fact first been brought by her father to Freud two years earlier, when she was sixteen and suffering from a cough and hoarseness; he had then "proposed giving her psychological treatment," but this suggestion was not adopted, since "the attack in question, like the others, passed off spontaneously" (p. 22). In the course of his treatment of Dora, Freud also learned of further hysterical—or hysterically connected—productions on her part, such as a feverish attack that mimicked appendicitis, a periodic limp, and a vaginal catarrh or discharge. Moreover, during the two-year interval between Dora's first visit and the occasion on which her father brought her to Freud a second time and "handed her over to me for psychotherapeutic treatment," Dora had "grown unmistakably neurotic" (p. 19) in what today we would recognize as more familiar manifestations of emotional distress. Dora was now "in the first bloom of youth—a girl of intelligent and engaging looks" (p. 23). Her character had, however, undergone an alteration. She had become chronically depressed and was generally dissatisfied with both herself and her family. She had become unfriendly toward the father, whom she had hitherto loved, idealized, and identified with. She was "on very bad terms" with her mother, for whom she felt a good deal of scorn. "She tried to avoid social intercourse, and employed herself—so far as she was allowed to by the fatigue and lack of concentration of which she complained—with attending lectures for women and with carrying on more or less serious studies"[3] (p. 23). Two further events precipitated the crisis which led to her being delivered to Freud. Her parents found a written note in which she declared her intention to commit suicide because "as she said, she could no longer endure her life." Following this there occurred one day "a slight passage of words" between Dora and her father, which ended with Dora suddenly losing consciousness—the attack, Freud believed, was "accompanied by convulsions and delirious states," although it was lost to amnesia and never came up in the analysis.

Having outlined this array of affections, Freud dryly remarks that such a case "does not upon the whole seem worth recording. It is merely a case of 'petite hystérie' which the commonest of all somatic and mental symptoms ... More interesting cases of

---

[3] It is worth noting that Freud tells us nothing more about these activities.

hysteria have no doubt been published ... for nothing will be found in the following pages on the subject of stigmata of cutaneous sensibility, limitation of the visual field, or similar matters" (pp. 23-24). This disavowal of anything sensational to come is of course a bit of shrewd disingenuousness on Freud's part, for what follows at once is his assertion that he is going to elucidate the meaning, origin, and function of every one of these symptoms by means of the events and experiences of Dora's life. He is going, in other words, to discover the "psychological determinants" that will account for Dora's illnesses; among these determinants he lists three principal conditions: "... a psychical trauma, a conflict of affects, and ... a disturbance in the sphere of sexuality" (p. 24). And so Freud begins the treatment by asking Dora to talk about her experiences. What emerges is the substance of the case history, a substance which takes all of Freud's immense analytic, expository, and narrative talents to bring into order. I will again very roughly and briefly summarize some of this material.

Sometime after 1888, when the family had moved to B_____ (the health resort where the father's tuberculosis had sent them), an intimate and enduring friendship sprang up between them and a couple named K. Dora's father was deeply unhappy in his marriage and apparently made no bones about it. The K.'s too were unhappily married, as it later turned out. Frau K. took to nursing Dora's father during these years of his illness. She also befriended Dora, and they behaved toward one another in the most familiar way and talked together about the most intimate subjects. Herr K., her husband, also made himself a close friend of Dora's, going regularly for walks with her and giving her presents. Dora in her turn befriended the K.'s two small children, "and had been almost a mother to them." What begins to be slowly if unmistakably disclosed is that Dora's father and Frau K. had established a sexual liaison and that this relation had by the time of Dora's entering into treatment endured for many years. At the same time Dora's father and Frau K. had tacitly connived at turning Dora over to Herr K., just as years later her father "handed her over to me [Freud] for psychotherapeutic treatment." And Dora had herself, at least at first, behaved toward Frau K.'s children in much the same way that Frau K. had behaved toward her. Up to a certain point, then, the characters in this embroilment were virtually behaving as if they were walking in their sleep. In some sense everyone was conspiring to conceal what was going on; and in some yet further sense everyone was conspiring to deny that anything was going on at all. What we have here, on one of its sides, is a classical Victorian domestic drama, that is at the same time a sexual and emotional can of worms.

Matters were brought to a crisis by two events that occurred to Dora at two different periods of her adolescence. When she was fourteen Herr K. contrived one day to be alone with her in his place of business; in a state of sexual excitement, he "suddenly clasped the girl to him and pressed a kiss upon her lips" (p. 28). Dora responded with a "violent feeling of disgust," and hurried away. This experience, like those referred to in the foregoing paragraph, was never discussed with or mentioned to anyone, and relations continued as before. The second scene took place two years later in the summer when Dora was sixteen (it was just after she had seen Freud for the first time). She and Herr K. were taking a walk by a lake in the Alps. In Dora's words, as they come filtered to us through Freud, Herr K. "had the audacity to make her a proposal" (p. 25). Apparently he had begun to declare his love for this girl whom he had known so well for so long. "No sooner had she grasped Herr K.'s intention than, without letting him finish what he had to say, she had given him a slap in the face and hurried away" (p. 46). The episode as a whole will lead Freud quite plausibly to ask: "If Dora loved Herr K., what was the reason for her refusing him in the scene by the lake? Or at any rate, why did her refusal take such a brutal form, as though she were em-bittered against him? And how could a girl who was in love feel insulted by a proposal which was made in a manner neither tactless nor offensive?" (p. 38). It may occur to us to wonder whether in the extended context of this case that slap in the face was a "brutal form" of refusal; but as for the other questions posed by Freud, they are without question rhetorical in character.

On this second occasion Dora did not remain silent. Her father was preparing to depart from the Alpine lake, and she declared her determination to leave at once with him. Two weeks later she told the story of the scene by the lake to her mother, who relayed it—as Dora had clearly intended—to her father. In due course Herr K. was "called to account" on this score, but he

... denied in the most emphatic terms having on his side made any advances which could have been open to such a construction. He had then proceeded to throw suspicion upon the girl, saying that he had heard from Frau K. that she took no interest in anything but sexual matters, and that she used to read Mantegazza's *Physiology of Love* and books of that sort in their house on the lake. It was most likely, he had added, that she had been over-excited by such reading and had merely 'fancied' the whole scene she had described [p. 26].

Dora's father "believed" the story concocted by Herr—and Frau—K., and it is from this moment, more than two years before she came to Freud for treatment, that the change in Dora's character can be dated. Her love for the K.'s turned into hatred, and she became obsessed with the idea of getting her father to break off relations with them. She saw through the rationalizations and denials of her father and Frau K., and had "no doubt that what bound her father to this young and beautiful woman was a common love-affair. Nothing that could help to confirm this view had escaped her perception, which in this connection was pitilessly sharp ..." (p. 32). Indeed, "the sharp-sighted Dora" was an excellent detective when it came to uncovering her father's clandestine sexual activities, and her withering criticisms of her father's character—that he was "insincere,... had a strain of [baseness] in his character,... only thought of his own enjoyment,... had a gift for seeing things in the light which suited him best" (p. 34)—were in general concurred in by Freud. As he also agreed that there was something in her embittered if exaggerated contention that "she had been handed over to Herr K. as the price of his tolerating the relations between her father and his wife"[4] (p. 34). Nevertheless, the cause of her greatest embitterment seems to have been her father's "readiness to consider the scene by the lake as a product of her imagination. She was almost beside herself at the idea of its being supposed that she had merely fancied something on that

[4] Later on, Freud adds to this judgment by affirming that "Dora's father was never entirely straightforward. He had given his support to the treatment so long as he could hope that I should 'talk' Dora out of her belief that there was something more than a friendship between him and Frau K. His interest faded when he observed that it was not my intention to bring about that result" (p. 109).

occasion" (p. 46). And although Freud was in his customary way skeptical about such impassioned protestations and repudiations—and surmised that something in the way of an opposite series of thoughts or self-reproaches lay behind them—he was forced to come to "the conclusion that Dora's story must correspond to the facts in every respect" (p. 46). If we try to put ourselves in the place of this girl between her sixteenth and eighteenth years, we can at once recognize that her situation was a desperate one. The three adults to whom she was closest, whom she loved the most in the world, were apparently conspiring—separately, in tandem, or in concert—to deny her the reality of her experience. They were conspiring to deny Dora her reality and reality itself. This betrayal touched upon matters that might easily unhinge the mind of a young person; for the three adults were not betraying Dora's love and trust alone, they were betraying the structure of the actual world. And indeed, when Dora's father handed her over to Freud with the parting injunction "Please try and bring her to reason" (p. 26), there were no two ways of taking what he meant. Naturally, he had no idea of the mind and character of the physician to whom he had dealt this leading remark.

Two other persons round out the cast of characters of this late-Victorian romance. And it seems only appropriate that they should come directly from the common stock of Victorian literature and culture, both of them being governesses. The first of these was Dora's own governess, "an unmarried woman, no longer young, who was well-read and of advanced views" (p. 36). This woman "used to read every sort of book on sexual life and similar subjects, and talked to the girl about them," at the same time enjoining Dora to secrecy about such conversations. She had long since divined the goings-on between Dora's father and Frau K. and had in the past tried in vain to turn Dora against both Frau K. and her father. Although she had turned a blind eye to this side of things, Dora very quickly penetrated into the governess's real secret: she, too, was in love with Dora's father. And when Dora realized that this governess was actually indifferent to her—Dora's—welfare, she "dropped her." At the same time, Dora had to dimly realize that there was an analogy between the governess's behavior in Dora's family and Dora's behavior in relation to the children of the K.'s and Herr K. The second governess made her appearance during

Dora's last analytic hour; the appearance was brilliantly elicited by
Freud, who remarked that Dora's decision to leave him, arrived at,
she said, a fortnight beforehand, "'sounds just like a maidservant
or a governess—a fortnight's warning'" (p. 105). This second
governess was a young girl employed by the K.'s at the time of
Dora's fateful visit to them at the Alpine lake some two years
before. She was a silent young person, who seemed totally to ignore
the existence of Herr K. Yet a day or two before the scene at the
lake she took Dora aside and told her that Herr K. had approached
her sexually, had pleaded his unhappy cause with her, had in fact
seduced her, but had quickly ceased to care for her. He had, in
short, done to her what in a day or two he was going to try to do
again with Dora. The girl said she now hated Herr K., yet she did
not go away at once, but waited there hoping Herr K.'s affections
would turn again in her direction. Dora's response at the lake and
afterward was in part a social one—anger at being treated by Herr
K. as if she were a servant or governess; but it was also in part a
response by identification, since she, too, did not tell the story at
once but waited perhaps for something further from Herr K. And
when, after the two-week interval, she did tell the story, Herr K.
did not renew "his proposals but ... replied instead with denials
and slanders" (p. 108) in which he was aided and abetted by Dora's
father and Frau K. Dora's cup of bitterness was full to overflowing,
as the following two years of deep unhappiness and deepening
illness undeniably suggest.

II

Dora began treatment with Freud sometime in October, 1900,
for on the fourteenth of that month Freud writes Fliess that "I have
a new patient, a girl of eighteen; the case has opened smoothly to
my collection of picklocks" (1887-1902, Letter 139). According to
this statement the analysis was proceeding well, but it was also not
proceeding well. The material produced was very rich, but Dora
was there more or less against her will. Moreover, she was more
than usually amnesic about events in her remote past and about her
inner and mental life—a past and a life toward which Freud was
continually pressing her—and met many or even most of his interpretations with statements such as "I don't know," and with a

variety of denials, resistances, and grudging silences. The analysis found its focus and climax in two dreams. The first of these was the production by Dora of a dream that in the past she had dreamed recurrently.[5] Among the many messages concealed by it, Freud made out one that he conveyed to his patient: " '. . . you have decided to give up the treatment,' " he told her, adding, " 'to which, after all, it is only your father who makes you come' " (p. 70). It was a self-fulfilling interpretation. A few weeks after the first dream, the second dream occurred. Freud spent two hours elucidating it, and at the beginning of the third, which took place on December 31, 1900, Dora informed him that she was there for the last time. Freud pressed on during this hour and presented Dora with a series of stunning and outrageously intelligent interpretations. The analysis ended as follows: "Dora had listened to me without any of her usual contradictions. She seemed to be moved; she said good-bye to me very warmly, with the heartiest wishes for the New Year, and—came no more" (pp. 108-109). Dora's father subsequently called on Freud two or three times to reassure him that Dora was returning, but Freud knew better than to take him at his word. Fifteen months later, in April, 1902, Dora returned for a single visit; what she had to tell Freud on that occasion was of some interest, but he knew that she was done with him, as indeed she was.

Dora was actuated by many impulses in breaking off the treatment; prominent among these partial motives was revenge—upon men in general and at that moment Freud in particular, who was standing for those other men in her life who had betrayed and injured her. He writes rather ruefully of Dora's "breaking off so unexpectedly, just when my hopes of a successful termination of the treatment were at their highest, and her thus bringing those hopes to nothing—this was an unmistakable act of vengeance on her part" (p. 109). And although Dora's "purpose of self-injury" was also served by this action, Freud goes on clearly to imply that

[5] Since this dream will be referred to frequently in what is to come, it may be helpful to the reader if I reproduce its wording: "A house was on fire. My father was standing beside my bed and woke me up. I dressed quickly. Mother wanted to stop and save her jewel-case; but Father said: 'I refuse to let myself and my two children be burnt for the sake of your jewel-case.' We hurried downstairs, and as soon as I was outside I woke up" (p. 64).

he felt hurt and wounded by her behavior. Yet it could not have been so unexpected as all that, since as early as the first dream, Freud both understood and had communicated this understanding to Dora that she had already decided to give up the treatment.[6] What is suggested by this logical hiatus is that although Dora had done with Freud, Freud had not done with Dora. And this supposition is supported by what immediately followed. As soon as Dora left him, Freud began writing up her case history—a proceeding that, as far as I have been able to ascertain, was not in point of immediacy a usual response for him. He interrupted the composition of *The Psychopathology of Everyday Life* (1901) on which he was then engaged and wrote what is substantially the case of Dora during the first three weeks of January, 1901. On January 25 he wrote to Fliess that he had finished the work the day before and added, with that terrifying self-confidence of judgment that he frequently revealed, "Anyhow, it is the most subtle thing I have yet written and will produce an even more horrifying effect than usual" (p. 4). The title he had at first given the new work— "Dreams and Hysteria"—suggests the magnitude of ambition that was at play in him. This specific case history, "in which the explanations are grouped round two dreams.... is in fact a continuation of the dream book. It further contains solutions of hysterical symptoms and considerations on the sexual-organic basis of the whole condition" (p. 4). As the provisional title and these further remarks reveal, it was to be nothing less than a concentrated synthesis of Freud's first two major works, *Studies on Hysteria* (Breuer and Freud, 1893-1895) and *The Interpretation of Dreams* (1900), to which there had been added the new dimension of the "sexual-organic basis," that is, the psychosexual developmental stages that he was going to represent in fuller detail in the *Three Essays on the Theory of Sexuality* (1905b). It was thus a summation, a new synthesis, a crossing point, and a great leap forward all at once. Dora had taken her revenge on Freud, who in turn chose not to behave in kind. At the same time, however,

[6] It is also permissible to question why Freud's hopes for a successful termination were at that moment at their highest—whether they were in fact so, and what in point of fact his entire statement means. We shall return to this passage later.

Freud's settling of his account with Dora took on the proportions of a heroic inner and intellectual enterprise.

Yet that account was still by no means settled, as the obscure subsequent history of this work dramatically demonstrates. In the letter of January 25, 1901, Freud had written to Fliess that the paper had already been accepted by Ziehen, joint editor of the *Monatsschrift für Psychiatrie und Neurologie*, by which he must mean that the acceptance did not include a reading of the piece, which had only been "finished" the day before. On February 15, in another letter to Fliess, he remarks that he is now finishing up *The Psychopathology of Everyday Life*, and that when he has done so, he will correct it and the case history—by which he apparently means that he will go through one last revision of the manuscripts and then "send them off, etc." That "etc." is covering considerable acreage. About two months later, in March, 1901, according to Ernest Jones, Freud showed "his notes of the case"—whatever *that* may mean—to his close friend, Oscar Rie. The reception Rie gave to them was such, reports Freud, that "I thereupon determined to make no further effort to break down my state of isolation"[7] (Jones, 1953, p. 362). That determination was less than unshakable, and on May 8, 1901, Freud wrote to Fliess that he had not yet "made up his mind" to send off the work. One month later he made up his mind and sent it off, announcing to Fliess that "it will meet the gaze of an astonished public in the autumn" (p. 4). But nothing of the sort was to occur, and what happened next was, according to Jones (1955, p. 256), "entirely mysterious" and remains so. Freud either sent it off to Ziehen, the editor who had already accepted it, and then having sent it, asked for it back. Or he sent it off to another magazine altogether, the *Journal für Psychologie und Neurologie*, whose editor, one Brodmann, refused to publish it, basing his outright rejection, it has been surmised, on the grounds of the improprieties and indiscretions that would be perpetrated by such a publication (Jones, 1955, p. 255f.). The upshot of all those circlings and countercirclings was that Freud returned the manuscript to a drawer for four more years. And when he did at last send

---

[7] Oscar Rie was a pediatrician who had earlier worked as Freud's assistant at Kassowitz's Institute for Children's Diseases; he became a member of Freud's intimate circle, was a partner at the Saturday night tarock games, and was at the time the Freud family physician.

it into print, it was in the journal that had accepted it in the first place.

But we are not out of the darkness and perplexities yet, for when Freud finally decided in 1905 to publish the case, he revised the work once again. As James Strachey remarks, "There is no means of deciding the extent" of these revisions, meaning no certain, external, or physical means. Strachey nonetheless maintains that "All the internal evidence suggests . . . that he changed it very little" (p. 5). According to my reading, Strachey is incorrect, and there is considerable internal evidence that intimates much change. But this is no place to argue such matters, and anyway, who can say precisely what Strachey means by "little" or what I mean by "much"? There is one further touch of puzzlements to top it all off. Freud got the date of his case wrong. When he wrote or rewrote it, either in January, 1901, or in 1905, he assigned the case to the autumn of 1899 instead of 1900. And he continued to date it incorrectly, repeating the error in 1914 in the "History of the Psycho-Analytic Movement" and again in 1923 when he added a number of new footnotes to the essay on the occasion of its publication in the eighth volume of his *Gesammelte Schriften.* Among the many things suggested by this recurrent error is that in some sense he had still not done with Dora, as indeed I think we shall see he had not. The modern reader may be inclined to remark that all this hemming and hawing about dates and obscurities of composition, questions of revision, problems of textual status, and authorial uncertainties of attitude would be more suitable to the discussion of a literary text—a poem, play, or novel—than to a work of "science." If this is so, one has to reply to this hypothetical reader that he is barking up the wrong discourse, and that his conception of the nature of scientific discourse—particularly the modes of discourse that are exercised in those disciplines which are not preponderantly or uniformly mathematical or quantitative— has to undergo a radical revision.

The final form into which Freud casts all this material is as original as it is deceptively straightforward. It is divided into five parts. It opens with a short but extremely dense and condensed series of "Prefatory Remarks." There follows the longest section of the work, called "The Clinical Picture" ("*Der Krankheitszustand*"). In this part Freud describes the history of Dora's family and of how he got to know them, presents an account of Dora's symptoms and how they seemed to have been acquired, and informs the reader of the process by which she was brought to him for treatment. He also represents some of the progress they had made in the first weeks of the treatment. Throughout he intersperses his account of Dora's illness and treatment with excursions and digressions of varying lengths on an assortment of theoretical topics that the material of the case brought into relevant prominence. The third part of the essay, "The First Dream," consists of the reproduction in part of the analysis of Dora's recurrent dream. Part of it is cast in dramatic dialogue, part in indirect discourse, part in a shifting diversity of narrative and expository modes, each of which is summoned up by Freud with effortless mastery. The entire material of the case up to now is reviewed and re-enacted once more: new material ranging from Dora's early childhood through her early adolescence and down to the moment of the analysis is unearthed and discussed, again from a series of analytic perspectives and explanatory levels that shift about so rapidly that one is inclined to call them rotatory. The fourth part, "The Second Dream," is about the final three sessions of the treatment, and Freud invents yet another series of original compositional devices to present the fluid mingling of dramatic, expository, narrative, and analytic materials that were concentrated in the three hours. The final part of the essay, "Postscript," written indeed after the case was officially "closed" but at an utterly indeterminate set of dates, is true to its title. It is not a conclusion in the traditional sense of neatly rounding off through a final summary and a group of generalizations the material dealt with in the body of the work—although it does do some of that. It is rather a group of added remarks, whose effect is to introduce still further considerations, and the work is brought to its proper end by opening up new and indeterminate avenues of exploration; it closes by giving us a glimpse of unexplored mental vistas in whose light presumably the entire case that has gone before would be transfigured yet again.

The general form, then, of what Freud has written bears certain suggestive resemblances to a modern experimental novel. Its narrative and expository course, for example, is neither linear nor rectilinear; instead, its organization is plastic, involuted, and heterogeneous, and follows spontaneously an inner logic that seems frequently to be at odds with itself; it often loops back around itself and is multidimensional in its representation of both its material and itself. Its continuous innovations in formal structure seem unavoidably to be dictated by its substance, by the dangerous, audacious, disreputable, and problematical character of the experiences being represented and dealt with, and by the equally scandalous intentions of the author and the outrageous character of the role he has had the presumption to assume. In content, however, what Freud has written is in parts rather like a play by Ibsen, or more precisely, like a series of Ibsen's plays. And as one reads through the case of Dora, scenes and characters from such works as *Pillars of Society*, *A Doll's House*, *Ghosts*, *An Enemy of the People*, *The Wild Duck*, and *Rosmersholm* rise up and flit through the mind. There is, however, this difference. In this Ibsen-like drama, Freud is not only Ibsen, the creator and playwright; he is also and directly one of the characters in the action, and in the end suffers in a way that is comparable to the suffering of the others.

What I have been reiterating at excessive length is that the case of Dora is first and last an extraordinary piece of writing, and it is to this circumstance in several of its most striking aspects that we should direct our attention. For it is a case history, a kind or genre of writing—a particular way of conceiving and constructing human experience in written language—which in Freud's hands became something that it never was before.[8]

III

The ambiguities and difficulties begin with the very title of the work, "Fragment of an Analysis of a Case of Hysteria." In what sense or senses is this piece of writing that the author describes as "a detailed report of the history of a case" (p. 7) a fragment? Freud himself supplies us with a superabundant wealth of detail on this count. It is a fragment in the sense that its "results" are "incom-

---

[8] Freud's chief precursors in this as in so much else are the great poets and novelists. There are a number of works of literature that anticipate in both form and substance the kind of thing that Freud was to do. I shall mention only one. Wordsworth's small masterpiece "Ruth" can in my judgment be most thoroughly understood as a kind of proto-case history; as a case history, so to speak, before the fact.

plete." The treatment was "broken off at the patient's own wish," at a time when certain problems "had not . . . been attacked and others had only been imperfectly elucidated." It follows that the analysis itself is "only a fragment," as are "the following pages" of writing which present it (p. 12). To which the modern reader, flushed with the superior powers of his educated irony, is tempted to reply: How is it that this fragment is also a whole, an achieved totality, an integral piece of writing called a case history? And how is it, furthermore, that this "fragment" is fuller, richer, and more complete than the most "complete" case histories of anyone else? But there is no more point in asking such questions of Freud—particularly at this preliminary stage of the proceedings—than there would be in posing similar "theoretical" questions to Joyce or Proust. And indeed Freud has barely begun.

The work is also fragmentary, he continues, warming to his subject, because of the very method he has chosen to pursue; on this plan, that of nondirectional free association, "everything that has to do with the clearing-up of a particular symptom emerges piecemeal, woven into various contexts, and distributed over widely separated periods of time" (p. 12). Freud's technique itself is therefore fragmentary; his way of penetrating to the microstructure—the "finer structure" as he calls it—of a neurosis is to allow the material to emerge piecemeal. At the same time these fragments only *appear* to be incoherent and disparate; in actuality they eventually will be understood as members of a whole. Still, in the present instance the results were more than usually unfinished and partial, and to explain what in the face of such difficulties he has done, he resorts to one of his favorite metaphorical figures:

> . . . I had no choice but to follow the example of those discoverers whose good fortune it is to bring to the light of day after their long burial the priceless though mutilated relics of antiquity. I have restored what is missing, taking the best models known to me from other analyses; but, like a conscientious archaeologist, I have not omitted to mention in each case where the authentic [facts] end and my constructions begin [p. 12].[9]

___

[9] From almost the outset of his career, images drawn from archaeology worked strongly in Freud's conception of his own creative activity. In *Studies on*

Here the matter has complicated itself one degree further. The mutilated relics or fragments of the past also remain fragments; what Freud has done is to restore, construct, and reconstruct what is missing—an activity and a group of conceptions that introduce an entirely new range of contingencies. And there is more of this in the offing as well.

Furthermore, Freud goes on, there is still another "kind of incompleteness" to be found in this work, and this time it has been "intentionally introduced." He has deliberately chosen not to reproduce "the process of interpretation to which the patient's associations and communications had to be subjected, but only the results of that process" (pp. 12-13). That is to say, what we have before us is not a transcription in print of a tape recording of eleven weeks of analysis but something that is abridged, edited, synthesized, and constructed from the very outset. And as if this were not enough, Freud introduces yet another context in which the work has to be regarded as fragmentary and incomplete. It is obvious, he argues, "that a single case history, even if it were complete and open to no doubt, cannot provide an answer to *all* the questions arising out of the problem of hysteria" (p. 13). One case of hysteria, in short, cannot exhaust the structure of all the others. And so in this sense too the work is a particle or component of a larger entity or whole. It nevertheless remains at the same time a whole in itself and has to stand by itself in its own idiosyncratic way—which is to be simultaneously fragmentary and complete. Thus, like a modernist writer—which in part he is—Freud begins by elaborately announcing the problematical status of his undertaking and the dubious character of his achievement.

Even more, like some familiar "unreliable narrator" in modernist fiction, Freud pauses at regular intervals to remind the reader of

---

Hysteria (Breuer and Freud, 1893-1895), Freud remarks that the procedure he followed with Fräulein Elisabeth von R. was one "of clearing away the pathogenic psychical material layer by layer, and we liked to compare it with the technique of excavating a buried city." In a closely related context, he observes that he and Breuer "had often compared the symptomatology of hysteria with a pictographic script which has become intelligible after the discovery of a few bilingual inscriptions." And his way of representing the "highly involved trains of thought" that were determinants in certain of the hysterical attacks of Frau Cäcilie was to compare them to "a series of pictures with explanatory texts" (pp. 139, 129, 177).

this case history that "my insight into the complex of events composing it [has] remained fragmentary" (p. 23), that his understanding of it remains in some essential sense permanently occluded. This darkness and constraint are the result of a number of converging circumstances, some of which have already been touched on and include the shortness of the analysis and its having been broken off by Dora at a crucial point. But it also includes the circumstance that the analysis—any analysis—must proceed by fragmentary methods, by analyzing thoughts and events bit by discontinuous bit. Indeed, at the end of one virtuoso passage in which Freud demonstrates through a series of referential leaps and juxtapositions the occurrence in Dora's past of childhood masturbation, he acknowledges that this is the essence of his procedure. "Part of this material," he writes, "I was able to obtain directly from the analysis, but the rest required supplementing. [And, indeed, the method by] which the occurrence of masturbation in Dora's case [has been] verified has ... shown us that material belonging to a single subject can only be collected piece by piece at various times and in different connections" (pp. 80-81). The method is hence a fragmentary construction and reconstruction which in the end amount to a whole that simultaneously retains its disjointed character—in sum it resembles "reality" itself, a word that, as writers today like to remind us, should always be surrounded by quotation marks.

At the same time, however, Freud protests too much in the opposite direction, as when he remarks that "It is only because the analysis was prematurely broken off that we have been obliged in Dora's case to resort to framing conjectures and filling in deficiencies" (p. 85). At an earlier moment, he had asserted that "if the work had been continued, we should no doubt have obtained the fullest possible enlightenment upon every particular of the case" (p. 12). We shall return later to these and other similar remarks, but in the present connection what they serve to underscore is Freud's effort to persuade us, and himself, of how much more he could have done—an effort which, by this point in the writing, the reader is no longer able to take literally.[10] And this tendency to

---

[10] In later years, and after much further experience, Freud was no longer able to make such statements. In "Inhibitions, Symptoms and Anxiety" (1926) he writes: "Even the most exhaustive analysis has gaps in its data and is insufficiently documented" (p. 107).

regard such assertions with a certain degree of skepticism is further reinforced when at the end of the essay—after over one hundred pages of dazzling originality, of creative genius performing with a compactness, complexity, daring, and splendor that seem close to incomparable in their order—he returns to this theme, which was, we should recall, set going by *the very first word* of his title. He begins the "Postscript" with a statement whose modesty is by now comically outrageous. "It is true," he writes, "that I have introduced this paper as a fragment of an analysis; but the reader will have discovered that it is incomplete to a far greater degree than its title might have led him to expect" (p. 112). This disclaimer is followed by still another rehearsal of what has been left out. In particular, he writes, he has "in this paper left entirely out of account the technique," and, he adds, "I found it quite impracticable . . . to deal simultaneously with the technique of analysis and with the internal structure of a case of hysteria." In any event, he concludes, "I could scarcely have accomplished such a task, and if I had, the result would have been almost unreadable" (p. 112). And if the reader is not grateful for these small mercies, Freud goes on a few pages later to speak of this essay as a "case of whose history and treatment I have published a fragment in these pages" (p. 115). In short, this fragment is itself only a fragment of a fragment. If this is so—and there is every reason to believe that Freud is seriously bandying about with words—then we are compelled to conclude that in view of the extreme complexity of this fragment of a fragment, the conception of the whole that Freud has in mind is virtually unimaginable and inconceivable.

We are then obliged to ask—and Freud himself more than anyone else has taught us most about this obligation—*what else* are all these protestations of fragmentariness and incompleteness about? Apart from their slight but continuous unsettling effect upon the reader, and their alerting him to the circumstances that there is an author and a series of contingencies behind the solid mass of printed matter that he is poring over, ploughing through, and browsing in, as if it were a piece of nature and not a created artifact—apart from this, what else do these protestations refer to? They refer in some measure, as Freud himself indicates in the postscript, to a central inadequacy and determining incompleteness that he discovered only after it was too late—the "great defect" (p. 118) of the case was to be located in the undeveloped, misdeveloped, and equivocal character of the "transference," of the relation between patient and physician in which so much was focused. Something went wrong in the relation between Freud and Dora or—if there are any analysts still reading—in the relation between Dora and Freud. But the protestations refer, I believe, to something else as well, something of which Freud was not entirely conscious. For the work is also fragmentary or incomplete in the sense of Freud's self-knowledge, both at the time of the actual case and at the time of his writing it. And he communicates in this piece of writing a less than complete understanding of himself, though like any great writer, he provides us with the material for understanding some things that have escaped his own understanding, for filling in some gaps, for restoring certain fragments into wholes.

How else can we finally explain the fact that Freud chose to write up this particular history in such extensive detail? The reasons that he offers in both the "Prefatory Remarks" and the "Postscript" aren't entirely convincing—which doesn't of course deny them a real if fractional validity. Why should he have chosen so problematic a case, when presumably others of a more complete yet equally brief kind were available? I think this can be understood in part through Freud's own unsettled and ambiguous role in the case; that he had not yet, so to speak, "gotten rid" of it; that he had to write it out, in some measure, as an effort of self-understanding—an effort, I think we shall see, that remained heroically unfinished, a failure that nonetheless brought lasting credit with it.

IV

If we turn now to the "Prefatory Remarks," it may be illuminating to regard them as a kind of novelistic framing action, as in these few opening pages Freud rehearses his motives, reasons, and intentions and begins at the same time to work his insidious devices upon the reader. First, exactly like a novelist, he remarks that what he is about to let us in on is positively scandalous, for "the complete elucidation of a case of hysteria is bound to involve the revelation of . . . intimacies and the betrayal of . . . secrets" (p. 8). Second, again like a writer of fiction, he has deliberately chosen persons, places, and circumstances that will remain obscure; the scene is laid not in metropolitan Vienna but "in a remote provincial town."

He has from the beginning kept the circumstances that Dora was his patient such a close secret that only one other physician—"in whose discretion I have complete confidence"—knows about it. He had "postponed publication" of this essay for "four whole years," also in the cause of discretion, and in the same cause has "allowed no name to stand which could put a non-medical reader upon the scent" (p. 8). Finally, he has buried the case even deeper by publishing it "in a purely scientific and technical periodical" in order to secure yet another "guarantee against unauthorized readers." He has, in short, made his own mystery within a mystery, and one of the effects of such obscure preliminary goings-on is to create a kind of Nabokovian frame—what we have here is a history framed by an explanation which is itself slightly out of focus.[11]

Third, he roundly declares, this case history is science and not literature: "I am aware that—in this city, at least—there are many physicians who (revolting though it may seem) choose to read a case history of this kind not as a contribution to the psychopathology of neuroses, but as a *roman à clef* designed for their private delectation" (p. 9). This may indeed be true; but it is equally true that nothing is more literary—and more modern—than the disavowal of all literary intentions. And when Freud does this again later on, toward the end of "The Clinical Picture," the situation becomes even less credible. The passage merits quotation at length.

I must now turn to consider a further complication to which I should certainly give no space if I were a man of letters engaged upon the creation of a mental state like this for a short story, instead of being a medical man engaged upon its dissection. The element to which I must now allude can only

---

[11] One is in a position now to understand rather better the quasi-meretricious fits of detestation that overtake Nabokov whenever Freud's name is mentioned. That "elderly gentleman from Vienna" whom Nabokov has accused of "inflicting his dreams upon me" was in fact a past master at all the tricks, ruses, and sleights-of-hand that Nabokov has devoted his entire career to. The difference is this: that in Freud such devices are merely a minor item in the immense store of his literary resources.

Nabokov's revenge has been such cuties as "Dr. Sig Heiler," "Sigismund Lejoyeux," and one "Dr. Froit of Signy-Mondieu-Mondieu." At an entirely different level an analogous relation existed between Charlie Chaplin and W. C. Fields. The latter often tried to get his own back on the comic genius by calling him "that god-damned juggler" along with similar phrases of endearment.

serve to obscure and efface the outlines of the fine poetic
conflict which we have been able to ascribe to Dora. This
element would rightly fall a sacrifice to the censorship of a
writer, for he, after all, simplifies and abstracts when he
appears in the character of a psychologist. But in the world of
reality, which I am trying to depict here, a complication of
motives, an accumulation and conjunction of mental activities
—in a word, overdetermination—is the rule [pp. 59-60].

In this context it is next to impossible to tell whether Freud is up to
another of his crafty maneuverings with the reader or whether he is
actually simply unconscious of how much of a modern and
modernist writer he is. For when he takes to describing the difference between himself and some hypothetical man of letters and
writer of short stories he is in fact embarked upon an elaborate
obfuscation. That hypothetical writer is nothing but a straw man;
and when Freud in apparent contrast represents himself and his
own activities, he is truly representing how a genuine creative
writer writes. And this passage, we must also recall, came from the
same pen that only a little more than a year earlier had written
passages about Oedipus and Hamlet that changed for good the
ways in which the civilized world would henceforth think about
literature and writers.[12] What might be thought of as this sly
unliterariness of Freud's turns up in other contexts as well.

[12] Some years earlier Freud had been more candid and more innocent about
the relation of his writing to literature. In *Studies on Hysteria* he introduces his
discussion of the case of Fräulein Elisabeth von R. with the following disarm-
ing admission: "I have not always been a psychotherapist. Like other neuro-
pathologists, I was trained to employ local diagnoses and electro-prognosis,
and it still strikes me myself as strange that the case histories I write should read
like short stories and that, as one might say, they lack the serious stamp of science.
I must console myself with the reflection that the nature of the subject is evidently
responsible for this, rather than any preference of my own. The fact is that local
diagnosis and electrical reactions lead nowhere in the study of hysteria, whereas a
detailed description of mental processes such as we are accustomed to find in the
works of imaginative writers enables me, with the use of a few psychological
formulas, to obtain at least some kind of insight into the course of that affection.
Case histories of this kind are intended to be judged like psychiatric ones; they
have, however, one advantage over the latter, namely an intimate connection
between the story of the patient's sufferings and the symptoms of his illness—a
connection for which we still search in vain in the biographies of other psychoses"
(Breuer and Freud, 1893-1895, pp. 160-161).

If we return to the point in the "Prefatory Remarks" from which we have momentarily digressed, we find that Freud then goes on to describe other difficulties, constraints, and problematical circumstances attaching to the situation in which he finds himself. Among them is the problem of "how to record for publication" (p. 10) even such a short case—the long ones are as yet altogether impossible. We shall presently return to this central passage. Moreover, since the material that critically illuminated this case was grouped about two dreams, their analysis formed a secure point of departure for the writing. (Freud is of course at home with dreams, being the unchallenged master in the reading of them.) Yet this tactical solution pushes the *entire problematic* back only another step further, since Freud at once goes on to his additional presupposition, that only those who are already familiar with "the interpretation of dreams"—that is, *The Interpretation of Dreams* (1900), whose readership in 1901 must have amounted to a little platoon indeed—are likely to be satisfied at all with the present account. Any other reader "will find only bewilderment in these pages" (p. 11). As much as it is like anything else, this is like Borges—as well as Nabokov. In these opening pages Freud actively and purposefully refuses to give the reader a settled point of attachment, and instead works at undercutting and undermining his stability by such slight manipulations as this: i.e., in order to read the case of Dora which the reader presumably has right in front of him, he must also first have read the huge, abstruse, and almost entirely unread dream book of the year before. This off-putting and disconcerting quality, it should go without saying, is characteristically modern; the writer succumbs to no impulse to make it easy for the reader; on the contrary, he is by preference rather forbidding, and does not extend a cordial welcome. But Freud has not yet finished piling Pelion upon Ossa, and he goes on to add for good measure that the reader really ought to have read *Studies on Hysteria* as well, if only to be confounded by the differences between this case and those discussed at such briefer length there. With this and with a number of further remarks about the unsatisfactory satisfactory character of what he has done and what is to come, Freud closes this frame of "Prefatory Remarks," leaving what audience he still has left in a bemused, uncertain, and dislocated state of mind. The reader has been, as it were, "softened up" by his first encounter with this unique expository and narrative authority; he is thoroughly off balance and is as a consequence ready to be "educated," by Freud. By the same token, however, if he has followed these opening few pages carefully, he is certainly no longer as prepared as he was to assert the primacy and priority of his own critical sense of things. He is precisely where Freud—and any writer—wants him to be.

At the opening of part I, "The Clinical Picture," Freud tells us that he begins his "treatment, indeed, by asking the patient to give me the whole story of his life and illness," and immediately adds that "the information I receive is never enough to let me see my way about the case" (p. 16). This inadequacy and unsatisfactoriness in the stories his patients tell is in distinct contrast to what Freud has read in the accounts rendered by his psychiatric contemporaries, and he continues by remarking that "I cannot help wondering how it is that the authorities can produce such smooth and [exact] histories in cases of hysteria. As a matter of fact the patients are incapable of giving such reports about themselves." There is an immense amount beginning to go on here. In the first place, there is the key assumption that everyone—that every life, every existence—has a story, to which there is appended a corollary that most of us probably tell that story poorly. There follows at once Freud's statement of flat disbelief in the "smooth and exact" histories published by his colleagues who study hysteria. The implications that are latent in this negation are at least twofold: (a) these authorities are incompetent and may in some sense be "making up" the histories they publish; (b) real case histories are neither "smooth" nor "exact," and the reader cannot expect to find such qualities here in the "real" thing. Furthermore, the relations at this point in Freud's prose between the words "story," "history," and "report" are unspecified, undifferentiated, and unanalyzed, and in the nature of the case contain and conceal a wealth of material.

Freud proceeds to specify what it is that is wrong with the stories his patients tell him. The difficulties are in the first instance formal shortcomings of *narrative:* the connections, "even the ostensible ones—are for the most part incoherent," obscured and unclear; "and the sequence of different events is uncertain" (p. 16). In short, these narratives are disorganized, and the patients are unable to tell a coherent story of their lives. What is more, he

states, "the patients' inability to give an ordered history of their life
in so far as it coincides with the history of their illness is not merely
characteristic of the neurosis. It also possesses great theoretical
significance" (pp. 16-17). Part of this significance comes into view
when we regard this conjecture from its obverse side, which Freud
does at once in a footnote.

> Another physician once sent his sister to me for psychothera-
> peutic treatment, telling me that she had for years been treated
> without success for hysteria (pains and defective gait). The
> short account which he gave me seemed quite consistent with
> the diagnosis. In my first hour with the patient I got her to tell
> me her history herself. When the story came out perfectly
> clearly and connectedly in spite of the remarkable events it
> dealt with, I told myself that the case could not be one of
> hysteria, and immediately instituted a careful physical exami-
> nation. This led to the diagnosis of a not very advanced stage
> of tabes, which was later on treated with Hg injections . . . with
> markedly beneficial results [pp. 16-17].

What we are led at this juncture to conclude is that Freud is
implying that a coherent story is in some manner connected with
mental health (at the very least, with the absence of hysteria), and
this in turn implies assumptions of the broadest and deepest kind
about both the nature of coherence and the form and structure of
human life. On this reading, human life is, ideally, a connected
and coherent story, with all the details in explanatory place, and
with everything (or as close to everything as is practically possible)
accounted for, in its proper causal or other sequence. And in-
versely, illness amounts at least in part to suffering from an
incoherent story or an inadequate narrative account of oneself.

Freud then describes in technical detail the various types and
orders of narrative insufficiency that he commonly finds; they
range from disingenuousness both conscious and unconscious to
amnesias and paramnesias of several kinds and various other means
of severing connections and altering chronologies. In addition, he
maintains, this discomposed memory applies with particular force
and virulence to "the history of the illness" for which the patient
has come for treatment. In the course of a successful treatment, this
incoherence, incompleteness, and fragmentariness are progressive-

ly transmuted, as facts, events, and memories are brought forward into the forefront of the patient's mind.

> The paramnesias prove untenable, and the gaps in his memory are filled in. It is only towards the end of the treatment that we have before us an intelligible, consistent, and unbroken case history. Whereas the practical aim of the treatment is to remove all possible symptoms and to replace them by conscious thoughts, we may regard it as a second and theoretical aim to repair all the damages to the patient's memory [p. 18].

And he adds as a conclusion that these two aims "are coincident"—they are reached simultaneously and by the same path.[13] Some of the consequences that can be derived from these tremendous remarks are as follows. The history of any patient's illness is itself only a substory (or a subplot), although it is at the same time a vital part of a larger structure. Furthermore, in the course of psychoanalytic treatment, nothing less than "reality" itself is made, constructed, or reconstructed. A complete story—"intelligible, consistent, and unbroken"—is the theoretical, created end story. It is a story, or a fiction, not only because it has a narrative structure but also because the narrative account has been rendered in language, in conscious speech, and no longer exists in the deformed language of symptoms, the untranslated speech of the body. At the end—at the successful end—one has come into possession of one's own story. It is a final act of self-appropriation, the appropriation by oneself of one's own history. This is in part so because one's own story is in so large a measure a phenomenon of language, as psychoanalysis is in turn a demonstration of the degree to which language can go in the reading of all our experience. What we end with, then, is a fictional construction which is at the same time satisfactory to us in the form of the truth, and as the form of the truth.

---

[13] There is a parodic analogue to this passage of some contemporary significance. It is taken from the relatively esoteric but influential field of general systems theory, one of whose important practitioners suffered from severe disturbances of memory. Indeed, he could hardly remember anything. He nonetheless insisted that there was nothing wrong with his memory; in fact, he went on to argue, he had a perfect memory—it was only his retrieval system that wasn't working. In the light of such a comment, it is at least open to others to wonder whether other things as well weren't working.

No larger tribute has ever been paid to a culture in which the various narrative and fictional forms had exerted for centuries both moral and philosophical authority, and which had produced as one of its chief climaxes the great bourgeois novels of the nineteenth century. Indeed we must see Freud's writings—and method—as themselves part of this culmination, and at the same moment, along with the great modernist novels of the first half of the twentieth century, as the beginning of the end of that tradition and its authority. Certainly the passages we have just dealt with contain heroic notions and offer an extension of heroic capabilities if not to all men then to most, at least as a possibility. Yet we cannot leave this matter so relatively unexamined, and must ask ourselves how it is that this "story" is not merely a "history" but a "case history" as well. We must ask ourselves how these associated terms are more intimately related in the nexus that is about to be wound and unwound before us. To begin to understand such questions, we have to turn back to a central passage in the "Prefatory Remarks." Freud undertakes therein to "describe the way in which I have overcome the *technical* difficulties of drawing up the report of this case history" (p. 9). Apparently the "report" and the "case history" referred to in this statement are two discriminable if not altogether discrete entities. If they are, then we can further presume that, ideally at any rate, Dora (or any patient) is as much in possession of the "case history" as Freud himself. And this notion is in some part supported by what comes next. Freud mentions certain other difficulties, such as the fact that he "cannot make notes during the actual session . . . for fear of shaking the patient's confidence and of disturbing his own view of the material under observation" (p. 9). In the case of Dora, however, this obstacle was partly overcome because so much of the material was grouped about two dreams, and "The wording of these dreams was recorded immediately after the session" so that "they thus afforded a secure point of attachment for the chain of interpretations and recollections which proceeded from them" (p. 10). Freud then writes:

The case history itself was only committed to writing from memory after the treatment was at an end, but while my recollection of the case was still fresh and was heightened by my interest in its publication. Thus the record is not absolutely—phonographically—exact, but it can claim to possess a high degree of trustworthiness. Nothing of any importance has been altered in it except in some places the order in which the explanations are given; and this has been done for the sake of presenting the case in a more connected form [p. 10].

Such a passage raises more questions than it resolves. The first sentence is a kind of conundrum in which case history, writing, and memory dance about in a series of logical entwinements, of possible alternate combinations, equivalences, and semiequivalences. These are followed by further equivocations about "the record," "phonographic" exactitude, and so forth—the ambiguities of which jump out at one as soon as the terms begin to be seriously examined. For example, is "the report" the same thing as "the record"; and if "the record" were "phonographically" exact, would it be a "report"? Like the prodigious narrative historian that he is, Freud is enmeshed in an irreducible paradox of history: that the term itself refers both to the activity of the historian—the writing of history—and to the objects of his undertaking, what history is "about." I do not think, therefore, that we can conclude that Freud has created this thick context of historical contingency and ambiguity out of what he once referred to as Viennese *Schlamperei.*

The historical difficulties are further compounded by several other sequential networks that are mentioned at the outset and that figure discernibly throughout the writing. First, there is the virtual Proustian complexity of Freud's interweaving of the various strands of time in the actual account; or, to change the figure, his geological fusing of various time strata—strata which are themselves at once fluid and shifting. We observe this most strikingly in the palimpsestlike quality of the writing itself; which refers back to *Studies on Hysteria* of 1893-1895; which records a treatment that took place at the end of 1900 (although it mistakes the date by a year); which then was composed in first form during the early weeks of 1901; which was then exhumed in 1905 and was revised and rewritten to an indeterminable extent before publication in that year; and to which additional critical comments in the form of footnotes were finally appended in 1923. All of these are of course held together in vital connection and interanimation by nothing else than Freud's consciousness. But we must take notice as well of the copresence of still further different time sequences in Freud's presentation—this copresence being itself a historical or novelistic circumstance of some magnitude. There is first the connection established by the periodically varied rehearsal throughout the account of Freud's own theory and theoretical notions as they had developed up to that point; this practice provides a kind of running applied history of psychoanalytic theory as its development is refracted through the embroiled medium of this particular case. Then there are the different time strata of Dora's own history, which Freud handles with confident and loving exactitude. Indeed, he is never more of a historical virtuoso than when he reveals himself to us as moving with compelling ease back and forth between the complex group of sequential histories and narrative accounts with divergent sets of diction and at different levels of explanation that constitute the extraordinary fabric of this work. He does this most conspicuously in his analytic dealings with Dora's dreams, for every dream, he reminds us, sets up a connection between two "factors," an "event during childhood" and an "event of the present day—and it endeavours to re-shape the present on the model of the remote past" (p. 71). The existence or re-creation of the past in the present is in fact "history" in more than one of its manifold senses. And such a passage is also one of Freud's many analogies to the following equally celebrated utterance.

> Men make their own history, but they do not make it just as they please; they do not make it under circumstances chosen by themselves, but under circumstances directly encountered, given and transmitted from the past. The tradition of all the dead generations weighs like a nightmare on the brain of the living. And just when they seem engaged in revolutionising themselves and things, in creating something that has never yet existed, precisely in such periods of revolutionary crisis they anxiously conjure up the spirits of the past to their service and borrow from them names, battle cries and costumes in order to present the new scene of world history in this time-honored disguise and this borrowed language [Marx, 1852, p. 15].

And just as Marx regards the history-makers of the past as sleep-walkers, "who required recollections of past world history in order to drug themselves concerning their own content," so Freud similarly regards the conditions of dream formation, of neurosis itself, and even of the cure of neurosis, namely, the analytic experience of transference. They are all of them species of living past history in the present. If the last of these works out satisfactorily, then a case history is at the end transfigured. It becomes an inseparable part of an integral life history. Freud is of course the master historian of those transfigurations.[14]

V

We cannot in prudence follow Freud's written analysis of the case in anything like adequate detail. What we can do is try to trace out the persistence and development of certain themes. And we can try as well to keep track of the role—or some of the roles—played by Freud in the remainder of this case out of whose failure this triumph of mind and of literature emerged. At the very beginning, after he had listened to the father's account of "Dora's impossible behavior," Freud abstained from comment, for, he remarks, "I had resolved from the first to suspend my judgement of the true state of affairs till I had heard the other side as well" (p. 26). Such a suspension inevitably recalls an earlier revolutionary project. In describing the originating plan of *Lyrical Ballads*, Coleridge (1817, Volume 2, p. 6) writes that it "was agreed that my endeavours should be directed to persons and characters supernatural, or at least romantic; yet so as to transfer from our inward nature a human interest and a semblance of truth sufficient to procure for these shadows of imagination that willing suspension of disbelief for the moment, which constitutes poetic faith." We know very well that Freud had a more than ordinary capacity in this direction, and that one of the most dramatic moments in the prehistory of psychoanalysis had to do precisely with his taking on faith facts that turned out to be fantasies. Yet Freud is not only the reader suspending judgment and disbelief until he has heard the other side of the story; and he is not only the poet or writer who must induce a similar process in himself if he is

[14] Erik H. Erikson has waggishly observed that a case history is an account of how someone fell apart, while a life history is an account of how someone held together.

to elicit it in his audience. He is also concomitantly a principal, an actor, a living character in the drama that he is unfolding in print before us. Moreover, that suspension of disbelief is in no sense incompatible with a large body of assumptions, many of them definite, a number of them positively alarming. I think that before we pursue any further Freud's spectacular gyrations as a writer, we had better confront the chief of these presuppositions.

They have to do largely with sexuality and in particular with female sexuality. They are brought to a focus in the central scene of Dora's life (and case), a scene that Freud "orchestrates" with inimitable richness and to which he recurs thematically at a number of junctures with the tact and sense of form that one associates with a classical composer of music (or with Proust, Mann, or Joyce). Dora told this episode to Freud toward the beginning of their relation, after "the first difficulties of the treatment had been overcome." It is the scene between her and Herr K. which took place when she was fourteen years old—that is, four years before the present tense of the case—and that acted, Freud said, as a "sexual trauma." The reader will recall that on this occasion Herr K. contrived to get Dora alone "at his place of business" in the town of B_____, and then without warning or preparation "suddenly clasped the girl to him and pressed a kiss upon her lips." Freud then asserts that "This was *surely* just the situation to call up a *distinct* feeling of sexual excitement in a *girl* of *fourteen* who had *never before* been approached. But Dora had at that moment a violent feeling of disgust, tore herself free from the man, and hurried past him to the staircase and from there to the street door" (p. 28; all italics are mine). She avoided seeing the K.'s for a few days after this, but then relations returned to "normal"— if such a term survives with any permissible sense in the present context. She continued to meet Herr K., and neither of them ever mentioned "the little scene." Moreover, Freud adds, "according to her account Dora kept it a secret till her confession during the treatment" (p. 28), and he pretty clearly implies that he believes this.

This episode preceded by two years the scene at the lake that acted as the precipitating agent for the severe stage of Dora's illness; and it was this later episode and the entire structure that she and others had elaborated about it that she had first presented to Freud, who continues thus:

In this scene—second in order of mention, but first in order of time—the behaviour of this child of fourteen was already entirely and completely hysterical. I should without question consider a person hysterical in whom an occasion for sexual excitement elicited feelings that were preponderantly or exclusively unpleasurable; and I should do so whether or no the person were capable of producing somatic symptoms [p. 28].

As if this were not enough, he proceeds to produce another rabbit out of his hat. In Dora's feeling of disgust an obscure psychical mechanism called the "reversal of affect" was brought into play; but so was another process, and here Freud introduces—casually and almost as a throwaway—one more of his grand theoretical-clinical formulations, namely, the idea of the *"displacement* of sensation,"* or, as it has more commonly come to be referred to, the "displacement upwards." "Instead of the genital sensation which would certainly have been felt by a healthy girl in such circumstances, Dora was overcome by the unpleasurable feeling which is proper to the tract of mucous membrane at the entrance to the alimentary canal—that is by disgust" (p. 29). Although the disgust did not persist as a permanent symptom but remained behind residually and potentially in a general distaste for food and poor appetite, a second displacement upward was the resultant of this scene "in the shape of a sensory hallucination which occurred from time to time and even made its appearance while she was telling me her story. She declared that she could still feel upon the upper part of her body the pressure of Herr K.'s embrace" (p. 29). Dipping into the hat once again, and taking into account certain other of Dora's "inexplicable"—and hitherto unmentioned—"peculiarities" (such as her phobic reluctance to walk past any man she saw engaged in animated conversation with a woman), Freud "formed in my own mind the following reconstruction of the scene. I believe that during the man's passionate embrace she felt not merely his kiss upon her lips but also the pressure of his erect member against her body. The perception was revolting to her; it was dismissed from her memory, repressed, and replaced by the innocent sensation of pressure upon her thorax, which in turn derived an excessive intensity from its repressed source" (pp. 29-30). This repressed source was located in the erotogenic oral zone, which in Dora's case had undergone a developmental deformation from the period of infancy. And thus, Freud concludes, "The pressure of the erect member probably led to an analogous change in the corresponding female organ, the clitoris; and the excitation of this second erotogenic zone was referred by a process of displacement to the simultaneous pressure against the thorax and became fixed there" (p. 30).

This passage of unquestionable genius contains at the same time something questionable and askew. In it Freud is at once dogmatically certain and very uncertain. He is dogmatically certain of what the normative sexual response in young and other females is, and asserts himself to that effect. At the same time he is, in my judgment, utterly uncertain about where Dora is, or was, developmentally. At one moment in the passage he calls her a "girl," at another a "child"—but in point of fact he treats her throughout as if this fourteen-, sixteen-, and eighteen-year-old adolescent had the capacities for sexual response of a grown woman—indeed, at a later point he conjectures again that Dora either responded, or should have responded, to the embrace with specific genital heat and moisture. Too many determinations converge at this locus for us to do much more than single out a few of the more obvious influencing circumstances. In the first instance, there was Freud's own state of knowledge about such matters at the time, which was better than anyone else's but still relatively crude and undifferentiated. Second, we may be in the presence of what can only be accounted for by assuming that a genuine historical-cultural change has taken place between then and now. It may be that Freud was expressing a legitimate partial assumption of his time and culture when he ascribes to a fourteen-year-old adolescent— whom he calls a "child"—the normative responses that are ascribed today to a fully developed and mature woman.[15] This supposition is borne out if we consider the matter from the other end, from the

---

[15] Freud may at this point be thinking within an even more historically anachronistic paradigm than the one that normally applied in the late-Victorian period or in the Vienna of the time. In both pre- and early-industrial Europe sexual maturity was commonly equated—especially for women—with reproductive maturity, and both were regarded as coterminous with marriageability. Ironically it was Freud more than any other single figure who was to demonstrate the inadequacy and outmodedness of this paradigm. See Gagnon and Simon (1973, p. 296).

standpoint of what has happened to the conception of adolescence in our own time. It begins now in prepuberty and extends to—who knows when? Certainly its extensibility in our time has reached well beyond the age of thirty. Third, Freud is writing in this passage as an advocate of nature, sexuality, openness, and candor—and within such a context Dora cannot hope to look good. The very framing of the context in such a manner is itself slightly accusatory. In this connection we may note that Freud goes out of his way to tell us that he knew Herr K. personally and that "he was still quite young and of prepossessing appearance" (p. 29).[16] If we let Nabokov back into the picture for a moment, we may observe that Dora is no Lolita, and go on to suggest that *Lolita* is an anti-*Dora*.

Yet we must also note that in this episode—the condensed and focusing scene of the entire case history—Freud is as much a novelist as he is an analyst. For the central moment of this central scene is a "reconstruction" that he "formed in my own mind." This pivotal construction becomes henceforth the principal "reality" of the case, and we must also observe that this reality remains Freud's more than Dora's, since he was never quite able to convince her of

[16] There is a fourth influencing circumstance that deserves to be mentioned. Freud appears to have worked in this case with a model in mind, but it turned out that the model either didn't fit or was the wrong one. In the case of "Katharina" in *Studies on Hysteria*, Freud had performed a kind of instant analysis with a fair degree of success. Katharina was the eighteen-year-old daughter of the landlady of an Alpine refuge hut that Freud had climbed to one summer's day. This "rather sulky-looking girl" had served Freud his meal and then approached him for medical advice, having seen his signature in the Visitors' Book. She was suffering from various hysterical symptoms—many of which resembled those that afflicted Dora—and the story that came out had to do with attempted sexual seductions by her father, followed by her actually catching her father in the act with a young cousin—a discovery that led to the separation and divorce of the parents. The symptoms and the experiences seemed very closely connected, and as Freud elicited piecemeal these stories from her she seemed to become "like someone transformed" before his eyes. He was very pleased and said that he "owed her a debt of gratitude for having made it so much easier for me to talk to her than to the prudish ladies of my city practice, who regard whatever is natural as shameful" (Breuer and Freud, 1893-1895, pp. 125-134). The circumstances of her case and of Dora's are analogous in a number of ways, but Dora was no rustic Alpine *Jungfrau* who spoke candidly and in dialect (which Freud reproduces); she was in truth one of the prudish ladies of his city practice who was frigid then and remained so all her life.

the plausibility of the construction; or, to regard it from the other pole of the dyad, she was never quite able to accept this version of reality, of what "really" happened. Freud was not at first unduly distressed by this resistance on her side, for part of his understanding of what he had undertaken to do in psychoanalysis was to instruct his patients—and his readers—in the nature of reality. This reality was the reality that modern readers of literature have also had to be educated in. It was conceived of as a *world of meanings*. As Freud put it in one of those stop-you-dead-in-your-tracks footnotes that he was so expert in using strategically, we must at almost every moment "be prepared to be met not by one but by several causes—by *overdetermination*" (p. 31). Thus the world of meanings is a world of multiple and compacted causations; it is a world in which everything has a meaning, which means that everything has more than one meaning. Every symptom is a concrete universal in several senses. It not only embodies a network of significances but also "serves to represent several unconscious mental processes simultaneously" (p. 47). By the same token, since it is a world almost entirely brought into existence, maintained, and mediated through a series of linguistic transactions between patient and physician, it partakes in full measure of the virtually limitless complexity of language, in particular its capacities for producing statements characterized by multiplicity, duplicity, and ambiguity of significance. Freud lays particular stress on the ambiguity, and is continually on the lookout for it, and brings his own formidable skills in this direction to bear most strikingly on the analyses of Dora's dreams. The first thing he picks up in the first of her dreams is in fact an ambiguous statement, with which he at once confronts her. While he is doing so, he is also letting down a theoretical footnote for the benefit of his readers.

> I laid stress on these words because they took me aback. They seemed to have an ambiguous ring about them.... Now, in a line of associations ambiguous words (or, as we may call them, 'switch-words') act like points at a junction. If the points are switched across from the position in which they appear to lie in the dream, then we find ourselves on another set of rails;

and along this second track run the thoughts which we are in search of but which still lie concealed behind the dream [p. 65].[17]

As if this were not sufficient, the actual case itself was full of such literary and novelistic devices or conventions as thematic analogies, double plots, reversals, inversions, variations, betrayals, etc.—full of what the "sharp-sighted" Dora as well as the sharp-sighted Freud thought of as "hidden connections"—though it is important to add that Dora and her physician mean different things by the same phrase. And as the case proceeds Freud continues to confront Dora with such connections and tries to enlist her assistance in their construction. For example, one of the least pleasant characteristics in Dora's nature was her habitual re-proachfulness—it was directed mostly toward her father but radiated out in all directions. Freud regarded this behavior in his own characteristic manner. "A string of reproaches against other people," he comments, "leads one to suspect the existence of a string of self-reproaches with the same content" (p. 35). Freud accordingly followed the procedure of turning back "each [simple] reproach on to the speaker [herself]." When Dora reproached her father with malingering in order to keep himself in the company of Frau K., Freud felt "obliged to point out to the patient that her present ill-health was just as much actuated by motives and was just as tendentious as had been Frau K.'s illness, which she had understood so well" (p. 42). At such moments Dora begins to mirror the other characters in the case, as they in differing degrees all mirror one another as well.

Yet the unity that all these internal references and correspon-dences point to is not that of a harmony or of an uninflected linear series. And at one moment Freud feels obliged to remark that

---

[17] Such a passage serves to locate Freud's place in a set of traditions in addition to those of literature. It is unmistakable that such a statement also belongs to a tradition that includes Hegel and Marx at one end and Max Weber and Thomas Mann somewhere near the other. It was Weber who once remarked that "the interests of society are the great rails on which humanity moves, but the ideas throw the switches" (1915, p. 252). And Mann for his part regularly gave off such observations as: " 'Relationship is everything. And if you want to give it a more precise name, it is ambiguity' " (1947, p. 47).

... my experience in the clearing-up of hysterical symptoms
has shown that it is not necessary for the various meanings of
a symptom to be compatible with one another, that is, to fit
together into a connected whole. It is enough that the unity
should be constituted by the subject-matter which has given
rise to all the various phantasies. In the present case, moreover,
compatibility even of the first kind is not out of the question. . . .

We have already learnt that it quite regularly happens
that a single symptom corresponds to several meanings *simultaneously*. We may now add that it can express several meanings *in succession*. In the course of years a symptom can change
its meaning or its chief meaning, or the leading role can pass
from one meaning to another [p. 53].

To which it may be added that what is true of the symptom can
also be true of the larger entity of which it is a part. The meaning
in question may be a contradictory one; it may be constituted out
of a contradictory unity of opposites, or out of a shifting and
unstable set of them. Whatever may be the case, the "reality" that
is being both constructed and referred to is heterogeneous, multidimensional, and open-ended—novelistic in the fullest sense of the
word.

Part of that sense, we have come to understand, is that the
writer is or ought to be conscious of the part that he—in whatever
guise, voice, or persona he chooses—invariably and unavoidably
plays in the world he represents. Oddly enough, although there is
none of his writings in which Freud is more vigorously active than
he is here, it is precisely this activity that he subjects to the least
self-conscious scrutiny, that he almost appears to fend off. For
example, I will now take my head in my hands and suggest that his
extraordinary analysis of Dora's first dream is inadequate on just
this count. He is only dimly and marginally aware of his central
place in it (he is clearly incorporated into the figure of Dora's
father), comments on it only as an addition to Dora's own ad-
dendum to the dream, and does nothing to exploit it (pp. 73f.).
Why he should choose this course is a question to which we shall
shortly return. Instead of analyzing his own part in what he has
done and what he is writing, Freud continues to behave like an
unreliable narrator, treating the material about which he is writing

as if it were literature but excluding himself from both that treatment and that material. At one moment he refers to himself as someone "who has learnt to appreciate the delicacy of the fabric of structures such as dreams" (p. 87), intimating what I surmise he incontestably believed, that dreams are natural works of art. And when in the analysis of the second dream we find ourselves back at the scene at the lake again; when Dora recalls that the only plea to her of Herr K. that she could remember is "You know I get nothing out of my wife"; when these were precisely the same words used by Dora's father in describing to Freud his relation to Dora's mother; and when Freud speculates that Dora may even "have heard her father make the same complaint ... just as I myself did from his own lips" (pp. 98, 106)—when a conjunction such as this occurs, then we know we are in a novel, probably by Proust. Time has recurred, the repressed has returned, plot, double plot, and counterplot have all intersected, and "reality" turns out to be something that for all practical purposes is indistinguishable from a systematic fictional creation.

Finally, when at the very end Freud turns to deal—rudimentarily as it happens—with the decisive issue of the case, the transferences, everything is transformed into literature, into reading and writing. Transferences, he writes, "are new editions or facsimiles" of tendencies, fantasies, and relations in which "the person of the physician" replaces some earlier person. When the substitution is a simple one, the transferences may be said to be "merely new impressions or reprints": Freud is explicit about the metaphor he is using. Others "more ingeniously constructed ... will no longer be new impressions, but revised editions" (p. 116). And he goes on, quite carried away by these figures, to institute a comparison between dealing with the transference and other analytic procedures. "It is easy to learn how to interpret dreams," he remarks, "to extract from the patient's associations his unconscious thoughts and memories, and to practise similar explanatory arts: for these the patient himself will always provide the text" (p. 116). The startling group of suppositions contained in this sentence should not distract us from noting the submerged ambiguity in it. The patient does not merely provide the text; he also *is* the text, the writing to be read, the language to be interpreted. With the transference, however, we move to a different degree of difficulty and onto a different level of explanation. It is only after the transference has been resolved, Freud concludes, "that a patient arrives at a sense of conviction of the validity of the connections which have been constructed during the analysis" (p. 117). I will refrain from entering the veritable series of Chinese boxes opened up by that last statement, and will content myself by proposing that in this passage as a whole Freud is using literature and writing not only creatively and heuristically—as he so often does—but defensively as well.

The writer or novelist is not the only partial role taken up unconsciously or semiconsciously by Freud in the course of this work. He also figures prominently in the text in his capacity as a nineteenth-century man of science and as a representative Victorian critic—employing the seriousness, energy, and commitment of the Victorian ethos to deliver itself from its own excesses. We have already seen him affirming the positive nature of female sexuality, "the genital sensation which would certainly have been felt by a healthy girl in such circumstances" (p. 29), but which Dora did not feel. He goes a good deal further than this. At a fairly early moment in the analysis he faces Dora with the fact that she has "an aim in view which she hoped to gain by her illness. That aim could be none other than to detach her father from Frau K." Her prayers and arguments had not worked; her suicide letter and fainting fits had done no better. Dora knew quite well how much her father loved her, and, Freud continues to address her,

> I felt quite convinced that she would recover at once if only her father were to tell her that he had sacrificed Frau K. for the sake of her health. But, I added, I hoped he would not let himself be persuaded to do this, for then she would have learned what a powerful weapon she had in her hands, and she would certainly not fail on every future occasion to make use once more of her liability to ill-health. Yet if her father refused to give way to her, I was quite sure she would not let herself be deprived of her illness so easily [p. 42].

This is pretty strong stuff, considering both the age and her age. I think, moreover, that we are justified in reading an overdetermination out of this utterance of Freud's and in suggesting that he had motives additional to strictly therapeutic ones in saying what he did.

In a related sense Freud goes out of his way to affirm his entitlement to speak freely and openly about sex—he is, one keeps forgetting, the great liberator and therapist of speech. The passage is worth quoting at some length.

> It is possible for a man to talk to girls and women upon sexual matters of every kind without doing them harm and without bringing suspicion upon himself, so long as, in the first place, he adopts a particular way of doing it, and, in the second place, can make them feel convinced that it is unavoidable. . . . The best way of speaking about such things is to be dry and direct; and that is at the same time the method furthest removed from the prurience with which the same subjects are handled in 'society', and to which girls and women alike are so thoroughly accustomed. I call bodily organs and processes by their technical names . . . *J'appelle un chat un chat.* I have certainly heard of some people—doctors and laymen—who are scandalized by a therapeutic method in which conversations of this sort occur, and who appear to envy either me or my patients the titillation which, according to their notions, such a method must afford. But I am too well acquainted with the respectability of these gentry to excite myself over them. . . .
>
> . . . The right attitude is: *'pour faire une omelette il faut casser des oeufs'* [pp. 48-49].

I believe that Freud would have been the first to be amused by the observation that in this splendid extended declaration about plain speech (at this point he takes his place in a tradition coming directly down from Luther), he feels it necessary to disappear not once but twice into French. I think he would have said that such slips—and the revelation of their meanings—are the smallest price one has to pay for the courage to go on. And he goes on with a vengeance, immediately following this passage with another in which he aggressively refuses to moralize in any condemnatory sense about sexuality. As for the attitude that regards the perverse nature of his patient's fantasies as horrible—

... I should like to say emphatically that a medical man has no business to indulge in such passionate condemnation.... We are faced by a fact; and it is to be hoped that we shall grow accustomed to it, when we have [learned to] put our own tastes on one side. We must learn to speak without indignation of what we call the sexual perversions ... The uncertainty in regard to the boundaries of what is to be called normal sexual life, when we take different races and different epochs into account, should in itself be enough to cool the zealot's ardour. We surely ought not to forget that the perversion which is the most repellent to us, the sensual love of a man for a man, was not only tolerated by a people so far our superiors in cultivation as were the Greeks, but was actually entrusted by them with important social functions [pp. 49-50].

We can put this assertion into one of its appropriate contexts by recalling that the trial and imprisonment of Oscar Wilde had taken place only five years earlier. And the man who is speaking out here has to be regarded as the greatest of Victorian physicians, who in this passage is fearlessly revealing one of the inner and unacknowledged meanings of the famous "tyranny of Greece over Germany."[18] And as we shall see, he has by no means reached the limits beyond which he will not go.

How far he is willing to go begins to be visible as we observe him sliding almost imperceptibly from being the nineteenth-century man of science to being the remorseless "teller of truth," the character in a play by Ibsen who is not to be deterred from his "mission." In a historical sense the two roles are not adventitiously related, any more than it is adventitious that the "truth" that is told often has unforeseen and destructive consequences and that it can

[18] "When the social historian of the future looks back to the first half of the twentieth century with the detachment that comes with the passage of time, it will by then be apparent that amongst the revolutionary changes to be credited to that period, two at least were of vital importance to the development of humanism: the liberation of psychology from the fetters of conscious rationalism, and the subsequent emancipation of sociology from the more primitive superstitions and moralistic conceptions of crime. It will also be apparent that this twin movement towards a new liberalism owed its impetus to the researches of a late-Victorian scientist, Sigmund Freud, who first uncovered the unconscious roots of that uniquely human reaction which goes by the name of 'guilt' ..." (Glover, 1960, p. ix).

rebound upon the teller. Sometimes we can see this process at work in the smallest details. For instance, one day when Freud's "powers of interpretation were at a low ebb," he let Dora go on talking until she brought forth a recollection that make it clear why she was in such a bad mood. Freud remarks of this recollection that it was "a fact which I did not fail to use against her" (p. 59). There can be no mistaking the adversary tone, however slight, of this statement. It may be replied that Freud is writing with his customary dry irony; yet this reply must be met by observing that irony is invariably an instrument with a cutting edge. But we see him most vividly at this implacable work in the two great dream interpretations, which are largely "phonographic" reproductions of dramatic discourse and dialogue. Very early on in the analysis of the first dream, Freud takes up the dream element of the "jewel-case" and makes the unavoidable symbolic interpretation of it. He then proceeds to say the following to this Victorian maiden who had been in treatment with him for all of maybe six weeks:

> 'So you are ready to give Herr K. what his wife withholds from him. That is the thought which has had to be repressed with so much energy, and which has made it necessary for every one of its elements to be turned into its opposite. The dream confirms once more what I had already told you before you dreamt it—that you are summoning up your old love for your father in order to protect yourself against your love for Herr K. But what do all these efforts show? Not only that you are afraid of Herr K., but that you are still more afraid of yourself, and of the temptation you feel to yield to him. In short, these efforts prove once more how deeply you loved him' [p. 70].

He immediately adds that "Naturally Dora would not follow me in this part of the interpretation," but this does not deter him for a moment from pressing on with further interpretations of the same order; and this entire transaction is in its character and quality prototypical for the case as a whole. The Freud we have here is not the sage of the Berggasse, not the master who delivered the incomparable *Introductory Lectures* (1916-1917), not the tragic Solomon of "Civilization and Its Discontents" (1930). This is an earlier Freud, the Freud of the Fliess letters, to certain passages of which I would now like to turn.

In May, 1895, Freud writes to Fliess to tell him why he has not been writing to him. Although he has been overburdened with work, patients, etc., he is aware that such excuses are in part pretexts.

> But the chief reason was this: a man like me cannot live without a hobby-horse, a consuming passion—in Schiller's words a tyrant. I have found my tyrant, *and in his service I know no limits*. My tyrant is psychology; it has always been my distant, beckoning goal and now, since I have hit on the neuroses, it has come so much the nearer [Freud, 1887-1902, Letter 24; italics mine].

Three weeks later he writes to Fliess to inform him that he has started smoking again after an abstinence of fourteen months "because I must treat that mind of mine decently, or the fellow will not work for me. I am demanding a great deal of him. Most of the time the burden is superhuman" (Letter 25). In March of the next year he tells Fliess that "I keep coming back to psychology; it is a compulsion from which I cannot escape" (Letter 43). A month later he communicates the following:

> When I was young, the only thing I longed for was philosophical knowledge, and now that I am going over from medicine to psychology I am in the process of attaining it. I have become a therapist against my will; I am convinced that, granted certain conditions in the person and the case, I can definitely cure hysteria and obsessional neurosis [Letter 44].[19]

[19] One might have thought that such a passage would have at least slowed the endless flow of nonsense about Freud's abstention from philosophical aspirations. To be sure, Freud is himself greatly responsible for the phenomenon. I am referring in part to the famous passage in "Inhibitions, Symptoms and Anxiety" (1926):

"I must confess that I am not at all partial to the fabrication of *Weltanschauungen*. Such activities may be left to philosophers, who avowedly find it impossible to make their journey through life without a Baedeker of that kind to give them information on every subject. Let us humbly accept the contempt with which they look down on us from the vantage-ground of their superior needs. But since *we* cannot forgo our narcissistic pride either, we will draw comfort from the reflection that such 'Handbooks to Life' soon grow out of date and that it is precisely our short-sighted, narrow and finicky work which obliges them to appear in new editions, and that even the most up-to-date of them are nothing but attempts to find a substitute for the ancient, useful and all-sufficient Church

And in May of 1897, he writes: "No matter what I start with, I always find myself back again with the neuroses and the psychical apparatus. It is not because of indifference to personal or other matters that I never write about anything else. Inside me is a seething ferment, and I am only waiting for the next surge forward" (Letter 62). This is the Freud of the case of Dora as well. It is Freud the relentless investigator pushing on no matter what. The Freud that we meet with here is a demonic Freud, a Freud who is the servant of his *daimon*. That *daimon* in whose service Freud knows no limits is the spirit of science, the truth, or "reality" —it doesn't matter which; for him they are all the same. Yet it must be emphasized that the "reality" Freud insists upon is very different from the "reality" that Dora is claiming and clinging to. And it has to be admitted that not only does Freud overlook for the most part this critical difference; he also adopts no measures for dealing with it. The demon of interpretation has taken hold of him, and it is this power that presides over the case of Dora.

In fact, as the case history advances, it becomes increasingly clear to the careful reader that Freud and not Dora has become the central character in the action, Freud the narrator does in the writing what Freud the first psychoanalyst appears to have done in actuality. We begin to sense that it is his story that is being written and not hers that is being retold. Instead of letting Dora appropriate her own story, Freud became the appropriator of it. The case history belongs progressively less to her than it does to him. It may be that this was an inevitable development, that it is one of the typical outcomes of an analysis that fails, that Dora was under any

Catechism. We know well enough how little light science has so far been able to throw on the problems that surround us. But however much ado the philosophers may make, they cannot alter the situation. Only patient, persevering research, in which everything is subordinated to the one requirement of certainty, can gradually bring about a change. The benighted traveller may sing aloud in the dark to deny his own fears; but, for all that, he will not see an inch further beyond his nose" (p. 96).

This is splendid and spirited writing; but I cannot resist suggesting that Freud is using philosophy here as a kind of stalking horse and that the earlier passage is in some senses closer to his enduring meaning. What Freud meant there by "philosophical knowledge" was knowledge or comprehension of the veritable nature of reality itself, and I do not believe he ever abandoned his belief in such knowledge. In any case, too much has been made—on both sides—of the "antagonism" between psychoanalysis and philosophy.

circumstances unable to become the appropriator of her own history, the teller of her own story. Blame does not necessarily or automatically attach to Freud. Nevertheless, by the time he gets to the second dream he is able to write: "I shall present the material produced during the analysis of this dream in the somewhat haphazard order in which it recurs to my mind" (p. 95). He makes such a presentation for several reasons, most of which are legitimate. But one reason almost certainly is that by this juncture it is his *own* mind that chiefly matters to him, and it is *his* associations to her dream that are of principal importance.

At the same time, as the account progresses, Freud has never been more inspired, more creative, more inventive; as the reader sees Dora gradually slipping further and further away from Freud, the power and complexity of the writing reach dizzying proportions. At times they pass over into something else. We have already noted that at certain moments Freud permits himself to say such things as: if only Dora had not left "we should no doubt have obtained the fullest possible enlightenment upon every particular of the case" (p. 12); or that there is in his mind "no doubt that my analytic method" can achieve "complete elucidation" of a neurosis (p. 24); or that "It is only because the analysis was prematurely broken off that we have been obliged ... to resort to framing conjectures and filling in deficiencies" (p. 85). Due allowance has always to be made for the absolutizing tendency of genius, especially when as in the case of Dora the genius is writing with the license of a poet and the ambiguity of a seer. But Freud goes quite beyond this. There are passages in the case of Dora which, if we were to find them, say, in a novel, would prompt us to conclude that either the narrator or the character who made such an utterance was suffering from *hubris;* in the context of psychoanalysis one supposes that the appropriate term would be *chutzpah.* For example, after elucidating the symbolism of the jewel-case and Dora's reticule, Freud goes on to write:

> There is a great deal of symbolism of this kind in life, but as a rule we pass it by without heeding it. When I set myself the task of bringing to light what human beings keep hidden within them, not by the compelling power of hypnosis, but by observing what they say and what they show, I thought the

task was a harder one than it really is. He that has eyes to see and ears to hear may convince himself that no mortal can keep a secret. If his lips are silent, he chatters with his finger-tips; betrayal oozes out of him at every pore. And thus the task of making conscious the most hidden recesses of the mind is one which it is quite possible to accomplish [pp. 77-78].

This, we are forced to recall, is from the Freud who more than anyone else in the history of Western civilization has taught us to be critically aware of fantasies of omniscience, and who on other occasions could be critical of such tendencies in himself. But not here where the demon of interpretation is riding him, riding him after Dora, whom it had ridden out. And it rides him still further, for he follows the passage I have just quoted with another that in point of mania quite surpasses it. Dora had complained for days on end of gastric pains. Freud quite plausibly connected these sensations with a series of other events and circumstances in her life that pointed to a repressed history of childhood masturbation. He then continues:

It is well known that gastric pains occur especially often in those who masturbate. According to a personal communication made to me by Wilhelm Fliess, it is precisely gastralgias of this character which can be interrupted by an application of cocaine to the 'gastric spot' discovered by him in the nose, and which can be cured by the cauterization of the same spot [p. 78].

At this juncture we have passed beyond interpretation and are in the positive presence of demented and delusional science. This passage was almost certainly written in 1901 as part of the first draft of the text; but it must remain a matter of puzzlement that neither in 1905, when he published the revised version, nor at any time thereafter did Freud think it necessary to amend or strike out those mythological observations.[20]

[20] It is pertinent to the present discussion to add that on at least one occasion in 1895 Freud directly addressed Fliess as "Demon" or "You Demon." (*"Daimonie warum schreibst Du nicht? Wie geht es Dir? Kümmerst Du Dich gar nicht mehr, was ich treibe?"*) Furthermore, the treatment described by Freud in the foregoing paragraph was administered by Fliess to Freud himself on several occasions during the 1890's. Throughout that decade Freud suffered at irregular intervals

Anyone who goes on like this—and as Freud has gone on with Dora—is, as they say, asking for it. *Chutzpah's* reward is poetic justice. When Dora reports her second dream, Freud spends two hours of inspired insight in elucidating some of its meanings. "At the end of the second session," he writes, "I expressed my satisfaction at the result" (p. 105). The satisfaction in question is in large measure self-satisfaction, for Dora responded to Freud's expression of it with the following words uttered in "a depreciatory tone: 'Why, has anything so very remarkable come out?' " That satisfaction was to be of short duration, for Dora opened the third session by telling Freud that this was the last time she would be there—it was December 31, 1900. Freud's remarks that "Her breaking off so unexpectedly, just when my hopes of a successful termination of the treatment were at their highest, and her thus bringing those hopes to nothing—this was an unmistakable act of vengeance on her part" (p. 109) are only partly warranted. There was, or should have been, nothing unexpected about Dora's decision to terminate; indeed, Freud himself on the occasion of the first dream had already detected such a decision on Dora's part and had communicated this finding to her. Moreover, his "highest" hopes for a successful outcome of the treatment seem almost entirely without foundation. The case, as he himself presents it,

---

from migraine headaches and colds. He applied cocaine locally (one supposes that he took a healthy sniff), permitted Fliess to perform a number of nasal cauterizations, and at one point seems to have undergone minor surgery of the turbinate bone in the nasal passage at Fliess's hands.

The pertinence of the displacement of Freud's relation to Fliess into the case of Dora becomes clearer if we recall that in this friendship—certainly the most important relation of its kind in his life—Freud was undergoing something very like a transference experience, without wholly understanding what was happening to him. In this connection, the case of Dora may also be regarded as part of the process by which Freud began to move toward a resolution of his relation with Fliess—and perhaps vice versa as well.

That relation is still not adequately understood, as the documents that record it have not been fully published. As matters stand at present, one has to put that relation together from three sources: (1) *The Origins of Psychoanalysis* (Freud, 1887-1902); this volume contains some of Freud's letters to Fliess, many of them in fragmentary or excerpted form, plus drafts and notes of various projects; (2) Jones's (1953, 1955, 1957) *The Life and Work of Sigmund Freud;* and (3) Schur's (1972) *Freud: Living and Dying.* The last work provides the fullest account yet available, but does not stand by itself and must be supplemented by material drawn from the other two sources.

provides virtually no evidence on which to base such hopes—Dora
stonewalled him from the beginning right up to the very end. In
such a context the hopes of success almost unavoidably become a
matter of self-reference and point to the immense *intellectual*
triumph that Freud was aware he was achieving with the material
adduced by his patient. On the matter of "vengeance," however,
Freud cannot be faulted; Dora was, among many other things,
certainly getting her own back on Freud by refusing to allow him
to bring her story to an end in the way he saw fit. And he in turn is
quite candid about the injury he felt she had caused him. "No one
who, like me," he writes, "conjures up the most evil of those half-
tamed demons that inhabit the human breast, and seeks to wrestle
with them, can expect to come through the struggle unscathed"
(p. 109).

This admission of vulnerability, which Freud artfully manages
to blend with the suggestion that he is a kind of modern combination of Jacob and Faust, is in keeping with the weirdness and
wildness of the case as a whole and with this last hour. That hour
recurs to the scene at the lake, two years before, and its aftermath.
And Freud ends this final hour with the following final interpretation. He reminds Dora that she was in love with Herr K.; that she
wanted him to divorce his wife; that even though she was quite
young at the time she wanted " 'to wait for him, and you took it
that he was only waiting till you were grown up enough to be his
wife. I imagine that this was a perfectly serious plan for the future
in your eyes' " (p. 108). But Freud does not say this in order to
contradict it or categorize it as a fantasy of the adolescent girl's
unconscious imagination. On the contrary, he has very different
ideas in view, for he goes on to tell her:

> 'You have not even got the right to assert that it was out of the
> question for Herr K. to have had any such intention; you have
> told me enough about him that points directly towards his
> having such an intention. Nor does his behaviour at L_____
> contradict this view. After all, you did not let him finish his
> speech and do not know what he meant to say to you' [p. 108].

He has not done with her yet, for he then goes on to bring in the
other relevant parties and offers her the following conclusion:

'Incidentally, the scheme would by no means have been so impracticable. Your father's relation with Frau K. . . . made it certain that her consent to a divorce could be obtained; and you can get anything you like out of your father. Indeed, if your temptation at L_____ had had a different upshot, this would have been *the only possible solution for all the parties concerned*' [p. 108; italics mine].

No one—at least no one in recent years—has accused Freud of being a swinger, but this is without question a swinging solution that is being offered. It is of course possible that he feels free to make such a proposal only because he knows that nothing in the way of action can come of it; but with him you never can tell—as I hope I have already demonstrated. One has only to imagine what in point of ego strength, balance, and self-acceptance would have been required of Dora *alone* in this arrangement of wife-and-daughter-swapping to recognize at once its extreme irresponsibility, to say the least.[21] At the same time we must bear in mind that such a suggestion is not incongruent with the recently revealed circumstance that Freud analyzed his own daughter. Genius makes up its own rules as it goes along—and breaks them as well. This "only possible solution" was one of the endings that Freud wanted to write to Dora's story; he had others in mind besides, but none of them were to come about. Dora refused or was unable to let him do this; she refused to be a character in the story that Freud was composing for her, and wanted to finish it herself. As we now know, the ending she wrote was a very bad one indeed.[22]

[21] Fifteen years later, when Freud came to write about Ibsen, the character and situation that he chose to analyze revealed the closest pertinence to the case of Dora. In "Some Character-Types Met with in Psycho-Analytic Work" he devotes a number of pages to a discussion of Rebecca West in *Rosmersholm*. Rebecca, the new, liberated woman, is one of those character types who are "wrecked by success." The success she is wrecked by is the fulfillment—partly real, partly symbolic—in mature life of her Oedipal fantasies, the precise fulfillment that Freud, fifteen years earlier, had been capable of regarding as the "only solution" for Dora, as well as everyone else involved in the case (see 1916, pp. 324-331).

[22] For what happened to Dora in later life, see Deutsch (1957). The story is extremely gruesome. For some further very useful remarks, see Erikson (1964, pp. 166-174).

VI

Let us move rapidly to a conclusion long overdue. In this extraordinary work Freud and Dora often appear as unconscious, parodic refractions of each other. Both of them insist with implacable will upon the primacy of "reality," although the realities each has in mind differ radically. Both of them use reality, "the truth," as a weapon. Freud does so by forcing interpretations upon Dora before she is ready for them or can accept them. And this aggressive truth bounds back upon the teller, for Dora leaves him. Dora in turn uses her version of reality—it is "outer" reality that she insists upon—aggressively as well. She has used it from the outset against her father, and five months after she left Freud she had the opportunity to use it against the K.'s. In May of 1901 one of the K.'s children died. Dora took the occasion to pay them a visit of condolence—

> ... and they received her as though nothing had happened in the last three years. She made it up with them, she took her revenge on them, and she brought her own business to a satisfactory conclusion. To the wife she said: 'I know you have an affair with my father'; and the other did not deny it. From the husband she drew an admission of the scene by the lake which he had disputed, and brought the news of her vindication home to her father. Since then she had not resumed her relations with the family [p. 121].

She told this to Freud fifteen months after she had departed, when she returned one last time to visit him—to ask him, without sincerity, for further help, and "to finish her story" (p. 120). She finished her story, and as for the rest, Freud remarks, "I do not know what kind of help she wanted from me, but I promised to forgive her for having deprived me of the satisfaction of affording her a far more radical cure for her troubles" (p. 122).

But the matter is not hopelessly obscure, as Freud himself has already confessed. What went wrong with the case, "Its great defect, which led to its being broken off prematurely," was something that had to do with the transference; and Freud writes that "I did not succeed in mastering the transference in good time" (p. 118). He was in fact just beginning to learn about this therapeutic phenomenon, and the present passage is the first really important one about it to have been written. It is also in the nature of things heavily occluded. Instead of trying to analyze at what would be tedious length its murky reaches, let me state summarily my sense of things. On Dora's side the transference went wrong in several senses. In the first place, there was the failure on her part to establish an adequate positive transference to Freud. She was not free enough to respond to him erotically—in fantasy—or intellectually—by accepting his interpretations: both or either of these being prerequisites for the mysterious "talking cure" to begin to work. And in the second, halfway through the case a negative transference began to emerge, quite clearly in the first dream. Freud writes that he "was deaf to this first note of warning," and as a result this negative "transference took me unawares, and, because of the unknown quantity in me which reminded Dora of Herr K., she took her revenge on me as she wanted to take her revenge on him, and deserted me as she believed herself to have been deceived and deserted by him" (p. 119). This is, I believe, the first mention in print of the conception that is known as "acting out"—out of which, one may incidentally observe, considerable fortunes have been made.

We are, however, in a position to say something more than this. For there is a reciprocating process in the analyst known as the countertransference, and in the case of Dora this went wrong too. Although Freud describes Dora at the beginning of the account as being "in the first bloom of youth—a girl of intelligent and engaging looks" (p. 23), almost nothing attractive about her comes forth in the course of the writing. As it unwinds, and it becomes increasingly evident that Dora is not responding adequately to Freud, it also becomes clear that Freud is not responding favorably to this response, and that he doesn't in fact like Dora very much.[23] He doesn't like her negative sexuality, her inability to surrender to her own erotic impulses. He doesn't like her "really remarkable achievements in the direction of intolerable behavior" (p. 75). He

---

[23] Dora seems indeed to have been an unlikable person. Her death, which was caused by cancer of the colon, diagnosed too late for an operation, "seemed a blessing to those who were close to her" (Deutsch, 1957, p. 167). And Deutsch's informant went on to describe her as " 'one of the most repulsive hysterics' he had ever met."

doesn't like her endless reproachfulness. Above all, he doesn't like her inability to surrender herself to him. For what Freud was as yet unprepared to face was not merely the transference, but the countertransference as well—in the case of Dora it was largely a negative countertransference—an unanalyzed part of himself.[24] I should like to suggest that this cluster of unanalyzed impulses and ambivalences was in part responsible for Freud's writing of this great text immediately after Dora left him. It was his way—and one way—of dealing with, mastering, expressing, and neutralizing such material. Yet the neutralization was not complete; or we can put the matter in another way and state that Freud's creative honesty was such that it compelled him to write the case of Dora as

[24] That the countertransference was not entirely negative is suggested in tu. very name that Freud chose to give to his patient in writing this case history. In *The Psychopathology of Everyday Life*, Freud tries to explain how this "one name . . . was determined." He unconsciously took it, he says, from his "sister's nursemaid," whose real name was Rosa, but who, Freud had only recently learned, was called Dora because his "sister could take the name 'Rosa' as applying to herself as well." Freud felt pity for such " 'poor people' " who " 'cannot even keep their own names,' " and the next day, he states, when he was "looking for a name for someone *who could not keep her own*, 'Dora' was the only one to occur to me." He connects this circumstance as well with an unspecified one of the two governesses in the case of Dora, another "person employed in someone else's house" (1901, p. 241).

There is no reason to doubt this interpretation. It is, however, in my opinion, incomplete. For the names Dora and Rosa occur in close juxtaposition in another context that was important for Freud. That context is Freud's favorite novel by Dickens, *David Copperfield*. Like David, Freud was born with or in a caul—an augury of a singular destiny. On at least one occasion, Freud described his father as a Micawber-like figure. The first book he sent as a gift to Martha Bernays shortly after they had met was a copy of *David Copperfield*.

Dora, of course, was David Copperfield's first love and first wife. She is at once a duplication of David's dead mother and an incompetent and helpless creature, who asks David to call her his "child-wife." She is also doomed not to survive, and Dickens kills her off so David can go on to realize himself in a fuller way. The Rosa in *David Copperfield* is another representation of thwarted and deformed female sexuality. Rosa Dartle, who is also "employed in someone else's house," is one of Dora's completing counterparts, as she has been as well the object of some kind of obscure sexual molestation at the hands of Steerforth, with whose mother she continues to live and suffer.

One could go on indefinitely with such analogies, but the point should be sufficiently clear: in the very name he chose, Freud was in a manner true to his method, theory, and mind, expressing the overdeterminations and ambivalences that are so richly characteristic of this work as a whole.

For other relevant biographical material, see Jones (1953, pp. 2, 4, 104, 174).

he did, and that his writing has allowed us to make out in this remarkable "Fragment" a still fuller picture. As I have said before, this fragment of Freud's is more complete and coherent than the fullest case studies of anyone else. Freud's case histories are a new form of literature—they are creative narratives that include their own analysis and interpretation. Nevertheless, like the living works of literature that they are, the material they contain is always richer than the original analysis and interpretation that accompany it; and this means that future generations will recur to these works and will find in them a language they are seeking and a story they need to be told.

REFERENCES

Breuer, J., & Freud, S. (1893-1895), Studies on Hysteria. *Standard Edition*, 2. London: Hogarth Press, 1955.

Coleridge, S. T. (1817), *Biographia Literaria*, 2 vols., ed. J. Shawcross. New York and London: Oxford University Press, 1907.

Deutsch, F. (1957), A Footnote to Freud's "Fragment of an Analysis of a Case of Hysteria." *Psychoanal. Quart.*, 26:159-167.

Erikson, E. H. (1964), Psychological Reality and Historical Actuality. *Insight and Responsibility*. New York: Norton, pp. 159-215.

Freud, S. (1887-1902), *The Origins of Psychoanalysis: Letters to Wilhelm Fliess, Drafts and Notes, 1887-1902*. New York: Basic Books, 1954.

―――― (1900), The Interpretation of Dreams. *Standard Edition*, 4 & 5. London: Hogarth Press, 1953.

―――― (1901), The Psychopathology of Everyday Life. *Standard Edition*, 6. London: Hogarth Press, 1960.

―――― (1905a), Fragment of an Analysis of a Case of Hysteria. *Standard Edition*, 7:3-122. London: Hogarth Press, 1953.

―――― (1905b), Three Essays on the Theory of Sexuality. *Standard Edition*, 7:125-243. London: Hogarth Press, 1953.

―――― (1914), On the History of the Psycho-Analytic Movement. *Standard Edition*, 14:7-66. London: Hogarth Press, 1957.

―――― (1916), Some Character-Types Met with in Psycho-Analytic Work. II. Those Wrecked by Success. *Standard Edition*, 14:316-331. London: Hogarth Press, 1957.

―――― (1916-1917), Introductory Lectures on Psycho-Analysis. *Standard Edition*, 15 & 16. London: Hogarth Press, 1963.

―――― (1926), Inhibition, Symptoms and Anxiety. *Standard Edition*, 20:75-172. London: Hogarth Press, 1959.

―――― (1930), Civilization and Its Discontents. *Standard Edition*, 21:57-145. London: Hogarth Press, 1961.

Gagnon, J. H., & Simon, W. (1973), *Sexual Conduct: The Social Sources of Human Sexuality*. Chicago: Aldine.

Glover, E. (1960), *The Roots of Crime*. New York: International Universities Press.

Barnaby B. Barratt, Ph.D.

Freud's Psychology as Interpretation

Freud's psychology is proving remarkably difficult to relegate to history. For Freud's proponents, his theories still represent the *opus magnum* of the social sciences; for the anti-Freudians, they present a recurrent challenge. Despite the rapid expansion of psychology, Freudianism retains a provocative allure partly because, being little understood and much maligned, it has never been properly assimilated into the main body of the discipline. To a certain extent, that is because the majority of mainstream psychologists fail to comprehend the metaphorical level on which psychoanalytic concepts are articulated. Moreover, they misconstrue the object and the intentions of the psychoanalytic endeavor. Despite an immense critical and explicatory literature, Freud's psychology is continually being reread and re-evaluated. Its epistemological status is still a matter for debate and its fundamentals are still open to reinterpretation. Although it may be virtually unattainable, a definitive assessment of Freudianism might augur its obsolescence. What is the mode of discourse appropriate for such an assessment, and within what epistemological and philosophical framework does Freud's psychology reach its apotheosis?

The protracted and wearisome debate over Freud within the English-speaking world has largely concerned the scientific status of psychoanalysis (see, for example, Pumpian-Mindlin, 1952; Hook, 1959). The sterility of this debate is self-evident: argument over whether Freud's psychology is pretheoretical science, pseudo-

I would like to thank Dr. Margaret A. Boden of the University of Sussex and Dr. Peter H. Wolff of Harvard University for their comments on earlier drafts of this paper.

science, or mysticism has little advanced us toward that mature and balanced appreciation which characterizes historical perspective and transcendence. Freudianism is not a positivist or empiricist doctrine; the criticisms of Nagel (1959), Farrell (1961), and others are unanswerable on their own grounds, and it has to be conceded that Freud's theories are not scientific statements in this particular sense (see Popper, 1957, 1963). However, this concession has no necessary implications for the truth of Freud's propositions and it does not diminish their value, impact, and heuristic relevance. Despite the systematizing work of Freudians such as Rapaport (1959), the controversial problem of the epistemological status of Freud's psychology has not been resolved. Freudianism involves a mixed mode of discourse, and there is a tension between its causal explanations and its interpretations. Historically, this epistemological mixture has animated the psychoanalytic movement. What is needed, therefore, is a careful examination of the way in which certain epistemologies, familiar and unfamiliar, are represented within the Freudian stock. This does not so much involve an investigation of the genealogy of Freud's ideas as an informed and dialectically critical rereading of his work.

With a few notable exceptions, it cannot be said that the debate about psychoanalysis within the Anglo-American social sciences has contributed to this task: indeed, much of this debate has served to obfuscate rather than illuminate these issues. However, a number of writers have noted the creative tensions within Freud's work: these include the tensions between general and clinical theories (Rapaport, 1959), between explanation and "mere description" (Rubinstein, 1967), between science and "intuitive existentialism" (Yankelovich and Barrett, 1970), between mechanistic and humanistic images (Holt, 1972), between metapsychology and clinical theory (Klein, 1973), and, as I shall elaborate, between causal explanation and interpretation. Despite these insights, the Anglo-American debate about Freud's status as a scientist and about the testability of his propositions has taken place almost entirely within the framework of logical empiricism.[1] Few thinkers have seriously

[1] I follow Radnitzky's (1968a) use of the term *logical empiricism* to cover a number of Anglo-Saxon schools of metascience. Radnitzky uses this term as roughly equivalent to the German generic label *analytische Wissenschaftstheorie*; it covers "analytic" philosophies such as Popperianism, ordinary-language philos-

questioned whether this particular metascientific framework is appropriate. Preceded by Tauber and Green (1959), Szasz (1962), and a few others, Rycroft has tentatively argued that Freud's procedure was "not the scientific one of elucidating causes *but* the semantic one of making sense" (1966, p. 14, my emphasis). This argument implies that "making sense" is not a scientific endeavor as such and thus relegates to a nonscientific position many social scientists, including psychologists from von Uexküll to Laing. I am going to bypass the thorny problem of defining "science" because I believe that Rycroft was onto something more fundamental than terminology: namely, that Freud's psychology might be considered not only as if a natural science within the discourse of logical empiricism but as a hermeneutic-dialectical discipline within a Continental metascientific framework.[2]

In *Freud and Philosophy: An Essay on Interpretation* (1970), Paul Ricoeur invites us to forgo evaluation of Freud's psychology as a natural science and to consider it as a hermeneutic system; he elaborates various aspects of this thesis in a subsequent anthology entitled *The Conflict of Interpretations* (1974). Ricoeur views Freudianism as a set of rules for the interpretation of the words and symbols that constitute human existence; thus Freud created "a mediating *science of meaning* which is irreducible to the immediate *consciousness of meaning*" (Ricoeur, 1974, p. 149). This perspective on Freudianism is inherent in certain traditions of European think-

---

ophy, formalism, and even pragmatism. The common feature of this group is that all accept some principle of empiricism, and thus are closely allied to the methodological framework of the natural sciences.

[2] I follow Radnitzky's (1968b) use of the term *hermeneutic-dialectical* to cover a number of Contintental schools of metascience, including the traditions of phenomenology, existentialism, critical theory, philology, and, as Ricoeur argues, Freudianism. Hermeneutic-dialectical disciplines are perhaps confined to the study of humans and of society. Radnitzky's essential distinction, which I think is valuable, is between the logical-empiricist and the hermeneutic-dialectical approaches to the study of human phenomena. Although Radnitzky's work must be read for a proper understanding of this distinction, he partially encapsulates it in this passage: "... the genealogy of problems dealt with by logical-empiricism goes towards increasing the precision and clarity of the problems and to a lesser extent of problem solutions. The genealogy of the problems dealt with by the hermeneutic-dialectical tradition goes towards increasing emancipation and transparence: the self-awareness of human agents that helps them to emancipate themselves from the hypostatized forces of society and history ..." (1968b, p. 3). See footnote 1.

ing; Radnitzky, for example, in his commentary upon Habermas's work, argues that "what Freud *de facto* did was to produce a shift in the tradition of psychology by introducing a way of studying phenomena which is *primarily* hermeneutic" (1968b, p. 55).[3] Ricoeur's own intellectual background derives from Husserlian phenomenology with the particular French influences of Marcel and Merleau-Ponty, and from a remarkably extensive knowledge covering Wittgenstein's work, English linguistic philosophy, the epistemological tradition of Hegel and Heidegger, and various schools of philology and Biblical exegesis. As Ihde (1971) has described, Ricoeur's own investigations have developed from an eidetic or structural phenomenology concerned with the problems of consciousness and human will (Ricoeur, 1965, 1966) toward a hermeneutic phenomenology concerned with symbols, myths, and the problems of religious faith (Ricoeur, 1967, 1970, 1974). Throughout his work, Ricoeur expresses a deep respect for the "mysteries" of human existence. His wish is to contribute to a grand philosophy of language by conjoining psychoanalysis and various phenomenologies. This philosophy is ultimately directed toward a "reconciled ontology"; it is an ontotheological design which will, supposedly, reconstitute our faith in the "sacred." Ricoeur's philosophical and religious aspirations are a distant and, in my judgment, misguided ambition; his interest in Freudianism, however, is relevant here and now. Although one may disagree profoundly with Ricoeur's inclinations, his work on psychoanalysis, which includes both a reading of Freud and a philosophical thesis, is of considerable importance. Ricoeur places himself in the company of intellectuals such as Dalbiez (1936), Flugel (1945), Marcuse (1955), and Rieff (1959) in that he introduces a new and stimulating per-

[3] As this essay proceeds, it will become evident to some readers that my own thinking about the epistemology of Freud's psychology and about Ricoeur's work has been influenced by my reading of certain of the critical theorists of the Frankfurt School. For example, this is apparent, later in the essay, in my references to the relationship between epistemology and human interests, and to the grounding of psychoanalytic knowledge on a commitment to human liberation. Although this essay focuses on the problems of interpretation and presents a critique of Ricoeur's position, I do point to the possibility of a rather different epistemological formulation, in the direction of the view of psychoanalysis as a form of critical theory. Within the scope of this essay, I could neither elaborate this view nor discuss its implications; I intend to devote a subsequent essay to this task.

spective on Freudianism. His reading of Freud is a brilliant and self-sufficient work which richly rewards intensive study. In this paper, I would like to outline and evaluate what I perceive as the main directions of Ricoeur's philosophical thesis, following its three successive stages. These he refers to as the "epistemological," "reflective," and "dialectical" moments (1970, p. 473).[4] They involve, respectively, an examination of the epistemological status of Freudian psychology, the positioning of Freud's work within a tradition of reflective thinking, and an attempt to reconstitute Freudianism as a cornerstone of an affirmative and eschatological philosophy. I intend to present Ricoeur's ideas in a highly condensed form, and I shall argue that although those of us concerned with psychoanalytic epistemology can learn much from Ricoeur, we must refuse the ontotheological route which he takes in the last moment of his thesis.

Ricoeur views Freud's psychology as a hermeneutic system directed toward the double meanings, the symbolism, of human existence. Hermeneutics concerns "the rules that preside over an exegesis, that is, over the interpretation of a particular text, or of a group of signs that may be viewed as a text" (p. 8). This interpretation is "a work of understanding that aims at deciphering symbols" (p. 9). What are the symbols with which Freud is concerned? Freud understands human existence as comprising a number of different modalities of communication in which desire is expressed. Ideally, these modalities are congruent: speech complementing action and nonverbal expression, for example. However, their integration may be imperfect: actions and expressions may contradict verbal output, and so forth. Dreams, parapraxes, and neurotic symptoms are indicative of such discrepancies (see Freud, 1900, 1901, 1917). Human self-understanding is limited to the intentional aspects of language, and so persons both express and misunderstand themselves in these discrepancies. The central theme of Freud's psychology is that of the split-off personality in which the "language" of the unconscious is alienated from the structure of conscious intentions. Symbols both mediate this alienation and reflect it in their plurivocality. Interpretation is essential because of

---

[4] Hereafter, unless otherwise indicated, all page numbers identifying quotations refer to Ricoeur's *Freud and Philosophy* (1970).

the complexity of the intentional structure of human symbols whereby "a direct, primary, literal meaning designates, in addition, another meaning which is indirect, secondary, and figurative and which can be apprehended only through the first" (Ricoeur, 1974, pp. 12-13). Ricoeur characterizes the intrasymbolic relationship between meanings as that of analogy, thus linking the semantic duality of the symbol with "the analogy of the physical and the existential" (p. 17). By means of decoding or deciphering, Freudian psychology explicates the semantic structure of plurivocal symbols; this work of elucidation involves interpretation along the lines of Biblical exegesis or literary criticism. Its purpose is to retrieve alienated and subjectively incomprehensible communications to consciousness, thus reintegrating the discrepant categories of the split-off personality (see Freud, 1917, 1940).

Freud's interpretative psychology employs a hermeneutic model resembling that of certain philological methods (see Freud, 1940). He explicitly compared interpretation in psychoanalysis to a work of translation and to scriptural explanation (Freud, 1900, 1913, 1923). In this respect Freud was not an innovator: Ellenberger (1970) has traced his debt to the literature of "unmasking" and to its exponents such as Maury and Delaye, as well as to the oneirologists such as Scherner and Hervey de Saint-Denis. Freud's originality lies in his distinction between manifest and latent content and in his use of free association in the application of systematic interpretation to therapy. He extended the concept of a text to include any set of signs that might be understood as such. There are, of course, several important distinctions between Freudian analysis and philological investigation. Orthodox hermeneutics aims at the comprehension of human symbols in general, whereas psychoanalysis aims at the understanding of alienated and idiomatic personal communications. Psychoanalytic interpretation is essentially part of a reflective process undertaken in an intersubjective context, whereas orthodox hermeneutics involves propositions about an external realm of objects. Further, whereas traditional philology takes the intentional structure of consciousness as its basis and regards textual distortions as impediments, Freud gave the inadequacies of the apparent text a central inferential role in that he regarded distortions and omissions as expressions of intention. Freudian interpretation is applied to symbolic fragments, the meaning of which is opaque to consciousness, and thus Freud, by investigating the realm of personal meaning *beyond* consciousness, challenges the Cartesian tradition of the *cogito*.

Ricoeur regrets that "there is no general hermeneutics, no universal canon for exegesis, but only disparate and opposed theories concerning the rules of interpretation" (pp. 26-27). Polarizing this opposition for the sake of clarity, he suggests that "according to the one pole, hermeneutics is understood as the manifestation and restoration of a meaning . . . a proclamation, . . . according to the other pole, it is understood as a demystification, as a reduction of illusion. Psychoanalysis at least on a first reading, aligns itself with the second understanding of hermeneutics" (p. 27). Initially, Freudianism does not explicate phenomena so much as challenge the illusions which are endemic to the consciousness of a split-off personality. This demystification demands a suspicious mode of thought: Freud takes his place as one of the triumvirate of the school of suspicion. He shares with Marx and Nietzsche a decision "to look upon the whole of consciousness primarily as 'false' consciousness" (p. 33) and a "general hypothesis concerning both the process of false consciousness and the method of deciphering" (p. 34) for which it calls. Moreover, they each adopt an implicit conception of authenticity as the goal of demystification. For Freud, the reduction of illusions is propaedeutic to the reappropriation of meaning, the attainment of true discourse, which involves the proclamative style of interpretation; ". . . what Freud desires is that the one who is analyzed, by making his own the meaning that was foreign to him, enlarge his field of consciousness, live better, and finally a little freer" (p. 35). Ricoeur sees within Freudianism an immanent reconciliation between the two styles of hermeneutics, and he argues that Freud's psychology should be understood as a mode of dialectical reflection that is intimately related to the interpretation of human symbols within the context of an intersubjective debate through which the subject retrieves personal meaning.

How do the substantive aspects of Freud's psychology—the first topography, the structures of the second topography, and the energy economics—fit into the hermeneutic perspective on Freudianism? Ricoeur insists that we recognize the primacy of the hermeneutic over the objectivistic in Freud's psychology. He would argue that the topographies—the partitioning of psychical phenomena into unconscious, preconscious, and conscious, and into id, ego, and superego—constitute characteristics of the intersubjective psychoanalytic debate, and presumably also of Freud's own self-analysis, rendered as a model of the mental apparatus. Thus the topographies must be understood in terms of this debate rather than the other way around. Ricoeur does not make the foolish claim that Freudian metapsychology is historically derived from psychoanalytic experience; rather, it is suggested that even though these models may, in certain respects, have been brought to the psychoanalytic situation, this situation remains epistemologically prior. Freud's desire to transpose hermeneutic insights into an objectivistic framework is readily understandable, given his personal training and given that he belonged to the intellectual era which gave birth to the Vienna Circle, and to a milieu in which the natural sciences were revered as the sole discipline of knowledge and as constituting a world view which excluded all others. Ellenberger (1970) has demonstrated Freud's debt to philosophers of the unconscious such as Carus, von Hartmann, Schopenhauer, and Nietzsche, as well as his debt to Helmholtzian psychology, to Meynert's brain mythology, to Exner's neurophysiology, and to Brücke's misguided ideas about energetics. The predominant *Zeitgeist* partially diverted Freud from his revolutionary contribution in hermeneutic reflection toward Machian positivism.

Freud's unfinished "Project for a Scientific Psychology" (1895) constitutes his manifesto for a biomechanistic model of the human psyche. Although Freud eventually destroyed all his personal copies of the "Project," the physicalism of the energy economics was never entirely eliminated from his work. It poses a particular problem for theorists who wish to regard Freudianism purely as a theory of communication, reflection, and interpretation. Ricoeur formulates this problem aptly when he writes:

> ... as I see it, the whole problem of Freudian epistemology may be centralized in a single question—how can the economic explanation be *involved* in an interpretation dealing with meanings; and conversely, how can an interpretation be an *aspect* of the economic explanation? It is easier to fall back on a disjunction: either an explanation in terms of energy, or an

understanding in terms of phenomenology. It must be recognized, however, that Freudianism exists only on the basis of its refusal of that disjunction [p. 66].

Thus Ricoeur neatly encapsulates the major difficulty involved in regarding Freud's psychology as a hermeneutic system. Before moving to an examination of the way in which he tries to resolve this difficulty—that is, to a discussion of the way in which Ricoeur views Freudianism neither as a natural science nor as a phenomenology—I would like to comment upon his attitude toward the energetics and hermeneutics of Freud's theory.

Unlike many of those who have reinterpreted Freudianism, Ricoeur sees the energy-economy model as an indispensable part of psychoanalytic theory. In this respect, he disputes Jacques Lacan's rereading of Freud, which has had a seminal influence upon contemporary psychoanalytic theory in France (see Lacan, 1966; Wilden, 1968, 1972; Bär, 1974). Lacan defines the unconscious as the "discourse of the Other" and describes it as "structured like a language"; influenced by Jakobson and Lévi-Strauss, Lacan insists that we approach Freud's work as a theory of language in which the primary process is regarded not as a "free flow of energy" but as a "free flow of meaning," and in which condensation and displacement are understood in terms of the relations of "metaphor" and "metonymy" respectively. In Lacan's rereading of Freud, the energetics are displaced by linguistics. Ricoeur, however, argues that the linguistic conception of the unconscious "only makes sense in conjunction with the economic concepts of Freudian theory; instead of replacing the Freudian topographic and economic points of view, it parallels that point of view in every respect" (pp. 395-396). Taking off from a critique of Laplanche and Leclaire's (1961) work on Lacan's theory of metaphoric relations and the unconscious, Ricoeur demonstrates the failure of this theory to account adequately for the processes of repression which divide the unconscious from the conscious. The energy model, Ricoeur argues, is necessary to Freudianism, for "the only thing that guarantees the separation of the systems is the economic explanation" (p. 403). Thus "the function of the energy metaphors is to account for the disjunction between meaning and meaning" (p. 394), and energy has its place at "the intersection of desire and language" (p. 395).

Ricoeur concludes that Lacan's "interpretation of repression as metaphor shows that the unconscious is related to the conscious as a particular kind of discourse to ordinary discourse; but the economic explanation is what accounts for the separation of the two discourses" (p. 403).

Thus we arrive at a profound problem in Ricoeur's reading of Freud. Ricoeur points to a major difficulty in Lacan's totalization of the linguistic approach to Freudianism. His solution to this difficulty is to assert "the irreducibility of the economic to the linguistic point of view" (p. 402), arguing that: "the linguistic interpretation does not constitute an alternative to the economic explanation" (p. 396) but should parallel it. Yet Ricoeur insists that "the economics are accessible only in their relation to hermeneutics," and indeed that relations of energy can only be understood as relations of meaning, there being "no economic process to which there cannot be found a corresponding linguistic aspect" (p. 403). Thus, to defend his thesis that Freudianism is primarily a hermeneutic system, Ricoeur (pp. 63-114) seeks to demonstrate that there is a correlation between energetics and hermeneutics within Freud's psychology insofar as the connection between forces can be linked to experienced relations between meanings.

Ricoeur's solution to the difficulty of Lacanian theory is less than satisfactory. For every analyst knows that, if taken literally, Freud's ideas about the hydraulics of psychical processes are indefensible. Contemporary neurobiology, physiology, and psychiatry have irrevocably discredited these notions. Ricoeur acknowledges, with Freud, that the energy economics are part of psychoanalytic "mythology," and argues that "it may be that the entire matter must be redone, possibly with the help of energy schemata quite different from Freud's" (p. 395). This acknowledgment, however, is not a solution. Although he promotes a hermeneutic approach to Freudianism, Ricoeur correctly pinpoints a defect in Lacan's attempt to understand Freud's psychology as a theory of language; for he recognizes that "the symbolism of the unconscious is not *stricto sensu* a linguistic phenomenon" (p. 399). Thus Ricoeur finds it necessary to retain, in some unspecified yet nonliteral sense, Freudian energetics even though he is aware that this retention poses an epistemological problem (see p. 395). In my judgment, this is as untidy as it is unconvincing; it is no more than a rather feeble attempt to circumvent a major difficulty. Wilden (1968, 1972) has suggested an alternative means by which Lacanian theory might be corrected; he criticizes the French overextension and misuse of the concept of "language," and argues that a communicational-systemic approach is more appropriate since it can properly account for relations between information and energy. This approach seems to have much to offer, and it is to be regretted that it has not been further explored by those theorists who are advocating a fresh rereading of the Freudian texts.

Ricoeur views psychoanalysis as a "unique and irreducible form of praxis" (p. 418). He makes a careful distinction between Freud's psychology and the homologous system of Husserlian phenomenology, and between Freudianism and the disciplines of the natural sciences.

Freud's psychology is not phenomenological, even though "no reflective philosophy has come as close to the Freudian unconscious as the phenomenology of Husserl and certain of his followers, especially Merleau-Ponty and De Waelhens" (p. 376). Four related areas—method, theme, theory of language, and intersubjectivity— cover the convergences and divergences between psychoanalysis and phenomenology.

The phenomenological method of "reduction" shares some features of psychoanalytic technique insofar as it involves "the dispossession of immediate consciousness as origin and place of meaning" (p. 376). However, Freud's "archeological" method of interpretation by which unconscious purposes are rendered accessible has no counterpart in phenomenology. As Ricoeur puts it, "the suspicion analysis professes about the illusions of consciousness is different from the suspension of the natural attitude. If phenomenology is a modification of the Cartesian doubt about existence, psychoanalysis is a modification of the Spinozist critique of free will" (pp. 390-391). The theme of intentionality might also seem to link phenomenology and psychoanalysis. Quoting Vergote, Ricoeur points out that Freud and Husserl, the heirs of Brentano, both define the psychical not in terms of consciousness but in terms of meaning, psychical meaning being dynamic and historical. Husserl writes about the "passive genesis" of meaning and posits a perceptual model of unconscious processes as the center of intentions, that is, as a source of meaning. This conception resembles Freudian theory; yet, as Ricoeur shows, Husserl, lacking the archeological technique of psychoanalysis, could not go as far as Freud in theorizing about the unconscious. Thus the Freudian "semantics of desire is the concrete realization of that which Husserl glimpsed under the old title of association, but of whose intentional significance he was perfectly aware; in short, phenomenology talks about passive genesis, the meaning that comes about apart from me, but psychoanalysis concretely shows it" (pp. 381-382). Hence "the unconscious of phenomenology is the preconscious of psychoanalysis, that is to say, an unconscious that is descriptive and not yet topographic" (p. 392).

For both phenomenology and psychoanalysis the reality of language is the meaning of behavior; both investigate the intentional structure of verbal and nonverbal acts. However, Ricoeur argues that here too there is a divergence, since phenomenology employs a more limited conception of language than does Freudianism. Perhaps most important, psychoanalysis and phenomenology share an emphasis on intersubjectivity, both in a theoretical and a technical sense. They both propose that "*all* our relationships with the world have an intersubjective dimension" (p. 386). Ricoeur argues that Freud's models are, in certain essential respects, grounded in intersubjectivity. For example, "the whole dialectic of roles within the second topography expresses the internalization of a relation of opposition" (p. 387) which is set up in the intersubjective field; further, "the discourse of the unconscious becomes meaningful only in the interlocutory discourse of analysis" (p. 388). Ricoeur argues that "the theme of intersubjectivity is undoubtedly where phenomenology and psychoanalysis come closest to being identified with each other, but also where they are seen to be most radically distinct" (p. 406). This distinction lies in the fact that phenomenology has no equivalent to the work of psychoanalysis, that is, to the processes of resistance, transference, and repetition which are the mainstays of Freudian technique.

For Ricoeur, Freud's psychology is approximated by phenomenology but goes beyond it. Psychoanalysis cannot, therefore, seek epistemological legitimacy by reformulating itself to become a species of phenomenology. If Freud's hermeneutic theory cannot turn to phenomenology, should it be judged within the epistemological framework of the natural sciences? Ricoeur's explicit and much emphasized answer is that Freud's interpretative psychology, because its work is with human meanings, is wholly incommensurable with natural science. Indeed, Ricoeur applauds the work of theorists such as Skinner (1956), Nagel (1959), and Scriven (1959), who variously criticize Freudianism as a scientific position, and states his belief that "psychoanalysis is not a science of observation; it is an interpretation, more comparable to history than psychology" (p. 345). Elsewhere he asserts that:

> ... psychoanalysis does not satisfy the standards of the sciences of observation, and the "facts" it deals with are not verifiable by multiple independent observers. The "laws" it formulates cannot be converted into relationships of variables ... Properly speaking, there are no "facts" in psychoanalysis in the sense that experimental science understands "facts." This is why its theory is not a theory in the same way that the theory of gases in physics and the theory of genes in biology are [1974, p. 186].

Although expressing some sympathy with their aims, Ricoeur rejects all attempts to reformulate psychoanalytic insights into the categorical framework of logical empiricism: the behaviorist transmogrifications, the functionalism of ego psychology, and the operational reconversions by theorists both inside and outside the psychoanalytic movement (e.g., Kubie, 1952; Ellis, 1956; Madison, 1961). He argues that "this assimilation of psychoanalysis to observational science does not satisfy the psychologist and does not respect the peculiar constitution of psychoanalysis" (p. 352).

Why is Ricoeur adamant that Freud's psychology, considered as a hermeneutic system, is incompatible with natural science? Ricoeur argues that Freudianism deliberately and systematically cultivates the ambiguous in that it places plurivocal symbols at the center of a reflective process: "... symbols, by reason of their analogical texture, are opaque, non-transparent ... in epistemological terms, their opacity can only mean equivocity" (p. 41). Psychoanalysis is concerned with a personal and unique structure of double meanings which is not translatable into the terminology of multiple causation. Freudianism, because it is concerned with the relations between meanings, does not employ the discourse of physical causation but the discourse of allegory, metaphor, analogy, and so forth. The structure and content of personal meaning are contextually bound and, in certain respects, privatized; comprehension of them is tied to processes of reflection and self-formation. Although there may be similarities between cases, psychoanalysis can offer no fixed universal interpretations. These similarities constitute types, like Weberian ideal types, which Freudianism merely uses as "the intellectual instruments of an understanding focused upon singularity" (p. 374). They are nomothetic regularities, like the regularities of history, but, Ricoeur argues, they are not equivalent to the general laws of the natural sciences. The end product of psychoanalysis is an understanding of the meaning of almost incomprehensible symbols. The knowledge acquired in this way has little external relevance because of the virtual identity of its subject and object: hermeneutics in psychology aims not at increased public knowledge but at an advance in self-understanding. According to Ricoeur, this is an idiographic process in that its truth is enclosed within the communication of the intersubjective situation; a psychoanalytic proposition can be adopted, criticized, improved, or ignored, but it cannot be treated like a hypothesis in the natural sciences. Thus Ricoeur sets up a radical dichotomy between hermeneutic and logical-empiricist knowledge systems, that is, between the acquisition of an interpretative understanding and of a physicocausal explanation.

The epistemological dichotomy which Ricoeur establishes has three aspects. Firstly, it stems from his narrow perception of the natural sciences as necessarily mechanistic and atomistic, as inevitably involving linear determinate models of causality, as demanding public observation, and as unable to deal with the idiographic. In this respect, it is significant that he seems to identify scientific psychology with behaviorist operationalism. Secondly, Ricoeur's position relates to the real difficulties surrounding the role of reflective thinking within the discourse of logical empiricism and of the natural sciences. Ricoeur refers to this obliquely when he writes about "the inability of a psychology of positivist inspiration to furnish an equivalent of the relations of signifier to signified that place psychoanalysis among the hermeneutic sciences" (p. 358). Thirdly, the extremism of Ricoeur's divorce of knowledge through interpretative understanding and knowledge through physico-causal explanation leads him to fail to confront adequately the crucial problems of *reduction* and *validation.* It is to these twin problems that I shall now turn.

Ricoeur believes that exegetical interpretation and the explanation of the natural sciences are completely independent and irreducible. This is "the distinction Brentano, Dilthey, and Husserl had in mind when they sharply distinguished between understanding of the psychical or the historical, and explanation of nature" (p. 363). Thus Ricoeur follows the influences of the neo-Kantians who posit a split between the dialectical social world and a nondialectical nature. His view of Freudian hermeneutics has some similarity to Winch's (1958) aprioristic sociology in that he follows the Weberian distinction between the acquisition of an interpretative understanding and the provision of a causal explanation, although unlike Weber (1922) he does not regard the former as necessarily incomplete and inferior to the latter. Freud's psychology elucidates the purposive structure of personal meaning; "Freud's originality consists in maintaining that the strange phenomena which had previously been left to physiology are explainable in terms of intentional ideas" (p. 361). Ricoeur claims that "Freud's notions are *logically irreducible* to physicalist terms" (p. 361, my emphasis). Contrary to Peters's (1954, 1958) reductionist theory of motivation, Ricoeur follows Toulmin (1954) and Flew (1954) in asserting "that an explanation through motives is irreducible to an explanation through causes, that a motive and a cause are completely different" (p. 360). This assertion need not be debated here since Ricoeur's thesis does not depend upon the motive-cause distinction. Rather, he argues that psychoanalytic epistemology should not be rescued by trying "to simplify analytic discourse by assigning it entirely to the realm of motives and not of causes" (p. 361), for Freud's psychology involves "a mixed discourse that falls outside the motive-cause alternative" (p. 363). Ricoeur summarizes his point of view when he writes that:

> . . . the statements of psychoanalysis are located neither within the causal discourse of the natural sciences nor within the motive discourse of phenomenology. Since it deals with a psychical reality, psychoanalysis speaks not of causes but of motives; but because the topographic field does not coincide with any conscious process of awareness, its explanations resemble

causal explanations, without, however, being identically the same, for then psychoanalysis would reify all its notions and mystify interpretation itself [p. 360].

That Freudian interpretation of the intentional structure of individual meaning cannot *logically be translated* into an explanation at the level of physicocausality is a perfectly acceptable argument. However, following Boden's (1970, 1972) distinction between logical and empirical reduction in psychology,[5] we must ask whether Ricoeur is also implying that the objects of Freudian hermeneutics —the intentions and symbols—are also *empirically irreducible* to neurobiological processes. Ricoeur does not confront this question squarely and maintains a position of admitted ambiguity. He seems to suggest that no physiological data could possibly have any relevance to a Freudian interpretation. Such a suggestion is counterintuitive. For technically, we know that psychosomatic symptoms and their remission may be used within the course of an analysis to corroborate or call into question an interpretation; and theoretically, since human beings *are* biological systems, one cannot conceive of human communications and purposes as existing entirely independently of physical processes. For this reason, one would expect some sort of systematic correlation between them. If one allows for the possibility of empirical reduction, one may, for example, accept Speisman's (1965) neat experiment as suggestive evidence in favor of Freudian theory. Ricoeur, however, would probably deny the relevance of such data. The exciting quality of Ricoeur's thesis—the idea that Freud's psychology might be regarded most appropriately as a hermeneutic system and that, as such, its propositions cannot be translated into physicocausal hypotheses—is marred by his extremism. This extremism consists of an undefended and almost certainly untenable antireductionism. It leads Ricoeur to a related failure: the failure to elaborate any clear standards by which hermeneutic propositions might be validated.

---

[5] Boden argues against logical reductionism and for empirical reductionism. For example, she writes that ". . . psychological subjects *are*, under an alternative description, purely physical systems of a certain sort. The intentional description and the physical description are logically distinct, and are not intertranslatable. Nevertheless, the features of intentionality may [*in principle*] be explained by a purely causal account, in the sense that they may be shown to be totally dependent upon physical processes" (1970, p. 200).

The natural sciences have reasonably well-established proce-dures of verification and refutation, even though these are not without problems, as the controversies within philosophy of science and sociology of knowledge surely demonstrate. Since Ricoeur tells us that hermeneutic accounts are in no way reducible to the explanations of the natural sciences, the onus is upon him to explain the procedure of validation within an interpretative disci-pline. As Farrell (1964) and Home (1966) have pointed out, moti-vational accounts raise particular epistemological problems for psychology; since Ricoeur argues that psychoanalytic discourse falls outside of the motive-cause distinction, we may anticipate that he will have to confront similar and perhaps more serious problems in proposing that Freud's psychology be viewed as a hermeneutic system. Sherwood (1969) has confronted the problems surrounding the criteria for evaluation of psychoanalytic "narratives" and sug-gests that appropriateness, adequacy, and predictive accuracy are important. Ricoeur might agree that appropriateness and adequacy are necessary aspects of a good interpretation, but he denies that psychoanalysis can provide public predictions. Yet, as Eagle (1973) has suggested, the criterion of empirical verification, accuracy, or testability is the most important if a discipline is to be scientific in the established naturalistic sense. This criterion Ricoeur explicitly rejects. Although he expresses concern about "the legitimacy of seeking the semantic structure of double-meaning and with the legitimacy of taking this structure as the privileged object of inter-pretation" (p. 9), that is, with the legitimacy of the hermeneutic enterprise as such, Ricoeur fails to confront the question of stan-dards of interpretation. He offers no clear criteria of hermeneutic validation. The implications and the reasons for this failure will become evident later.

The problem of standards of validation is common to other hermeneutic theories, as Ricoeur perhaps recognizes when he men-tions that "the problem of a technique of interpretation has more kinship with the question asked by Schleiermacher, Dilthey, Max Weber, and Bultmann than with the problems of even the tamest behaviorism" (1974, p. 187). The methodology by which an inter-pretation is generated is not that by which a natural scientist infers a material relationship. A cynic might argue that the hermeneutic technique is aptly portrayed in Pareto's characterization of a pseudoscientific method: from a particular datum, the idea is to draw a certain conclusion; the quest is not for this conclusion, which is known in advance, but simply for a way of getting from the datum to the conclusion (Pareto, 1916; see Cioffi, 1970). Freud (1933) defended his nonoperational formulations by comparing his psychology with astronomy, a science based on observation rather than experiment. As has been pointed out elsewhere, the comparison is inappropriate, for astronomy involves observation of predicted events under controlled conditions, whereas psychoanalysis, dealing with meanings, can offer no controlled observation on the instrumental level because it functions on an intersubjective level. In this context, the application of Gaussian statistics or, as Meehl (1970) proposes, of Bayesian calculation to Freud's psychology is inappropriate. Ricoeur even suggests that psychoanalysis is, in a certain sense, an antitechnique or antitechnology in counterposition to the natural sciences because, operating within the field of language, it eschews the manipulation of matter and serves to free humans for projects other than that of domination over nature (1974, pp. 177-195). This attitude relates to Ricoeur's attack upon the concept of adaptation and upon an entire school of American psychoanalysts, such as Hartmann, Klein, and Rapaport, for their attempt to transform psychoanalytic ideas into concepts acceptable to the natural sciences. From Ricoeur's perspective, Freudianism involves a fragile and personal intersubjective process concerned with elucidating the semantics of human desire; the end product of this process is the expansion of consciousness and the continuation of arrested self-formative processes through interpretative reflection.

For two reasons, psychoanalysis cannot furnish data for prediction or for manipulative transformation and control. Firstly, as Scriven (1959) points out, Freud's psychology can make only "normic statements" that concern certain lawlike regularities of psychical processes but that are not of the nature of cause and effect. Employing the Hegelian distinction, one can argue that the phenomena with which psychoanalysis is concerned involve the causality of fate rather than the causality of nature. The invariance of human life history or of the structure of personal meaning is, in a certain sense, existentially created; it is not the lawful invariance of physical events. Freud's psychology requires this distinction because therapeutic progress is held to depend upon the dissolution of existentially created invariance by the power of hermeneutic reflection. For example, the phenomenon of an interpretation producing the immediate remission of a hysterical paralysis, a tick, or a period of impotence is not easily explained solely in terms of physiochemical causes and the laws of neurobiological processes. The distinction is a necessary heuristic which seems justifiable so long as the concept of existential invariance is not elevated into something mystical and wholly autonomous from natural law: the idea of "free will" need not imply indeterminism. There is a second reason why Freud's psychology cannot be predictive: if the context of the psychoanalytic debate does involve "open system" *dialectical* processes, then one cannot expect neat predictions to be generated from this context as they might be from an investigation within a "closed," linear, and mechanistic system. Thus the refusal of psychoanalysts to offer public, testable predictions is entirely legitimate.

Ricoeur's perspective liberates Freudianism from the evaluative stringencies to which it has previously been subjected. Psychoanalysis is a potentially interminable debate involving interpretative intersubjective processes of reflection. It has little external validity because there can be no definite demarcation between the subject and object of its knowledge. Thus far, I can accept Ricoeur's epistemological thesis. However, a number of questions about Freudian hermeneutics remain. How are rival interpretations within the psychoanalytic context to be adjudicated? What are the canons of hermeneutic exegesis? Although public criteria for the validation of psychoanalytic knowledge may not be feasible, the need for interpretative standards and rules is exigent. Ricoeur insists that "it is one thing to be capable of empirical verification, and another thing to render possible a historical interpretation" (p. 375). He suggests that "the only radical way to justify hermeneutics is to seek in the very nature of reflective thought the principle of a *logic of double meaning,* a logic that is complex but not arbitrary, rigorous in its articulations but irreducible to the linearity of symbolic logic" (p. 48); elsewhere he argues that this logic of plurivocality is "no longer a formal logic but a transcendental logic. It is established at the level of conditions of possibility: not the conditions of the objectivity of a nature, but the conditions of the appropriation of our desire to be" (1974, p. 19). However, Ricoeur fails to elaborate upon these assertions; moreover, the call for a transcendental logic of double meaning does not answer the question of hermeneutic validation. The only indication Ricoeur provides as to what constitutes a good interpretation is that "the concepts of analysis are to be judged according to their status as conditions of the possibility of analytic experience, insofar as the latter operates in the field of speech" (p. 375). Although this is not a solution, it reveals an important facet of Ricoeur's attitude toward the problem of interpretative standards.

It becomes evident that Ricoeur does not really recognize the necessity of establishing criteria by which rival interpretations within psychoanalysis might be adjudicated. Indeed, at one point, having asked the question, "How can the conflict of rival interpretations be arbitrated?," he suggests that such problems are "not properly considered in a fundamental hermeneutics, and this by design: this hermeneutics is intended not to resolve them but to dissolve them" (1974, p. 10). Implicitly and subtly, Ricoeur seems to identify truth and the movement of psychoanalytic interpretation; for psychoanalysis is "a *well-determined* experience, which *unfolds* in a dual relationship" (1974, p. 190, my emphasis). The implications of this notion will be examined in the course of my later discussion of Ricoeur's attempt to reconstitute Freudianism within the framework of an eschatological philosophy. Ricoeur implies that it does not even matter if an interpretation is inconsistent with the facts, for "in analysis, the real history is merely a clue to the figurative history through which the patient arrives at self-understanding; for the analyst, the important thing is this figurative history" (p. 369). In this way, Ricoeur circumvents the question raised by interpretations which are efficacious yet wrong, and wholly ignores the manifold problems of suggestibility and remystification raised by the hermeneutic approach to Freudianism. This defect in Ricoeur's thesis is serious.

The hermeneutic perspective on Freud's psychology is not to be abandoned because of Ricoeur's failure to establish standards and rules for the validation of interpretations. Although it is not the purpose of this paper, the task of explicating such criteria is exigent. It is wholly unsatisfactory to assume, as Ricoeur seems to do, that truth somehow emerges by necessity within the psychoanalytic situation. It would be equally unsatisfactory to suggest that truth is to be discerned solely on the basis of personal resonance, or to argue that idiographic interpretations are to be validated by reference to certain fixed universal types, which actually are not the proper concern of the psychoanalytic endeavor. Freud's psychology as a hermeneutic system does imply a set of criteria for the arbitration of conflicting interpretations. Such a set constitutes an epistemology which, like all epistemologies, connects with certain human interests. The psychoanalytic process aims at a recollection by which the latent meaning of a distorted text and of the distortions themselves is discovered. Although nonadoption of an interpretation does not constitute refutation, an interpretation is valid if successfully adopted, that is, if it leads to further valid interpretations, to increased self-understanding, and to the continuation of self-formative processes. In a certain sense, interpretations are adjudicated by the subject to whom they pertain, and thus meaning is created when subject and analyst mutually agree about the lucidity of a particular narrative. To a limited extent, this embroils one in the "hermeneutic circle," comparable to Anselm's concept of postcritical faith: one must believe before one can understand, understand before one can believe (see p. 28). Ricoeur might be rescued from the errors of his epistemological thesis if one were to argue that an interpretation is valid if it is consistent with the facts and if it implies an advance in critical self-understanding which motivates the continuation of self-formative processes which had been arrested; a good interpretation contributes to the task of consciousness, that is, the creation of authentic discourse. This is not the public standard of "cure" but the personal, intersubjective criterion of insight and the appropriation of meaning. In sum, interpretations are adopted for their emancipatory value. This epistemology is not fully formulated, nor is it without problems, but it is, I believe, an improvement upon Ricoeur's position, which merely states that psychoanalytic hermeneutics should be directed toward "the conditions of possibility of a semantics of desire" (p. 375, emphasis removed). The question of knowledge is inextricably and unavoidably bound to the question of human interests and the grounding of knowledge.

With Ricoeur, we must recognize that Freudianism is intimately connected to processes of interpretative reflection. The end point of psychoanalysis and the starting point of Freud's psychology is reflection by which persons free themselves from that split-off state in which sections of their communication had become alienated from consciousness and in which they had become objects for themselves. What is the place of this form of knowledge within the discourse of logical empiricism and of the natural sciences? Radnitzky shows that it is not that logical-empiricist disciplines cannot cope with hermeneutics but rather that their "official methodology makes it impossible for them to deal with philologies and hence their methodology makes self-reflection impossible" (1968b, p. 77). Ricoeur regards Freudian hermeneutics as a development of the reflective tradition in European philosophy. This tradition is not concerned with the experience of immediate self-consciousness and, indeed, is critical of the idea that knowledge is necessarily limited to such experience. Reflective thought aims at self-understanding and the stimulation of self-formative processes; it is "the appropriation of our effort to exist and our desire to be by means of works which testify to this effort and this desire" (Ricoeur, 1974, p. 329, emphasis removed). In this sense, the reflective tradition goes beyond a critique of knowledge and moves toward the recuperation of authentic and integrated discourse.

The archeological method of hermeneutics distinguishes Freud's psychology from other forms of reflective investigation. Freudianism begins with the dispossession of consciousness, that is, the rejection of immediate meaning, and aims at achieving a fuller reappropriation of personal meaning through an interpretative understanding of the unconscious. This understanding is circumscribed by its constitution; its knowledge is relative to the rules of interpretation which determine it, to the intersubjective context in which it is generated, and to the transference language in which it is expressed. Moreover, as has been suggested, psychoanalytic knowledge either depends upon a transcendental logic, as Ricoeur proposes, or, as I have indicated, upon its grounding in emancipatory human interests. Ricoeur argues that the Freudian topographies result from reflective thinking that employs a hermeneutic archeology; they are justified "by the tactic of dispossession through which reflection counters the spell of false consciousness" (p. 439). Similarly, Ricoeur argues that Freud's economic point of view is "the discourse appropriate to an archeology of the subject" (p.

440). Although I do not intend to rediscuss the matter, this argument involves the important distinction between human desire and the languages in which it is represented, and returns us to Ricoeur's thesis concerning Freud's conjunction of hermeneutics and energetics. The archeological moment of reflective thinking, Ricoeur suggests, generates the substantive features of Freud's psychology: the topographies and the energy economics. Ricoeur concludes that we must understand "the Freudian metapsychology as an adventure of reflection; dispossession of consciousness is its path, because the act of becoming conscious is its task" (p. 439).

Freud's psychology is a mode of reflective investigation employing a hermeneutic archeology. Through the interpretation of human symbols, Freudianism challenges the illusions of immediate consciousness: its demystifying hermeneutics constitutes a potent and profound critical theory. However, Ricoeur wishes to argue that psychoanalysis is more than this: Freud's psychology can also be proclamative. He writes that:

> ... if the subject is to attain its true being, it is not enough for it to discover the inadequacy of its self-awareness, or even to discover the power of desire that posits it in existence. The subject must also discover that the process of "becoming conscious," through which it *appropriates* the meaning of its desire and effort, does not belong to it, but belongs to the *meaning* that is formed in it. The subject must mediate self-consciousness through spirit or mind, that is through the figures that give a telos to this "becoming conscious" [p. 459].

Ricoeur finds within Freudianism, particularly within Freud's writings on culture, an immanent reconciliation between demystifying and proclamative hermeneutics. Beyond the critical archeology he perceives a teleology. From an investigation of the epistemology of interpretation, Ricoeur shifts his concern toward an ontology of understanding. Ricoeur, as a theologian of the Judaeo-Christian tradition, wishes to graft hermeneutics onto phenomenology and to recast psychoanalysis within a eschatological system, so that he may establish a pathway to purified faith and a basis for a renewal of religious hope, a hope that is founded on the promise of something "sacred." While Ricoeur is correct to point to the role of psychoanalysis in that reappropriation of meaning that goes beyond mystification, he greatly overemphasizes and misconceives this aspect, ignoring its fundamental limitations and its authentic foundations. In my judgment, this part of Ricoeur's thesis constitutes an abuse of the intentions of the psychoanalytic effort; those who accept the hermeneutic perspective have good reasons to reject the way in which Ricoeur exploits this epistemology. It is to this affirmative moment in Ricoeur's thesis that I shall now turn.

While admitting that Freud (1918) expressly stated that his psychology constitutes an analysis and not a synthesis, Ricoeur wishes to demonstrate that "if Freudianism is an explicit and thematized archeology, it relates of itself, by the dialectical nature of its concepts, to an implicit and unthematized teleology" (p. 461). He elaborates this thesis by comparing Freud's critical hermeneutics with Hegelian phenomenology. This comparison takes off from Hyppolite's (1946, 1957) research on the Hegelian aspects of Freudianism and from an understanding of Hegel's *The Phenomenology of Mind* (1807) which seems to have been influenced by Kojeve (1947). Ricoeur argues that Hegel's theory of the structure and development of "spirit" or mind inverts and complements psychoanalytic theory. Hegelianism and Freudianism have a certain similarity inasmuch as each involves a movement of interpretation in which a particular form is understood through another form. The explicit content of Hegel's philosophy concerns a teleological process by which consciousness is achieved, that is, the way in which the self of an authentic self-consciousness is posited. The theme of this philosophy is the Hegelian dialectic, that is, a progressive synthetic movement in which each form obtains its meaning from that which follows it and thus consciousness or "spirit" is advanced. Like Freudianism, the Hegelian content and theme concern the vicissitudes of human desire. The Freudian archeology challenges immediate false consciousness by means of a regressive analytic movement in which each form obtains its meaning from its antecedent. On the basis of this similarity, Ricoeur proceeds to conjugate Freud and Hegel and to subsume them within his grand philosophy.

Ricoeur does not deny that his conjugation of Freud and Hegel may depend upon an "overinterpretation" of Freud (p. 473), and he admits that the psychoanalytic teleology which he proposes is "evident only in a reading of Freud coupled with a reading of Hegel" (p. 473). However, he does attempt to demonstrate that an implicit teleology is evident at three levels within Freud's psychology: in concepts which Freud employs nonreflectively; in concepts such as identification which are in some way "out of harmony with the dominant conceptualization of psychoanalysis" (p. 473); and in concepts such as sublimation which present certain unresolved difficulties within Freudian theory. The intersubjective debate of psychoanalysis resembles the Hegelian dialectic of relations between master and slave: the former ends with the parity of two consciousnesses, the latter with a process of mutual recognition. Similarly, Ricoeur shows that "all the phases of the libido are phases of the reduplication of self-consciousness" (p. 475) which Hegel described. Moreover, he argues that Freud's ideas about identification and about the genesis of the superego, which are in some ways discordant with the main body of psychoanalytic theory, resemble Hegel's ideas about the development of human desire from processes of "reduplication of consciousness," that is, in a certain sense, from intersubjective interaction. Finally, Ricoeur attributes the series of unresolved problems within the Freudian theory of human desire which are presented by the concept of sublimation to the implicit teleology of this concept. In this way, Ricoeur suggests that Freud and Hegel share a dialectic and that their theories are structurally homologous. There are indeed certain interesting resemblances between Freudian psychology and the Hegelian phenomenology; the relationship between their dialectics deserves further exploration, for it is intricate and important. However, the equation that Ricoeur proposes—discovering Freudianism in Hegelianism and vice versa—involves a number of problems, some of which Ricoeur chooses to overlook.

Is the dialectic of Freudianism as closely homologous to that of Hegelianism as Ricoeur believes? The resemblances can be deceptive. As Ricoeur points out, Freud and Hegel do share the theme of the constitutive nature of consciousness. Moreover, like Hegelianism, Freudianism is a dialectical theory which rejects the positivist epistemology based upon an insurmountable and antidialectical dichotomy between the subject and object of knowledge: as I have already indicated, psychoanalysis cannot be objectivistic because there can be no defined demarcation between its epistemological subject and object. There are, however, profound differences in the alternatives to positivism espoused in these two theories. Hegel presents an affirmative metaphysical system; he assumes that the only true knowledge is the self-knowledge of the infinite subject and that the traditional subject-object dichotomy can be overcome on the basis of the ultimate primacy of the absolute subject. The Hegelian dialectic is directed toward this state of knowledge, which Hegel conceptualizes as the "absolute idea"; truth is identified with the unfolding of historical forms. The teleology of this identity theory of knowledge allows for the ultimate acquisition of absolute truth. Psychoanalytic knowledge is dialectical, but it does not constitute an absolutist metaphysics. It is true that there is a gross and confusing resemblance between the process of psychoanalysis and the epistemology of Hegelianism. In the course of an analysis, a subject reappropriates sections of communication and desire which had become objectified through pathological mechanisms of splitting or alienation. Hence the consequent integration appears to be directed toward a quasi-Hegelian identity of subject and object. However, this resemblance depends upon an illegitimate conflation of the aims of personality change and epistemology. Freud posits an ongoing dialectical tension between the subject and object of psychoanalytic hermeneutics without making the teleological assumption of their ultimate identity. Freudian psychology may implicitly suggest the possibility of a synthesis, but this does not mean that it has the teleology of an identity theory; the psychoanalytic effort is not directed toward a reconciled totality that is the accomplishment of a transcendental consciousness, but is epistemologically grounded in its concrete commitment to reason and human emancipation.

Ricoeur realizes that there can be no simple unification of Freudian and Hegelian theories; his equation, which reads Freud into Hegel and finds Hegel in Freud, is more subtle and sophisticated. Ricoeur's theological design requires that Freud be conjoined with Hegel and that the product be subsumed within the foundations of an eschatological philosophy. The first stage of this design involves the unification of Freudian archeology and Hegelian teleology; however, Ricoeur finds that this unification depends upon certain amendments. Freudian theory is amended in that Ricoeur rejects Freud's conceptions of the "realism of the unconscious" (p. 431); I shall not debate this issue here. Hegelianism is even more remarkably transformed in that Ricoeur, remaining loyal to contemporary phenomenology, abstains from the idea of epistemological closure or finality and rejects Hegel's idealist conception of the "absolute idea." In this way, Ricoeur returns to Kant, adopting a Kantian attitude toward the limits of reason; moreover, it may be noted that the theological question to which Ricoeur's investigations are directed, the question of *hope*, is formulated in an essentially Kantian fashion. Ricoeur's Hegelianism, or quasi Hegelianism, is transcendental, teleological, and affirmative, but shorn of its metaphysical implications. Epistemologically, this standpoint is highly complex and, as I shall indicate, seems to contain a number of contradictions which Ricoeur fails to confront satisfactorily.

Ricoeur unifies Freud and Hegel by recasting them within a quasi-Hegelian dialectic. He suggests that the critical archeology of Freudianism is complemented by a teleology which does not have the defined epistemological end point of an absolutist metaphysics. Thus Ricoeur can employ it as part of an ontological theology which is eschatological and transcendental but in which hope for something "sacred" displaces faith in the absolute. While I can agree with Ricoeur that Freudianism is not an absolutist doctrine in the Hegelian sense, I contest his idea that Freud's psychology is teleological and affirmative. The movement of psychoanalytic knowledge has no epistemological terminus; indeed, Freud abstains from the idea that absolute reason is attainable within existing or potential conditions. No analyst or analysand is or can be the repository of absolute knowledge even about a single personality. Freud's psychology is not founded on the assumption of an ultimate attainment of a reconciled totality, yet it avoids relativistic resignation by its grounding in liberatory human interests. It is true that psychoanalysis implies something more than a critical archeology; Freud's (1933) prescription that "Where id was, there ego shall be" does suggest a recuperative process not wholly accounted for by demystifying hermeneutics construed in a narrow sense. However, this need not imply a teleology. Indeed, I find it impossible to accept Ricoeur's argument that his conjunction of Freud and Hegel is somehow teleological yet does not assume the attainment of epistemological closure; his references to a transcendental logic and to the *promise* that he finds within human symbols are by no means convincing. Ricoeur's thesis seems to express a theologically motivated conviction that, epistemologically, progress within the psychoanalytic context is in some way inevitable and guaranteed. Despite his overt disavowal of the Hegelian metaphysics, Ricoeur seems to identify truth and the movement of interpretation in psychoanalysis, just as Hegel identifies truth and the course of history. Ricoeur's description of psychoanalysis as an experience which *unfolds* is illuminating in this respect, as it implies a necessary and indivertible movement of revelation. This attitude connects with Ricoeur's almost complete failure to establish criteria of hermeneutic validation, that is, standards by which rival interpretations within the psychoanalytic situation might be adjudicated; this failure was discussed earlier. Ricoeur does try to show, mainly on the basis of Freud's writings on culture, that the psychoanalytic teleology he proposes can be found concretely within the semantic overdetermination of symbols. In attempting this, he employs somewhat modified concepts of "symbol" and "overdetermination" to which Shope (1973) has directed some thoughtful criticism; indeed, Ricoeur admits that "Freud would reject our interpretation of overdetermination" (p. 498). For Ricoeur, the hermeneutic investigation of symbols furnishes an intimation of the "sacred"; his unification of Freud and Hegel provides a teleological philosophy upon which he intends to develop a proclamative eschatology. This unification involves a conversion of Freudianism which is not only a violation of the theoretical foundations of Freud's psychology but also seriously travesties the intentions of the psychoanalytic effort. I do not intend to pursue Ricoeur's ontotheological design any further because, as I have indicated, I find the enterprise itself and the Hegelianized reading of Freud upon which it rests both misconceived and unconvincing. I shall therefore now turn to a summary of the divergences between Ricoeur's perspective and my own.

I maintain that the foundations and the intentions of the psychoanalytic endeavor are to be understood neither through a reading of Hegel nor, as Ricoeur proposes, through a quasi Hegelianism which is teleological and affirmative, although allegedly relieved of its metaphysical character. Rather, Freud's psychology should be understood in terms of the materialist critique of Hegel. My standpoint, which I hope to expand upon elsewhere, is that psychoanalysis is essentially a dialectical and materialistic hermeneutics which constitutes a powerful critical theory; I challenge the attempt to reformulate Freudianism within a teleological and affirmative philosophy. Ricoeur wants hermeneutics to create the basis for an eschatology because he perceives critical theory in itself as nothing more than iconoclastic. He assumes that the alternatives are nihilism or a reconstitution, renewal, and reappropriation of religious hope, that is, the establishment of a "purified faith" based on that promise of the "sacred" which is supposedly bestowed upon us by the hermeneutics of human symbols. Ricoeur fails to recognize that there is a third direction in which reflective effort might proceed, namely that of critical theory as sufficient in itself by virtue of its grounding in emancipatory commitment. Although critical theory is not affirmative, positive, or teleological, it is not necessarily nihilistic. Ricoeur's thesis subverts the psychoanalytic effort, for in Ricoeur's hands, Freud's psychology is turned away from the real world of human suffering and concrete social processes. Freudianism concerns the discourse of personal meaning; Ricoeur correctly gives a privileged position to the plurivocality of symbols, yet he does so in such a way as to sever the meaning of human symbols from their social and historical context. Instead of searching for basic mediating categories by which to relate personal meaning to this context, Ricoeur wishes to find within the structure of human symbols an intimation of the enigmatic and ineffable by which he can arrive at an ontology of affirmation; in this way, Ricoeur allows theological *hope* to defuse the inherent tension of the Freudian dialectic. Ricoeur views the synthesis that is implied by the psychoanalytic archeology as the guaranteed product of a transcendental consciousness; he asserts that the reconciliation to which the alleged teleology of Freudianism is directed provides its own transcendental logic. The belief, concomitant upon Ricoeur's identification of truth and the unfolding of psychoanalytic interpretations, that progress is indivertible leads to a certain quietism: Ricoeur's philosophy can be affirmative even though human reality is not, hope for the "sacred" is possible in the face of alienation, true consciousness might be attained without social transformation. In this way, Ricoeur annuls the driving force of critical theory, that is, its commitment to human liberation. For Ricoeur, the hermeneutics of symbols offers an individual peace which abrogates the

concrete struggle toward reason and authenticity that is at the
heart of the psychoanalytic effort.

The truth of Freud's psychology does not lie in an anticipated
future but in a process of critical reflection upon origins. Freud
eschews the metaphysics of finality; the Freudian dialectic is essentially unclosed and incomplete. Its tension is not to be alleviated.
The synthesis which psychoanalysis implies is not the result of a
transcendental consciousness but is rooted in real social processes;
reason cannot become affirmative without social transformation.
The confirmation of the Freudian dialectic lies not within onto-
theology, as Ricoeur's eschatological thesis suggests, but, to borrow
a concept, within the realm of the historicopractical. The implicit
conception of a reconciled totality is generated within the labor of
critical reasoning; Freud's psychology does not have its grounding
within the symbolic discourse of the individual but within that
which impels the effort to understand this discourse, that is, the
struggle for human emancipation. This struggle is the driving force
that maintains the tension of the Freudian dialectic. If properly
understood, the psychoanalytic effort to decipher the personal
meaning of symbolic discourse leads not to the "sacred" but to a
fundamental confrontation with human social relations and history. The commitment to liberatory human interests, which ani-
mates the effort toward this confrontation, itself comprises the
grounding of psychoanalytic knowledge.

What can be salvaged from Ricoeur's thesis on Freudianism?
Ricoeur presents a brilliant and sensitive reading of Freud's psychology. The paradox of his thesis is that, although his scholarly
reading of Freud's theory greatly enriches our understanding of it,
his philosophical thesis leads us toward and then diverts us from a
definitive assessment of the epistemological position of psychoanalysis. The thesis does, however, succeed in clearing the ground for
such an assessment; for Ricoeur launches a fundamental attack on
the widely held assumption that the natural sciences constitute the
only legitimate mode of discourse within which to evaluate Freudianism. I consider this to be Ricoeur's most significant contribution; its importance cannot be overemphasized. Freud's psychology
is not a positivist doctrine nor is it to be understood within the
metascientific framework of logical empiricism. It is most appropriately regarded as primarily a hermeneutic discipline. There is an

epistemological tension within psychoanalysis which has implications for all other human sciences. In one sense this is a tension between explanation at the level of purposive structure and at the level of physicocausality. In another sense it is a tension between meaning and facticity. In yet another sense it is a tension between two *Weltanschauungen* for, as Radnitzky (1968a, 1968b) shows, the logical-empiricist and hermeneutic-dialectical approaches to the study of humans are rooted in different styles of philosophy. There is a crucial distinction between the acquisition of an interpretative understanding and the provision of a physicocausal explanation; the purposive discourse concerned with human motives and meanings is not translatable into the discourse of physicocausality. Psychology needs to incorporate both modes of discourse, and hermeneutics can make a substantive and essential contribution to the understanding of human systems. I can readily accept Apel's (1967) argument that the human sciences should involve an interplay between hermeneutic-dialectical and naturalistic discourse, that is, in another sense, between hermeneutics and empirics. These approaches should be complementary. In my judgment, part of the solution to the crises facing contemporary social sciences, particularly the mainstream of Anglo-American psychology, lies in the explication of the way in which these modes of discourse could be related complementarily. The psychoanalytic movement might have represented *par excellence* that interplay which should be the hallmark of all human sciences. The movement has not been distinguished in this way, partly because Freud himself did not clarify his juxtapositioning of discourses and partly because his successors did not fully recognize this feature of his psychology. Both critics and advocates have inhibited a fuller appreciation and deeper evaluation of Freudianism by their preoccupation either with its status within the framework of logical empiricism or with the richness of its insights. In this respect, Ricoeur's thesis is an excellent antidote to the sterile Anglo-American debate over Freudianism.

It is an antidote but it is not an answer. For the extremism of Ricoeur's thesis leads to its downfall. Adopting a neo-Kantian viewpoint, Ricoeur assumes the diametric opposition of hermeneutic and natural-scientific discourse; his thesis on Freud's psychology involves a wholesale rejection of the latter. For him, philosophical enterprise is sovereign to science, his conception of which is overly narrow and unreflective. This extremism results in untidy thinking about the problematic relationship between the energy and the language of human desire. It leads Ricoeur into an untenable antireductionism and connects with his parallel failure to confront satisfactorily the question of validation within a knowledge system that is primarily hermeneutic. As I have suggested, Ricoeur can be rescued from these difficulties. The Freudian conjunction of energetics and linguistics demands a fuller and more systematic exploration, informed perhaps by the insights of biocybernetics and semiology. The distinction between logical and empirical reductionism enables us to articulate the epistemological plane of the phenomena under consideration and hence to define the appropriate mode of discourse. Standards for adjudication between rival interpretations in the psychoanalytic context can be formulated; in part, this formulation will involve an explication of the human interests in which Freud's psychology is grounded. It is understood that these standards will not be equivalent to the objectivistic verificational criteria of public prediction, control, and testability to which physicocausal hypotheses are subjected. However, interpretations should not counter the realm of facts; hermeneutics cannot be wholly autonomous from empirics in the way that Ricoeur suggests. Rather, as I have suggested, they should be complementary, in such a way that there can be an interplay between the knowledge of the natural sciences and that of hermeneutic-dialectical disciplines. Modified in these ways, the epistemological moment of Ricoeur's thesis could contribute to an improved comprehension of Freudian theory and the nature of psychoanalytic knowledge.

Ricoeur defends Freud's psychology both against vulgar Freudianism and against attacks from the disciplines of logical empiricism. He emphasizes that the central concern of Freud's theory is not with facts but with meaning; perhaps no one, Ricoeur writes, "has contributed as much as Freud to breaking the charm of *facts* and opening up the empire of *meaning*" (1974, p. 146). Unlike the natural sciences, which ultimately have recourse to mathematics and logic, disciplines concerned with human meaning lack such direct appeal to rationality; their epistemological locus is inevitably closer to the human interests in which they are grounded. This does *not* imply that hermeneutic disciplines are unscientific. Ricoeur argues that Freudianism is a creative offshoot of the reflective tradition in European thinking; its distinctive feature is its powerful interpretative method which reveals, through the investigation of human symbols, alienated sections of personal meaning beyond immediate false consciousness. Ironically, Freud's use of quasi-naturalistic concepts, as in the topographies and energy economics, enabled him to advance the field of reflective investigation, as Ricoeur shows in the course of his comparison of psychoanalysis and Husserlian phenomenology; the mixed discourse of Freudianism is not just a source of difficulty for social scientists interested in psychoanalysis, it is the mainspring of Freud's originality. The reflective moment of Ricoeur's thesis helps us to locate Freud's psychology in the field of intellectual endeavor to which it properly belongs.

Ricoeur points to the hermeneutic tension between demystification and proclamation or recuperation, and tries to fashion the latter aspect of Freud's psychology into a teleology by conjoining Freud with a quasi-Hegelian phenomenology. Ricoeur employs this teleology in his attempt to reconstitute psychoanalytic hermeneutics as a part of a theology directed toward an ontology of affirmation. This moment of Ricoeur's thesis undermines the foundations and goals of the psychoanalytic effort; here one cannot speak of "rescuing" his thesis. I have argued that Ricoeur's conjugation of Freud and Hegel is unconvincing and illegitimate; moreover, I have sketched the reasons for my strong dissent from Ricoeur's reformulation of Freud's psychology and from his ontotheological aspirations. I would argue that Freudianism constitutes a critical theory, not an affirmative philosophy; the Freudian dialectic is not teleological but resists finality because of its constitution as a struggle, impelled by a particular emancipatory commitment. As I have indicated, epistemology is inevitably tied to human interests. Psychoanalysis is primarily an interpretative system bound by an epistemology which is not that of logical empiricism or the natural sciences; its effort is toward an advance in human self-understanding and formation. Freud's psychology is a mode of reflective investigation empowered by demystifying hermeneutics which are inextricably tied to the struggle for reason, authenticity, and human liberation.

REFERENCES

Apel, K.-O. (1967), Analytic Philosophy of Language and the 'Geisteswissen-schaften.' *Foundations of Language; Suppl. Series 5.* Dodrecht: Reidel.

Bär, E. S. (1974), Understanding Lacan. *Psychoanalysis and Contemporary Science,* 3:473-544. New York: International Universities Press.

Boden, M. A. (1970), Intentionality and Physical Systems. *Phil. Sci.,* 37:200-214.

────── (1972), *Purposive Explanation in Psychology.* Cambridge, Mass.: Harvard University Press.

Cioffi, F. (1970), Freud and the Idea of a Pseudo-Science. In: *Explanation in the Behavioural Sciences,* ed. R. Borger & F. Cioffi. London: Cambridge University Press, pp. 471-499.

Dalbiez, R. (1936), *Psychoanalytical Method and the Doctrine of Freud,* trans. T. F. Lindsay. New York: Longmans Green, 1941.

Eagle, M. (1973), Sherwood on the Logic of Explanation in Psychoanalysis. *Psychoanalysis and Contemporary Science,* 2:331-337. New York: Macmillan.

Ellenberger, H. F. (1970), *The Discovery of the Unconscious: A History of Dynamic Psychiatry.* New York: Basic Books.

Ellis, A. (1956), An Operational Reformulation of Some Basic Principles of Psychoanalysis. In: *Minnesota Studies in the Philosophy of Science,* Vol. 1. *The Foundations of Science and the Concepts of Psychology and Psychoanalysis,* ed. H. Feigl & M. Scriven. Minneapolis: University of Minnesota Press, pp. 131-154.

Farrell, B. A. (1961), Can Psychoanalysis Be Refuted? *Inquiry,* 4:16-36.

────── (1964), The Criteria for a Psychoanalytic Interpretation. In: *Essays in Philosophical Psychology,* ed. D. Gustafson. New York: Doubleday, pp. 299-323.

Flew, A. (1954), Psychoanalytic Explanation. In: *Philosophy and Analysis,* ed. M. Macdonald. New York: Philosophical Library, pp. 139-148.

Flugel, J. C. (1945), *Man, Morals and Society.* New York: International Universities Press.

Freud, S. (1895), Project for a Scientific Psychology. *Standard Edition,* 1:295-397. London: Hogarth Press, 1966.

────── (1900), The Interpretation of Dreams. *Standard Edition,* 4 & 5. London: Hogarth Press, 1953.

────── (1901), The Psychopathology of Everyday Life. *Standard Edition,* 6. London: Hogarth Press, 1960.

────── (1913), The Claims of Psycho-Analysis to Scientific Interest. *Standard Edition,* 13:165-190. London: Hogarth Press, 1955.

────── (1917), Introductory Lectures on Psycho-Analysis. *Standard Edition,* 15 & 16. London: Hogarth Press, 1963.

────── (1918), Lines of Advance in Psycho-Analytic Therapy. *Standard Edition,* 17:159-168. London: Hogarth Press, 1955.

────── (1923), Remarks on the Theory and Practice of Dream-Interpretation. *Standard Edition,* 19:109-121. London: Hogarth Press, 1961.

────── (1933), New Introductory Lectures on Psycho-Analysis. *Standard Edition,* 22:5-182. London: Hogarth Press, 1964.

────── (1940), An Outline of Psycho-Analysis. *Standard Edition,* 23:144-207. London: Hogarth Press, 1964.

Hegel, G. W. F. (1807), *The Phenomenology of Mind,* trans. J. B. Baillie. New York: Harper & Row, 1967.

Holt, R. R. (1972), Freud's Mechanistic and Humanistic Images of Man. *Psychoanalysis and Contemporary Science*, 1:3-24. New York: Macmillan.
Home, H. J. (1966), The Concept of Mind. *Internat. J. Psycho-Anal.*, 47:42-49.
Hook, S., ed. (1959), *Psychoanalysis, Scientific Method and Philosophy*. New York: New York University Press.
Hyppolite, J. (1946), *Genèse et Structure de la Phénoménologie de l'Esprit de Hegel*, 2 vols. Paris: Aubier-Montaigne.
———— (1957), Phénoménologie de Hegel et Psychanalyse. *Psychanal.*, 3:17-32.
Ihde, D. (1971), *Hermeneutic Phenomenology: The Philosophy of Paul Ricoeur*. Evanston, Ill.: Northwestern University Press.
Klein, G. S. (1973), Is Psychoanalysis Relevant? *Psychoanalysis and Contemporary Science*, 2:3-21. New York: Macmillan.
Kojève, A. (1947), *Introduction to the Reading of Hegel,* trans. J. H. Nichols. New York: Basic Books.
Kubie, L. S. (1952), Problems and Techniques of Psychoanalytic Validation and Progress. In: *Psychoanalysis as Science*, ed. F. Pumpian-Mindlin. Stanford, Cal.: Stanford University Press, pp. 46-124.
Lacan, J. (1966), *Ecrits*. Paris: du Seuil.
Laplanche, J., & Leclaire, S. (1961), L'Inconscient. *Les Temps Modernes*, No. 183:81-129.
Madison, P. (1961), *Freud's Concept of Repression and Defense: Its Theoretical and Observational Language*. Minneapolis: University of Minnesota Press.
Marcuse, H. (1955), *Eros and Civilization: A Philosophical Inquiry into Freud*. Boston: Beacon.
Meehl, P. E. (1970), Some Methodological Reflections on the Difficulties of Psychoanalytic Research. In: *Minnesota Studies in the Philosophy of Science*, 4, ed. M. Radner & S. Winokur. Minneapolis: University of Minnesota Press, pp. 403-416.
Nagel, E. (1959), Methodological Issues in Psychoanalytic Science. In: *Psychoanalysis, Scientific Method and Philosophy*, ed. S. Hook. New York: New York University Press, pp. 38-56.
Pareto, V. (1916), *The Mind and Society*, Vol. 1, trans. A. Bongiorno & A. Livingston. New York: Harcourt Brace, 1935.
Peters, R. S. (1954), Cure, Cause and Motive. In: *Philosophy and Analysis*, ed. M. Macdonald. New York: Philosophical Library, pp. 148-154.
———— (1958), *The Concept of Motivation*. London: Routledge & Kegan Paul.
Popper, K. (1957), Philosophy of Science: A Personal Report. In: *British Philosophy in the Mid-Century* [1st ed.], ed. C. A. Mace. London: Allen & Unwin, pp. 155-191.
———— (1963), *Conjectures and Refutations*. London: Routledge & Kegan Paul.
Pumpian-Mindlin, E., ed. (1952), *Psychoanalysis as Science: The Hixon Lectures on the Scientific Status of Psychoanalysis*. Stanford, Cal.: Stanford University Press.
Radnitzky, G. (1968a), *Anglo-Saxon Schools of Metascience*. Göteborg: Scandinavian University Books.
———— (1968b), *Continental Schools of Metascience*. Göteborg: Scandinavian University Books.
Rapaport, D. (1959), The Structure of Psychoanalytic Theory. *Psychol. Issues*, Monogr. No. 6. New York: International Universities Press, 1960.
Ricoeur, P. (1965), *Fallible Man*, trans. C. Kelbley. Chicago: Regnery.
———— (1966), *Freedom and Nature: The Voluntary and the Involuntary*, trans.

E. Kohák. Evanston, Ill.: Northwestern University Press.

————— (1967), *Symbolism of Evil*, trans. E. Buchanan. New York: Harper & Row.

————— (1970), *Freud and Philosophy: An Essay on Interpretation*, trans. D. Savage. New Haven: Yale University Press.

————— (1974), *The Conflict of Interpretations: Essays in Hermeneutics*, ed. D. Ihde. Evanston, Ill.: Northwestern University Press.

Rieff, P. (1959), *Freud: The Mind of the Moralist*. New York: Viking.

Rubinstein, B. B. (1967), Explanation and Mere Description: A Metascientific Examination of Certain Aspects of the Psychoanalytic Theory of Motivation. In: Motives and Thought: Psychoanalytic Essays in Honor of David Rapaport, ed. R. R. Holt. *Psychol. Issues*, Monogr. No. 18/19:20-77. New York: International Universities Press.

Rycroft, C. (1966), Causes and Meaning. In: *Psychoanalysis Observed*, ed. C. Rycroft. London: Constable, pp. 7-22.

Scriven, M. (1959), Psychoanalytic Theory and Evidence. In: *Psychoanalysis, Scientific Method and Philosophy*, ed. S. Hook. New York: New York University Press, pp. 226-251.

Sherwood, M. (1969), *The Logic of Explanation in Psychoanalysis*. New York: Academic Press.

Shope, R. K. (1973), Freud's Concepts of Meaning. *Psychoanalysis and Contemporary Science*, 2:276-303. New York: Macmillan.

Skinner, B. F. (1956), Critique of Psychoanalytic Concepts and Theories. In: *Minnesota Studies in the Philosophy of Science*, Vol. 1. *The Foundations of Science and the Concepts of Psychology and Psychoanalysis*, ed. H. Feigl & M. Scriven. Minneapolis: University of Minnesota Press, pp. 77-87.

Speisman, J. C. (1965), Autonomic Monitoring of Ego Defense Process. In: *Psychoanalysis and Current Biological Thought*, ed. N. S. Greenfield & W. C. Lewis. Madison: University of Wisconsin Press, pp. 227-244.

Szasz, T. S. (1962), *The Myth of Mental Illness*. London: Secker & Warburg.

Tauber, E. S., & Green, M. R. (1959), *Prelogical Experience*. New York: Basic Books.

Toulmin, S. (1954), The Logical Status of Psychoanalysis. In: *Philosophy and Analysis*, ed. M. Macdonald. New York: Philosophical Library, pp. 132-139.

Weber, M. (1922), *Wirtschaft und Gesellschaft*, 4th ed. Mohr: Tubingen, 1956.

Wilden, A. (1968), *The Language of the Self*. Baltimore: Johns Hopkins Press.

————— (1972), *System and Structure: Essays in Communication and Exchange*. London: Tavistock.

Winch, P. (1958), *The Idea of a Social Science*. London: Routledge & Kegan Paul.

Yankelovich, D., & Barrett, W. (1970), *Ego and Instinct*. New York: Random House.

Bruce F. McKeown, M.A.

Identification and Projection in Religious Belief: A *Q*-Technique Study of Psychoanalytic Theory

Studies in the psychology of religion often refer to the important role of projection of nonreligious objects upon religious symbols. Understanding religion in this manner is neither new nor unique; analyses of projective behavior date back to Socrates. Among the studies suggesting a psychology of religion in this light, and perhaps the most intensive for its time, was the work of Ludwig Feuerbach (1841) in which he considered religion to be "human nature reflected, mirrored in itself. . . . Where, therefore, feeling is not depreciated and repressed . . . there also is religious power and significance already conceded to it, there also is it already exalted to that stage in which it can mirror and reflect itself, in which it can project its own image as God. God is the mirror of man" (p. 63). According to Feuerbach, God becomes "that which has essential value for man, which he esteems the perfect, the excellent, in which he has true delight" (p. 63); "what a man declares concerning God, he in truth declares concerning himself" (p. 29); and "Man—this is the mystery of religion—projects his being into objectivity. . . . It is true that man places the aim of his actions in God, but God has no other aim of action than the moral and eternal salvation of man: thus man has in fact no other aim than himself. The divine activity is not distinct from the human" (pp. 29-30). Anticipating Freud's statements on religion, Feuerbach concluded that religion was a dream, fantasy, or illusion expressing man's helpless and dependent condition as well as providing an imaginative gratification of the wish to overcome that situation.

Feuerbach's anthropological critique of religion as projection (see also Kamenka, 1970) led him to comment further upon religion as a source of alienation ("religion is the disuniting of man from himself"), and these interests, including his desire to study man as man unencumbered by fiction and myth, have been noted by many as having been an influence upon Karl Marx (see, e.g., Coser, 1971; Lichtheim, 1964; Meszaros, 1970; Zeitlin, 1967), an influence recognized by Marx himself (1844). Gaining inspiration from Feuerbach and other young Hegelians, Marx believed that Feuerbach was the only philosopher to provide a seriously critical approach to the embattled Hegelian dialectic, to have founded a genuine materialism by insisting upon the social relationships of man to man, and to have pointed to the alienating consequences of philosophy as well as religion (see Marx, 1844-1845, pp. 69-70). Feuerback failed, however, to "conceive the sensible world as *practical*, human sense activity." Marx wrote (1844-1845): "Feuerbach resolves the essence of religion into the essence of man. But the essence of man is not an abstraction inherent in each particular individual. The real nature of man is the totality of social relations. . . . Feuerbach therefore does not see that the 'religious sentiment' is itself a social product, and that the abstract individual whom he analyses belongs to a particular society" (pp. 68-69).

Nonetheless, Marx, like Feuerbach, was concerned with the effects of religion upon the consciousness of people. Like property, money, and wage labor, religion is an alienating intermediary between people because the more activity people expend in the world of things, the more powerful become those objects at the expense of a richer inner life. "It is just the same as in religion. The more of himself man attributes to God, the less he has left in himself" (1844-1845, p. 170). Furthermore, in the Marxian view religion is a facade, a part of the ideological superstructure through which the downtrodden masses project their real needs and wishes while submitting themselves to the manipulations of self-serving ruling classes. However valuable religion, especially Christianity, may have been for historical transition, it too would succumb to the inevitable changes in other more basic areas of life. Marx asked (1848), "Does it require deep intuitions to comprehend that man's ideas, views, and conceptions, in one word, man's consciousness, changes with every change in the condition of his material existence, in his social relations and his social life?" (pp. 51-52). It is in the final posthistorical period of communism that man will be in accord with nature, understand the true significance of his existence, and end his self- and social alienation by eradicating the misperceived need to attribute and project human nature onto nonhuman objects.

Like Feuerbach, Marx was interested in the psychological nature of religion (the alienating influence of projection), but was concerned more with the sociopolitical implications of religious belief and practice and evidently did not intend to develop a comprehensive psychology of religion. The Feuerbachian-Marxian thesis of religion as projection, however, has been incorporated into many psychologies of religion, and since the turn of this century the number of writings on the topic has been large. It is not the purpose of this paper to review this extensive literature (for a summary see Spinks, 1963; also Homans, 1970), but rather to discuss the psychoanalytic perspective on religion and provide an empirical test of some of its fundamental assumptions, emphasizing the dynamics of identification and projection and their roles in religious behavior.

THE FREUDIAN HYPOTHESIS

Among the early studies of religion perhaps the most important is *The Varieties of Religious Experience* by William James (1902). James's work was based primarily on writings by and about religious personalities, interpreted according to psychological principles. With the wisdom of nearly 70 years' hindsight, Thouless (1971) notes that although many of the limitations of an early psychology can be seen in James's book, it did lay the foundations for a scientific study of religion. Of particular interest has been James's notion of "religious experience," which he defined more broadly than had been the tradition, so that one could speak of the religious dimension of a variety of behaviors (see Capps, 1974).

Writing at the same time as James, Freud was explicating the outlines of psychoanalysis, which he believed would provide a comprehensive explanation of human behavior. In bringing to light the unconscious Freud and other psychoanalysts thought man could better understand the determinants of his behavior, thereby contributing to the adjustments necessary for a more rational and fuller life. The writings of Freud and his disciples, as well as the reinterpretations and revisions of that body of thought, are voluminous, and there are many treatments detailing the essential propositions (see, e.g., Fromm, 1950, 1963; Jung, 1938; Moxon, 1921; Schroeder, 1929). The writings of Freud and his disciples on the topic of religion have been of continuing interest, and it is a topic to which Freud himself made several controversial but important contributions.

Freud's first major statement on religion was not a treatise on religion as such, but its main line of argument was used repeatedly in his explicitly religious studies. In *Totem and Taboo* (1913) he speculated about how primitive religions began in the seemingly universal practice of totemism. The meaning of totemism was primarily symbolic, the totem being some sacred animal killed and eaten once a year at the totemistic feast. The feast, furthermore, was the symbolic acting out of the ancient unconscious hostility of the sons toward their father in the primal horde. The sons conspired against their father in order to fulfill their incestuous desires for the mother, but the father's murder generated such guilt that they were unable to take the father's place. To prevent future occurrences of that kind, the totem feast (representing the father's murder) was instituted so that later generations would be reminded of the original act. On the basis of this "just so" story Freud developed his general ideas about civilization and the growth of social institutions. The account of the totem and the taboo was not intended as a complete delineation of contemporary religion; however, as will be described below, the conclusions drawn from the study of primitive societies were applied to fully developed religions.

Although Freud and others believed that the totem was part of a prereligious stage of development ("totemism . . . the first form in which religion was manifested in human history" [Freud, 1937-1939, p. 83]), it was also thought that higher forms of religion could not unfold until primitive man had made an important distinction which is brought into focus by Rank and Sachs (1913):

So long as the division into internal and external world, ego and non-ego, had not been fully elaborated, the knowledge that the psychic reality produced by hallucinatory means is different from objective reality perceived by the senses could not become fixed. . . . With progressive adaptation to reality, the previous feeling of omnipotence, based on the mingling of objective with psychic reality, had to be in large part renounced and this feeling now saved itself in the field of endopsychic gratification in phantasy life [p. 73].

The murderous act of which the totem is symbolic marked the onset of instinctual repression (and hence civilization); it resulted, likewise, in psychic tensions and anxieties which were eventually projected onto the outer world so that "the animate beings who arose on a basis of this view and peopled the outer world became demons, to whom one ascribed the will and the power to do harm" (Rank and Sachs, p. 74). The resulting progression led from demon belief to magic and witchcraft, spiritualism, mythology, and finally the transformation of demons into gods. With the gods came identifiable religious cults and rites permitting and facilitating the "renunciation of the gratification of socially hostile instincts: [the rituals'] essence lies in their allowing, partly in the myth creating phantasy, partly by cultistic and ritualistic practice, the forbidden acts represented in this phantasy" (Rank and Sachs, pp. 76-77). Religion, therefore, is a response to an all-pervasive and underlying sense of guilt, and founded on the repression of instinct. Moxon (1921) summarized the psychoanalytic position in this manner:

. . . religion appears no longer either as an inexplicable miracle of divine grace or as a rational device of crafty and greedy priests. In certain conditions of life and culture, religion is as natural a product of the psyche as poetry, phantasy and other means of diversion from painful work. . . . Religious belief gives a symbolic satisfaction for hidden impulses, lowly emotions and primitive ideas. The psycho-analysts have proved that in religion the wish is verily father to the thought [p. 92].

Freud's other and more specific writings concerning religion de-emphasize individual psychology and broaden into the perspective of social psychology. In "The Future of an Illusion" (1927) he is more interested in the social purposes and dysfunctions of religions than in their psychic origins, although he does provide an overview of religion as a psychological construct (infantilism, wish fulfillment, and displacement). Freud's conception of religion as an illusion is in keeping with the general thesis he propounded in *Totem and Taboo*. Like Moxon, Freud believed that religious ideas are the fulfillments of the oldest and strongest wishes of mankind. "The secret of their strength lies in the strength of those wishes. As we already know, the terrifying impression of helplessness in childhood aroused the need for protection—for protection through love—which was provided by the father; and the recognition that this helplessness lasts throughout life made it necessary to cling to the existence of a father, but this time a more powerful one" (1927, p. 30). One may, then, relieve one's tensions by recourse to belief in a divine Providence (an image of the father), continuation of life after death, and the establishment of a structure of morality. "It is an enormous relief to the individual psyche if the conflicts of its childhood arising from the father-complex—conflicts which it has never wholly overcome—are removed from it and brought to a solution which is universally accepted" (p. 30). The significance of religion as an illusion is that wish fulfillment is its main motivating factor and in that regard enables one to disregard one's problems in a troubled reality (for a debate between Freud and one of his contemporaries, a Protestant minister, see Freud and Pfister [1909-1939]).

Freud's major work specifically related to the development and interpretation of religion is *Moses and Monotheism* (1937-1939), which traces the history of the Jewish faith in a manner analogous to the ideas expressed in *Totem and Taboo*. According to Freud, Moses was not Jewish but was an Egyptian living at the time of Akhenaten. A noble, distinguished, and ambitious man, Moses had identified with the rule of Akhenaten's faction, which had instituted a monotheistic faith. Following Akhenaten's death, however, a reaction set in with the new rulers, and Moses, caught in a political-theological split, was unwilling to accept the new leadership and faced a personal crisis. "When the king died and the reaction set in, he saw all his hopes and prospects destroyed; if he was not prepared to abjure all the convictions that were so dear to him, Egypt had nothing more to offer him—he had lost his country" (p. 28). Moses envisioned himself perpetuating the monotheistic practices in a new nation, and consequently found his following among certain Semitic tribes settled in an Egyptian border province of which he may have been governor. Moses made their acquaintance, established himself as their leader, and eventually undertook their exodus from Egypt. "In complete contrast to the Biblical tradition, we may presume that this Exodus took place peacefully and unpursued. The authority of Moses made this possible and at that time there was no central administration which might have interfered with it" (p. 29). Freud further postulated that the Jewish tribes, known later as the people of Israel, at a certain time accepted a new religion, but neither in Egypt nor at the base of a mountain in the Sinai; their conversion took place at Meribaht-Kadesh, which was south of Palestine. At that time the Jewish people incorporated the worship of Jahweh, a god borrowed from neighboring tribes.

At this juncture in his discussion Freud drew a distinction between two persons known as Moses. One Moses, the son-in-law of the Midianite priest Jethro, performed religious functions by mediating between Jahweh and the Jews.

> We cannot dispute the impression that this Moses of Kadesh and Midian, to whom tradition could actually attribute the erection of a brazen serpent as a god of healing, is someone quite other than the aristocratic Egyptian inferred by us, who presented the people with a religion in which all magic and spells were proscribed in the strictest terms. Our Egyptian Moses is no less different, perhaps, from the Midianite Moses than is the universal god Aten from the demon Yahweh in his home on the Mount of God [p. 36].

Then what became of the Egyptian Moses? Freud accepted an argument made by others that during the Exodus the Egyptian was murdered and his religion abandoned.

> Moses, deriving from the school of Akhenaten, employed no methods other than did the king; he commanded, he forced his faith upon the people. The doctrine of Moses may have been even harsher than that of his master.... Moses, like Akhenaten, met with the same fate that awaits all enlightened despots. The Jewish people under Moses were just as little able to tolerate such a highly spiritualized religion and find satisfaction of their needs in what it had to offer as had been the

Egyptians of the Eighteenth Dynasty.... those who had been dominated and kept in want rose and threw off the burden of the religion that had been imposed on them.... the savage Semites took fate into their own hands and rid themselves of their tyrant [p. 47].

Following his death the religion of the Egyptian Moses was integrated with the religion of the Moses at Kadesh, and the content and form of the Jewish faith resulted from that synthesis.

The Egyptian's murder had continuing effects upon the Jewish people, and it is in this respect that the similarities and differences between the theses of *Moses and Monotheism* and of *Totem and Taboo* become important and clear. As Reid (1972) notes, the reaction of the primal sons to their father's death was remorse—the expression of love for the murdered father which eventually led to his deification. Moses' death, on the other hand, was very different; the people denied they had murdered their liberator and in so doing also denied his ethical commandments. Thus, according to Reid, there are two fundamental differences between the deaths of Moses and the primal father.

First, Moses, unlike the primal father, freed his people from bondage and, second, he practiced the ethical standards and commands (the instinctual repressions) expected of his followers, also unlike the primal father. The primal father was, in a sense, deserving of his fate—the sons' hostile feelings could be justified; but that was not the case in the relationship between Moses and his people. They had freely and willingly followed him from Egypt, and Moses himself practiced the reunuciations imposed upon the Jews. As Reid puts it,

No matter how much they hated him, they could not justify their murdering him.... The psychic results of a crime which *cannot* be justified (the murder of Moses) differ from the psychic results of a crime which *could* be justified (the murder of the primal father). We must therefore qualify the statement that Moses was "an eminent substitute." The essential ambivalence of the father-son relationship was lacking [p. 17].

In his interpretation of *Moses and Monotheism*, Reid concludes that whereas the death of the primal father generated remorse, the death of Moses created such feelings of guilt that they were immediately repressed ("forgotten"). "Such guilt has no recourse but repression. And so it was with the Israelites" (p. 24).

When Freud stated that the murder of Moses was "forgotten," he did not mean that the event had no impact on the Jewish people or that the crime was irrelevant to the growth of Judaism. Forgotten means repressed, and the significance of the repressed crime was its return to consciousness later on ("the return of the repressed") in the form of religious rite and tradition. Reverting from his social psychology to individual psychology, Freud explained the nature of the return of the repressed and its influence upon the development of religion:

> We are now assuming that this process was being repeated then for the second time. When Moses brought the people the idea of a single god, it was not a novelty but signified the revival of an experience in the primaeval ages of the human family which had long vanished from men's conscious memory. But it had been so important and had produced or paved the way for such deeply penetrating changes in men's life that we cannot avoid believing that it had left behind it in the human mind some permanent traces, which can be compared to a tradition.
>
> We have learnt from the psycho-analyses of individuals that their earliest impressions, received at a time when the child was scarcely yet capable of speaking, produce at some time or another effects of a compulsive character without themselves being consciously remembered. We believe we have a right to make the same assumption about the earliest experiences of the whole of humanity [1937-1939, pp. 129-130].

For Freud, the emergence of the memory of the crime resulted in the conception of a single great God—a memory, no matter how distorted, that simply *"must* be believed." Because it was distorted it was a delusion, and yet "in so far as it brings a return of the past, it must be called the *truth"* (p. 130).

Reid acknowledges Freud's discussion of the "latency period" between the death of Moses and the return of the repressed, but diverges from Freud on how that return stimulated a new religion. He wonders why Freud did not consider the developments in historical terms. "The importance of the murder of Moses then, is not as Freud states, that in historical times a group of otherwise undifferentiated people murdered an 'eminent father substitute' and so re-experienced the emotional conditions of the primal murder" (p. 24). If one accepts Reid's distinction between the consequences of the death of the primal father (remorse) and of Moses (guilt), then one understands how the guilt of the act re-emerged as well. Attempting to expiate their guilt, "the people accepted ever more severe restrictions on their instinctual drives" (p. 25). Reid also writes: ". . . Freud discusses *individual* development. He does not follow it with the expected application to the historical conditions which occasioned the return of the repressed guilt among the Jews" (p. 26). Those conditions included the deportation to and exile in Babylonia of a large number of Jews and their eventual return from exile. Reid's amplification of Freud's brief discussion of the latency period may be summarized as follows:

(1) The latency period was anticathectic. The Jews were prosperous and successful; their good fortune prevented the repressed from rising to the surface. "Freud's dictum can be applied here: 'As long as things go well with a man, his conscience is lenient and lets the ego do all sorts of things' " (p. 26). However, the deportation to Babylonia was critical enough to reverse the effects of the anticathexis. The Jewish people fell on hard times and their misfortune led them to search their souls, express remorse for past sins, and impose abstinences and punishments upon themselves.

(2) Freud's second condition was the reinforcement of instinctual elements connected to the repressed (as represented in the stage of puberty). According to Reid's historical explanation,

> The "instinctual elements" attached to the repressed guilt for the murder of Moses were, simply, the instincts which the laws of Moses had sought to subdue [e.g., the Ten Commandments]. . . . Proximity to the less inhibited, idolatrous, luxury-prone Babylonians was the second condition favoring the return of the repressed guilt: witness of the instinctual freedom denied them by Moses and which had been the direct cause of their murdering him "reminded" them of the deed [p. 27].

(3) Finally, "if at any time in recent experience impressions or experiences occur which resemble the repressed . . . closely . . . they are able to awaken it" (Freud, 1937-1939, p. 95). Reid dis-

covers that this indeed happened historically: the Persians, victorious over the Babylonians, permitted the Jewish exiles to return to their "promised land." That event "could not have failed to impress upon those exiles that they were experiencing a startling repetition of the great deed of liberation some eight hundred years earlier. . . . The repressed guilt for the murder of Moses now rose decisively in the people" (p. 28). Thus in these three conditions and events one sees the manner in which the memory of the murder of Moses returned and became the seed of the Jewish faith.

Freud concludes *Moses and Monotheism* with a brief discourse on Judaism's development and the Jewish unwillingness to accept the Messiah of Christianity. He writes that the essence of Moses' death was the killing of the Great Father. People need an authority they can admire and to whom they can submit, and it is the longing for the father which persists from childhood. "And now it may begin to dawn on us that all the characteristics with which we equipped the great man are paternal characteristics, and that the essence of great men for which we vainly searched lies in this conformity" (p. 109). Moses provided the appropriate father figure for the Jewish people: "There can be no doubt that it was a mighty prototype of a father which, in the person of Moses, stooped to the poor Jewish bondsmen to assure them that they were his dear children" (p. 110). It was the identification of Moses with God that generated the psychic problems for them, for they had killed God and that memory drove them to establish the great systems of ethics and religious experiences. Moses became the recipient of their projected collective superego, a conclusion with which Zeligs (1973) concurs ("Being both leader and prophet, he served too as the 'voice of God,' thus symbolizing the *collective superego*" [p. 217]). The death of Moses, later understood as the death of God, was both a burden from which the Jews could not be relieved and an act kept alive by the prophets and for which the Law was created (as a means for helping to alleviate the burden). As Freud put it in *Moses and Monotheism*, "These ethical ideas cannot . . . disavow their origin from the sense of guilt felt on account of a suppressed hostility to God. They possess the characteristic—uncompleted and incapable of completion—of obsessional neurotic reaction-formations; we can guess, too, that they serve the secret purposes of punishment" (1937-1939, pp. 134-135).

Freud furthermore believed that the plight of the Jewish people spread beyond themselves; their peculiar awareness of guilt was generalized throughout the Mediterranean area and was eventually expressed in the Christian writings, especially those of Saul of Tarsus (Paul): ". . . 'the reason we are so unhappy is that we have killed God the father.' And it is entirely understandable that [Paul] could only grasp this piece of truth in the delusional disguise of the glad tidings: 'we are freed from all guilt since one of us has sacrificed his life to absolve us'" (p. 135). The Messiah concept eventually replaced the covenant with God in importance, and the murder, difficult in itself to resolve, became ever more distorted and was replaced by the idea of original sin. As taught by Paul, original sin could be overcome only by salvation through means other than the Jewish Law. Thus the grounds were laid for a new religion. The identification of Jesus with the expected Messiah and his ultimate sacrifice provided the avenue for Jewish reconciliation with God. The identification also created the conditions in which the ancient reconciliation of father with son could be achieved (Jesus as a totem). What was originally a "Father religion" had become a "Son religion." Freud noted that those refusing to accept the new doctrine remained Jews but they have also continually suffered the reproach, "They killed God." Freud concluded *Moses and Monotheism* without explaining the Jewish rejection of Christianity, but suggested that the issue is another fruitful area for study, a cue which Reid fortunately picked up.

Reid continues with a discussion of the Jewish burden of guilt from which they longed to be free. The prophets provided intellectual assurances of God's interest in His people but those assurances were insufficient to appease the guilt. In addition, the prophets offered an eschatological element (the hope of a Messiah) which continued to be forceful in Jewish thought. The Messiah, in the popular view (which is central for Reid; see pp. 31-32), was to be the anointed, righteous king, fulfilling specific prophecies and reigning in final judgment over all who had subjected the people to the miseries of life. However, "the idea of the Messiah as either the 'suffering servant' . . . or as the 'son of man' . . . did not play a dominant part in the popular conception of the Messiah" (p. 32), although they were the essential images associated with Jesus of Nazareth. As Reid reminds us, Jesus, upon revealing himself to his disciples, charged them to secrecy about himself and his mission. The charge was given for a very specific reason. The Jews were awaiting a Messiah who would absolve them once and for all of their guilt for the murder of Moses. Jesus' self-conception, on the other hand, was completely opposite to the popular image of the expected savior; he was in no sense the fulfillment of their wish. Reid offers an interesting statement of the result:

> If the conception of the Messiah was indeed born of the guilt for the murder of Moses, it was born of the hope for the expiation of that unresolved guilt. Then, the new deliverer could under no circumstances suffer as had his predecessor. The people wanted another chance. This time, when the great deliverer should come, they would not, as they had done to Moses, murder him. They would, therefore, *prove* to Yahweh that they finally earned their deliverance from guilt [p. 33].

Jesus was an unacceptable Messiah because not only did he not fulfill the conscious desire for worldly sovereignty, he did not fulfill the unconscious role of a Messiah—that is, "he would not suffer" (p. 34). Accepting Jesus was to continue admitting to the original murder and guilt, not to resolve it.

The psychoanalytic position on religion, therefore, can be summarized as follows: religion is an illusion that nonetheless contains historical truth. Freud wrote in "The Future of an Illusion," ". . . the primal father was the original image of God, the model on which later generations have shaped the figure of God. Hence the religious explanation is right. . . . And the displacement of man's will on to God is fully justified. . . . Thus religious doctrine tells us the historical truth . . . whereas our rational account disavows it" (1927, p. 42). "God" is the continuation of a father imago displaced into a supernatural realm where one's protection and security can be assured. In *Moses and Monotheism* Freud connected primitive and nonprimitive man on the basis of the universal need for a father figure:

> We understand how a primitive man is in need of a god as creator of the universe, as chief of his clan, as personal protector. This god takes his position behind the dead fathers, about whom tradition still has something to say. A man of later

days, of our own day, behaves in the same way. He, too, remains childish and in need of protection, even when he is grown up; he thinks he cannot do without support from his god [1937-1939, p. 128].

Much of the significance of religion, of the "truth of religion," is thereby reflected in the belief in one God and the relationship of the child to his father. "Now that God was a single person, man's relations to him could recover the intimacy and intensity of the child's relation to his father" (Freud, 1927, p. 19). Likewise, Farrell (1955) discusses the relationship between religion and stages of psychological development, arguing somewhat like Freud that should a child fixate in a parent-dependent stage his future behavior will be based on regression to that stage, even when he has learned responses appropriate for his age that should modify the regressive behavior. "Since he cannot any longer exhibit this dependent behaviour towards his parents, he unconsciously displaces it on to parent-substitutes. Since the father is the dominant parent-figure in our culture, the important displacement that occurs will be on to a new father figure" (p. 188).

Parent images are evident in Christianity ("God the Father," "Mary, mother of God") and, as Farrell notes, in secular religions such as Marxism (Marx, Lenin, and at one time a third part of a trinity, Stalin). The religious act, such as praying to our Father in Heaven or engaging in communion (the totem feast), "satisfies the deeper needs of the person who is consciously ignorant of its meaning" (Moxon, 1921, p. 94; see also Tillich, 1960, pp. 79-81, and Reik, 1923). Ultimately, for some theorists religion is essentially sexual in origin (Moxon), and neurotic (Rubins, 1955), but as mentioned earlier these understandings become more meaningful when the concepts of identification, projection, and displacement are introduced in order to understand how the religious sentiment is originally established.

EMPIRICAL RESEARCH AND THE
PSYCHOANALYTIC HYPOTHESES

Numerous investigations into the concepts and processes discussed above have been conducted, but the available evidence is ambiguous about whether the psychoanalytic explanation of religion, as presented by Freud and others, is supported. Some studies reinforce the idea of the Oedipal conflict as the driving force in religious development, whereas in others that interpretation is rejected in favor of alternative theories. It should be noted that in the following discussion I have not attempted an extensive review of the research, but rather have tried to indicate the scope and method of research consistent with the data gathered for this paper and reported below.

Relying on scalar measures to test projection in religious behavior, Siegman (1961) deduced three hypotheses from psychoanalytic theory: (1) feelings and concepts concerning God should resemble those of the father; (2) fear of God is a projection of the castration complex and thus fear should be greater among men than women; (3) religious people should display a greater tendency to project than nonreligious people. His results failed to support the first and third hypotheses and provided only tentative support for the second. It is noteworthy that Siegman found insignificant correlations between the measures of religious belief and observance and the indices of projection, and he remarks that "It has to be admitted that none of the tests which were used . . . to measure projection are completely satisfactory. Each of the tests, however, measures some aspect of projection with some degree of validity" (p. 76). The problems of validity are of course important, especially in studies of this kind; if "projection" and "identification" are not being tapped, or only slightly so, then one has little basis upon which to speculate. The importance of proper method in this respect is crucial in empirical studies of psychoanalytic processes— when projection is being studied the subjects should be projecting. Nevertheless, the paucity of his results did not deter Siegman from doubting the validity of the projection hypothesis. Indeed, he attempted to explain his meager findings by referring to perceptual and learning theory. Suffice it to say that the hypothesis of projection as a dynamic of religious behavior is not refuted by poor results gained from questionable measures of the phenomenon.

Others have taken a more promising approach, examining the association between parental images and images of God. These researchers have undertaken to examine the psychological processes by employing those very processes in the research. Gorsuch (1968), tying together the work of Spilka, Armatas, and Nussbaum (1964) and Osgood, Suci, and Tannenbaum (1957), used adjective ratings and found a variety of differing perceptions of the Deity (although all related to a general underlying factor characterized as "traditional Christianity"). Gorsuch suggested that further research might delve into the sources of influence that give rise to the conceptualizations of God as expressed through the adjectives. Subsequently, Vergote et al. (1969) compared parental and God images by paying particular attention to differences between maternal and paternal characteristics. Their cross-cultural study revealed that the image of God is generally more paternal than maternal, although in the American sample the symbol was seen in somewhat more maternal terms.

Similar results have been found in two studies by Nelson using the Q technique. Nelson and Jones (1957) explored the application of the technique to religion and especially to the object of God. More explicitly, they were interested in knowing if "God" was indeed the projection of the father image. Sixteen subjects Q-sorted 60 descriptive statements in four different conditions of instruction, describing in turn "God," "mother," "father," and "Jesus." The intercorrelations revealed that the mother object correlated more strongly with God and Jesus, and Nelson and Jones concluded that the mother image is more influential in determining deity concepts than the father. In a follow-up study Nelson (1971), rejecting the Freudian position, sought to test the Adlerian hypothesis that the concept of God correlates with that of the preferred parent. His results confirmed those of earlier studies (Nelson and Jones, 1957; Godin and Hallez, 1964; Strunk, 1959). In spite of a general tendency to prefer the mother, God was identified with the parent preferred by the subject. Nelson concluded that "there is no support for Freud's idea of the concept of God as the projection of the attitude toward one's father" (p. 49).

Nelson's results do not necessarily support his conclusion, however. For instance, he does not state that his sample of subjects (37 males, 47 females) was a random selection. Now it is important to note that Q technique does not require the subject sample to be a statistically random one; the crucial problem lies in the selection of statements (the statement sample) and the various conditions of instruction under which the Q sorting takes place. Nelson nevertheless drew conclusions based on the number and nature of parental preferences (e.g., "There was a general tendency to prefer the mother. This tendency was greater for the males than the females"; p. 48). Furthermore, and more important, the differences in the mean correlations between God and father and God and mother for those subjects with no parental preference were very small (no greater than .03), a finding nonsupportive of the Nelson and Jones study in which "God" was the mother.

The value of Nelson's studies lies less in what he considers an invalidation of Freud's thesis than in providing additional support for the varieties of identifications that can develop in the psychology of object relations. That is to say, the associations made between the concepts of God and the "preferred parent" reinforce the thesis that perceptions of religious objects are still in large part the result of identifications with primary objects projected upon secondary objects and religious symbols. Indeed, one can point to a number of studies in which the same dynamics as those studied by Nelson and Jones are considered and which are also supportive of Freud's major contentions. Rizzuto (1974), for example, reported two clinical case studies in which the God symbol was closely connected to the father image. Her main conclusion, however, was that the elements forming the image of God originate in the early object representations of childhood which are internalized and eventually have a life of their own.

The remainder of this paper provides a more thorough investigation than that of Nelson and Jones, Rizzuto, and others, of the roles played by identification and projection in the formation of religious concepts. Particular attention is given to primary and secondary (religious) object formation. The intent is neither to prove nor disprove Freud's fundamental assertions but rather to understand more fully the way in which religious objects or symbols become meaningful to the persons who hold them.

A STUDY OF IDENTIFICATION AND PROJECTION IN RELIGIOUS BELIEF

Perceptions of and ideas about God, Jesus, the Biblical prophets, one's conscience, and religion in general are expected to be congruent with the identifications made between the primary objects of childhood and important secondary objects. Studies that rest on this assumption have dealt with the meanings given to political objects, for example (see Thomas, 1970), and in a recent and important paper delineating the rules for intensive analysis of single cases Baas and Brown (1973) have demonstrated how displacements from the primary objects to the domains of secondary objects may be studied empirically.

If displacement and projection occur between the self and immediate primary objects (e.g., one's mother and father), secondary objects (such as one's grandmother or best friend), and political objects (symbols, concepts, persons), then one can infer that they function in other substantive areas as well, including the religious realm (see Baas and Brown for the principles underlying this supposition). Although the observation of these processes is indirect, psychoanalysts have devised a variety of means to study objectively what are essentially subjective experiences, means which include free association, projective tests, and play therapy. The use of each device assumes that manifest behavior is rooted in the unconscious, often disguised by defensive and coping techniques. The research or therapeutic task is to interpret the behavior in terms of the underlying dynamics generating or supporting the subject's or client's overt behavior. Investigative techniques, therefore, must include some type of *facilitating operation* to make objective the subjective. As Baas and Brown have written,

> We are forced to deal with representations of phenomena because we can rarely deal directly with the phenomena themselves. The physicist, after all, does not deal directly with gravity or electricity, but with readings from recording devices. The devices serve to *transform* the unknowable phenomenon into a more readily accessible medium, and it is hoped that whatever is essential to an understanding of the unknowable phenomenon will appear as an invariant in the conceptual representation of it, undistorted (or minimally so) by the process of transformation [1973, p. 176].

The data used in this study were collected through a procedure which taps the processes of displacement, identification, and projection. Q technique (Stephenson, 1953) was selected as highly suitable for the study. The Q sorting of statements contains both a conscious component (the physical ranking of items) and an unconscious component (the resulting interrelationships, unknown to the subject, between the items described in the various sortings). Consequently, one can

> ... take issue with [the] view that Q technique is of little importance in psychoanalytically-oriented research since, presumably, it only deals with conscious materials. A subject, while Q sorting, may be entering into projection, denial, transference, and all manner of dynamic activities. In this sense, the sorting of statements shares certain characteristics with the behavior of a patient describing figures in a dream, although the latter is no doubt less subject to conscious awareness. When the therapist notes the relationship between the dream-like figure and the client's mother, he is noting a relationship which, in our methodology, is presented to us in the form of a correlation coefficient. There is, therefore, a similarity between factor analysis and certain inferential aspects of psychoanalysis [Baas and Brown, 1973, p. 182, fn. 10].

Unlike previous research in the psychology of religion (e.g., Nelson and Jones, 1957), the present study provides a wider universe of stimuli which, when their descriptions are correlated and factor analyzed, present more clearly the associations between religious and nonreligious objects and the dynamics that led to those associations.

PROCEDURE

Six subjects, all of whom came from conservative Protestant backgrounds, were chosen for study. One male and one female were selected to represent each of three religious types: two subjects who had remained close to the church both doctrinally and experientially; two who had moved away from the church, attended infrequently, and had reservations about some theological issues; and two who had cut themselves off entirely from their churches and were self-designated atheists or agnostics. For one reason or another three subjects (the two agnostics and the very religious male) completed so few Q sorts that they were not included in the analysis. The three subjects who completed the task are described below.

Each subject was presented with 50 adjectives typed on separate cards; the adjectives were systematically drawn from a listing of personality traits (Anderson, 1968) so as to include three kinds of traits: those commonly perceived as (a) socially commendable, (b) neutral, and (c) uncommendable. Adjective traits with explicitly religious or moral connotations (e.g., "ethical") were excluded. Each subject described 24 objects (Table 1), by rank-ordering the 50 adjectives from "most like" to "most unlike" each

TABLE 1

SELF, PRIMARY, AND RELIGIOUS OBJECT DOMAINS

Self Domain

Myself (ego)
What I would like to be (ego ideal)
Person I was taught to be (superego)
Myself when I felt the most religious
Myself when most depressed
Myself when I felt the most guilty
Myself when I felt the most sorrowful
Myself when I felt God was angry with me

Primary Objects Domain

My father
My mother
The person I distrust the most
Mother, when she and I had our worst falling-out
Father, when he and I had our worst falling-out
The person I hate the most
My best friend
The person I most admire

Religious Objects Domain

The best example of a Christian (an actual person)
The ideal Christian
God
Jesus Christ
The person who best exemplifies a sinner
Satan
Jesus at the time of the crucifixion
God, when I felt He was angry with me

object according to the quasi-normal forced-choice distribution shown in Table 2, placing three of the adjectives most like the object being described under $+4$, the four next most like the object under $+3$, and so forth, until the continuum was completed. Adjective traits neither like nor unlike the object were placed under 0.

The 24 objects representing each subject's object world were selected to represent three different domains: Self, Primary Objects, and Secondary or Religious Objects. The objects were also typed on slips of paper and placed in individual envelopes numbered from 1 to 24; their descriptions, as provided in the subjects' Q sorts, were completed in one month. Each description was a variation of a common condition of instruction; for example, "Describe your *self*—by distributing the 50 adjectives from 'most like me' $(+4)$ down to 'most unlike me' (-4)." To avoid the possibility of response set, the subjects were instructed to shuffle the adjectives between each sorting; none of the subjects completed more than two sortings on any given day.

The Q sorts were intercorrelated, producing a 72 x 72 correlation matrix which was factor analyzed using the principal components method with communalities placed in the diagonal of the correlation matrix; in the example of the illustrative single case, only the subject's Q-sort descriptions were correlated and analyzed. The number of factors with eigenvalues greater than one were extracted and given a varimax rotation to simple solution.

AN ILLUSTRATIVE SINGLE CASE—SUBJECT M

To illustrate the way in which identifications and projections can function in religious belief, a summary is presented of a single

TABLE 2

CONTINUUM FOR ADJECTIVE Q SORTS

	(most unlike)							(most like)	
Value	-4	-3	-2	-1	0	$+1$	$+2$	$+3$	$+4$
Frequency	3	4	6	7	10	7	6	4	3 (N=50)

case. Although one should avoid generalizing from the *specifics* of one person to another, the single-case approach is instructive when fundamental *principles* are involved; indeed, the most interesting and theoretically rewarding discoveries in fields seemingly as far apart as psychoanalytic and behaviorist psychology have come from studies of only one subject's, patient's, or laboratory animal's behavior. In this instance, as with the combined analysis, it is suggested that the psychodynamics giving rise to religious identifications and meanings cut across individual idiosyncrasies and lend support to the psychoanalytic view of religion as reviewed earlier.

Subject M is a 27-year-old married woman employed as a social worker and marriage counselor. She has a bachelor's degree in sociology and is completing a master's degree in higher educational counseling. Her undergraduate education was received in a private liberal arts college associated with a Protestant denomination. While living at home Mrs. M attended the same conservative church as her parents and of the denomination that supports her college. At present, however, she frequently attends Protestant churches other than that in which she was reared. Mrs. M describes her theological positions as "liberal" and her social and political beliefs as "liberal" also.

The factor structure of Mrs. M's object world (Table 3) shows that her 24 Q sorts were organized in essentially three different ways. Her first factor can be identified as a "good objects" factor, defined by the description of her mother. Included in the factor are other objects perceived to be characteristic of her ideal world (the ideal Christian, her ego ideal, and the best example of a Christian) and others held in high esteem (the most admired person, her best friend). Two important religious objects, God and Jesus, are also included in the factor. One should also note the location of Mrs. M's self-concept, indicating some congruence between her self-image and the good aspects of her interpersonal world. In general, the factor can be described, by referring to the factor scores of the adjective traits, as warm ($+4$), honorable ($+3$), and conscientious ($+4$); her conceptions of self and her "good objects" are accepted in an environment of trust ($+3$) and patience ($+3$). The objects in the factor are defined as not being unhappy (-3), irresponsible (-4), thoughtless (-4), cynical (-3), or malicious (-4).

TABLE 3

FACTOR MATRIX: SUBJECT M

Object Descriptions	Factors[a]		
	1	2	3
Mother	(78)	−08	−22
Best example of Christian	(76)	−12	−13
Person most admired	(75)	−08	−24
Jesus Christ	(74)	−11	−31
When most religious	(74)	−11	−30
Crucified Christ	(74)	−14	−20
Best friend	(68)	−16	05
Ideal Christian	(68)	−32	−34
Ideal self	(67)	−11	−29
Person taught to be	(67)	−33	−21
Self	(62)	−24	−17
God	(61)	35	−30
Father	(57)	−09	07
Angry God	14	(69)	−15
Angry mother	02	(68)	02
Angry father	−14	(65)	−04
Person hated the most	−16	(64)	16
Best example of a sinner	−35	(51)	36
When most depressed	−10	−05	(62)
Self—when God was angry	−10	08	(59)
When most sorrowful	(42)	(−54)	27
Person distrusted	(−50)	(53)	38
Satan	(−46)	(52)	09
Guilty self	(−52)	−07	(57)

[a] Decimals have been omitted. Factor loadings ±.40 are significant $p < .01$.

The second factor reinforces the relationships found in the first; in it are the "bad objects" of an angry God and both angry parents, along with two despised persons, the most hated and the best example of a sinner. Unlike Factor 1 objects, Factor 2 objects were described as quite unloving and nonaccepting; they are strict (+3), demanding (+4), domineering (+4), self-centered (+3), and not tolerant (−4), patient (−3), or trusting (−4). The definitions of these objects are like a small child's reaction to and perception of adults when he is unable to have his own way, and the angry God is the target of those projections. In that manner the angry God becomes the angry parents writ large.

The "depressed" third factor contains only two objects with pure loadings—the depressed self and the self when God is angry. Like the identifications found in Factor 2, the relationship between the religious and nonreligious is clear; depression provides the behavioral clues for her feelings when she believes she has acted contrary to God's expectations. The relationship is further supported by the third variable in the factor: the guilty self (mixed negatively with Factor 1). The guilty self and the self when God is angry are nearly one and the same, as might be expected, and it is evidently not difficult for the subject to identify her sense of guilt with what displeases God. When depressed or feeling guilty Mrs. M appears cynical ($+3$), insecure ($+4$), and self-centered ($+4$), and is neither clever (-3) or shrewd (-3; "you can't fool God"), nor honorable (-3) or trusting (-4). As it turns out, one discovers from the descriptions of Factor 2 objects that Mrs. M's perceptions of the angry God and parents and the two other bad objects are the receptacles for the displacements of her own bad qualities.

The positions of the remaining objects, mixed on at least two of the three factors, are in keeping with the previous discussion. For example, Mrs. M's conceptions of Satan and the person most distrusted are negative and opposite (bipolar) to the good objects of Factor 1 but positive on Factor 2. The guilty self is the exact opposite of the happy, good self but, as mentioned above, similar to her self when depressed and feeling the wrath of God. The position (bipolarity) of the guilty self on the first factor deserves emphasis because it points to an important dynamic relationship suggesting that the good and ideal object identifications (mother, the good Christian, Jesus, best friend, ideal self, God, father, and the like) are defenses against becoming the guilty person she would rather avoid, and yet "being guilty" is not that difficult because it is part of the self (even if it is bipolar), ideal self, and the other good objects relations. Mrs. M does not, so to speak, need to change factors (i.e., rearrange or create new identifications) to experience guilt. By and large, her object world is divided into the good, in which the mother is central, and from whom she has learned the cues for the interpretation of Christian ideals; the bad, including the angry God related to her angry parents; and her ugly, depressed, and guilty self.

THE COMBINED ANALYSIS

The single case discussed above has indicated that psychological dynamics of identification, projection, and displacement do function in a person's signification of religious objects and experience. To reiterate, the precise nature of the identifications and projections is idiosyncratic; however, both theory and evidence strongly suggest that underlying processes are similar across people. Persons whose religious training and experience differ from those of Mrs. M or the other two subjects studied here (Mr. S and Miss A) may develop differing religious orientations, but one can suspect that the dynamics by which their religious objects are given meaning is the same.

The testing for the communality of the subjects' experiences and the uniformity of psychological processes revealed a variety of relationships, although all 72 object descriptions fell into five basic patterns. The results (see Table 4), which bear out the findings of the single case study, can be summarized as follows:

Factor 1: Predominant in this factor are the loadings of "good, friendly objects." Subject A (described in footnote 2, Table 4) sets the standard in her descriptions. Jesus Christ, much more than God, is the one religious symbol identified with, and takes on the characteristics of the good objects. The ego ideal for all three subjects helps to determine the nature of the Christ symbol.

Factor 2: Factor 2 objects are essentially from the self domain, generally depressed and sorrowful. The objects of Miss A are interesting although confusing. The factor can be interpreted in this manner: the similarity of the Q sorts of subjects M and S to those of A reflect the mode of experience missing in their sorrowful or bad selves when matched with the highly Christian example of Miss A. If that is so, M and S are experiencing some of the regret they have for severing themselves from their traditional Christian roots.

Factor 3: Factor 3 is a bad objects factor. It contains eight of the nine angry parents and Gods. As in the single case of Mrs. M, the evidence overwhelmingly supports the proposition that

TABLE 4

FACTOR MATRIX: COMBINED Q SORTS

Object Descriptions	S^b	1	2	3	4	5
				Factors[a]		
Best example of a Christian	A	(89)	13	-03	-16	14
Ideal self	A	(89)	00	-06	00	15
Ideal self	S	(84)	-17	-04	-11	12
Best friend	A	(82)	11	-10	-05	28
Person most admired	A	(80)	-13	06	31	15
Jesus Christ	A	(75)	16	10	-34	10
Person most admired	M	(72)	-02	-05	-27	06
Best friend	M	(67)	-22	02	-38	09
Best example of a Christian	S	(66)	08	-01	-20	38
Crucified Christ	S	(64)	02	09	-38	31
Self	S	(63)	01	-18	-26	28
Best friend	S	(62)	29	-01	11	30
God	M	(58)	-15	38	-38	27
When most religious	A	(50)	-31	-06	-37	29
Person most hated	A	(-71)	-24	24	39	19
Guilty self	A	(-58)	38	07	35	38
When most sorrowful	A	32	(71)	04	-36	-01
Self	A	22	(67)	24	-29	16
When most depressed	S	-36	(64)	08	-06	08
Self—when God was angry	M	-36	(64)	-02	02	-24
When most sorrowful	S	35	(63)	-18	-35	04
Self—when God was angry	S	-16	(61)	25	30	-03
Crucified Christ	A	23	(56)	-11	-36	-02
Father	A	21	(43)	18	-27	36

Angry father	M	01	−14	(89)	−03	−09
Angry God	A	13	−02	(86)	−03	−11
Angry God	M	08	01	(78)	−10	−12
Angry mother	M	−08	−04	(75)	−17	−21
Angry mother	S	−14	−19	(73)	−22	16
Angry father	A	−06	08	(72)	05	21
Angry God	S	01	−37	(65)	20	25
Angry father	S	−38	−30	(55)	16	21
Satan	A	−01	−31	08	(80)	−06
Satan	S	−26	−29	14	(73)	−16
Best example of a sinner	S	−30	02	12	(73)	02
Satan	M	−22	−30	18	(72)	03
Best example of a sinner	M	−06	17	30	(67)	03
Person hated the most	S	−15	16	26	(62)	27
Crucified Christ	M	34	31	−03	(−63)	−16
Person taught to be	A	26	25	14	(−59)	38
Father	S	30	19	01	−20	(45)
Self—when God was angry	A	−18	31	−02	17	(−63)
When most depressed	M	(−60)	(54)	07	09	−31
Angry mother	A	(−64)	(44)	34	04	14
When most depressed	A	(−59)	(61)	04	14	09
God	S	(48)	−27	(57)	−14	32
God	A	(52)	−11	(62)	−17	08
Self	M	(66)	−04	−07	(−54)	20
Ideal self	M	(78)	−10	−09	(−44)	05
Person taught to be	M	(44)	01	07	(−65)	26
Father	M	(67)	−13	07	(−40)	02
Best example of a Christian	M	(71)	02	00	(−45)	06
When most religious	M	(56)	−07	−08	(−45)	16
Mother	M	(46)	−08	30	(−45)	15

TABLE 4 (continued)

Object Descriptions	S^b	Factors[a]				
		1	2	3	4	5
Ideal Christian	M	(48)	00	-05	(-65)	-01
Jesus Christ	M	(68)	-24	01	(-46)	09
Person taught to be	S	(47)	07	-05	(-62)	24
Ideal Christian	S	(56)	-03	06	(-70)	12
Jesus Christ	S	(69)	-13	15	(-40)	22
Ideal Christian	A	(42)	13	07	(-75)	08
Person hated the most	M	(-41)	07	39	62	-09
Person distrusted	S	(-50)	-03	13	73	00
Person distrusted	A	(-55)	-30	03	52	08
Best example of a sinner	A	(-66)	-17	06	(62)	-07
Mother	S	(55)	-03	11	-39	(44)
Person most admired	S	(49)	-13	26	-31	(55)
When most sorrowful	M	-13	(52)	-15	(-45)	10
Mother	A	-24	(54)	-17	(-56)	11
Guilty self	S	(-53)	(50)	-02	21	(-42)
Guilty self	A	(-45)	(60)	-05	-04	(-50)
Person distrusted	M	(-56)	12	(40)	(44)	00
When most religious	S	(43)	11	-02	(-49)	(57)

[a] Decimals have been omitted. Factor loadings ±.40 are significant $p < .01$.

[b] Subject S is a 27-year-old married male working toward a Ph.D. in clinical psychology. Individual analysis of his data reveals weak relationships with his parents; he expresses a certain dissatisfaction with his self-image. He is "liberal" and an infrequent churchgoer. Miss A is single, 20 years old, and in college. She is very conservative and religious, and identifies strongly with her father.

an angry God is the angry parent writ large. It might be noted, too, that in the cases of Mr. S and Miss A the straight descriptions of God are mixed in this factor with the good objects of Factor 1; this relationship sheds light on the phrase "God-fearing."

Factor 4: The bad objects in this factor are different from those in Factor 3. Located here are the bad and hated objects and symbols, both personal and religious (Satan); mixed negatively with the factor are many of the good objects. "Satan" incorporates and represents all those projections and displacements of qualities not found in the examples of one's parents, oneself, ego ideal, and superego.

Factor 5: The fifth factor reflects person-specific aspects, mainly those of Mr. S. In that respect, the objects may be reflecting the quite different situation experienced by S in the home in relation to his parents. Both Mrs. M and Miss A were involved in much stronger and more positive relationships with their parents during childhood.

THE TRUTH OF RELIGION:
"WHAT A FRIEND WE HAVE IN JESUS"

The results of religious research conducted in light of psychoanalytic theory have been confusing and often contradictory. The frustration with and rejection of the theory by some investigators have been due in part to testing the literal statements and fictions of Freud without attempting to understand whether the *principles* of psychoanalytic processes are valid, even though exact formulations by Freud and other pioneers may miss the mark. I believe that the research reported above supports several of the fundamental hypotheses of psychoanalysis; and also that the procedures adopted for the study reflect more than casual associations between perceptions of self, others, and religious imagos, revealing some basic dynamics of identification, projection, and displacement. However, it is not enough to show that people do make identifications which are in turn projected onto religious symbols; the crucial questions revolve around the understandings and insights one can tease out and the meanings that can be attributed.

The most striking conclusion to be drawn is not unlike that found in *Moses and Monotheism:* the significance of accepting Jesus as the Messiah is the transformation of the Jewish faith from a Father religion to a Son religion. The meaning of Christianity is provided in the identifications by Christians with the Son of God, not with the Father. It would appear that this result has been taken to an extreme; that is, God has been put out of sight in religious experience, a development that reinforces the thesis of the "God-is-dead" theologians. The positive religious identifications of all three subjects are consistently with Jesus and, more important, these identifications are in terms of the parents and friends perceived as more like Christ than like God. This tendency is supported by current trends in interpreting the meaning of Jesus. He is the suffering servant; He is kind and patient, neither aggressive nor domineering. The punishing symbol is never the Son but always the Father. These perceptions may be understood by referring to Freud's totem analogy but they can also be interpreted on different grounds. Religious socialization in Christianity stresses its unique Christ-like character; the image of God is almost too abstract to comprehend, but when it is, it is understood in negative terms. Christians may indeed be Jews in self-persecution for killing their Father and attempting to expiate their guilt in the goodness of Christ. Jesus is more concrete, more accessible, more loving. He is, as the gospel song goes, our best friend. The Christian identifies with a friendly symbol and, it turns out, does so by making Him his peer; the buddy relationship with Jesus among the "Jesus freaks" is a natural outcome. God, on the other hand, remains somewhere in the great unknown, breaking through only when the person believes he has done wrong and the superego is in stress.

Long ago William James wrote: "... it is clear that between what a man calls *me* and what he simply calls *mine* the line is difficult to draw. We feel and act about certain things that are ours very much as we feel and act about ourselves" (1890, p. 291). James's insight is applicable to religious belief in the same way that Freud believed religion contained a historical truth. The empirical study of religion discloses that in the religious personality the sense of the Other is intimately enclosed in the sense of Self; the psychoanalyst understands that in terms of projective identification and the believer in terms of supernatural acts. Either way, the reality cannot be denied.

REFERENCES

Anderson, N. H. (1968), Likableness Ratings of 555 Personality-Trait Words. *J. Pers. Soc. Psychol.*, 9:272-279.

Baas, L. R., & Brown, S. R. (1973), Generating Rules for Intensive Analysis: The Study of Transformations. *Psychiatry*, 36:172-183.

Capps, D. (1974), Contemporary Psychology of Religion: The Task of a Theoretical Reconstruction. *Soc. Res.*, 41:362-383.

Coser, L. A. (1971), Karl Marx. In: *Masters of Sociological Thought*. New York: Harcourt Brace Jovanovich, pp. 43-87.

Farrell, B. A. (1955), Psychological Theory and the Belief in God. *Internat. J. Psycho-Anal.*, 36:187-204.

Feuerbach, L. (1841), *The Essense of Christianity*. New York: Harper & Row, Torchbooks, 1957.

Freud, S. (1913), Totem and Taboo. *Standard Edition*, 13:1-161. London: Hogarth Press, 1955.

—— (1927), The Future of an Illusion. *Standard Edition*, 21:5-56. London: Hogarth Press, 1961.

—— (1937-1939), Moses and Monotheism. *Standard Edition*, 23:7-137. London: Hogarth Press, 1964.

—— & Pfister, O. (1909-1939), *Psychoanalysis and Faith: The Letters of Sigmund Freud and Oskar Pfister*. New York: Basic Books, 1963.

Fromm, E. (1950), *Psychoanalysis and Religion*. New Haven: Yale University Press.

—— (1963), *The Dogma of Christ and Other Essays on Religion, Psychology and Culture*. Greenwich, Conn.: Fawcett.

Godin, A., & Hallez, M. (1964), Parental Images and Divine Paternity. In: *From Religious Experience to a Religious Attitude*, ed. A. Godin. Brussels: Lumen Vitae Press, pp. 79-110.

Gorsuch, R. L. (1968), The Conceptualization of God as Seen in Adjective Ratings. *J. Sci. Study Rel.*, 7:56-64.

Homans, P. (1970), *Theology after Freud*. New York: Bobbs-Merrill.

James, W. (1890), *The Principles of Psychology*, Vol. 1. New York: Dover, 1950.

—— (1902), *The Varieties of Religious Experience*. London: Longmans, Green.

Jung, C. G. (1938), *Psychology and Religion*. New Haven: Yale University Press.

Kamenka, E. (1970), *The Philosophy of Ludwig Feuerbach*. London: Routledge & Kegan Paul.

Lichtheim, G. (1964), *Marxism: An Historical and Critical Study*. New York: Praeger.

Marx, K. (1844), *The Economic and Philosophic Manuscripts of 1844*. New York: International Publishers, 1964.

—— (1844-1845), *Selected Writings in Sociology and Social Philosophy*, ed. T. B. Bottomore & M. Rubel. New York: McGraw-Hill, 1956.

———— (1848), *Communist Manifesto*. Chicago: Regnery (Gateway Edition), 1954.

Meszaros, I. (1970), *Marx's Theory of Alienation*. New York: Harper & Row.

Moxon, C. (1921), Religion in the Light of Psycho-Analysis. *Psychoanal. Rev.*, 8:92-98.

Nelson, M. O. (1971), The Concept of God and Feelings toward Parents. *J. Individ. Psychol.*, 27:46-49.

———— & Jones, E. M. (1957), An Application of Q-Technique to the Study of Religious Concepts. *Psychol. Rep.*, 3:293-297.

Osgood, C. E., Suci, G. J., & Tannenbaum, P. H. (1957), *The Measurement of Meaning*. Urbana: University of Illinois Press.

Rank, O., & Sachs, H. (1913), The Significance of Psychoanalysis for the Humanities. Chap. III. Theory of Religion. *Amer. Imago*, 21:73-84, 1964.

Reid, S. (1972), *Moses and Monotheism:* Guilt and the Murder of the Primal Father. *Amer. Imago*, 29:11-34.

Reik, T. (1923), One's Own and the Foreign God. *Amer. Imago*, 25:3-15, 1968.

Rizzuto, A.-M. (1974), Object Relations and the Formation of the Image of God. *Brit. J. Med. Psychol.*, 47:83-99.

Rubins, J. L. (1955), Neurotic Attitudes toward Religion. *Amer. J. Psychoanal.*, 15:71-81.

Schroeder, T. (1929), The Psychoanalytic Approach to Religious Experience. *Psychoanal. Rev.*, 16:361-376.

Siegman, A. W. (1961), An Empirical Investigation of the Psychoanalytic Theory of Religious Behavior. *J. Sci. Study Rel.*, 1:74-78.

Spilka, B., Armatas, P., & Nussbaum, J. (1964), The Concept of God: A Factor Analytic Approach. *Rev. Rel. Res.*, 6:28-36.

Spinks, G. S. (1963), *Psychology and Religion*. Boston: Beacon.

Stephenson, W. (1953), *The Study of Behavior*. Chicago: University of Chicago Press.

Strunk, O., Jr. (1959), Perceived Relationships between Parental and Deity Concepts. *N. Y. Univ. Psychol. Newsletter*, 10:222-226.

Thomas, D. B. (1970), Political Perceptions among Radicals and Moderates: An Intensive Study. Unpublished master's thesis, Kent State University.

Thouless, R. H. (1971), *An Introduction to the Psychology of Religion*, 3rd ed. Cambridge, Eng.: Cambridge University Press.

Tillich, P. (1960), The Religious Symbol. In: *Symbolism and Religion in Literature*, ed. R. May. New York: Braziller, pp. 75-98.

Vergote, A., Tamayo, A., Pasquali, L., Pattyn, M.-R., & Custers, A. (1969), Concept of God and Parental Images. *J. Sci. Study Rel.*, 8:79-87.

Zeitlin, I. M. (1967), *Marxism: A Re-examination*. New York: Van Nostrand.

Zeligs, D. F. (1973), Moses and Pharoah: A Psychoanalytic Study of Their Encounter. *Amer. Imago*, 30:192-219.

4 Therapeutic Process and Outcome

Leo Goldberger, Ph.D., Roger Reuben, M.A.,
and George Silberschatz, M.A.

Symptom Removal in Psychotherapy:
A Review of the Literature

In the continuing search for the optimal treatment of specific psychological disturbances, an objective examination of the claims of psychodynamically oriented therapists is of great importance. A review of the psychotherapy outcome literature was undertaken to answer the question: How effective is psychodynamic psychotherapy in the treatment of certain specified disorders as judged by the criterion of symptom removal?

The sharpest criticism of psychodynamically oriented therapy has long come from the behavior therapists. But these two contending schools of thought have largely ignored each other's writings, and only rarely have they addressed themselves to identical issues in therapy research. Where the behavior therapist focuses explicitly on symptom removal as the criterion of the success of a given treatment, the criterion of the psychotherapist (insight or analytically oriented) is a more global "resolution of personality problems." These differing perspectives are of course of a fundamental nature, since they grow out of two quite different theories of psychopathology. Nevertheless, one might expect past research to shed some light on the effectiveness of psychotherapy in removing symptoms.

Prepared under National Institute of Mental Health Contract No. PLD-10686-74 and Grant No. 5 PO1 MH 22916-03. We are indebted to Drs. Morris B. Parloff, Benjamin B. Rubinstein, Daniel Shapiro, and Theodore Shapiro for their helpful suggestions.

It is fairly well accepted today that behavior therapy is a valuable treatment modality, especially for certain circumscribed behavioral symptoms—compulsive rituals, phobias (for example, Isaac M. Marks's [1969] impressive research reports), and certain sexual dysfunctions (impotence/frigidity) (Masters and Johnson, 1970; Kaplan, 1974; and others).

But it is one thing to claim that behavior therapy is highly successful in removing certain circumscribed behavioral symptoms and another to imply (a) that psychodynamic psychotherapy is singularly unsuccessful in accomplishing the same thing or (b) that symptom removal is equatable with superior over-all adjustment ("mental health," "happiness," "personality integration," "better interpersonal relations").

A discussion of the "success" or "efficacy" of a particular treatment modality must contend with the problem of the *criterion* of successful outcome. Our discussion rests on the premise that we need not choose between symptom removal and personality adjustment as *the* criterion of successful outcome: symptom removal *and* personality integration should both be assessed. Since symptoms have been traditionally conceptualized as the *signs* or *indicators* of emotional difficulty and not the difficulty itself, it is natural that, in most psychotherapy outcome studies, change is discussed in terms of psychodynamic criteria, and little attention is devoted to change in terms of symptomatic criteria. Clearly, the case for the effectiveness of psychodynamic psychotherapy ought not to rest on symptom removal as the sole criterion of change.

In this paper, we review only those studies in which psychotherapy outcome *is* assessed (either focally or incidentally) in terms of symptom removal. This focus on symptom removal permits a direct comparison between psychotherapy and behavior therapy, albeit on a narrow and very selective base. Wherever possible, our inquiry is extended to a consideration of the effectiveness of psychotherapy in terms of more global outcome criteria.

LIMITS OF THE LITERATURE SEARCH

All systematic *quantitative* outcome studies of *individual psychotherapy* with *adults* suffering from any of the following *symptom categories* were reviewed: (1) compulsions (including obsessional symptoms), (2) sexual dysfunction[1] (primarily impotence/frigidity), (3) phobias, (4) hysteria (conversion and anxiety hysteria), and (5) anxiety neurosis (primarily anxiety state). The reason for selecting these specific syndromes is that behavior therapists have generally claimed success in treating phobias (e.g., Marks, 1969), compulsive rituals (e.g., Wolpe, 1969), and sexual dysfunction (e.g., Masters and Johnson, 1970). Anxiety neurosis and hysteria were included so that the traditionally acclaimed therapeutic strength of psychodynamic psychotherapy would also be represented.

We selected only those studies which made reference, either focally or incidentally, to the outcome of the psychotherapy by the criterion of symptom removal. In general, any research report that made specific reference to hysterics, compulsives, phobics, etc., and included information about the course of the symptom as a result of psychotherapy, was reviewed.

In the present review, the focus was exclusively on individual psychotherapy. We excluded research on guidance and educational therapies whose main function is to provide information. Also excluded were chemotherapy, behavior therapy, shock therapy, occupational therapy, and laboratory analogues, unless a comparison with psychotherapy was involved.

In order to find the studies that satisfied our criteria, we searched through hundreds of references from various sources. The present report includes studies reviewed in the four most comprehensive reviews to date on psychotherapy outcome: Luborsky (1971), Luborsky and Spence (1971), Bergin (1971), and Luborsky, Singer, and Luborsky (1975). In addition, we also searched the bibliographies of Meltzoff and Kornreich (1970), Eysenck (1966), and the NIMH bibliography of *Research on Individual Psychotherapy*, prepared by Strupp and Bergin in 1967. We also reviewed Volumes 1-10 of the *Annual Survey of Psychoanalysis* and Volumes

[1] It should be noted that the sexual dysfunction group was included on purely heuristic grounds and in no way implies a disregard for the significant psychoanalytic distinction between a neurotic symptom proper and an inhibition of function. The latter is a clinical feature that may or may not be embedded in a neurosis, and, indeed, may be quite independent of neurosis.

11-24 of the *Annual Review of Psychology*. And finally, we availed ourselves of the topic index filing system of the New York Psychoanalytic Institute library.

In addition to the quantitative literature, the following case studies were reviewed: Chatterjee (1966), Chatterji (1964), Jaffe (1971), Segal (1958), Tausend (1956), Wahl (1968), Godenne (1966), Little (1968), Niederland (1958), Philippopoulos (1967), and Wangh (1959). These single case studies were not included in the analysis of the data because we believed that such simple summations of positive versus negative results would probably yield a biased, unrepresentative view of the general improvement rate in the treatment of any particular symptom. Usually a case is reported in order to establish or illustrate a theoretical or technical concept or issue, not to provide data on psychotherapy outcome. Moreover, traditionally case study reports are of treatment successes rather than failures. For both these reasons, we decided not to include case studies in the systematic investigation of psychotherapy outcome, though they are cited in Table 1 (see below). (It is noteworthy that out of the hundreds of references checked only *19* quantitative studies met the criteria for inclusion in the present review. This small yield strikingly reflects the peripheral role assigned to symptom removal in the evaluation of psychotherapy outcome.)

PROBLEMS IN INTERPRETING OUTCOME DATA

Bergin (1971) has alerted us to the pitfalls of the "objective" interpretation of psychotherapy outcome data. For example, he reanalyzed the data Eysenck (1952) obtained from various psychoanalytic institutes and arrived at a very different improvement rate than did Eysenck: 91% improved compared to Eysenck's 39%![2] The point is not who is "right" and who is "wrong," but rather that this disparity should sensitize us to the ambiguous nature of the data and remind us that the same data readily lend themselves to a variety of interpretations. One of the problems that arose per-

---

[2] The major source of this discrepancy stemmed from Eysenck's inclusion of psychotics and dropouts as treatment failures. Eysenck also applied a more stringent criterion for successful outcome than did Bergin.

sistently in the interpretation of outcome data centered on symptom removal.

At first glance it may appear that the question, "What happened to the presenting symptom following psychotherapy?", can be answered with "present" or "absent." But symptoms rarely "disappear" completely. More typically, they become less "intense," less "pervasive," or to put the matter somewhat differently, patients learn to cope with their symptoms more effectively. In short, symptom "removal" is a relative matter. In analyzing the data, we used a rather stringent criterion for classifying a case as "symptom-free." If a particular study had categories such as "cured," "much improved," "improved," "slight improvement," and "no change," we counted only those cases in the "cured" and "much improved" categories as reflecting symptom removal.[3] The "improved" cases may reflect only a minimal amount of improvement, with no meaningful symptomatic relief, and were therefore excluded. On the other hand, to exclude the "much improved" cases might be too stringent a criterion. This is a somewhat arbitrary solution but not an unreasonable one in the circumstances.[4]

Another problem was the issue of psychotherapy dropouts. Here we adopted Bergin's approach rather than Eysenck's (see above), and excluded dropouts from our tabulations. As Bergin has said, "I consider it an unfair test of a method to count against it all cases where it is not fully applied" (1971). It should be noted that the exclusion of dropouts leads to a somewhat higher improvement rate.

ANALYSIS OF THE REVIEW DATA

Thirty-one entries (studies) derived from 19 separate research

[3] Obviously it may be open to question whether the designation "cured," and particularly the expression "much improved," mean the same thing in all of the studies. For the purpose of the present paper we have *assumed* that they do, at least in a rough sort of way. We are of course also aware that "cure" is a problematical term altogether; our usage here simply follows tradition which conceives of "cure" in relative terms.

[4] If the study explicitly addressed itself to outcome in terms of symptom removal, we naturally followed the criteria established by the investigator. It is only in the studies in which we had to ferret out this information ourselves from the data presented that we followed the procedure outlined above.

projects were reviewed and classified. Diagnostic categories, information about sample size, treatment modalities, setting, duration, presence or absence of control group and follow-up, and percentage improvement were considered.[5] Percentage improvement figures correspond to the number of cases that may be regarded as symptom-free according to the criteria of the investigator. (That is, as noted in the previous section, we were essentially guided by the criteria established by the various investigators in defining a case as symptom-free, though we collapsed the designations "symptom-free," "cured" and "much improved" into a single category.) A second set of percentage improvement figures indicates the number of cases that showed improvement in over-all personality functioning for those studies in which this information was also provided. All subsequent analyses are based on the data presented in Table 1 (p. 520).

One way to analyze the data is to count the number of *studies* that yield improvement rates at certain specified levels (see Table 2, p. 528). Seven of the 31 studies report improvement rates below 50% and 24 studies report improvement rates above 50%. Eleven studies report improvement rates above 75%. Inspection of the data according to diagnostic group reveals that three of the six studies of phobias report improvement rates of less than 50%, whereas three of the six anxiety neurosis studies report improvement rates above 75%. Of the remaining categories, eight of the nine studies of compulsions report better than 50% improvement rates, and all six of the hysteria studies report improvement rates of over 50%. This first analysis of the data indicates that the improvement rate for phobias is lower than the improvement rates for the other symptom categories.

Another way to analyze the data is to count *all cases* in all studies and calculate the percentage of patients who were symptom-free following psychotherapy (see Table 3, p. 529). The mean improvement rate for all cases across symptom categories is 64.4%. The improvement rate for phobias, 50.5%, is again considerably lower than the improvement rates for the other four categories.

---

[5] We considered rating the "adequacy" of the studies according to the criteria and rating scheme proposed by Luborsky, Singer, and Luborsky (1975), but owing to the already small number of studies included in the present review, such further refinement would have precluded meaningful conclusions.

BRIEF VERSUS LONG-TERM PSYCHOTHERAPY

There are obvious disadvantages to combining studies with very different treatment durations. In one study the average duration of treatment was 10 sessions, whereas many other studies cite data from psychoanalyses of an average duration of over two years. In order to test the differences in therapeutic effect we arbitrarily divided treatment modalities into two groups: (1) those which lasted less than six months (short-term psychotherapy), and (2) longer treatments combined (long-term psychotherapy) (see Table 4, p. 530).

It must be emphasized that, given the small number of cases available in making this comparison, the generalizability of our findings is limited. Phobias and sexual dysfunction show greater improvement with short-term psychotherapy, whereas compulsions and anxiety neuroses show greater improvement with long-term psychotherapy. An examination of the nature of these symptom groups yields one possible, though very superficial, explanation for these results. Sexual dysfunction and phobias, at least some of them, are more circumscribed and less pervasive (in personality functioning and behavior) than are anxiety neurosis and obsessive-compulsive disorders. It may therefore not be surprising to find that the more circumscribed symptoms are more responsive to brief, symptom-focused treatment. (But this explanation is admittedly simplistic. Certainly, from a psycho-analytic standpoint one would require a much more careful explication of the therapist-patient interaction, its transference aspects and its unconscious meanings. Phobic avoidances and sexual inhibitions may be especially susceptible to dissolution—because of the tacit permission granted by the therapist to engage in "forbidden" instinctual activities and fantasies—in a therapeutic context that tends to emphasize direct and active approaches to symptoms and that tends to leave transference aspects of the relationship unanalyzed.)

PSYCHOANALYSIS VERSUS PSYCHOTHERAPY

The results can be further analyzed by comparing the data according to different therapeutic modalities. Improvement rates

Table 1
Phobia

| Author(s)/Year | N | Treatment | | Average Duration | C.G.* | F.† | %I. (s.r.)‡ | %I. (p.a.)§ | Comments |
		Mode	Setting						
Schjelderup (1955)	5	Psychoanalysis	Private	3 years	No	Yes	60% 3/5	40% 2/5	See below
Rosenbaum, Friedlander, & Kaplan (1956)	8	Analytically oriented psychotherapy	Clinic	1 year	No	No	25% 2/8	12.5% 1/8	See below
Tausend (1956)	1	Psychoanalysis	Private	3 years +	No	No	1/1	—	—
Segal (1958)	1	Psychoanalysis	Private	1½ years	No	Yes	1/1	—	—
Wangh (1959)	1	Psychoanalysis	Private	5 years	No	No	1/1	—	—
Errara & Coleman (1963)	19	Brief psychotherapy	Clinic	12 sessions	No	Yes	21% 4/19	—	See below
Roberts (1964)	38	Inpatient Psychotherapy Hospital stay	Clinic	Brief	No	Yes	55.3% 21/38	—	See below
Gerz (1966)	29	Logotherapy	—	Brief	No	Yes	76% 22/29	—	See below
Gelder, Marks, & Wolff (1967)	42	Desensitization N=16; Group therapy N=16; Individual psychotherapy N=10	Clinic	Desensitization 9 mos.; Group therapy 18 mos.; Individual psychotherapy 12 mos.	No	Yes	See below	30% 3/10	See below

| Little (1968) | 1 | Psychoanalysis | Private | 2 years + | No | No | 1/1 | — |

*Control group   †Follow-up   ‡Symptom removal   §Personality adjustment

Re Gelder, Marks, & Wolff (1967): — % Improvement (symptom removal): Desensitization 56%, 9/16
Group Therapy 12.5%, 2/16
Individual Therapy 30%, 3/10

Comments

Schjelderup (1955): 60% symptom removal; 40% personality reintegration (2 out of 5).

Rosenbaum, Friedlander, & Kaplan (1956): The study seems quite good over-all, but with only 8 phobic patients no conclusions can be drawn.

Errara & Coleman (1963): The only conclusion that might reasonably be drawn is that brief psychotherapy (average of 12 sessions) did not help these patients with their symptoms. Although several patients showed varying degrees of improvement, only one patient's *symptom* disappeared completely. Records of cases and follow-up generally good.

Roberts (1964): At follow-up (1½ years to 18 years), 21 of 38 patients were able to leave their homes, not restricted in travel. Not clear what kind of treatment or how long patient was treated.

Gerz (1966): Seems like a very weak study based largely on subjective impressions (no "objective" criterion measures). Drugs used as adjunct.

Gelder, Marks, & Wolff (1967): Desensitization produced significantly more rapid results (i.e., after 6 months of treatment, more symptomatic improvement than Individual or Group Therapy). As time went on, the differences in improvement were less between Desensitization and Individual and Group Therapy. Desensitization seemed to have produced greater improvement than others at follow-up, but the differences were statistically insignificant.

TABLE 1 (continued)

OBSESSIONS—COMPULSIONS

| Author(s)/Year | N | Treatment | | Average Duration | C.G.* | F.† | % I. (s.r.)‡ | % I. (p.a.)§ | Comments |
		Mode	Setting						
Coriat (1917)	12	Psychoanalysis	—	4-6 mos.	No	No	92% 11/12	—	—
Fenichel (1930)	71	Psychoanalysis	Clinic	6 mos. or longer	No	No	62% 47/71	62% 47/71	—
Jones (1936)	17	Psychoanalysis	Clinic	6 mos. or longer	No	No	47% 8/17	47% 8/17	—
Alexander (1937)	7	Psychoanalysis	Clinic	6 mos. or longer	No	No	57% 4/7	57% 4/7	—
Knight (1941)	6	Psychoanalysis	Clinic	6 mos. or longer	No	No	66% 4/6	66% 4/6	—
Schjelderup (1955)	5	Psychoanalysis	Private	4 years	No	Yes	100% 5/5	80% 4/5	See below
Rosenbaum, Friedlander, & Kaplan (1956)	4	Analytically oriented psycho-therapy	Clinic	1 year	No	No	75% 3/4	25% 1/4	See below
Niederland (1958)	1	Psychoanalysis	Private	—	No	Yes	1/1	—	—
Chatterjee (1966)	1	Psychoanalysis	Private	850 sessions	No	No	—	—	See below
Gerz (1966)	6	Logotherapy	—	Brief	No	Yes	67% 4/6	—	See below

					*Control Group	†Follow-up	‡Symptom removal	§Personality adjustment
Sifneos (1966)	—	Brief dynamically oriented psychotherapy	Clinic	—	—	Yes	—	—	See below
Solyom, Garza-Perez, Ledwidge, & Solyom (1972)	10	Paradoxical Intention; Brief psychotherapy	Clinic (3 Outpatient; 7 Inpatient)	6 weeks	No	Yes	50% 5/10	—	See below

*Control Group   †Follow-up   ‡Symptom removal   §Personality adjustment

Comments

Schjelderup (1955): All cases had complete symptom removal and 4 out of 5 (80%) underwent personality reintegration.

Rosenbaum, Friedlander, & Kaplan (1956): Small number of compulsives.

Chatterjee (1966): Symptom removal and characterological change.

Gerz (1966): Weak study. Drugs used as adjunct.

Sifneos (1966): No basic characterological changes were achieved. Evidence of new learning and over-all improvement with some symptomatic relief.

Solyom, Garza-Perez, Ledwidge, & Solyom (1972): At follow-up, no symptom substitution was found.

TABLE 1 (continued)
SEXUAL DYSFUNCTION

Author(s)/Year	N	Treatment			C.G.*	F.†	% I. (s.r.)‡	% I. (p.a.)§	Comments
		Mode	Setting	Average Duration					
Jones (1936)	8	Psychoanalysis	Clinic	6 mos. or longer	No	No	37.5% 3/8	—	See below
Chatterji (1964)	1	Psychoanalysis	Private	4 years	No	No	—	—	—
Philippopoulos (1967)	1	Analytic therapy	Private	3½ years	No	No	—	—	—
Cooper (1968)	54	Psychotherapy	Clinic	1 year +	No	No	37% 20/54	—	See below
Ellison (1968)	100	Insight therapy	Hospital & Private	10 sessions	No	Yes	87%	—	—
Ovesey & Meyers (1968)	3	Psychoanalysis	Private	3-6 years	No	Yes	100%	—	—
O'Connor & Stern (1972)	96	Psychoanalysis N=61; Psychotherapy N=35	Clinic	Psychoanalysis 2 years +; Psychotherapy 2 years or less	No	No	68% 65/96	—	—

*Control Group †Follow-up ‡Symptom removal §Personality adjustment

Comments

Jones (1936): Patients diagnosed as impotent.

Cooper (1968): Over-all response to therapy was poor. Impotence with acute onset cases responded well. Premature ejaculation cases responded poorly. The authors cite evidence suggesting that "limiting" constitutional factors might be responsible for generally poor results, that is, the symptom may not be entirely of psychogenic origin.

ANXIETY NEUROSIS

| Author(s)/Year | N | Treatment | | | C.G.* | F.† | % I. (s.r.)‡ | % I. (p.a.)§ | Comments |
		Mode	Setting	Average Duration					
Fenichel (1930)	3	Psychoanalysis	Clinic	6 mos. or longer	No	No	33% 1/3	33% 1/3	—
Kessel & Hyman (1933)	8	Psychoanalysis	Clinic	6 mos. or longer	No	No	75% 6/8	75% 6/8	—
Alexander (1937)	1	Psychoanalysis	Clinic	6 mos. or longer	No	No	1/1	1/1	—
Knight (1941)	12	Psychoanalysis	Clinic	6 mos. or longer	No	No	75% 9/12	75% 9/12	—
Miles, Barrabee, & Finesinger (1951)	62	Psychotherapy	Clinic	27 sessions	No	Yes	58% 36/62	58% 36/62	See below
Schjelderup (1955)	10	Psychoanalysis	Private	2 years	No	Yes	100% 10/10	80% 8/10	—
Rosenbaum, Friedlander, & Kaplan (1956)	23	Analytically oriented psycho-therapy	Clinic	1 year	No	No	74% 17/23	34.8% 8/23	—

*Control Group †Follow-up ‡Symptom removal §Personality adjustment

Comments

Miles, Barrabee, & Finesinger (1951): Follow-up at 2 to 12 years.

TABLE 1 (continued)

HYSTERIA

Author(s)/Year	N	Treatment Mode	Setting	Average Duration	C.G.*		% I. (s.r.)‡	% I. (p.a.)§	Comments
Coriat (1917)	16	Psychoanalysis	—	4-6 mos.	No	No	94% 15/16	—	See below
Fenichel (1930)	106	Psychoanalysis	Clinic	6 mos. or longer	No	No	62% 66/106	62% 66/106	—
Kessel & Hyman (1933)	1	Psychoanalysis	Clinic	6 mos. or longer	No	No	100% 1/1	100% 1/1	—
Jones (1936)	31	Psychoanalysis	Clinic	6 mos. or longer	No	No	54% 17/31	54% 17/31	—
Alexander (1937)	10	Psychoanalysis	Clinic	6 mos. or longer	No	No	50% 5/10	50% 5/10	—
Knight (1941)	5	Psychoanalysis	Clinic	6 mos. or longer	No	No	80% 4/5	80% 4/5	—
Rosenbaum, Friedlander, & Kaplan (1956)	7	Analytically oriented psychotherapy	Clinic	1 year	No	No	85% 6/7	42.8% 3/7	—
Godenne (1966)	1	Insight-oriented psychotherapy	Private	About 1 year	No	Yes	—	—	See below

Study	N	Treatment	Setting	Duration	*Control Group	†Follow-up	‡Symptom removal	§Personality adjustment	Comments
Wahl (1968)	1	Psychoanalysis	Private	400 hours	No	No	—	—	See below
Jaffe (1971)	1	Psychoanalysis	Private	3 years	No	Yes	1/1	1/1	See below

*Control Group †Follow-up ‡Symptom removal §Personality adjustment

Comments

Coriat (1917): Phobias were not referred to as such; rather they were called "anxiety hysteria."

Godenne (1966): Patient's symptoms (recurring stupors) were completely removed. Patient was also doing much better in school, socialized more, and was able to express anger overtly (rather than sulk).

Wahl (1968): Very impressive case. Patient experienced extreme back and neck pains for about 2½ years before entering treatment. She had been totally bedridden. Analysis cured her symptoms and brought about personality reintegration.

Jaffe (1971): The symptoms (prolonged episodes of all-encompassing anxiety) were completely removed.

TABLE 2

PERCENTAGE IMPROVEMENT REPORTED IN 31 STUDIES

	Phobias	Compul-sions	Sexual Dysfunc-tion	Anxiety Neurosis	Hysteria	Total
Below 50% Improvement	3	1	2	1	0	7
50%-66% Improvement	2	3	0	1	3	9
66%-75% Improvement	0	2	1	1	0	4
Above 75% Improvement	1	3	2	3	2	11
Total	6	9	5	6	5	31

Improvement Rate	Number of Studies
Below 50%	7
Above 50%	24

Improvement Rate	Number of Studies
Below 50%	7
Above 66%	15

for classical psychoanalysis compared to all other psychotherapies (including psychoanalytically oriented psychotherapy) are presented in Table 5 (p. 531).

The results indicate that, compared to psychotherapy, psychoanalysis yields higher improvement rates for the three symptom categories and is appreciably more effective in the treatment of anxiety neurosis as well. The latter finding may be accounted for by examining the nature of this diagnostic category. In anxiety neurosis, anxiety is "free-floating" or detached from specific situational contexts or intrapsychic conflicts. As a result, an

TABLE 3

PERCENTAGE OF PATIENTS REPORTED IMPROVED IN 31 STUDIES

	Phobias	Compulsions	Sexual Dysfunction	Anxiety Neurosis	Hysteria	Total
No. Pts. Improved	55	91	178	80	114	518
Total No. of Pts.	109	138	261	119	176	803
% of Pts. Improved	50.5%	65.9%	68.2%	67.2%	64.8%	64.5%

unstructured, nonsymptom-focused therapeutic approach is necessary in treating this syndrome.

Proponents of psychoanalysis might claim that these findings show psychoanalysis to be a more effective therapeutic modality than psychotherapy. However, given the absence of adequate controls of such relevant variables as duration and frequency of treatment, criteria for patient selection, and therapist experience level, such a claim lacks empirical support. Further controlled studies are necessary for a comparison of the differential effectiveness of psychoanalysis and psychotherapy in removing symptoms.

SYMPTOM REMOVAL AND
OVER-ALL PERSONALITY ADJUSTMENT

Although the primary focus of the present report has been on symptom removal, data were also collected on over-all personality adjustment following psychotherapy. These data are presented in Table 6 (p. 532) for the symptom groups of phobia, compulsion, anxiety neurosis, and hysteria. None of the studies on sexual dysfunction and only three of the phobia studies cited data on personality adjustment; in contrast, most of the studies of compulsions and all of the anxiety neurosis and hysteria studies provide this information.

The average improvement rate for all symptom groups is 58%. This rate is somewhat lower than the 64.4% reported for symptom

TABLE 4

A COMPARISON OF PERCENTAGES OF PATIENTS REPORTED IMPROVED
IN LONG-TERM AND SHORT-TERM PSYCHOTHERAPY

	Phobias	Compul-sions	Sexual Dysfunc-tion	Anxiety Neurosis	Hysteria	Total
All Studies						
No. of Pts. Improved	55	91	178	80	114	518
Total No. of Pts.	109	138	261	119	176	803
% of Pts. Improved	50.5%	65.9%	68.2%	67.2%	64.8%	64.5%
Long-term Psychotherapy (6 mos. or longer)						
No. of Pts. Improved	8	82	91	44	114	339
Total No. of Pts.	23	122	161	57	176	539
% of Pts. Improved	34.8%	67.2%	56.5%	77.2%	64.8%	62.9%
Short-term Psychotherapy (less than 6 mos.)						
No. of Pts. Improved	47	9	87	36	—	179
Total No. of Pts.	86	16	100	62	—	264
% of Pts. Improved	54.7%	56.3%*	87.0%*	58.1%*	—	67.8%

* Based on one study

removal. Some studies report symptomatic improvement without significant personality change, but no studies report the reverse. The improvement rate for phobias, in terms of personality adjustment, is again the lowest of all the symptom categories.

TABLE 5

A Comparison of Percentages of Patients Reported Improved in Psychoanalysis and Psychotherapy

	Phobias	Compul- sions	Sexual Dysfunc- tion	Anxiety Neurosis	Hysteria	Total
All Studies						
No. of Pts. Improved	55	91	178	80	114	518
Total No. of Pts.	109	138	261	119	176	803
% of Pts. Improved	50.5%	65.9%	68.2%	67.2%	64.8%	64.5%
Psychoanalysis						
No. of Pts. Improved	3	79	53	27	108	270
Total No. of Pts.	5	118	72	34	169	398
% of Pts. Improved	60.0% *	66.9%	73.6%	79.4%	63.9%	67.8%
Psychotherapy						
No. of Pts. Improved	52	12	125	53	6	248
Total No. of Pts.	104	20	189	85	7	405
% of Pts. Improved	50.0%	60.0%	66.1%	62.3%	85.7%	61.2%

* Based on one study

A COMPARISON OF BEHAVIOR THERAPY WITH PSYCHOTHERAPY

Only one study directly compared behavior therapy with psychotherapy. This investigation, by Gelder, Marks, and Wolff (1967), not only compares behavior therapy with psychotherapy[6]

[6] The study compares behavior therapy, individual psychotherapy, and group psychotherapy, but our discussion is limited to the first two.

TABLE 6

PERCENTAGE OF PATIENTS REPORTED IMPROVED
IN RESOLUTION OF PERSONALITY PROBLEMS

	Phobias	Compulsions	Anxiety Neurosis	Hysteria	Total
No. of Pts. Improved	6	7	69	96	239
Total No. of Pts.	23	9	119	160	301
% of Pts. Improved	26.1%	77.8%	57.9%	60.0%	58.0%

There were no data for patients suffering from sexual dysfunction.

but also applies both types of outcome criteria (symptom removal and personality adjustment) to each treatment group. We believe that this approach provides a promising design for future psychotherapy outcome studies and is therefore worthy of discussion and criticism.

The Gelder et al. study is an attempt to determine what kind of therapy is most effective in treating phobic disorders. Forty-two patients were randomly assigned to three different treatment groups: 16 to group therapy, 16 to desensitization sessions, and 10 to individual psychotherapy. For each therapeutic procedure outcome was assessed by the criteria of both social adjustment and symptom removal. Improvement was assessed by the patient, the therapist, and an outside rater, and interjudge reliabilities between raters were obtained. On the average, desensitization lasted for nine months and individual psychotherapy lasted for about a year. Improvement was rated every six weeks by the therapist and the patient, and every six months by an independent rater. All patients were interviewed by a psychiatric social worker after the final ratings; the follow-up period between end of treatment and final rating was nine months for desensitization and six months for individual psychotherapy.

The results indicate that in the course of treatment, phobias improved more rapidly with desensitization than with individual psychotherapy, and this difference was found to be statistically significant for both patients' and psychiatrists' ratings. After six months of treatment patients and psychiatrists again rated desensitization as better than psychotherapy. At the end of therapy, no significant difference between the two forms of treatment was found for either psychiatrists' or patients' ratings, nor were significant differences reported at the time of follow-up. Nine of the 16 patients in the desensitization group and three of the 10 patients receiving psychotherapy were rated as "much improved" symptomatically. In terms of social adjustment, only the category of "leisure adjustment" improved faster with desensitization than with psychotherapy. Improvement in relationships was found for both treatment groups.

As stated earlier, the basic design of the Gelder et al. study is a sound one; its implementation, however, was seriously flawed. The investigation was carried out with a very small number of subjects ($N=42$), and the individual psychotherapy group ($N=10$) was 40% smaller than the desensitization group ($N=16$). Although the investigators made an attempt to match patients in the treatment groups, such important variables as sex, chronicity and intensity of phobic disorder, type of phobia, and therapist experience level were not adequately controlled. Another major flaw was that the duration of individual psychotherapy was "artificially limited" to about one year. The investigators themselves concede that "longer treatment might have helped some patients more" (referring to the individual psychotherapy group). We believe that because the psychotherapy group received incomplete or "artificially limited" treatment, the comparison between the two treatment groups is not meaningful.

SUMMARY AND IMPLICATIONS FOR FUTURE RESEARCH

What broad conclusions can we draw from this review? One is that psychotherapy is moderately successful in removing symptoms. An average of 64.4% of total cases were symptom-free following psychotherapy. This improvement rate is appreciable, though somewhat lower than the improvement rates characteristically cited by behavior therapists.

The rate of improvement in terms of personality adjustment was 58%. In most instances in which patients were helped with their symptoms, they also benefited from psychotherapy in terms of over-all functioning. There were no instances in which patients benefited generally but retained their symptoms.

We recommend that future psychotherapy outcome research be much more specific in describing patients' presenting problems, the type and duration of treatment, and the criteria for outcome. We suggest that, wherever possible, a control group be used to allow for a more definitive demonstration that therapeutic changes are a result of the treatment and not of extraneous variables. Ideally, such controls should encompass the specific as well as the so-called "nonspecific" factors in psychotherapy (see Strupp, 1973); the nonspecific factors being those that inhere in the so-called "good" human relationship that forms the background of the more "technical" aspects involved in the management of the psychodynamic factors in therapy. We also recommend that future research pursue follow-up data in greater depth, to permit an assessment of the fate of the symptom, and to allow for the scrutiny of possible symptom substitutions, characterological changes, and a determination of over-all personality functioning.

REFERENCES

Alexander, F. (1937), *Five Year Report of the Chicago Institute for Psychoanalysis (1932-1937)* and *Supplement to the Five Year Report.*

Bergin, A. E. (1971), The Evaluation of Therapeutic Outcomes. In: *Handbook of Psychotherapy and Behavior Change: An Empirical Analysis,* ed. A. E. Bergin & S. Garfield. New York: Wiley.

Chatterjee, T. K. (1966), A Case of Obsessional Neurosis. *Samiska,* 20:169-176.

Chatterji, N. (1964), A Case of Psychosexual Impotence. *Samiksa,* 18:27-41.

Cooper, A. J. (1968), A Factual Study of Male Potency Disorders. *Brit. J. Psychiat.,* 114:719-731.

Coriat, I. (1917), Some Statistical Results of the Psychoanalytic Treatment of the Psychoneuroses. *Psychoanal. Rev.,* 4:209-216.

Ellison, C. (1968), Psychosomatic Factors in the Unconsummated Marriage. *J. Psychosomat. Res.,* 12:61-65.

Errara, P., & Coleman, J. V. (1963), A Long-Term Follow-Up Study of Neurotic Phobic Patients in a Psychiatric Clinic. *J. Nerv. Ment. Dis.,* 136:267-271.

Eysenck, H. J. (1952), The Effects of Psychotherapy: An Evaluation. *J. Consult. Psychol.,* 16:319-324.

——— (1966), *The Effects of Psychotherapy.* New York: International Science.

Fenichel, O. (1930), *Ten Years of the Berlin Psychoanalytic Institute (1920-1930).*

Gelder, M. G., Marks, I. M., & Wolff, H. (1967), Desensitization and Psychotherapy in the Treatment of Phobic States: A Controlled Inquiry. *Brit. J. Psychiat.*, 113:53-73.

Gerz, H. O. (1966), Experience with the Logotherapeutic Technique of Paradoxical Intention in the Treatment of Phobic Obsessive-Compulsive Patients. *Amer. J. Psychiat.*, 123:548-553.

Godenne, G. D. (1966), Report of a Case of Recurring Hysterical Pseudo-Stupors. *J. Nerv. Ment. Dis.*, 141:670-677.

Jaffe, D. S. (1971), The Role of Ego Modification and the Task of Structural Change in the Analysis of a Case of Hysteria. *Internat. J. Psycho-Anal.*, 52:375-393.

Jones, E. (1936), *Decennial Report of the London Clinic of Psycho-Analysis (1926-1936)*.

Kaplan, H. S. (1974), *The New Sex Therapy*. New York: Brunner/Mazel.

Kessel, L., & Hyman, H. T. (1933), The Value of Psychoanalysis as a Therapeutic Procedure. *J. Amer. Med. Assn.*, 101:1612-1615.

Knight, R. P. (1941), Evaluation of the Results of Psychoanalytic Therapy. *Amer. J. Psychiat.*, 98:434-446.

Little, R. B. (1968), Resolution of Oral Conflicts in a Spider Phobia. *Internat. J. Psycho-Anal.*, 49:492-494.

Luborsky, L. (1971), Factors Influencing the Outcome of Psychotherapy: A Review of Quantitative Research. *Psychol. Bull.*, 75:145-185.

———— Singer, B., & Luborsky, L. (1975), Comparative Studies of Psychotherapies: Is It True that Everyone Has Won and All Must Have Prizes? *Arch. Gen. Psychiat.*, 32:995-1008.

———— & Spence, D. P. (1971), Quantitative Research on Psychoanalytic Psychotherapy. In: *Handbook of Psychotherapy and Behavior Change: An Empirical Analysis*, ed. A. E. Bergin & S. Garfield. New York: Wiley.

Marks, I. M. (1969), *Fears and Phobias*. New York: Academic.

Masters, W. H., & Johnson, V. E. (1970), *Human Sexual Inadequacy*. Boston: Little, Brown.

Meltzoff, J., & Kornreich, M. (1970), *Research in Psychotherapy*. New York: Atherton.

Miles, H. W., Barrabee, E. L., & Finesinger, J. E. (1951), Evaluation of Psychotherapy with a Follow-Up Study of 62 Cases of Anxiety Neurosis. *Psychosomat. Med.*, 13:83-105.

Niederland, W. (1958), The Psychoanalysis of a Severe Obsessive-Compulsive Neurosis. *Bull. Philadelphia Assn. Psychoanal.*, 8:83-93.

O'Connor, J. F., & Stern, L. O. (1972), Results of Treatment in Functional Sexual Disorders. *N. Y. State J. Med.*, 72:1927-1934.

Ovesey, L., & Meyers, H. C. (1968), Retarded Ejaculation. *Amer. J. Psychother.*, 22:185-201.

Philippopoulos, G. S. (1967), The Analysis of a Case of Frigidity. *Psychother. Psychosomat.*, 15:220-230.

Roberts, A. H. (1964), Housebound Housewives: A Follow-Up Study of a Phobic Anxiety State. *Brit. J. Psychiat.*, 110:191-197.

Rosenbaum, M., Friedlander, J., & Kaplan, S. M. (1956), Evaluation of Results of Psychotherapy. *Psychosomat. Med.*, 18:113-132.

Schjelderup, H. K. (1955), Lasting Effects of Psychoanalytic Treatment. *Psychiatry*, 18:109-133.

Segal, H. (1958), Fear of Death: Notes on the Analysis of an Old Man. *Internat. J. Psycho-Anal.*, 39:178-181.

Sifneos, P. E. (1966), Psychotherapy for Mild Obsessional Neuroses. *Psychiat. Quart.*, 40:271-282.

Solyom, L., Garza-Perez, J., Ledwidge, B. L., & Solyom, C. (1972), Paradoxical Intention in the Treatment of Obsessive Thoughts: A Pilot Study. *Comprehensive Psychiat.*, 13:291-297.

Strupp, H. H. (1973), Toward a Reformulation of the Psychotherapeutic Influence. *Internat. J. Psychiat.*, 11:263-365.

———— & Bergin, A. E. (1967), *Research on Individual Psychotherapy.* Washington, D.C.: National Institute of Mental Health.

Tausend, H. (1956), Psychoanalysis of a Case of Agoraphobia. *Samiksa*, 10:175-200.

Wahl, C. W. (1968), Psychoanalysis of a Case of Muscular Dystonia. *Psychoanal. Quart.*, 37:239-260.

Wangh, M. (1959), Structural Determinants of a Phobia. *J. Amer. Psychoanal. Assn.*, 7:675-695.

Wolpe, J. (1969), *The Practice of Behavior Therapy.* New York: Pergamon.

Fred Pine, Ph.D.

On Therapeutic Change:
Perspectives from a Parent-Child Model

Freud's early faith in the value of catharsis (Breuer and Freud, 1893-1895) as a mechanism of therapeutic change gave way to emphasis on insight and working through (Freud, 1914), processes that require considerable cognitive effort, the achievement of affective conviction, and repeated relearning, reconviction, and testing over time. Though these processes are in the foreground of those through which change is achieved in psychoanalysis, other processes are also present in the background. In this paper I shall deal with some of those background factors. Interestingly, when we turn beyond classical psychoanalytic treatment to work with more seriously ill patients with deficient ego functioning, many of those background factors come into the foreground as instruments of change.

Drawing from a parent-child model, I shall address aspects of the facilitation of development as these apply to issues of therapeutic change. Specifically, the role of identification with and other internalizations from the analyst/therapist is discussed, as is the role of safety (in the therapy and in the parent-child relationship) that permits change or development, respectively, to take place (Sandler, 1960). Since it seems unlikely that developmental processes that have not taken place earlier can always take place in the context of therapy, issues of reversibility of psychopathology, and of critical periods as well, are inevitably raised.

I wish to express my appreciation to Drs. Theodore Shapiro and David Schecter for their comments on an earlier draft of this paper.

While some analytic writers have discussed treatment from points of view related to the one to be pursued here (see Alexander, 1956; Blanck and Blanck, 1974; Mahler and Furer, 1960; Silverman, 1976; Winnicott, 1955), by and large these issues are not treated extensively in the more classically oriented psychoanalytic literature. The interpersonal theorists (Sullivan, 1940, 1953; Fromm-Reichmann, 1950, 1959) often come closer; but I shall, in contrast to them, try to relate my discussion to the distinctly intra-psychic-historical viewpoint of psychoanalysis. Strupp's (1973) paper on the relative roles of nonspecific interpersonal factors versus specific technical factors in bringing about therapeutic change contains a thought-provoking analysis of issues quite similar to the ones to be treated here; however, the whole thrust of his paper, the way the ideas are put together, is radically different from my own emphasis. And finally, Loewald's (1960) paper on the integrative value of the patient's object relationship to the analyst and of the analytic process itself, though couched in more theoretical terms, is also a forebear of the present paper. Like Loewald, I am attempting to understand some of the "silent" features of analytic technique as it currently exists. Unlike Loewald, however, I shall also raise specific issues of technique, and ways of thinking about the development of technique, for supportive and child therapies—in this case by drawing on developmental considerations.

The several ideas to be advanced here all grew out of experiences in developmental studies and in work with severely disturbed patients. The mechanisms for bringing about change that I shall discuss can all come under the heading of "good parenting"—that is, they parallel what good parents *are* for the child or *do* for the child. But this umbrella concept—"good parenting"—may obscure rather than clarify what I wish to say. For the analyst/therapist is not a parent to his patients, and I am not proposing that he behave like one; nor (except literally in child treatment) is the patient a child, and I am certainly not proposing that he be treated like one. Instead, I shall propose that aspects of the therapeutic process can be understood by drawing on our knowledge of the facilitative role of the parent in the development of the child.

Considerations regarding the facilitation of growth, including elements of identification and of safety in a relationship, are relevant to the classical process of psychoanalysis as well as to other therapies, as I shall discuss below, so it is interesting to consider why psychoanalysis has been relatively remiss in formalizing them. Historical reasons are not hard to find. Freud's and Breuer's early discovery of transference, and Breuer's experience of it as a danger (Jones, 1953), from early on led to a tendency to keep the patient-analyst relationship "pure." Further, the history of criticism of psychoanalysis as nothing but "suggestion" has led to a leaning over backward to deny the real power of the analyst in the patient's life. Additionally, clinical experience with short-lived transference cures supports skepticism about the power of the relationship alone, without insight, to lead to lasting change. And perhaps most pervasive in its impact has been the *drive* bias of psychoanalytic theory; in early psychoanalytic theory, object relationships were seen largely as carried by drives; the "object" was indeed defined by its end-point position in the search for gratification. Only more recently has the independent, facilitative, and indispensable role in the growth process of the primary (mothering) object been given systematic theoretical attention (Mahler, Pine, and Bergman, 1975; Winnicott, 1965).

I have said that the technical issues that I shall discuss can be compared to what good parents "are for the child" or "do for the child." For clarity in exposition, I shall retain this distinction between the passive ("are") and the active ("do"). By the term "passive" I refer to modes of impact upon the patient that are inevitably consequent upon the therapist's mere *presence*—his reliability and consistent commitment to what is beneficial for the patient. I focus on these modes of impact in an attempt to understand relatively "silent" aspects of the effect of all therapies, including psychoanalysis. By the term "active," I refer to specific technical *interventions* that a therapist undertakes, tailored to a particular patient at a particular time. A focus on these interventions and their rationale may enable us to generate hypotheses regarding further interventions in work with ego-deficient patients.

In the following, I shall begin with the passive processes and then turn to the active ones, though the distinction between them is not always sharp and I use it solely as an expository device. In pursuing my topic, I shall draw on ideas and experiences from insight therapy and psychoanalysis, from supportive therapy, from work with children, and from work with ego-deficient patients of any age. Over-all, the intent of this paper is to contribute to a more complete rationale for psychological treatment and for its modes of impact upon the patient.

THE PRESENCE OF THE THERAPIST

Psychological treatment can be viewed as the relation of one person to another where a part of the task is to enable the patient to take in, and make into his own, what is "given" by the therapist. There is of course more to the process than this but, for heuristic purposes, let us adopt that point of view for the moment. It is a formulation that provides a natural link to "parenting," where the establishment of a relationship and the influence of and input to one by the other (there, parent to child) is at the center of the process. In psychological treatments, as in parent-child relations, the ways in which the other becomes significant for the self (the problem of object relations) and the ways in which what is in the other becomes part of the "me" (the problem of internalization) are at the core. The further question, in what areas and under what conditions can developmental processes that have not taken place earlier still take place in the therapeutic relationship, is of obvious significance for psychological treatments as well. It is a question that touches on the reversibility of psychopathology, on critical periods, and on "silent" effects of therapy; it is the question that underlies much of the clinical discussion in the present paper.

Psychoanalysis, and the therapies that stem from it, quite rightly view treatment rather differently from the way just stated. In much of the clinical theory of psychoanalysis, the technical treatment goals of insight and working through tend to appear as eminently rational, indeed expressly tailored to the nature of the problem. Valid though this view may be, it obscures other equally valid points. In general, by defining problems and solutions within their own terms and framework, theories tend to be self-validating, and this is true of psychoanalysis no less than of others. Let me clarify.

The clinical theory of psychoanalysis has had much to say about interruptions of the developmental process. Among these interruptions are: fixation or regression in the libidinal sphere; developmental failures in the ego sphere, including reliance on primitive and maladaptive defenses; trauma that leads to unending repetition of the past; and excessive cathexis of primitive parental imagos which insures that all later object relationships will be colored by issues of omnipotence and powerlessness, irrational authority and weakness, idealization and disillusionment.

But beyond the *formulation* of these interruptions of the developmental process, the implicit *rationale* of psychoanalytic technique has been derived from a conception of the pathogenic consequences of such interruptions. Thus, whether the aim of analysis is expressed in topographic terms (to make the unconscious conscious) or in structural terms ("Where id was, there ego shall be"—Freud, 1933, p. 80) or in genetic terms (the uncovering and reconstruction of the past), the essential aim of the work has been to bring these residues of the past into awareness as a way of reducing their psychopathological sequelae. Already in *The Interpretation of Dreams* Freud wrote: "As a result of the unpleasure principle, then, the [primary process] is totally incapable of bringing anything disagreeable into the context of its thoughts" (1900, p. 600). Instead, such "disagreeable" content is subject to processes of displacement and condensation which eventuate in dreams, slips, jokes, and, from a clinically more significant standpoint, symptoms and, in part, pathological character traits. The aim of treatment is to allow the "disagreeable" content into consciousness; once there, it can be dealt with in new ways.

Hypotheses regarding technique, and conceptions concerning its mode of impact, can, however, also be derived from a psychoanalytic theory of *normal development*, and not only from the clinical theory of its *interruptions*. A fair degree is known about how development takes place, some of which has been contributed by psychoanalysis, but all of which can be profitably related to the distinctive psychoanalytic point of view, a view which brings focus to a wide range of clinical psychopathological and normal developmental issues. Many of these ideas refer to the *facilitation* of normal development. Such concepts as "good-enough mothering" (Winnicott, 1960) and the establishment of basic trust or "confident expectation" (Benedek, 1938), with recognition of the mother-child relationship that is requisite for that, are relevant here; Mahler's

(1965) emphasis on the development of the child's ego functions in the matrix of the mother-child relationship is also to the point. All of these concepts point to the role of the actual parent, and later internal representations, in the development of the child. This paper focuses on the implications, for therapy, of a parent-child model, and developmental considerations stemming from such a model are the ones that I would like to highlight.

In the remainder of this section I shall try to show something about the developmental learning that takes place in therapy and about the context of object relationship (both present and historical) in which this occurs. I shall do this in turn for classical psychoanalysis, child therapy, and supportive therapy.

PSYCHOANALYTIC THERAPY

In the literature on classical psychoanalysis, the patient-analyst relationship has been discussed in terms of the therapeutic alliance; but discussion of this alliance leans more toward its role in making the work of analysis possible (this work conceived of as insight and working through) than toward its intrinsic role in bringing about change. Beyond this, however, most patients who have undergone psychoanalysis feel that they have learned and gained from the contact with the analyst, from the kind of person he or she is and the way he or she functions—quite aside from the insights gained in the analysis. And I say the kind of person the analyst "is" rather than "seems to be" to emphasize, in Greenson's (1967) terms, the *reality* aspects of the relationship. I am not speaking here of major transference-based perceptions nor even of what Alexander (1956) calls the "corrective emotional experience." Rather, I refer to part-identification with aspects of the analyst's style, values, or way of thinking, pervasively evident to the analysand during the analytic process; specific, though incidental, educative moments; moments of the analyst's confirmation of the analysand's subjective reality; and beyond these the important context of safety in the analysis, to which I shall return below. None of this alters the centrality of the role of insight and working through in the analytic process; nor am I advocating any extra-analytic "friendliness" in the patient-analyst relationship. Identification and impacts of the object relationship inevitably occur in the analytic process as it is classically carried on because processes in the patient are receptive to them, indeed create them.

It is my impression that all of the above is self-evident to analysts *during the time* they themselves are patients, though, ironically, they often lose the clear perception of this about their own patients when they are sitting behind the couch rather than lying upon it. I think there are at least two reasons for this. First is the analyst's theoretical and personal preference for seeing insight as the effective agent of change; while I share this theoretical leaning, I see no reason why it should keep us from also seeing other aspects of the process. The second reason for analysts' being more clear about, for example, identificatory and educative aspects of the process when they are the patient than when they are the analyst is that many of these processes do not enter either the sphere of conflict or the sphere of verbalization. Although the patient experiences these processes, often with a feeling of their great impact, he rather seldom expresses this experience to the analyst. The relative neglect of such phenomena says more about the belief systems of analysts than about the truths of analysis.

Just as so-called "supportive" therapies are likely to include "interpretive" aspects, as I shall discuss below, so too the reverse. Insight treatment inevitably includes aspects that stem from the patient-analyst relationship itself and these are one source of patient change. When Alexander developed such observations into his concept of the "corrective emotional experience," he aroused considerable opposition. This was in part because of the tone of manipulation and play acting in his recommendation that the therapist "can also consciously and planfully replace [his own personality reactions] with attitudes which are favorable in promoting what is the essence of the whole therapeutic process— the corrective emotional experience" (1956, p. 100). Interestingly, though, an *earlier* idea of Alexander's does not imply role playing. He wrote: "Emotional and intellectual support is to some degree present in all forms of treatment. It results from the therapeutic situation itself, independently of the special techniques employed, provided the therapist instills confidence in his patient and listens with benevolent understanding to his patient's complaints" (1948, p. 274). This is what I refer to as the effect of the "mere presence" of the therapist.

I would like to pursue this idea and specify it further in my own way in what follows. The ideas are not new; I wish only to draw them together in the context of certain inevitable learnings that take place in the analytic situation, drawing on those that have their undoubted origins in the universal parent-child relationship. I shall discuss (1) some general modes of impact of one person upon another as these are expressed in analysis and (2) the analytic context of safety.

1. There are certain modes of impact of one person upon another that are, I believe, active throughout the life cycle; as such, they are present in the early parent-child relationship and also in the analytic situation. I shall mention three that are closely related. First, the patient makes certain *identifications* with aspects of the analyst's functioning; that is, what was experienced as other comes to be part of the self (Schafer, 1968). These identifications may be with a tone of voice, a form of humor, an attitude of calm under adversity, a habit of questioning "why" about oneself, a style of expression, an interest or avocation. These become "silently" part of the patient's functioning, sometimes with an awareness of their origin accompanied by an inner sense of relatedness, sometimes without such an awareness; sometimes they are lasting, sometimes short-lived (see Schecter, 1968). Second, the *educative role* of the analyst—far more significant in child analysis—is not absent in adult work if for no other reason than that the patient won't let it be. That is, the role of authority (parent, teacher) in education is ever of significance, and information given by the awesome authority of the analyst has a high likelihood of being taken in. This applies not only to the dynamically linked information of the insight process but also to attitudes about behavioral options, modes of functioning in the real world, that now and then are intentionally or unintentionally embedded in interpretive comments—or that are found there by the patient hungry for them. And third, the analyst seems not only to clarify but to *confirm the inner reality* of the patient. For many patients, and at times for all patients, the analyst's statement or restatement of what the patient already knows or has said confirms it, gives it the impact of the awesome authority of the analyst. These are all functions inevitably served by the parent for the child (object of

identification, educator, source of confirmation) and are processes of interpersonal impact that have no "critical period" of effect— i.e., they are active throughout life in relationships in which there is an authority differential between the participants: parent and child, analyst and patient.

There is a key aspect of the analytic process which ensures that a shaping role is played by the analyst for the patient, a broad aspect that draws from each of the three features described above. It stems from the role of speech in analysis. The medium of psychoanalysis conveys a powerful message to the patient. Five years or so of training in the use of words, in certain habits of thought, in modes of delay and the control of action—all part and parcel of the analytic process—have a shaping influence on the patient (see Loewenstein, 1956; T. Shapiro, 1970). Ironically, that this is sometimes less true than we would wish with certain patients is a testament to the lasting power of the identifications with the old parental styles, now also built into the structural and psychodynamic arrangements within the particular patient.

2. The second feature of analysis that I would like to discuss is what I shall call the analytic "context of safety." Another of Alexander's views that aroused opposition was that the fact of a difference between the analyst and the parent is the "essential therapeutic agent" (1956, p. 41) in analysis. There is an ambiguity here. "Essential" may mean "more important than insight," but it need not. "Essential" can also mean "basic to the rest"—that is, setting the conditions under which all the rest, including insight, can take place. If one wrote that in order for a patient to gain from analysis it is essential that he come to his sessions, no one would object; that does not mean that coming to sessions is the "essential therapeutic agent." Here, as regards coming to sessions, the point is banal. But as regards the nature of the analytic relationship, it is not at all banal. For the nature of that relationship provides a context of safety in which growth can take place. The analyst *is* different from the parent, *without* manipulation or play acting. And this *is* essential to all the rest of what takes place.

Children can develop, and so can adults, more successfully if their environment is reasonably stable and reasonably trustworthy; if the environment enriches, makes demands, and spurs them on, so much the better. The analytic situation provides all of this. It is within that context that the work of insight regarding urges, affects, fantasies, and conflicts can go on. Numerous writers are currently working in this area. Bowlby (1969) gives primacy to the attachment of the child to the mother—as a given, not by association with oral needs. Mahler (1965) discusses the child's growth in the matrix of the mother-child relationship. White (1963) argues that exploration, the development of competence, the use of the ego's "independent energies," takes place given reasonable safety in the child's life; in the face of internal drive tension, these ego energies are washed over; the drive pressures are more imperious, demanding first attention. In general, "good-enough mothering" (Winnicott, 1960) allows development to proceed.

It is easy not to notice this. Especially when it is working smoothly, it is "invisible." Perhaps because Sullivan worked with psychotic patients he early saw the absence of these core object attachments and turned to the technical importance of interpersonal relationships. Freud's patients (and most patients considered suitable for analysis—there is selective screening here!) had a reasonable stability in their core attachments from infancy and early childhood. Given that, given the basic inner context of object relatedness and some degree of trust, center stage is readily seized by drive-linked fantasies and conflicts. But work with a ghetto population, or disorganized families, or institutionalized infants (Provence and Lipton, 1962) makes clear that in the *absence* of that early context of safety, *it* is what takes center stage in therapeutic work or developmental progress (or lack of it).

The point is that the analytic setting, like the average expectable environment (Hartmann, 1939) that includes good-enough mothering, provides a context of safety in which the rest (the child's growth on the one hand, or the analysand's communication, developing insight, and trying out of change on the other) can take place. Like Lewin's "dream screen" (1946), the breast on which the dream is projected, but here in a broader context of basic attachment, the analysis, like the child's growth, is acted upon the solid stage of safety in a relationship. Without the stage, which we too easily take for granted (when it is there), the action would not take place.

CHILD PSYCHOTHERAPY

Let us look briefly at child therapy from a similar standpoint. In the psychological treatment of a young and growing child, especially a treatment of some length, the child begins to endow the therapist with functions more typically reserved for the parent. This does not involve the therapist's behaving in parentlike ways (though I shall later suggest that hypotheses regarding technical innovations for ego-deficient patients can be stimulated by an understanding of the actual behavior of the "good-enough" parent); rather it involves the uses the child makes of the therapist. Beyond this, the therapeutic "context of safety" has a special place in child therapy as well as the general role that I have already mentioned.

Childhood is a time of the relatively rapid emergence of new intrapsychic and behavioral modes of function. These developing capacities of the child (ego functions, sublimations, modes of object relationship and of adaptation), whatever their built-in maturational components, grow in the matrix of the mother-child relationship and of adaptation), whatever their built-in matura-least four implications: (1) that new capacities are modeled after those of the mother (or father); (2) that they may be used (practiced, developed, perfected) in the relationship to her/him; (3) that, when used elsewhere, they may be shared with her/him in verbal exchange when the child brings them home, gathering permission and support for his new achievements outside the home and making them part of his relations to the parents; and (4) that they come to serve functions, often multiple functions, in the context of the relationships to the parents as well as intrapsychically, and thus become part of the more permanent psychic repertoire. My general point is, however, that for the growing child in long-term therapy, all of this inevitably takes place in the *relationship with the therapist* as well as in the one with the *parent*.

Beyond this specific position of the child therapist in the development of the child (which coexists peacefully with the therapist's interpretive role) is the specific facilitation of the emergence of new functions provided by the context of safety of the treatment relationship. The degree to which the mother-child relationship is benign or malignant determines the degree to which progressive new capacities on the one hand or survival techniques on the other will emerge from the child's potential repertoire. Work with severely disturbed children from multiproblem families makes clear the many survival mechanisms that *can* emerge in the child as he attempts to cope with overwhelming stress (see Malone, 1966). In childhood, with its rapidly developing new modes of function, the therapeutic context of safety permits not only the process of exploration and the risks of change but also the emergence of healthier adaptive modes at each developmental step, when new modes are necessarily emerging in any event.

Let me mention one other feature of child therapy which, though not as closely tied to issues of internalization and object relationship as those already discussed, nonetheless sets the therapist in a position of inevitable overlap with the parental function vis-à-vis the growth process. The child's psychological equilibrium is regularly disrupted as a consequence of the growth process itself—of new environmental demands from without and of new needs and capacities within. The therapist is thus working with a system in disequilibrium. And, while at times it may be hard to keep pace with the growth process, to attune ourselves to emerging changes, it is nonetheless true that there is a distinct advantage to working with systems in disequilibrium. Too fixed, too satisfied, too well-defended a system is less amenable to change; that is why anxiety in the patient is such a help to therapeutic work—it is a sign of disequilibrium. Crisis theorists (Lindemann, 1956; Caplan, 1960) have shown that a person in crisis is susceptible not only to a *breakdown* of his traditional mode of functioning but to *influence* toward new, more constructive re-equilibration. Blos (1963) makes a similar point about the constructive potentials of the growth crisis of adolescence. The long-term therapist of the growing child, like the "long-term parent," is inevitably present and therefore in a position to deal with those periods of disequilibrium—*during* the disequilibrium.

SUPPORTIVE PSYCHOTHERAPY

When we turn to the question of therapeutic change in supportive therapies, the parent-child model is particularly relevant. Let us begin by asking: What is supported in supportive therapy? At the least, the presence of an interested therapist "supports" the brittle or severely ill patient's *ties to human objects* and capacities for the *maintenance of defense*. The presence and interest of the therapist (like the presence and interest of the parent for the child) does these things almost automatically. Rapaport (1957) drew upon Piaget's (1936) concept of "nutriment" to advance the argument that certain psychological structures (and it seems to me that object relationships and defenses are among them) require a sustained "stimulus nutriment"—i.e., a continued input of stimuli—for their maintenance. Rapaport originally applied these proposals to studies of stimulus deprivation in an attempt to explain the alteration of function that emerged in those conditions. For the isolated and brittle patient, the therapist's presence provides the nutriment for the continuance of an object tie and the maintenance of defense.

The conditions under which a continuing need for stimulus input of this kind can gradually be replaced by internalization remains a question for supportive therapy. However, a detour into the child's early history suggests some relevant developmental considerations and points to the clarifying role of events that take place between child and caretaker.

The young infant is fully dependent upon the physical presence of its mother for its survival. This dependence comes to expand beyond the need for physical care to the need for her presence to provide a feeling of safety and satisfaction. "Separation anxiety" and "stranger anxiety" are concepts that speak to the other side of that comfort. But the actual presence of the mother is not forever required. We speak of the development of "libidinal object constancy" to refer to the child's achievement of an internal representation of the mother *which he can use* (for comfort, for control) *in the way he can use the actual mother* (Pine, 1974a). This is a gradual achievement; it is never total; but most of us achieve it to a fair degree. Thus, developmentally, ongoing interaction with the real external object is replaced to a degree, and in some ways, by internalization. So too, optimally, in supportive therapy, though the questions how and under what conditions remain unclear.

Now what of defense? The same is true. Conceiving defense

broadly as the control of impulse and/or of unpleasant affect, we are reminded that the mothering one is an "auxiliary ego" for the infant—an external source of those defense functions that will later spring from inner sources. In research on normal development (Pine, 1971), I was struck by the usefulness (borrowing from Spitz, 1946) of the concept of "anaclitic defense"—defense in which the child stills anxiety by making actual contact with the actual mother—a phenomenon especially found (not surprisingly) in relation to anxiety over separation. But this, too, is later replaced (more or less, and by most of us) by internal defense processes.

A critical question for supportive therapy is: How does the need for continued stimulus input (the therapist's presence as nutriment) change into internalization, whereby the patient can sustain object relationships and his own inner defense processes relatively autonomously? Though the answer is not readily at hand, we should recall that it is also by no means clear precisely when an interpretation in insight therapy will be taken in by the patient in a way that can produce constructive and inner-determined modification of function. Issues of internalization are relevant there, too. The "brilliant" and awesome interpretation in a first session, or the controlling and powerful interpretation of an overbearing analyst, may be internalized in ways quite different from the insight that develops slowly, with the patient's participation, in the context of an ongoing therapeutic alliance. But once we raise questions about internalization of interpretations on the one hand, or internalization of object representations or defense processes on the other, the parent-child relationship, the initial locus of internalization processes, becomes relevant as a source of understanding.

To sum up: I have been discussing aspects of technique and of therapeutic change from the point of view of a psychoanalytic developmental theory. In particular, I have tried to show the relevance, for a rationale of therapeutic change, of a psycho-analytic theory of *facilitation* of development to complement the more usual clinical theory of *interruption* of development. I have focused principally on clinical phenomena that can be understood in terms of the patient's relationship to the analyst/therapist, identifications with him or other internalizations from him, and the general therapeutic context of safety that permits all of the rest of treatment (both exploration and development or change) to go on. I have pointed especially to developmental phenomena that do not have a critical period after which they are inoperative but which, at least to some degree and in some areas, operate throughout life. As such, they are in the foreground of some therapies, though in the background of all.

I have not attempted to develop a systematic theory of technique based upon these concepts. To do so, I believe, would be not only overambitious but inherently flawed, since I believe these points of contact between technique and the parent-child relation go only so far, and no further, in enlightening us about technique. Instead, my aim has been twofold: to expand (not replace) our rationale of technique and therapeutic change, and to raise questions regarding the areas and times in the life cycle when processes central to early development (especially internalization and developmental facilitation) are still operative and therefore relevant for therapy as well. So far I have focused on the "mere presence" of the therapist with this twofold aim in mind. I shall turn now to the "actions" of the therapist with similar aims. Here I shall discuss specific technical interventions that the therapist undertakes, tailored to the individual patient, and generated by a conception of the role of the "good parent." I shall focus principally on child therapy and so-called supportive therapies. I hope that the clinical examples will contribute to our thinking about the opportunities for and the limitations of reversibility of developmental failure.

THE "ACTIONS" OF THE THERAPIST

In a paper on "Ego Disturbances," Redl (1951) wrote: "This short paper . . . sets itself a limited task: to lure the practitioner into becoming much more impressed with the need to be very specific in the use of the term 'ego disturbance' and to stimulate the clinician to seek a much wider repertoire of techniques whenever he is confronted with the task of 'ego support' " (p. 273). He then illustrated *specific* areas of deficient functioning that may require *specific* kinds of intervention. Harrison and McDermott, who reprinted this paper in their volume on *Childhood Psychopathology,* introduced it with the following editorial comment: "Teasing out the precise aspect of ego function requiring specific differential therapeutic attention in lieu of global support for a vaguely defined 'weak ego' transforms an impossible task into a difficult one" (1972, p. 532). My route to the work to be described below has been similar, and my intent comparable: confronted by "impossible" therapeutic situations, I have tried to think about them in ways that would transform them into something merely "difficult."

Technical variations of the kind that grew out of Redl's work with delinquent adolescents, like some of the variations I have used with severely disturbed patients (that I shall describe below), may or may not warrant being referred to by Eissler's (1953) term "parameters." Eissler referred to variant techniques within the context of an essentially classical psychoanalytic therapy, variant techniques themselves subject to later analysis. But sometimes the variant may be larger than what is classical, so to speak, and then we should speak of alternative therapeutic modalities rather than parameters as such. I mean to address the whole range here, including greater and lesser variations from "classical" technique.

One is more impressed with the need for technical variations in work, like Redl's, with nonanalyzable patients; and the examples I shall draw upon stem from such work. In my own experience, there have been three routes to thinking about such technical variations. In each, work with "impossible" clinical situations became merely "difficult" as I drew on my interest in developmental theory to catalyze technical variations and new thought. First was my experience for a couple of years in assuming responsibility for the supervision and teaching of work with difficult, multiproblem, intrapsychically chaotic, socioeconomically distressed, and environmentally overstimulated children and their families in our municipal hospital clinic. The work was frustrating and painful, and I found that the only way to keep at it was to meet it as an intellectual challenge, to draw stimulation and satisfaction from the attempt to let experience, theory, and at times novel techniques guide it, a process that often yielded a better therapeutic outcome as well. Second was my experience with some of my own patients over the years, patients in whom chronic and severe deficiencies of ego functioning were slow to alter and with whom, within the context of reasonably orthodox therapeutic procedures, I found myself making technical variations focused on specific aspects of the psychopathology. And third has been my involvement in varying ways with my colleagues, Drs. Margaret Mahler and Manuel Furer and Ms. Anni Bergman, over the past dozen years, whose work with symbiotic psychotic children (Mahler, 1968; Mahler and Furer, 1960; Bergman, 1971; Bergman and Furer, 1974) includes comparable efforts to deal with "impossible" psychopathology by creating variations in technique within the context of sophisticated, psychoanalytically guided treatment.

Before going to the clinical examples, an aside is in order to clarify the personal ideology underlying this work. It seems to me that a therapist who is "psychoanalytically oriented" is psychoanalytically oriented in whatever he or she does, though just *what* he does (especially beyond the range of the "average expectable analyzable patient") should vary with the patient's psychic structure. Technical variations, too, even major ones, can be "psychoanalytically oriented." Although the terms "psychoanalytically oriented psychotherapy" and "insight therapy" are often used synonymously, such an equation is actually a usurpation of the former term, implying that insight therapy has drawn on the vast contributions of psychoanalysis whereas supportive therapy has not. It is as though the latter is a mindless wasteland, not guided by a theory of human functioning. Psychoanalysis has status, and naming has power; and one result of contrasting psychoanalytically oriented (insight) therapy with supportive therapy has been that psychoanalytic theoretical considerations have only very slowly been applied to the work of supportive therapy.

I would propose instead two parallel terms: psychoanalytically oriented *insight* therapy and (equally) psychoanalytically oriented *supportive* therapy. They may of course be, alternatively, "psychodynamically oriented" or "family oriented" or "behaviorally oriented" or whatever one's theory—but they remain parallel. For if we genuinely operate with a theory of human development, structure, and change, such as psychoanalysis (among others) provides, then all of our thinking, no matter what the problem, no matter who the patient, is influenced by—i.e., "oriented" by—that theory. It is true in considerable degree that insight therapy, far more than supportive therapy, draws upon—is oriented by—

psychoanalytic *technique*, but both can be equally oriented by psychoanalytic *theory* more generally—in particular its conceptions of development and change on the one hand, and of psychic structure and human thought, affect, and drive processes on the other. In the following discussion I have drawn upon psychoanalytic *developmental* theory to elucidate aspects of technique in supportive therapy and in work with ego-deficient patients.

The clinical illustrations given below are not necessarily novel. They are intended as examples not so much of new approaches as of the application of psychoanalytically enriched parent-child considerations to the creation of developmentally forwarding strategies for use with particular patients at particular points in their therapy. The examples are certainly not to be viewed as a "new" method of therapy. They are merely clinical *moments*, technical *bits*, which took place between therapist and patient in the context of complex, multifaceted therapeutic relationships that also included considerable interpretive work of a reasonably familiar kind.

Indeed, no therapy is ever totally "supportive" in the sense that no exploratory and interpretive work whatsoever goes on, and this is certainly true of the cases I am going to describe. And, contrariwise, as I tried to show earlier, there is no such thing as a "pure" insight therapy in which the mere presence of another, the analyst, does not lead to the "supportive" stabilization of defenses and of object relationships, or in which the analytic context of safety does not provide the setting for risking change. Discussions of the two, supportive and insight therapies, often take the approach that they are counter*posed*—i.e., in some *opposition* to one another. I believe, however, that in actuality they are counter*poised*—i.e., in some *balance* with one another. In any event, the "supportive" therapies that I have in mind are complex affairs, intellectually taxing, including flexibility and variation in techniques, and also including many moments of interpretive work. In describing them, I shall try to show how the particular technical *acts* of the therapist or the *form* of his or her presence had their therapeutic impact, and I shall relate them to developmental, parent-child issues.

Let me begin with a fairly simple and not unusual clinical vignette, but one that represents my first awakening to the phenomena I wish to discuss. Some years ago, I was seeing a 16-year-old boy in psychotherapy. He had been brought to treatment after having drawn a much younger boy into performing fellatio on him. As I got to know him, it became clear that in that incident and elsewhere he acted on impulse, without plan or anticipation of consequence, in an almost haphazard way, without the impulse itself appearing to have a very powerful impelling force (see D. Shapiro, 1965). Just as his planfulness was deficient, so too was his whole cognitive and affective life rather vacant and undifferentiated. Raised by a depressed mother, abandoned by his father, this was the developmental outcome, though the specific formative steps were not known to me.

In the second year of therapy, the following incident took place: Robert was telling me about a high school dance to which he had gone. "All the other guys were dancing with girls, except me . . . But I wasn't angry." Should I point out the denial of anger? My past contact with him amply justified that interpretation; in his life he never had "gotten," and once again at the dance he wasn't "getting"; he was chronically angry. For some reason (I do not know it very precisely now and I doubt if I knew it any more precisely then) I chose not to. Instead I said: "Perhaps, like you say, you weren't angry. Perhaps you were envious; perhaps you were wishing that you could be dancing too." He lit up, and that moment between us became important for us both. It was the start of my later "teaching" him further, not only to help him develop and use differentiated affects, but to help develop other ego functions as well (anticipation and planning, verbalization, judgment)—to fill the vacant and undifferentiated psyche with the tools of ego function.

For me, though I did not know it at that moment in 1957, the incident was the start of this paper—a long-range effect. For Robert, the effect was more immediate. When I introduced him to his envy in that situation I believe I did several things: I showed him that a certain unarticulated inner sensation, vaguely and confusedly experienced, was indeed an identifiable affective state, known to others and therefore socially shared and somewhat more acceptable; I helped prevent a process (signalled by the "I wasn't angry") whereby all of his feelings would typically get caught up in the flow of his anger, thereby losing their specificity and their differentiated signal value for him; and I believe that, through words, through the naming of emotional states (Katan, 1961; see T. Shapiro, 1974), I aided the control function—words providing a moment of recognition and delay in which discomfort over a feeling might have a chance of being handled in ways other than through denial or immediate discharge through action.

At a level a bit more removed from the concrete clinical data, just what had happened? Following Anna Freud's (1927) comments about psychoanalytic work with children, I believe that I had shifted for the moment from an interpretive mode to something that was an amalgam of an educative and an interpretive one. Though Katan's (1961) paper had not yet been written, its later publication helped me to understand that the naming of feelings has an important role to play in normal development as well. And in her paper, it is clear that that function is ordinarily carried out by the empathic parent.

Let me highlight one point: in this instance, I believe, the developmental function served by the naming of feelings helped this adolescent in much the same way as it helps a growing child; its "critical period" of effect, so to speak, had not passed. Some kinds of learning can be taken in from the "benevolent parent" at any point in the life cycle.

Let me give another example. This one is more recent and, in contrast to the work with Robert, involved a more explicit and conscious attempt to draw on developmental formulations to deal with a specific deficit in ego function that was making therapeutic advance impossible. The clinical situation was one of failure in the development of the signal function of anxiety.

How does signal anxiety ordinarily develop? Presumably, the infant, experiencing distress, has repeated experiences of gratification (or termination of distress). At some point, the distress begins to be associated with these previous experiences of relief; memory thus comes into play and there is a capacity to anticipate relief once again. In these moments of delay, where distress is held in abeyance (because of the anticipation of relief) and therefore does not escalate, it seems to me probable that the opportunity for higher-order defenses (at first simply the "defense" of calling mother) can develop. In contrast, for the child for whom relief is not forthcoming, the beginning of distress is a "signal" only of the previously unrelieved distress, a memory that accelerates the escalation to panic next time around.

Emmy[1] was a child who could neither use the affect signal to call inner defenses into play nor rely on her capacity to terminate distress. At the age of nine, there was a clear deficiency in the process: anxiety signal → defense → control of anxiety. She was almost totally unable to tolerate affective discomfort. A spark of anxiety would rapidly escalate to a conflagration of panic—indicative of a borderline ego organization (Pine, 1974b; Rosenfeld and Sprince, 1963). That is, anxiety did not function as a signal that brought an array of defenses to the fore; all it signified, so to speak, was that panic was on the way. How then to talk? Any but bland or neutral words set off screaming or physical flight from the office, in a reaction that we were convinced was well beyond her capacity to control. Months went by in quiet play, but the talk situation did not change. As in a phobia, so too with the panic: the potential affect storm was such that the danger situation was avoided at all costs and steps toward new understanding or mastery could not be made.

It seemed to us that aid, in the form of a break in the cycle of anxiety → panic → flight, had to come from the outside, just as it does in the course of development when the parent's ministrations still the anxiety and substitute for the inner defenses that are not yet functional. What the therapist did, in steps and in varying combinations, at times by written note and at times by speech, was to tell Emmy such things as the following: "In about a minute" (or, "After the game of checkers") "I'm going to ask you a question" (this, to alert her anticipatory function); and he might add: "I'll only ask one question and then I'll stop and we'll play again" (this, to let her see a *terminus* of the threat and to let her see that the therapist would aid in bringing it to a halt); or later: "After the game, I want to talk for about five minutes" (he might lay his watch down where she could see it), "but if it's too hard, just say 'no more' and we'll stop" (this, to give her some active control over the danger). Overall, the therapist attempted to titrate the stimulus load for the patient; he also helped her achieve a more active anticipatory

[1] Dr. Robert Hansler was the therapist in this case, under my supervision, and I wish to thank him for allowing me to use this material.

capacity to combat her more usual passive experience in the face of affect storms. Emmy became much more able to talk in these bits though, as you can imagine, this was—like a single area of interpretation in psychoanalysis—only a small part of the work.

This entire process is not unlike the situation in which a therapist may say to an impulsive adolescent or adult patient, "After this session, because of what we talked about, you may have the urge to . . ."—saying this as a way of helping the patient with defective control functions to anticipate and control an impulse (as Emmy had to have help in controlling the affect). This was, by the way, another important part of the work with Robert (whom I described above)—the therapist's warning filling in for the historically unsaid and the (in any event) uninternalized parental "Don't." In addition to providing aid for the anticipatory function, such a warning provides a model for causal thinking (feelings lead to actions, actions have consequences, thought can lead to controls)—a kind of thinking that is often absent in such patients (D. Shapiro, 1965). How fully *this* can be internalized by older patients in the course of treatment, when it has not been accomplished earlier, is less clear to me; but my impression is that it is only minimally possible.

Let me give a third example drawn from child therapy, an example drawn from a different area of development. The capacity to hold "disagreeable" contents in consciousness is a developmental achievement of enormous consequence. In admittedly simplistic terms, it permits us to think adaptively about such contents and forestalls their (potential) proliferating effect outside of awareness and/or the need for the maintenance of repressive defenses against them. With adult patients we have learned that such repressed fantasies have already had a widespread effect and, technically in analysis, we approach them by *listening*, by letting the patient tell us, so that gradually we are able to understand the fantasies in all or many of their ramifications.

But some parents of young children don't behave that way. One parent may say: "I know you're angry at me, and I'm angry at you, but you still have to do what I told you to." Another says: "Boys have penises and girls have vaginas, and they are both different." Another says: "We adopted you because we saw you and we knew we would love you." Simple statements all, but unmentionable by certain *other* parents. And I suspect that such differences (from the outside) foster or counteract other tendencies (inside the child) which ultimately make for differences in what is thinkable and what is unthinkable or unmentionable for a particular child.

The therapist of the child patient can stand in either place—as an analytic therapist with a "wait and learn" attitude toward relatively unavailable content, or as a parent-educator who explains certain difficult-to-think-about matters in order to foster the growth process. The former, "wait and learn," leads to rich and complex understanding; but it is our familiar analytic procedure and, since I have nothing new to add to it, I will not discuss it further here. But I would like to give a clinical example of the more active parentlike intervention, with its general developmental and precise clinical rationale in this case.

Susanna[2] came to therapy at the age of eight, bright, winning, yet with an abstracted, faraway air. She was referred by her school which reported two things about her: that her faraway quality seriously interfered with her peer relationships, and that she periodically engaged in a form of aggressive activity, quite out of character for her, which gave them serious concern. The activity, seemingly coming out of the blue and having a driven, repetitive quality, involved her plowing aggressively, at full steam, through a crowd of her schoolmates, bowling them over, knocking them aside. In the history-taking, one fact stood out: although this child's development had been relatively free of accidents and illness, she had been hit by a truck at 18 months, and hit so severely that everyone, parents and physicians alike, viewed it as miraculous that she lived (and lived without any physical sequelae of the accident). While the accident itself was not available to Susanna's memory, she was quite aware of the (accurate) family view of the miraculousness of her survival.

Her psychotherapy could not help focusing on this accident because of what she brought to the sessions. Almost without exception, every session began with some kind of behavioral enactment of the accident—often in an abstracted, and equally often in an odd, somehow off-center, way. And it quickly became apparent

² Dr. Jean Tinsdale was the therapist in this case, under my supervision, and I wish to thank her for allowing me to use this material.

that her plowing through her schoolmates, trucklike, knocking them over, was yet another enactment of the same thing. In the office she would, for example, drop to the floor suddenly, as though dead, or beep like a truck horn at the most unlikely (unanticipated, caught-by-surprise) moments.

In the course of the therapeutic work, the therapist had occasion again and again to link these behaviors to the accident. Susanna responded at first with curiosity and then with recognition; but after a while she became rather fed up with talk of the accident, continued her enactments, and got annoyed at these "translations" of them. Considering the extent to which this material dominated the therapy, it was impressive how little was learned about its connection to her wishes, object relationships, and character structure; mainly we saw repetition in fantasy—the point-by-point correspondence of the enactments with the accident (though there were variations on the theme which revealed the developing magical notions of mastery especially). Susanna functioned remarkably well in her life; the traumatic residue of the accident seemed to have been quite compartmentalized, appearing with a faraway quality in her various play enactments, but not touching many other areas. Blos (1963), in discussing late adolescent development, speaks of a kind of ideal outcome in which derivatives of early traumata get remade into constructive life tasks (for example, a sickly Teddy Roosevelt who becomes an outdoorsman and soldier). For Susanna, the residue of the trauma seemed cut off from much of the rest of her life—not affecting many areas but also kept unmodified by subsequent experience.

The therapeutic work was governed by the effort to help Susanna "talk out" ideas relating to the accident, quite apart from whether ramifications of the accident in her fantasy life were ever expressed. (This was not a preformed approach; it grew in response to the material that she did, and *didn't*, bring into the sessions.) Much as the proverbial postsurgery patient wants to "show you my operation" and talk about it, and much as some sensitive parents may encourage talking and retalking about traumatic incidents as a way of working through the stimulation that could not be mastered all at once, so too with Susanna. And the result was striking. The two school-linked presenting problems dropped away, and Susanna developed new age-appropriate interests (bicycle riding and skating) which, in the clinical material, were clearly the heirs of the enactments of the truck accident (another moving vehicle). By their pleasure and age-appropriateness, and by the fact that the old enactments dropped away when these new interests arrived, they seemed to signal that the developmental process had been freed (Winnicott, 1971) and that the old trauma had entered the mainstream of her functioning in such a way as to power constructive activities rather than, in a compartmentalized way, undergo endless repetition.

In these brief case reports I have tried to illustrate fairly small sections of complex and multifaceted therapies, sections that can have light shed on them, I believe, by an examination of their relation to aspects of the functioning of the "good parent." Let me turn now to a somewhat more extended report of the treatment of a young woman in a therapy that could variously be considered insight-oriented or supportive. It is the latter aspect that I wish to focus upon. Though not created out of theory, the therapeutic power of its supportive aspects became comprehensible to me when I examined it in terms of a developmentally oriented dynamic theory.

I first met Carrie some years ago, when she was 16 years old—a complex, bright, sensitive, but chaotic and impulse-ridden adolescent who was capable of genuine loyalty, concern for others, and receptiveness in an object relationship; but she was virtually incapable of preventing herself from rushing into action to escape even the least amount of affective discomfort. Raised in Ireland by a borderline foster mother (who foster-cared numerous children), and with the periodic presence of a man whom she believed to be her true father (and who later disappeared), she was, during her early teens, before she and her foster mother emigrated to the United States, given the hurtful "gift" of information that the man was not her true father and that her actual mother was a prostitute who had "given her away."

Carrie had periodic difficulties with her school and other community agencies, as well as with her foster mother, and she eventually came to a neighborhood settlement-house clinic where she was referred for psychotherapy. I saw her once, then twice a week for about two and a half years before the therapy terminated abruptly, to resume some years later in a very different form. In that first period of therapy, the work was rich but erratic. When working well, she would, with a mix of stammering and hesitant yet passionate and strong expression, work on aspects of her pained relationships to her various parents and even, at times, on her defensive style of flight, action, and chaos that overrode painful affect. But she often missed her sessions, sometimes for weeks at a time, and work on one issue in the therapy in a sustained way over several sessions was rare.

The interruption of the therapy came about as follows: her attachment to her male therapist had all along been difficult for her to manage, and interpretive work did no more than forestall the next anxiety-ridden flight from her strong feelings. In particular, her transference longings for the therapist-as-good-mother and her erotic fantasies about the therapist-as-Oedipal-father both, in turn, precipitated flight from the therapeutic relationship. The flight led her into relationships first with a man who was clearly a substitute for the therapist (a destructive and inappropriate relationship that she was able to give up upon interpretation and major control imposed by the therapist) and later with a young man, close to her own age, who was not at all an inappropriate partner.

Into that relationship, however, the psychopathology of both mothers—her foster mother and his mother—came like an invasion. First his, then her, mother made clear their interest in having "the children" sleep together premaritally under the watchful and delighted eyes of the respective mothers (who seemed to be in competition with one another in this regard). Carrie thought, indeed *knew*, that the whole thing was bizarre, but she was caught in the web of her attachment to the young man, her sexual excitement, her entanglement with her mother, and her flight from the therapist—and could not easily extricate herself. But then she did. The young couple, then 18, left both mothers to live together, Carrie left therapy, and I did not hear from her again for a few years. So ended the first phase.

It is now 18 years since I first met Carrie. We still have a therapeutic relationship that is of great importance to her. The interim steps were these:

After a few years without contact, I received a phone call from her. This call set the pattern for our contacts over the next eight years. She would call, say she wanted to see me, set an appointment, and fail to show up. This occurred about once a year. After the first few episodes, I began to talk to her over the phone about her obvious wish and fear regarding seeing me, her paralysis with that, and, after a while, urged that she consider seeing someone else, perhaps a female therapist. She refused to do that, whatever support or interpretation was given, even though she recognized her inability to get herself in to see me. During those phone calls I did learn, however, that she had had out-of-wedlock twins in the interim and had continued the chaotic, action-oriented, trouble-prone style of her life.

And then came a series of calls (which eventuated in our resuming contact), a severe depression, and a brief period of disorganization. A crisis had come over her children. The father of the twins was making a move to take them out of the country with him. But beyond that, Carrie was torn between her awareness that she could not take care of the children (because of her need for action to escape unpleasant feelings, and hence a need to get out of the home, generally at unpredictable times, and away from them) and, on the other hand, her enormous guilt over subjecting them to the same cycle of abandonment and loss that she had been through. At that period she did come to see me a few times, and we talked on the phone often; I helped her to accept her inability to care for the twins at that time, to allow a relative to care for them, to visit and not abandon them, and to tolerate (by anticipation) her guilt. The immediate crisis past, again began phone calls and broken appointments.

At that point, about five years ago now, I made a new arrangement. I held an hour each week for her. It was "her hour," whether she used it or not. It was always there. She understood that, because she so often failed to show up, I would not hold this hour in my private office where I spent time only to see regularly scheduled patients, but that I would hold it at my hospital office where I could always use the time at my desk if she did not come. There was never any fee. She understood that I might schedule cancelable appointments in her hour, but never permanent ones. She would be spared the embarrassment, and I the annoyance, of broken appointments ... and we have kept this arrangement for five years. Carrie periodically calls *during* her hour or calls about the possibility of coming to her next scheduled hour. She calls about six to 10 times a year and comes two or three times a year; but we often discuss real issues at least for a while on the phone. Whenever I am going to be away for any reason during that hour, I always drop her a note in advance so that she won't call or arrive to find me absent. And with this arrangement, Carrie has settled down. For the first time she has held a job for over two years; her panics are more manageable; she is not skirting the edge of asocial trouble; and she visits her children and cares for them deeply. She is quite aware that her life is far from perfect, and she has mothering and schooling ambitions that she may yet fulfill; but she is functioning with more stability than I have ever seen in her.

What happened? I would like to describe what I attempted to do when I *did* see her, and what I believe happened when I *did not* see her but when "her hour" was nonetheless reliably there.

In the (occasional) sessions there have been two main areas of work. First, I have tried to help her identify her feelings and to anticipate her action tendencies, to "lend" her control and the tools for control, much as I have described in some of the other brief case reports. Central to this work has been genuine insight and uncovering regarding her inability to tolerate painful feeling, and linked to a critical, painful, imagined memory of "my mother giving me away, selling me, like a piece of meat." The agony and tears of this and other remembrances produce an instantaneous and driven need to "appear happy" by an array of actions and giddy affect. And second, we have worked on the interrelated issues of guilt over her children, the realities of her own capacities for care, and the guilt-depression storms that lie in the wake of this.

But that work is the regular stuff of psychotherapy, here half "supportive" and half "insight oriented," the two in a comfortable relationship in one unified "therapy." More germane to the current paper is the rest of the work: the sessions that are there for her, used or not. It is my impression that these have served an important function for the patient. The unconditional availability of the hour (and of the place where and the person with whom it would take place) gave her a home base. It anchored her. This young woman (now 34), whose past is uncertain to her, has one place where she knows she can always "go home again." And I use those words deliberately. The developing child, in early steps away from the mother, in adolescent ventures with friends, and in later more or less independent adult existence, "knows" (in an inner if not totally realistic sense) that he or she has a parental home to go back to— something which, whatever the ambivalence, makes, I believe, separation more possible, and something which is felt as an acute reality loss with the death of the parents and the loss of the parental home, the home of one's childhood.

Beyond that, I believe the conditions of our arrangement gave Carrie *control* over her approach and distancing in relation to the therapist (something desirable but not always achieved by the child in relation to the parent)—whether this was linked at any one moment to the oral longings or the sexual attraction in that approach-distancing conflict. And with that control, approach would not be *required,* and distancing would not lead to *loss.* Developmentally, the parent who can be reliably there, yet not intrusive, cedes the child a like control.

In one of our recent phone conversations, Carrie told me that she feels she is finally growing up. Though she hadn't seen me for months, she had kept in touch with me by phone and was feeling close to me. As we were saying goodbye, she thanked me "for being around," by which I believe she was expressing her own recognition of the importance of a home base.

CONCLUDING REMARKS

In this paper I have attempted to illustrate (a) how considerations stemming from the parent-child relationship can enrich our understanding of some of the sources of therapeutic change in both insight and supportive therapies, and (b) how technical variations in work with ego-deficient patients can be generated by parallel considerations. The intent has been to supplement our understanding by focusing on phenomena that are in the background of classical analysis (where insight and working through are in the foreground), but which come into the foreground in work with ego-deficient patients.

It is an interesting aside to consider the verbal process of classical psychoanalysis from a developmental standpoint as well. For patients who have achieved early self-differentiation and object attachment, and in whom internal processes of defense and cognitive function are reasonably well elaborated, it may be precisely the speech-and-explanation modality that accords with their developmental receptiveness and needs (personal communication, Dr. Wagner Bridger). For such patients speech maintains an optimal contact and distance from the analyst (see Stone, 1961) and permits the articulation and integration of vague impulse-affect states (see Loewald, 1960).

But to return to the main topic of the present paper: From a developmental perspective, the ideas put forth here all have to do with object relations and internalization, with what one person does for or provides for another, and how what is done or provided by the other can facilitate change in or be taken in by another. The degree to which, and the areas in which, a "critical period" phenomenon characterizes human functioning are by no means clear. Whether and in what areas developmental processes that have been missed at their proper time for synthesis remain forever unavailable is not something that we have clear knowledge about. This is the problem of reversibility of psychopathology couched in developmental language. Human developmental phenomena are endlessly complex, and it seems likely that we are dealing not with problems of an either-or nature, but with instances of many partial, faulty, or unstable developments remaining as potentials even when initial learning and development have not taken place.

To take a simple instance, the educative function of the naming of feelings: it seems to be usable by patients at any point in the life cycle, and whether or not there is individual historical precedent for it; it has no single critical period after which it is functionless. But even far more severe and complex disturbances can sometimes be "corrected" when later experiences provide part of what has been missed. Thus, the astonishingly deprived and developmentally stunted infants in institutions described by Provence and Lipton (1962) made remarkable (though incomplete) recoveries when they enter good foster homes. And some of the symbiotic psychotic children described by Mahler and her colleagues (Mahler, 1968; Mahler and Furer, 1960; Bergman and Furer, 1974) were able to make at least some use of a corrective symbiotic experience even at a developmentally delayed point in their life cycles.

I am not here making a plea for more therapeutic optimism.

My own experience with patients with severely stunted development by no means justifies this. I am suggesting only that (1) attention to developmental, parent-child issues in all treatment can enrich our understanding of how change takes place; (2) attention to what parents are for or do for their children may provide us with hypotheses about technical variations for patients with relatively intractable ego deficit; and (3) attention to the conditions and areas in which learning and internalization that normally occur earlier can *still* occur later will help us to develop further theoretical understanding of human development while we simultaneously learn about therapeutic technique.

REFERENCES

Alexander, F. (1948), *Fundamentals of Psychoanalysis*. New York: Norton.
───── (1956), *Psychoanalysis and Psychotherapy*. New York: Norton.
Benedek, T. (1938), Adaptation to Reality in Early Infancy. *Psychoanal. Quart.*, 7:200-214.
Bergman, A. (1971), "I and You": The Separation-Individuation Process in the Treatment of a Symbiotic Child. In: *Separation-Individuation: Essays in Honor of Margaret S. Mahler*, ed. J. B. McDevitt & C. F. Settlage. New York: International Universities Press, pp. 325-355.
───── & Furer, M. (1974), Child Psychosis: A Review of Mahler's Theory and Some Recent Developments and Thoughts. Paper presented at meeting of the American Orthopsychiatric Association, San Francisco, Calif.
Blanck, G., & Blanck, R. (1974), *Ego Psychology: Theory and Practice*. New York: Columbia University Press.
Blos, P. (1963), *On Adolescence*. Glencoe, Ill.: Free Press.
Bowlby, J. (1969), *Attachment and Loss*, Vol. 1. *Attachment*. New York: Basic Books.
Breuer, J., & Freud, S. (1893-1895), Studies on Hysteria. *Standard Edition*, 2. London: Hogarth Press, 1955.
Caplan, G. (1960), Patterns of Parental Response to the Crisis of Premature Birth. *Psychiatry*, 23:365-374.
Eissler, K. (1953), The Effect of the Structure of the Ego on Psychoanalytic Technique. *J. Amer. Psychoanal. Assn.*, 1:104-143.
Freud, A. (1927), Four Lectures on Child Analysis. *The Writings of Anna Freud*, 1:3-69. New York: International Universities Press, 1974.
Freud, S. (1900), The Interpretation of Dreams. *Standard Edition*, 4 & 5. London: Hogarth Press, 1953.
───── (1914), Remembering, Repeating, and Working-Through. *Standard Edition*, 12:145-156. London: Hogarth Press, 1958.
───── (1933), New Introductory Lectures on Psycho-Analysis. *Standard Edition*, 22:5-182. London: Hogarth Press, 1964.
Fromm-Reichmann, F. (1950), *Principles of Intensive Psychotherapy*. Chicago: University of Chicago Press.

———— (1959), *Psychoanalysis and Psychotherapy.* Chicago: University of Chicago Press.
Greenson, R. R. (1967), *The Technique and Practice of Psychoanalysis*, Vol. 1. New York: International Universities Press.
Harrison, S. I., & McDermott, J. F., eds. (1972), *Childhood Psychopathology.* New York: International Universities Press.
Hartmann, H. (1939), *Ego Psychology and the Problem of Adaptation.* New York: International Universities Press, 1958.
Jones, E. (1953), *The Life and Work of Sigmund Freud*, Vol. 1. New York: Basic Books.
Katan, A. (1961), Some Thoughts about the Role of Verbalization in Early Childhood. *The Psychoanalytic Study of the Child*, 16:184-188. New York: International Universities Press.
Lewin, B. D. (1946), Sleep, the Mouth, and the Dream Screen. *Psychoanal. Quart.*, 15:419-434.
Lindemann, E. (1956), The Meaning of Crisis in Individuals and Family Living. *Teachers Coll. Rec.*, 57:310-315.
Loewald, H. W. (1960), On the Therapeutic Action of Psychoanalysis. *Internat. J. Psycho-Anal.*, 41:16-33.
Loewenstein, R. (1956), Some Remarks on the Role of Speech in Psychoanalytic Technique. *Internat. J. Psycho-Anal.*, 37:460-468.
Mahler, M. S. (1965), On the Significance of the Normal Separation-Individuation Phase. In: *Drives, Affects, Behavior*, Vol. 2, ed. M. Schur. New York: International Universities Press, pp. 161-169.
———— (1968), *On Human Symbiosis and the Vicissitudes of Individuation*, Vol. 1. *Infantile Psychoses.* New York: International Universities Press.
———— & Furer, M. (1960), Observations on Research Regarding the Symbiotic Syndrome of Infantile Psychosis. *Psychoanal. Quart.*, 29:317-327.
———— Pine, F., & Bergman, A. (1975), *The Psychological Birth of the Human Infant.* New York: Basic Books.
Malone, C. A. (1966), Some Observations on Children of Disorganized Families and Problems of Acting Out. In: *A Developmental Approach to Problems of Acting Out*, ed. E. N. Rexford. New York: International Universities Press, pp. 22-41.
Piaget, J. (1936), *The Origins of Intelligence in Children.* New York: International Universities Press, 1952.
Pine, F. (1971), On the Separation Process: Universal Trends and Individual Differences. In: *Separation-Individuation: Essays in Honor of Margaret S. Mahler*, ed. J. B. McDevitt & C. F. Settlage. New York: International Universities Press, pp. 113-130.
———— (1974a), Libidinal Object Constancy: A Theoretical Note. *Psychoanalysis and Contemporary Science*, 3:307-313. New York: International Universities Press.
———— (1974b), On the Concept "Borderline" in Children: A Clinical Essay. *The Psychoanalytic Study of the Child*, 29:341-368. New Haven: Yale University Press.
Provence, S., & Lipton, R. (1962), *Infants in Institutions.* New York: International Universities Press.
Rapaport, D. (1957), The Theory of Ego Autonomy: A Generalization. In: *Collected Papers*, ed. M. M. Gill. New York: Basic Books, 1967, pp. 722-744.

Redl, F. (1951), Ego Disturbances. In: *Childhood Psychopathology*, ed. S. I. Harrison & J. F. McDermott. New York: International Universities Press, 1972, pp. 532-539.

Rosenfeld, S., & Sprince, M. P. (1963), An Attempt to Formulate the Meaning of the Concept "Borderline." *The Psychoanalytic Study of the Child*, 18:603-635. New York: International Universities Press.

Sandler, J. (1960), The Background of Safety. *Internat. J. Psycho-Anal.*, 41:352-356.

Schafer, R. (1968), *Aspects of Internalization*. New York: International Universities Press.

Schecter, D. (1968), Identification and Individuation. *J. Amer. Psychoanal. Assn.*, 16:48-80.

Shapiro, D. (1965), *Neurotic Styles*. New York: Basic Books.

Shapiro, T. (1970), Interpretation and Naming. *J. Amer. Psychoanal. Assn.*, 18:399-421.

—— (1974), The Development and Distortions of Empathy. *Psychoanal. Quart.*, 43:4-25.

Silverman, L. (1976), The Unconscious Symbiotic Fantasy as a Ubiquitous Therapeutic Agent. Paper presented at meeting of the American Psychoanalytic Association, Baltimore, Md.

Spitz, R. (1946), Anaclitic Depression. *The Psychoanalytic Study of the Child*, 2:313-342. New York: International Universities Press.

Stone, L. (1961), *The Psychoanalytic Situation*. New York: International Universities Press.

Strupp, H. H. (1973), Toward a Reformulation of the Psychotherapeutic Influence. *Internat. J. Psychiat.*, 11:263-327.

Sullivan, H. S. (1940), *Conceptions of Modern Psychiatry*. New York: Norton.

—— (1953), *The Interpersonal Theory of Psychiatry*. New York: Norton.

White, R. W. (1963), Ego and Reality in Psychoanalytic Theory. *Psychol. Issues*, Monogr. No. 11. New York: International Universities Press.

Winnicott, D. W. (1955), Metapsychological and Clinical Aspects of Regression within the Psychoanalytical Set-up. *Collected Papers*. New York: Basic Books, 1958, pp. 278-294.

—— (1960), Ego Distortion in Terms of True and False Self. *The Maturational Processes and the Facilitating Environment*. New York: International Universities Press, 1965, pp. 140-152.

—— (1965), *The Maturational Processes and the Facilitating Environment*. New York: International Universities Press.

—— (1971), *Therapeutic Consultations in Child Psychiatry*. New York: Basic Books.

5   Adaptation and Stress

Judith Godwin Rabkin, Ph.D., and
Elmer L. Struening, Ph.D.

Social Change, Stress, and Illness:
A Selective Literature Review

The object of this paper is to review the research literature concerning observed relationships between social change, stress, and the onset of illness. The framework within which these findings are considered represents an integration of components derived from Freud's early considerations of external trauma and reactive illness, later psychosomatic formulations, and contemporary stress theory.

It has long been recognized that changes in the social environment often heighten the person's vulnerability to stress and stress-related diseases. Even when existing social conditions are difficult, their alteration, especially when rapid, frequently generates stress. As Hippocrates observed, "Those things which one has been accustomed to for a long time, although worse than things which one is not accustomed to, usually give less disturbance."

Despite recognition of the role of social factors in the onset of illness, adequate documentation was limited for many years. Even today questions about selective vulnerability remain unanswered, such as why some people become ill when exposed to difficult social events whereas others do not, and why some groups are more susceptible than others to illness in the presence of social change.

Until recently in the history of medicine, considerations about selective vulnerability were secondary in importance to the need to account for and control the infectious diseases that were the major causes of mortality. The illness model generated by the germ theory in the nineteenth century led to the diligent search for a single etiological factor and a specific antidotal cure or "magic bullet."

However, it has been increasingly recognized that this approach is comparatively ineffective in accounting for and controlling the chronic diseases that today predominate in industrial societies. In an effort to develop a more appropriate multicausal conceptualization of disease, attention is being increasingly devoted to the social context in which illness occurs, and one important element of this context is social change.

I. THEORETICAL BACKGROUND

Before turning to a review of empirical evidence regarding the relationship between social change and illness onset, we shall consider two major approaches that have been widely employed as conceptual frameworks for research in the field: psychosomatic and stress theory. The historical correspondence between these two approaches has been variously presented, and is more a matter of viewpoint than of fact. In the stress literature, Scott and Howard (1970) reviewed eight basic conceptual models used to explain the phenomena of stress. Among these models are Hans Selye's, Harold Wolff's, and the "psychosomatic model of stress" associated with Dunbar and with Alexander and his colleagues. Moss (1973) also included the "psychosomatic-psychoanalytic" model in his review of stress models. From this point of view, psychosomatic theory is subsumed under the general stress rubric.

Conversely, Reiser (1975), in his review of the historical phases of psychosomatic theory, identifies its roots in psychoanalytic theory, since psychosomatic theory was first formulated by analysts. However, he regards the psychoanalytic point of view as having been eclipsed by the stress model *within* the framework of psychosomatic theory. He believes it is the stress model which today occupies the forefront or growing edge of psychosomatic theory and research.

In addition to these reciprocal views of psychosomatic theory as one of the several stress models, and the stress concept as one of several phases of psychosomatic theory, a third option is to regard the two approaches as historically independent traditions which have gradually converged in their efforts to identify, describe, and evaluate the contributions made by nonmedical factors to the timing of illness episodes and their distributions within and across populations. Following this latter organizational scheme, the independent, distinctive, early stages of psychosomatic specificity theory and of stress theory will be presented, followed by a review of the nonspecific theory of disease causation endorsed in broad outline by contemporary proponents of both perspectives.

INITIAL POSITION: PSYCHOSOMATIC THEORY

The history of psychosomatic theory and research falls into three broad phases, the first of which was initiated by Freud. As historians of the field are fond of observing, psychoanalysis began with the study of a psychosomatic phenomenon: conversion. Freud's studies of hysteria served to bridge the dichotomy between mind and body that had characterized nineteenth-century philosophic and scientific thought, and illuminated the psychological origins of certain somatic symptoms. Freud initially used the term "conversion" in his first paper on the defenses, entitled "the Neuro-Psychoses of Defence" and published in 1894. He defined conversion as a process whereby an "incompatible idea is rendered innocuous by its *sum of excitation* being *transformed into something somatic*" (p. 49). Symptom choice was regarded as a function of three factors: the suitability of the organ for symbolic expression of a psychic conflict, qualifications of the defense mechanisms, and somatic or psychic trauma (Deutsch, 1959). In this way drive and defense aspects were seen to contribute to the choice and timing of a given somatic symptom. However, the only body parts accessible for use in conversion were thought to be those capable of mental representation. Any body experience that could be perceived consciously or unconsciously would be potentially capable of being associated with other mental content and therefore could be used as a "body language" to symbolize and express hidden conflicts and wishes.

After Freud's early work on conversion, interest in the area declined, and it was not until the 1930's that renewed attention was devoted to psychosomatic clinical phenomena.[1] During this

[1] As Lipowski (1968) has observed, the term "psychosomatic" has been used in many contexts: psychosomatic medicine, movement, approach, research, disorder, symptoms, theory. In addition to the psychosomatic clinical theory and

second phase, extending to the mid-1950's (Reiser, 1975), the psychosomatic specificity theory, derived from psychoanalytic concepts, predominated in the thinking and research of psychosomatic medicine. During this period, Flanders Dunbar (1943) formulated a variety of "psychosomatic profiles" of personality types associated with different illness patterns, and attention was focused on identifying and describing repressed conflicts that led ultimately to organic manifestations. Not only was symptom choice regarded as largely psychologically determined, but a specific conflict was believed to cause specific cell and tissue damage (Deutsch, 1959). Other theorists believed that the illness itself was both the symbolic expression and consequence of developmental experiences and the ego's attempts to cope with intrapsychic conflict (Reiser, 1968).

As Knapp (1975) has noted, the classical formulation of emotional specificity was developed by Franz Alexander and his colleagues at the Chicago Institute. Using the physiological knowledge of their time (which was far more meager than it is today), they developed a set of hypotheses characterizing illnesses which came to be known as the seven psychosomatic disorders: bronchial asthma, neurodermatitis, rheumatoid arthritis, hypertension, ulcerative colitis, peptic ulcer, and thyrotoxicosis. According to their model, three components together determined illness: organ vulnerability; psychological patterns of conflict and defense formed early in life (both of which could be influenced by constitutional factors); and the precipitating life situation. Despite the tripartite nature of this model, they concentrated almost exclusively on the second component, the emotional "constellations" or personality patterns that were presumed to be differentially associated with the seven "psychosomatic" diseases. In this theory of psychosomatic specificity, each constellation was seen as consisting of a central conflict pattern together with the primary

---

research touched on here are the equally important research areas of neurophysiological and neuroendocrine mediating mechanisms, psychophysiological research, and developmental studies, which do not fall within the scope of the current review. Even within the area of psychosomatic clinical theory there are significant contributions, such as those of Schur and Deutsch, regarding ego regression and illness which have been excluded here in order to focus on the role of individual differences in personality constellations and their relation to illness.

defenses employed against it. Thus, for example, the central conflict culminating in bronchial asthma stems from impulses that threaten one's attachment to one's mother, which lead in turn to fear of maternal abandonment; the asthmatic symptom is interpreted as a repressed expiratory cry for the lost mother (Masserman, 1955).

During this period, analysts working within the psychosomatic framework asked their medical colleagues to refer for psychoanalysis patients suffering from one of the seven diseases they were studying. Combined medical and psychological studies led them to conclude that, within disease categories, these patients resembled one another in personality type more than they resembled members of the general population. Beginning in 1953, Alexander and his colleagues conducted an extensive study of 83 patients diagnosed as having a psychosomatic disease. Each was interviewed at length. Interview transcripts, from which medical references were deleted, were given to four or more analysts, each of whom was asked to make a diagnosis on the basis of the transcript. Accurate diagnoses were made by analysts more often than by a group of internists, and at a level exceeding that expected by chance (41% of the diagnoses were correct). These findings were interpreted as supporting the specificity theory that "a patient with a vulnerability of a specific organ or somatic system and a characteristic psychodynamic constellation develops the corresponding disease when the turn of events in his life is suited to mobilize his earlier established central conflict and break down his primary defenses against it" (Alexander, French, and Pollock, 1968, p. 11).

In recent years, the specificity theory has been criticized from several points of view, although selected aspects are still used in both clinical and research settings. First, the retrospective design commonly used creates the possibility that, instead of having a causal influence on the disease process, the observed personality characteristics may have developed *in reaction* to the disease or *in reaction* to the patient's predisposition earlier in his life (Reiser, 1966). Second, although lip service was paid to the role of the external precipitating situation in illness onset, the patient's social context was not adequately considered. Third, the process by which psychological conflicts created organic lesions was not delineated, nor were physiological mechanisms analyzed in any detail. Since the introduction of the specificity theory, significant and extensive findings have been made in the field of psychoneuro-endocrinology. Indeed, in a recent editorial in *Psychosomatic Medicine* entitled "Are 'Psychosomatic' Diseases Diseases of Regulation?" Weiner (1975) enumerates evidence to suggest that four of the diseases traditionally regarded as psychosomatic are characterized by specific disturbances of physiological regulatory mechanisms that may constitute a predisposing risk factor.

Furthermore, as Reiser (1975) has pointed out, there are at least three stages in the natural history of any disease: that preceding the clinical appearance of the disorder, the actual onset, and the period following establishment of the disease process. Factors associated with disease onset are not necessarily relevant to an understanding of the mechanisms involved in establishing predisposition. Psychosomatic specificity theory concerns the issue of individual psychological predisposition, but neglects other components related to predisposition as well as consideration of the subsequent stages of disease.

In addition to these theoretical criticisms, a practical issue arose: medical patients who consulted internists were seldom interested in psychoanalysis as their sole treatment, and few were actually suitable analytic candidates (Engel, 1968). In addition, treatment of psychosomatic disorders by psychoanalysis or other psychotherapeutic methods did not produce good enough results to warrant a regimen of exclusively psychological treatment, as Kaplan (1975) has pointed out. As a result, the study of psychological factors associated with disease patterns has moved from the clinical treatment setting to the hospital bedside, experimental laboratory, and community for further development and elucidation.

The specificity theory has become less popular, and in standard textbooks of psychiatry it has been presented with declining enthusiasm over the past 20 years. While proponents of the theory may continue to believe that "it has been clearly established that organic manifestations can be the result of repressed unconscious conflicts" (Deutsch, 1959), prevailing opinion seems more accurately expressed by Kolb, in his textbook overview, who writes that "most psychiatrists now agree that the conception of a personality pattern specific to each psychosomatic disorder has no sound foundation" (1973, p. 450). Recent critical reviews of the seven "psychosomatic" disorders tend to stress multiple etiology, reject the dominance of psychogenesis, and call for refinement of methodology. Indeed, there is no longer widespread agreement that there exists a subset of disorders that are specifically psychosomatic, even though the diagnostic category of "psychophysiologic disorders" still remains in the American Psychiatric Association's *Diagnostic and Statistical Manual of Mental Disorders*, defined as "physical disorders of presumably psychogenic origin." While the notion of personality characteristics as predisposing risk factors continues to be studied, as discussed in the last section of this paper, the specificity theory of Alexander and his colleagues is today regarded as overinclusive in some respects and too narrow in its purely intrapsychic focus.

At present, research investigators working within the psychosomatic framework continue to be active and productive. The scope of their work has extended far beyond the scope of those who were earlier preoccupied with psychosomatic disorders. As Lipowski (1968) has observed, there is no logical reason to exclude any disease from the province of psychosomatic research "since its goal is to elucidate and integrate the biological, psychological and social components of any medical event" (p. 398).

INITIAL POSITION: STRESS THEORY

In 1935, Hans Selye articulated his concept of stress as a syndrome or set of nonspecific physiological reactions by the organism to various noxious environmental agents of a physical or chemical nature. His formulation was largely responsible for the introduction of the concept of stress into the scientific vocabulary, and inaugurated 40 years of research and theoretical developments conducted with accelerating enthusiasm on an international scale in numerous branches of the medical, and later social, sciences.

In very general terms, Selye defined stress as "the state manifested by a specific syndrome which consists of all the nonspecifically induced changes within a biological system" (1956, p. 54). The syndrome, called the General Adaptation Syndrome or GAS, is a particular configuration of physiological processes and states which occurs in the same over-all pattern in response to many different kinds of external stimuli or stressors, and is species-wide in form. The GAS entails three sequential phases: alarm, resistance, and exhaustion, modeled after Cannon's observations. These phases represent the body's adaptation to a stressor, and are intended to maximize effective resistance to it. If the adaptation is not effective, it may contribute to the development of many diseases, which Selye refers to as diseases of adaptation. They are not specific outcomes, nor are they caused solely by the failure of the adaptation process. Disease etiology is seen as multiply determined, and disease outcomes may cover the spectrum of acute and chronic disorders.

For many years Selye has pursued the effect of stressors on the organism's physiological state, in both animal and human studies. As a physician and endocrinologist, his major contributions concern the identification and description of glandular changes, primarily of adrenal functioning, and the process of inflammation as major characteristics of the GAS. While he has broadened his initial concept of noxious environmental agents to include *any* demand on the organism that exceeds a certain level of intensity (1974), his model and his research address chemical, physical, and organic agents rather than symbolic conditions and events. Emphasis is placed on the universal quality of the GAS, rather than on individual differences in response to stressors.

The Concept of Generalized Susceptibility

As psychosomatic theorists moved away from the specificity theory, and as stress theorists sought to broaden Selye's formulations to include social as well as physical stressors, an overlapping body of theoretical and empirical observations emerged which may be referred to as a nonspecific theory of disease causation. Representative major contributors include Harold G. Wolff, classified as both a stress and a psychosomatic theorist, Schmale and Engel, who are primarily identified with psychosomatic theory, and Cassel, who is associated with stress theory and epidemiological research. Following a brief summary of their respective views, a general etiological conception of illness will be offered which seems to represent current thinking among proponents of both theoretical approaches.

Selye's stress concept has been extended and broadened by others to include its application as a mediating variable in regulating the impact of social and interpersonal experiences on the well-being of the individual (Mason, 1975). A major contributor to this theoretical evolution was Harold G. Wolff who, with Hinkle, established the Human Ecology Laboratory at Cornell Medical School in 1954 to study the effects of environmental changes on health. Wolff's contributions were both theoretical and empirical; his research with Hinkle is reviewed in a later section. He defined stress as a "dynamic state within the organism in response to a demand for adaptation . . . since life itself entails constant adaptations, living creatures are continually in a state of more or less stress" (1968). Rejecting the psychosomatic specificity hypothesis, he believed that man's social environment and past experience, including biological factors and life events, have a small influence upon the form illness takes but a major influence on its timing and course. Further, he did not accept the idea of a specific category of psychosomatic disorders, but instead regarded each as having multiple causes, with interaction among the environment, the host, and an agent, following the standard epidemiological paradigm. In short, Wolff endorsed a general, nonspecific conception of the role played by stress in the onset of illness.

In their analysis of social and personal factors associated with illness, Engel, Schmale, and their colleagues (Adamson and Schmale, 1965; Schmale and Engel, 1967; Schmale, Meyerowitz, and Tinling, 1970; Schmale and Iker, 1966; Engel, 1968) have concentrated on the transitional phase between health and illness, the setting in which illness occurs. They have conceptualized a psychological state to which they have assigned a cumbersome label, the "giving up-given up" syndrome, and which seems basically equivalent to the experience of demoralization. It is regarded as a transitional ego state, ushered in by failure of previously effective defenses and coping devices and marked by awareness of this failure. The person feels helpless in the sense that a significant loss, either impending, actual, or symbolic, is seen as irreversible, accompanied by the perception of being less competent and less secure in social roles and relationships. The "given up" stage may or may not follow. At present, nothing is known about the mechanisms through which this complex might contribute to somatic change. Engel, Schmale, and colleagues believe that the experience of this syndrome reflects a psychobiological state which facilitates the clinical appearance of disease (Schmale and Iker, 1966) and is, indeed, the most common setting in which all diseases appear. Within this framework they have gathered supporting evidence from studies of the onset of psychological symptoms and the development of cervical cancer. In general, they believe that the giving up-given up syndrome acts as a facilitating factor which permits disease to appear when it does, but, unlike earlier psychosomatic theorists, they regard this psychological orientation as unrelated to choice of disease entity.

In contrast to the theorists mentioned so far, who were physicians concerned with patient care and treatment as well as research based largely on the clinical method, Cassel is an epidemiologist who is professionally concerned with disease distribution in populations and whose focus is a group or community. He has devoted considerable attention to the literature on both animal and human studies of social conditions, and the social changes that have been associated with the health status of various populations. Observing the wide variety of pathological conditions that emerge following changes in the social milieu, Cassel has concluded that the monoetiological, specific model of disease causation, historically derived from the germ theory of illness, is not appropriate. "A conclusion more in accordance with the known evidence would be that ... variations in group relationships, rather than having a specific etiological role, would enhance susceptibility to disease in general" (1974, p. 1042). This concept of *generalized susceptibility* is in direct contrast to the concept of psychosomatic specificity, whose proponents hypothesized a specific, personal set of characteristics associated with a particular disease outcome. In brief, Cassel's focus, like that of other social epidemiologists, is on the influence of position in the social structure and social support systems, or changes in structure and support systems, on disease susceptibility.

In summary, within both the psychosomatic and stress literatures in the last 25 years, theorists and research scientists have devoted considerable attention to the correspondence between social relationships, social conditions, and life changes on the one hand, and consequent manifestations and distributions of various diseases on the other. The notion of socially induced stress as a precipitating factor in chronic diseases is at present gaining wide acceptance among scientists in the natural and social sciences. It is becoming recognized that stress can be one of the components of any disease, not just of the seven "psychosomatic" entities. As Dodge and Martin (1970) have expressed it, "the diseases of our times, namely the chronic diseases, are etiologically linked with excessive stress and in turn this stress is a product of specific socially structured situations inherent in the organization of modern technological societies" (p. 3). Even susceptibility to microbial infectious diseases is seen as a function of environmental conditions culminating in physiological stress on the person, rather than as due simply to his exposure to an external source of infection (Dubos, 1965).

Those who are engaged in the formulation of a revised etiological model generally associate illness onset with at least five potentially relevant factors. These are: the presence of stressful environmental conditions; perception by the person that such conditions are indeed stressful; his relative ability to cope with or adapt to these conditions; his genetic predisposition to a disease; and the presence of a disease agent.

In this context it is seen that the stress concept does not explain why some people are more susceptible to illness than others. Stress does not cause disease. Like "anxiety" and "instinct," it is a broad and general descriptive concept. Its utility derives from its role in identifying productive lines of research in the study of disease etiology, encompassing external events influencing individuals and populations, and also their appraisals and interpretations of such events. Accordingly, we will turn to a consideration of the body of research that has concentrated on the correspondence between social change, stress, and illness onset.

In the following review, we focus on the nature of social environmental changes and their effects on the health of human populations. Two categories of change, one consisting of events affecting large groups, and the other consisting of life events and changes of a primarily personal nature, will be considered in turn. A third section encompasses three sets of variables—formal properties of the stressful events, individual characteristics, and the nature of available social buffers—that together mediate the perception and impact of the stressful event and influence the probability that illness will occur in given circumstances of social change.

Definition

In this literature review, we consider the following sequence of conditions: social stressors → mediating factors → stress response → illness onset. The term *social stressors* refers to widespread social changes such as migration, and personal life changes such as bereavement, which alter a person's social setting. A more specific definition of this term is proposed by Holmes and Rahe (1967), who define as social stressors any set of circumstances whose advent signifies or requires change in the person's ongoing life pattern. According to this conception, exposure to social stressors does not *cause* disease, but may alter the person's susceptibility at a particular time, and as such serves as a precipitating factor.

Mediating factors include those characteristics of the stressful event, of the person, and of his social-support system that influence his perception of stressors and so serve to modify their impact. These variables include long-term predisposing factors which heighten the person's risk of becoming ill, such as high serum cholesterol in relation to myocardial infarction. Other mediating variables may make the person less vulnerable to the experience of stress, such as prior experience with the stressor. In general, consideration of mediating variables contributes to an understanding of differential sensitivities to social stressors.

Stress response is the organism's response to stressful conditions, consisting of a pattern of physiological and psychological reactions, both immediate and delayed. *Illness onset* is defined by the appearance of clinical symptoms of disease. *Predisposing* factors refer to long-standing behavior patterns, childhood experiences, and durable personal and social characteristics that may alter the person's susceptibility to illness. *Precipitating factors*, in contrast, influence the timing of illness onset and refer, for the most part, to more or less transient current conditions or characteristics. *Chronic disease* refers very generally to syndromes which are of long duration and which are noninfectious. It is the chronic diseases rather than the acute, infectious ones that are usually thought to be particularly influenced by the experience of stress.

II. STRESSORS:
CHANGES IN THE SOCIAL ENVIRONMENT

Changes of social environment may occur at different structural levels: national, statewide, community, family, or individual. At one extreme, wartime conditions or radical fluctuations in the national economy touch the lives of whole populations, albeit differentially. At the other, events such as bereavement or job loss affect only the individual. The study of social change falls generally into two categories. The first, to be reviewed in this section, concerns the impact of widespread processes of social change on the health of populations. Investigators working within sociological, psychiatric, epidemiological, and social-psychological frameworks typically compare illness rates before and after the introduction of social change within one population, or compare rates for those who experienced change and those who did not. Aggregate data are usually employed, so that findings are primarily applicable to groups rather than individuals. The second category of change in the social environment concerns life events that occur on an individual basis. This research field, which will be reviewed in the following section, focuses on the number and nature of life changes in a specified time period before illness onset, and is usually based on individual reports. Both of these categories of social change are regarded as precipitating factors rather than necessary or sufficient causes of disease.

Categories of widespread social change that have been associated with heightened levels of social stress include sudden disasters, evolving "progressive" conditions, geographic mobility and migration, and social disorganization which itself is often a product of the other processes. Cassel (1973, 1975) suggests that these conditions or processes have in common a lack of feedback to the individual regarding what behaviors are desirable and acceptable, and it is this failure of communication that constitutes the source of stress in social change. Groen (1971) has noted that each kind of change requires coping, adaptation, defense, and repair; if these processes are inadequately carried out, the experience of stress is exacerbated. Jaco (1970) has commented on the association between social change and mental illness, referring to social change as a general mental-health hazard. Evidently, both gradual and rapid social change can constitute a source of stress when traditional support systems are undermined and new ones are not immediately available.

Varieties of social change can be grouped in two major classes. Sometimes change is due to movement by the individual, as in the case of migration. In other instances, the individual remains where he is but others leave and arrive, or prevailing customs are modified by processes such as industrialization, urbanization, and urban renewal or deterioration. These two classes of social change will be considered in turn.

Migration and geographic mobility have long been recognized as factors associated with increased rates of mental illness and chronic physical disorders. Much work has been devoted to the relationship between migration and mental illness (see Struening, Rabkin, and Peck, 1970, for a review of the literature). Almost all studies show higher rates of psychiatric hospitalization for migrant and immigrant groups than for other population groups. Although a wide range of intervening variables has been found to contribute to these high rates, there remains an association between migration and hospitalization that cannot be entirely accounted for by characteristics of the migrant group. Accordingly, in efforts to identify those conditions leading to increased risk of psychiatric hospitalization for immigrant groups, investigators have turned to analyses of their interactions with the receiving society. They have considered such phenomena as the extent of cultural discrepancy, various conditions in the new society, and pressures for assimilation. It has been found that migrants settling in urban areas containing a high proportion of earlier migrants of similar origins adjust more easily than those moving into areas containing few other migrants or those of dissimilar background, and that the transition from rural to urban is more difficult than that from one urban setting to another (Srole et al., 1962; Fried, 1964, 1966). Some aspect of the transition from one society to another apparently constitutes a hazardous situation leading to increased risk for psychiatric hospitalization. Thus stress seems most intense for those migrants whose original culture differs radically from the new, where there are no familiar groups to join and thus modify the impact of change, and where the receiving society most actively emphasizes rapid assimilation.

Migrants also seem more vulnerable than other groups to

infectious and chronic diseases. Geographically mobile men have higher rates of coronary heart disease than geographically stationary men when such variables as diet, smoking, and family history are controlled (Graham and Reeder, 1972). Job transfers entailing geographical moves have also been studied in relation to health. Willmuth, Weaver, and Donlan (1975) compared company medical records of 148 transferred workers and 148 controls matched for age, sex, and job description. Using analysis of variance, they found that transferred workers, especially those below professional rank, made significantly more visits to the company nurse for minor illnesses and complaints, though no differences were found with respect to episodes of major illness. Drolet (cited in Wolff, 1968, p. 192) observed that the Irish who immigrated to America in the nineteenth century were materially better off than those who remained behind, yet their death rate from tuberculosis in New York City was 100% higher than the rate reported in Dublin during the same period.

High blood pressure has also been associated with migration. Cassel (1970) cited 22 studies in which "primitive" populations living in small cohesive societies were found to have low blood pressure that did not change with age. When members of such societies migrated to areas where they were exposed to Western culture, they were found to have high blood-pressure levels and to exhibit the positive relationship between age and blood pressure found among Western populations. Despite methodological flaws in many of these studies (such as nonstandardized measurements, observer variation, selective rather than representative samples), the frequency with which the same findings have been reported by different investigators for widely disparate groups suggests that the phenomenon is a real one.

In animal studies, it has been observed that the more dominant animals show the least effects of, and the subordinate ones the most extreme responses to, socially disruptive conditions of many kinds. Perhaps among humans too social rank in part determines the health consequences of socially disruptive experiences. Cassel (1974) has proposed that future studies of illness patterns among migrants should distinguish between those who assume subordinate positions in the host countries and those who take on positions of prestige and power.

In sum, movement into new and unfamiliar environments evidently contributes to increased susceptibility to both psychological and physical disorders. This may not be apparent immediately after the transition has been made, and indeed may not materialize at all in many instances, but the risk is present.

Social change also occurs when prevailing social environments are altered by processes such as industrialization, urbanization, urban renewal, or radical economic change. Processes of this nature are gradual compared to the sudden shifts incurred by migration or natural disasters. They too, however, have the effect of dissolving former social-support systems, leaving people unprotected and unprepared for the new experiences to which they are exposed.

Increased rates of a wide variety of diseases have been associated with the effects of social transformations. Tyroler and Cassel (1964) designed a study for measuring mortality rates from coronary heart disease in populations that were themselves stable but whose social situation was changing in varying degrees. They classified North Carolina counties according to their degrees of urbanization in 1950 and 1960, and found a strong relation between increased urbanization and mortality rates from heart disease; the more urbanized the county, the higher the mortality rates.

In another North Carolina study, Cassel and Tyroler (1961) compared Appalachian mountaineers who were the first in their families to engage in industrial work with co-workers from the same ethnic stock and mountain coves whose parents had worked in the factory before them. They selected a stratified random sample of 265 first-generation white male factory workers aged 20 to 50 and 125 co-worker controls matched for age and over-all health status. Their dependent variables were scores on the Cornell Medical Index and morbidity rates based on periods of three or more consecutive days of sick leave, for which doctors' notes were required. From cross-tabulations of their data, they found that a greater proportion of first-generation workers complained of somatic symptoms, and in more organ systems, than did second-generation workers of the same age in the same factory. Although no statistical tests were performed, such a trend is suggested in their tables. The authors cautioned that their sample was an unusual one and therefore the results are not necessarily applicable to the general population. However, they did regard their findings as supporting the hypothesis that cultural change is associated with patterns of illness.

Using a very different design, Syme, Borhani, and Buechley (1965) and Syme (1975) also found a relationship between "cultural mobility" (to use their term) and illness. They compared demographic and occupational data of 80 white males identified in a community survey as having coronary heart disease, and 80 controls. Using chi-square tests, they found higher coronary heart disease rates among men of foreign-born (and presumably lower-status) parentage who had gone to college than among those who had not, and also as compared to college graduates of native parentage. This difference was not itself regarded as a causal factor but as a reflection of a more general phenomenon which might indeed contribute to heightened risk.

In the two studies described, social change from one generation to the next was regarded as a factor contributing to increased susceptibility to illness. Social changes experienced in the course of their own youth has been associated with higher rates of psychological impairment in a southern community survey of young black adults. Schwab, McGinnis, and Warheit (1973) administered a 317-item questionnaire to 322 adults and found disproportionate rates of both psychological and physical disorders among black respondents, with particularly high rates among those under 30. The authors concluded rather speculatively that these high rates seem a product of the rapid sociocultural changes that southern black communities have experienced in the last 20 years, as well as of intergenerational conflicts about values, roles, and beliefs. Neither the data analysis, which consisted of cross-tabulations and percentages, nor the authors' discussion, provide more than tentative evidence to support their notion of the relation between rapid social change and susceptibility to illness. Such studies considered cumulatively, however, do offer grounds for further pursuit of this hypothesis.

Urban renewal programs have also been associated with psychosocial stress and increased vulnerability to illness. As Levy and Rowitz (1973) observed, urban renewal causes the breakdown of old communities and the disruption of established systems of social support, especially for older people. In their study of psychiatric hospitalization rates by neighborhood in Chicago, they found that "it is precisely those areas of the city which are undergoing rapid and drastic social change which appear to create the highest rates of psychiatric casualties" (1973, p. 155).

Conditions of economic adversity have been associated with higher rates of mental illness in an elaborate series of analyses by Brenner (1973). Comparing fluctuations in the national economy, as measured by employment rates, with New York State hospital admission rates over a 120-year period, he explored the general hypothesis that "as economic activity decreases and the economy contracts, *overall* social stress increases and therefore mental hospitalization should increase" (p. 7). He found that, when age, sex, and diagnosis are controlled, a powerful relationship is continuously observable between changes in the economy and admission rates: over the last 60 years the correlation between the two measures ranged between $-.80$ and -1.00. Like many other investigators of stress and illness, he observed that once stress appears, group cohesiveness plays an important part in preventing psychiatric hospitalization. He concluded that the single largest population at risk for psychiatric hospitalization consists of those whose way of life is threatened by temporary or chronic economic instability.

The eventual outcome of insufficient adaptation to pervasive social change can be social disintegration. This may be brought about by heavy migration, cultural confusion, natural disasters, or any other massive assault on the prevailing social system. As Leighton (1971) has defined it, the process of disintegration is characterized by such factors as defects in the patterns of communication, leadership and followership, and cooperation. Failures occur in such basic functions as provision of food, shelter, and clothing, maintenance of law and order, the care of children, and the satisfaction of emotional needs. On the basis of their Yoruba and Stirling County studies, he and his colleagues concluded that "The small community is a system such that the greater the disintegration, the greater the failure in community functions and the greater their malfunctioning, the more adverse the effect on the mental health of its members" (1971, p. 118).

Cassel (1973) has reviewed the literature and found studies to demonstrate that, in addition to its association with increased incidence of mental disorder, social disorganization is related to higher rates of tuberculosis, stroke mortality, coronary heart disease, and hypertension. Neser, Tyroler, and Cassel (1971) correlated aggregate measures of social breakdown (such as percentage of one-parent families, percentage of out-of-wedlock births, rates of males sentenced to prison and road camps) and stroke mortality rates by county in North Carolina over a nine-year period. They found a regular rise in mortality rates for stroke in the black population as levels of social disorganization increased. Wolff (1968) cites a graphic example concerning American Navahos who were transferred from their homeland to reservations a few miles away in essentially the same physical environment but in a setting of social disorganization. Shortly thereafter an "appalling" increase in mortality from tuberculosis occurred. The same phenomenon occurred among Bantus who moved to Johannesburg.

Narrowing one's focus from the community as a system to the family as a system, parallel findings have been reported regarding the level of organization and health status of its members. Mutter and Schliefer (1966), in a study of children's somatic illness, found that families of sick children were more disorganized and had experienced more life changes than families of healthy children. Kosa and Robertson (1969) also noted that chronic family disorganization has been associated with increased susceptibility to illness.

COMMENT

As a group, most studies of societal changes and consequent health status of populations suffer from a variety of methodological weaknesses. The populations studied are seldom systematically selected, so findings cannot be readily generalized. In many instances, such as migration studies, the samples are inevitably self-selected, and the same is true of factory workers or college graduates who are the first in their families to undertake such ventures. Even when sampling is handled well, the data available to investigators are often limited, both because suitable instruments may be lacking and because information about large groups is difficult to obtain. Further, with the exception of the studies of Brenner and Levy and Rowitz mentioned above, the statistical analyses of these epidemiological data are often limited, failing to account for multiple factors and influences on outcome measures and instead relying on simple tabulations and nonparametric tests. In addition, it is seldom possible for social scientists to conduct prospective studies of the health consequences of social change, and the typical retrospective design is subject to the usual difficulties in differentiating between precipitating and outcome variables. Other deficiencies include lack of replication studies and of long-term cumulative research programs which alone can provide the basis for reasonably certain conclusions.

Nevertheless, as these selected investigations are intended to show, evidence is accumulating that major changes in the social environment can increase susceptibility to a broad spectrum of chronic diseases. These changes can take many forms, as reviewed above, but all share the property of weakening or destroying the web of interpersonal relationships that formerly constituted the individual's social-support and feedback systems. In the absence of this social buffer, the individual's vulnerability to illness seems to be enhanced.

III. STRESSORS:
PERSONAL CHANGES AND LIFE-EVENTS RESEARCH

Over the past 25 years, attention has been devoted to the role of stressful life events in the etiology of various diseases. Derived from Cannon's early observations of bodily changes related to emotions and Adolph Meyer's interest in the life chart as a tool in medical diagnosis, the field was launched at a 1949 conference on Life Stress and Bodily Disease sponsored by the Association for Research in Nervous and Mental Diseases. Since then, several groups of investigators have adopted this general framework in independent long-term projects. Their work has evoked widespread interest and, in addition to extensive professional publications, has appeared in both general medical magazines such as *Medical World News* (1971; Leff, 1975) and the popular press (*Time*, 1971).

In general, the purpose of life-events research is to demonstrate a temporal association between a recent increase in the number of social events which require adaptive responses from the person involved, and the onset of illness. The underlying assumption is that such events serve as precipitating factors, influencing the timing but not the type of illness. The onset of mental as well as physical disorders and accidents has been studied in both retrospective and prospective designs within the life-events framework.

Most investigators working in this area have adopted, in its original or a modified form, a 43-item checklist developed by Holmes and Rahe and their colleagues (1967). The checklist items are intended to represent fairly common situations concerning family, personal, occupational, and financial events that require or signify a change in adjustment. On the Social Readjustment Rating Scale, on a scale of 1 to 100, death of spouse is weighted as 100, marriage as 50, a change in recreation as 19, a vacation as 12. This and comparable checklists, usually covering the previous six to 24 months, are typically used as the measure of stressful life events. Modified forms have been developed for specific populations such as children, college students, and athletes, but in general the format has remained consistent.

The most elaborate and extensive program of life-events research has been conducted by Rahe, Holmes, and Gunderson and their colleagues. Their work, originally largely based on Naval shipboard personnel, has been extended on an international basis and has evoked considerable comment in the literature, both positive and critical. A brief description of their approach and representative findings is intended to illustrate the kinds of research, and major issues and problems, in this area.

In their early retrospective studies, Rahe and his colleagues (1972) asked over 2,000 Navy personnel to report their life changes and illness histories during the previous 10 years. The number of illness episodes was related to scores on the Social Readjustment Rating Scale (SRRS); these scores are referred to as life-change units or LCUs. In general, those who recorded up to 150 LCUs a year reported good health for the following year. When annual LCU scores were between 150 and 300, about half the respondents reported illness in the next year. When annual LCU scores exceeded 300, as they did for a small proportion of the respondents, illness followed in 70% of the cases, and furthermore tended to entail multiple episodes.

In prospective studies of 2,500 American Naval personnel aged 17 to 30, life events occurring in the six months before shipboard tours of duty were compared with shipboard medical records of the six-month cruise. Respondents were grouped into quartiles based on their precruise LCU scores, and mean illness rates for each group were significantly different ($p = .01$). When this study was repeated with a sample of 821 Norwegian sailors, comparable results were obtained (Rahe et al., 1974). Another study of life changes and illness experienced by the entire 1,005-man crew of a battleship on combat duty off Vietnam yielded a similar correspondence (Rubin, Gunderson, and Arthur, 1971).

Numerous other studies by a variety of investigators have similarly demonstrated statistically significant associations between number and intensity of life events and the probability of specific near-future illnesses (see Holmes and Masuda, 1974, and Rahe, 1972, for extensive lists of references). In both retrospective and prospective investigations, positive relationships have been found between mounting life change and such diverse conditions as sudden cardiac death, myocardial infarctions, accidents, athletic injuries, tuberculosis, leukemia, multiple sclerosis, diabetes, and the entire gamut of minor medical complaints (Antonovsky and Kats, 1967; Bramwell et al., 1975; Rahe et al., 1964; Rahe, 1972; Rahe and Lind, 1971; Selzer and Vinokur, 1974; Theorell and Rahe, 1971). Nixon's phlebitis has been attributed to the cumulative pressures of his final months in office (Brody, 1974). High scores on checklists of life events have also been repeatedly associated with mental symptoms and disorders, and such scores have been found to differentiate between psychiatric and other samples (Dekker and Webb, 1974; Jaco, 1970; Markush and Favero, 1974; Myers et al., 1972; Paykel, 1974; Paykel, Prusoff, and Myers, 1975; Uhlenuth and Paykel, 1973).

It has been further noted that life events may be related to the course of illness and recovery, whatever the etiology of the primary disease (Kagan and Levi, 1974). In addition, periodic analyses of life events may serve to monitor and help predict the course of illness, as demonstrated in a posthospital follow-up of mental patients by Michaux et al. (1967).

At the present time, it seems reliably established that stressful life events commonly precede the onset of a wide variety of physical and mental disorders in populations. The sheer number of these reports, the variety of populations studied, and the range of disorders involved, together suggest that the life-events checklist is a useful and meaningful tool for predicting illness and, more generally, for learning more about illness vulnerability and onset. However, closer scrutiny of both methodological and theoretical issues, as well as the actual data that have been reported, uncovers a host of serious issues.

The most immediate issue, and one which has received only cursory attention from investigators in the area, concerns the size and practical significance of the correlation between the number and nature of life events and subsequent episodes of illness. The vast majority of life-events investigators have, until very recently, relied on statistical methods of the most rudimentary nature to analyze this relationship. Between-group differences comparing either populations differing in health status or differing in LCU scores are often reported only in precentages, or else exclusively in terms of statistical significance (p levels). However, the authors usually fail to point out that, considering the very large sample sizes used in life-events research, almost any relationship will be statistically significant—i.e., reflect a correspondence not attributable to chance alone—even in the absence of any practical utility.

When studies are examined for reports of obtained correlation coefficients between number of life events and number of illness episodes, they are often conspicuously missing. When present, they are typically below .30. In Rahe's Naval data, for example, correlation coefficients between life events and illness were consistently around .12 (Rahe et al., 1974), and other investigators have reported equally low, albeit statistically significant, correlation coefficients (e.g., Bieliauskas and Webb, 1974; Gersten et al., 1974; Markush and Favero, 1974). In other words, recent life events account for perhaps 10 % of the variance in illness onset, and often considerably less. In practical terms, then, life-events scores taken by themselves are not effective predictors of the probability of future illnesses.

It seems likely that stronger relationships between life events and episodes of illness would be obtained if the psychometric properties of the measuring instrument were improved and the outcome criteria refined. Although few studies of the reliability and validity of life-events checklists have been published, available evidence suggests weaknesses in both of these respects (Rahe, 1974).

Another potential source of error concerns the possibility that a given life event and a sequential illness are both products of the same phenomenon, so that one cannot definitely be said to precede or precipitate the other. This problem may arise when the cause and effect of a life event are both at least partial results of the person's own behavior, as, for example, in the case of a college student who drops out of school and then manifests symptoms of mental illness. Although the problem of clearly differentiating between life change and observed outcome has not been ignored in the literature, satisfactory solutions have not yet been achieved. According to Hudgens (1974), 29 of 43 events on the SRRS checklist are often the symptoms or consequences of illness, and as such represent possible sources of contamination.

In addition to such potential sources of error, several investigators have wondered whether life-events checklist scores are actually associated with illness onset or, rather, with care-seeking behavior (Mechanic, 1974a; 1976). Since care-seeking behavior—i.e., medical records—is frequently used as the operational definition of illness onset in college populations, Naval shipboard studies, and elsewhere, the issue is not easily resolved. Cadoret et al. (1972) and Hudgens (1974), in their studies of life events and mental depression, both suggest that mounting life changes precipitate psychiatric hospitalization, not the appearance of symptoms. It must be noted that this distinction between illness onset and treatment-seeking behavior may apply to disorders of gradual onset and those which are often untreated, such as colds and headaches. The issue is, however, irrelevant to the association of life changes with rates of accidents, suicide, mortality, and acute severe illness such as myocardial infarctions. It is perhaps in the realm of social change and mental disorder that most care is required in handling this issue.

Investigators using the life-events approach have differences of opinion about the nature of the events to be included in checklists (Hough, Fairbank, and Garcia, 1976). Though the various instruments in use have overlapping items, they vary in length, content, number of positive versus negative items, and number of items over which respondents have no control (such as "death of a friend"). Most checklists selectively emphasize events of young adulthood, undesirable events, and subjectively evaluated events; this emphasis may make it difficult to interpret findings when different groups are being compared (Holmes and Masuda, 1974; Dekker and Webb, 1974; Uhlenuth et al., 1974). The "common" events represented on life-events checklists may be largely irrelevant to specific groups, or certain groups may experience far fewer changes than are usually reported (Kellam, 1974; Wershow and Reinhart, 1974). B. P. Dohrenwend (1974) has concluded that there really are several domains of life events, and those to be sampled must depend on the goals of a given study.

Considerable attention has been devoted to the question whether an event must be negative to evoke stress. In their original work, Holmes and Rahe (1967) scaled life events in terms of "the intensity and length of time necessary to accommodate to a life event, regardless of its desirability." B. S. Dohrenwend (1973) also endorses this position, which is supported by extensive clinical work on normal life crises such as engagement and marriage (Rapoport, 1963). Gersten et al. (1974), however, disagree, as does Selye (1976), whose most recent definition of stress is "the nonspecific response of the body to any demand" (p. 55).

In addition to questions regarding item selection and scoring, another issue in life-events research that warrants further attention is the possibility of an interaction between social changes and other factors, such as the availability of social-support systems to serve as buffers for the person affected. Cassel has observed that deficient support systems will not in themselves contribute to illness susceptibility in the absence of social stressors. The converse is also probable: social stressors in the presence of strong social-support systems will have only minor effects on health. An excellent illustration of the value of measuring the interactions of these sets of variables is provided by Nuckolls, Cassel, and Kaplan (1972), who studied life changes and social supports for women during pregnancy, in relation to complications in later pregnancy and delivery. Neither the life-change score alone nor the social-support score alone was related to complications. When the two scores were considered jointly, however, significant findings emerged: 90% of the women with high life-change scores and *low* social-support scores had one or more complications, whereas only 33% of women with equally high life-change scores but with *high* social-support scores had any complications. The social-support scores were irrelevant in the absence of high life-change scores. These results clearly document the need for a broader approach to the study of life events and illness; counting the number of events in a given period is valuable but not sufficient.

A final issue to be raised concerns the composition of the samples used in many life-events studies. Wershow and Reinhart (1974) refer to the common failure to "disaggregate groups," as in the study in which patients in a dermatology clinic and patients with coronary heart disease are together classified as suffering from chronic disorders, or when responses of subjects with vastly different backgrounds and life styles are combined for analysis. In recent publications, some of these distinctions have been taken into consideration. In general, however, more care needs to be taken in the selection of representative respondents in order to facilitate interpretation of findings and their generalization to groups beyond the sample being studied.

It must be noted that extensive critical appraisals of life-events studies are possible primarily because of the relatively large and coherent body of research that has been published in this area. The fact that different groups of investigators have produced coordinated and cumulative research findings over many years provides critics with an adequate picture of how far work has progressed, what are current deficiencies and weaknesses, and what remains to be done.

The field of life-events research, like that of psychotherapy research, seems to evoke almost as much critical commentary as empirical data. However, in life-events research, communication channels are evidently effective. The quality of recent work far surpasses that of earlier studies, and many suggestions have been incorporated into research programs. Increasing numbers of studies are prospective in design, and investigators are concerning themselves with sample selection, seeking appropriate and relevant items in their checklists, trying to refine their outcome criteria, and using multivariate statistical methods in data analyses.

We would conclude that the life-events approach to the measurement of stress and subsequent illness offers a method that is attractive in its simplicity, directness, ease of data collection, and commonsense appeal or "face validity." By now it has been demonstrated sufficiently often that some relationship exists between life changes and illness, accounting for a small proportion of the variance associated with illness onset. Instead of repeatedly reanswering the question whether life events play a precipitating role in illness onset, the next steps in the development of this field entail examination of the circumstances in which such effects are enhanced or minimized.

IV. MEDIATING FACTORS:
CONTRIBUTIONS OF STRESSOR, INDIVIDUAL, AND
SOCIAL-SUPPORT VARIABLES

Some people develop chronic diseases and mental disorders after exposure to stressful conditions, whereas others do not. Indeed, most people do not become disabled even when terrible things happen to them, as Hudgens (1974) has observed. Exposure to stressors alone is almost never a sufficient explanation for illness in ordinary human experience, and other factors that influence their impact require consideration. These may be grouped in three broad categories, which will be reviewed in turn: characteristics of the stressful situation, individual biological and psychological attributes, and characteristics of buffering social-support systems available to the individual.

Before turning to a review of these mediating factors, it is important to emphasize both their cumulative impact and the relationships among them. That is, the more severe the external situation, the less significant are social and individual characteristics in determining the likelihood and nature of response. When conditions are harsh enough, as in some wartime situations, prolonged sensory-deprivation experiences, or concentration-camp internment, breakdown is virtually universal, and individual variations are reflected only in the length of time before the reaction occurs, and perhaps in subsequent recovery time. In contrast, when the stressful situation is comparatively less severe, social supports and individual characteristics contribute to an understanding of why some people become ill and others do not.

Finally, although it seems probable that exceptional, atypical, extreme environmental conditions can induce disability in those so exposed even if they do not possess social or personal deficits, vulnerability alone, in the absence of stressful conditions, does not in itself precipitate or cause chronic disease or mental disorder.

1. STRESSOR CHARACTERISTICS

Formal characteristics of stressors that have been associated with the probability of disease occurrence include their intensity, magnitude (departure from baseline conditions), duration, unpredictability, and novelty.

One way to measure *intensity* is to evaluate perceived or actual rates of change. Lauer (1974) studied perceived and actual rates of societal and personal change in relation to reported anxiety levels among 678 college students ranging in age from 17 to 52 years. Despite the weakness of his measures, several of which were represented by only one item, he found a significant positive correlation between the perceived rate of societal change and the experience of anxiety and stress as measured by the Taylor Manifest Anxiety Scale. Respondents who felt that "the world we live in is changing so fast it leaves me breathless at times" had higher anxiety-stress scores than other respondents. This relationship was even stronger when the perceived change was regarded as undesirable. Further, while both societal and personal changes were significantly related to stress level, the contribution of the former was greater. This study, then, offers tentative evidence regarding the role of the rate, scope, and desirability of change, as contributors to the experience of psychological stress.

Magnitude can be evaluated in terms of extent of departure from "average" conditions. The magnitude of stressful events directly corresponds to its impact on the person. It is now widely agreed that sufficient stress will induce an acute stress reaction in all so exposed, regardless of variations in predisposition. There has been less consensus concerning the long-term or permanent physiological and psychological alterations induced by stressful events. However, recent evidence from longitudinal studies of concentration-camp survivors has shown that profound and protracted stress may have permanent effects on all (Horowitz, 1976).

Concerning more or less ordinary experiences of living, Wyler, Masuda, and Holmes (1971) found a significant relationship between the magnitude of prior life changes and the seriousness of chronic illness in a sample of 232 medical and psychiatric patients. They reported a Spearman rank-order correlation coefficient (rho) of .73 between scores on a Seriousness of Illness Rating Scale and the Schedule of Recent Experience covering the two years preceding the onset of illness.

Studies of the effects of extreme environments, such as prisoner-of-war or concentration camps, also show a linear correspondence between the magnitude of the stressor and the extent of the disorders, both acute and chronic. For example, Eitinger (1971), in a study of Norwegian concentration-camp survivors 12 to 15 years after World War II, found some kind of mental disturbance in 99% of his sample. Further, the severity of conditions of imprisonment was correlated with the likelihood of subsequent development of both somatic and mental disabilities. Similarly, Arthur (1974) reported that, in the decade after release, mortality rates among former American prisoners of war who were interned in Japan were 60% higher than those of prisoners of war released from German camps where conditions were significantly less severe, and more than double those of nonprisoner G.I. controls. Survivors of Japanese camps (in which more than 33% died, compared to less than 1% in German camps) in subsequent years had grossly inflated illness rates as well, based on Veterans Administration hospital records. Wolff (1968) noted that these illness rates were closely related to the amount of stress experienced. While the average illness rate among survivors of Japanese camps was double that of controls, it was seven times as great among those who experienced the most extreme hardships. Postwar illnesses occurred in all organ systems, and deaths were from causes as varied as cancer, accidents, and tuberculosis. Hocking (1970) observed that there were differential rates of disorder even within the horrendous Nazi concentration-camp system; prewar internment was not as devastating as wartime imprisonment. Even during the war there was a difference in conditions and impact of camps designed for detention and those designed for extermination.

In the face of the most extreme conditions, all who were exposed and who survived were disabled, many for life. Among the one in 600 who survived Nazi extermination camps, who were exposed to physical maltreatment, and prolonged undernutrition as well as psychological brutality, both short- and long-term sequelae were profound and pervasive. In such contexts, the biological, nutritional, and psychological insults are interwoven so that their differential effects are unidentifiable.

Behavioral reactions to extreme conditions tend to be remarkably similar, even stereotyped. Acute symptoms following exposure to natural disasters tend to be uniform, and the disabilities of concentration-camp survivors have been delineated as a specific pattern, the "K-Z" syndrome, encompassing biological as well as mental disabilities. In addition, a more general effect, that of premature aging, has been described among survivors of Hiroshima. It has been observed that their mortality and morbidity patterns are consistent with those of persons 15 or 20 years older than their actual age (Wolff, 1968).

Over-all, we may conclude that the magnitude of the stressful event is positively related to the extent of disability brought about, and that the more extreme the stressful situation, the more variance is accounted for by the stressor rather than by social, biological, or individual characteristics. As Hocking expressed it, "when individuals are subjected to a prolonged threat to their survival, the evidence suggests that pre-existing personality characteristics, resulting from inherited and early environmental experiences, are replaced by a universal and basic biological reaction" (1970, p. 21). Furthermore, long-term behavioral abnormalities have been reported from many different countries as occurring in people who were subjected to quite different types of environmental stress, although exceptions have been reported (Antonovsky, 1974). It seems that many of those who were exposed to prolonged biologically and psychologically stressful situations "never regain their former state of physical, social and psychologic well-being" (Hocking, 1970, p. 20).

The nature of the relationship between the *duration* of stressors and illness varies. While prolonged exposure often induces more severe or pervasive illness, as demonstrated in animal studies of electroshock and ulcer development, this is not always the case. As

Susser (1968) reported in a review of mental illness and World War II combat conditions, the highest rate of disorder among English bomber crews occurred early in the standard tour of 30 sorties. Evidently some men were predisposed to stress reactions and their vulnerability was manifested soon after exposure.

When the magnitude of a stressful event is sufficient to evoke a response in all who are exposed, duration can be the critical factor in differentiating among individual responses. Sensory deprivation seems to be the only condition so far identified which, in the absence of a hostile context, physical assault, or nutritional deprivation, brings about psychological disturbance in all who experience it. There is wide variation in the ability of people to tolerate such conditions; some can endure many days of isolation while others cannot stand it for more than a few hours. Studies of those with low and high tolerance for reduced sensory stimulation have not identified any personality differences. Factors found to make isolation more tolerable include previous exposure to such conditions, knowledge of the proposed duration of isolation, and the provision of simple tasks to be done by the subjects.

In the psychoanalytic literature, Kris (1956) and Khan (1963) have both considered the differential impact of exposure to brief and prolonged stressful situations. Kris spoke of shock trauma, defined as a single dramatic experience, in contrast to strain trauma, described as "the effect of long-lasting situations which may cause traumatic effects by the accumulation of frustrating tensions" (1956, p. 73). Khan's notion of cumulative trauma is analogous to Kris's concept of strain: both are gradual, silent, invisible, and insidious processes which serve to bias or warp personality development over time, which are cumulative in effect and apparent only in retrospect. Kris observed that, in the analytic situation, patients' recollections of the stressful impact of a single event may actually represent an ongoing strain extending over a period of time.

In summary, the duration of a stressful situation is variable in its effects. In some instances, a brief but intense experience can have devastating impact, whereas in other situations duration influences response and so makes a significant contribution to the understanding of differential reactions to a stressful situation.

Unpredictable events have a more adverse effect than those which are anticipated or for which people are prepared on the basis of prior experience. On the basis of animal studies, Miller (1975) noted that learning what to expect and when to expect it enables the individual to differentiate between dangerous and safe periods and to develop appropriate coping mechanisms which reduce the actual danger, the fear response, and the eventual stress reaction. In contrast, unanticipated or unpredictable events evoke a sense of helplessness which magnifies the stress reaction. In their study of behavioral responses to noise, Glass and Singer (1972) found that the inability to control or even anticipate the occurrence of loud noise in a laboratory setting enhanced its negative effect on behavior. They observed impairments in frustration tolerance, proofreading performance, and ability to resolve cognitive conflict after exposure to episodes of unpredictable noise.

In his studies of surgical patients, Janis (1958) observed that those who realistically anticipated the stressful nature of impending surgery dealt with the situation competently. In contrast, those with low anticipatory fear due to defensive denial or simply lack of information were unprepared for the stressful experience and displayed notably more emotional disturbance postoperatively. Janis concluded that "if a normal person is given accurate prior warning of impending pain and discomfort, together with sufficient reassurances so that fear does not mount ... [excessively], he will be less likely to develop acute emotional disturbances than a person who is not warned" (1974, p. 140). As in other contexts, realistic anticipation of and preparation for stressful events seem to modify their adverse impact.

Novelty enhances the impact of stressful events. As noted above, prior experience facilitates tolerance for the experience of sensory isolation. Cassel (1970) also concluded that previous experience with a potential stressor can markedly influence the intensity and appropriateness of response to it.

Finally, as the life-events literature has demonstrated, numerous stressors operating simultaneously or in sequence have greater impact than stressors that occur separately. As Coleman (1973) points out, in general systems theory this is called "overloading," and it has been found that the behavioral capabilities of an organism tend to drop dramatically with even a mild degree of overloading.

COMMENT

The literature concerning the dimensions of stressful situations that mediate their impact on individuals is derived from such diverse sources that a general critical appraisal is unwarranted. Some of the work, such as Miller's animal studies of the roles of prior experience and the fear response on stress reactions, Glass and Singer's noise research, and sensory-deprivation investigations, represent conventional, well-executed laboratory studies with clearly defined independent and dependent variables. On the other hand, much of the work concerning the magnitude and duration of stressors has been, of necessity, retrospective in design, using samples of convenience and ad hoc measures of change in the absence of pre and post indices. As such, information gathered about survivors of prisoner-of-war and concentration camps is more like the reports of cultural anthropologists than those of behavioral scientists. As it happens, however, the consequences of extreme stressors are usually so profound that the findings are meaningful as they stand.

Cumulatively, these findings suggest that the formal properties of stressors constitute a significant source of variation affecting the influence of the stressor on individuals. Their effect seems to be reciprocally related to that of other potential etiological agents, including biological and psychological predispositions, availability of social supports, and the nature of personal resources. In the extreme case, however, the magnitude and intensity of the stressor may render negligible the contributions of these other predisposing factors and may represent conditions sufficient to cause severe disabilities, both physiological and psychological, in previously intact persons. While Hudgens (1974) may argue convincingly that he has never seen evidence that "life stress can cause madness in a person previously of sound mind," this argument seems to apply only to the "average expectable environment" (Hartmann) and not to ultimate stressors such as concentration-camp conditions.

2. INDIVIDUAL CHARACTERISTICS AS MEDIATING VARIABLES

As Mechanic has observed, we cannot anticipate the impact of events on a person "while only knowing the dimensions of the challenge he faces; we also must know a good deal about his capacities to deal with these situations" (1976, p. 2). Factors that influence individual reactions to stressful events include the person's perception of these events, the range and relevance of his coping skills, and generalized personality style.

A critical factor in evaluating the impact of stressful events on the person is his perception of stress. Personal characteristics determine his perception and appraisal of the significance of potentiality harmful, challenging, or threatening events. It is this cognitive process which differentiates a stressor from a stimulus and which determines the nature of the stress reaction and subsequent coping activities (Groen, 1971; Jacobs, Spilken, and Norman, 1969).

As Lazarus (1971) has pointed out, the essential difference between the healthy and unhealthy, the successful and unsuccessful, is less a matter of avoiding stressful conditions than of coping adequately with them. Adaptive coping behavior depends on the accurate appraisal of prevailing conditions, including judgments about the degree of threat and the significance of the goal that may be endangered, identification of the agent of harm, viability of alternative courses of action and social or situational constraints on particular methods of response (Lazarus, 1970). Only after such judgments are made can appropriate action occur.

Following the Dohrenwends' (1970) conceptualization, the perception of stress is mediated by two broad categories of variables: one concerns personal or "internal" factors; the other, interpersonal or external factors. Personal factors include such variables as biological and psychological sensitivity thresholds, intelligence, verbal skills, morale, personality type, psychological defenses, past experience, and a sense of mastery over one's fate (B. S. Dohrenwend and Dohrenwend, 1970; Rahe, 1974; Wolff, 1968). Demographic characteristics such as age, education, income, and occupation may also contribute to the person's evaluation of stressful conditions and his response to them (Uhlenuth et al., 1974).

The effects of most personal variables in mediating stressful conditions are fairly obvious: those with more skills, assets, and resources, more versatile defenses and broader experience, tend to fare better. In general, the more competence a person has demonstrated in the past, the more likely that he will cope adaptively with a current stressor. And the more experience he has had previously with a particular stressor, the more probable that his present response will be effective (Miller, 1975).

The correspondence of personality type to stress reactions and disease vulnerability is less clear-cut. As we noted in the introductory section, the subject has been of major interest among those concerned with the psychosomatic approach. Over the years, investigators have proposed several models to account for the impact of intrapsychic factors on bodily function, including the concept of organ inferiority (Adler), specific emotional conflicts as determinants of disordered function in a particular organ (Alexander), and personality constellations associated with specific psychosomatic disorders (Dunbar).

With the passage of time and the accumulation of experience, these approaches to the understanding of personality and illness have become less popular. Investigators who have continued to work within this tradition have turned their attention to the delineation of broader life styles and behavior patterns rather than specific intrapsychic constellations and conflicts. A major focus within this framework has been the study of personal correlates of premature coronary heart disease, myocardial infarction, and sudden death. Increased risk of myocardial infarction has been identified with particular personality characteristics for many years. Dunbar (1943) regarded the attempt to surpass or subdue authority as the area of focal conflict for coronary patients, whom she described as compulsively striving, hard-working, disciplined, and characterized by extreme repression of spontaneous impulses. Subsequent writers have developed this notion more broadly (Wolf, 1971), and the coronary-prone person is now seen as someone who differs in degree rather than in kind from others. Rosenman and Friedman (Friedman and Rosenman, 1974; Rosenman et al., 1975), who have spent many years conducting retrospective and prospective studies, write of Type A and Type B behavior patterns. Type A behavior is associated with the aggressive, ambitious, competitive, time-pressured, high-geared person who emphasizes work rather than family life and whose goal seems to be the acquisition of personal power. Data from the prospective Western Collaborative group study showed that, after eight and one-half years of follow-up, the Type A person is twice as likely to experience premature myocardial infarction as is the more relaxed, easygoing Type B (Syme, 1975). Other writers have referred to Type A behavior as the "Sisyphus syndrome," work addiction or workaholism. As Theorell and Rahe (1974) have pointed out, it is not known whether genetic traits or early childhood experiences are largely responsible for this style of functioning, nor has it even been clearly identified as a factor of etiological importance in the onset of myocardial infarction. However, information about the social and psychological characteristics of cardiac patients has already been found to be extremely important in their rehabilitation. This finding underlines the utility of Reiser's (1975) observations, mentioned earlier, regarding the three phases of the disease process.

The individualism and competitiveness that seem to be the hallmarks of the coronary-prone person are often regarded as distinctively American in style, and as antithetical to traditional Japanese cultural values. It has been suggested that this difference may be in some way related to the widely different rates of heart disease in Japan, whose rate of 50/100,000 is the lowest among industrialized nations, and in America, where the rate of 350/100,000 is one of the world's highest. A study of CHD rates among 4,000 Japanese men living in California, conducted by Marmor, Syme, and Winkelstein (see Blakeslee, 1975), offers some evidence in support of this hypothesis. They found that the Japanese-Americans who plunged most fully into the American life style have five times the heart-disease rate found among those who continued to maintain Japanese cultural norms and who live quiet, noncompetitive lives as members of tightly knit social networks.

In general, as exemplified in this brief discussion of studies of the behavior of the coronary-prone person, distinctive behavioral and characterological styles have been observed to occur more often among those who subsequently develop certain chronic diseases, and as such they may serve as predisposing factors. The extensive research on clustering of life events in association with myocardial infarction and sudden cardiac death does not contradict these findings, since such life events apparently serve as triggering or precipitating elements influencing the timing rather than the risk of such illness.

Instead of seeking to identify specific personality constellations associated with high sensitivity to social change and illness, as earlier psychosomatic investigators attempted to do, several investigators working within the stress framework have concentrated on generalized emotional responsiveness as a critical variable. Such responsiveness or sensitivity, in contrast to emotional insulation or shallowness, can be said to characterize a person's response style to various situations.

An early study concerning this dimension was conducted by Wolf and Ripley (1947), who identified the qualities of emotional detachment and suppression as significant survival factors among American prisoners of war in Japanese prison camps during World War II. Two groups of prisoners displayed these qualities: those who were mature and well-adjusted and who could adapt to the rigorous conditions of the prison camp, and psychopaths whose chronic emotional shallowness proved to be a critical asset in this context.

Ford and Spaulding (1973) also found that personality style was strongly related to levels of coping ability in contending with the stresses of being a prisoner of war. Their sample consisted of the 82 surviving crew members of the *U.S.S. Pueblo* who were incarcerated in North Korea for 11 months in 1968-1969. They found, as have others in studies of World War II prison-camp survivors, that those with dependent and obsessional character styles fared less well than others. Those who adapted most effectively were described as having "confident self-identity."

Hinkle and Wolff (1957), working with an interdisciplinary team, interviewed and evaluated for 16 hours each 100 men and women who had been born and raised in China, who came here to graduate school after the war, and who, because of the changed political situation in China, were unable to return home. They had all experienced physical dislocations and hardships during the social upheavals which have occurred in China during the last 40 years, but for the group as a whole these experiences were more or less equal. Hinkle and Wolff found that the distribution of illness among these Chinese was not random. Over a period of years, some members had far more episodes of illness than others, and some were ill much less often than the group average. Hinkle and his colleagues (1974) were impressed by a quality they called *emotional insulation* which characterized the healthier members of the group. Major losses and life changes which might be expected to evoke profound emotional reactions in most people seemed to have had little effect on them. This quality seems equivalent to the emotional detachment identified by Wolf and Ripley.

The work of Janis (1974) substantiates these observations regarding an association between a generalized heightened sensitivity and greater disturbance in reaction to stressful events. He and his colleagues have observed that a person will overreact to any sign of danger "if his predispositional tendencies include a low threshold for anxiety arousal to a broad class of threat stimuli" (p. 164). He has used an inventory of somatic anxiety symptoms as an index of such chronic high anxiety. On the basis of studies of response to fear-arousing messages, he has developed an "inter-action hypothesis" to the effect that the optimal level of fear arousal is generally lower for highly anxious and defensive person-alities than for the less anxious and defensive. Accordingly, chroni-cally anxious people are generally less able to accept realistic de-scriptions of future stressful events intended to prepare and strengthen their coping abilities unless their fears are allayed, and in general they are more apt to react negatively to stressful events.

Kosa and Robertson (1969) carry this analysis one step further when they suggest the likelihood of an interaction between personality characteristics and a particular kind of stressor. Perhaps it is not a specific personality characteristic as such that facilitates effective coping in all stressful situations, but the degree to which the personality is congruent with a particular social condition. They refer to findings showing that first-borns, who are often described as more dependent, suffer more under conditions of social isolation than others.

On the basis of these observations, which represent a selective rather than exhaustive review of work in this area, it may be concluded that a variety of personal characteristics contribute to the manner and effectiveness with which the person responds to stressful circumstances. Who one is influences how one perceives and reacts to social and personal events and changes.

3. External Mediating Factors: Social Supports and Social Position

Another broad set of contingencies, or mediating factors, in the stress equation, which may be considered social or transactional in nature, concerns the nature of the buffers and supports accessible to the individual in his social environment. Included in this category are factors such as social position and social supports, one's ease of access to helping resources, social influence and social class, amount of family support, community attitudes, subcultural processes, and prevailing group morale. Many of these social characteristics are included, to a greater or lesser degree, in the analysis of social position and social supports that will be reviewed here in some detail to exemplify the effect of external or social buffers on susceptibility to disease.

The social positions that individuals or groups occupy in a community can materially influence their experience of stress, and consequently their vulnerability to a broad range of chronic diseases. Cassel (1973), Caplan (1974), and Mechanic (1974b) have independently observed that stress may be reduced for those who are effectively embedded in social networks or support systems. These networks serve multiple functions: they provide their members with consistent feedback and communications of what is expected of them, supports and assistance with tasks, evaluations of their performance, and appropriate rewards. These functions augment the individual's strengths and facilitate his mastery of his environment.

The disruption or absence of membership in an enduring social network has been identified as a predisposing factor to the experience of stress. Three such categories—those of *social isolation*, *social marginality* (minority membership), and *status inconsistency*—will be considered here.

Urban sociologists have recognized for years that deteriorating areas of the central city containing shabby businesses, many rooming houses, and an unstable, transient population of single adults, have disproportionately high rates of disorders, both physical and psychological (Faris and Dunham, 1939). More recently, the condition of social isolation has been delineated as a major factor in increased risk for disease. While the argument has been presented that psychiatric patients often choose to live alone and move about frequently as a device for protecting themselves against involvement in disruptive family relationships (Gerard and Houston, 1953), there is also considerable evidence to suggest that those who live alone without being involved with other people or organizations *for this very reason* have a high vulnerability to a variety of chronic diseases.

In his classic studies of "hospitalism," Spitz (1946) demonstrated that infants become ill and even die in the absence of maternal or other social ties. More recently, investigators have described reversible growth failure in children exposed to chronic maternal deprivation (Schmale, Meyerowitz, and Tinling, 1970). It is now recognized that a generalized "failure to thrive" among institutionalized children is often associated with a lack of meaningful relationships to other people.

Adults who live alone, with no family, kin, neighbors, or any meaningful group attachment, cohesion, or affiliation, are more susceptible to tuberculosis (Holmes, 1956), multiple accidents, alcoholism, psychiatric hospitalization with a diagnosis of schizophrenia, and suicide (Holmes, 1956; Cassel, 1970; Linsky, 1970; Levy and Rowitz, 1973). Parkes, Benjamin, and Fitzgerald (1969), in an aptly entitled study called "Broken Heart," found among nearly 4,500 widowers in the year following their bereavement a mortality rate 40% above that of married men of the same age. They cited an investigation of Rees and Lutkins in which mortality rates among 900 widows and widowers were 10 times greater than for matched controls. Clayton (1974, 1975), in a prospective study, found more physical and psychological symptoms but no increase in mortality rates among 109 widows and widowers during their first year of bereavement. Her data also suggested that younger widows and widowers showed more depressive symptoms and were more apt to require medical hospitalization than either matched married controls or older widows and widowers. Over-all, there seems good reason to agree with Parkes (1970) and Kiritz and Moos (1974) that major bereavements are potential causes of ill health. Generally, the absence of social supports or group membership evidently enhances susceptibility to conditions that elicit physiological stress responses which in turn lead to the development of various manifestations of chronic disease.

While social isolation represents perhaps the most extreme example of impairment of one's position in the community, marginal social status, due to membership in a low-status group or in one that is in a numerical minority in the area, has also been associated with increased health risks. Linsky (1970) found that members of low-status ethnic minorities who displayed deviant behavior were more apt to be psychiatrically hospitalized than were other persons who displayed similar behavior. The sheer numerical size of a given group, referred to in the literature as ethnic density, has been found to be significantly related to psychiatric hospitalization rates: as a given ethnic group constitutes a smaller proportion of the total population in a particular area, rates of diagnosed mental illness increase, both in comparison to the rates for other ethnic groups in that area and to the rates for members of the same ethnic group in neighborhoods where they constitute a significant proportion or majority. This observation has been made with respect to Chinese in Canada (Murphy, 1961), French and English minorities in neighboring Quebec towns (Sydiaha and Rootman, 1969), Italians in different Boston areas (Mintz and Schwartz, 1964), and black and white residents of various census tracts in Baltimore (Klee et al., 1967). Since these findings are independent of ethnicity as such, it is evidently the variable of ethnic density or sparsity which generates the conditions that culminate in psychiatric hospitalization. Presumably, the smaller the community of ethnically similar members, the less social support is available to any one of them. Equivalent findings have been noted for socially marginal groups with respect to physical diseases such as tuberculosis (Holmes, 1956).

A third form of marginality or impairment of one's position in the community is related to status inconsistency. This sociological term refers to the situation of a person who occupies two or more distinct social statuses or roles that involve incompatible social expectations. The person with status inconsistency can be considered "a particular type of marginal man," as Lenski (1954) phrased it in an early application of the concept. For both individuals and groups, an approximation of its prevalence can be obtained from analysis of various combinations of statuses in terms of their compatibility. For example, as Dodge and Martin (1970) explain, mother-married-adult are three compatible statuses representing a pattern of status integration, whereas mother-unmarried-adolescent are incompatible ones. The person described by the latter set presumably experiences more conflict, since conformity to the demands of one status would interfere with those of another.

Status inconsistency can also occur when one's achieved status is not concordant with one's ascribed status. For example, inconsistencies between occupational level and educational level, or between lack of employment and age, also represent conditions of status inconsistency. Dodge and Martin suggest that the degree to which people usually occupy two statuses simultaneously provides an operational measure of their compatibility.

Research investigators have reasoned that chronic emotional stress results from a lack of fit among social, structural, and personality elements as reflected in measures of status incongruence. This socially induced stress is presumed to play a predisposing or precipitating (triggering) role in the onset of chronic physical and emotional disorders. Studies exploring the stressful effects of status incongruence have been conducted both with individuals, in survey format, and with populations, using aggregate data derived from public records.

In an elaborate research program, Kahn and his colleagues (Kahn et al., 1961; Kahn and French, 1970) conducted a series of studies of role conflict in industrial settings. They developed measures based on observer ratings to assess the degree of conflict associated with various industrial positions. Persons occupying roles rated high in conflict were found to score significantly higher on checklists of medical symptoms than did workers occupying roles without conflict.

Other studies of individuals have dealt with observed discrepancies between education and income level, or education and occupational rank, which were presumed to generate role conflict. As such, they are one step removed from the direct individualized ratings of this variable which Kahn and his colleagues were able to carry out. While a few investigators failed to find an association between status incongruence and measures of health (for example, Meile and Haese, 1969), several have successfully demonstrated one, using different kinds of samples and measures of health (Abramson, 1966; Jackson, 1962; King and Cobb, 1958).

Hinkle (1974) and his colleagues at the Human Ecology Study Program at Cornell analyzed the medical careers of 2,600 semi-skilled employees who worked continuously for the New York City Telephone Company for 20 years. Admittedly, this group of people is atypical in terms of their geographical and employment stability, and consequent lack of exposure to social change. They found an enormous range in the number of illness episodes recorded, ranging from fewer than 5 days of sickness absence a year to an average of 50 days a year for every year for 20 years. The people with the greatest amount of disability had more different illness syndromes, more organ systems involved, and diseases arising from a greater number of apparent causes. In comparing the very healthy and the very frequently ill, Hinkle found that the healthy workers were people whose social backgrounds, aspirations, and interests coincided with their present circumstances, whose family, educational, and occupational statuses were congruent. This was not the case for the frequently ill workers, whose educational or family status was often inappropriately high for the kind of work they were doing. While Hinkle did not invoke the concept of status inconsistency in his conceptual analysis, his findings lend themselves to such an interpretation.

Although the foregoing studies all focused on status incongruity in which current income or occupational level was lower than educational level, the reverse pattern of inconsistency has also been found to be related to increased incidence of illness. Christenson and Hinkle (1961) studied two groups of men currently employed as managers in the same company. One group was college-educated and from a middle-class background; the other consisted of noncollege graduates who were hired as skilled craftsmen and later advanced to managerial status. The latter group, whose occupational achievements had outstripped their educational level, had a far greater number of illnesses of all sorts, both major and minor, physical and emotional, long-term and short-term, affecting every organ. Cassel (1970) has interpreted these findings to suggest that exposure to unfamiliar situations leads to increased susceptibility to disease, but they can also be considered from the point of view of stress generated by status incongruence.

Comment

Findings regarding the deleterious effects on physical and psychological well-being of social isolation and social losses such as bereavement are cumulatively persuasive. Whether social isolation causes or contributes to the onset of illness is perhaps not conclusively demonstrable, since the possibility exists that a prior condition or factor causes or contributes both to the social pathology of isolation and to the somatic or psychological pathology that follows. In addition, those who experience social isolation are in a sense self-selected, although this argument does not apply to the experience of bereavement. Nevertheless, the relationship between these variables seems substantial, and has been demonstrated effectively in varying groups.

The concept of social marginality as a precipitator of illness has been explored largely in relation to psychological disorder. Numerous studies of ethnic groups constituting minorities in their neighborhoods suggest that minority status *in itself* is associated with higher rates of major mental disorder. Again the problems of self-selection arise: people who accept minority status, at least when they do so willingly, are by definition unlike otherwise similar people who choose to live in neighborhoods where they constitute a majority. It has not been established whether the observed relationship between minority status and mental illness prevails when the minority residents are new arrivals in a community, presumably upwardly mobile; whether they are the less competent or elderly who are left behind in transitional neighborhoods where those who can, depart; or in stable neighborhoods with a small, permanent minority group. The question may also be asked if it makes a difference whether minority members are dispersed throughout a neighborhood or are concentrated in an enclave. It would be interesting to know whether the relative social position of a minority is related to the health status of its members in areas where significant social differences are observable. Does it matter if the minority is substantially better off or less well off than the majority? Further exploration of physical health differences between minority and majority groups in the same neighborhood may extend the generality of the relationships. These issues are not meant to detract from the validity of the reported findings, but are suggested as areas for future exploration.

The research findings concerning status inconsistency and illness, based on both aggregate and clinical samples, are interesting because of their number and because similar phenomena have been observed using diverse approaches. Some of the results are more compelling than others, at least in terms of their face validity. For example, it is difficult to imagine the mechanism whereby inconsistency between the mother's education and the father's occupational rank is associated with higher probability of rheumatoid arthritis in their female offspring, as reported in one study. On the other hand, observations of clustering of illnesses in people who are dissatisfied and unhappy about their life circumstances, while based on unrepresentative samples, seems somehow more plausible.

In general, various investigators have demonstrated an association between the prevalence of different chronic diseases and disruptions of the individual's position in his social environment. As Cassel (1975) observed, both animal and human studies suggest that "the presence of another particular animal of the same species may, under certain circumstances, protect the individual from a variety of stressful stimuli." To this we would add the further conclusion that the individual's position in his social network and the degree of consistency in this position also mediate his response to social stressors.

SUMMARY

It has been shown that a wide array of major social changes may enhance the vulnerability of populations and individuals to stress and illness. Their impact is affected both by the nature of social buffers or support systems available, and by characteristics of the stressful event and of the individual that further modify the effects of exposure to social stressors. While we cannot yet predict on an individual basis who will become ill, or what predisposing and precipitating factors and necessary conditions for illness onset, or what symptoms, will be manifested, we are learning to identify populations at risk.

REFERENCES

Abramson, J. H. (1966), Emotional Disorder, Status Inconsistency and Migration. *Milbank Mem. Fund Quart.*, 44:23-48.

Adamson, J., & Schmale, A. (1965), Object Loss, Giving Up, and the Onset of Psychiatric Disease. *Psychosom. Med.*, 27:557-576.

Alexander, F., French, T., & Pollock, G. (1968), *Psychosomatic Specificity*, Vol. 1. Chicago: University of Chicago Press.

Antonovsky, A. (1974), Conceptual and Methodological Problems in the Study of Resistance Resources and Stressful Life Events. In: *Stressful Life Events*, ed. B. S. Dohrenwend & B. P. Dohrenwend. New York: Wiley, pp. 245-258.

—— & Kats, R. (1967), The Life Crisis History as a Tool in Epidemiological Research. *J. Health Soc. Behav.*, 8:15-21.

Arthur, R. (1974), Extreme Stress in Adult Life and Its Psychic and Psychophysiological Consequences. In: *Life Stress and Illness*, ed. E. Gunderson & R. Rahe. Springfield: Thomas, pp. 195-207.

Bieliauskas, L., & Webb, J. (1974), The Social Readjustment Rating Scale: Validity in a College Population. *J. Psychosomat. Res.*, 18:115-123.

Blakeslee, S. (1975), Study of Japanese-Americans Indicates Stress Can Be a Major Factor in Heart Disease. *The New York Times*, August 5, p. 15.

Bramwell, S. T., Masuda, M., Wagner, N., & Holmes, T. (1975), Psychosocial Factors in Athletic Injuries. *J. Human Stress*, 1:6-20.

Brenner, M. H. (1973), *Mental Illness and the Economy*. Cambridge: Harvard University Press.

Brody, J. (1974), Nixon's Attacks of Phlebitis Believed Linked to Stress of Watergate Events. *The New York Times*, October 31, p. 33.

Cadoret, R, Winokur, G., Dorzab, J., & Baker, M. (1972), Depressive Disease: Life Events and Onset of Illness. *Arch. Gen. Psychiat.*, 26:133-136.

Caplan, G. (1974), *Support Systems and Community Mental Health*. New York: Behavioral Publications.

Cassel, J. (1970), Physical Illness in Response to Stress. In: *Social Stress*, ed. S. Levine & N. Scotch. Chicago: Aldine, pp. 189-209.

—— (1973), The Relation of the Urban Environment to Health: Implications for Prevention. *Mt. Sinai J. Med.*, 40:539-550.

—— (1974), An Epidemiological Perspective of Psychosocial Factors in Disease Etiology. *Amer. J. Pub. Health*, 64:1040-1043.

—— (1975), Social Science in Epidemiology: Psychosocial Processes and "Stress" Theoretical Formulation. In: *Handbook of Evaluation Research*, Vol. 1, ed. E. L. Struening & M. Guttentag. Beverly Hills, Calif.: Sage, pp. 537-549.

—— & Leighton, A. (1969), Epidemiology and Mental Health. In: *Mental Health Considerations in Public Health*, ed. S. E. Goldston. Washington, D.C.: Public Health Service.

—— & Tyroler, H. (1961), Epidemiological Studies of Culture Change I. Health Status and Recency of Industrialization. *Arch. Envir. Health*, 3:25-33.

Christenson, W., & Hinkle, L. (1961), Differences in Illness and Prognostic Signs in Two Groups of Young Men. *J.A.M.A.*, 177:247-253.

Clayton, P. (1974), Mortality and Morbidity in First Year of Widowhood. *Arch. Gen. Psychiat.*, 30:747-750.

—— (1975), The Effect of Living Alone on Bereavement Symptoms. *Amer. J. Psychiat.*, 132:133-137.

Coleman, J. (1973), Life Stress and Maladaptive Behavior. *Amer. J. Occup. Ther.*, 27:169-180.

Dekker, D., & Webb, J. (1974), Relationships of the Social Readjustment Rating Scale to Psychiatric Patient Status, Anxiety and Social Desirability. *J. Psychosomat. Res.*, 18:125-130.

Deutsch, F., ed. (1959), *On the Mysterious Leap from the Mind to the Body*. New York: International Universities Press.

Dodge, D., & Martin, W. (1970), *Social Stress and Chronic Illness*. Notre Dame, Ind.: University of Notre Dame Press.

Dohrenwend, B. P. (1974), Problems in Defining and Sampling the Relevant Population of Stressful Life Events: In: *Stressful Life Events*, ed. B. S. Dohrenwend & B. P. Dohrenwend. New York: Wiley, pp. 275-312.

Dohrenwend, B. S. (1973), Life Events as Stressors: A Methodological Inquiry. *J. Health Soc. Behav.*, 14:167-175.

———— & Dohrenwend, B. P. (1970), Class and Race as Status-Related Sources of Stress. In: *Social Stress*, ed. S. Levine & N. Scotch. Chicago: Aldine, pp. 111-140.

Dubos, R. (1965), *Man Adapting*. New Haven: Yale University Press.

Dunbar, F. (1943), *Psychosomatic Diagnosis*. New York: Hoeber.

Eitinger, L. (1971), Acute and Chronic Psychiatric and Psychosomatic Reactions in Concentration Camp Survivors. In: *Society, Stress and Disease*, Vol. 1, ed. L. Levi. London: Oxford University Press, pp. 219-230.

Engel, G. (1968), The Psychoanalytic Approach to Psychosomatic Medicine. In: *Modern Psychoanalysis*, ed. J. Marmor. New York: Basic Books, pp. 251-273.

Faris, R., & Dunham, H. W. (1939), *Mental Disorders in Urban Areas*. Chicago: University of Chicago Press.

Ford, C., & Spaulding, R. (1973), The *Pueblo* Incident. *Arch. Gen. Psychiat.*, 29:340-343.

Freud, S. (1894), The Neuro-Psychoses of Defence. *Standard Edition*, 3:45-61. London: Hogarth, 1962.

Fried, M. (1964), Effects of Social Change on Mental Health. *Amer. J. Orthopsychiat.*, 34:3-28.

———— (1966), The Role of Work in a Mobile Society. In: *Planning for a Nation of Cities*, ed. S. B. Warner. Cambridge: M.I.T. Press, pp. 81-104.

Friedman, M., & Rosenman, R. (1974), *Type A Behavior and Your Heart*. New York: Knopf.

Gerard, D., & Houston, L. (1953), Family Setting and the Social Ecology of Schizophrenia. *Psychiat. Quart.*, 27:90-101.

Gersten, J., Langer, T., Eisenberg, J., & Orzek, L. (1974), Child Behavior and Life Events: Undesirable Change or Change Per Se? In: *Stressful Life Events*, ed. B. S. Dohrenwend & B. P. Dohrenwend. New York: Wiley, pp. 159-170.

Glass, D., & Singer, J. (1972), *Urban Stress: Experiments on Noise and Social Stressors*. New York: Academic.

Graham, S., & Reeder, L. (1972), Social Factors in the Chronic Diseases. In: *Handbook of Medical Sociology*, 2nd ed., ed. H. Freeman, S. Levine, & L. Reeder. Englewood Cliffs, N.J.: Prentice-Hall, pp. 63-107.

Groen, J. (1971), Social Change and Psychosomatic Disease. In: *Society, Stress and Disease*, Vol. 1, ed. L. Levi. London: Oxford University Press, pp. 91-109.

Hinkle, L. (1974), The Effect of Exposure to Culture Change, Social Change and Changes in Interpersonal Relationships on Health. In: *Stressful Life Events*, ed. B. S. Dohrenwend & B. P. Dohrenwend. New York: Wiley, pp. 9-44.

———— & Wolff, H. G. (1957), Health and the Social Environment: Environmental Investigations. In: *Explorations in Social Psychiatry*, ed. A. Leighton, J. Clausen, & R. Wilson. New York: Basic Books, pp. 105-137.

Hocking, F. (1970), Extreme Environmental Stress and Its Significance for Psychopathology. *Amer. J. Psychother.*, 24:4-26.

Holmes, T. H. (1956), Multidiscipline Studies of Tuberculosis. In: *Personality, Stress and Tuberculosis,* ed. P. J. Sparer. New York: International Universities Press, pp. 65-152.

———— & Masuda, M. (1974), Life Change and Illness Susceptibility. In: *Stressful Life Events,* ed. B. S. Dohrenwend & B. P. Dohrenwend. New York: Wiley, pp. 45-72.

———— & Rahe, R. (1967), The Social Readjustment Rating Scale. *J. Psychosomat. Res.,* 11:213-218.

Horowitz, J. (1976), *Stress Response Syndromes.* New York: Aronson.

Hough, R., Fairbank, D., & Garcia, A. (1976), Problems in the Ratio Measurement of Life Stress. *J. Health Soc. Behav.,* 17:70-82.

Hudgens, R. (1974), Personal Catastrophe and Depression. In: *Stressful Life Events,* ed. B. S. Dohrenwend & B. P. Dohrenwend. New York: Wiley, pp. 119-134.

Jackson, E. (1962), Status Consistency and Symptoms of Stress. *Amer. Sociol. Rev.,* 27:469-480.

Jaco, E. (1970), Mental Illness in Response to Stress. In: *Social Stress,* ed. S. Levine & N. Scotch. Chicago: Aldine, pp. 210-227.

Jacobs, M., Spilken, A., & Norman, M. (1969), Relationship of Life Change, Maladaptive Aggression and Upper Respiratory Infection in Male College Students. *Psychosomat. Med.,* 31:31-44.

Janis, I. (1958), *Psychological Stress: Psychoanalytic and Behavioral Studies of Surgical Patients.* New York: Wiley.

———— (1974), Vigilance and Decision Making in Personal Crises. In: *Coping and Adaptation,* ed. G. Coelho, D. Hamburg, & J. Adams. New York: Basic Books, pp. 139-175.

Kagan, A., & Levi. L. (1974), Health and Environment—Psychosocial Stimuli: A Review. *Soc. Sci. Med.,* 8:225-241.

Kahn, R., & French, J. (1970), Status and Conflict: Two Themes in the Study of Stress. In: *Social and Psychological Factors in Stress,* ed. J. McGrath. New York: Holt, Rinehart & Winston, pp. 238-263.

———— Wolfe, D., Quinn, R., Snock, J., & Rosenthal, R. (1961), *Organization Stress: Studies in Role Conflict and Ambiguity.* New York: Wiley.

Kaplan, H. (1975), Psychophysiological Disorders. In: *Comprehensive Textbook of Psychiatry—II,* Vol. 2, 2nd ed., ed. A. M. Freedman, H. Kaplan, & B. Sadock. Baltimore: Williams & Wilkins, pp. 1628-1631.

Kellam, S. (1974), Stressful Life Events and Illness: A Research Area in Need of Conceptual Development. In: *Stressful Life Events,* ed. B. S. Dohrenwend & B. P. Dohrenwend. New York: Wiley, pp. 207-214.

Khan, M. M. (1963), The Concept of Cumulative Trauma. *The Psychoanalytic Study of the Child,* 18:286-306. New York: International Universities Press.

King, S., & Cobb, S. (1958), Psychosocial Factors in the Epidemiology of Rheumatoid Arthritis. *J. Chronic Dis.,* 7:466-475.

Kiritz, S., & Moos, R. (1974), Physiological Effects of Social Environments. *Psychosomat. Med.,* 36:96-114.

Klee, G., Spiro, E., Bahn, A., & Gorwitz, K. (1967), An Ecological Analysis of Diagnosed Mental Illness in Baltimore. In: *Psychiatric Epidemiology and Mental Health Planning,* ed. R. Monroe, G. Klee, & E. Brody. Psychiatric Research Report 22, American Psychiatric Association, pp. 107-148.

Knapp, P. (1975), Current Theoretical Concepts in Psychophysiological Medicine. In: *Comprehensive Textbook of Psychiatry—II*, Vol. 2, 2nd ed., ed. A. M. Freedman, H. Kaplan, & B. Sadock. Baltimore: Williams & Wilkins, pp. 1631-1637.

Kolb, L. (1973), *Modern Clinical Psychiatry*, 8th ed. Philadelphia: Saunders.

Kosa, J., & Robertson, L. (1969), The Social Aspects of Health and Illness. In: *Poverty and Health*, ed. J. Kosa, A. Antonovsky, & I. Zola. Cambridge, Mass.: Harvard University Press, pp. 35-68.

Kris, E. (1956), Recovery of Childhood Memories in Psychoanalysis. *The Psychoanalytic Study of the Child*, 11:54-88. New York: International Universities Press.

Lauer, R. (1974), Rate of Change and Stress: A Test of the "Future Shock" Hypothesis. *Social Forces*, 52:510-516.

Lazarus, R. (1970), Cognitive and Personality Factors Underlying Threat and Coping. In: *Social Stress*, ed. S. Levine & N. Scotch. Chicago: Aldine, pp. 143-164.

——— (1971), The Concepts of Stress and Disease. In: *Society, Stress and Disease*, Vol. 1, ed. L. Levi. London: Oxford University Press, pp. 53-58.

Leff, D. (1975), Stress-Triggered Organic Disease in This Year of Economic Anxiety. *Med. World News*, 16:72-81.

Leighton, A. H. (1971), Psychiatric Disorder and Social Environment: An Outline for a Frame of Reference. In: *Psychiatric Disorder and the Urban Environment*, ed. B. Kaplan. New York: Behavioral Publications, pp. 20-67, 117-139.

Lenski, G. (1954), Status Crystallization: A Non-vertical Dimension of Social Status. *Amer. Sociol. Rev.*, 19:405-413.

Levy, L., & Rowitz, L. (1973), *The Ecology of Mental Disorder*. New York: Behavioral Publications.

Linsky, A. (1970), Who Shall Be Excluded: The Influence of Personal Attributes in Community Reaction to the Mentally Ill. *Soc. Psychiat.*, 5:166-171.

Lipowski, Z. (1968), Review of Consultation Psychiatry and Psychosomatic Medicine. *Psychosomat Med.*, 30:395-422.

Markush, R., & Favero, R. (1974), Epidemiological Assessment of Stressful Life Events, Depressed Mood, and Psychophysiological Symptoms—A Preliminary Report. In: *Stressful Life Events*, ed. B. S. Dohrenwend & B. P. Dohrenwend. New York: Wiley, pp. 171-190.

Mason, J. (1975), A Historical View of the Stress Field. *J. Human Stress*, 1:6-12.

Masserman, J. (1955), *The Practice of Dynamic Psychiatry*. Philadelphia: Saunders.

Mechanic, D. (1974a), Discussion of Research Programs on Relations between Stressful Life Events and Episodes of Physical Illness. In: *Stressful Life Events*, ed. B. S. Dohrenwend & B. P. Dohrenwend. New York: Wiley, pp. 87-97.

——— (1974b), Social Structure and Personal Adaptation: Some Neglected Dimensions. In: *Coping and Adaptation*, ed. G. Coelho, D. Hamburg, & J. Adams. New York: Basic Books, pp. 32-46.

——— (1976), Stress, Illness and Illness Behavior. *J. Human Stress*, 2:26.

Medical World News (1971), Down the Road to Clinical Depression. Jan. 22, p. 41.

Meile, R., & Haese, P. (1969), Social Status, Status Incongruence and Symptoms of Stress. *J. Health Soc. Behav.*, 10:237-244.

Michaux, W., Gansereit, K., McCabe, O., & Kurland, A. (1967), The Psycho-pathology and Measurement of Environmental Stress. *Community Mental Health J.*, 3:358-372.

Miller, N. (1975), The Role of Learning in Physiological Responses to Stress. Paper presented at Kittay Scientific Foundation Third International Symposium on Psychopathology of Human Adaptation.

Mintz, N., & Schwartz, D. (1964), Urban Ecology and Psychosis: Community Factors in the Incidence of Schizophrenia and Manic-Depression among Italians in Greater Boston. *Internat. J. Soc. Psychiat.*, 10:101-117.

Moss, G. (1973), *Illness, Immunity and Social Interaction*. New York: Wiley.

Murphy, H. B. (1961), Social Change and Mental Health. *Milbank Mem. Fund Quart.*, 39:385-445.

Mutter, A., & Schliefer, M. (1966), The Role of Psychological and Social Factors in the Onset of Somatic Illness in Children. *Psychosomat. Med.*, 28:333-341.

Myers, J., Lindenthal, J., Pepper, M., & Ostrander, D. (1972), Life Events and Mental Status: A Longitudinal Study. *J. Health Soc. Behav.*, 13:398-406.

Neser, W., Tyroler, H., & Cassel, J. (1971), Social Disorganization and Stroke Mortality in the Black Population of North Carolina. *Amer. J. Epidemiol.*, 93:166-175.

Nuckolls, C., Cassel, J., & Kaplan, B. (1972), Psycho-Social Assets, Life Crises and the Prognosis of Pregnancy. *Amer. J. Epidemiol.*, 95:431-441.

Parkes, C. (1970), The Psychosomatic Effects of Bereavement. In: *Modern Trends in Psychosomatic Medicine*, Vol. 2, ed. O. W. Hill. New York: Appleton-Century-Crofts, pp. 71-80.

——— Benjamin, B., & Fitzgerald, R. (1969), Broken Heart: A Statistical Study of Increased Mortality among Widowers. *Brit. Med. J.*, 1:740-743.

Paykel, E. (1974), Life Stress and Psychiatric Disorder: Applications of the Clinical Approach. In: *Stressful Life Events*, ed. B. S. Dohrenwend & B. P. Dohrenwend. New York: Wiley, pp. 135-150.

——— Prusoff, B., & Myers, J. (1975), Suicide Attempts and Recent Life Events. *Arch. Gen. Psychiat.*, 32:327-333.

Rahe, R. (1972), Subjects' Recent Life Changes and Their Near-Future Illness Reports. *Ann. Clin. Res.*, 4:250-265.

——— (1974), The Pathway between Subjects' Recent Life Changes and Their Near-Future Illness Reports: Representative Results and Methodological Issues. In: *Stressful Life Events*, ed. B. S. Dohrenwend & B. P. Dohrenwend. New York: Wiley, pp. 73-86.

——— Floistad, I., Bergan, T., Ringdal, S., Gerhardt, R., Gunderson, E., & Arthur, R. (1974), A Model for Life Changes and Illness Research. *Arch. Gen. Psychiat.*, 31:172-177.

——— & Lind, E. (1971), Psychosocial Factors and Sudden Cardiac Death: A Pilot Study. *J. Psychosomat. Res.*, 15:19-24.

——— Meyer, M., Smith, M., Kjaer, G., & Holmes, T. (1964), Social Stress and Illness Onset. *J. Psychosomat. Res.*, 8:35-44.

Rapoport, R. (1963), Normal Crises, Family Structure and Mental Health. *Family Process*, 2:68-80.

Reiser, M. (1966), Toward an Integrated Psychoanalytic-Physiological Theory of Psychosomatic Disorders. In: *Psychoanalysis—A General Psychology*, ed. R. Loewenstein, L. Newman, M. Schur, & A. Solnit. New York: International Universities Press, pp. 570-582.

———— (1968), Psychoanalytic Method in Psychosomatic Research. *Internat. J. Psycho-Anal.*, 39:231-235.

———— (1975), Changing Theoretical Concepts in Psychosomatic Medicine. In: *American Handbook of Psychiatry*, Vol. 4, 2nd ed., ed. S. Arieti. New York: Basic Books, pp. 477-500.

Rosenman, R., Friedman, M., Brand, R., Jenkins, D., Strauss, R., & Wurm, M. (1975), Coronary Heart Disease in the Western Collaborative Group Study. *J.A.M.A.*, 233:872-877.

Rubin, R., Gunderson, E., & Arthur, R. (1971), Life Stress and Illness Patterns in the U.S. Navy-V. Prior Life Change and Illness Onset in a Battleship's Crew. *J. Psychosomat. Res.*, 15:89-94.

Schmale, A., & Engel, G. (1967), The Giving Up-Given Up Complex Illustrated on Film. *Arch. Gen. Psychiat.*, 17:135-145.

———— & Iker, H. (1966), The Affect of Hopelessness and the Development of Cancer. *Psychosomat. Med.*, 28:714-721.

———— Meyerowitz, S., & Tinling, D. (1970), Current Concepts of Psychosomatic Medicine. In: *Modern Trends in Psychosomatic Medicine*, Vol. 2, ed. O. W. Hill. New York: Appleton-Century-Crofts, pp. 1-25.

Schwab, J., McGinnis, N., & Warheit, G. (1973), Social Psychiatric Impairment: Racial Comparisons. *Amer. J. Psychiat.*, 130:183-187.

Scott, R., & Howard, A. (1970), Models of Stress. In: *Social Stress*, ed. S. Levine & N. Scotch. Chicago: Aldine, pp. 259-278.

Selye, H. (1956), *The Stress of Life*. New York: McGraw-Hill.

———— (1974), *Stress without Distress*. Philadelphia: Lippincott.

———— (1976), *The Stress of Life*, rev. ed. New York: McGraw Hill.

Selzer, M., & Vinokur, A. (1974), Life Events, Subjective Stress and Traffic Accidents. *Amer. J. Psychiat.*, 131:903-906.

Spitz, R. (1946), Hospitalism: A Follow-up Report. *The Psychoanalytic Study of the Child*, 2:113-117. New York: International Universities Press.

Srole, L., Langer, T., Michael, S., Opler, M., & Rennie, T. (1962), *The Midtown Manhattan Study*. New York: McGraw-Hill.

Struening, E. L., Rabkin, J., & Peck, H. (1970), Migration and Ethnic Membership in Relation to Social Problems. In: *Behavior in New Environments*, ed. E. Brody. Beverly Hills, Calif.: Sage, pp. 57-87.

Susser, M. (1968), *Community Psychiatry*. New York: Random House.

Sydiaha, D., & Rootman, I. (1969), I. Ethnic Groups within Communities: A Comparative Study of the Expression and Definition of Mental Illness. *Psychiat. Quart.*, 43:131-146.

Syme, S. (1975), Social and Psychological Risk Factors in Coronary Heart Disease. *Mod. Conc. Cardiovascular Dis.*, 44:17-22.

———— Borhani, N., & Buechley, R. (1965), Cultural Mobility and Coronary Heart Disease in an Urban Area. *Amer. J. Epidemiol.*, 82:334-346.

Theorell, T., & Rahe, R. (1971), Psychosocial Factors and Myocardial Infarction. I. An Inpatient Study in Sweden. *J. Psychosomat. Res.*, 15:25-31.

———— ———— (1974), Psychosocial Characteristics of Subjects with Myocardial Infarctions in Stockholm. In: *Life Stress and Illness*, ed. E. Gunderson & R. Rahe. Springfield: Thomas, pp. 90-104.

Time (1971), The Hazards of Change. March 1, p. 54.

Tyroler, H., & Cassel, J. (1964), Health Consequences of Culture Change: The Effect of Urbanization on Coronary Heart Mortality in Rural Residents of North Carolina. *J. Chronic Dis.*, 17:167-177.

Uhlenuth, E., Lipman, R., Balter, M., & Stern. M. (1974), Symptom Intensity and Life Stress in the City. *Arch. Gen. Psychiat.*, 31:759-764.

———— & Paykel, E. (1973), Symptom Intensity and Life Events. *Arch. Gen. Psychiat.*, 28:473-477.

Weiner, H. (1975), Are "Psychosomatic" Diseases Diseases of Regulation? (Editorial) *Psychosomat. Med.*, 37:289-290.

Wershow, H., & Reinhart, G. (1974), Life Change and Hospitalization—A Heretical View. *J. Psychosomat. Res.*, 18:393-401.

Willmuth, L., Weaver, L., & Donlan, S. (1975), Utilization of Medical Services by Transferred Employees. *Arch. Gen. Psychiat.*, 32:85-88.

Wolf, S. (1971), Patterns of Social Adjustment and Disease. In: *Society, Stress and Disease*, Vol. 1, ed. L. Levi. London: Oxford University Press, pp. 5-6.

———— & Ripley, H. (1947), Reactions among Allied Prisoners of War Subjected to Three Years of Imprisonment and Torture by the Japanese. *Amer. J. Psychiat.*, 104:180-193.

Wolff, H. G. (1968), *Stress and Disease*, 2nd ed., ed. S. Wolf and H. Goodell. Springfield: Thomas.

Wyler, A., Masuda, M., & Holmes, T. (1971), Magnitude of Life Events and Seriousness of Illness. *Psychosomat. Med.*, 33:115-122.

Name Index

625

CONTENTS OF VOLUMES 1-4